Nationalist, Realist, and Radical:

Three Views of American Diplomacy

Nationalist, Realist, and Radical:

Three Views of American Diplomacy

JERALD A. COMBS
San Francisco State College

Harper & Row, Publishers
New York, Evanston, San Francisco, London

Nationalist, Realist, and Radical:

Three Views of American Diplomacy

Standard Book Number: 06-041348-4

Library of Congress Catalog Card Number: 73-181544

For My Mother and Father
Margaret and Arthur Combs

Contents

Nationalist, Realist, and Radical:

Three Views of American Diplomacy

Introduction

Is the United States a ruthless imperialist power? Radicals say so and demand a thorough change. Is the United States simply a misguided country, overestimating its own virtue and power, naïvely intervening in foreign affairs it does not understand and cannot control? Senator J. William Fulbright claims this is so and argues for a less arrogant and more realistic policy. Or is America a wise and courageous nation, defending its democratic values and those of its friends against the aggression of the world's assorted tyrants? The President argues that this is true and urges us to continue on our present path. The debate rages in the halls of Congress. It screams from newspaper headlines and television broadcasts. It tears apart the universities. It haunts the minds of the young men we send to fight in the service of American foreign policy.

Strange as it may seem, the debate has penetrated even the studies of America's historians. For many years they have been examining America's past diplomacy, looking for trends and principles, for successes and failures that would throw light on the country's present predicament. Their work has done much to shape the political debate now going on.

For the past decade or so, the three most important interpretations emerging from the work of America's diplomatic historians have been exactly those enunciated by President Nixon, by Senator Fulbright, and by the Radical movement. One group of historians holds that past American policy has generally been well intentioned, realistic, and successful. A second group credits United States policy with good intentions but criticizes it for excessive zeal and failure to recognize the realities of power and interest in world affairs. A third group condemns past American policy as being rapaciously self-interested, expansive, and aggressive. Each of these historical schools has developed a large and respectable body of literature to support and illustrate its point of view. These three interpretations have come to be known by a welter of different terms, but for purposes of this book I have chosen to call them the Nationalist, the Realist, and the Radical. Since today's political debate is based so firmly on the interpretations and evidence supplied by these three histori-

cal schools, a knowledge of them is vital to every American's political as well as historical understanding.

Each chapter of this book contains a sample of the Nationalist, Realist, and Radical interpretation of a major event or trend in American diplomatic history. Most of the essays were written by leaders of their respective schools. Occasionally, however, an essay was selected not because the author subscribed to a school's overall perspective but because his work happened to coincide with it at a particular point. I want to emphasize that if I use a historian's work to represent the Radical perspective, I do not mean to represent that historian as a political revolutionary.

The essays in each section have been arranged in a sequence intended to provide the most coherent dialogue between them, not to give any particular viewpoint preferential treatment. It is my hope that a careful study and comparison of these interpretations will help lead to reasoned discourse and a peaceful resolution of America's foreign-policy problems.

one
The Overall
Perspective

Realist

Realist historians believe that American foreign policy has been naïve, overly idealistic, and moralistic. These historians argue that Americans have foolishly regarded peace and goodwill among nations as the natural state of things. According to this view, Americans have regarded war as an unnatural aberration produced by the machinations of monarchs and dictators. Americans seem to believe that if only democratic governments could be established throughout the world, war would disappear. Because the people fight and pay for their nation's wars, they would be far less anxious to open hostilities than their leaders, who reap the glory. Open markets and a free flow of communication would further guarantee understanding and mutual dependency among nations, inhibiting war to an even greater extent.

For many years, according to the Realists, the United States hoped to bring about such conditions in the world by exemplifying the benefits of democracy and by abstaining from the power politics of a feuding Europe in order to preserve America's own peace, liberty, and prosperity. Americans attributed the success of this isolationist policy to their own sagacity, ignoring the role of the European balance of power that kept the only nations capable of threatening American interests and security too busy with one another to bother the United States.

When this European balance broke down in the twentieth century and the United States was threatened, Americans reacted violently. They embarked on crusades, confident that the nation was powerful enough to purge the world of evil and warlike autocrats. They hoped that, once having made the world "safe for democracy," the United States could af-

ford to ignore world politics again, leaving a peaceful democratic world to govern its own affairs.

Realists regard America's extreme oscillation between righteous isolation and crusading intervention as a foolish and tragic policy. They argue that a more realistic attitude toward foreign affairs is essential for the survival of the United States and the world. They ask Americans to accept a degree of conflict among nations as a natural result of differing interests and not ordinarily the product of evil leaders or undemocratic systems. The Realists believe that in most cases human beings can only ameliorate such conflicts, not eliminate them. This is best done, they say, by establishing and maintaining a balance of power among nations. It would then be in the interest of all nations to settle their differences peacefully, for if they were to make war they would have opponents with equal or superior power. Even the balance of power, of course, would not prevent all wars, Realists admit. But in the case of war, ideology and military strategy should be strictly limited to the political goal of re-establishing a balance of power. Realists desperately fear emotional crusades for total victory, crusades that destroy the balance of power and leave chaos, which in turn only invites further aggression and bloodshed.

Thus, the Realists support a foreign policy less influenced by the moralistic emotions of the people and more responsive to professional diplomats who understand the realities of international politics. These professionals would set limited goals for the nation, goals based squarely on national interest. They would balance these goals carefully with the power available to achieve them. Although such a policy would require acknowledgment and acceptance of conflict, selfishness, and power in international affairs, Realists believe it would offer a far better chance for peace, international stability, and the growth of democracy and prosperity than the utopian goals and delusions of omnipotence that have plagued American diplomacy in the past.

The Realist critique of American foreign policy originated with men like theologian Reinhold Niebuhr; British historian E. H. Carr; career diplomats George Kennan and Louis Halle; journalist and philosopher Walter Lippmann; geographer Nicholas J. Spykman; and a group of historians and political scientists associated with Hans J. Morgenthau at the University of Chicago. It became especially influential after World War II, when memories of Munich and Auschwitz and fears of Stalinist Russia made past American isolationism and hopes for universal peace and democracy seem dangerous pipe dreams.

In the following selection, Hans J. Morgenthau illustrates the Realist point of view by briefly surveying the history of American diplomacy. Professor Morgenthau is the director of the Center for the Study of American Foreign and Military Policy at the University of Chicago, the Albert A. Michelson Distinguished Service Professor of Political Science and Modern History at the University of Chicago, and the Leonard Davis Distinguished Professor of Political Science at the City University of New York. Two of Morgenthau's books, In Defense of the National Interest and Politics Among Nations, did much to develop and popularize the Realist view.

In Defense
of the
National Interest

Hans J. Morgenthau

[Except during the era of the Founding Fathers, the classic age of American statecraft, what has passed for American foreign policy has been] either improvisation or—especially in our century—the invocation of some abstract moral principle in whose image the world was to be made over. Improvisation was largely successful, for in the past the margin of American and allied power has generally exceeded the degree to which American improvidence has failed the demands of the hour. The invocation of abstract moral principles was in part hardly more than an innocuous pastime; embracing everything, it came to grips with nothing. In part, however, it was a magnificent instrument for marshaling public opinion in support of war and warlike policies —and for losing the peace. The intoxication with moral abstrac-

From In Defense of the National Interest by Hans J. Morgenthau, pp. 4–24, 25–33. Copyright 1950, 1951 by Hans J. Morgenthau. Reprinted by permission of Alfred A. Knopf, Inc.

tions, which as a mass phenomenon started with the Spanish-American War and which in our time has become the prevailing substitute for political thought, is indeed one of the great sources of weakness and failure in American foreign policy. Much will have to be said about this later.

Still it is worthy of note that underneath this political dilettant-ism, which is nourished by improvidence and a sense of moral mission, there lives an almost instinctive awareness of the perennial interests of the United States. This has been especially true with regard to Europe and the Western Hemisphere, for in these regions the national interest of the United States has always been obvious and clearly defined.

THE NATIONAL INTEREST OF THE UNITED STATES

In the Western Hemisphere we have always endeavored to preserve the unique position of the United States as a predominant power without rival. We have not been slow in recognizing that our predominance was not likely to be effectively threatened by any one American nation or combination of nations acting without support from outside the hemisphere. This peculiar situation has made it imperative for the United States to isolate the Western Hemisphere from the political and military policies of non-American nations. The interference of non-American nations in the affairs of the Western Hemisphere, especially through the acquisition of territory, was the only way in which the predominance of the United States could have been challenged from within the hemisphere itself. The Monroe Doctrine and the policies implementing it express that permanent national interest of the United States in the Western Hemisphere.

Since a threat to our national interest in the Western Hemisphere can only come from outside it—historically, from Europe—we have always striven to prevent the development of conditions in Europe which would be conducive to a European nation's interfering in the affairs of the Western Hemisphere or contemplating a direct attack upon the United States. These conditions would be most likely to arise if a European nation, its predominance unchallenged within Europe, could look across the sea for conquest without fear of being menaced at the center of its power; that is, in Europe itself.

It is for this reason that the United States has consistently—

the War of 1812 is the sole major exception—pursued policies aiming at the maintenance of the balance of power in Europe. It has opposed whatever European nation—be it Great Britain, France, Germany, or Russia—was likely to gain that ascendancy over its European competitors which would have jeopardized the hemispheric predominance and eventually the very independence of the United States. Conversely, it has supported whatever European nation appeared capable of restoring the balance of power by offering successful resistance to the would-be conqueror. While it is hard to imagine a greater contrast in ways of thinking about matters political than that between Alexander Hamilton and Woodrow Wilson, in this concern for the maintenance of the balance of power in Europe—for whatever different reasons— they are one. It is with this concern that the United States has intervened in both World Wars on the side of the initially weaker coalition, and has pursued European policies so largely paralleling those of Great Britain; for from Henry VIII to this day Great Britain has had a single objective in Europe: the maintenance of the balance of power.

Asia has vitally concerned the United States only since the turn of the century, and the relation of Asia to our national interests has never been obvious or clearly defined. In consequence, our policies in Asia have never as unequivocally expressed our permanent national interest as have the hemispheric and European policies; nor have they commanded the bipartisan support the latter have largely enjoyed. In addition, they have been subjected more fully to moralistic influence than the European and hemispheric policies. Yet underlying the confusions, reversals of policy, and moralistic generalities of our Asiatic policy since McKinley, one can detect a consistency that reflects, however vaguely, the permanent interest of the United States in Asia. And this interest is again the maintenance of the balance of power. The principle of the "open door" in China expresses this interest. Originally its meaning was purely commercial, but when other nations, especially Japan, threatened to close the door to China not only commercially but also militarily and politically, the "open door" was interpreted to cover the territorial integrity and political independence of China for not commercial but political reasons. However unsure the United States has been in its Asiatic policy, it has always assumed that the domination of China by another nation would lead to so great an accumulation of power as to threaten the security of the United States.

THE AMERICAN EXPERIENCE IN FOREIGN AFFAIRS

Wherever American foreign policy has operated, political thought has been divorced from political action. Even where our long-range policies reflect faithfully, as they do in the Americas and in Europe, the true interests of the United States, we think about them in terms that have at best but a tenuous connection with the actual character of the policies pursued. We have acted on the international scene, as all nations must, in power-political terms; but we have tended to conceive of our actions in non-political, moralistic terms. This aversion to seeing problems of international politics as they are, and the inclination to view them in non-political and moralistic terms, can be attributed both to certain misunderstood peculiarities of the American experience in foreign affairs and to the general climate of opinion in the Western world during the better part of the nineteenth and the first decades of the twentieth centuries. Three of these peculiarities of the American experience stand out: the uniqueness of the American experiment; the actual isolation, during the nineteenth century, of the United States from the centers of world conflict; and the humanitarian pacifism and anti-imperialism of American ideology.

The uniqueness of the American experiment in foreign policy resides in two elements: the negative one of distinctness from the traditional power-political quarrels of Europe, and the positive one of a continental expansion that created the freest and richest nation on earth, apparently without conquest or subjugation of others.

When the founders of the republic broke out our constitutional ties with Britain, they were convinced that this meant the beginning of an American foreign policy distinct from that of Europe. As Washington's Farewell Address put it: "Europe has a set of primary interests, which to us have none, or a very remote relation. Hence she must be engaged in frequent controversies, the causes of which are essentially foreign to our concerns. Hence, therefore, it must be unwise in us to implicate ourselves, by artificial ties, in the ordinary vicissitudes of her politics, or the ordinary combinations and collisions of her friendships or enmities." In 1796, European politics and power politics were identical; there were no other power politics but those engaged in by the princes of Europe. "The toils of European ambition, rivalship, interest, humor or caprice" were all that the American eye could discern of the international struggle for power. The retreat from European politics, as proclaimed by Washington, could therefore be taken to mean retreat from power politics as such.

The expansion of the United States up to the Spanish-American War seemed to provide conclusive proof of both the distinctness and the moral superiority of American foreign policy. The settlement of the better part of a continent by the thirteen original states—an act of civilizing rather than of conquering—appeared essentially different from, and morally superior to, the imperialistic ventures, wars of conquest, and colonial acquisitions with which the history of other nations was replete. Yet what permitted this uniqueness in American expansion was not so much political virtue as the contiguity of the sparsely settled object of conquest with the original territory of departure. As was the case with Russia's simultaneous eastward expansion toward the Pacific, the United States, in order to expand, did not need to cross the oceans and fight wars of conquest in strange lands, in the manner of the other great colonizing nations. Furthermore, the utter political, military, and numerical inferiority of the Indian opponent tended to obscure the element of power, which was no less real though less obtrusive in our continental expansion than in the expansionist movements of other nations. Thus what actually was the fortuitous conjunction of two potent historic accidents could take on in the popular imagination the aspects of an inevitable natural development, a "manifest destiny," confirming the uniqueness of American foreign policy in its freedom from those power-political blemishes that degrade the foreign policies of other nations.

Yet American isolation from the European tradition of power politics was more than a political program or a moralistic illusion. In the matter of involvement in the political conflicts centering in Europe, and the commitments and risks implied in such involvement, American isolation was an established political fact until the end of the nineteenth century. This actuality was a result of deliberate choice as well as of the objective conditions of geography. Popular writers might see in the uniqueness of America's geographic position the hand of God unalterably prescribing the course of American expansion as well as isolation, but more responsible observers, from Washington on, were careful to emphasize the conjunction of geographic conditions and of a foreign policy choosing its ends in the light of geography and using geographic conditions to attain those ends. Washington referred to "our detached and distant situation" and asked: "Why forego the advantages of so peculiar a situation?" When this period of American foreign policy drew to a close, John Bright wrote to Alfred Love: "On your continent we may hope your growing millions may henceforth know nothing of war. None can assail you; and you are anxious to abstain from mingling with the quarrels of other nations."

From the shores of the North American continent, the citizens of the new world watched the strange spectacle of the struggle for power unfolding in distant Europe, Africa, and Asia. Since for the better part of the nineteenth century their foreign policy enabled them to keep the roles of spectators, what was actually the result of a passing historic configuration appeared to Americans as a permanent condition, self-chosen as well as naturally ordained. At worst they would continue to watch the game of power politics played by others. At best the time was near when, with democracy established everywhere, the final curtain would fall and the game of power politics would no longer be played.

Aiding in the achievement of this goal was conceived to be part of America's mission. Throughout our history, the national destiny of the United States has been understood in anti-militaristic, libertarian terms. Whenever that national mission finds a non-aggressive, abstentionist formulation, as in the political philosophy of John C. Calhoun, it is conceived as the promotion of domestic liberty. Thus we may "do more to extend liberty by our example over this continent and the world generally, than would be done by a thousand victories." When the United States, in the wake of the Spanish-American War, seemed to desert this anti-imperialist and democratic ideal, William Graham Sumner restated its essence: "Expansion and imperialism are a grand onslaught on democracy . . . expansion and imperialism are at war with the best traditions, principles, and interests of the American people." Comparing the tendencies of European power politics with the ideals of the American tradition, Sumner thought with Washington that they were incompatible. Yet, as a prophet, he saw that with the conclusion of the Spanish-American War America was irrevocably committed to the course that was engulfing Europe in revolution and war.

To understand the American mission in such selfless, humanitarian terms was all the easier because the United States, in contrast to the other great powers, was generally not interested—at least outside the Western Hemisphere—in particular advantages definable in terms of power or of territorial gain. Its national interest was exhausted by the preservation of its predominance in the Western Hemisphere and the balance of power in Europe and Asia. And even this interest in general stability rather than special advantage was, as we know, not always clearly recognized.

Yet while the foreign policy of the United States was forced, by circumstance if not by choice, to employ the methods, shoulder the commitments, seek the objectives, and run the risks, from which it had thought itself permanently exempt, American political thought continued to uphold that exemption at least as an ideal. And that ideal was supposed to be only temporarily beyond the reach of the American people, because of the wickedness and stupidity of either American or, preferably, foreign statesmen. In one sense, this ideal of a free, peaceful, and prosperous world, from which popular government had forever banished power politics, was a natural outgrowth of the American experience. In another sense, this ideal expressed in a particularly eloquent and consistent fashion the general philosophy that dominated the Western world during the better part of the nineteenth century. This philosophy rests on two basic propositions: that the struggle for power on the international scene is a mere accident of history, naturally associated with non-democratic government and therefore destined to disappear with the triumph of democracy throughout the world; and that, in consequence, conflicts between democratic and non-democratic nations must be primarily conceived not as struggles for mutual advantage in terms of power but as fights between good and evil, which can only end with the complete triumph of good, and with evil wiped off the face of the earth.

The nineteenth century developed this philosophy of international relations from its experience of domestic politics. The distinctive characteristic of this experience was the domination of the middle classes by the aristocracy. The political philosophy of the nineteenth century identified this aristocratic domination with political domination of any kind, and concluded that by ending aristocratic domination one could abolish all political domination. After the defeat of aristocratic government, the middle classes developed a system of indirect domination. They replaced the traditional division into the governing and governed classes and the military method of open violence, characteristic of aristocratic rule, with the invisible chains of economic dependence. This economic system operated through a network of seemingly equalitarian legal rules which concealed the very existence of power relations. The nineteenth century was unable to see the political nature of these legalized relations, considering them to be essentially different from what had gone, so far, under the name of politics. Therefore, politics in its aristocratic—that is, open and violent—form was identified with politics as such. The struggle, then, for political power, in domestic as well as in international affairs, appeared to be only a historic accident, coincident with autocratic government and bound to disappear with the disappearance of such government.

It is easy to see how this general climate of opinion in the Western world nourished similar tendencies that the specific experiences of American history had planted in the American mind. Thus it is not an accident that nowhere in the Western world was there greater conviction and tenacity in support of the belief that involvement in power politics is not inevitable but only accidental, and that nations have a choice between power politics and another kind of foreign policy conforming to moral principles and not tainted by the desire for power. Nor is it by accident that this philosophy of foreign policy found its most dedicated and eloquent spokesman in an American President, Woodrow Wilson.

THE THREE PERIODS OF AMERICAN FOREIGN POLICY

The Realistic Period

The illusion that a nation can escape, if it wants to, from power politics into a realm where action is guided by moral principles rather than by considerations of power is deeply rooted in the American mind. Yet it took more than a century for that illusion to crowd out the older notion that international politics is an unending struggle for power in which the interests of individual nations must necessarily be defined in terms of power. Out of the struggle between these two opposing conceptions, three types of American foreign policy have emerged: the realistic—thinking and acting in terms of power—represented by Alexander Hamilton; the ideological—thinking in terms of moral principles but acting in terms of power—represented by Thomas Jefferson and John Quincy Adams; and the moralistic—thinking and acting in terms of moral principles—represented by Woodrow Wilson. To these three types, three periods of American foreign policy roughly correspond, the first covering the first decade of the history of the United States as an independent nation, the second covering the nineteenth century to the Spanish-American War, and the third covering the half century after that war. This division of the history of American foreign policy—as will become obvious in our discussion—refers only to prevailing tendencies, without precluding the operation side by side of different tendencies in the same period.

It illustrates both the depth of the moralistic illusion and the original strength of the opposition to it that the issue between these two opposing conceptions of foreign policy was joined at the very beginning of the history of the United States, was decided in favor of the realistic position, and was formulated with unsurpassed simplicity and penetration by Alexander Hamilton. The memorable occasion was Washington's proclamation of neutrality in the War of the First Coalition against revolutionary France.

In 1792, the War of the First Coalition had ranged Austria, Prussia, Sardinia, Great Britain, and the United Netherlands against revolutionary France, which was tied to the United States by a treaty of alliance. On April 22, 1793, Washington issued a proclamation of neutrality, and it was in defense of that proclamation that Hamilton wrote the "Pacificus" and "Americanus" articles. Among the arguments directed against the proclamation were three derived from moral principles. Faithfulness to treaty obligations, gratitude toward a country that had lent its assistance to the colonies in their struggle for independence, and the affinity of republican institutions, were cited to prove that the United States must side with France. Against these moral principles, Hamilton invoked the national interest of the United States:

> There would be no proportion between the mischiefs and perils to which the United States would expose themselves, by embarking in the war, and the benefit which the nature of their stipulation aims at securing to France, or that which it would be in their power actually to render her by becoming a party.
>
> This disproportion would be a valid reason for not executing the guaranty. All contracts are to receive a reasonable construction. Self-preservation is the first duty of a nation; and though in the performance of stipulations relating to war, good faith requires that its ordinary hazards should be fairly met, because they are directly contemplated by such stipulations, yet it does not require that extraordinary and extreme hazards should be run. [Hamilton argues that we should not enter the war out of gratitude for past favors from France.]
>
> Indeed, the rule of morality in this respect is not precisely the same between nations as between individuals. The duty of making its own wel-

fare the guide of its actions, is much stronger upon the former than upon the latter; in proportion to the greater magnitude and importance of national compared with individual happiness, and to the greater permanency of the effects of national than of individual conduct. Existing millions, and for the most part future generations, are concerned in the present measures of a government; while the consequences of the private actions of an individual ordinarily terminate with himself, or are circumscribed within a narrow compass.

.   .   .

An examination into the question how far *regard to the cause of Liberty* ought to induce the United States to take part with France in the present war, is rendered necessary by the efforts which are making to establish an opinion, that it ought to have that effect. In order to a right judgment on the point, it is requisite to consider the question under two aspects.

I. Whether the cause of France be truly the cause of Liberty, pursued with justice and humanity, and in a manner likely to crown it with honorable success.

II. Whether the degree of service we could render, by participating in the conflict, was likely to compensate, by its utility to the cause, the evils which would probably flow from it to ourselves.

If either of these questions can be answered in the negative, it will result, that the consideration which has been stated ought not to embark us in the war. . . .

The certain evils of our joining France in the war, are sufficient dissuasives from so intemperate a measure. The possible ones are of a nature to call for all our caution, all our prudence.

To defend its own rights, to vindicate its own honor, there are occasions when a nation ought to hazard even its existence. Should such an occasion occur, I trust those who are most averse to commit the peace of the country, will not be the last to face the danger, nor the first to turn their backs upon it.

But let us at least have the consolation of not having rashly courted misfortune. Let us have to act under the animating reflection of being engaged in repelling wrongs, which we neither sought nor merited; in vindicating our rights, invaded without provocation; in defending our honor, violated without cause. Let us not have to reproach ourselves with having voluntarily bartered blessings for calamities.

But we are told that our own liberty is at stake upon the event of the war against France—that if she falls, we shall be the next victim. The combined powers, it is said, will never forgive in us the origination of those principles which were the germs of the French revolution. They will endeavor to eradicate them from the world.

If this suggestion were ever so well founded, it would perhaps be a sufficient answer to it to say, that our interference is not likely to alter the case; that it would only serve prematurely to exhaust our strength.

Must a nation subordinate its security, its happiness, nay, its very existence to the respect for treaty obligations, to the sentiment of gratitude, to sympathy with a kindred political system? This was the question Hamilton proposed to answer, and his answer was an unequivocal "no." To the issues raised by the opposition to Washington's proclamation of neutrality Hamilton unswervingly applied one standard: the national interest of the United States. He put the legalistic and moralistic arguments of the opposition, represented by Madison under the pseudonym "Helvidius," into the context of the concrete power-situation in which the United States found itself on the international scene, and asked: If the United States were to join France against virtually all of Europe, what risks would the United States run, what advantages could it expect, what good could it do to its ally?

The Ideological Period

Considerations such as these, recognized for what they were, guided American foreign policy for but a short period; that is, as long as the Federalists were in power. *The Federalist* and Washington's Farewell Address are their classic expression. Yet we have seen that these considerations, not recognized for what they were or even rejected, have determined the great objectives of American foreign policy to this day. During the century following their brief flowering, their influence has persisted, under the cover of those moral principles with which from Jefferson onward American statesmen have liked to justify their moves on the international scene. Thus this second period witnessed a discrepancy between political thought and political action, yet a coincidence in the intended results of both. What was said of Gladstone could also have been said of Jefferson, John Quincy Adams, Grover Cleveland, Theodore Roosevelt, the war policies of Wilson and of Franklin D. Roosevelt: what the moral law demanded was by a felicitous coincidence always identical with what the national interest seemed to require. Political thought and political action moved on different planes, which, however, inclined to merge in the end.

John Quincy Adams is the classic example of the political moralist in thought and word, who cannot help being a political realist in action. Yet even in Jefferson, whose dedication to abstract morality was much stronger and whose realist touch in foreign affairs was much less sure, the moral pretense yielded often, especially in private utterance, to the impact of the national interest upon native good sense.

Thus during the concluding decade of the Napoleonic Wars Jefferson's thought on international affairs was a reflection of the ever changing distribution of power in the world rather than of immutable moral principles. In 1806, he favored "an English ascendancy on the ocean" as being "safer for us than that of France." In 1807, he was by the logic of events forced to admit:

I never expected to be under the necessity of wishing success to Buonaparte. But the English being equally tyrannical at sea as he is on land, & that tyranny bearing on us in every point of either honor or interest, I say "down with England" and as for what Buonaparte is then to do to us, let us trust to the chapter of accidents. I cannot, with the Anglomen, prefer a certain present evil to a future hypothetical one.

However, in 1812, when Napoleon was at the pinnacle of his power, Jefferson hoped for the restoration of the balance. Speaking of England, he said:

It is for the general interest that she should be a sensible and independent weight in the scale of nations, and be able to contribute, when a favorable moment presents itself, to reduce under the same order, her great rival in flagitiousness. We especially ought to pray that the powers of Europe may be so poised and counterpoised among themselves, that their own security may require the presence of all their forces at home, leaving the other quarters of the globe in undisturbed tranquility.

In 1814, again compelled by the logic of events, he came clearly out against Napoleon and in favor of a balance of power which would leave the power of Napoleon and of England limited, but intact.

Surely none of us wish to see Bonaparte conquer Russia, and lay thus at his feet the whole continent of Europe. This done, England would be but a breakfast; and, although I am free from the visionary fears which the votaries of England have effected to entertain, because I believe he cannot effect the conquest of Europe; yet put all Europe into his hands, and he might spare such a force to be sent in British ships, as I would as leave not have to encounter, when I see how much trouble a handful of British soldiers in Canada has given us. No. It cannot be to our interest that all Europe should be reduced to a single monarchy. The true line of interest for us, is, that Bonaparte should be able to effect the complete exclusion of England from the whole continent of Europe, in order, as the same letter said, "by this peaceable engine of constraint, to make her renounce her views of dominion over the ocean, of permitting no other nation to navigate it but with her license, and on tribute to her, and her aggressions on the persons of our citizens who may choose to exercise their right of passing over that element." And this would be effected by Bonaparte's succeeding so far as to close the Baltic against her. This success I wished him the last year, this I wish him this year; but were he again advanced to Moscow, I should again wish him such disasters as would prevent his reaching Petersburg. And were the consequences even to be the longer continuance of our war, I would rather meet them than see the whole force of Europe wielded by a single hand.

Similarly, in 1815, Jefferson wrote:

For my part, I wish that all nations may recover and retain their independence; that those which are overgrown may not advance beyond safe measures of power, that a salutary balance may be ever maintained among nations, and that our peace, commerce, and friendship, may be sought and cultivated by all.

It was only when, after 1815, the danger to the balance of power seemed to have passed that Jefferson allowed himself again to indulge in the cultivation of moral principles divorced from political exigencies.

From this tendency, to which Jefferson only too readily yielded, John Quincy Adams was well-nigh immune. We are here in the presence of a statesman who had been reared in the realist tradition of the first period of American foreign policy, who had done the better part of his work of statecraft in an atmosphere saturated with Jeffersonian principles, and who had achieved the merger of these two elements of his experience into a harmonious whole. Between John Quincy Adams's moral principles and the traditional interest of the United States there was hardly ever a conflict. The moral principles were nothing but the political interests formulated in moral terms, and vice versa. They fit the interests as a glove fits the hand. Adams's great contributions to the tradition of American foreign policy—freedom of the seas, the Monroe Doctrine, and Manifest Destiny—are witness to this achievement.

In the hands of Adams, the legal and moral principle of the freedom of the seas was a weapon, as it had been two centuries earlier when Grotius wielded it on behalf of the Low Countries, through which an inferior naval power endeavored to safeguard its independence against Great Britain, the mistress of the seas. The Monroe Doctrine's moral postulates of anti-imperialism and mutual non-intervention were the negative conditions for the safety and enduring greatness of the United States. Their fulfillment secured the isolation of the United States from the power struggles of Europe and, through it, the continuing predominance of the United States in the Western Hemisphere. Manifest Destiny was the moral justification as well as the moral incentive for the westward expansion of the United States, the peculiar American way—foreordained by the objective conditions of American existence—of founding an empire, the "American Empire," as one of the contemporary opponents of Adams's policies put it.

The Utopian Period

Jefferson and John Quincy Adams stand at the beginning of the second period of American thought on foreign policy, both its most eminent representatives and the heirs of a realist tradition that continued to mold political action, while it had largely ceased to influence political thought. At the beginning of the third period, McKinley leads the United States as a great world power beyond the confines of the Western Hemisphere, ignorant of the bearing of this step upon the national interest, and guided by moral principles completely divorced from the national interest. When at the end of the Spanish-American War the status of the Philippines had to be determined, McKinley expected and found no guidance in the traditional national interests of the United States. According to his own testimony, he knelt beside his bed in prayer, and in the wee hours of the morning he heard the voice of God telling him—as was to be expected—to annex the Philippines.

This period initiated by McKinley, in which moral principles no longer justify the enduring national interest as in the second, but replace it as a guide for action, finds its fulfillment in the political thought of Woodrow Wilson. Wilson's thought not only disregards the national interest, but is explicitly opposed to it on moral grounds. "It is a very perilous thing," he said in his address at Mobile on October 27, 1913,

to determine the foreign policy of a nation in the terms of material interest. It not only is unfair to those with whom you are dealing, but it is degrading as regards your own actions. . . . We dare not turn from the principle that morality and not expediency is the thing that must guide us, and that we will never condone iniquity because it is most convenient to do so. . . .

Yet in his political actions, especially under the pressure of the First World War, Wilson could not discount completely the national interest of the United States, any more than could Jefferson before him. Wilson's case, however, was different from Jefferson's in two respects. For one thing, Wilson was never able, even when the national interest of the United States was directly menaced, to conceive of the danger in other than moral terms. It was only the objective force of the national interest, which no rational man could escape, that imposed the source of America's mortal danger upon him as the object of his moral indignation. Thus Wilson in 1917 led the United States into war against Germany for the same reasons, only half-known to himself, for which Jefferson had wished and worked alternately for the victory of England and France. Germany threatened the balance of power in Europe, and it was in order to remove that threat—and not to make the world safe for democracy—that the United States put its weight into the Allies' scale. Wilson pursued the right policy, but he pursued it for the wrong reasons.

Not only, however, did Wilson's crusading fervor obliterate awareness of the traditional interest of the United States in maintaining the European balance of power, to be accomplished through the defeat of Germany; it also had politically disastrous effects, for which there is no precedent in the history of the United States. Wilson's moral objective required the destruction of the Kaiser's autocracy, and this happened also to be required by the political interests of the United States. The political interests of the United States required, beyond this immediate objective of total victory, the restoration of the European balance of power, traditional guarantor of American security. Yet it was in indignation at the moral deficiencies of that very balance of power, "forever discredited," as he thought, that Wilson had asked the American people to take up arms against the Central Powers! Once military victory had put an end to the immediate threat to American security, the very logic of his moral position —let us remember that consistency is the moralist's supreme virtue—drove him toward substituting for the concrete national interest of the United States the general postulate of a brave new world where the national interest of the United States, as that of all other nations, would disappear in a community of interests comprising mankind.

Consequently, Wilson considered it to be the purpose of victory not to restore a new, viable balance of power, but to put an end to the balance of power once and forever. "You know," he told the English people at Manchester on December 30, 1918, that the United States has always felt from the very beginning of her history that she must keep herself separate from any kind of connection with European politics, and I want to say very frankly to you that she is not now interested in European politics. But she is interested in the partnership of right between America and Europe. If the future had nothing for us but a new attempt to keep the world at a right poise by a balance of power, the United States would take no interest, because she will join no combination of power which is not the combination of all of us. She is not interested merely in the peace of Europe, but in the peace of the world.

Faced with the national interests of the great Allied powers, Wilson had nothing to oppose or support them with but his moral principles, with the result that the neglect of the American national interest was not compensated for by the triumph of political morality. In the end Wilson had to consent to a series of uneasy compromises, which were a betrayal of his moral principles —for principles can, by their very nature, not be made the object of compromise—and which satisfied nobody's national aspirations. These compromises had no relation at all to the traditional American national interest in a viable European balance of power. Thus Wilson returned from Versailles a compromised idealist, an empty-handed statesman, a discredited ally. In that triple failure lies the tragedy not only of Wilson, a great yet misguided man, but of Wilsonianism as a political doctrine.

Yet Wilson returned unaware of his failure. He offered the American people what he had offered the Allied nations at Paris: moral principles divorced from political reality. "The day we have left behind us," he proclaimed at Los Angeles on September 20, 1919,

was a day of balances of power. It was a day of "every nation take care of itself or make a partnership with some other nation or group of nations to hold the peace of the world steady or to dominate the weaker portions of the world." Those were the days of alliances. This project of the League of Nations is a great process of disentanglement.

WILSONIANISM, ISOLATIONISM, INTERNATIONALISM— THREE FORMS OF UTOPIANISM

Whereas before Paris and Versailles these moral principles rang true with the promise of a new and better world, afterwards they must have sounded rather hollow and platitudinous to many. Yet what is significant for the course American foreign policy was to

take in the interwar years is not so much that the American people rejected Wilsonianism, but that they rejected it by ratifying
the denial of the American tradition of foreign policy which was
implicit in the political thought of Wilson. We are here indeed
dealing with a tragedy not of one man, but of a political doctrine
and, as far as the United States is concerned, of a political tradition. The isolationism of the interwar period could delude itself
into believing that it was but the restorer of the early realistic
tradition of American foreign policy. Did it not, like that tradition,
proclaim the self-sufficiency of the United States within the Western Hemisphere? Did it not, like that tradition, refuse to become
involved in the rivalries of European nations? The isolationists of
the twenties and thirties did not see—and this was the very essence of the policies of the Founding Fathers—that both the isolated and the preponderant position of the United States in the
Western Hemisphere was not a fact of nature, and that the freedom from entanglements in European conflicts was not the result
of mere abstention on the part of the United States. Both benefits
were the result of political conditions outside the Western Hemisphere and of policies carefully contrived and purposefully executed in their support. For the realists of the first period, isolation
was an objective of policy, and had to be striven for to be
attained. For the isolationists of the interwar period, isolation was
a natural state, and only needed to be left undisturbed in order
to continue forever. Conceived in such terms, it was the very ne-
gation of foreign policy.

Isolationism, then, is in its way as oblivious to political reality
as is Wilsonianism—the internationalist challenge, to which it
thought to have found the American answer. In consequence,
they are both strangers not only to the first, realistic phase of
American foreign policy, but to its whole tradition. Both refused
to face political reality either in realistic or ideological terms.
They refused to face it at all. Thus isolationism and Wilsonianism
have more in common than their historic enmity would lead one
to suspect. In a profound sense they are brothers under the skin.
Both are one in maintaining that the United States has no interest in any particular political and military configuration outside
the Western Hemisphere. While isolationism stops here, Wilsonianism asserts that the American national interest is not somewhere in particular, but everywhere, being identical with the interests of mankind itself. Both refuse to concern themselves with
the concrete issues upon which the national interest must be as-

serted. Isolationism stops short of them, Wilsonianism soars beyond them. Both have but a negative relation to the national interest of the United States outside the Western Hemisphere. They
are unaware of its very existence. This being so, both substitute
abstract moral principles for the guidance of the national interest, derived from the actual conditions of American existence.
Wilsonianism applies the illusory expectations of liberal reform to
the whole world, isolationism empties of all concrete political
content the realistic political principle of isolation and transforms
it into the unattainable parochial ideal of automatic separation.

In view of this inner affinity between isolationism and Wilsonianism, it is not surprising that the great debate of the twenties
and thirties between internationalism and isolationism was carried on primarily in moral terms. Was there a moral obligation for
the United States to make its contribution to world peace by joining the League of Nations and the World Court? Was it morally
incumbent upon the United States, as a democracy, to oppose
Fascism in Europe and to uphold international law in Asia? Such
were the questions raised in that debate, and the answers depended upon the moral position taken. The question central to
the national interest of the United States, that of the balance of
power in Europe and Asia, was hardly ever faced squarely, and
when it was faced it was dismissed on moral grounds. Mr. Cordell Hull, Secretary of State of the United States from 1933 to
1944, and one of the most respected spokesmen of internationalism, summarizes in his *Memoirs* his attitude toward this central
problem of American foreign policy:

> I was not, and am not, a believer in the idea of balance of power or
> spheres of influence as a means of keeping the peace. During the First
> World War I had made an intensive study of the system of spheres of in-
> fluence and balance of power, and I was grounded to the taproots in
> their iniquitous consequences. The conclusions I then formed in total op-
> position to this system stayed with me.

When internationalism triumphed in the late thirties, it did so in
the moral terms of Wilsonianism. That in this instance the moral
postulates inspiring the administration of Franklin D. Roosevelt
happened to coincide with the exigencies of the American national interest was again, as in the case of Jefferson and of the
Wilson of 1917, due to the impact of a national emergency upon
innate common sense, and to the strength of a national tradition
that holds in its spell the actions of even those who deny its va-

lidity in words. However, as soon as the minds of the American leaders, freed from these inescapable pressures of a primarily military nature, turned toward the political problems of the Second World War and its aftermath, they thought and acted again as Wilson had acted under similar circumstances. That is to say, they thought and acted in moral terms, divorced from the political conditions of America's existence.

The practical results of this philosophy of international affairs, as applied to the political problems of the war and postwar period, were therefore bound to be quite similar to those which had made the Allied victory in the First World War politically meaningless. Conceived as it was as a "crusade"—to borrow from the title of General Eisenhower's book—against the evil incarnate in the Axis powers, the purpose of the Second World War could only be the destruction of that evil, brought about through the instrumentality of "unconditional surrender." Since the threat to the Western world emanating from the Axis was conceived primarily in moral terms, it was easy to imagine that all conceivable danger was concentrated in that historic constellation of hostile powers and that with its destruction political evil itself would disappear from the world. Beyond "unconditional surrender" there was to be, then, a brave new world after the model of Wilson's, which would liquidate the heritage of the defeated nations—evil and not "peace-loving"—and establish an order of things where war, aggressiveness, and the struggle for power itself would be no more. Thus Mr. Cordell Hull could declare on his return in 1943 from the Moscow conference that the new international organization would mean the end of power politics and usher in a new era of international collaboration. Three years later, Mr. Philip Noel-Baker, then British Minister of State, echoed Mr. Hull by stating in the House of Commons that the British government was "determined to use the institutions of the United Nations to kill power politics, in order that by the methods of democracy, the will of the people shall prevail."

With this philosophy dominant in the West—Mr. Churchill provides almost the sole, however ineffective, exception—the strategy of the war and of the peace to follow could not help being oblivious to those considerations of the national interest which the great statesmen of the West, from Hamilton through Castlereagh, Canning, and John Quincy Adams, to Disraeli and Salisbury, had brought to bear upon the international problems of their day. War was no longer regarded as a means to a political end. The only end the war was to serve was total victory, which is another way of saying that the war became an end in itself. Hence, it became irrelevant how the war was won politically, as long as it was won speedily, cheaply, and totally. The thought that the war might be waged in view of a new balance of power to be established after the war, occurred in the West only to Winston Churchill—and, of course, it occurred to Joseph Stalin. The national interest of the Western nations was, then, satisfied in so far as it required the destruction of the threat to the balance of power emanating from Germany and Japan; for to that extent the moral purposes of the war happened to coincide with the national interest. However, the national interest of the Western nations was jeopardized in so far as their security required the creation of a new viable balance of power after the war.

How could statesmen who boasted that they were not "believers in the idea of balance of power"—like a scientist not believing in the law of gravity—and who were out "to kill power politics," understand the very idea of the national interest which demanded, above all, protection from the power of others? Thus it was with deep and sincere moral indignation that the Western world, expecting a utopia without power politics, found itself confronted with a new and more formidable threat to its security as soon as the old one had been subdued. There was good reason for moral indignation, however misdirected it was. That a new balance of power will rise out of the ruins of an old balance and that nations with political sense will avail themselves of the opportunity to improve their position within it, is a law of politics for whose validity nobody is to blame. Yet they are indeed blameworthy who in their moralistic disdain for the laws of politics endanger the interests of the nations in their care.

The Overall Perspective

Radical

Radical historians see American diplomatic history in a very different light than do Realists. They believe that American foreign policy, far from being too idealistic, has been realistic and self-interested to the point of rapaciousness. The United States, they claim, has always been an aggressive, expansionist, and imperialist power. Like all capitalist countries, it has required expansion abroad to prevent economic stagnation at home and a consequent move by the American people for a revolutionary redistribution of the nation's wealth. At times the American people themselves have supported expansion for their own economic benefit. At other times they have been enlisted in aggressive expansionist crusades by a power elite that convinced them that their security and democratic ideals were at stake. Actually, of course, this power elite was seeking new markets and resources to benefit itself. In both cases, the result has been an aggressive, imperialist, realistic foreign policy from the time of the nation's founding to the present day.

Until the twentieth century, America's expansion was primarily intracontinental. Its victims were Indians, Spaniards, and Mexicans. As the frontier dwindled, the United States placed new emphasis on overseas markets. The Old Left, represented by socialists like Scott Nearing, expected the United States to conquer foreign nations to provide these markets. The New Left, however, argues that the United States has developed a "new imperialism." America dominates foreign markets through its economic power, intervening militarily only when revolutionaries threaten to overturn the pliable governments that welcome American trade and capital.

According to Radical historians, the United States has become the chief antirevolutionary and antiprogressive power in the world. The nation's policy, they believe, must be reversed if the poorer peoples of the world are ever to have a chance for prosperity and democracy. Radical historians argue that this reversal can take place only if the United States provides an "open door at home" (Charles A. Beard's phrase). Economic expansion could be produced by redistributing the nation's wealth, providing the lower classes with greatly enhanced purchasing power. Increased demand would bring increased production, and America's prosperity would no longer depend on ever-expanding overseas markets. This would eliminate the major motive for imperialism and war and set the stage for a cooperative, peaceful, and progressive American foreign policy.

The origins of this interpretation of American diplomatic history lie, of course, with Marx and Lenin. J. A. Hobson, a turn-of-the-century English economist and historian, has also been extremely influential. The most important American historians subscribing to this view have been associated with the University of Wisconsin: older historians such as Charles A. Beard and Fred Harvey Harrington and younger men who have been

*students or friends of William Appleman Williams. These younger histori-
ans, many of whom are just coming to prominence, include Gar Alpero-
witz, Walter LaFeber, Lloyd Gardner, Gabriel Kolko, and Thomas McCormick.*

*A general history of America's past imperialism and a prescription for
its correction are described in the following essay by William Appleman
Williams. For many years, Williams's writings were all but ignored by the
historical profession. But his work, and that of the younger historians he
has influenced, is now making its way into the mainstream of historical
publication. The war in Vietnam and the rise of the New Left have obviously been major factors in bringing about renewed interest in the Radical view of American diplomatic history. Doctor Williams is now a professor of history at Oregon State University.*

The Great Evasion

William Appleman Williams

Marx never prepared a separate, formal study of capitalist foreign relations, and no one has ever collected his scattered discussions of the subject into one co-ordinated volume. V. I. Lenin's famous essay on *Imperialism* is a significant document in its
own idiom, but it has little value as a basis for evaluating Marx.
The same is true of the neglected study by Nikolai Bukharin, *Imperialism and World Economy,* although it provides a somewhat
better outline of Marx's own ideas. It seems wise, therefore, to
review the main elements of Marx's analysis as he offered it in
his own studies of capitalism.

One of the central features of capitalism, Marx argued, was its
splitting of the economy into two principal parts. This "cleavage
between town and country" was not complete, of course, but the

Reprinted by permission of Quadrangle Books from *The Great Evasion* by William Appleman Williams, pp. 31–50, 51. Copyright © 1964 by William Appleman
Williams.

reciprocal relationship between them was heavily imbalanced in favor of the town, or Metropolitan, sector. Marx was here following Adam Smith, the master theorist of capitalism, as well as the facts he gathered in his own study of the system. This was one of the most important instances in which the theory and the practice of capitalism coincided.

Another such example involved the continued expansion of the marketplace, first within a country and then beyond its boundaries. The never-ending necessity to accumulate additional surplus value, or capital, a process which was essential for the system as well as to the individual businessman, meant that this market "must, therefore, be continually extended." Without such expansion the economic system would stagnate at a certain level of activity, and the political and social system based upon it would suffer severe strains leading either to a caste society upheld by force or to revolution. Hence "the real task of bourgeois society," Marx explained, "is the establishment of the world market . . . and a productive system based on this foundation."

As it crossed the national boundary, this process transformed "the cleavage between town and country" into "the colonial system." The town became the developed, industrial Metropolis, while the country became the backward, underdeveloped society. It follows both logically and from the evidence that the periodic crises created and suffered by capitalism intensified the drive to expand the market. "The conquest of new markets and the more thorough exploitation of the old ones," Marx pointed out, served as the principal means whereby the internal crisis in the Metropolis "seeks to balance itself."

Concerning both the normal and the crisis situations, Marx was typically succinct and non-euphemistic in describing the central feature of this expansion of the marketplace. "The favored country recovers more labor in exchange for less labor." It is worth re-emphasizing, moreover, that Adam Smith reached the identical conclusion, and based his entire theory and strategy of capitalist success on this essentially imbalanced relationship between the Metropolis and the country society.

Such expansion of the marketplace is directly and explicitly relevant to an understanding of American foreign relations. It offers, to begin with, a good many insights into the major periods of American diplomacy. The first of these eras began in the middle of the eighteenth century and culminated in the 1820's. The increasing British efforts after 1750 to control and limit the exist-

ing American marketplace, its further agrarian expansion westward, and its increasing share in international trade, led to a
confrontation with the colonists that lies at the heart of the American Revolution.

Similar British attempts to restrict American territorial expansion after independence had been won, and to set limits upon
America's international trade (which antagonized the surplus-pro-
ducing farmers as well as other groups), promoted and accelerated and intensified the nationalism which led to the War of 1812.
And the American push into the Floridas, and into the trans-Mississippi region, was obviously expansionist in origin and purpose.
The vision of a great trade with South America and Asia, while
not as central to these movements as the concern for land, was
nevertheless a significant part of the continuing pressure to expand the marketplace that culminated in the Trans-Continental
Treaty of 1819 with Spain.

Throughout this period, moreover, the same underlying thrust
to expand the marketplace defined the basic character of American policy toward the Indians. The drive to dispossess the natives of their land, and the campaign to remove all restrictions on
trade with the various tribes, combined to drive the Indians further westward while at the same time subverting any efforts to
integrate them as full citizens into the white man's society and
weakening their ability to resist further encroachments.

In a similar way, Marx's emphasis on the expansion of the marketplace offers major—and in many respects still unexploited—
perceptions concerning the struggle between various elements of
the country during the 1840's and 1850's to organize the marketplace along one of three alternate axes: a North-South, a
South-West, or a North-West alliance. The psychology of fear that
became so apparent in all sections of the nation on the eve of
the Civil War, for example, is directly related to this increasingly
intense conflict.

Farmers in the region north of the Ohio River not only manifested an active desire to control the national government and
the Western territories for their own benefit, but developed a corresponding antagonism toward other groups and regions which
appeared to be blocking their attempts to win that predominance.
Southerners expressed similar hopes and fears, as did still other
groups in the Northeastern part of the country. As the economic
integration between the Northeastern "town" and the food-pro-
ducing Northwestern "country" became stronger than an earlier

relationship between the Eastern Metropolis and the Southern raw material producing "country," Southerners increasingly defined themselves as members of a potentially independent system sustained and strengthened through connections with non-American Metropolitan areas.

The formerly regional conflicts thus gradually changed into a struggle between two giant sections over the issue of which was to control the trans-Mississippi West. Both blocs viewed that area as what today would be called an underdeveloped, potentially neocolonial resource that would guarantee their respective prosperity and security. At bottom, both sections viewed slavery as an economic phenomenon that would determine the outcome of the marketplace struggle for final victory. Ultimately, of course, slavery became both a symbol of that conflict and a moral and ideological banner for both sides. If slavery be said to have caused the Civil War, however, it must also be said that it did so more in its economic sense than in its moral respect. For the general response to the abolitionist minority (both positive and negative) was grounded in the economic fears of Northerners and Southerners who saw themselves first of all as combatants in a desperate struggle to control the continental marketplace.

The postwar conflicts between the Eastern Metropolis and the Southern and Western agrarian sectors of the economy can most fruitfully be approached as a clear illustration of the validity of the emphasis placed on "the cleavage between town and country" by Smith and Marx. This provides by far the most accurate guideline to any understanding and interpretation of the Granger, Alliance, and Populist movements. Even a viable psychological interpretation of these protest movements must be grounded upon such a structural analysis.

The general drive to expand the marketplace during these same years of the late nineteenth century provided the primary energy for the American economic move outward into Europe, Africa, Latin America, and Asia. That expansion has been sustained and intensified in the twentieth century. Nobody but Americans thrust world power upon the United States. It came as a direct result of this determined push into the world marketplace. John D. Rockefeller's comment on the policy of Standard Oil typifies the attitude of both centuries. "Dependent solely upon local business," he explained in 1899, "we should have failed years ago. We were forced to extend our markets and to seek for export trade."

Since the farmer was a capitalist entrepreneur (a vital consideration often neglected or discounted in narrowly psychological interpretations of his behavior), Marx's analysis provides an insight into the policies and actions of the agrarians that most commentators have overlooked. If Marx is correct, that is, then the evidence ought to reveal the farmers participating in the expansionist movement as their production outran domestic consumption. The documents show precisely that: the American farmer's concern with overseas markets played a significant part in initiating and sustaining the momentum of the idea and the practice of such expansion.

Beginning in the early 1880's, the farmers' turn to export markets led directly to diplomatic encounters with England, France, Austria-Hungary, and Germany. It also prompted specific urban business interests, such as the railroads, the flour millers, the meat packers, and the implement manufacturers, to follow the lead of the farmers and undertake their own expansionist efforts. And, more generally, urban business leaders increasingly looked to agricultural export figures as a reliable index of general economic activity.

Politicians likewise responded, and the campaign for reciprocity treaties drew almost as much support from certain agrarian groups (as with Secretary of State James G. Blaine's efforts in 1890 to win reciprocity agreements with Cuba and other food-importing nations) as from the manufacturers. This involvement in the world marketplace also played a central role in the agrarian campaign for unlimited coinage of silver at a ratio of 16 to 1. The farmers, and their leaders like William Jennings Bryan, argued that free coinage would free America from economic control by Great Britain and other European powers and give the United States economic supremacy in the world marketplace. This militant and expansive economic nationalism, which stemmed directly from the experience of the farmers in having to deal through Liverpool and London, not only provided a surprising amount of support for building a new and big navy and taking Hawaii, but was a very significant factor in the coming of the Spanish-American War.

Marx's particular emphasis on foreign policy as a way to generate recovery in the context of economic crisis is also verified by American behavior. The trans-Appalachian depression that developed between 1808 and 1811, and which hit the farmers hard, had a direct causative connection with the agitation that elected the War Hawks and led to the War of 1812. Expansion into Mexico began in the downturn after the War of 1812, and matured into an imperial clash ultimately involving war during the panics and the depression of the late 1830's. The same pattern appears in the late 1860's and the 1870's, though it is somewhat camouflaged by taking the form, at least primarily, of the North's extension of its economic control over the South and the West.

Americans again began to react more explicitly and generally to depressions by turning to economic expansion during the business troubles of the 1880's, a decade when surplus production began to pose a problem in some industries as well as in agriculture. This response crystallized during the panic and depression of the 1890's and prompted the appearance of a good many general theories about the necessity of such expansion. Such ideas played a double role: they served as an explanation of what was happening, and they offered a solution for the difficulties of the system. As a result, they were a primary causative force in the imperial expansion of the period.

This emphasis on overseas economic expansion, through both exports and investments, was an integral part of the New Deal program for recovery from the Great Depression. And it was the central theme of the discussions during 1943–1945 concerning the best way to handle the depression that was expected to develop at the end of World War II. The same approach has been increasingly emphasized during the series of postwar recessions. The New Frontier's stress on the expansion of exports and the creation of regional markets tied to the American system is candidly explained and defended as a solution for the specific difficulties of the domestic economy and the more general problems incident to the breakdown of the nineteenth-century imperial system.

Marx recognized and understood that the imperial relationship that evolved out of such economic expansion could take several forms. One of these is colonialism, which involves the seizure or conquest of empty, or lightly populated, real estate and the subsequent transfer of other people into the new area. It is accompanied by direct and extensive controls over the new society, as well as over the displaced or conquered population. Americans take great pride, of course, in denying any colonial blemish upon their historical record. This case is debatable even if colonialism is defined or thought of, as it usually is by Americans, as involving action across the open sea.

But there is no serious justification for making the crossing of water a necessary condition of colonialism. The essential definition is the control of territory and resources, and the displacement, re-establishment, and control of human beings. American policy toward the Indian, and toward the Negro from 1650 to 1863, certainly satisfies those criteria and therefore belies the assertion that the United States has never been a colonial power. It is customary and accurate to talk about the Negro during those years as a slave, but slavery is only the most extreme form of colonial exploitation. In any event, the Negro was transported across the sea in the course of being colonized.

There was also a significant degree of colonialism involved in the economic and political controls exercised by the American Metropolis over the Western territories. Jefferson's attitude toward the non-English settlers in the region acquired through the Louisiana Purchase is symbolic, not only of the discrepancy between his rhetoric and his policy, but also of the general attitude of the East toward the new settlements across the mountains. The foreigners could acquiesce or leave, Jefferson announced; otherwise force would be used against them.

The process by which the settlements beyond the Appalachians were ultimately accepted as full members of the federal commonwealth does not offer as great an exception to the usual colonial pattern as latter-day Americans are inclined to assume. For one thing, the final agreement to admit such areas as states was not achieved without overt resistance by the territories against being treated as colonies. The agitation of the 1780's, for example, had a great deal to do with overcoming Easterners who wanted to handle the trans-Appalachian region as a colony in the traditional British manner.

In the final plan, moreover, the Metropolis was given many explicit controls over a territory until it was admitted as a state, and these opened the way for outsiders to establish their power and authority in less formal ways. It often took a generation (if not longer) for the new state to break free of the resulting institutionalized influence. Nor was statehood granted by the Metropolis with any noticeable dispatch. After the Civil War, for example, only two territories (Nebraska and Colorado) gained legal equality during a period of twenty-four years. As might be imagined, this artificial and protracted delay reinforced and intensified other causes involved in the West's antagonism and resistance toward outsiders.

A second kind of imperial relationship that Marx recognized and discussed is the form of administrative colonialism evolved by the British in India during and after the 1850's. This pattern is characterized by the effective control by an outside minority, through force and the threat of force, of alien territory and population, and by its concurrent establishment of economic predominance. It does not involve, as with colonialism per se, the large-scale transfer of population under the direction and control of the Metropolis. There is emigration from the Metropolis, but it is strictly limited both in numbers and direct function. Its object is to provide a military force in being in support of the leadership necessary for the effective control and management of the political economy of the subject society. The emigrants thus comprise an absolute and a relatively small group of army and naval personnel, political administrators, and economic directors. The success of the system, and of the agents of the Metropolis, is measured by the degree to which absentee control of crucial decisions is institutionalized within a framework of native self-government in local affairs, and routinely maintained domestic political and social peace.

American administrative colonialism appears most classically in the cases of Cuba and the Philippines. All the features of the system were apparent: the colony's own internal cleavage between town and country, its imbalanced, limited, and skewed development, and the improvement purchased at the price of drastic costs in human and material resources, and in harmful consequences to the social fabric itself. The same pattern, with variations appropriate to the circumstances, has emerged in American relations with Liberia and many Latin-American countries, such as Nicaragua and Guatemala. And the current American relationships with Okinawa, South Korea, and Vietnam follow the main outlines of such administrative colonial empire.

The third principal form of the imperial relationship emerges in the evolution of the inherent nature of the marketplace connection between a Metropolis and a backward, underdeveloped region or society. It arises out of the imbalance between the two societies which produces the situation so aptly described by Adam Smith: "The revenue of a trading and manufacturing country must, other things being equal, always be much greater than that of one without trade or manufactures. . . . A country without trade and manufactures is generally obliged to purchase, at the expense of a great part of its rude produce, a very small part of

the manufactured produce of other countries." Or as described
by Karl Marx: "The favored country recovers more labor in exchange for less labor." Or, to phrase it in the language of our
own time, the price received by the underdeveloped country for
its goods and services does not suffice to pay for the goods and
services it requires to initiate and sustain its own development.
For that matter, in many cases the prices set by the Metropolis
for such goods decline so much that the loss to the underdeveloped country is not even made up by grants or loans provided by
the Metropolis.

Even under the most favorable circumstances, therefore, the
gap between the rich and the poor remains constant or de-
creases only in tiny and sporadic increments. At worst (and more
usually), the increases take the form of creeping impoverishment
in the poorer nation. Or, as Marx put it, in a kind of increasing
misery and increasing proletarianization. It is essential to realize
that, whatever the evidence indicates as to increasing misery
within the Metropolis, the facts of the world capitalist marketplace support Marx's analysis. He was correct. The poor are
poorer and more miserable.

While force is periodically employed, and formal agents from
the Metropolis occasionally take a direct hand in managing the
affairs of the weaker society, neither action is a routine, institutionalized part of this variant of the imperial relationship. British
historians have recently used the phrases, "the imperialism of
free trade" and "informal empire," to describe this pattern, and
their suggestions seem astute, accurate, and convenient. As
Marx clearly understood, the system evolves from the basic capitalist conception of the market and the marketplace as the Metropolis expands into the backward area.

The marketplace is an integrated, two-way relationship involving access to raw materials as well as export markets for goods,
services, and investment capital. Marx understood these reasons
that lay behind the expansionist arguments developed by American farmers and industrial leaders. They pointed out the marginal
utility of foreign operations and explained why it was rational to
sell at a loss overseas in order to avoid the economic and social
costs of shutting down when the domestic demand was satisfied.
In addition to saving capital and avoiding labor unrest, such
practices offered an effective strategy for entering and winning
control of foreign markets.

American foreign relations since 1895 provide the central historical illustration of this kind of imperial expansion. The informal empire of the United States in the twentieth century offers an example of the character, dynamism, and consequences of the capitalist marketplace that is even purer in form and substance than the one provided by British expansion after the middle of the nineteenth century. The famous Open Door Notes of 1899 and 1900 were consciously and brilliantly formulated on the assumption that America possessed the necessary and overwhelming economic power vis-à-vis other advanced industrial powers, as well as the weaker, poorer countries, and on the conviction that Adam Smith was correct in holding that such strength would enable the United States to control the world marketplace if it was defined as a fair field with favor to none.

Given this belief in the fundamental economic preponderance of their system, American policy-makers designed their imperial strategy with a view to creating and maintaining the conditions which would enable their nation's power to produce the desired economic and political victories. Since they viewed war as the great disrupter of economic progress, and as the nightrider of political and social regression, their broad objective was to establish rules of the game which would prevent the struggle in the marketplace from becoming a trial by arms.

The Open Door Notes sought to do this in Asia (and, later, in other regions, such as Africa) by committing America's industrial rivals to the following principles of policy and action: (1) a prohibition on further division and colonization of such areas as China; (2) existing and subsequent regulations within established spheres of interest to apply equally to all competitors; and (3) equal opportunity to be afforded to all rivals in all future economic activity.

While the strategy did not succeed in preventing subsequent wars, it is crucial to realize that the United States entered such conflicts to defend and to re-establish the Open Door Policy. In an important degree, moreover, America was drawn into those wars because of antagonisms arising out of the effectiveness of its performance within the limits set by the principles of the Open Door Policy. This was true in the positive sense of American economic penetration and influence in the world marketplace after 1900, as well as in the negative sense that the Open Door Policy appeared to competitors as an obstacle to their own progress. In this respect, at any rate, the policy was effective enough in its actual or potential economic operation to subvert its political and military objectives.

The evolution and adoption of the Open Door Policy involved one of the truly majestic ironies of American—and perhaps even Western—history. Men like Theodore Roosevelt and Henry Cabot Lodge initially favored a vigorous kind of administrative colonialism as the proper strategy of American expansion. Not unjustly, therefore, they came to be known as Imperialists. Their critics and opponents, men like Andrew Carnegie, William Jennings Bryan, and Edward Atkinson, claimed and were known by the label of Anti-Imperialists. This likewise was true and fair enough as a description of their position on traditional colonialism, or even formal and extensive administrative colonialism.

But the Anti-Imperialists were actually men who understood and advocated the very kind of informal empire that Adam Smith and Karl Marx maintained was created by the inherent imbalance of the marketplace relationship between the advanced industrial Metropolis and the poor, backward, agrarian societies. To begin with, the Anti-Imperialists argued that the economic and other institutional requirements of colonialism or widespread administrative colonialism would slow down and limit the accumulation of capital at home, would progressively limit essential bourgeois freedoms, and would breed social unrest. They added that such a strategy of expansion would also encourage and sustain resistance movements in the dependencies and lead to wars with other advanced nations. Taken together, such consequences would be very apt to subvert economic and political liberty at home, and might even bring about the destruction of the empire itself. To avoid such dangers, yet enjoy the necessary expansion of the marketplace, the Anti-Imperialists rested their strategy of empire on the very principle that Adam Smith advanced.

The Anti-Imperialists and Smith were correct. The Open Door Policy worked magnificently for half a century—surely as effectively as the European forms of colonialism and administrative colonialism. American economic power expanded throughout the world, into the other advanced countries as well as into the underdeveloped regions (including European colonies and spheres of interest), and came ultimately and literally to dominate the world capitalist marketplace. And, measured either in absolute terms or relatively against the performance of the older patterns of empire, the United States was required to employ but small amounts of force between 1900 and 1950 in order to maintain its imperial relationship with the weaker countries. Within the assumptions of the system, American economic power was deployed with considerably more astuteness, and managed with more finesse and sophistication, than either its advocates or its critics are often prone to admit. In addition to the huge profits returned to the United States, the result was the creation of a pattern of domestic politics within the "country" side of the empire that sustained pro-American rulers in power for the great majority of the years since 1900.

But Karl Marx was also correct. The inherent drive within the advanced countries to accumulate capital and to expand and control the marketplace, and the resulting increasing proletarianization and misery in the subject half of the empire, had led to more and increasingly violent conflict. American entry into World War I was at bottom predicated upon the conclusion, reached by both top economic and high political leaders, that the United States could not risk being excluded from what appeared to be the probable reorganization of the world marketplace on terms that would seriously restrict, if not actually subvert, the operation of the Open Door Policy.

Both the Allies and the Central Powers had made it clear by 1916 that they would transform a military and political victory into an economic system strongly favorable to themselves. Wilson's emphasis on his famous Fourteen Points, and his insistence on the Covenant of the League of Nations, involved far more than transcendental idealism. Those programs were designed to apply the axioms of the Open Door Policy to the world and, through the crucial Article X of the Covenant, to guarantee their observance for an indefinite future. The same considerations, even more explicitly avowed, lie at the heart of American involvement in World War II and the Cold War.

America's increasing opposition to Germany and Italy began not with the attacks on Czechoslovakia or Poland, but in connection with basic Axis economic policy (such as barter agreements in place of open marketplace transactions) as early as 1933, and in response to German penetration of Latin-American economic affairs during that decade. Germany's increasing resort to force to extend the sway of such ideas and policies, and others including racial persecution, carried the economic and ideological conflict into the military arena before Japan's attack on Pearl Harbor. From the very beginning, moreover, American leaders openly acknowledged that the tension with Japan was created by the decision to uphold and enforce the principles of the Open Door Policy in China and southeastern Asia in the face of Japanese expansion.

Antagonism toward the Soviet Union involved the same issues in an even more central and unqualified manner. This struggle, which had begun in 1917 and 1918, involved an outright rejection by the Soviets of the cardinal principles of the capitalist marketplace. The United States never fully reconciled itself to this withdrawal by Russia from the capitalist world. In the more narrow and explicit sense, this opposition manifested itself at the end of World War II in an openly proclaimed American determination to preserve and institutionalize the principles of the Open Door Policy in northeastern Asia and in eastern Europe. The Soviet Union's avowed willingness to negotiate particular and more limited rights for the capitalist world in those regions was never explored in any serious, sustained manner. The United States defined the choice as lying between an acceptance of the principles of the Open Door Policy or a condition of opposition and antagonism.

None of this means (in any of the three instances) that the United States entered upon war simply to make money. Certain freedoms and liberties are essential to capitalists and capitalism, even though capitalists and capitalism are not essential to freedom and liberty. There is no discrepancy, therefore, in going to war for a free marketplace and going to war to defend, secure, and even extend the particular freedoms and liberties associated with such a marketplace political economy. But if either war had been fought solely for those freedoms and liberties, then the condition of the underdeveloped part of the world would have been quite different as early as 1920. And its circumstances would have changed much more rapidly, and with considerably less violence against the advanced Metropolitan countries, after the victory in 1945.

Hence none of these actions involved either a series of terrible conspiracies or a kind of narrow, crude economic motivation or determinism on the part of American leaders or their constituency. All parties had a sincere and practical commitment to the kind of freedom inherent in the Open Door Policy per se, and in the informal empire constructed by the United States between 1898 and 1950. The issue is not how bad or evil Americans were, but rather the far more profound and human theme of their tragic inability to realize their desire for peace and freedom so long as they declined to modify seriously the principles of possessive individualism that lie at the heart of capitalism.

As far as America's informal empire itself is concerned, the case of Cuba serves perfectly—if horribly—to illustrate the validity of Marx's analysis. Or, for that matter, the accuracy of Adam Smith's argument. To Marx's axiom about who takes more labor from whom, add his principle that "violent eruptions are naturally more likely to occur in the extremities of the bourgeois organism than in its heart," and top it off with his conclusion that the ideals of the capitalist fight a generally losing battle with the economic axioms of the system. The result is a definition of, and a set of major insights into, the principal features of Cuban-American relations from 1895 to the present. Marx was not primarily concerned to predict when the convulsion would occur, or who would ride its first wave. He was engaged in explaining what would happen, and why it would occur, if the Metropolis continued to act on the principles of the marketplace in its relationships with a colonial or otherwise dependent society. The origins and evolution of the Cuban Revolution, and the nature and course of its confrontation with the United States, verify the central themes of his analysis.

The Cuban missile crisis of 1962 offers an international example of Marx's fundamental argument that a change in the forces of production ultimately causes a change in the relations of production. In the confrontations of war and cold war, of course, the means of production are ultimately defined in military terms. During the years that the United States enjoyed a monopoly or a significant advantage in nuclear weapons, from 1945 to 1955, it unilaterally established and in large measure maintained the ground rules for international relations in the atomic age.

There were exceptions, particularly in China, that provided clear warnings that this vast preponderance of productive power did not provide the United States with an ability to control every situation. The policy was based on a far too narrow, and even typically marketplace, definition of power. It provided an excellent illustration of the way in which the mind concerned with commodities discounts the significance of people. The instruments of power were confused with the sources of power.

The signs indicating the dangers in this outlook were largely ignored until the Russians developed the same productive forces and the same instruments of power. Even then, however, the evidence continued to be generally discounted for a considerable period. Americans continued to make a fetish of producing the commodity of the atom and hydrogen bombs, arguing quite irrationally that the power to kill everybody twice or thrice gave them more security than only being able to do so once. The situation took on the characteristics of a macabre extension of the national attitude toward buying multiple automobiles. Thorstein Veblen might have discussed the phenomenon under the heading of the urge to conspicuous annihilation.

Then came the Cuban Revolution. It was an example of the impotence of nuclear supremacy that could not be evaded or rationalized away. American control of the island had been too obvious for too long a time, and the absurdity of vaporizing the revolution in order to save trade and investments was so evident as to be humorous despite the frustration. Americans sensed, when they did not realize it more explicitly, that the revolution was the product of their own administrative colonialism and informal empire. Even the Pavlovian exercises in explaining it as the work of a communist conspiracy were feeble and generally unimpressive examples of casuistry.

The first direct attempt to destroy the revolution employed the strategy of using conventional weapons inside what was thought to be the womb of safety provided by nuclear predominance. But the strength of the revolution foiled that American effort to combine superficial morality and rhetorical righteousness with secret malice. The subsequent nuclear showdown with the Russians was a direct consequence of that unsuccessful effort to square the circle. Cuban leaders became convinced that the United States would try again with vastly greater forces. This may not have been true, but they declined to risk their revolution on the word of an American administration that had already acted differently than it had talked.

On the surface, it is true, the productive forces of the United States emerged triumphant in the resulting confrontation with the Soviet Union. "The other fellow blinked," as the story goes. But as Secretary of State Dean Rusk later acknowledged, the United States for the first time caught a glimpse of the true nature of nuclear reality. The Soviets withdrew their missiles, but the United States gradually realized that it, the world's greatest Metropolis, had become a colony. A colony, that is to say, of the vast forces of production that it had created and put on the marketplace.

For in a profound sense, the increasing recognition of the necessity of co-existence that dates from the Cuban missile crisis stands as proof of Marx's central thesis that the productive forces will ultimately determine the relations of production. No single entrepreneur can impose his will on the economic marketplace if he is blocked by an element of comparable strength, save at a price so dear as to be self-destructive. Neither can one superpower impose its will upon the international nuclear marketplace if it is matched by another superpower, save at the cost of the very influence it is seeking to enlarge. There is considerable evidence, moreover, that one of the main reasons Soviet leaders placed their weapons in Cuba was to dramatize this truth to the United States.

It is conceivable that, despite that encounter, the United States will continue trying to prove Marx wrong by sustaining the essential structure and attitudes of the Cold War. That approach reveals a powerful inherent propensity to devolve into nuclear war. It is a dynamism that is not effectively checked, let alone redirected, by mere changes in the rhetoric or the means employed in connection with the existing policy. Even if the policy somehow avoided nuclear war, America would not really have proved that Marx was wrong. Another decade of cold war, even more sophisticated and more gentlemanly cold war, would destroy capitalism in any meaningful—let alone American—sense. The result would be a form of non-violent, totalitarian state managerialism that would make C. Wright Mills's power elite look like the founding fathers of Jacksonian Democracy. . . .

In the realm of foreign affairs, at least, the United States has not proved that Karl Marx was wrong. America has been a colonial power. America has practiced administrative colonialism on a significant scale. America has built an informal empire of massive proportions. And America is now face to face with the proof of Marx's thesis that such empires create their own increasingly effective opposition both from within and from without.

The Overall Perspective

Nationalist

The Nationalist school of American diplomatic historians is convinced that the United States has made relatively few mistakes in the conduct of its foreign policy over the past centuries. These historians believe that American foreign policy has nicely combined a realistic concept of the nation's self-interest with an idealistic and generous support of the just aspirations of other nations for self-determination, democracy, and prosperity. The Nationalists reject the Radicals' charges that the United States has been an aggressive, imperialist nation. They also disagree with the Realists' charge that this country has contributed much to war and turmoil by its misguided idealistic crusades.

Nationalist historians, for instance, regard the Monroe Doctrine as an excellent example of realism and idealism in American foreign policy. By opposing European intervention in Latin America, the United States helped protect the Latin nations' right to self-determination. At the same time that the Monroe Doctrine fulfilled these idealistic ends, it also served the interests of the United States. Latin American markets and resources, formerly monopolized by European colonial powers, were now available to us. In addition, the only nations capable of threatening American security, until very recently the European powers, were denied a foothold in the Western Hemisphere.

Since the Nationalists regard past American policy as highly successful, they reject the Realists' charge that this policy has been adversely affected by the interference of the uninformed and moralistic masses. At the same time they reject the Radicals' argument that American policy has been the product of a power elite that has manipulated the emotions of the people.

The Nationalist school is the oldest of those under discussion and has dominated the writing of diplomatic history since the beginning of America's concern with foreign affairs. Until the 1920s, Nationalist history was bombastic and ultrapatriotic. Since that time it has become more scholarly, more cosmopolitan, and more objective. The leading historians of this school are Samuel Flagg Bemis, Herbert Feis, Ernest May, Arthur Link, and Dexter Perkins. Their view is the one that predominates in most American history textbooks.

In the following essay, Dexter Perkins gives a brief survey of American diplomatic history, taking care to answer the criticisms of the Realists and the Radicals. Notice particularly the emphasis on the combination of realism and idealism infusing the policies of the American government. Perkins is a professor emeritus at the University of Rochester and the leading authority on the Monroe Doctrine.

Foreign Policy and the American Spirit

Dexter Perkins

[Perkins begins by admitting the Realist contention that United States foreign policy is extraordinarily dependent on popular opinion.]

This does not mean that the United States is necessarily in the position where it cannot bargain on a decent basis or that it is forced by public opinion to demand all and concede nothing in a diplomatic negotiation. It has backed down more than once. In 1844 the campaign cry of the Democracy was "fifty-four forty or fight," but we compromised on the forty-ninth parallel. In 1895 Grover Cleveland demanded that Great Britain arbitrate the Guiana boundary dispute with Venezuela, but the terms of submission gave to the British a large part of what they had been demanding. Although President Franklin D. Roosevelt talked of unconditional surrender, it was possible to assure the Japanese in 1945 that they would not be deprived of their Emperor. Even in the violent climate of 1950 and 1951, the Truman administration, though exposed to constant attacks for its "weakness," was able to make many concessions in the negotiations with the Communists in Korea, until it came to the issue of the prisoners of war. We have not been as inflexible as we are sometimes accused of being by Europeans.

Nonetheless, there is a danger that a diplomacy influenced by public sentiment may be less pliant than that of the professional diplomats. The record of the United States does not demonstrate this; but the special circumstances of our own time, the very sharpness of the contrast between democracy and totalitarianism, suggest that we may here encounter a real danger. To embroider this point, however, would lead us into the field of prophecy, not of history.

Another characteristic of American diplomatic history is the

Reprinted from Dexter Perkins, *Foreign Policy and the American Spirit*, pp. 8–15, 92–105. © 1957 by Cornell University. Used by permission of Cornell University Press.

importance that has been attached to general principles. This, too, springs from the popular character of American diplomacy. The mass of men have neither the knowledge nor the inclination to understand a complex diplomatic problem in all its various ramifications. They can judge only in the large, fixing the mood and general objectives; and policy, to be made intelligible to them, must be stated in broad terms. It is a sound instinct that has made the greatest of American statesmen do this very thing. Washington, of course, did this, in the Farewell Address; Monroe did it in the famous message of 1823; so, too, did his successors in the evolution of the celebrated doctrine; so, too, did Woodrow Wilson in his great war speeches; so, too, did Harry Truman in the pronouncement of March, 1947. American foreign relations are shot through with general ideas. These general ideas are usually affected with a moral content. That democracy is the best form of government and is of universal application, that aggression is immoral, and the notion that nations must act on ethical principle are among the most usual of these ideas. Indeed it is doubtful whether the statesmen of any other country are so given to moral homilies as our own. Read the correspondence of Cordell Hull with Admiral Nomura and you will see a prime—indeed, an unrivaled—example of this kind of thing; but there are many others. The strongly moralistic emphasis in American diplomacy is somewhat irksome to Europeans, who often put it down as hypocrisy. But it is really nothing of the kind. It is a reflection of a kind of naïveté that exists in the general public and that springs from an imperfect understanding of the play of forces which determines the intercourse of nations.

In dwelling on this point, on the importance of large ideas, I do not wish to be understood as saying that the American people have often become slaves to general theories. On the contrary, their natural impulse to generalize has been offset, time and again, by the strongly pragmatic streak in the national character. Monroe defied Europe in the name of general principle in 1823, but when asked to make an alliance by one of the South American states, he not only declined but made it clear that he would not act without Great Britain. Polk was wise enough to declare that the Monroe Doctrine applied with greatly increased force to the North American continent, but to turn his gaze away from the Anglo-French blockade of the Argentine. The Monroe Doctrine, in fact, was really applied only in the area of the Caribbean, where it was closely associated with the security interests of the United

States. And it was conveniently transformed when expediency suggested that a unilateral pronouncement carried with it a kind of arrogant assumption of superiority distasteful to the states of Latin America. In the same way the attachment of the United States to democracy has not prevented it from dealing with other governments of quite a different stripe when its interests have demanded such action. It cheered Kossuth but kept out of the European revolutions of the forties; it enjoyed good relations with an imperial China and imperial Russia; it has always been ready to deal with dictatorships in the New World, dictatorships of the personal type; and it seems to see no obstacle today to closer relations with Yugoslavia or with Spain. Nor, to take a third illustration of its attitude toward general principles, does it today interpret collective security in a fixed way. The Latin-American engagements implementing the Charter of the United Nations call for one kind of action; the Atlantic Pact for another; the Pacific Pact for yet another. The empirical spirit is usually there to temper the generalizations—this is by no means to say that the generalizations have no influence on policy.

Another element in American foreign policy, profoundly related to the national temperament and to the play of public opinion, is the strongly pacific bent in the American philosophy. No one in his senses could accuse the Americans of being a militarist people. Of course they have had their moments of jingoism; they were spoiling for war with Spain in the late nineties. But they have not as a rule glorified war, and they have been peculiarly susceptible to the dream of peace.

Let us look at each side of the coin, as I have just presented it. One of the remarkable evidences of the nonmilitaristic temper is the way in which the Americans have tended to think ill of their wars after these wars have happened. Every struggle in which the United States has engaged has had its revisionist historians. The War of 1812, we are told, was not a war to resist Britain on the sea, but a war with an imperialist impulse behind it; the war with Mexico was a war of aggression; the war of 1898, so we are assured, might have been avoided if President McKinley had stressed more fully the scope of Spanish concession; our entry into the war of 1917 was due to our partiality for the Allies, to the inept diplomacy of the Wilson administration, to the pressure of commercial and financial interest, and to the wicked machinations of British propaganda; the war of 1941 was a deep-laid plot on the part of Franklin D. Roosevelt, who deliberately plunged the country into an unnecessary conflict. I am not endorsing these views, you understand; indeed I dissent from most of them. But the fact that they exist, and carry some weight, is a most interesting commentary on the American spirit.

There are many other signs of the peace-loving spirit in the history of American foreign relations. There is, for example, the emphasis again and again placed on alternatives to war. There is the legal approach, for example, which is rather distinctively American and which is associated with our constitutional forms at home. The concrete example of this approach lies in American advocacy of a world court. It is true that there was much opposition to this idea, as well as advocacy of it. But in few other countries was the juridical settlement of international disputes taken as seriously as it is in the United States. Another evidence of the same temper is to be found in the Kellogg-Briand pact. I do not believe that a proposal to outlaw war by promises, a general engagement to do so, could possibly have emanated from any European chancellery. Yet it came naturally to the Americans, and the pact itself was ratified with scarcely a dissenting vote. Other examples are easy to cite: the emphasis placed on the Covenant of the League in 1919 and on the Charter of the United Nations in 1945. We must not judge the League in the light of the opposition it aroused. We must think of it in its world setting and remember its American origin. And it seems likely that the League's successor has nowhere warmer support than in the United States.

The matters I have been discussing have to do with peace viewed from the institutional or legal side. But one of the most striking evidences of the peace-loving spirit in this country lies in the rapid demobilization which has followed quickly on victory in our two great wars of the twentieth century. A more sophisticated people, or a more brutal one, would have recognized immediately the vast bargaining power that we possessed in the victorious legions of 1918 and 1945. Yet we quickly threw much of that bargaining power away; and though voices are raised in lamentation today by our numerous retrospective critics, there were few to oppose the action which we took at the time.

Closely connected with the pacific spirit is the American attitude toward imperialism. Of course we have had imperialistic impulses—for example, the impulse to extend our political power over alien peoples. But our imperialism has always been imperialism with an uneasy conscience. It has always been associated with the notion that some day we will grant self-rule to those whom we have dominated. And during the last twenty years we have not only abandoned the policy of intervention in the affairs of New World states, but have, by two solemn protocols, bound ourselves not to intervene. I know of no such act of abnegation on the part of any other nation.

Because this is our point of view, we take a critical attitude of the imperialism of others. We pressed for concessions on the part of the British to India and of the Dutch to Indonesia; we pressed for concession on the part of the French in Tunisia. We associate ourselves with anti-imperialist policies in the Near East. And in this the diplomats undeniably have the support of majority opinion.

Before I leave the question of imperialism, I want to inject one special word. Despite our policies with regard to Latin America, the word imperialism is constantly on the lips of our enemies; and since they cannot fairly say that we are governing anyone else directly, they like to speak of economic imperialism. I want to raise the question whether any such term has exact content *and meaning.* Without political control can a country be truly imperialistic? Of course economic strength confers bargaining power and influence. But it does not confer domination. And imperialism means domination. I find it a little difficult to see how real imperialism can function without active political intervention.

On the other hand, we must not imagine, of course, that all is sweetness and light in the foreign policy of the United States, historically considered, or that we have always been moved by pacific instincts. The combative spirit has more than once expressed itself in American diplomacy, notably in the forties and fifties and in the period just preceding the Spanish-American War; and certainly the war temper grew between 1915 and 1917 and between 1939 and 1941.

The pacific spirit and the anti-imperialistic spirit have not been the only expressions of the foreign policy of the United States. It is worth noting that, historically speaking, the Americans have often given a very wide definition to the concept of security. This wide definition was never more evident than in the famous message of 1823, in which President Monroe declared that any intervention on the part of European powers in the New World would be dangerous to our peace and safety. In the first quarter of the twentieth century the Philippines came within our defense zone, and they have remained there ever since. The national definition of a security interest was again enlarged in the period of the

First World War, when to many persons the collapse of British naval power and the victory of Germany were thought to present a definite challenge to the United States. And the broad definition of American security has never been better illustrated than in the enunciation of the Truman Doctrine, which proclaims the purpose of the United States to assist all peoples threatened by alien control. Such statements as those of Monroe and Truman are characteristic of American foreign attitudes, in the breadth of their generalization, in the instinct for bold and sweeping assertion. But characteristic, too, is the American instinct for the practical, the retreat from theory when retreat becomes convenient or necessary. This has been very well illustrated of late in the policy asserted with regard to Korea. We began by invoking the doctrine of collective security in favor of the South Korean Republic, in our eyes the legal government of Korea. But we quickly modified any purpose of unifying all the country and entered into negotiations for an armistice which would have left Korea divided. We negotiated with the aggressor, of course, on the condition that he cease from aggression, but without thought of further punishment. Do not misunderstand me; I am not saying that this policy was wrong. I merely illustrate the manner in which theory and practice unite in the development of American foreign policy.

This union of opposites is, it seems to me, a very genuine source of strength. A diplomacy that rests upon the people must speak to the people. It can speak best in large and sweeping generalizations, which appeal to the heart as well as to the head, which can be understood—or perhaps I should say felt—by the great body of the voters. But the doctrinaire pursuit of a broad objective may very easily conflict with the practical realities of the moment, may sacrifice the national interest—whatever that illusive phrase may mean. In the United States the people have rarely objected to the modification of theory in the face of unpleasant facts. They have rarely insisted upon policies which were, in their upshot, disastrous for the United States (though of course our revisionist historians might challenge this observation). On the whole, such a diplomacy as ours is sufficiently realistic to deal with the actual world and sufficiently idealistic to derive great strength from its idealism. It makes mistakes—who does not?—but compare those mistakes with the mistakes of the dictators, with the insensate ambition of Adolf Hitler, with the cruel vanity of Mussolini, perhaps even with the calculating and sinister ambitions of Moscow. On this last, of course, we have not the true historical perspective today, and we may not have it for a long time to come. But in one fact we can take some pride. Our diplomacy is not only well adapted to, indeed the expression of, our national temperament, but it reflects the desire for a wider union of peoples. It serves America in a broader context than that of isolationism. It appeals to American idealism, but it is based on the genuine need we have today for a wide association of peoples in the face of the monster of the Kremlin.

.   .   .

Nowhere has [America's] sense of guilt about [its] wars manifested itself more explicitly or more tangibly than in the national historiography. Repeatedly, historians have reviewed the record of one after another of America's wars, and have been so prone to assign war-responsibility to their own government that the term "revisionists" has become a standard designation for the writers who devote themselves to refuting the patriotic explanation of our part in wars, recent or remote.

In saying that this applies to all our wars, we should perhaps make an exception of the American Revolution. To suggest that the Revolution was a mistake, that the breach in the unity of the English-speaking peoples ought to have been avoided, that the cause of the dispute was too trivial to justify a resort to arms, has not been characteristic of the writers of history, though now and again an ardent Anglophile may have put forward such views.

But with the War of 1812 we reach a part of our history on which the revisionists have been at work. It is, for example, the thesis of Professor J. W. Pratt that the real purpose of the war was imperialistic, that a coalition of the South and West, with their eyes on Florida and Canada respectively, sought to bring the country into the conflict. It has been pointed out by other writers that the war was simply foolish: a war for neutral rights, it can be argued, is in its essence rather futile. You cannot vindicate such rights by fighting. You can only increase the dangers and perils to which your own commerce is exposed. Further, in this second conflict with Great Britain, the struggle ended without the faintest recognition of any of the principles for which the United States contended.

The argument that the War of 1812 was useless can also be supported on the ground that the Madison Administration, which was entirely unprepared for the waging of the struggle, endangered national unity by leading the nation into war, since there was bitter opposition in New England—opposition so extreme that it even led to some talk of secession. The whole business, it has been argued, was a mistake, and it would have been better if the nation had never taken up arms.

Such, at least, is one thesis with regard to 1812. This is not to say, be it understood, that this thesis is a correct one; it is merely to say that these are samples of the highly critical views of a past war that seem to crop up in the United States.

Let us look next at the war with Mexico. Here the critical view has again and again been put forward, and is, of course, contemporary with the conflict itself. The action of President Polk, we have more than once been told, was highly provocative; he instructed General Taylor in the winter of 1846 to occupy territory which was in dispute between Mexico and the United States; Taylor himself behaved badly by blockading the Mexicans across the Rio Grande at Matamoras; and the Mexicans were thus goaded into armed action. Polk's real objective was conquest, and the war ended in our acquisition of California and the Southwest. It was a true war of aggression, and should be so regarded.

A similar interpretation has grown up with regard to the Spanish-American War of 1898—an interpretation perpetuated in that brilliant book by Walter Millis, "The Martial Spirit." According to this view, the Spanish government had virtually conceded the essential American demands in April of 1898; it had agreed to suspend the policy of concentration camps in Cuba, which had shocked American opinion; and it had indicated its willingness to grant an armistice to the Cuban insurgents. But President McKinley, who had in Theodore Roosevelt's picturesque phrase, "no more backbone than a chocolate éclair," gave slight emphasis to these concessions in his message to Congress, and in the prevailing temper of American public opinion, that body lost little time in declaring war. Thus, through the weakness of an American President (so runs the argument or the implication) the country was launched into an unnecessary conflict.

The same tendency of historians to regard a resort to arms as futile was manifest on a still larger scale after World War I. At the distance of about a decade from the end of the struggle, American revisionists made themselves heard with a new theory of the events of 1914–17. Matter-of-fact citizens had for the most part assumed that Germany's challenge to the United States on the high seas had been the cause of America's taking up arms.

But the case was restated in a wholly different way. The policy of the United States was shaped (so it was contended) by considerations of a very different kind. British propaganda directed American opinion; President Wilson never honestly carried out a policy of neutrality. Moreover, the Administration was influenced by a desire to extend American trade. The munitions traffic produced profits that gave the United States a stake in the cause of the Allies; so, too, did Allied loans. Thus, economic forces afford the true explanation for the policy pursued—a policy confused and tortuous, and never candidly set forth.

World War II is only a few years behind us, but already the revisionist thesis has again been put forward, and from the pen of one of the most eminent, most respected, and most respectable of American scholars. The late Charles A. Beard has told us, in his book published a few years ago, precisely how it happened. President Roosevelt, it appears, committed himself to a policy of peace in the electoral campaign of 1940, but in 1941 he so shaped events that war, both with Germany and with Japan, became virtually inevitable. In regard to the war in Europe, he secured from Congress the so-called Lend-Lease Enactment, under the pretense that this measure of assistance to Great Britain would prevent our entry into war; he then extended aid to include first patrols and then convoys at sea; he instructed the American Navy to take action which would almost inevitably provoke the Germans to war; he misrepresented as an act of defense the famous episode of the destroyer *Greer,* which at the time it was attacked by a German submarine was following that submarine and reporting its position to British vessels and air patrols; he sought a showdown at the very time that he was professing to avoid it, and the showdown came.

In his relations with Japan, the Beard argument continues, President Roosevelt was no less ingenious; he extended aid to the Chinese government with which the Tokyo regime was at war; he applied economic pressure against that regime; he put aside the offer of a personal conference with Prince Konoye, the Japanese Minister in the summer and early autumn of 1941; he declined to accept proposals for a *modus vivendi* in November of 1941; by his action he encouraged the Japanese to make the "sneak attack" on Pearl Harbor, which indeed was more or less foreseen. Moreover, the war into which he led the United States is now revealed as a futility; for while it destroyed the power of Hitler and of militarist Japan, it left a new and more dangerous totalitarian state in a position of supreme power. It brought, not peace, but a situation more dangerous and troubled than ever. And, in attempting to challenge the Soviet Union, the United States is embarking upon a policy so sweeping and so perilous as to offer a new illustration of the dangers of ambitious policies such as those we have recently pursued.

If we were to put together the generalizations that have been stated in the preceding paragraphs, we would come to the conclusion that the foreign policy of the United States has been almost uniformly inept; that every war in which this country has been engaged was really quite unnecessary or immoral or both; and that it behooves us in the future to pursue policies very different from those pursued in the past. What are we to think of these revisionist theories? To what degree do they rest upon a sound basis and furnish a foundation for action?

In the first place, it is to be said that no one of these explanations of America's wars can be wholly accepted by the scientific scholar. Take, for example, the War of 1812. It may be true that one of the motives of that conflict was American imperialism. Not all students of the period assign to this motive the important place that was given it by Professor Pratt, but let us grant for the moment its significance. It still remains true that other factors can be brought into the account; it seems unreasonable to suppose that British violation of American rights on the high seas is to be set completely aside as one of the elements in bringing about American action. The measurement of a nation's opinion, the exact determination of the why of great events, is in all cases a very difficult matter; but it is more rational and more scientific to assume that a variety of forces was operating than to lay exclusive emphasis on some single factor.

It is easy, too, to declare that the War of 1812 was a futility; but Albert Gallatin, one of the wisest statesmen of his time, did not so regard it. "The war," he wrote, "has been productive of evil and good, but I think the good preponderates. . . . The war has renewed and reinstated the national feelings and character which the Revolution had given, and which were daily lessened. The people have now more general objects of attachment. . . . They are more Americans; they feel and act more as a nation; and I hope that the permanency of the Union is thereby better secured." Look at the matter from another point of view. It is true that the United States did not secure from Great Britain any recognition of its point of view with regard to impressments or its neutral rights at sea; but it is not true that the nation did not profit from the war. The connection of the Indian tribes of the Old Northwest with Britain was definitely broken; and whether it be a direct effect of the war or not, it can be said with some confidence that the British Foreign Office treated the United States with far more consideration after the Peace of Ghent than before.

It is difficult to defend wholeheartedly the attitude of President Polk in connection with the Mexican war; but any judgment of that period that fails to emphasize the fact that Polk sought, apparently in good faith, a peaceful settlement with Mexico, and that this settlement was rejected by the Mexicans themselves, does not rest upon sound grounds. Polk was *ready* to come to terms without acquiring California or New Mexico; greater wisdom on the part of those in authority in Mexico City would probably have prevented war. And it might well be asked of those who have judged the diplomacy of the rigid Tennessean most harshly if they would wish to undo what he actually did.

The war with Spain illustrates another aspect of the problem of moral judgment on America's wars. It would have been more candid and more courageous of President McKinley if he had underlined the important nature of the concessions made by Spain when he reported to Congress; but to assume that if he had done so, war would have been prevented, is a purely gratuitous assumption. For how do we know that the Cuban insurgents would have accepted the armistice that Spain was ready to offer; what interests would they have had in so doing? After all, they wanted not autonomy but independence; and their best chance of independence lay precisely in American intervention. And how can we be sure that a Congress that had already lashed itself into a passion against Spain, and a nation that had been for more than a year open to the incitements of a yellow press, would have paid much heed to the President's pronouncement even if it had been more emphatically made?

It is, of course, possible to argue, as Professor S. F. Bemis does, that the imperialist courses into which the United States was launched as a result of the war with Spain were a mistake; but here again one may well avoid too sharp a judgment. For it is possible to point out the consequences of the decisions taken in 1898, while it is not possible to set up anything more than a hypothesis as to what would have happened if the decisions then made had been different. One has a right, of course, to deplore the entry of the United States into the affairs of the Far East—

then or now; but to argue that without the war with Spain that entry would never have occurred is to indulge in pure assumption.

The revisionist judgment of World War I seems to this writer particularly and grossly unscientific—save in one respect. It ought today to be candidly admitted that the Administration of Woodrow Wilson adopted a double standard in the enforcement of the traditional principles of neutrality—that it was rigorous in dealing with Germany and generously lax in dealing with Great Britain—but it ought also to be admitted by every student that this partiality was in large measure a reflection of the drift of American opinion itself. Beyond this, in my judgment, it is impossible to go. Who can prove that British propaganda produced this partiality? Who can measure the effect of that propaganda as compared with the effect of some other elements in the situation, of the influence, for example, of the fact that it was Germany and Austria that first declared war, of the influence of the German violation of Belgian neutrality, of the influence of the general assumption that Britain and France were democratic nations, and that the Central Powers were certainly far less so?

And, to go further, by what process of reasoning can it be established that the Administration of Woodrow Wilson, with its far from cordial attitude towards American business interests, was directly affected by the desire to promote those interests? How, for that matter, can it be demonstrated that the economic well-being of the United States was better promoted by entrance into the conflict than it would have been by the continuation of a policy of neutrality? How can it be shown that if the Germans had not afforded a provocation to war with their resumption of the submarine warfare in the winter of 1917, it would have been possible for the American government to abandon its neutrality, especially in view of the fact that as late as January 22, 1917, the President was still talking of a peace without victory?

There is something to be said for our participation in World War I not only from the viewpoint of causes, but also from the viewpoint of results. Discount the menace presented by Imperial Germany, if you will. Ignore the argument that without the intervention of the United States the German government would have been able to bring Britain to her knees, that German naval power would have been supreme, and that the page of German ambition, written so bold and large by Adolf Hitler, would have been inscribed in the decade of the 'twenties, instead of in the 'thirties. Even when all this is left out of the reckoning, there remain some favorable results of World War I. The world of 1919, the world of Allied victory, was a relatively secure world, and one which was still to enjoy a decade of great prosperity and material advance; the aspirations of many national groups were satisfied to a remarkable degree; and a temporary reconciliation of the two great secular enemies, France and Germany, was brought to pass in the Treaties of Locarno. As a matter of fact, the war of 1917–18 opened up the fairest opportunities for a Europe free from the menace of a predatory ambition, and it is certainly not wholly irrational to maintain, as did Mr. Lloyd George in his memoirs, that, had the statesmen of the postwar period been equal to their opportunities, the Treaty of Versailles might have ushered in a long period of peace. Of course, this, too, is assumption; but it is assumption sufficiently reasonable to make one think twice about the contrary hypothesis that our entry into World War I was simply a gigantic mistake.

Again we come to World War II. We must examine it in some detail. Is it true that President Roosevelt "lied us into war"? Let us look at the record. The public opinion polls, imperfect as they are as a guide, suggest no such conclusion. They show that the American people, indifferent at first to the struggle in Europe, or perhaps foolishly optimistic as to the prospects of victory for the democratic nations, became genuinely aroused after the Fall of France, and that a great body of public sentiment was increasingly in favor of aid to the democracies, even at the risk of war. For example, as early as June, 1940, when people were polled on the question as to whether the President was right in making it possible for Great Britain and France to buy models of airplanes that were being used by our army and navy, the affirmative view was taken by 80 per cent of those questioned. This percentage was only slightly affected by partisan affiliation, 85 per cent of the democrats being so recorded, and 76 per cent of the Republicans. When the destroyer-bases transaction was under discussion in August, it was approved by 60 per cent of those polled, and disapproved by only 37 per cent, and this vote, it should be emphasized, was taken before the deal was consummated, and at a time, therefore, when there was no incentive to support it as a national commitment irrevocably taken. By November of 1940, after the national election, the question was put, "If it appears that England will be defeated by Germany and Italy unless the United States supplies her with more food and materials, would you be in favor of giving more help to England?" and 90 per cent of those polled responded in the affirmative.

The Lend-Lease Bill came before Congress in the winter of 1941. In four successive samplings of public opinion, the percentage in favor of the measure was always twice as great as those opposed, with still more giving a qualified approval. Further, the implementation of the bill by authorizing convoys (a measure not taken until July) was already approved by 55 per cent in June, with only 38 per cent in the negative. When, indeed, the issue was defined in terms of a possible British defeat, the percentage in favor of the action increased to 71 per cent with only 21 per cent opposed. Similarly, in the fall, the arming of American merchant ships was approved by 72 per cent against 21 per cent, and the shooting of German warships on sight by 62 per cent to 28 per cent.

Many of the most important steps in the Roosevelt policy towards Germany were made the basis of legislative action. The adoption of national conscription in time of peace (surely some index of the concern of the American people with the menace of National Socialism) was adopted in the House of Representatives by a vote of 232 to 124, and in the Senate by a vote of 47 to 25 (almost two to one). Lend-Lease, after a prolonged debate that gave ample time for the expression of the public judgment, was passed by a vote of 317 to 71 in the House, and 60 to 31 in the Upper Chamber. The arming of American merchant ships in the fall was approved by a vote of 259 to 138 in the House, and, with an amendment ending the exclusion of American ships from the war zones, in the Senate by 50 to 37. Though the amended measure had a close call in the House, 212 to 194, it was nonetheless enacted. Such figures make it absurd to assume that the President was acting contrary to American public opinion, or that his own sounding of the alarm (a fact to be conceded) struck no responsive chord in the breasts of his compatriots. An additional point to be noted is that, on almost every vote, the defections in the ranks of the Democrats were fewer than those in the ranks of the Republicans; in other words, that where party allegiance did not operate, the drift was towards and not away from the Chief Executive.

There are other facts that deserve to be considered in any assessment of public opinion. The Republican nominating convention was one of those rare conventions in which the practiced players of the political game were persuaded to nominate a candidate whose strength amongst the professionals was by no means great. The foremost contenders in the months preceding the convention were Senator Taft, who took the isolationist viewpoint with his usual courage, and Thomas E. Dewey, who was at that time busily carrying water on both shoulders. Yet the nominee was Wendell Willkie. Willkie stood for a policy not very different from that of the President himself, and had as early as April declared for aid to the Allies. The formation of the Committee to Defend America by Aiding the Allies took place in May of 1940, and the roster of its membership discloses a strong nonpartisan support for a policy of intervention. It is certainly not very scientific to ignore these facts in an assessment of the policy of the Administration; honest students of the period, especially those who believe that the foreign policy of a democracy must take its shape from the opinion of the people, cannot fail to accord them a very vital significance.

It is not possible to speak so categorically with regard to our relations with Japan. There were, for example, no important votes in Congress to serve as the basis for a judgment. Yet here, too, there can easily be established a connection between the broad lines of the Roosevelt policy and the sentiments of the people. From as early as June, 1939, for example, 72 per cent of those questioned as to their sympathies in the war between Japan and China declared their sympathies were with China. When the Vandenberg Resolution was brought forward in the summer of 1939, calling for the denunciation of our trade treaty with Japan, 82 per cent of those polled believed that we should refuse to sell her any more war materials. When President Roosevelt forbade the shipment of scrap iron to Japan, 96 per cent of those questioned approved his action. By February of 1941, 60 per cent thought the interests of the United States would be threatened by the seizure of Singapore and the Dutch East Indies, though only 39 per cent were as yet ready to risk war. And by November of 1941, 64 per cent thought the United States should take steps to prevent Japan from becoming more powerful, even if this meant risking war with Japan.

These facts may not be decisive, but they certainly indicate that a powerful body of opinion was behind Roosevelt's actions. Furthermore, unless one is disposed to maintain that we had no interests worthy of protection in the Orient, the Philippines included, there was ample reason to look askance on Japanese policy, and on the multiplied aggressions of the Tokyo government. Consider the record: the Amau statement of 1934, and the doctrine of a Greater East Asia, the denunciation of the naval treaties, the fortification of the Pacific Islands, the war with China, the acquisition of Jehol, the occupation of northern Indo-China, the tri-partite alliance with the Axis, and the occupation of southern Indo-China.

In the revisionist gospel, these acts are of no significance. Attention is fixed on the American riposte to them, on loans to China, on the denunciation of the commercial treaty of 1911, on the severance of trade relations. By a curiously inverted logic, these acts are made provocative, and the acts of Japan appear as the expression of a legitimate national interest. Just how reasonable is such an approach? Just how reasonable is it to suppose that, under any administration, the country would have observed complacently the advance of Japan, and its alliance with German imperialism?

The revisionists also turn to the results of the war, and declare that we are now confronted by a danger greater than that which we attempted to destroy. They blandly assume that in Europe the two totalitarian giants would have bled each other white, and that in Asia we would have been able to live with an imperialist Japan. But how can they prove any such hypothesis? How do they know that Hitler would have been defeated? How do they know that Japan, inflamed by victory, would have kept her hands off the Philippines? To assert such things is to assume a degree of omniscience that is denied to mortal man. It is to brush aside as of no importance the assumptions (and they were assumptions, it is to be frankly admitted) which actually governed conduct, and received wide currency, in 1941. In international affairs, it can be argued, one meets one danger at a time, and the fact that a new peril presents itself is not proof, or anything like proof, of the unreality of the peril that preceded.

What, then, are we to think of revisionism? In the first place, it may be stated categorically that we will always have it with us. The evidence is conclusive that it lies deep in the temperament of the American people, with their innate dislike of violence, their instinct for re-examination of their own motives, the partisan impulses that prompt to criticism, the disillusionments that come with victory. The revisionists, moreover, will always have a great advantage with the unsophisticated and the naïve. For every war leaves many discontents behind, and it is always comfortable to trace these discontents to the war itself. It is easy to accept an hypothesis, if one wants to accept it; and revisionism is, in essence, merely the presentation of hypotheses, hypotheses that are bound to appear attractive to at least some segment of public opinion.

It is also fairly clear that, within narrow limits, revisionism may make for better history. Its challenge to the conventional view is not wholly without utility; it protects us against the nationalistic, or the chauvinistic, approach; it stimulates reflection as to the bases of our own policy; it tends to raise the question, the useful question, as to whether our own diplomatic action is unduly rigid and more concerned with theories than with the national interests, clearly understood and soundly and thoughtfully interpreted.

On the other hand, it must always have its dangers. It is sheer intellectual levity to imagine that, in matters so complex as international relations, we can accurately trace the consequences of an alternative course of action which never happened. It may, moreover, be actually harmful. The revisionist theory of the war of 1917–18 had only one obvious result: it encouraged the great militarist states to imagine that they could count on the indifference of the United States to the realization of their nefarious ambitions. A revisionist theory of World War II might well have the same result. It suggests that we can be secure if we abdicate our role as a world power; it suggests that we can and ought to watch the growth of a new totalitarianism without apprehension, without ever reacting emotionally against it, and that such an attitude can be indefinitely prolonged without any snapping of the nerves, without one of those indefinable changes of national mood which lead to the final acceptance of a challenge.

Revisionism rests, too, upon a very doubtful interpretation of human nature. Revisionists are often motivated by a dislike, perhaps even a noble dislike, of a resort to force. But, in fact, no institution is so deeply ingrained in human nature as war, and the attempt to flee from this fact is no solution of an age-old problem. No generation ought to be clearer on this point than our own; for when did great states ever submit to more humiliation, or watch with greater complacency the building up of aggression than did the states of Western Europe in the 'thirties? If this painful period shows anything, it shows that in the face of ruthless ambition, the pacific spirit will in time be undermined, in the very nature of the case; and that a nation which begins with appeasement is likely to end with war. This is, no doubt, an unpleasant truth; but it seems to have a good many facts to support it; and to treat all war as a gigantic mistake is not to advance materially the preservation of peace.

The matter, indeed, can be put in a nutshell. Behind revisionism often lies the spectre of appeasement, the assumption that the will to avoid war is sufficient to prevent war. The problem is more complex. When it is recognized to be such, the chances of avoiding conflict will be enhanced.

two
Origins
of American
Diplomatic
Principles

Nationalist

How did the United States develop its principles of foreign policy? For that matter, what are the principles of American foreign policy? Naturally, the Nationalists, Realists, and Radicals disagree over which principles have guided the United States in foreign affairs. The Radicals seek the roots of American imperialism. The Realists look for the sources of America's excessive idealism. The Nationalists, believing that American foreign policy has been realistic, idealistic, and successful all at the same time, search for the origins of the principles that have made this so.

Max Savelle, a professor of history at the University of Illinois at Chicago Circle, maintains that there have been six basic principles guiding American policy through most of its history. According to the following essay, what are these principles? Are they indebted mostly to New World experience or to America's European heritage? Do they seem both realistic and benevolent? Have they been followed consistently enough to be considered principles of American policy? If so, is this because of the historical experiences cited by Professor Savelle or because later situations just happened to require similar responses?

Savelle is the author of many books, his most recent being The Origins of American Diplomacy, *which is in part an expansion of the following article.*

The Colonial Origins of American Diplomatic Principles

Max Savelle

In a survey of the "permanent bases" of American diplomacy, published a few years ago, Mr. John W. Davis lists six doctrines which, as he says, "seem to have run with reasonable persistence throughout the course of American diplomacy." These are, according to Mr. Davis, the doctrine of isolation, the Monroe Doctrine, the doctrine of non-intervention, the freedom of the seas, the open door, and the pacific settlement of disputes. The first four Mr. Davis classifies as "negative" principles; the other two he calls "positive." For the purposes of this paper, Mr. Davis's classification will be used.

Now, in the words of Mr. James Brown Scott, "the foreign policy of a state or nation necessarily pre-supposes its existence as

From Max Savelle, "The Colonial Origins of American Diplomatic Principles," *Pacific Historical Review*, Vol. III, No. 3 (1934), 334–350. © 1934 by the Pacific Coast Branch, American Historical Association. Reprinted by permission of the Branch.

a political body." Historians of American foreign policy have, therefore, generally begun their story with the appointment of a Committee of Secret Correspondence by the second Continental Congress and the sending of Silas Deane abroad as the agent of the colonies on the eve of American independence. Deane and the American commissioners who followed him to Europe went with instructions which show that the basic principles of subsequent American diplomacy were already well developed in the minds of the American leaders in the Congress. Whence came the diplomatic principles embodied in the instructions of the American representatives abroad? Were they formulated, as it were, out of nothing, and without antecedents, to meet the need of the moment, or did they have some other, more remote origin? It is the purpose of this paper to suggest that the ideas underlying the permanent bases of American diplomacy were already old, even traditional, long before the time of American independence; that those ideas are as old as European settlement in America, because they arose out of needs which were inherent in the geographic situation of the colonies here; and that they developed simultaneously in America and in Europe, out of the intercolonial relations of English, Spanish, Dutch and French colonies, on the one hand, and out of the adaptation of European diplomacy to the new international situation presented by the appearance of colonial empires in the western hemisphere, on the other.

The doctrine of isolation, the first of these basic principles, probably dates from the beginning of Anglo-Saxon colonization in North America. The idea of escape from the entanglements of Europe, international, moral, religious and economic, appears in the thinking of the earliest permanent settlers, especially those who built their homes on the shores of Massachusetts Bay. "There never was a generation," wrote Increase Mather in 1677, "that did so perfectly shake off the dust of Babylon both as to ecclesiastical and civil constitution, as the first generation of Christians that came into this land for the gospel's sake." William Bradford and Edward Winslow both express this feeling in explaining the move of the Pilgrims from Leyden to America, and the same theme is repeated again and again in the history of Massachusetts Bay. The Massachusetts General Court, for example, in 1651 reminded Oliver Cromwell that it was to escape Europe that the founders of that colony came to America, and justified their feeling on the ground that "We know not any country more peaceable and free from Warre . . ." than this. Francis Daniel Pastorius, speaking, perhaps, for thousands of the Germans who came to the middle colonies in the next century, expressed the same feeling when he said that "After I had sufficiently seen the European provinces and countries, and the threatening movements of war, and had taken to heart the dire changes and disturbance of the Fatherland, I was impelled through a special guidance from the Almighty, to go to Pennsylvania."

This deeply rooted feeling of escape from the turmoil of Europe, an escape guaranteed by three thousand miles of ocean, is the negative side of the colonial doctrine of isolation. The doctrine also had its positive side, which took the form of refusal, on occasion, to be drawn into European conflicts. Thus, for example, during the first Anglo-Dutch war, Governor Peter Stuyvesant of New Netherland proposed to the New England Confederation that the English and Dutch colonies maintain a policy of neutrality in the war between their "Nations in Europe." At the same time, Massachusetts, who did not share Connecticut's prospect for territorial gain at the expense of the Dutch, was blocking the entrance of the New England Confederation into the war, because, as it seemed to the Massachusetts General Court, "it was most agreeable to the gospel of peace which we profess, and safest for these colonies at this season, to forbeare the use of the sword."

The real reason for these actions by New Netherland and Massachusetts was probably less the gospel of peace than the fact that there was a very profitable intercolonial trade going on between them, which must inevitably have suffered in war. Their isolation was thus based largely upon self-interest; but the ideas inherent in the action are, none-the-less, the basic ideas of the doctrine of isolation, as subsequently developed. The geographic situation of the English and Dutch colonies not only took them outside the stream of European conflict, in this case, but had actually created interests for them which made for the maintenance of peace.

Nor was this an isolated case. Similar situations arose, from time to time, during the intercolonial wars of the eighteenth century; and the unwillingness of such colonies as New Jersey and Pennsylvania to contribute men or money for those wars, because their interests were not directly involved, is notorious. Furthermore, as a part of the doctrine of the two spheres, the principle of American isolation from European conflict was recognized and encouraged by the mother countries by treaty, as, for example, in the Anglo-French treaty of Whitehall, of 1686.

John Adams expressed no new idea, therefore, when he formulated the American doctrine of isolation in 1776, to the effect that "we should make no treaties of alliance with any European power . . . [but] that we should separate ourselves, as far as possible and as long as possible, from all European politics and wars." Rather, he was expressing in terms of high policy a sentiment which was already a tradition in the American colonies, based upon a deep-seated feeling of escape from Europe and a strong tendency, encouraged by European diplomacy, to avoid becoming entangled in European conflict, whenever it was to their interest to do so.

Similarly, the ideological origins of the Monroe Doctrine, which is complementary to that of isolation, are to be traced far back into the beginnings of the colonial period. The basic theme in the Monroe Doctrine is the idea that "the political system of the allied powers [of Europe] is essentially different . . . from that of America . . . [and] we should consider any attempt on their part to extend their system to any portion of this hemisphere as dangerous to our peace and safety." This is, in itself, a re-statement of the old international doctrine that America is a new world, separate and distinct from Europe, to which the European system of politics and diplomacy does not apply. In expressing his doctrine, Monroe thus falls back upon the older European principle of the two spheres, which had found both doctrinal expression and contractual implementation before the end of the sixteenth century.

As early as 1532, Francisco de Vittoria proclaimed the inviolability of America. It is true, of course, that Vittoria's argument is very different from that of Monroe. Vittoria based his principle upon the fact that the Indians had a civilization of their own, were the rightful owners of the new lands, and, therefore, could not legally be dispossessed, whereas Monroe based his doctrine upon the existence of an European-American civilization in America which had developed since the beginning of European settlement. They do have, however, a common premise, and that is that America is a new, different and independent world, over which Europe has no legal right to extend its control.

Vittoria's philosophical pronouncement of the doctrine of the two spheres was not, however, the interpretation of that doctrine carried into the practice of European diplomacy. The early diplomatic application of this principle is to be seen, rather, in the practical dogma that "there is no peace beyond the Line." That is to say, to the diplomatists of the sixteenth and seventeenth centuries, Europe was one world and America, lying beyond the Line, was another; and piracy, territorial plundering, or intercolonial wars might take place in that new sphere without disturbing the peace and friendly relations of the mother countries in Europe. Likewise, under certain treaties, the reverse was true.

Such was the principle of the two spheres inherent in the oral agreement with regard to colonial affairs between French and Spanish diplomats in Cateau-Cambrésis, in 1559, and embodied in many subsequent treaties, notably the Anglo-Spanish treaty of 1604. This was also the principle underlying the Anglo-French treaty of Whitehall, of 1686. In this latter case, however, the doctrine is a doctrine of peace, not war. For Article XVII of this treaty provides that hostilities between the French and English colonies in America shall not be made a cause of war between the mother countries, and Article XVIII provides that war between England and France shall not be a cause of war in America; but that "true and firm peace and neutrality shall continue in America between the . . . French and English nations, in the same manner as if no rupture had occurred in Europe."

The clearest example, perhaps, of the legal embodiment of the doctrine of the two spheres is the Hispano-Portuguese treaty of 1750. Not only is it provided in this treaty that the Spanish and Portuguese colonies shall remain neutral in case of war between the two nations in Europe, but, also, the treaty provides that, should either party to the treaty make an alliance with a third nation, the party making such an alliance, nevertheless, will not permit its ally to use its American ports or territories as bases of operations against the other party to the treaty or its colonies. In other words, even though enemies in Europe, they are to remain effectual allies for the maintenance of the *status quo* in America. This treaty is significant, not only as showing the importance of the doctrine of the two spheres in European diplomacy, but, also, because it shows that the diplomats of Spain and Portugal, at least, were coming to think of the territorial *status quo* in America as fixed, and not subject to further change.

It thus seems clear that the principle of the two spheres was well established when John Adams and his colleagues embodied the idea in the form of treaties prepared for the American representatives abroad, in 1776. The interpretation now given to this principle, however, was new. Hitherto, the European treaties based upon the doctrine of the two spheres had legalized a system for America which was distinct from the system of Europe, in matters of commerce, territories, and war. But Adams went one step farther, and, while assuming the basic principle of the two spheres, claimed for the young United States a deciding voice in the disposition of territories in North America still in the possession of Great Britain.

At this point, a new factor enters into any consideration of the old doctrine of the two spheres. Basically, the doctrine remains the same; but henceforth affairs in the western sphere are not to be determined by the diplomats of Europe. On the contrary, there has now appeared in the western world a new and independent nation which may be expected to assume a decisive position in affairs pertaining to America. It was only a short step further that Monroe was to go, when, the Spanish colonies having, in the meantime, achieved their independence, he proclaimed the predominant interest of the United States, not only in any territorial change that might, in the future, take place, but in blocking, once and for all, the possibility of further change in the direction of extending European possessions in the entire western hemisphere.

It should be borne in mind, of course, that Monroe did not, necessarily, draw upon European precedents to justify his interpretation of the doctrine of the two spheres. The ingrained American sentiment of isolation produced, in its normal growth, the determination not only to stay out of European complications, but, also, to keep European complications out of America. The doctrine of isolation is the negative American aspect of the principle of the two spheres; the Monroe Doctrine is the positive American aspect of that same principle. It is sufficient for us to note that both the European doctrine of the two spheres and the American doctrine of isolation, culminating in the Monroe Doctrine, have a common origin and kinship in the elemental facts of the geography of the new world.

In a similar, if, perhaps, a more local and specific sense, the principle of non-intervention may be said to have grown out of the exigencies of colonial life in America. Perhaps the earliest opportunity for interference in the affairs of another nation or colony, and an occasion which demands the formulation of a policy, presented itself to the Commonwealth of Massachusetts Bay

in the struggle of Charles de la Tour and the Sieur d'Aulnay
Charnisé for the control of Acadia, in the fourth and fifth decades
of the seventeenth century. [Savelle goes on to show that when
the Governor of Massachusetts agreed to aid one side of a dispute in Acadia, the people of the colony forced him to recant.
The people warned the Governor, "He that loseth his life in an
unnecessary quarrel dyes the Devill's martyr."]

Out of this same episode with La Tour and d'Aulnay may be
seen arising the beginnings of American diplomatic interest in
the freedom of the seas. From the first, New England's major interests lay upon the sea; and when d'Aulnay protested against
the Massachusetts trade with La Tour and threatened to seize
the "Bastonnais" ships, the magistrates sent him a "sharp answer," asserting the right of the English colonists to travel the
seas freely, trading with whomsoever they would.

.   .   .

Turning now to the "positive" doctrines of American foreign
policy, we find their evolution may be traced to similar beginnings. The principle of the freedom of trade, which now goes
under the name of the "open door," goes back at least to that
day in 1541 when Francis I expostulated against the Hispano-Portuguese monopoly of the land and commerce of the world: *"Le
soleil luit pour moi comme pour les autres; je voudrais bien voir
la clause du Testament d'Adam qui m'exclut du partage du
monde."*

But this principle, too, has an independent origin in the needs
and the experiences of the British colonies in the new world. As
early as 1627 we find the Pilgrim governors at Plymouth negotiating with an emissary from the Dutch colony of New Amsterdam
for "mutual commerce and trading in such things as our countries afford." And the chief provision in the treaty between the
Commonwealth of Massachusetts and Governor d'Aulnay, of Acadia, in 1644, was that "it shalbe lawfull for all their people, aswell
French as English, to trade each with other . . . provided al-
wayes that the governor and Majestrates [of Massachusetts]
aforesaid bee not bound to restrayne their Merchants from trade-
ing with the[ir] ships with what people soever, whether French or
others, in what place soever inhabiting." Here is a guarantee of
the open door in Acadia; for one of the specific aims of this
treaty, so far as Massachusetts was concerned, was to prevent

the closing of the lucrative trade between the Boston merchants and La Tour, d'Aulnay's rival.

A similar treaty was made at Jamestown, in the year 1660, between the English colony of Virginia and the Dutch colony of New Netherland, in flat defiance of the British Navigation Act of 1651. And the freedom of trade provided by the treaty of Jamestown was further established, in Virginia, by legislation, in the Act of March, 1660, to the effect that "all strangers of what Xpian nation soever in amity with the people of England shall have free liberty to trade with us, for all allowable commodities . . . and shall have equall right and justice with our own nation in all courts of judicature." If England closed the door to Virginia, Virginia itself would open the door, to the Dutch and to all others, by treaty and by act of Assembly. Thus did the colony defy the mother country because the colony's economic interests ran counter to those of England; thus, also, did Virginia give expression to a principle, which Virginia was not able to maintain, it is true, in the face of the later Acts of Trade, but which has remained one of the permanent bases of American foreign policy.

Meanwhile, the "most favored nation" clause, itself a diplomatic lever for opening closed commercial doors, was making its appearance in European diplomacy, and was embodied in the Anglo-French commercial treaty of Utrecht. This principle, too, was adopted for its own use by the United States, and embodied in the Franco-American commercial treaty of 1778; but it was inserted there only because it was found impossible to get from France that unrestricted freedom of commerce with France and the French colonies which was the dearest wish of the young American nation, whose past growth and whose future prosperity were predicated upon an expanding commerce.

Finally, the principle of peaceful settlement of disputes, as all these other permanent bases, has its origins both in the practices of European diplomacy with regard to the colonies and in the experiences of the colonies themselves. As early as 1655, Oliver Cromwell made a treaty with France which dealt, in part, with the issues raised in the informal war then going on between the two countries and with the seizure of Acadia by Major Sedgwick's expedition in 1654. This treaty provided for the establishment of a joint claims commission, composed of three appointees on each side, which was empowered, also, to settle the dispute with regard to the ownership of Acadia. In case the commissioners failed to agree, the disputes between the two countries were to be submitted to the city of Hamburg for arbitration. The provisions for arbitration were not carried out; but the principle of the arbitration of colonial disputes was clearly recognized, and was embodied later, notably in the Anglo-French treaty of Whitehall, 1686.

Meanwhile, in the colonies themselves, this principle had been established by the intercolonial treaty of Hartford, 1650. For two decades the boundary line between the English and the Dutch in Connecticut and Long Island had been in dispute. Various suggestions had been made, on both sides, that the dispute be settled by arbitration, but no action was taken until Peter Stuyvesant journeyed to Hartford in 1650 and negotiated with the Commissioners of the United Colonies a treaty which provided for the determination of the boundary by four commissioners, two to be appointed on each side.

Thereafter, the principle of settlement of colonial disputes by arbitration or joint commission was given lip-service in the treaties of Whitehall (1686), Utrecht (1713), and Aix-la-Chapelle (1748); and an attempt was actually made to settle the dispute over the Acadian boundary by peaceful methods after 1749. This attempt collapsed, however, with the outbreak of the Seven-years War, and, apparently, there is no record of a successful application of this method of settling intercolonial disputes after the treaty of Hartford. The principle was, none-the-less, recognized; and it was embodied, as a principle by no means new, in the Jay Treaty of 1794, upon the basis of which certain disputes between the United States and Great Britain were actually settled.

Origins of American Diplomatic Principles

Realist

Realists find the principles that have guided American policy in the past to be unrealistic rather than successful. They wonder how the United States became so utopian in its beliefs. Why does this nation exaggerate its own strength? What brings it to fight total war for total victory without regard for the balance of power or the postwar settlement? Why has the United States been so distrustful of professional military skills and so willing to rely on civilian minutemen? In the next two selections, Daniel J. Boorstin and Felix Gilbert seek the origins of these and other principles they believe have led the United States down mistaken paths.

Do these principles necessarily contradict those accepted by Max Savelle and the Nationalists? When there are incompatibilities, which viewpoint seems most nearly correct? When the principles do not contradict one another, which ones seem most important in the formation of past and present American foreign policy? To what extent and in what ways do these principles differ from those of European nations? Why did such differences come about?

Daniel J. Boorstin is director of the National Museum of History and Technology of the Smithsonian Institution. He received a Bancroft Prize in 1959 for the book from which this essay was extracted. Felix Gilbert is a professor of history at the Institute for Advanced Study in Princeton, New Jersey.

The Americans: The Colonial Experience

Daniel J. Boorstin

DEFENSIVE WARFARE AND NAÏVE DIPLOMACY

The period during which the American colonies were founded is generally described as the Age of Limited Warfare in Europe. From about the time in the early 17th century when the Puritans settled Massachusetts Bay until the French Revolutionary Wars

From Daniel J. Boorstin, *The Americans: The Colonial Experience*, 1964, pp. 345–349, 351–352, 356, 357–358, 362. Reprinted by permission of Random House.

near the end of the 18th century, Europe showed notable restraint. After the bloodbath of the religious wars, the "Enlightened Age" offered Europe a relief, less from the fighting itself
than from its worst horrors. War was moderated less through efforts to abolish it than through the growth of formal rules of warfare and by the specialization of the military function. Since the
restraints which made wars less destructive also made them less
decisive, European history during the colonial period was a story
of continual indecisive warfare. "Now it is frequent," Daniel
Defoe remarked in 1697, as the War of the Dutch Alliance drib-
bled out, "to have armies of fifty thousand men of a side stand at
bay within view of one another, and spend a whole campaign in
dodging, or, as it is genteelly called, observing one another, and
then march off into winter quarters. The difference is in the max-
ims of war, which now differ as much from what they were formerly as long perukes do from piqued beards, or as the habits of
the people do now from what they then were. The present max-
ims of war are—

Never fight without a manifest advantage,
And always encamp so as not to be forced to it.

And if two opposite generals nicely observe both these rules, it is
impossible they should ever come to fight."

Battles tended to take place on large open fields, where the
customary rules and formations could be obeyed. At the opening
of a battle, the opposing forces were set up like men on a chess-
board; each side usually knew what forces the other possessed,
and each part of an army was expected to perform only specific
maneuvers. Sneak attacks, irregular warfare, and unexpected
and unheralded tactics were generally frowned on as violations
of the rules. "This way of making war," Defoe succinctly put it,
"spends generally more money and less blood than former wars
did." Though armies increased, casualties declined. In the year
1704, which witnessed decisive battles of the War of the Spanish
Succession, only 2000 British soldiers and sailors died in action
and no more than 3000 died of wounds, disease, or other causes
connected with the war.

Such moderation would have been impossible if the waging of
wars had not become a specialized occupation from which the
mass of the people felt removed. War had become the task of
warriors, whose functions were as separated from those of the

common man as were the tasks of the learned barrister, the doctor of physick, or the cleric. Officers of opposing sides enjoyed the fraternity of all professionals and of the international European aristocracy: between engagements they wined and entertained one another with balls, concerts, and dinner parties. Usually aristocratic professionals, they were drawn from the nobility and the upper classes, for whom the duty of military service to their prince remained a relic of feudal days. Private soldiers, who had not yet acquired the kudos of "fighting for their country," were few by modern standards and tended more and more to be the dregs of society. Driven to recruit from the jails and taverns, the sovereign preferred, if he could afford it, to fill his ranks with such mercenary professionals as the Swiss or the Hessians.

War, then, was not an encounter fought by two fully mobilized communities and hallowed by patriotism. Military engagements occurred not in the rubble of factories and cities, but usually on a military playing field, a plain at some distance from the populace. There the "rules of warfare" were neatly and scrupulously followed, with the least possible interference to the peaceful round of household, farm, and fair. Commanders would no more have undertaken a battle in thick underbrush or woods, at night, or in bad weather, than a modern professional baseball team would consent to play in dense woods on a wet day. There were exceptions, but surprisingly few.

From the middle of the 17th until near the end of the 18th century, European war was merely an instrument of policy. It was not waged to exterminate another people or to change their ways of life or their political or economic institutions. Usually it was the effort of one ruling prince to extend his territory, to vindicate his honor, or to secure a commercial advantage from an opposing sovereign, who was likely to be his cousin. Objectives were much more limited than they had been during the religious wars of the 16th and early 17th centuries.

The pan-European character of the aristocratic literary culture provided the common ideas out of which grew a specialized literature defining the just occasions and proper limits of warfare. During most of this period, the leading handbook was Grotius' *De jure belli ac pacis* (On the Law of War and Peace), 1625–31, which set up authoritative "rules" for civilized nations; it was displaced in the later 18th century by Vattel's *Le droit des gens* (The Law of Nations), 1758, which made some changes but still assumed that civilized nations were bound in peace or war by certain natural regulations.

The American Indian who lay in wait for the earliest colonists had, unfortunately, not read Grotius or Vattel. He had no international aristocracy, nor was he persuaded of the advantages of limited warfare that was waged only during clear weather in open fields. He had his own weapons and his own ways, the ways of the forest. He was not accustomed to pitched battles nor to the trumpet-heralded attack. The Indian bow, unlike the matchlock, was silent, accurate, and capable of rapid fire even in wet weather; the tomahawk was a more versatile weapon than the fifteen-foot pike. When the Indian captured an enemy he did not obey Grotius' laws of war by taking prisoners and seeking to exchange them. On the contrary, massacre and torture were his rule; he thought nothing of flaying his enemy or bleeding him to death with jabs of pointed sticks. The Rev. Joseph Doddridge observed the savage attacks in Western Virginia in the later 18th century:

The Indian kills indiscriminately. His object is the total extermination of his enemies. Children are victims of his vengeance, because, if males, they may hereafter become warriors, or if females, they may become mothers. Even the fetal state is criminal in his view. It is not enough that the fetus should perish with the murdered mother, it is torn from her pregnant womb, and elevated on a stick or pole, as a trophy of victory and an object of horror to the survivors of the slain. If the Indian takes prisoners, mercy has but little concern in the transaction. He spares the lives of those who fall into his hands, for the purpose of feasting the feelings of ferocious vengeance of himself and his comrades, by the torture of his captive.

This American scene created a new type of adventure literature —stories of Indian captivities—which recounted the suffering and heroism of ordinary settlers, their wives, and children.

The Indian was omnipresent; he struck without warning and was a nightly terror in the remote silence of backwoods cabins. The New England settlers, Cotton Mather recalled, felt themselves "assaulted by unknown numbers of devils in flesh on every side"; to them the Indians were "so many 'unkennell'd wolves.'" Every section of the seacoast colonies suffered massacres. The bloody toll of the Virginia settlements in 1622, and again in 1644, was never forgotten in the colony. In Virginia in 1676, Nathaniel Bacon's Rebellion expressed the demand of western settlers for more aid against the Indians. We have already seen how the Indian massacres of the mid-18th century sharpened the crisis of the Quaker government of Pennsylvania. Such nightmares shaped the military policy of settlers until nearly the end of the 18th century. The Indian menace, which haunted the fringes of settlement through the whole colonial era, remained a terror to the receding West well into the 19th century. Not until ten years after the massacre of Custer's force in 1876, when the few remaining Indians had been removed to Indian Territory or to reservations, did the Indian threat disappear.

The Indian was not the only menace. Parts of the English colonies suffered intermittent threats of invasion by European powers —the French, the Dutch, or the Spanish. While England remained relatively safe from foreign invasion from the time of the Armada (1588) at least until the time of Napoleon, the earliest settlers of Virginia were often in terror that the Spanish massacre of the Huguenots at Fort Caroline in Florida might be repeated in their own province. More than once the pioneer settlers of Jamestown raised the alarm that Spanish ships were coming up their rivers; they anxiously watched every approaching sail in fear that it might bring invaders. Boston was alarmed by the approach of La Tour in a French ship of 140 tons in 1643, and on numerous later occasions had reason to fear attack from some European force. Even the pacifism of Pennsylvania Quakers was strained by the appearance of Spanish ships in the very harbor of the city.

Such threats forced whole communities to huddle together in time of danger. The garrison house, built as a common dwelling and refuge during Indian raids, became a symbol of the unlimited nature of warfare in America.

.   .   .

Thus war had become an institution for the citizenry as well as the warriors. The colonials were in the habit of defending themselves on neighboring ground instead of employing professionals on a distant battlefield. Just as everybody in America was somewhat literate but none was greatly literary, everybody here was a bit of a soldier, none completely so. War was conducted without a professional army, without generals, and even without "soldiers" in the strict European sense. The Second Amendment to the Federal Constitution would provide: "A well regulated Militia, being necessary to the security of a free State, the right of the people to keep and bear Arms, shall not be infringed."

The distinctive American experience would, of course, make

difficulties whenever Americans would be arrayed in war or diplomacy against Europeans, for in Europe the professional army with its aristocratic officer class had made war a sophisticated, attenuated activity. To that sophistication there were two aspects. On the one hand, specialization of the soldier's function had made possible the limitation of warfare. On the other hand, it made possible a sophisticated diplomacy by which sovereigns used professional armies to serve their trivial or devious purposes and under which an uninterested populace lightly allowed their "nation" (i.e., the professional soldiery) to be committed to battle. A professional army was casually sent wherever the sovereign wished for imperial, dynastic, or commercial strategy. European war by the 18th century was far removed from the naïve defense of the hearth: specialized fighters were trained to kill for reasons they did not understand and in distant lands for which they had no love. As the 18th century wore on, such wars of policy commanded more and more of the blood and treasure of Europe. But these wars were barely intelligible, much less defensible, among colonial Americans, to whom war was the urgent defense of the hearth by everybody against an omnipresent and merciless enemy. Americans would long find it hard to understand the military games played by kings, ministers, and generals who used uniformed pawns on distant battlefields, or the diplomatic games in which such wars were only interludes.

.   .   .

The militia system itself, with its axiom that every man was a trained and ready-armed soldier who would instantly spring to the defense of his country, encouraged the belief—which often proved a dangerous illusion—that the community was always prepared for its peril. In a country inhabited by "Minute Men" why keep a standing army? At the time of the first World War, William Jennings Bryan would boast that when the President called, a million freemen would spring to arms between sunrise and sunset. His belief was based on the obsolete assumption that the very conditions of American life produced men who were always ready to fight. The fear of a standing army, which by European hypothesis was the instrument of tyrants and the enslaver of the peoples, reenforced opposition to a professional body of men-in-arms. Moreover, so long as the men-in-arms were merely civilians temporarily distracted from their regular peaceful occupations, so long as there was no professional group concerned for its own prestige, few American politicians dared urge the advantages of a professional army.

The long-standing American myth of a constantly prepared citizenry helps explain why Americans have always been so ready to demobilize their forces. Again and again, our popular army has laid down its arms with dizzying speed, only to disperse into a precarious peace. This rhythm of our life began in the earliest colonial period. The people sprang quickly to arms: for example, on the night of September 23, 1675, during King Philip's War, an alarm at a town thirty miles out of Boston brought twelve hundred militiamen under arms within an hour. As soon as an alarm was past, an expedition over, or a campaign ended, militiamen showed the same speed in disbanding.

.   .   .

HOME RULE AND COLONIAL "ISOLATIONISM"

The militia had arisen to defend farms, homes, and towns, not to serve as pawns in anyone's grand strategy. When threatened by unpredictable bands of marauding Indians, colonists saw no sense in sending men off to fight in some distant place, while leaving their own homes unprotected. Anyway, there was seldom a battlefront in Indian warfare. From the very beginning, therefore, Americans thought of military defense in the most direct and simple terms. They did not think of men marching off to battle, but of a man standing, gun in hand, beside his neighbors to fend off the enemy attacking his village. Settlers were ready enough to build a stockade, a garrison house, or a fort for their own town, but they were reluctant to maintain a fort at some distance—however strategic it might be for their own defense.

Some of the crucial defenses of the colonies were never built, simply because the nearby towns could not afford the expense of an adequate fortification and remote towns were not enough interested. For example, Castle Island commanded the channel by which vessels had to approach Boston, and a strong, continuously-maintained fort there would have protected the whole colony. But repeated efforts to persuade outlying towns to bear their share of the expense were unsuccessful; the Island fortification lacked a permanent garrison, was never fully manned, and periodically fell into decay. The burden of maintaining it, when it was maintained at all, was assumed by Boston and a few adjacent towns. The same story could be told of Virginia and the southern colonies, where the danger of coastal invasion by foreign powers and by pirates was constant. At Jamestown, for example, the fortification had so decayed by 1691 that it could not even be used as a depot for supplies. Because the coastal defenses of the colonies required the largest investment, the most cooperation and planning, and the greatest support from remote places, they proved to be the weakest link in the colonial military scheme. For such defense, colonists came to rely on guard-ships arriving fully manned from England.

Perhaps the dominant fact about the relationship of the colonies to each other was this reluctance of any one colony to send its militia to join in the defense of its neighbor. The "burgher guard," or local militia, of New Amsterdam, which had been first mustered during the Indian War of 1644, was unwilling even to go outside the city limits. When New York or South Carolina fought in their own defense, they automatically defended the other colonies, but this was the consequence of their more exposed geographic situation; it was not due to any cooperative or farsighted spirit. Nevertheless, no colony hesitated to use its neighbors. For a long time Virginia regularly sent a messenger to New York and New England to bring back word on the movements of the hostile French and the northern Indians—never to see whether help was needed in the North, but simply to be forewarned against a possible attack on themselves. A large proportion of the intercolonial communications consisted of explanations, more or less diplomatic, of why each dared not, or could not afford, to send its militia outside its own borders.

. . . Under the new Federal Constitution, declarations of war were possible only through a cumbersome and time-consuming legislative process, in full public view. The after-image of the early American vision remained. And the American people retained a strong and often disorganizing hand on their nation's foreign policy.

To the Farewell Address: Ideas of Early American Policy

Felix Gilbert

John Adams was a member of the committee entrusted with the preparation of the Model Treaty [suggested instructions to American diplomats during the Revolution], and he was assigned to draft this document. Adams must be considered as the chief architect of the Model Treaty and its accompanying instructions. He had given much thought to the subject before he entered upon this task. In March 1776, evidently influenced by Paine's *Common Sense,* he had set down on paper his ideas as to the "connection we may safely form" with France and arrived at the following formula: "1. No political connection. Submit to none of her authority, receive no governors or officers from her. 2. No military connection. Receive no troops from her. 3. Only a commercial connection; that is, make a treaty to receive her ships into our ports; let her engage to receive our ships into her ports; furnish us with arms, cannon, saltpetre, powder, duck, steel." How fundamental these ideas were for him can be deduced from the fact that they also appear in letters which he wrote in the spring of 1776. He urged the necessity of sending ambassadors to foreign courts "to form with them, at least with some of them, commerical treaties of friendship and alliance"; and when the dangers to American freedom of an alliance with a foreign power were pointed out to him, he stressed that in recommending foreign alliances, he was thinking only of a contractual safeguard of America's trade relations. "I am not for soliciting any political connection, or military assistance, or indeed naval, from France. I wish for nothing but commerce, a mere marine treaty with them."

The Model Treaty was intended to realize the ideas which John

From "Novus Ordo Seculorum," in Felix Gilbert, *To the Farewell Address: Ideas of Early American Policy* (copyright © 1961 by Princeton University Press; Princeton Paperback, 1970), pp. 49–50, 54–58, 59–66, 72–75. Reprinted by permission. Footnotes have been omitted.

Adams had previously developed—namely, that alliance did not imply a political bond and that America's contacts with outside powers should be limited to trade relations.

. . .

The striking thing about the Model Treaty and the accompanying instructions is that, although the Americans were in a desperate situation in which they looked anxiously for foreign help, their leaders insisted on proposals which were entirely alien to the spirit of the diplomatic practice of the time.

II

It was a long journey from the simple brick building of the State House in Philadelphia, with its unpretentious wood paneling, to the palaces of Paris and Versailles, abounding in marble and rosewood, chinoiseries, mirrors, and silk. How did the American leaders have the courage to proffer to the French government, ensconced in eighteenth-century splendor, a treaty which challenged all the diplomatic traditions of which France was the foremost practitioner?

The Americans were convinced of the immense value of the offer which they made to France: the ending of the English monopoly of trade with North America. The consequence would be not only to increase French economic prosperity, but also to weaken England, France's old rival. The Americans may have somewhat overestimated the extent to which the opening of the American ports to the ships of all nations would revolutionize the European state system. But in the American view, France would gain such far-reaching advantages that America had a right to determine the nature of the relationship which, in the future, should exist between America and the European powers.

The Model Treaty with which the Americans formulated their concept of this relationship shows the impact of the program which Paine had set forth in *Common Sense*. The Model Treaty and the accompanying instructions were designed to keep America out of European struggles and to secure for her peace and freedom by making all European powers interested partners in American trade. But behind these documents there lay an attitude which leads beyond the image which Paine had given of America's role in foreign policy. Paine's ideas are products of the age in which he was born, of the Enlightenment; but in *Common*

Sense, he did not share its optimism. To Paine, the world, with the exception of America, was rotten and lost. "Freedom hath been hunted around the globe. Asia and Africa have long expelled her, Europe regards her like a stranger, and England hath given her warning to depart." America was to be preserved as the last bulwark of liberty, "an asylum for mankind." This censure of Europe corresponded to feelings deeply rooted in America's colonial past and facilitated the acceptance of the ideas of *Common Sense* in America. But American intellectual life was also strongly imbued with the spirit of the Englightenment. Although most Americans may have agreed with Paine's condemnation of Europe's political and social life as it existed at the time, not all of them shared Paine's gloomy prognostications for Europe's future; many were in accord with the Enlightenment belief in progress and were convinced that a new and better age in the history of the human race was approaching. They believed the American Revolution had started a great experiment; they felt they were setting a pattern which the rest of the world would follow. Thus the Model Treaty had a double face. It was intended, on the one hand, as an instrument to achieve an independent existence for America, secure from the corrupting influence of Europe. On the other hand, by eliminating purely political issues like territorial settlements, by focussing on the regulation of commercial relations, and by placing them on such a liberal basis that the arrangements between France and America could easily be extended to the nations of the whole world, the Americans transformed the Model Treaty into a pattern for all future diplomatic treaties. The Americans entered the European scene as the representatives of the diplomacy of a new era. They did not feel confronted by an entirely hostile world. They might find little sympathy for their ideas with the rulers of France, who thought in terms of traditional diplomacy. But they felt they had many friends: their allies were all the progressive minds of Europe, the writers and thinkers whom we now call "the philosophes."

The philosophes' ideas on foreign policy and diplomacy throw light on the broad background from which the American views on this topic developed. The philosophes confirmed the Americans in their outlook on diplomacy and, for a number of years, were an important factor in determining the course of American foreign policy; finally, they infused a lasting idealistic element into the American attitude toward foreign affairs.

The views of the philosophes both on foreign policy and on domestic policy were based on the conviction that history had reached the end of a long and tortuous development; the contrasts and conflicts of the past would now be resolved in a great synthesis, and a permanent order could be accomplished. The confidence of the philosophes in the near approach of a golden age had its foundation in a peculiar constellation of historical factors. [One of these factors was the growing awareness of the importance of non-European parts of the globe.]

.   .   .

This feeling that one civilization now encompassed the whole world was reinforced by the astounding growth of economic interdependence. In the centers of European civilization, people could rely on having a regular supply of goods from all over the world: sugar from the West Indies, tea and china from the Far East, coffee and chocolate from the Americas and Africa. The barriers that existed seemed artificial and ephemeral in comparison with the fine net by which the merchants tied the individuals of the different nations together like "threads of silk." As Sédaine says in his famous comedy Le philosophe sans le savoir, the merchants—whether they are English, Dutch, Russian, or Chinese—do not serve a single nation; they serve everyone and are citizens of the whole world. Commerce was believed to bind the nations together and to create not only a community of interests but also a distribution of labor among them—a new comprehensive principle placing the isolated sovereign nations in a higher political unit. In the eighteenth century, writers were likely to say that the various nations belonged to "one society"; it was stated that all states together formed "a family of nations," and the whole globe a "general and unbreakable confederation."

The social force which carried this development was the bourgeoisie. In the eighteenth century, its members became conscious of being a main prop of social life; they felt entitled to have all obstacles to the development of their interests eliminated. The philosophes gave the claims of this class an ideological form. They did for the bourgeoisie what intellectuals usually do when a new and rising class wants to break the restraints which keep it in a subordinate position. Then intellectuals identify the cause of a class with the cause of the human race in general and explain that the fight is . . . for freedom against tyranny, rather than for special interests against privileges and suppression by a ruling group. The triumph of the new class is to be a victory of humanity, the final solution of all historical conflicts.

.   .   .

If the ideas of the philosophes on foreign policy have been studied less than those on domestic policy, this one-sidedness of modern interests corresponds to the order of value which the philosophes themselves assigned to these two fields of political activity. Their thesis was that the great role which foreign affairs played in the political life of their time was one of the most fundamental evils of the existing political system. D'Argenson has most succinctly formulated this basic attitude of the philosophes with regard to the relationship between domestic and foreign affairs. "The true purpose of the science called politics is to perfect the interior of a state as much as possible. Flatterers assure the princes that the interior is there only to serve foreign policy. Duty tells them the opposite."

The philosophes directed a systematic attack against the view which regarded foreign policy as the center and culmination of political activities. They assailed the entire concept of man which complements this philosophy of power politics that stresses the qualities of physical prowess, honor, and obedience. The high evaluation of military virtues is a "dangerous prejudice, a carryover from barbarism, a remnant of the former chaos." "True fame consists not in the glory which the stupidity of the people connects with conquests and which the still more stupid historians love to praise to the point of boring the reader"; if the right name were to be given to conquests "which for so long have been praised as heroism," they would be called crimes.

The existing methods of diplomacy were so much geared towards power politics and war that they could never serve the opposite purpose—the preservation of peace. The main target of the philosophes was the assumption that the only possibility and guarantee for peace lay in the maintenance of a balance of power among the states. There is hardly a philosophe and reformer who does not inveigh against the idea of balance of power, "this favorite idea of newspapers and coffee-house politicians." This idea, "reducing the whole science of politics to knowledge of a single word, pleases both the ignorance and the laziness of the ministers, of ambassadors and their clerks." In contrast to the ostensible aim of promoting peace, balance of power had, it was said, always done harm to a system of lasting peace and was opposed to it. The reason was that "the system of balance of power is a system of resistance, consequently of disturbance, of shocks and of explosions." With the overthrow of this central concept of eighteenth-century diplomacy, the other concerns of the traditional diplomacy were also reevaluated and shown up in their futility and dangerousness. According to the philosophes, the conclusion of treaties and alliances, the most significant activity of eighteenth-century diplomacy, would not serve to establish friendly relations among states; treaties are nothing but "temporary armistices" and alliances "preparations for treason." Even when they are called defensive alliances, they are "in reality always of an offensive nature." Diplomatic activity, thus being identical with double-dealing and pursuing purposes different from those it openly avows, needs to wrap itself in secrecy and has become an "obscure art which hides itself in the folds of deceit, which fears to let itself be seen and believes it can succeed only in the darkness of mystery." Secrecy, therefore, is not—as the diplomats pretend—necessary for the efficient fulfillment of their functions; it only proves that they are conspirators planning crimes. Diderot, in a satirical piece entitled "Political Principles of Rulers," has summarized the views of the philosophes on the diplomacy of their time. "Make alliances only in order to sow hatred. . . . Incite wars among my neighbors and try to keep it going. . . . Have no ambassadors in other countries, but spies. . . . To be neutral means to profit from the difficulties of others in order to improve one's own situation." Though different writers made different aspects of diplomacy— secrecy or formality of etiquette—the chief butts of their criticism, they were all in agreement that diplomacy could not be reformed by redressing any single abuse. The evil inherent in diplomacy could be removed only by a complete change in the attitude of those who ruled. Foreign affairs showed most clearly the ills of a world not yet ruled by reason. "The blind passions of the princes" were the cause of wars, conquests, and all the miseries accompanying them. A favorite story of the eighteenth century illustrating the arbitrariness which dominated foreign policy was the story of the palace window: Louvois, fearing disgrace because Louis XIV had expressed displeasure with Louvois' arrangements concerning the construction of the windows of the Trianon, instigated the King to renew the war against the Hapsburgs in order to divert his attention from architectual matters. As long as foreign policy continued to be determined by passions, by whims and arbitrary proclivities, diplomacy could be nothing else but "the art of intrigue."

If one wants to reduce this whole complex of eighteenth-century ideas on diplomacy to a simple formula, it can be summarized as the establishment of a rule of reason. It is the same solution which the philosophes had for the problems of domestic policy. In view of the pre-eminence which they gave domestic over foreign affairs, they considered the introduction of a new and peaceful era in foreign policy dependent on a reorganization of domestic policy. It would even be enough to put the policy of France on a new basis. Since France was the hub in the wheel of European politics, the other nations would quickly follow the French lead; a new period in world history would begin.

Yet how could this change be effected? As much as the eighteenth-century reformers agreed on the basic concepts which we have sketched above, they differed on how their ideas could be realized. Some looked for a solution along conservative, others along radical, democratic lines.

Among those who had a more conservative outlook were the physiocrats. A great number of the philosophes—some in a more, others in a less orthodox way—belonged to the physiocratic school. Although today physiocracy is usually regarded as having propounded an original and important economic doctrine, the significance of physiocratic theories in the eighteenth century seemed to reach far beyond the economic sphere and to range over the entire structure of social and political life. The physiocrats called their political theory "economic policy," not because they were concerned solely with economic questions, but because, to them, economics and politics were identical. They believed that all political problems would be solved if the right economic principles were followed and the right economic measures adopted. The contrast to "economic policy" was the "old policy," the "false policy," or "power politics"; all of these terms were alternately used. "The essence of power politics consists of divergence of interests, that of economic policy of unity of interests—the one leads to war, frustrations, destruction, the other to social integration, co-operation, and free and peaceful sharing of the fruits of work." The physiocrats elaborated this contrast between "the old policy" and "the economic policy," between an "artificial" and a "natural" political situation, with great gusto and especially emphasized that, as a result of the artificiality of the "old policy," dealings had to be shrouded in secrecy and mystery. The diplomats had to be actors—"competitors in grimaces"—and each nation was barricaded behind its own frontiers, intent on making commercial treaties to its own advantage and to the disadvantage of its neighbor. In contrast, the new world in which the "economic policy" was to be realized would have an unrestricted exchange of goods. From mutual interdependence would emerge the realization that increase in one nation's wealth means increased wealth for all other nations, and that the interests of all nations are identical; consequently, there would be no advantage in enlarging one's own territory and combatting one's neighbor. A single measure, namely, the establishment of free trade, would bring about this miraculous change; it was up to the rulers of the states to take this one decisive measure. The physiocrats were favorites of many princes, and their faith in the power of reason was so strong that they believed in the probability of persuading the rulers of the states to make this change. They were no opponents of despotism; on the contrary, they were confident that the new order could be introduced quite easily with and by means of the prince's absolute power.

Other philosophes believed that the physiocrats were deceiving themselves by trusting in princely absolutism. These more radical thinkers saw despotism as an integral part of the old order which had to be overcome. The decisive step in establishing the new order was a change in political leadership; the people themselves had to take over control of political life. These writers were concerned with the problem of how to achieve an effective popular control of foreign policy. Condorcet, who was particularly interested in this question, constructed a mechanism which he considered suitable for this purpose. No convention between nations should be valid without approval of the legislative body. Moreover, as a further safeguard, he demanded that political treaties should be ratified by the single districts of a state. In case of an enemy attack, war might be declared, but only by the legislative; and a declaration of war would have to be followed immediately by new elections, which would give the people the opportunity to express their views on the war. Evidently Condorcet had no doubt that the people would always be peace-loving; the practical issue was to remove all obstacles to a direct expression of the popular will. Condorcet regarded diplomats as such an obstacle, as unnecessary middlemen. He had no use for them, nor for diplomatic arrangements establishing automatic obligations by which the freedom of action of a nation would be bound. "Alliance treaties seem to me so dangerous and so little useful that I think it is better to abolish them entirely in time of peace. They are only means by which the rulers of states precipitate the people into wars from which they benefit either by covering up their mistakes or by carrying out their plots against freedom, and for which the emergency serves as a pretext." The picture which the philosophes envisaged of the relations among nations after the rule of reason had been established was implied in their criticism of the existing foreign policy: the former would be the reverse of the latter. Foreign policy should follow moral laws. There should be no difference between the "moral principles" which rule the relations among individuals and "moral principles" which rule the relations among states. Diplomacy should be "frank and open." Formal treaties would be unnecessary; political alliances should be avoided particularly. Commercial conventions should refrain from all detailed regulations establishing individual advantages and privileges; they should limit themselves to general arrangements stating the fundamental rules and customs of trade and navigation. In such a world, the connection among the different states would rest in the hands not of governments but of individuals trading with each other.

If this picture of the foreign policy of the future was not very precise, there was a special reason. Foreign policy and diplomacy were regarded as typical phenomena of the *ancien régime,* they owed their importance to the fact that the rulers followed false ideals and egoistic passions instead of reason. The logical consequence was that in a reformed world, based on reason, foreign policy and diplomacy would become unnecessary, that the new world would be a world without diplomats.

.   .   .

[Gilbert also shows how America's foreign policy was derived from England's policy of "splendid isolation" and hopes for a balance of power in Europe.]

The foreign policy of the young republic, with its emphasis on commerce and on avoidance of political connections, has usually been explained as a policy of isolation. Unquestionably, the English background of the ideas which served in the formation of the American outlook on foreign policy contained an isolationist element. However, if we place the ideas which guided early American foreign policy beside those of the European philosophes, it becomes clear that the isolationist interpretation is one-sided and incomplete: American foreign policy was idealistic and internationalist no less than isolationist.

In many minds, these two motives can be found interwoven in such a way that neither of the two elements can be regarded as predominant. This was characteristic of Jefferson. He remained opposed to diplomacy, which he considered as "the pest of the peace of the world, as the workshop in which nearly all the wars of Europe are manufactured." In 1792, when a number of diplomatic nominations had been submitted to the Senate by Washington for approval, Jefferson suggested that diplomatic representatives should be sent by America only to those countries where geographic closeness or interests of commerce demanded a permanent representation; this meant to London, Paris, Madrid, Lisbon, and The Hague. Also, these appointments should be kept "on the lowest grades admissible." Later Jefferson wrote that "Consuls would do all the business we ought to have." Jefferson's inclination towards the adoption of what he called an "a-diplomatic system" sprang from his fear that America might become involved in European politics but, at the same time, he wanted to set an example to the entire world. Jefferson was convinced that the relations between nations in the future would take forms different from those of the diplomacy of the past. His belief in the emergence of a new spirit in international relations is beautifully expressed in a letter to Madison of August 28, 1789. Jefferson pleaded for acknowledging the duties of gratitude in America's relations to France: the often heard view that power and force ruled in the relations between nations "were legitimate principles in the dark ages which intervened between ancient and modern civilisation, but exploded and held in just horror in the 18th century. I know but one code of morality for man whether acting singly or collectively."

Thus, although the American outlook on foreign affairs contained two different elements, they could be combined; and then they reinforced each other. But they could also be contradictory. Then those who were concerned with foreign policy suddenly swerved from one extreme to the other. Unexpected resistance or obstacles might turn the utopian hopes for an imminent "reformation, a kind of protestantism, in the commercial system of the world" into its reverse: demand for complete withdrawal from any contact with the outside world. The Americans might have to "recall their Ministers and send no more," as Adams wrote; or they ought "to stand to Europe precisely on the footing of China," as Jefferson formulated it. Yet it was immediately argued that this was not possible, because it would mean that the Americans would have to "give up the most of their commerce, and live by their agriculture." It was "theory only." In such moments, the egoistic insistence on isolation appeared no less unrealistic than the altruistic counsels of internationalism.

This dilemma was reflected in an episode which happened at the time of the end of the War of Independence. Indignation about the brutal way in which England used her sea-power had led a number of European states to form a league of "armed neutrality," with the purpose of defending the right of neutrals on the sea. This policy not only corresponded to the general aims of the foreign policy of the United States but also raised the hope of gaining from these powers support in the struggle against Britain. Thus, the United States was anxious to join the league, but, because a belligerent power could hardly become a member of a league of neutrals, the American advances were rebuffed. When, with the signing of the preliminaries of peace, this obstacle was removed and the Netherlands urged America to participate actively in the policy of armed neutrality, Congress took another look at the possible practical consequences of such a policy; it was realized that the league would make the United States a member of a political bloc. Thus Congress, in a resolution which admitted that "the liberal principles on which the said confederacy was established, are conceived to be in general favourable to the interests of nations, and particularly to those of the United States," rejected further negotiations about entry into the league, because "the true interest of these states requires that they should be as little as possible entangled in the politics and controversies of European nations." The principle of avoiding political connections proved to be incompatible with progress toward freeing commerce, which was the great hope for overcoming power politics.

But as contradictory as isolationism and internationalism could sometimes prove themselves to be, these contrasts could be overlooked; and they could be regarded as compatible with each other because there was a common factor between them, though only of a negative character: isolationism existed in a sphere of timelessness; internationalism existed in the future. Neither existed in the world of the present. Thus the attitudes which the young republic had adopted had not yet satisfactorily solved the problem—either practically or theoretically—of how to chart a course in the world as it was.

Origins of American Diplomatic Principles

Radical

Radicals seek the origins of American imperialism because they regard it as the dominant principle of American diplomacy throughout the nation's history. Generally they find the origins of this national principle in two sources—the heritage of European imperialism and the necessities of capitalism. Richard Van Alstyne, the author of the following selection, is not truly a Radical historian. He does not see expansion as the inevitable product of capitalism. He believes, however, that America has been imperialistic and does an excellent job of tracing the historical origins of its imperialism. Many Radical historians have borrowed from Van Alstyne's work to support their own ideas. Obviously, Radicals consider the "unique" principles discussed in the previous essays to be either subsidiary concepts or outright myths.

Which of the principles ascribed to the United States by the Nationalists and Realists are contradicted by Van Alstyne's work? How do the others fit into the Radical perspective? What is the relative importance of the European heritage and the American experience in developing America's concept of empire?

Richard Van Alstyne is a professor of history emeritus at the University of Southern California and is presently distinguished professor of History at Callison College, University of the Pacific in Stockton, California.

The Rising American Empire

Richard Van Alstyne

The title of this book comes straight from George Washington. Even as early as March 1783 the United States was, to Washington, a 'rising empire'. The phrase describes precisely what he and his contemporaries had in mind, that is to say an *imperium* —a dominion, state or sovereignty that would expand in population and territory, and increase in strength and power. Benjamin Franklin had been speaking and writing in terms like these for nearly forty years. Nor was the example of ancient Rome overlooked. Speaking with revolutionary fervour, William Henry Drayton, one of South Carolina's leading planters who was also chief justice of that province, delivered himself in 1776 of the following:

> Empires have their zenith—and their descension to a dissolution. . . . Three and thirty years numbered the illustrious Days of the Roman greatness—Eight Years measure the Duration of the British Grandeur in meridian Lustre! How few are the Days of true Glory! . . . The British Period is from the Year 1758, when they victoriously pursued their Enemies into every Quarter of the Globe. . . . The Almighty . . . has made choice of the present generation to erect the American Empire. . . .
>
> And thus has suddenly arisen in the World, a new Empire, stiled the United States of America. An Empire that as soon as started into Existence, attracts the Attention of the Rest of the Universe; and bids fair, by the blessing of God, to be the most glorious of any upon Record.

The contrast between Washington's matter-of-fact way of expressing himself and Drayton's flamboyancy hardly needs a comment. Yet both men were moved by pride, and by a sense of future greatness, a conviction that the United States was the heir to, and the successor of, Britain in the New World. The declared purpose in fighting the War for Independence was to create a new empire or, to put the thought in words hardly familiar at the time, a new national state. Prior to the Seven Years War people had allowed to the term 'British Empire' only the limited meaning that the original Latin word 'imperium' conveyed, that is, a power or a sovereignty. But by 1760, under the influence of the sweeping victories over France, the meaning of the term had been broadened so that the emphasis was put upon territorial expanse and upon the people who inhabited it. This shift in meaning took place under the leadership of Chatham and the victorious Whigs, who desired to keep Canada; and Washington, Franklin and other Americans who had participated in this war and who ardently desired to eliminate the French and make North America a British continent, readily accepted the new interpretation. And so, with the coming of the Revolution and with the welding of the Thirteen Colonies into a new sovereign nation, the substitution of the phrase, 'American Empire', for British came easily and naturally. The Revolution also revived and strengthened the ancient Roman conception of patriotism and, through the zeal and passion of this feeling, it breathed life into the American imperium.

.   .   .

In the United States it is almost a heresy to describe the nation as an empire. The founders so regarded it, as I have shown, and the word continued to be accepted usage through the middle of the nineteenth century, but this has been largely overlooked. The concept of an American empire disappeared with the War between the States, but the consolidation of national power that followed that war meant that it was more than ever an actuality. The learned Dr. Richard Koebner has shown how and for what reasons people in both Britain and America came to deprecate the concept and its purely emotive derivative, 'imperialism'. With the appearance of protest and criticism against the island conquests of 1898 and against the alleged 'big stick' policies of Theodore Roosevelt, 'imperialism' became an epithet applied indiscriminately to various nations but to the United States only for the years 1898 to 1912. This period is torn out of context and given a unique frame of reference, leading to the profound historical fallacy that the United States under the influence of Theodore Roosevelt suffered an unfortunate temporary 'aberration' from its hallowed traditions, from which it subsequently recovered as from a sickness. From this arose the curious belief that only nations with island possessions are empires. The earlier ambition of the United States to expand its continental domain was not, according to one representative historian, imperialism, a truth only in the sense that the word itself was not coined until the 1870s. Then, by way of compounding the confusion, this writer adds: 'In reality, the extension of American rule over Indian tribes and their lands was imperialism—not recognized as such only because the Indians were so few in number as to be virtually swallowed'.

Here it might be pointed out that American foreign policy has a vocabulary all its own, consciously—even ostentatiously—sidestepping the use of terms that would even hint at aggression or imperial domination, and taking refuge in abstract formulae, stereotyped phrases, and idealistic clichés that really explain nothing. Phrases like 'Monroe Doctrine,' 'no entangling alliances', 'freedom of the seas', 'open door,' 'good neighbour policy,' 'Truman doctrine,' 'Eisenhower doctrine,' strew the pages of American history but throw little light on the dynamics of American foreign policy. Parrot-like repetition of these abstractions and other generalities produces an emotional reflex which assumes that American diplomacy is 'different', purer, morally better than the diplomacy of other powers. There is a strong pharisaical flavour about American diplomacy, easily detected abroad but generally unrecognized at home. No doubt it is a part of the cult of nationalism.

Consider, for instance, the implication behind the well-worn stereotype, 'The United States enforces the Monroe Doctrine'. My dictionary tells me that a doctrine is a teaching—its derivation is the Latin verb, *doceo*, 'I teach'. But actually as American diplomacy manipulates this phrase, the Monroe Doctrine has long since assumed the characteristics of positive law which the United States, the lord of the western hemisphere, applies from time to time as it sees fit. The particular application may or may not be benevolent—that depends on how it is interpreted; but there is no doubt that it is arbitrary. Furthermore, it is an interesting point, I think, that American diplomacy shows a preference for a term that is commonly identified with theological dogma.

The Monroe Doctrine has the additional authority of Canon Law behind it. To carry the analogy further, the United States assumes unto itself a function of the mediaeval Papacy: the prerogative of infallibility.

The quotation, 'wheresoever the Roman conquers, he inhabits', which is incorporated in the title of this first chapter, is from the Stoic philosopher, Seneca. I culled it from the pages of one of the greatest of historians, Edward Gibbon, in the opinion that it applies with equal truth to the American nation. The idea that America—the 'New World'—would be conquered and inhabited by people of English stock was native to the empire builders of Elizabethan England and bred into the minds of the early immigrants to Virginia and Massachusetts Bay. With the latter, especially with the Puritans who migrated with a sense of grievance against their homeland, it became an article of faith that they were in a new world, a new sphere. Expounded with particular force and clarity by the New England Puritans, who regarded themselves as founders of a new Israel in the North American wilderness, the doctrine of the two spheres became a fixation in the American mind prerequisite to the growth of nationalism. New England, which was 'God's American Israel' according to its Calvinist divines, assumed from the outset an attitude of political independence toward the mother country. The Great and General Court of Massachusetts--the pretentious title which the legislative assembly of that province bestowed upon itself—audaciously substituted an oath of allegiance to itself in place of the oath to the king.

The notion of a pre-emptive right to the continent was given legal affirmation by the first Colonial charters, which designated the Pacific Ocean, or South Sea as it was then called, as the western boundary of the several colonies. Those who drafted the charters could not have even dreamed of the immense distance from one sea to the other, but as knowledge of the interior began to appear the charters, far from being regarded as ridiculous, were invoked as 'proof' that the French, who had mastered the vastness of the Mississippi basin, were mere trespassers. To this legal fiction was added the argument that the continent belonged as of right to those who could colonize it. Thus the Virginia planter, Lewis Burwell, in 1751 made a sweeping denial of the right of anyone except the people of the Atlantic seaboard to appropriate the hinterland. To the Board of Trade in London Burwell wrote:

That, notwithstanding the Grants of the Kings of England, France or Spain, the Property of these uninhabited Parts of the World must be founded upon prior Occupancy according to the Law of Nature; and it is the Seating & Cultivating the soil & not the bare travelling through a Territory that constitutes Right; & it will be political & highly for the Interest of the Crown to encourage the Seating the Lands Westward as soon as possible to prevent the French.

Here is perhaps the first invocation of John Locke's law of nature as the basis for territorial claim, and the first linking of natural law to colonization as giving to the Anglo-Americans their claim of superior right to the interior. This concept of the right to colonize, premised upon an assumed ability to implement the right, thus begins to be part of the American mentality in the eighteenth century. John Quincy Adams and James Monroe, employing the same reasoning, gave the doctrine classic expression in 1823; and the Monroe Doctrine became the chosen ideological weapon of the United States in the nineteenth century for warning intruders away from the continent. Manifest destiny, the intriguing phrase utilized by historians to label the expansion of the United States in the nineteenth century, is merely the other side of the coin. It was characteristic of the nineteenth as well as of the eighteenth century, moreover, to assert the right before the actual work of colonization had begun. Burwell in 1751, like Monroe in 1823 and others that were to follow, was speaking of prospects, not of actual accomplishment. Looked at from the standpoint of the sum total of its history, the abstract formulae and principles being disregarded or at least discounted, the United States thus becomes by its very essence an expanding imperial power. It is a creature of the classical Roman-British tradition. It was conceived as an empire; and its evolution from a group of small, disunited English colonies strung out on a long coastline to a world power with commitments on every sea and in every continent, has been a characteristically imperial type of growth.

My reason, then, for invoking the heretical phrase, American Empire, is so that the United States can be studied as a member of the competitive system of national states with a behaviour pattern characteristic of an ambitious and dynamic national state. This approach gives precedence to foreign affairs over domestic affairs, reversing the customary practice of treating national history from the standpoint of the nation preoccupied with its own internal affairs and only incidentally looking beyond its borders.

In other words, it is a history of the American national state or, as I prefer, of the American Empire, rather than a history of the American people.

The attitude, predetermined in Elizabethan England, that the 'New World' belonged exclusively to the English as the people capable of colonizing and exploiting it was germinal in the formation of American ideas of empire. Even in their infancy both Virginia and Massachusetts revealed a conquering spirit, an eagerness to participate or even to assume the initiative, whenever possible, in warfare against their French and Spanish neighbours. The tiny French colonies of Port Royal in Acadia on the Bay of Fundy and of Quebec on the St. Lawrence, though far away, were none the less unwelcome. A raid on Port Royal in 1613 by Samuel Argall, a ship captain in the employ of the Virginia Company, was initiated at Jamestown; and in 1629 the Kirke brothers from London captured and sacked both Quebec and Port Royal. This aggression was fostered by London businessmen, its object being to break the slender French holds in North America and secure control of the St. Lawrence gateway. These first attacks on the French registered a common outlook between English commercial interests and American settlers which was to be of decisive importance in the long contest with France for dominion over North America. On the other hand, taking the view that good relations with France in Europe overrode colonial ambitions, Charles I made peace with that country and repudiated the conquests in the New World. This decision of the King, representative of the agrarian, Tory viewpoint, was the first in a long series of checks which were to restrain English foreign policy from giving blanket support to American ambitions. Only a few years later Governor John Winthrop of Massachusetts attempted an intrigue in the internal affairs of Acadia, apparently with the object of bringing it under the control of its larger Puritan neighbour; and again in 1654 Massachusetts seized the opportunity of open war between England and France to attack the Acadian settlements. The Boston Yankees were already putting the Acadians at a disadvantage in the offshore cod fisheries.

A running war at sea between French and English vessels, with raids and counter-raids on the New England and Acadian coasts, was the rule during the next half century. The object of Massachusetts was permanent conquest; the most that the French could do was to wage defensive warfare in the form of reprisals. Boston again got its opportunity in 1690, when it launched a full scale invasion of Acadia followed the next year by an unsuccessful attempt on Quebec. By this time the New England mind was coming to regard Quebec as an 'American Carthage' which must be destroyed. But the New England provinces were not by themselves strong enough to accomplish their aim, even with the support of New York which had its own reason for wanting to subjugate Canada; and so in 1707 the Americans made their first official appeal to London for help in overthrowing the French. The result was two expeditions in which the British employed naval forces in conjunction with provincial soldiers: one in 1709 for the conquest of Acadia, a second in 1711 for the subjugation of Canada. The first one succeeded but the second was a failure. In the meantime, as far back as 1686, fur traders from New York had driven a wedge into the French hinterland by penetrating as far inland as Michilimackinac on Lake Michigan; and an interest was shown in building a fort on the site of Detroit, calculated to cut in twain the long arc of empire the French were beginning to construct between Quebec and the mouth of the Mississippi.

.   .   .

All these signs of the Anglo-Americans pushing inward the doors of their empire drove the French to the conclusion by 1749 that a supreme effort was necessary to hold the line at the natural frontier. There followed six years of feverish arming in America, paralleled by a succession of diplomatic attempts at compromise on the part of London and Paris. The British Government talked in terms of returning to the *status quo* of 1713, and each side had its own idea of setting up neutral areas west of the mountains; but neither could convince the other that such arrangements would stick, nor could they agree on what actually was meant by the *status quo* of 1713. The crucial areas were: Acadia, western New York, the Ohio valley, and the coastal plain of the Gulf of Mexico where Spain shared with France in the desire to drive the Americans back to the Atlantic coast. In all four of these areas the French energetically pushed forward their programme of fort building. To their minds, if they lost the interior to the British, whose wealth and power were already gaining on them so rapidly, France's position in Europe would be jeopardized. This conclusion, that if Britain were to be kept from becoming the mistress of Europe she must be checked over-seas, was the compelling factor in the French hope of making forts and garrisons stand up against the rising tide of commerce and population. On the British side opinion was divided: a dis-position to compromise in such a way as to leave the interior to the French, manifested by such men as Sir Thomas Robinson, the Secretary of State; a more warlike attitude displayed by Lord Halifax and the Board of Trade, who were committed to the ex-panding mercantile empire and who therefore lent a ready ear to the arguments of the Americans.

Most expansive of these arguments were those set forth by Franklin in a pamphlet written in 1751, which he called *Observa-tions concerning the Increase of Mankind.* In this and in a sec-ond pamphlet which he put out three years later, Franklin shows himself both a precursor of T. R. Malthus and a disciple of Machiavelli. Prophesying that the colonial population would double itself every quarter of a century, Franklin demanded more living room and admonished the British that a prince 'that acquires new Territory, if he finds it vacant, or removes the Natives to give his own people Room' deserves to be remem-bered as the father of his nation. Past gains established the duty that Britain now owed her Colonies:

What an Accession of Power to the *British* Empire by Sea as well as by Land! What Increase of Trade and Navigation! What Numbers of Ships and Seamen! We have been here but little more than 100 years, and yet the force of our Privateers in the late War, united, was greater, both in Men and Guns, than that of the whole *British* Navy in Queen *Elizabeth's* Time. How important an Affair then to *Britain* is the present Treaty for settling the Bounds between her Colonies and the *French,* and how care-ful should she be to secure Room enough, since on the Room depends so much the increase of her People.

Then, after the Albany Congress in 1754, Franklin resumed his attack even more vigorously. Britain should establish two colo-nies west of the Alleghenies and south of the Lakes in order to prevent the 'dreaded juncture of the French settlements in Can-ada with those of Louisiana'.
Otherwise:

They [the French] will both in time of peace and war (as they have al-ways done against New England) set the Indians on to harass our fron-tiers, kill and scalp our people, and drive in the advanced settlers; and so, in preventing our obtaining more subsistence by cultivating of new lands, they discourage our marriages, and keep our people from increasing; thus (if the expression may be allowed) killing thousands of our children before they are born.

Graphically supporting these arguments were two maps of the continent, the first of their kind to be issued in England: that of Lewis Evans, first published in 1749 and re-issued in 1755, and that of John Mitchell, published in the latter year under commission from the board of Trade. Both Evans and Mitchell knew America first-hand, and their maps challenged the other map of the continent previously published—that by Delisle of Paris in 1718. Neither Evans nor Mitchell allowed for French claims west of the moutains and south of the lakes.

In the aftermath of war, when the whole of the eastern half of North America from Hudson Strait to the Gulf of Mexico had fallen to the British Empire, and when the seeds of internal discontent and revolution against the mother country sprouted in the Colonies, an ugly legend took hold in America that the colonists had been made the unwilling victims of British 'imperialism'. It is a commonplace to remark that post-war periods are periods of disillusionment, discontent and quarrelling among the victors; and the mutual recriminations that were exchanged across the Atlantic almost as soon as this war was over show that it ran true to form. Nor is it perhaps too much to say that the American Revolution registered the failure of the Peace of 1763, because it broke up the solidarity of the Empire for which the Great War had been fought. Historical distortions and misrepresentations come easily in an atmosphere thus poisoned. Even Benjamin Franklin distorted the picture of the war only three years after it was over. Franklin in 1766 actually declared before a committee of the House of Commons that the Americans had had no concern with the territorial disputes over North America, that until a British army was sent they had been 'in perfect peace with both French and Indians', that the conflict had been 'really a British war', and that the Americans had unselfishly come to Britain's assistance. What an astonishingly false statement for a man of Franklin's extraordinary intelligence.

The legend was popularized by revolutionary agitators and propagandists such as Tom Paine, the English Quaker who left his motherland in 1774 with a grudge. With a flourish Paine blamed England for all the past wars into which the Americans had been 'dragged', and promised eternal peace and prosperity as the reward of independence. And somehow or other the succession of wars between 1689 and 1763, in all of which American territorial questions had been major issues, went down in American history books as private wars of the kings of England. Such nomenclature as 'King William's War', 'Queen Anne's War', 'King George's War', and even 'The French and Indian War', does not make for good history. I have never succeeded in tracing the origin of these queer titles, though it seems probable that they belong to the legacy of republicanism and anti-British feeling left by the Revolution. The term 'French and Indian War', as a substitute for which the phrase 'Great War for the Empire' is indeed more meaningful, was actually first introduced in the early national period. All four of these terms survive to this day as living historical stereotypes, although the animus which inspired them has died. Nevertheless, the distortion they represent is as great as would be the case if the two world wars of the twentieth century were stamped respectively 'Woodrow Wilson's War' and 'Franklin Roosevelt's War'.

Yet, to state the antithesis of this legend by charging that the Americans 'dragged' Britain into war would be resorting to the other extreme. British commercial and speculative interests, well represented in the government by the Board of Trade, were thoroughly committed to a war for empire in North America. Certainly they were not prepared to see the French eliminate Britain from that continent, as Newcastle, the Secretary of State, himself declared. And the French insistence that the watershed be made the boundary, with no British trade or settlement to the west of it was regarded in this sense. On the other hand, British counterproposals rendered in March 1755 were so drastic as to require the French to demolish even their inner line of forts along the Great Lakes and in the Illinois country, thus leaving Canada and Louisiana protected only by a scrap of paper.

Meanwhile by 1754 the French, under the guidance of three very able governors—La Galissonnière and Duquesne—had so advanced their military positions southward from Lake Erie to the forks of the Ohio that they were ready to make good on their claims to the watershed. Encirclement, which the Board of Trade had apprehended as far back as 1721, now seemed real, especially after the French had repulsed a small force of Virginia militia under the twenty-two-year-old George Washington and driven him east of the mountains. When in October 1754 the British Government learned of Washington's defeat, it decided on sending an expeditionary force to retrieve the Ohio valley. The sending of this expedition in March 1755 meant that Great Britain for the first time was assuming responsibility for the defence of the Colonial frontier. It meant that she viewed the defence of that remote frontier as vital to her own defence as a great power. That is the real significance of General Braddock's tragic campaign in the Virginia wilderness.

.   .   .

We recall that the Board of Trade had urged in 1721 that the Acadians should be displaced by an English-speaking population. We recall too the hostility of Massachusetts toward the Acadians, and the ill-concealed eagerness of men like Governor Shirley to get rid of them. In the years just before the outbreak of the Great War, an irredentist movement developed among the Acadians which furnished a satisfactory pretext for deporting them. Subversive activities, incited by the fighting priest from Quebec, Père Le Loutre, who was notorious for organizing Indian raids on the frontier villages of New England, alarmed the authorities in Halifax who saw, or chose to see, a Trojan horse within their gates. Halifax itself, a British naval base, was an outpost of New England mercantile influence; and since the disappointment of seeing Louisbourg restored to France, Governor Shirley had never lost sight of the possibility of crowding out the Acadians with a colonizing population from New England. In September 1754 the Lieutenant-Governor of Nova Scotia, Charles Lawrence, and three members of his council, all from New England, asked the Board of Trade for authority to deport all Acadians who refused to take an unqualified oath of allegiance. At first only a limited deportation seems to have been planned; but in the months of crisis that followed, the decision was made to execute a mass eviction of the French-speaking population. Between 1755 and 1758 some 6000 to 10,000 Acadians were forcibly removed from their native land, while others fled into the wilderness. This created the necessary vacuum in good farm lands for which the New England leaders had been waiting; and in 1759 Governor Lawrence, confident that his province would prove attractive to the restless farming population of Massachusetts, Rhode Island and Connecticut, proclaimed the country open to speculators and settlers upon terms that, for liberality, could hardly be excelled anywhere. Any group of promoters might obtain possession of one or more townships of 100,000 acres each; and any individual settler might acquire as much as a thousand acres for himself, with fifty additional acres for each member of his family, free of quit rent or other obligation for ten years. An inundation of farming families, chiefly from the Connecticut valley, ensued during the next few years so that Nova Scotia—'New Scotland'—became in fact an extension of New England.

Among the most energetic of the promoters was an Alexander McNutt, a native of Ulster who had gone out to Virginia in 1753 and then on to Boston, where he identified himself with the firm of Apthorp & Hancock, engaged in the shipping and supply business under contract with the authorities at Halifax. McNutt in 1759 obtained an option on lands aggregating 817,500 acres; and in 1765 he was joined by Benjamin Franklin and certain Philadelphia capitalists, who obtained a grant of two more townships Franklin subsequently secured an allotment of 20,000 acres for himself in the hope of inducing emigrants to go from Pennsylvania. These men overshot the mark, however. McNutt went home to Ulster in search of prospective emigrants, but found his plans blocked by the Board of Trade, while Franklin abandoned his own project in favour of his older speculation in Ohio lands.

The Peace of Paris of 1763 fulfilled the fondest dreams of the American empire builders. The war had been fought, as Lord Shelburne put it, for the security of the British colonies in America, a sentiment with which Benjamin Franklin heartily concurred. But Franklin by no means stopped short with mere security, for he was now dreaming of a world empire. In 1760 he wrote to his friend Lord Kames:

No one can more sincerely rejoice than I do, on the reduction of Canada; and this not merely as I am a colonist, but as I am a Briton. I have long been of opinion, that the foundations of the future grandeur and stability of the British empire lie in America; and though, like other foundations, they are low and little seen, they are, nevertheless, broad and strong enough to support the greatest political structure human wisdom ever erected. . . . All the country from the St. Lawrence to the Mississippi will in another century be filled with British people. Britain itself will become vastly more populous, by the immense increase of its commerce; the Atlantic sea will be covered with your trading ships; and your naval power, thence continually increasing, will extend your influence round the whole globe, and awe the world! . . .

Post-war difficulties soon set in, however, rendered unavoidable by the profound changes wrought by the war and giving rise to the myth which we have already discussed. Franklin, as we have seen, was among the first to subscribe to the myth, the occasion being his opposition to the Stamp Act. But he and other empire-minded Americans did not really change their objectives. Rather, they were led to think more directly of 'a new Empire, stiled the United States of America'. American nationalism, separatist and isolationist by its inheritance, and strengthened by the new position of security achieved through the Great War for the Empire, henceforth began generating forces of defiance and resistance eventuating in a war for independence. Britain, on her part, found herself trying to function under a new, untried, and indeed unworkable concept of Empire solidarity and centralized authority. A Canadian historian, Harold A. Innis, has gone straight to the heart of the problems facing the post-war government of George III. As Professor Innis writes:

> The complexity of an empire including the West Indies and Newfoundland with strong influential groups of lobbyists in England, the colonies including Nova Scotia in possession of a powerful tradition of assemblies, a conquered territory in Quebec, and a charter company in Hudson Bay, imposed too severe a strain on the constitutional resources of Great Britain taxed by the addition of Scotland in 1707 and the corruption of parliament under Walpole and George III.

Nevertheless, in conclusion, it is beyond argument that the entire future of the embryonic American empire rested upon the triumph of 1763.

three
Foreign
Policies
of the Founding
Fathers

Realist

The Realists regard the age of the Founding Fathers as the golden age of American diplomacy. Some Realists, like Hans Morgenthau, credit all the Founding Fathers with the kind of hardheaded practicality this school would like to see predominate in current American foreign policy. But most members of this school hold that even the golden age of American diplomacy was marred by a great battle between realism and idealism, personified by the struggle between Alexander Hamilton and his rivals Thomas Jefferson and James Madison. In fact, this is the theme of one of the most influential books of the past twenty-five years, Reinhold Niebuhr's Irony of American History. *In this work, Niebuhr attacks the baneful influence on American history of Jefferson's supposed refusal to accept the role of evil in human affairs. Niebuhr regards Jefferson's belief that men are naturally good as the root of many of America's domestic and foreign problems over the past two centuries. At one time Niebuhr's ideas had a tremendous impact on all aspects of American culture and did much to bring about the rise of the Realist school of American diplomacy.*

In the following essay, Paul Varg of Michigan State University documents Niebuhr's thesis with a careful historical account of the epic battle between Jefferson and Hamilton over foreign policy. What is Varg's defi-

*nition of Realism? In what ways and in what specific instances did
Jefferson and Madison fail to live up to that definition? What evidence is
there to prove that Hamilton was more realistic than his rivals? Is there
a connection between the emphasis of Jefferson and Madison on commercial weapons and the American attitude toward trade discussed by
Felix Gilbert in the previous chapter?*

Foreign
Policies
of the Founding
Fathers

Paul A. Varg

Foreign policy questions during the presidency of George Washington became the focal point of political debate and contributed
in a major way to the rise of political parties. The Constitution
did not envision parties, and George Washington was strongly
averse to their becoming a part of the American political scene,
but as Joseph Charles has shown in *The Origins of the American
Party System,* the debate over foreign policy, culminating in the
crisis over the question of ratification of the Jay Treaty, brought
about the division of the people into two divergent groups.

It has usually been overlooked that the issues at stake in the
debate over that treaty emerged in the first session of the first
Congress. James Madison was then a leader in the House of
Representatives, and he sought to carry out what he deeply be-

lieved had been the mandate of the public in establishing the new government, namely a change from the helpless posture in foreign affairs to a position of effective bargaining. His program centered on commercial relations and sought to extend commerce with nations other than Great Britain and thereby to free the republic from being a mere appendage of the British economy. He viewed British economic influence by means of close commercial ties as exceedingly dangerous to the cherished republican ideals. James Madison is usually associated with the states rights position in domestic history, but he was a highly sensitive nationalist whose patriotism rested on a deep commitment to the principles of the Revolution.

His opponent in the long controversy was Alexander Hamilton, another nationalist, with whom he had been a colleague in the Constitutional Convention and with whom he joined, along with John Jay, in writing the *Federalist Papers*. They were on cordial terms at the convention and the views they expressed in their written defense of the Constitution show a close harmony. The split between them arose over Madison's foreign commercial policy. Thereafter Madison became an ardent opponent of the views expressed by Hamilton in the famous reports he prepared as Secretary of the Treasury. Hamilton expressed surprise when he found Madison opposing him on the measures he recommended and he recalled that his opponent had expressed sympathy with similar proposals in 1787. There is evidence that Madison's essential disagreement with Hamilton was on foreign policy rather than the domestic measures. A recent writer, E. James Ferguson, raises questions concerning the genuineness of Madison's opposition to Hamilton's funding measures and suggests that political expediency rather than considerations of justice caused Madison to oppose Hamilton's proposal. This conclusion, of course, lends added weight to the view that the basic cause of the split between the two ardent nationalists was a difference in foreign policy.

Their differences on foreign policy are more than adequate to explain the struggle that developed. These differences went down to the very roots where every serious debate over foreign policy issues must inevitably find itself. Hamilton was above all a realist who fatalistically accepted the existing framework, and dedicated himself to obtaining the best bargain possible. He did not object to the *realpolitik* of balance of power diplomacy, chose to regard treaties as convenient arrangements binding on the parties until they no longer served the purposes of one or the other, accepted British dominance as a simple fact of life, and dismissed as dangerous embarking on goals that the limited power of the country could scarcely hope to achieve. His own limited aim in foreign relations was to guarantee access to what he considered the prime need of a nation that desperately needed capital for the development of its tremendous resources so that it might one day emerge as a major power.

James Madison exemplifies the idealist in foreign policy. He spoke often of the rights of the republic and of what was just in international affairs but never felt it necessary to balance goals with the power available. At the base of his nationalism was a moralistic view that the new republic would be false to its mission in the world if it compromised its ideals. To remain true to its mission the nation must free itself from British dominance over the carrying trade and from the marketing of its goods through the British mercantile houses because British influence through these channels would strengthen monarchical principles and jade the lustrous principles of republicanism.

When the administration of George Washington took office in March, 1789, the basic dilemma confronting the nation was not yet clear. The United States was allied to France not only by treaty but by sentiment; it was tied to Great Britain in terms of markets, sources of manufactures, and credit. The rivalry of these two nations, soon to break forth in war, imposed on the new nation issues that threatened to tear it apart. In these issues lies the thread of American diplomacy from 1789 to 1812.

In the first session of Congress Madison presented a program for a commercial system that would give the United States economic independence. He explained that "the commerce between America and Great Britain exceeds what may be considered its natural boundary." British dominance, he said, was due to "the long possession of our trade, their commercial regulations calculated to retain it, their similarity of language and manners, their conformity of laws and other circumstances—all these concurring have made their commerce with us more extensive than their natural situation would require it to be."

Madison's program called for discriminatory tonnage duties on British ships. France and other nations that had entered into commercial treaties were to be rewarded with preferential rates. The opposition quickly pointed out that the higher rates on non-British ships could only mean higher prices on the goods Americans bought. Madison replied that the patriotism of Americans would cause them to make the necessary sacrifice, and that Americans could be induced to build a merchant marine in a short time as American ships would have an advantage over all foreign ships. He admitted that he would much prefer to see a completely free system. "But," he said, "we have maritime dangers to guard against, and we can be secured from them no other way than by having a navy and seamen of our own; these can only be obtained by giving a preference." "I admit it is a tax," he continued, "and a tax upon our produce; but it is a tax we must pay for the national security."

A nationalistic tone pervaded Madison's discourse on commerce. The economic advantages sought seemed at times less important than to command the respect of Great Britain. "We have now the power to avail ourselves of our natural superiority," he said, "and I am for beginning with some manifestation of that ability, that foreign nations may or might be taught to pay us that respect which they have neglected on account of our former imbecility." It was all important to show that "we dare exert ourselves in defeating any measure which commercial policy shall offer hostile to the welfare of America." He defended his program against the charge that it was a tax that the people would pay by asserting that his measures would "secure to us that respect and attention which we merit." Great Britain, he charged, "has bound us in commercial manacles, and very nearly defeated the object of our independence."

Madison's nationalism led him to place a high estimate on the strength of the new nation. He had no fear of British recriminations for "her interests can be wounded almost mortally, while ours are invulnerable." The British West Indies, he maintained, could not live without American foodstuffs, but Americans could easily do without British manufactures. This same faith led him to the conclusion "that it is in our power, in a very short time, to supply all the tonnage necessary for our own commerce."

Enamored with democratic ideals and absorbed with the need for markets for the ever richer flow of agricultural produce, James Madison set forth a foreign policy that would enable the new nation to carry on its experiment in republican principles and promote the economic well being of the farmers who constituted ninety per cent of the population. Like true agrarians they believed that the world lived by the produce of the farm; like true Americans they also believed that American farms were the most important in meeting the needs of the world's markets. Therein, they thought, lay the new nation's opportunity to influence world affairs.

Farmers had an eye for markets that would enter into competitive bidding for their ever expanding supplies. Dependence on Great Britain, they said, reduced them to a hostage of that country. British merchants took almost half of their exports and furnished three-fourths of the imports. Their patriotism rebelled at the sense of dependence that British economic connections fostered. How much better to trade with all the world. That others wanted their wheat, flour, and rice seemed self-evident. The other nations would gladly buy from them if only the dependence on British ships could be overcome. British ships funnelled everything through England's entrepôts, and then redistributed large amounts to other nations. How much better if a direct trade with consuming countries could be opened up. What a great advantage it would be if the United States could have its own merchant marine. That merchant marine would serve as a great nursery for seamen and would enable the nation to build a navy to protect the routes to markets. And what a sense of freedom would be imparted by the absence of the ubiquitous British creditor who stalked through the South collecting his debts. Virginians alone owed British merchants £2,300,000 (pounds sterling).

James Madison, and the new Secretary of State, Thomas Jefferson, who soon joined him, called for legislative measures to emancipate the country from economic bondage to Great Britain and the fostering of closer economic ties with other nations. France naturally attracted attention. Capable of absorbing large amounts of produce both at home and in her West Indies colonies, and also able to supply many of the needed manufactures, France seemed to offer the best counterpoise to England. Together the two nations could break the overwhelming British economic power that held Europe in its control.

The prospect took on a new glow when, in 1789, France embarked on revolution. Now it seemed that the two nations would complement each other politically as well as economically. Thomas Jefferson alone among foreign diplomats in Paris welcomed the event. "I have so much confidence in the good sense of man, and his qualifications for self-government," he wrote, "that I am never afraid of the issue where reason is left free to exert her force; and I will agree to be stoned as a false prophet if all does not end well in this country. Here is but the first chapter of the history of European liberty." To Madison he observed that members of the French Assembly looked to America as their model and viewed American precedents as they would the authority of the Bible, "open to explanation but not to question."

The kinship between the two nations received symbolic expression in Jefferson's assistance in the drafting of the Declaration of the Rights of Man. And in the last days of August, 1789, the leaders of the new government met in Jefferson's apartment to settle their differences on the degree of power to be exercised by the king. Four years later the French Jacobins made James Madison an honorary citizen of France. Madison gloried in the thought that France ignored the traditional national fences that had divided humanity into hostile camps.

On August 28, two days after the French presented to the world the Declaration of the Rights of Man, Jefferson wrote to Madison expressing the hope that the United States would take steps to assist France and not be content to place the French "on a mere footing with the English."

When of two nations, the one has engaged herself in a ruinous war for us, has spent her blood and money to save us, has opened her bosom to us in peace, and received us almost on the footing of her own citizens, while the other has moved heaven, earth, and hell to exterminate us in war, has insulted us in all her councils in peace, shut her doors to us in every port where her interests would admit it, libelled us in foreign nations, endeavored to poison them against the reception of our most precious commodities, to place these two nations on a footing, is to give a great deal more to one than to the other if the maxim be true that to make unequal quantities equal you must add more to the one of them than the other.

At first all classes and parts of the country hailed the Revolution. George Washington, after learning of the developments in France in the summer of 1789, expressed fear that it "is of too great a magnitude to be effected in so short a space" but what had taken place struck him as "of so wonderful a nature, that the mind can hardly realize the fact." If it should end as recent events indicated "that nation will be the most powerful and happy in Europe." Gouverneur Morris, who was in Paris, found it difficult "to guess whereabouts the flock will settle, when it flies so wild," but he too approved of the overthrow of the old order. He advised Washington: "I say, that we have an *interest* in the liberty of France. The leaders here are our friends. Many of them have imbibed their principles in America, and all have been fired by our example. Their opponents are by no means rejoiced at the success of our revolution, and many of them are disposed to form connexions of the strictest kind, with Great Britain."

The revolution in France merely strengthened convictions that Jefferson and Madison had held since 1783. As minister to France since 1785 Jefferson had worked industriously to promote commerce between the two countries. And when the new government took office in 1789 Madison earnestly believed that a leading motive in its establishment had been to achieve a degree of reciprocity with England and to extend the trade with other countries.

Congress did establish discriminatory duties on foreign ships, but it rejected Madison's proposal for further discrimination against ships of nations that had failed to enter into a commercial treaty. Those involved in trade saw no great hope of developing a trade with France, a nation they considered as staunch an adherent of the old exclusive mercantile system as the British. Madison would make his proposals another day when the country faced a dangerous foreign situation. By then he faced the hard fact that Alexander Hamilton had committed the nation to a foreign and domestic policy that ran directly counter to the most cherished ideals of the agrarians and tied the United States to England.

Hamilton boldly asserted that foreign policy must serve the ends set forth by national economic policy. Foreign capital constituted the great economic need of the United States, and, true to his principles, Hamilton fought desperately to make foreign policy an instrument for meeting that need. Concerning the value of foreign capital, he wrote that it ought to be "considered as a most valuable auxiliary, conducing to put in motion a greater quantity of productive labor, and a greater portion of useful enterprise, than could exist without it." In an underdeveloped country like the United States, "with an infinite fund of resources yet to be unfolded, every farthing of foreign capital" invested in internal improvements and in industry, "is a precious acquisition."

The value he placed upon it appeared in more eloquent fashion in the measures he put through. Capital would be available if the new nation demonstrated that it was friendly to capitalists and not ready to bend to the whims of an ignorant public guided by passion and by hostility to privileged classes. His program as the Secretary of the Treasury met all the requirements. Foreign, national domestic debts, and state debts were met with an alacrity that invited the fullest confidence of the creditor class. The funding system provided an opportunity for profitable investment guaranteeing to creditors an attractive rate of interest over a long period of time. The United States Bank added to the circulating media and thereby promoted business, but it had the added advantage of providing capitalists with a good investment opportunity. And Hamilton's leadership in the Washington administration approximated that of a British prime minister who steered Congress at will and reduced popular distempers to harmless frustration.

Hamilton's financial system necessitated a policy of friendship toward Great Britain. Only British capital could guarantee the economic leap that the Secretary of Treasury envisioned. Only duties on imports would meet the financial obligations the new government assumed, and three-fourths of the imports came from Great Britain. Any interruption of that trade would deprive the new government of its major source of revenue. National interest, then, dictated good relations with Great Britain.

The great danger facing Hamilton's financial structure lay in the anti-British feelings of the people and their readiness to accept revolutionary France as a sister nation fighting for the rights of man. Of these two hazards, the feeling of kinship for the French revolutionary leaders posed the greatest threat. Hamilton viewed with alarm the French messianic rhetoric and a mass psychological outburst in the name of liberty, equality and fraternity that suggested the immediate emancipation of mankind from the thralldom of the past. The French leaders startled the world with appeals to people everywhere to revolt against their masters. The powerful and deeply ingrained democratic sentiments of Americans provided a fertile soil for such appeals, and Hamilton lived in mortal dread of the excited multitude driving their representatives into a pro-French policy that would alienate the British and perhaps even pull the nation into partnership with France against Great Britain in war.

The fiscal party, as Jefferson dubbed Hamilton and his followers, worked zealously to portray revolutionary France as an international ogre. In this the indefatigable and brilliant Hamilton led the way. His first opportunity came in 1790 at the time of the Nootka Sound Affair. This international incident portended war between Great Britain and Spain and led Colonel Beckwith, the British representative in the United States, to sound out Hamilton as to what American policy might be in such a contingency.

George Washington, fearing that a British request for the right to march troops from Canada across to New Orleans was in the offing, anxiously asked Hamilton, John Adams, and Thomas Jefferson to give their opinions as to how such a request should be met.

The Secretary of Treasury seized the opportunity to prepare a lengthy and thoughtful memorandum on every aspect of foreign relations. A war between Great Britain and Spain would in all probability soon involve France, and this raised the question of the responsibilities of the United States under the treaty of 1778 with France. Hamilton's anxiety for the national interest, as he understood it, led him to shrug off the obligations to that country with the greatest of ease. Americans did not, he said, owe the French gratitude. The motive of France had been to injure England and help herself, not to benefit the Americans. He considered France "entitled . . . to our esteem and good-will." "These dispositions towards her," he said, "ought to be cherished and cultivated; but they are very distinct from a spirit of romantic gratitude, calling for sacrifices of our substantial interests, preferences inconsistent with sound policy, or complaisances incompatible with our safety."

Early in 1791 Jefferson proposed that some privilege be granted to France in return for a recent favor. Hamilton replied that such favors would prove temporary and would be interpreted by Great Britain as a manifestation of hostility toward her. This was only one of many such suggestions by Jefferson and Madison, and Hamilton accused them of "a womanish attachment to France and a womanish resentment against Great Britain."

.   .   .

What had been a rift became a deep cleavage in 1793. Two developments sharpened the differences. In February of that year Great Britain and France went to war and forced the United States to give careful thought to its obligations under the French alliance. The Washington administration no sooner came to grips with that issue than Citizen Genêt arrived with a proposal for a new commercial treaty and instructions to promote the use of American manpower, port facilities, and produce. The merchant group made shrewd use of both to strengthen their political hold.

In April Washington's cabinet debated the question of the relationship of the United States to the two belligerents. The issue was not neutrality as much as it was the kind of neutrality. Hamilton contended that the treaty with France was no longer binding. He argued that the justice of Louis' execution appeared doubtful, that it remained to be seen whether the new government would prove stable, that it was guilty of taking extreme measures and of being the aggressor in the war, that it had violated all rights in seeking to promote revolutions abroad, and that it was undertaking military and naval operations involving risks never contemplated at the time the treaty was negotiated. Hamilton, the advocate of *realpolitik,* held that a nation's first duty was to uphold its own interests and that treaty obligations must always be subordinate to that duty. Jefferson expressed disgust at the expediency of the Secretary of the Treasury. "Would you suppose it possible," he wrote to Madison, "that it should have been seriously proposed to declare our treaties with France void on the authority of an ill-understood scrap in Vattel and that it should be necessary to discuss it?"

Jefferson refused to throw off the treaty, but this did not prevent him from firmly resolving on a policy of neutrality. It must be a "manly neutrality" as opposed to Hamilton's "abject principles" and willingness to offer "our breech to every kick which Great Britain may choose to give." He was equally determined to stand firm against any French violations of American neutrality. "I wish," he wrote to James Monroe, "we may be able to repress the spirit of the people within the limits of a fair neutrality." A "fair neutrality" would yield no more privileges to France than to England. Jefferson gave the treaty with France a strict interpretation and narrowed the rights of that country to a minimum. He confided to Madison, "I fear that a fair neutrality will prove a disagreeable pill to our friends, tho' necessary to keep us out of the calamities of a war."

Jefferson's "fair neutrality" gained the support of President Washington. He issued a proclamation warning citizens against unneutral acts. The tone of the proclamation disturbed the incorruptible Madison whose sense of moral obligation winced at the sacrifice of principle to what appeared to be national self interest. He disliked the use of the term "impartial" in the President's proclamation. "Peace," wrote Madison, "is no doubt to be preserved at any price that honor and good faith will permit." "In examining our own engagements under the Treaty with France," he wrote, "it would be honorable as well as just to adhere to the sense that would at the time have been put on them." "The attempt to shuffle off the Treaty altogether by quibblings on Vattel is equally contemptible." The difference between Hamilton's approach to a treaty and the approach of Jefferson and Madison was symbolic of the wide gulf that separated their broader concept of foreign relations.

The Secretary of State soon complained that his colleagues in the administration leaned toward England. "We are going on here in the same spirit still," he wrote. "The Anglomania has seized violently on three members of our council," said the Secretary of State. Jefferson saw that the "natural aristocrats" of the larger towns, the merchants trading in British capital, the "paper men," and all the "old tories" supported the English side on every question. The farmers, tradesmen, mechanics, and merchants trading on their own capital took the other side. The same groups who supported Hamilton's fiscal policy followed him on the question of foreign affairs. Not all discerned the intimate relation between the recently adopted financial program and the question of what attitude to take toward Great Britain, but the connection by no means escaped such leaders in Congress as William Smith of South Carolina and Fisher Ames and Theodore Sedgwick of Massachusetts. Nor did the fact that domestic policy and foreign policy were essentially one and the same escape Jefferson and Madison. The latter saw in the "errors" of the administration a wound to national honor, a disregard of the obligations to France, and an injury to public feeling "by a seeming indifference to the cause of liberty." But it was not the cause of liberty in Europe alone but in the United States as well that both Jefferson and Madison had in mind. What they did not understand was that Hamilton put national interest above all other considerations.

.   .   .

On November 6, 1793, the British Crown ordered the seizure of all ships laden with goods, the produce of any colony belonging to France, or carrying provisions or other supplies for the use of French colonies. By early March the British held 250 American vessels in their possession in the West Indies alone and American captains found that numerous obstacles in the form of legal procedures barred the way to the British promise of compensation. Even Theodore Sedgwick, long a supporter of appeasement of the British, confided:

Such indeed are the injuries which we have received from Great Britain that I believe I should not hesitate on going to war, but that we must in that case be allied to France, which would be an alliance with principles which would prostitute liberty & destroy every species of security.

The central issue now changed from that of Madison's resolutions [for commercial duties against England] to the best way of gaining immediate relief. Madison's measures had been framed as a long term program for bringing a better balance into foreign relations. Now the situation had become so critical that Madison acknowledged that commercial measures were "not the precise remedy to be pressed in first order; but they are in every view & argument proper to make part of our standing laws till the principles of reciprocity be established by mutual arrangements." The real question now centered on what measures would be most likely to promote a successful negotiation.

Theodore Sedgwick took the lead in calling for a program of defense that included a standing army. He soon discovered that the advocates of Madison's proposals opposed every such defense measure. He wrote to his friend Ephraim Williams: "Is it not strange that at the moment these madmen are doing every thing in their power to irritate G.B. they are opposing every attempt to put our country in a posture of defense." The grounds of opposition to Sedgwick's defense measures lay in fear of a standing army that would be at the beck and call of the executive for purposes other than defense against foreign aggression. Madison suspected that the emphasis on defense had its origin in part in an effort to sidetrack his commercial proposals but that the main aim lay elsewhere. He wrote to Jefferson: "you understand the game behind the curtain too well not to perceive the old trick of turning every contingency into a resource for accumulating force in the government."

The agrarians preferred resolutions and economic weapons, but Madison's resolutions soon fell by the wayside as more extreme measures came forward. On March 26 the House, sitting as a committee of the whole, passed a resolution in favor of granting the President the power to lay an embargo for thirty days. A month later Congress laid an embargo on all foreign shipping for one month. Congress renewed the measure for another thirty days in April.

"Such madness, my friend, such madness! and yet many good men voted for it . . . ," wrote Sedgwick. A few weeks earlier Sedgwick had called for the defeat of "Madison's wild system" so that the country could prepare for defense. Such measures, argued the followers of Hamilton, would improve the position of the United States in negotiating. The opponents' proposals, Sedgwick believed, would "enlist her pride and insolence against us."

Late in March Jonathan Dayton, of New Jersey, introduced a resolution calling for the sequestration of all debts due from the citizens of the United States to subjects of Great Britain. William Giles supported the measure with the contention that only if the British people were brought to fear for their own interests would they exert pressure on their government to negotiate. Dayton's resolution failed to pass.

In April the battle raged on another front. President Washington appointed John Jay special envoy to Great Britain. No appointment would have proved popular with the Republicans who much preferred to take economic measures before entering upon negotiations. The naming of Jay convinced them that further appeasement was to be expected. Jay had been ready to agree to the closing of the Mississippi in 1786 in return for a commercial treaty with Spain. His critics predicted that he would yield to the merchants again and negotiate a treaty that sacrificed the true national interest. The Republican societies engaged at once in a campaign of vilification of the envoy. This did not deter the Senate, always on the side of the executive branch, from confirming the appointment.

.   .   .

[Jay proceeded to negotiate a treaty with England in 1794 that secured some but by no means all of the concessions to which most Americans felt entitled.] The essence of Jay's defense of the treaty lay in his explanation to Edmund Randolph. "Perhaps it is not very much to be regret ed that all our differences are merged in this treaty, without having been decided; disagreeable imputations are thereby avoided, and the door of conciliation is fairly and widely opened, by the *essential* justice done, and the conveniences granted to each other by the parties," he reflected. The treaty removed the most serious apprehensions concerning British intentions in the West. The two boundary disputes in the Northwest and the Northeast were to be settled by commissions. A *modus vivendi* assuring Americans of compensation for the losses on the high seas removed some of the ignitive quality from the controversy over neutral rights. The Hamiltonians, anxious about what war would do to the fiscal system and dreading a war in which they would inevitably become the allies of France considered these two as the great gains of the treaty.

.   .   .

The argument against the treaty rode high on nationalistic passions. The agrarians paid scant attention to British arguments on the issues involved. They viewed each point from the vantage of America and rejected every compromise. Only a British surrender on almost all points could have satisfied the agrarians. Their ethnocentric view made it easy to find nothing but evils in the treaty. Yet, their antagonism did not rise out of purely nationalistic considerations.

The Jay Treaty pinched the Jeffersonians at three points. It committed the United States not to establish discriminatory duties against the British. Thereby it forced the agrarians to lay aside their whole foreign policy program and to accept that of the opposition.

Secondly, the treaty offended the nationalistic and democratic sentiments of the agrarians. Jefferson lamented: "The rights, the interest, the honor and faith of our nation are so grossly sacrificed. . . ." He wrote to Madison: "Where a faction has entered into a conspiracy with the enemies of their country to chain down the legislature at the feet of both; where the whole mass of our constituents have condemned this work in unequivocal manner, and are looking to you as their last hope to save them from the effects of the avarice and corruption of the first agent. . . ." Both Jefferson and Madison believed that a majority of the people opposed the treaty and that the popular will had been denied. When it became clear that the House of Representatives would appropriate the funds for putting the treaty into effect, Madison attributed it to the pressure of business interests.

Jefferson's and Madison's denunciations of the treaty are also better understood if one takes into account that in their eyes the treaty surrendered a major principle in the "Law of Nations." That term—"Law of Nations"—had all the aura of the Age of Enlightenment. It had no well defined meaning and certainly few generally accepted points, but to Jefferson and Madison it connoted justice and reason. They never doubted that their own broad interpretation of neutral rights accorded with the "Law of Nations" and the welfare of mankind.

This approach, one of the central threads of their foreign policy from 1789 to 1812, owed something to the fact that American interests would have benefitted tremendously by a universal acceptance of their interpretation of neutral rights. It owed quite as much to an idealistic view of what would benefit mankind. They desperately wanted a world order in which the innocent bystander nations would not be made to suffer because a few major powers engaged in the folly of war. Jefferson and Madison overlooked the fact that Great Britain could not accept such an ideal without granting victory to its enemies.

In the situation confronting the United States in the spring of 1796 the surrender of the ideal had an additional and more grievous meaning for Jefferson's followers. To yield to British dictates on control of the seas meant that France would be denied access to American supplies. The United States would provide Great Britain with supplies at a time when the traditional friend, France, was struggling for liberty.

In September, 1796, George Washington delivered his Farewell Address. The President, finding himself amid the dissensions of heated party strife, had striven manfully to avoid falling into the hands of either faction. In 1793 he had, to a great degree, followed Jefferson's advice in meeting the dangers brought on by the war between Great Britain and France. Throughout the heated debates he had retained a sense of gratitude toward France and a sincere desire to deal with her justly. In the summer of 1795, he had resisted the pressure of Hamilton to ratify the Jay Treaty at once and had deliberated long before making his decision to ratify it. To be sure he could not participate in the feelings experienced by Jefferson and Madison because he did not share their philosophical outlook and their intense concern for their particular political ideals. On the other hand, he found it more difficult than Hamilton to make the concessions necessary to preserve harmony with Great Britain. The President found himself in an isolated position.

When the time came to deliver a farewell address, he called on Hamilton to draft it, and the message warned against party spirit and against a passionate attachment to one nation. To the more extreme elements in the more extreme Republican societies the counsel was applicable, but it scarcely applied to Jefferson and Madison whose pro-French feelings were rigorously subordinated to American nationalism.

Their nationalism posed a danger for they confused their American view of the world with their proclaimed universal view of justice and right reason. Their strong desire to make their republic an example of what could be achieved by noble aspiration set free to apply reason made them impatient and particularly so concerning Great Britain's financial influence and arbitrary dicta as to how far the seas were to be open to a free exchange of goods. That they were misunderstood, that their views were dubbed theoretical, is not surprising. Idealists in the realm of foreign affairs trying to establish a program that would reconcile national interests and idealistic considerations were to find themselves in a difficult position many times in the future.

In the heated controversy over the Jay Treaty a set of symbols emerged that transferred the argument from the realm of the rational to the irrational. Followers of Hamilton were quickly denounced as monocrats; followers of Jefferson and Madison were identified as the dangerous disciples of the French school of reason. In the pamphlet warfare parties became images of the British or French systems. It was not only that Jefferson and Madison differed from Hamilton in the measures to be pursued but that the opponents read into them steps in the direction of a society patterned after popular conceptions of France and England. The differences between the foreign policies of the Federalists and Republicans had little relationship to the stereotypes of partisan political rhetoric. These widened the gulf beyond that warranted by a rather undramatic difference over practical measures.

A difference in basic attitudes also contributed to the political warfare. Thomas Jefferson and James Madison had no fear of society falling victim to instability, of individuals and factions irresponsibly following the whim of the moment, or of the social fabric being torn apart by the passions of men. Their confidence in the good sense of the body politic made a significant difference. When they encountered human foibles or systems that appeared to favor one group in society or one nation they boldly presumed that it was their duty to enlighten the misled and to change the system.

The Federalists certainly benefitted more directly from the measures of Hamilton and the close association with Great Britain, but that alone does not explain their stand on the Jay Treaty. They saw the social fabric as a frail gauze in constant danger of being torn apart. The British structure was their model because it gave stability to society and an orderly financial system that emphasized contracts, law and order. They saw no reason to risk present advantages for an untried experiment in reordering the nation's economic relations with the outside world, especially when to do so would align the nation with France. Hamilton's arguments in favor of the Jay Treaty rested on an acceptance of the world as it was and not on a vague concept of the world as it ought to be. Madison judged the Jay Treaty in terms of American rights and interests without making any concessions to the hard and fast economic realities. Hamilton succeeded in putting the problem of relations with Great Britain on the shelf. His whole argument centered on prudence; Madison's argument centered on what he believed to be just American claims.

Realists usually go on to use the War of 1812 as proof of the failure of Republicans to understand the realities of foreign policy. When Jefferson became President, and war once more broke out between England and France, he was presented with the same choice that had faced the Federalists during the Jay Treaty crisis. Jefferson could accept a compromise treaty (the Monroe-Pinckney Treaty of 1806) or resort to commercial warfare to coerce further concessions from Great Britain. Convinced of the justice of America's position on neutral rights, angry at the impressment of American seamen, and confident that the United States had sufficient economic power to force Great Britain to back down, Jefferson chose the route of commercial warfare. His embargo, however, totally failed to win concessions from England.

When Madison assumed the Presidency, he continued to wage commercial warfare until its failure became so apparent and so humiliating that he was driven to declare war on Great Britain to protect the prestige of the United States and the reputation of his Republican party. Thus excessive attachment to "justice" and overestimation of America's power led to a tragic war that might well have been prevented by the Federalists' more realistic diplomacy.

See Bradford Perkins, Prologue to War; *Reginald Horseman,* Causes of the War of 1812; *and Roger Brown,* The Republic in Peril.

Foreign Policies of the Founding Fathers

Radical

William Appleman Williams does not regard the battle of Hamilton with Jefferson and Madison as one of realism versus idealism. He sees, rather, a contest between two opposing concepts of mercantilism. According to Williams, Hamilton sought a nation governed by a power elite. He also wanted a close alliance with Great Britain, even at the expense of much of America's independence, because the power of the Anglo-American combination would have enabled the United States to expand its markets and territories indefinitely.

Williams regards the policy of Jefferson and Madison as preferable to Hamilton's. They wanted a clean break with Great Britain, which would give the United States the chance to develop a peaceful and democratic society. Nevertheless, Williams believes, the vision of Jefferson and Madison contained a fatal flaw—capitalist expansion. Instead of maintaining a democratic and egalitarian society by redistributing goods to provide greater lower-class purchasing power and an internally expanding economy, Jefferson and Madison chose to protect private property. Thus they were left with no choice but to expand America's foreign trade and territorial frontier if they were to provide land and jobs for America's growing population. Without this expansion, wealth would have rapidly accumulated in the hands of a few, and equality and democracy would have disappeared.

Such a policy makes Jefferson and Madison anything but blind idealists. Their opposition to the Jay Treaty, according to Williams, was a realistic attempt to break the bonds of the British Empire. The War of 1812, the consequence of their policies, was "A Classic War for Trade and Territory" in which "Americans quite consciously and purposefully went to war for their export trade, for more land, and to check Britain's engrossing of the home market for manufactures." (Williams, Contours of American History, Cleveland, 1961, p. 193.)

In the following essay, how does Williams's analysis of Hamilton's policy compare with Varg's analysis? Is Williams's emphasis on the role of expansion in the policies of Jefferson and Madison proper? Was American policy at this time essentially defensive or offensive? Was trade or territory more important to Hamilton? To Jefferson and Madison?

The Age of Mercantilism

William Appleman Williams

Based upon the suggestion by Curtis P. Nettels that one of the consequences of British mercantilism was the creation "of a new mercantilist state on this side of the Atlantic," and upon recent re-evaluations of mercantilism by William D. Grampp, Gunnar Myrdal, Jacob Viner, Charles Wilson, and others, this essay advances the hypothesis that the central characteristic of American history from 1763 to 1828 was in fact the development and maturation of an American mercantilism. Let it be emphasized that the interpretation is offered as a hypothesis and no more—as an idea to be examined and tested, then accepted, modified, or rejected on the basis of its relevance and validity. . . . There is no intention, furthermore, even to imply that the approach as here stated offers final answers to all the vexing problems connected with understanding early American society. It is merely proposed that a re-examination of the era from this angle may lead to new insights, and hence contribute to a broader interpretation of the period.

At the outset, for example, the use of the concept of mercantilism restores to its properly central place the fact that Americans thought of themselves as an empire at the very beginning of their national existence—as part of their assertive self-consciousness which culminated in the American Revolution. Though it may seem surprising, especially when contrasted with the image of isolationism which has been accepted so long, in reality this early predominance of a pattern of empire thought is neither very strange nor very difficult to explain. Having matured in an age of empires as part of an empire, the colonists naturally saw themselves in the same light once they joined issue with the mother country.

Revolutionary leaders were confident of their ability "not only

Reprinted by permission from William Appleman Williams, "The Age of Mercantilism: An Interpretation of the American Political Economy, 1763 to 1828," *William and Mary Quarterly,* Vol. XV, No. 4 (October 1958), 419–437. Copyright by William Appleman Williams.

to take territory by the sword, but to hold and govern it under a colonial status." Long before the break with England, for example, Benjamin Franklin was a leader of those who entertained a "burning interest in westward expansion." At the threshold of the revolution he visualized an American Empire including Canada, the Spanish Floridas, the West Indies, and perhaps even Ireland. George Washington, John Adams, John Livingston, and Thomas Lee were among those who shared such conceptions of an American Empire. By the end of the war, such men as Silas Deane looked forward to the time when "Great Britain, America and Russia united will command not barely Europe, but the whole world united." And in 1789, after remarking that "it is well known that empire has been travelling from east to west," Congregational minister and geographer Jedidiah Morse concluded that "probably her last and broadest seat will be America . . . the largest empire that ever existed."

While the vigor, even cockiness, of such statements may be explained by the consciousness of having whipped the champion, the underlying emphasis on expansion and empire was an integral part of the general outlook of mercantilism, a conception of the world shared by most of the revolutionary generation. Though they revolted against British mercantilism, there is considerable evidence to suggest that early American leaders did not, as so often is assumed, rebel against the idea and practice of mercantilism itself. In stressing the role of natural-rights philosophy in the thinking of the leaders of the revolution, the traditional view of the American Revolution has slighted this key point.

An acceptance of natural law is not incompatible with mercantilism, as is indicated by John Locke's vigorous espousal of both systems. Much of the talk in America about natural rights, moreover, concerned what Thomas Paine called the "natural right" to one's own empire. And though they were willing to use Adam Smith's polemic in behalf of laissez faire as a weapon against British mercantilism (and against their domestic opponents), most Americans adhered firmly in their own practice to the principle that the state had to intervene in economic affairs. America's romance with Smith's laissez faire came later and was of relatively short duration. Hence it would appear that a better understanding of early American history depends in considerable measure upon a grasp of the nature and practice of American mercantilism as it developed between 1763 and 1825.

Traditionally thought of as little more than a narrow and selfish point of view held by the trading interest, mercantilism was in fact a broad definition and explanation of the world shared by most of Western Europe in the seventeenth and eighteenth centuries. In this sense it was the basic outlook of those who labored to build a dynamic balanced economy of agriculture and business organized on a capitalistic basis within a nationalistic framework. Depending upon their specific function and power at any given stage in the process, mercantilists argued among themselves over the best means to achieve and maintain such a system—and differed in their estimates of whether or not it had been established—but they agreed on the objective and upon the need to use the state as a tool.

Whether agrarian or urban, therefore, mercantilists were essentially nationalists who strove for self-sufficiency through increased domestic production and a favorable balance (and terms) of trade. Their emphasis on production and the control of export markets and sources of raw materials, rather than on consumption and economic interdependence, led them to fear surpluses as a sign of crisis and failure. Thus they dropped the old feudal restrictions on exports and replaced them with taxes on imports. Their greatest fear was a surplus of goods. In this respect, furthermore, mercantilism was reinforced—albeit in a backhanded and even unintentional way—by the broad ethical outlook of Puritanism (which frowned on luxury), even though mercantilism itself was a secular and almost amoral system. Likewise, the concept of a chosen people, so strong in Puritanism, also strengthened the secular and economic nationalism of mercantilism. Thus mercantilists constantly labored to build a tightly organized and protected national market and to increase their share of the world market. The key points in their program were integration at home and expansion abroad.

In the exuberant confidence of their victory over Britain, Americans tended to assume that each new state could survive and thrive as a mercantile empire unto itself. That attitude was not too surprising, for each of the new states appeared to enjoy the raw materials, labor supply, and trading facilities for a balanced economy. That estimate of the situation was supported and reinforced by the conviction, itself part of traditional theory, that a state could remain democratic in political and social life only if it were small and integrated, and by the experiences of the colonies in dealing with Great Britain's imperial policy after 1763. Yet the political outlook and faith contradicted certain basic tenets of mercantilism, which Americans also entertained, or assumed.

The first attempt to reconcile the conflict produced the Articles of Confederation. That instrument of government stressed the independence of the states as self-contained units of mercantilism and democratic republicanism, yet also established a central government for the purposes of war and, as in the case of Canada, future expansion. But specific postwar developments, such as the serious recession, the expansionist conflicts between the states, and the difficulties in dealing with other countries in economic affairs, combined to disillusion many Americans with their experiment in particularistic mercantilism.

Broadly speaking, the resulting movement toward a stronger central government grew out of internal and international economic difficulties analyzed and explained with the ideas of mercantilism. By 1785, for example, most of the states, including the agrarian ones, were switching from tariffs for revenue to tariffs for international retaliation and protection. Merchants demanded American navigation acts, artisans agitated for protection of their labor, and agricultural interests wanted help in balancing their political economy. Various groups of Americans who concerned themselves directly with the problem of strengthening the central government—and there were many who were preoccupied with local and immediate difficulties or opportunities—offered several proposals for handling the problem. Centered in New England, the smallest group favored establishing an aristocratic society at home and rejoining the British Empire as a contractual junior partner. Such men were not willing to return to colonial status, but they did favor economic and social reintegration. Most Americans opposed that solution, favoring instead either the delegation of more power to the central government under the Articles of Confederation or the substitution of an entirely new instrument of government.

A letter from James Madison to Thomas Jefferson in the spring of 1786 not only indicates that the agrarian as well as the urban interests favored one or the other of those last two approaches, but dramatizes the fundamental mercantilism of the entire movement. "A continuance of the present anarchy of our commerce," Madison explained, "will be a continuance of the unfavorable balance on it, which by draining us of our metals . . . [will bring our ruin]. In fact, most of our political evils may be traced up to our commercial ones, and most of our moral may to our political."

Against this background, the Constitution appears as an instrument of centralized national government framed in the classic manner by men thinking within the framework of mercantilism and blessed with the physical and human resources for a balanced economy. It provided the foundation for a national system of economics and politics and organized American strength for the struggle with other mercantile empires and for the conquest of less powerful peoples. The latter considerations were essential, for the Founding Fathers resolved the contradiction between the stress on expansion in mercantilism and the emphasis on a small state in existing democratic political theory by developing a theory of their own which held that democratic republicanism could be sustained by just such expansion. James Madison, often called the Father of the Constitution, provided the most striking formulation of this proposition, but Thomas Jefferson, John Adams, and other early leaders either shared or adopted it in one form or another within a reasonably short time.

Taking his cue from David Hume, the Englishman who attacked Montesquieu's argument that democracy was a system that could work only in small states, Madison asserted that a large state offered a much better foundation for republicanism. Institutional checks and balances could help, and were therefore necessary, but they were not enough in and of themselves. "Extend the sphere," he argued, "and you take in a greater variety of parties and interests; you make it less probable that a majority of the whole will have a common motive to invade the rights of other citizens; or if such a common motive exists, it will be more difficult for all who feel it to discover their own strength, and to act in unison with each other. . . ."

While it is possible to conclude from Madison's remarks that he had in mind a static conception of such a large state, three considerations would appear to weaken that reading of his thesis. First, Madison used the verb "extend" in its active, unlimited sense. Second, he was stating a general theory, not making an argument in behalf of a given territorial settlement. And third, he advocated and vigorously supported the continued expansion of the United States. It seems more probable, therefore, that Madison was proposing, *as a guide to policy and action in his own time,* the same kind of an argument that Frederick Jackson Turner formulated a century later, when he advanced his frontier thesis which explained America's democracy and prosperity as the result of such expansion.

Madison's theory became the key to an American mercantilism. Merchants and manufacturers who wanted their own empire found it convincing and convenient. And Jefferson's thesis that democracy and prosperity depended upon a society of landholding freemen was a drastically simplified version of the same idea. Edward Everett of Massachusetts captured the essence of the interpretation in his judgment that expansion was the *"principle* of our institutions." Additional support for this interpretation is offered by Madison's later prophecy (in 1828–29) that a major crisis would occur in about a century, when the continent was filled up and an industrial system had deprived most people of any truly productive property. In the event, Madison's fears proved true sooner than he anticipated. For in the crisis of the 1890's, when Americans *thought* that the frontier was gone, they advanced and accepted the argument that new expansion was the best—if not the only—way to sustain their freedom and prosperity.

Madison's original statement of the expansionist thesis was important for two reasons. First, it provided the theoretical basis for an American mercantilism combining commercial and territorial expansion with political democracy. Second, by thus re-emphasizing the idea of empire, and proposing expansion as the key to national welfare, Madison opened the way for a discussion of the basic questions facing American mercantilism. Those issues concerned domestic economic affairs, the kind of expansion that was necessary and desirable, and the means to accomplish such gains while the nation was young and weak.

Washington's Farewell Address formulated a bipartisan answer to the problem of basic strategy. The solution was to build a commercial empire (which included markets for agricultural surpluses) by avoiding political involvement in the European system, meanwhile retaining complete freedom of action to secure and develop a continental empire in the Western Hemisphere. Washington's proposition was classically simple: play from the strength provided by America's basic economic wealth and geographic location in order to survive immediate weakness and emerge as *the* world power. "If we remain one people, under an efficient government," he promised, "the period is not far off when we may defy material injury from external annoyance . . . when we may choose peace or war, as our interest, guided by justice, shall counsel." Sharing that objective, and quite in agreement with the strategy, Thomas Jefferson summed it all up a bit later in one famous axiom: "entangling alliances with none." And with the enunciation of the Monroe Doctrine, freedom of action became the avowed and central bipartisan theme of American foreign policy.

As a condition of that persuasive agreement, however, several serious conflicts had to be resolved. Perhaps they can be discussed most clearly by defining and considering them within the framework of the gradual defeat and amalgamation of the pro-British and pro-French minorities by a growing consensus in favor of an American mercantilism. Such an approach has the additional value of making it possible to organize the analysis around familiar personalities as symbols of certain ideas, functional groups, and special interests. Let it be posited, therefore, that the following men are key figures in the evolution of an American mercantilism: Timothy Pickering, John Adams, and John Quincy Adams of Massachusetts; Alexander Hamilton of New York; and James Madison, Thomas Jefferson, and John Taylor of Virginia.

In many respects, at any rate, Pickering and Taylor represented the nether fringes of American mercantilism. Pickering trod the trail from reluctant revolutionary to threatening secessionist in the name of a domestic merchant aristocracy functioning as a quasi-independent contractual member of the British Empire. His ideal was a central government charged with the responsibility (and armed with the power and authority) to establish and sustain a politically and socially stratified society and to provide the economic assistance (especially funded credit) that was necessary for the rationalized operations of overseas correspondents of British mercantilism and for domestic speculative ventures. Though Pickering and his supporters fit the traditional stereotype of mercantilists, they were in fact and function no more than the agents of British mercantilism. They were very successful agents, to be sure, but they did not view or define America in terms of its own mercantilism. Rather did they visualize it as a self-governing commonwealth of the British Empire. Hence it was only very late and with great reluctance, if at all, that they supported the measures necessary for a mercantilist state in America.

At the other extreme, John Taylor developed his program as a variation on a theme first stated by the French physiocrats. He emphasized the primacy of agriculture as narrowly as Pickering stressed the virtue and necessity of the merchant-trader-speculator. Taylor's tirades against funded debts and bank stock, and his soliloquies in praise of the noble farmer, seem alike in their total opposition to the principles of mercantilism. But in other respects his ideas were not so untainted by mercantilism as his rhetoric indicated. As with most other planters, for example, his theory of labor coincided at all essential points with the view held by British mercantilists. So, too, did his conception of the role of western lands in the economy of the seaboard "mother country."

With respect to foreign trade, moreover, Taylor was trapped by the weakness of the physiocrats in that area of economics. Ostensibly free traders, the physiocrats did not favor the navy essential to such a program. Taylor and other American imbibers of the physiocratic elixir awoke to discover that their vision did not correspond to reality. Taylor himself was not very adaptive, and ended his career in attacks on Jefferson and other agrarians who did develop an American mercantilism. But Taylor's position does dramatize the dilemma faced by the agrarians. The contradiction between theory and actuality confronted them with a rather apparent choice: either they could content themselves with slow economic stagnation or they could build an American maritime system, accept dependence upon a foreign naval power, or support an American industry. In that choice lies a key aspect of the rise of a mature American mercantilism; for it developed most consciously and was ultimately practiced most rigorously by the southern agrarians who are often assumed to have been most rabidly antimercantilist. If nothing else, the weakness of their ideal program drove them into mercantilism.

It is particularly important to keep that fact in mind when considering Hamilton, about whom the discussion of American mercantilism has billowed for so long. Joseph Charles was essentially correct in his view that "the standard works on Hamilton evade the main issues which his career raises," and his judgment remains relevant despite the plethora of centennial essays and biographies. The entire question of Hamilton's mercantilism has to be decided with reference to three points: the meaning and significance of the *Report on Manufactures,* his role in the Jay Treaty episode, and his plans to join in the further expansion of the British Empire in the Western Hemisphere. However difficult it may be to pin him down with an alternate characterization, Hamilton simply cannot be considered the fountainhead of American mercantilism unless those aspects of his career can be interpreted within the framework of mercantilist thought and action.

Since the *Report on Manufactures* is often accepted as proof, as well as evidence, of Hamilton's mercantilism, it is convenient to give first consideration to that document. In doing so, it seems wise to recall the chronology of his three state papers on economic affairs. Hamilton was commissioned as Secretary of the Treasury on September 11, 1789; and there followed the manifesto on public credit in January 1790, the report on a central bank in December 1790, and the paper on manufacturing in December 1791. Even the most cursory review of those dates catches the two-year delay between the reports on credit and manufacturers. That interval becomes even more striking when viewed in the context of other events.

It was Madison rather than Hamilton, for example, who gave more attention to protective duties on manufactures during the Constitutional Convention. That is still more illuminating since associations for the promotion of American manufactures had appeared in New York, Boston, Providence, and Baltimore as early as 1785; and resolutions for domestic goods had followed the next year from such additional and widely separated localities as Hartford, Germantown, Richmond, and Halifax (South Carolina). By 1789, furthermore, not only had the anti-Federalists picked up political support from such groups in New England, New York, and Pennsylvania, but the special session of Congress received numerous requests and petitions from various manufacturing societies.

Having passed an emergency revenue bill in the form of tariff legislation, the Congress then *ordered* Hamilton, on January 15, 1790, to prepare a specific report on manufactures. That makes his delay even more noticeable, whatever allowances may be granted for his other duties and the thoroughness of his research. As late as October 1791, moreover, the administration saw no need to increase the tariff of 1789. In matters of chronology, urgency, and emphasis, therefore, it seems clear that Hamilton gave priority to funding the debt and establishing the bank. Those operations represented precisely the needs and objectives of the merchants who were semiautonomous correspondents of British mercantilism, and who were fundamentally opposed to a strong American industry. Their economic, political, and social position would be threatened by a vigorous program of industrialization; for at the very least they would have to make drastic changes in their outlook and actions. Since Hamilton's personal and political position was based on his rapport with that group, it seems relevant to consider whether Hamilton's mercantilism was as thoroughgoing as historians have assumed it was.

In Hamilton's behalf, it can be argued with considerable validity that domestic industry had to have a sound credit system as a cornerstone. But that approach only raises the question of why Hamilton did not present his funding and bank programs as the means to achieve an independent balanced economy. Since he did not, the most relevant explanation would seem to be that Hamilton was in fact a mercantilist who was hamstrung by his political dependence upon the Federalists around Pickering. His association with Tench Coxe would serve to strengthen that analysis. The same argument could then be used to explain why Hamilton delayed his paper on manufactures for almost two years after the Congress had asked for it in January 1790.

The weakest point in that interpretation concerns Hamilton's response to Madison's resolution of January 3, 1794, that "the interests of the United States would be promoted by further restrictions and higher duties in certain cases on the manufactures and navigation of foreign nations employed in the commerce of the United States." Working through William Smith of South Carolina, Hamilton killed Madison's entire program which was designed to promote commercial and industrial independence. Instead, Hamilton's committee in the House reported in favor of more borrowing and further domestic taxes. For that matter, neither Hamilton nor the Federalist party acted to increase protection after 1792.

The explanation of Hamilton's action which does the most to sustain his reputation as an American mercantilist is not as generous to his standing as a reformed monarchist. For given the broad and vigorous agitation from manufacturing societies for greater protection, Madison's resolutions offered Hamilton a striking opportunity to widen the base of the Federalist party. That would have strengthened his hand against the pro-British group within the party and have enabled him to give substance to the *Report on Manufactures.* If it be said that Hamilton favored domestic excise taxes in preference to domestic manufacturing, then his mercantilism appears even more questionable. A stronger argument could be made by reference to Hamilton's known reservations about democracy, which would account for his refusal to court the manufacturers as a counterweight to the merchants around Pickering.

It may be, however, that Hamilton's vigorous opposition to

Madison's resolutions of 1794 derived in considerable part from the fact that Madison's program was aimed at Great Britain. Not only was that true in the immediate, particular sense, but it also was the case in that Madison's proposals pointed toward general economic independence. That approach to the question of Hamilton's mercantilism has the virtue of having considerable relevance to his role in Jay's Treaty. An American mercantilist could explain and defend Hamilton's basic attitude and maneuvers behind Jay's back by one or both of two arguments. First, England had to be courted while the United States built a navy. Second, Hamilton stressed the political side of mercantilism.

Neither of those explanations is very convincing: Hamilton always favored the Army over the Navy, and political mercantilism is such a contradiction in terms that it begs the entire issue. That interpretation becomes even less convincing when asked to account for the fact that at the end of his career Hamilton turned not toward manufacturing but in the direction of becoming a partner in Britain's imperial adventures in Latin America. Indeed, Hamilton's foreign policy does less to settle the question of his mercantilism than to recall the report in 1793 that "the English considered Hamilton, [Rufus] King, and [William] Smith, of South Carolina, as main supports of British interest in America. Hamilton, not Hammond, was their effective minister." Perhaps the most to be said of Hamilton's mercantilism is that it was latent and limited, for his actions belied his rhetoric.

As in many other contexts, it is Madison who emerges as the central figure in the development of an American mercantilism. While there are many illustrations, perhaps his resolutions of January 1794 provide the most illuminating evidence. Once again Charles points the way: "The program with which Madison began the first strategic moves against the Federalists was not one which could be called anti-Federalist, particularist, or States' rights." His plan was to combine landed expansion to the west with support for domestic manufacturing and an independent American commercial policy. Considered at the practical political level, it represented a bid to the growing numbers of dissident Federalists who opposed a one-way relationship with Britain. Some of those men eyed a bull market for domestic manufactures. Others thought of an expansionist foreign policy with the established states cast in the role of "mother country." Madison saw such groups as allies for the anti-Federalists, as well as the building blocks of an American mercantilism.

Madison's conception of an American mercantilism was possibly too comprehensive as well as too premature politically to be adopted by Congress in 1794, though it was extensively debated before being sidetracked by Hamilton and Smith. But it did serve as a keen analysis and program for the growing consensus among anti-Federalists. That drive toward economic independence manifested itself in the Non-Intercourse Bill introduced in the summer of 1794, a move which was defeated only by the vote of Vice-President John Adams. Equally significant is the fact that it was backed by congressmen from Pennsylvania and Delaware as well as by those from southern states. Madison's mercantilism picked up new allies very rapidly, and two subsequent events served as catalysts in the process. Considered in the order of their importance, they were Jay's Treaty and the last stage in the defection of John Adams from High Federalism.

Following so closely upon the narrow defeat of the Non-Intercourse Bill, Jay's Treaty added injury to frustration. The great majority of Americans reacted bitterly and vigorously. Already weakened by deep fissures, the Federalist party cracked open under the ensuing attack. It cost them key leaders in such states as New Hampshire and Pennsylvania and alienated unknown numbers of voters south of the Potomac. As one who had cast the deciding vote against the Non-Intercourse Bill only with great reluctance, John Adams provided temporary leadership for such Federalist dissidents.

Adams strengthened his position even more by refusing to go quietly along to war with France at the bidding of the High Federalists. The differences between Hamilton and Adams were numerous, but perhaps none is so important to an appreciation of the maturing American mercantilism as the contrast between Hamilton's passion for a large army and Adams' emphasis on an American navy. Hamilton's military policy was that of the British nabob in North America, while that of Adams represented American mercantilism. Against that background, and in the context of his deciding vote on the Non-Intercourse Bill of 1794, it is possible to appreciate the full impact of Jay's Treaty on Adams. He made peace with France and forced Pickering out of the cabinet.

Little wonder, then, that Jefferson was willing to give way in favor of Adams. But thanks to Madison, who had been organizing a party as well as projecting a theory and a program, Jefferson became President. Once in power, Jefferson and his supporters were prodded by necessity and spurred by their own visions of empire toward the full development of an American mercantilism. There are several explanations for this phenomenon. Among the most important, one might list the following: the foreign-trade dilemma inherent in physiocratic theory (which was intensified by the wars stemming from the French Revolution); the creative leadership provided by such men as Madison and Albert Gallatin (who made his own *Report on Manufactures* in 1810); the political necessities and expediences of unifying and sustaining a national party; and the maturing thought of Jefferson himself. But wherever one chooses to place the emphasis, the fact remains that the Jeffersonians in action were far more mercantilistic than the Federalists had been—even in theory and rhetoric.

As early as 1791, for that matter, Jefferson began to shift away from the physiocratic dogma of free trade. And by 1793 he concluded his *Report on Commercial Policy* with a series of retaliatory proposals that were as mercantilistic as any he criticized. Perhaps even more significant was his early ambivalence toward manufacturing, which he never condemned outright once and for all. Jefferson disliked cities and the factory system for what he judged their negative impact on politics and morals, and for the conditions and style of life they imposed upon human beings, but he never discounted the importance of home manufacturing and commerce. He could not afford to, either as the leader of agrarians beginning to produce surpluses for sale, or as one who sought and accepted support from the increasing number of urban groups of all classes who preferred an empire of their own to rejoining the British system. Even if Jefferson had not caught the intellectual flaw in physiocratic trade theory, its practical consequences were something he could not avoid. In substance, therefore, the Jeffersonians based their strength and their policies on the mercantilistic program of a balanced economy at home and a foreign policy of expansion.

Their strategy was to exploit the policy of neutrality initiated by Washington and continued by John Adams. To do so, Jefferson ultimately resorted to the intensely mercantilistic policies of the embargo and nonimportation against Britain and France. It was with obvious pride that he remarked, in 1809, that those policies "hastened the day when an equilibrium between the occupations of agriculture, manufactures, and commerce, shall simplify our foreign concerns to the exchange only of that surplus which we cannot consume [in return] for those articles of reasonable comfort or convenience which we cannot produce." Not even Madison ever provided a more classic statement of American mercantilism.

Quite in line with Jefferson's recommendations of the 1790's, and his actions between 1800 and 1809, his successors acted vigorously against such weaker opponents as the Barbary Pirates who threatened American trade. On a more general level, Jefferson's argument that American democracy depended upon a surplus of land was but another, even more overtly formulated, version of Madison's theory that extending the sphere was the key to controlling factions. Hence he and his followers initiated and encouraged such expansion wherever they could, as in Florida and to the West; and it was precisely Jefferson's general expansionist outlook which overrode his concern that the Louisiana Purchase was unconstitutional.

The Louisiana Purchase opened the way to apply the tenets of American mercantilism to the entire hemisphere. It also encouraged an explicit American formulation of the expansionist philosophy of history that was implicit in mercantilism. Americans began to call openly and militantly for further expansion whenever and wherever they encountered domestic or foreign difficulties. Indians and Spaniards had to be pushed out of the way or destroyed. Interference with exports had to be stopped, by war if necessary. Canada offered the solution to other domestic economic problems, and should be taken forthwith.

After 1807, when economic troubles appeared at home, that expansionist outlook and program focused on Great Britain as the chief offender against the American Empire. Growing out of an alliance of business and agrarian interests which favored war to relieve immediate difficulties and forestall future crises, the War of 1812 was a classic mercantilist conflict for trade and colonies. The Jeffersonians' earlier economic and maritime warfare, which almost secured the immediate objectives, and which had appeared capable of clearing the way for a general advance, was just as mercantilistic in nature. Though in many ways it failed to attain its avowed objectives, the War of 1812 was in no sense a strategic defeat for American mercantilism. If only in turning Americans to the west and the south, it focused the general spirit of expansion in a new and powerful manner. Perhaps even more significant, the stalemate strengthened the idea of an American System as opposed to the rest of the world. It was in the wake of the War of 1812, after all, that the vapors of Manifest Destiny gathered themselves for an explosion westward to the Pacific.

John Quincy Adams formulated his own concept of Manifest Destiny as early as 1796, when he assured President Washington that the American System would "infallibly triumph over the European system. . . ." Fifteen years later he defined America as "a nation, coextensive with the North American Continent, destined by God and nature to be the most populous and most powerful people ever combined under one social compact." He pushed overseas economic expansion just as vigorously. Even his harshest critics, the High Federalists of New England who wanted to re-enter the British Empire in some form or another, recognized his mercantilism. They called him one of the species of "amphibious politicians, who live on both land and water. . . ."

Both before and after he served as Secretary of State under President James Monroe, Adams devoted his energies to building such an American Empire. His rational program for a dynamic balanced economy at home was too demanding for his countrymen. They grew ever more enamored of a philosophy that assured them that expansion was the way to ease their dilemmas and realize their dreams. Hence they paid little heed to his proposals for domestic development or to his warning that America should go "not abroad in search of monsters to destroy." But to the extent that Adams wanted an empire big enough to sustain such a balanced economy, and to the degree that he partook of the expansionist elixir, he won support and influence. And, indeed, his very presence in the cabinet of Monroe was a symbol of the maturity of American mercantilism. Having broken with the old pro-British party to vote for the Louisiana Purchase and the measures of economic warfare against Europe, Adams became the leader of those business interests which supported territorial as well as commercial expansion.

In timing, authorship, and content, the Monroe Doctrine was the classic statement of mature American mercantilism. Seizing the opportunity presented by the decay of the Spanish Empire, Monroe and Adams moved quickly, decisively, and independently to give substance to Henry Clay's fervent exhortation to "become real and true Americans and place ourselves at the head of the American System." Adams caught the tone and meaning of the doctrine in his famous remark that it was time for America to stop bobbing along as a cock-boat in the wake of the British Empire. Acting in that spirit, he spurned Secretary George Canning's not-so-subtle suggestion that America join England in a joint guarantee of Latin American independence and a pledge against their own expansion in the region. Canning claimed high honors for having brought in the New World to redress the balance of the Old, but one would like to think that Adams enjoyed a hearty chuckle over such ability to put a rhetorical gloss on a policy defeat. For what Canning had done was to block the old empires only to be confronted by the challenge of a mature American mercantilism.

In the negative sense, the Monroe Doctrine was designed to check further European colonization in the Western Hemisphere. But Americans were quite aware of the positive implications of the strategy: it left the United States as the most powerful nation on the scene. America's ultimate territorial and commercial expansion in the New World would be limited only by its energies and its preferences—just as Washington had argued. The negative side of the Monroe Doctrine is the least significant feature about it: the crucial point is that it was, in the minds of its authors, in its language, and in its reception by Americans, the manifesto of an American Empire.

The Monroe Doctrine was the capstone of a system destined to succumb to its own success. For in broad historical perspective, the classic function of mercantilism was to build a system strong enough to survive the application of the principles of Adam Smith. Without an American mercantilism there could have been no Age of Jacksonian Laissez Moi Faire. Perhaps, indeed, the greatest tribute to the leaders of American mercantilism lies in the fact that their handiwork withstood the trauma of a civil war and the sustained shock of unrestrained and irrational exploitation for some seventy years—until it became necessary in the Crisis of the 1890's to undertake the building of a new corporate system.

Foreign Policies of the Founding Fathers

Nationalist

Nationalists argue that American foreign policy in the years of the Founding Fathers was highly successful. This success they ascribe not to Hamilton or Jefferson and Madison, but to Washington, Adams, Jay, and a group of influential moderates who borrowed ideas from both sides and trod a middle course. Nationalists regard Hamilton as less realistic

and Jefferson and Madison as less idealistic than the Realist school asserts. On the other hand, they regard American foreign policy as less expansive and more defensive than do the Radicals. In all, the Nationalists
see the foreign policy of this period as a nice blend of realism and idealism enlisted in the service of protecting the territorial integrity and
commercial rights of a new and threatened nation.

Nationalists praise George Washington and John Jay for preserving
the peace with Great Britain in the 1790s. They argue that John Adams's
break with his own party to preserve peace with France in 1798 was not
only correct but heroic. Although the policies of Jefferson and Madison
may come in for some criticism, the Nationalists regard the War of 1812
as having been inevitable, forced on the United States by Great Britain's
ruthless attacks on American ships and seamen.

In the following essay, what evidence is there of Jefferson's and Madison's realism? How important a role did expansion seem to play in their
policies? In what ways did Hamilton seem idealistic? In what ways did
domestic policies affect foreign policy during this period? Placing your-
self in Washington's shoes, what realistic alternative policies do you see
as having been available to the United States and which would you have
chosen?

The Jay Treaty: Political Battleground of the Founding Fathers

Jerald A. Combs

Hamilton was born in the West Indies about 1755, the illegitimate son of an impecunious Scottish laird who deserted his family when Hamilton was just a boy. At the age of eleven, Hamilton took a job as a clerk in a counting house to support himself and his destitute family. The circumstances of his birth and early life instilled in him a fierce desire to succeed. At fourteen, he wrote a close friend, "to confess my weakness, Ned, my ambition is prevalent." His ruthless ambition coupled with a profound intelligence and personal charm were the basic elements of his political success. Despite his small stature and slightness of build, his ambition took the form of desire for military glory. Even as a clerk in the West Indies, his main hope of escaping his fate had been a war that would enable him to join the army and leave the islands. Instead, a group of wealthy islanders who were impressed by his abilities sent him to King's College (later Columbia University) in New York to study medicine.

In New York Hamilton was quickly caught up by the revolutionary fervor. He wrote tracts supporting commercial retaliation against the British and went off gleefully to seek glory in the war that followed. After a stint as a captain of artillery, he became an aide to Washington. As such he had a chance to demonstrate his intelligence and literary ability, but he chafed at the lack of ac-

From Jerald A. Combs, *The Jay Treaty: Political Battleground of the Founding Fathers,* 1970, pp. 33–35, 40–47, 65, 70–81, 84–85, 103–104. Reprinted by permission of the University of California Press.

tion. His thirst for military glory would not let him rest. It goaded him to challenge fellow officers to duels, and to call to the retreating General Lee at Monmouth to join him in a two-man suicide stand against the British. When finally given a field command, he needlessly marched his men on the parapets before Yorktown in full sight and range of the British infantry. Finally, he prevailed on Washington to let him lead the charge on one of the two major redoubts defending Yorktown, a duty he performed with ability and relish.

Hamilton's thirst for glory had a profound effect on his domestic and foreign policies. He believed that the United States as a nation should seek the same glory, the same heroic stature, that he himself pursued throughout his life. He knew that the United States should avoid war for many years until the new nation could build the strength necessary to prosecute it successfully. But when a war with a weak opponent beckoned or when the naval power of Great Britain might join the United States in a more serious enterprise and give it a good chance for success, Hamilton could not restrain himself. After making formal gestures to save the peace with France in 1798, he welcomed the prospect of joining Britain in a war against the hated French Revolution. As the effectual commander of the American Army during the crisis, he actually considered joining the Latin-American revolutionary Miranda in a blow against Spain's Latin American colonies. He considered Julius Caesar to be the greatest man who had ever lived and obviously hoped to carve himself a similar reputation as a soldier-statesman. He even went to his death in a duel he disapproved of, withholding his fire while Aaron Burr killed him, because he feared that his refusal to fight would so affront popular prejudice that his chance of returning to political leadership and saving the country from Jeffersonian imbecility would be lost.

Alexander Hamilton dreamed of a United States "ascendant in the system of American affairs," with himself at the head of the ascendant nation. He wrote in *The Federalist:*

The world may politically, as well as geographically, be divided into four parts, each having a distinct set of interests. Unhappily for the other three, Europe by her arms and by her negociations, by force and by fraud, has, in different degrees, extended her dominion over them all. Africa, Asia, and America have successively felt her domination. The superiority, she has long maintained, has tempted her to plume herself as the Mistress of the World, and to consider the rest of mankind as created for her benefit. . . . Facts have too long supported these arrogant pretensions of the European. It belongs to us to vindicate the honor of the human race, and to teach that assuming brother moderation.

Although other Americans might also share the vision of a United States ascendant in the western hemisphere, they usually had in mind a much more pacific and informal supremacy. Hamilton's was a military and imperial vision. He demanded heroism, bloodshed, and a sacrifice of individual pleasures for national destiny. In fact, his whole domestic political system was designed to drag an unwilling populace onto his road to glory.

.   .   .

[Naturally, Hamilton opposed any measures that threatened his romantic vision.] After all, there was a chance that Great Britain would retaliate in kind rather than give in to commercial pressure. This would have been disastrous for Hamilton's system. The nation's entire credit structure, the basis of Hamilton's plans for national power, rested on the revenue derived from the tariff and tonnage duties charged on imports. These duties netted over six million dollars annually in all the years except one between 1791 and 1796. The amount garnered from internal sources in that period only once rose above six hundred thousand dollars. Since the annual interest alone on the nation's foreign and domestic debts was well above two million dollars and the expenses of the government totaled some six hundred thousand dollars, the income America derived from import duties was vital. Ninety percent of these imports came from Great Britain. Thus, a commercial war that shut off British trade might well bankrupt the United States. As Hamilton wrote Jefferson, "My commercial system turns very much on giving a free course to trade, and cultivating good humor with all the world. And I feel a particular reluctance to hazard any thing, in the present state of our affairs, which may lead to a commercial warfare with any power."

British trade supplied not only revenue but vital manufactures as well. This gave Hamilton yet another reason to oppose measures that might bring on a commercial war with Britain. . . . Hamilton reasoned that the United States was dependent on Britain for some basic elements of its internal stability and self-defense.

His solution was to avoid challenging Britain until the United States had developed internal sources of manufactures and revenue capable of sustaining the nation in an emergency. In his Re-

port on Manufactures, he laid plans to develop those internal resources that would ultimately enable the United States to
challenge England if it should become necessary.

Some historians have charged that Hamilton never contemplated true independence of England, but instead was driven by
the image of himself "at the head of an American-British empire
embracing most of the world." According to this view the Anglo-
American alliances periodically proposed by Hamilton were not
intended to be temporary, as Hamilton claimed, but permanent. It
has even been said that Hamilton never sought a balanced political economy which would render the United States economically
independent of England. As one historian puts it, Hamilton "never
pushed manufacturing as an integral part of the economy and in
fact opposed the efforts of others to accelerate its development."

This argument is based primarily on Hamilton's opposition to
the efforts of Jefferson and Madison to raise the tariff and tonnage rates against the British. Only raising these rates would
have provided adequate protection for nascent American manufactures against overwhelming competition from Great Britain, it
is maintained. Hamilton's use of an excise tax in preference to
higher tariffs against England is seen as tantamount to opposition to manufactures, a balanced economy, and true independence from Great Britain.

This argument dismisses several vital facts. First, it is clear
that Hamilton did favor protection for American manufactures. In
1790 he advised Congress to raise the duty on unwrought steel,
which, in an oversight, had been set too low to provide protection
for the industry rapidly growing in Pennsylvania. The tariff of
1792, which realized the purposes of his Report on Manufactures,
provided very adequate protection and at the same time lowered
the duties on certain raw materials for America's manufactures.
Yet it is correct to say that Hamilton refused to push these duties
to prohibitive heights. In Federalist No. 35, he had already outlined a few of his reasons for this; some persons imagined that
raising tariffs

can never be carried to too great a length; since the higher they are, the
more it is alleged they will tend to discourage an extravagant consumption, to produce a favourable balance of trade, and to promote domestic
manufactures. But all extremes are pernicious in various ways. Exorbitant
duties on imported articles would beget a general spirit of smuggling.
. . . They tend to render other classes of the community tributary in an
improper degree to the manufacturing classes to whom they give a

premature monopoly of the markets: They sometimes force industry out of its more natural channels into others in which it flows with less advantage. And in the last place they oppress the merchant, who is often obliged to pay them himself without any retribution from the consumer.

Hamilton had still other reasons for refusing to push for higher tariffs once the protective rates of 1792 had gone into effect. To develop its manufactures, the United States needed capital even more than protection. In his Report on Public Credit, Hamilton pointed out that a properly funded national debt would answer the purpose of money; for if people had confidence in its bonds, these bonds would pass in business transactions as specie, and trade, agriculture, and manufactures would be promoted by them. This great source of capital for the development of manufactures was dependent on the revenue derived from customs to support it. Higher duties indeed might have protected America's manufactures against competition; but by inducing British retaliation, they might also have destroyed the major source of capital on which those manufactures relied. A more subtle way to encourage manufactures without endangering the course of Anglo-American trade, Hamilton thought, was for the national government to furnish boundaries rather than enact prohibitive tariffs. Bounties would run little risk of triggering retaliatory duties, yet would enable American manufacturers to compete with the British. Though Congress did not accept the idea, it was a brilliant way for the United States to have its cake and eat it too. Hamilton offered a means of supplying large amounts of revenue and manufactures while developing America's internal sources of these commodities. Ultimately, this would render America economically self-sufficient. Meanwhile, Great Britain would be helping to develop the resources that would enable the United States to challenge her for supremacy in the western hemisphere.

Thus Hamilton thought that a commercial war would threaten his entire system, and he believed such a commercial war would be very likely if the United States enacted legislation discriminating against the British. Others might argue that since Great Britain was so dependent on American trade, she would give in without a fight. But if Hamilton had any hopes of this, they were dissolved in October 1789 when [George] Beckwith [an agent of Canada's Governor Dorchester] relayed to him a message from the British cabinet that Britain would retaliate. Beckwith said that the British ministers had had as their first purpose since the Revolutionary War "to hold the Nation high, in the opinion of the world. . . . You cannot suppose, that those who follow up such a system will be influenced by compulsory measures. Upon such minds their tendency must be diametrically opposite. The purposes of National glory are best attained by a close adherence to National honour, alike prepared to meet foreign friendship, and to repel foreign hostility." Those were sentiments Hamilton could understand. He told Beckwith that "before I came into office and since, I have acted under that impression."

A commercial war would be bad enough if it undermined the revenue and manufactures so desperately needed by the United States. But, Hamilton said, commercial warfare was also "productive . . . of dispositions tending to a worse kind of warfare." He thought that if Jefferson and Madison were allowed to pursue their course of commercial retaliation, "there would be, in less than six months, an open war between the United States and Great Britain." Great Britain, with its fleet and provinces bordering the United States, was capable of destroying America's commerce, drying up its sources of revenue and manufactures, mounting and supplying land attacks either from Canada or the sea, and bombarding America's port cities. At the very least, such a war would destroy the power base that Hamilton was building.

So Hamilton advocated great moderation to avoid war with Great Britain. Yet he also supported preparations for war. In *The Federalist* he had warned his countrymen,

Let us recollect, that peace or war, will not always be left to our option; that however moderate or unambitious we may be, we cannot count upon the moderation, or hope to extinguish the ambition of others. . . . To judge from the history of mankind, we shall be compelled to conclude, that the fiery and destructive passions of war, reign in the human breast, with much more powerful sway, than the mild and beneficent sentiments of peace; and, that to model our political systems upon speculations of lasting tranquility, is to calculate on the weaker springs of the human character.

Thus, nothing America could do would insure peace. Peaceful intentions and treaties of friendship were as straw. History gave "an instructive but afflicting lesson to mankind how little dependence is to be placed on treaties which have no other sanction than the obligations of good faith; and which oppose general considerations of peace and justice to the impulse of any immediate interest and passion." Some might argue that republics were exempt from the ambitions of monarchs that had caused previous wars, and that as the world became more republican, it would become more peaceful as well; Hamilton, however, laughed at the idea. "Have republics in practice been less addicted to war than monarchies?" he asked. "Are not the former administered by *men* as well as the latter? Are there not aversions, predilections, rivalships and desires of unjust acquisition that affect nations as well as kings? Are not popular assemblies frequently subject to the impulses of rage, resentment, jealousy, avarice, and of other irregular and violent propensities?"

Hamilton had equal scorn for those who hoped that commerce would breed peace and that nations would hesitate to fight such a valuable customer as the United States for fear of losing trade: "Has commerce hitherto done any thing more than change the objects of war? Is not the love of wealth as domineering and enterprising a passion as that of power or glory? Have there not been as many wars founded upon commercial motives, since that has become the prevailing system of nations, as were before occasioned b[y] the cupidity of territory and dominion?"

Since relations between nations were as subject to passion and interest as relations between individuals within a nation, so the solution was the same for both—power. And by power, Hamilton meant military power. He had little more confidence in commercial retaliation as a substitute for war than he had in commerce as a guarantor of peace. Joined to military power, commercial weapons might be useful in certain situations. However, Hamilton thought trade's major function was to support the true instruments of power, an army and a navy.

The major purpose of a navy, as Hamilton saw it, was to protect America's trade. To do this, the navy had to be an offensive one, with large ships capable of ranging throughout the world. He despised the idea of a defensive navy composed of gunboats to protect America's coast and privateers to harass foreign shipping. Such a navy would be incapable of protecting America's own commerce. It was a "novel and absurd experiment in politics, [to tie] up the hands of Government from offensive war" if America expected to be a commercial people, he said. Without a navy, "our commerce would be a prey to the wanton intermeddlings of all nations at war with each other; who, having nothing to fear from us, would with little scruple or remorse supply their wants by depredations on our property, as often as it fell in their way. The rights of neutrality will only be respected, when they are defended by an adequate power. A nation, despicable by its weakness, forfeits even the privilege of being neutral."

Obviously the United States was unable to build a navy that in a short time "could vie with those of the great maritime powers." But it could soon build one that "would at least be of respectable weight, if thrown into the scale of either of two contending parties. This would be more particularly the case in relation to operations in the West-Indies. A few ships of the line sent opportunely to the reinforcement of either side, would often be sufficient to decide the fate of a campaign, on the event of which interests of the greatest magnitude were suspended." Thus America could hope "ere long to become the Arbiter of Europe in America; and to be able to incline the ballance of European competitions in this part of the world as our interest may dictate." From there the United States could move on to the point where it no longer merely inclined the balance of European competitions, but maintained "an ascendant in the system of American affairs." Then the United States would "dictate the terms of the connection between the old and the new world."

Such a plan, however, would require a regular army as well as a navy. Though most Americans feared a standing army as a threat to internal liberty, Hamilton regarded it as a necessity for the defense of the nation: "The steady operations of war against a regular and disciplined army, can only be successfully conducted by a force of the same kind." Besides, regular armies,

though they bear a malignant aspect to liberty and oeconomy, . . . [render] sudden conquests impracticable, and . . . [prevent] that rapid desolation, which used to mark the progress of war, prior to their introduction. The art of fortification has contributed to the same ends. . . . Campaigns are wasted in reducing two or three frontier garrisons, to gain admittance into an enemy's country. Similar impediments occur at every step, to exhaust the strength and delay the progress of an invader. . . . Formerly an invading army would penetrate into the heart of a neighbouring country, almost as soon as intelligence of its approach could be received; but now a comparatively small force of disciplined troops, acting on the defensive with the aid of posts, is able to impede and finally to frustrate the enterprises of one much more considerable. The history of war [in Europe] is no longer a history of nations subdued and empires overturned, but of towns taken and retaken, of battles that decide nothing, of retreats more beneficial than victories, of much effort and little acquisition.

Hamilton admitted that even without a regular army, America's geographical isolation and its great expanse of territory probably rendered it secure from total conquest by a European nation, so long as the country was united behind the war. But an invasion of the United States under such conditions would destroy the power base Hamilton was attempting to erect. "The want of fortifications leaving the frontiers . . . open . . . would facilitate inroads. . . . Conquests would be easy to be made, as difficult to be retained. War therefore would be desultory and predatory. PLUNDER and devastation ever march in the train of irregulars."

Under such conditions, lack of a standing army might actually be more conducive to tyranny than the absence of one. "Safety from external danger is the most powerful director of national conduct," he warned. "Even the ardent love of liberty will, after a time, give way to its dictates. . . . To be more safe they, at length, become willing to run the risk of being less free."

Thus, Hamilton planned the development of power and greatness for the United States. With an army, a navy, internal sources of revenue and manufactures, a unified federal government, and leaders seeking the glory that was America's true national interest, the United States would become the leader of the western hemisphere, able to bid defiance to the rest of the world. But what for the present? The United States was dependent on British trade for the revenue and manufactures so necessary to build a military establishment. Hamilton told Beckwith it might be as much as fifty years before the United States had developed its military forces and internal resources sufficiently to attempt to incline the balance between European powers contending in America, let alone dictate terms between the old world and the new. Allowing for diplomatic exaggeration, this would leave America forced to follow a foreign policy of appeasement for the rest of Hamilton's life. Where would be the glory and greatness he sought so desperately for himself?

Alexander Hamilton could conceive of only one means by which the United States could undertake a glorious foreign policy in the immediate future without endangering the growth of the nation's domestic power base. That was to secure aid from the British; and from 1789 on Alexander Hamilton tried to maneuver the United States into an alliance with Great Britain. Such an alliance would not only guarantee peace with the one nation capable of seriously threatening America's growing power, but would enable the United States to undertake immediately the kind of exploits of which Hamilton dreamed [such as joint Anglo-American expeditions against Spanish territory in the western hemisphere].

.   .   .

A certain serenity of spirit set Jefferson and Madison apart from the rest of the founding fathers. The two Virginians had a pacific temperament, and their foreign and domestic policies reflected it. They were ambitious, but they were never driven by the intense, gnawing anxieties that dominated a man like Hamilton. Hamilton relished conflict; Jefferson and Madison hated it. Jefferson thought "social harmony the first of human felicities," while Madison longed for a government of "reason, benevolence, and brotherly affection." Hamilton was dashing and arrogant; Jefferson and Madison were calm and deferential. Hamilton was a dandy; Jefferson was careless of personal appearance, and Madison wore little but black. Hamilton strutted; Madison stooped and Jefferson shambled. Hamilton was the total public man; his goals were public and he considered all private interests subordinate to them. Jefferson and Madison were essentially private men; for them the purpose of government was not national glory, but the protection of individuals in the pursuit of legitimate private interests. Jefferson and Madison thought the United States should seek not wealth but simplicity, not power but liberty, not national glory but domestic tranquillity, not heroism but happiness.

Hamilton's search for glory subordinated domestic to foreign policy. At home he sought merely to build a power base for the ultimate source of national greatness—foreign affairs. The pursuit of national happiness undertaken by Jefferson and Madison reversed these priorities. Their domestic system would provide the essentials of happiness, such as liberty, justice, and domestic tranquillity; foreign policy would simply defend this system from foreign interference and supply the minimum of foreign trade and territory that might aid its purposes.

.   .   .

Jefferson and Madison were convinced that passive acceptance of aggression was more dangerous than resistance. "A coward is much more exposed to quarrels than a man of spirit," Jefferson claimed. "Weakness provokes insult and injury, while a condition to punish it often prevents it. . . . I think it to our interest to punis[h] the first insult: because an insult unpunished is the parent of many oth[ers]."

Jefferson and Madison were particularly convinced of the necessity to resist the policies of Great Britain. To a large extent this attitude was a result of adapting their ideas about human nature to the nature of relations between states. Hamilton, who regarded nations and individuals as instinctively selfish, was not particularly surprised or chagrined at Britain's policies. In his opinion, these policies were the result of natural selfishness and a mistaken view of British interests, rather than any fixed hatred of the United States. If England could be made to see that its true interests lay in conciliating rather than opposing the United States, its policy would change. Retaliation, however, *would* induce hostility; and then appeals to reason and self-interest would be useless, for men were ruled more by passion than by reason.

Jefferson and Madison were not so worried about the effects of retaliation upon Great Britain. They thought England was already as hostile as it was going to get, and that its policies were the result of passionate hatred rather than natural self-interest. They resented Great Britain's policies more than Hamilton did partly because they expected more of nations. Because Jefferson and Madison expected magnanimity as well as self-interest and hatred in foreign relations, they reacted more strongly against Britain's conduct than Hamilton did. England seemed intractably hostile, anxious to see the American experiment fail so that she could pick up the shattered pieces of the Union. The British insisted on identifying their interests with the destruction of the United States instead of seeing that their long-range interests were best served by matching America's virtuous regard for the rights and interests of others. Only avarice and passionate dislike of the United States could explain the blindness of the British to their true interests. "Nothing will bring them to reason but physical obstruction, applied to their bodily senses," Jefferson concluded. Failure of America to resist would convince the British that hostility ran no risk of punishment, inviting further aggressions not only from England, but from all nations "lest [Britain] should exclusively enjoy the superior and peculiar advantages, arising from her conduct."

Still other principles reflected in the domestic policy of Jefferson and Madison helped determine them to resist the policy of Great Britain. Their belief that economic independence was vital to human liberty and dignity led them to resent being bound "in commercial manacles" to England. So they tried to free the United States from financial dependence on England despite the material costs of such a policy. Their principle of checking and balancing superior power also dictated resistance to Great Britain, since she was the greatest power in the world of that time and the only nation capable of mounting a major military effort against the United States. Rather than joining Great Britain, as Hamilton was wont to do, they favored Britain's weaker opponents. Thus they continued to support the French alliance.

After the French Revolution, they were further inclined to support France because of their democratic sympathies and their belief that republics were more disposed to peace and friendly relations than monarchies or oligarchies. But the French Revolution did little more than confirm them in their earlier policy. The direction of that policy had been settled years before the French Revolution, when Madison and Jefferson both regarded England's form of government as a sort of half-way house between the absolutism of the French monarchy and the libertarian republicanism of the United States.

Most important to the foreign policy of Jefferson and Madison, however, was not the determination that the United States *should* resist the wrongs of foreign nations but that it *could* do so. Hamilton argued that the United States lacked the most basic elements of national power—an army, a navy, domestic manufactures, an extensive and invulnerable source of revenue, and a powerful central government. Had Jefferson and Madison accepted that argument, they would have been faced with the choice of appeasing Great Britain or building powers destructive of the domestic happiness, liberty, justice, and tranquillity that foreign policy was supposed to protect. They avoided this dilemma by rejecting Hamilton's concept of the nature and extent of power necessary for the United States to resist the wrongs of Great Britain and Spain. They judged that the United States did not need an army, manufactures, extensive national revenue, nor a consolidated government. They even came to reject the need for a navy, of which they themselves had been advocates prior to 1789. They did not do this because they were blind idealists who failed to balance goals with the power available. On the contrary, they balanced them very carefully. They simply thought the United States already had power of a nature and extent capable of securing America's foreign policy goals without endangering its domestic system.

Jefferson and Madison decided that there were only two areas where the United States might be required to defend its interests with force—its borders and its ships at sea. Regarding the borders, they thought the United States had little to fear. Certainly there was no need for a regular army to defend them. America's distance from the European nations whose colonies bordered its territory meant that "No European nation can ever send against us such a regular army as we need fear, and it is hard if our militia are not equal to those of Canada and Florida." Jefferson and Madison counted on America's tremendous population growth to achieve inevitably and peacefully whatever the United States wanted on its frontiers.

.   .   .

Jefferson and Madison thought there was far more danger of a major war on the sea than on the frontier. American power would soon be so overwhelming on the frontier that no one would dare resist the nation's just interests there. But the ocean was something else again. The determination of Americans to share in the world's shipping and commerce meant "Frequent wars without a doubt," as far as Jefferson was concerned. . . .

He realized, however, that "our people are decided in the opinion that it is necessary for us to share in the occupation of the ocean." Believing it the "duty in those entrusted with the administration of their affairs to conform themselves to the decided choice of their constituents," he determined "to share as large a portion as we can of this modern source of wealth and power." Still, he hoped to keep trade merely a "handmaiden to agriculture," carrying off America's surplus crops and bringing back only the vital supplies that the United States could not produce for itself.

If Jefferson and Madison saw the potential for war and depravity in trade, however, they also saw its potential for peace. Both realized that trade created a community of interest that might deter nations from war with one another for fear of losing valuable commerce. Both thought that an international system of free trade would exploit this community of interest to the maximum. When Jefferson and John Adams obtained a trade treaty with Prussia which approached their ideal of free trade, they wrote that they were leading the way to an "object so valuable to mankind as the total emancipation of commerce and the bringing together all nations for a free intercommunication of happiness."

The restrictions that England and the rest of Europe imposed on American trade after the Revolution soon convinced Jefferson and Madison that free trade was out of reach. In 1785 Madison wrote, "A perfect freedom [of trade] is the System which would be my choice. But before such a System will be eligible perhaps for the U.S. they must be out of debt; before it will be attainable, all other nations must concur in it." Since other nations did not concur, he reluctantly decided that the United States had to "retort the distinction."

Yet even commercial retaliation could be an instrument of peace, Jefferson and Madison believed. In fact, their whole policy toward England was dedicated to that proposition. They were convinced that commercial retaliation could avoid the danger of war brought on by appeasement while at the same time avoiding the war that would come as a result of military resistance. It would forcibly remind the British that their long range interest was in conciliating the United States and protecting the community of interest which their mutual trade afforded. It would enable the United States to challenge Great Britain immediately without building an army, a navy, domestic manufactures, extensive revenue, or a consolidated government.

Jefferson and Madison acknowledged that commercial war was a possible outcome of retaliation against England, though they thought it improbable. Jefferson said, "they will be agitated by their avarice on one hand, and their hatred and their fear of us on the other. The result of this conflict of d[irty passions] is yet [to be] awaited." Madison avowed that, "If we were disposed to hazard the experiment of interdicting the intercourse between us and the Powers not in alliance, we should have overtures of the most advantageous kind tendered by those nations." Still he considered British counterretaliation possible. Like Jefferson, however, he did not fear its effects. He told the first Congress in 1789, "We soon shall be in a condition, we now are in a condition to wage a commercial warfare with that nation. The produce of this country is more necessary to the rest of the world than that of other countries is to America." He was not afraid that America would suffer in the contest, for England's "interests can be wounded almost mortally, while ours are invulnerable."

Hamilton, of course, thought this was nonsense. He believed the United States desperately needed British manufactures and the revenue derived from duties on British trade to support American credit. Jefferson and Madison rejected this notion. In their opinion, the United States was almost totally self-sufficient, producing all the three essentials of life—food, clothing, and shelter. British imports were not necessities, but "gewgaws." The value of these luxuries exceeded that of American exports to England, and the resulting imbalance of trade drained America of its sorely needed capital. "For my part I think that the trade with Great Britain is a ruinous one to ourselves; and that nothing would be an inducement to tolerate it but a free commerce with their West Indies; and that this being denied to us we should put a stop to the losing branch," Jefferson maintained.

A commercial war then would simply do what the United States ought to do of its own accord—cut down Anglo-American trade. It was British credit and America's thirst for luxuries that made British trade important to the United States, and both were harmful. "Fashion and folly is plunging [Americans] deeper and deeper into distress," said Jefferson. "We should try whether the prodigal might not be restrained from taking on credit the gewgaw held out to him on one hand, by seeing the keys of a prison in the other." Madison agreed. He thought, however, that the difficulty in collecting American debts would probably check the propensity of European merchants "to credit us beyond our resources, and so far the evil of an unfavorable balance will correct itself. But the Merchants of Great Britain if no others will continue to credit us at least as far as our remittances can be strained, and that is far enough to perpetuate our difficulties unless the luxurious propensity of our own people can be otherwise checked."

Thus, the credit extended by the British to American merchants which Hamilton thought vital to the volume of American trade and to the revenue derived from it, Jefferson and Madison thought a temptation to ruin. "It is much to be wished that every discouragement should be thrown in the way of men who undertake to trade without capital; who therefore do not go to the market where commodities are to be had cheapest, but where they are to be had on the longest credit. The consumers pay for it in the end, and the debts contracted, and bankruptcies occasioned by such commercial adventures, bring burthen and disgrace on our country. . . . Yet these are the actual links which hold us whether we will or no to Great Britain," said Jefferson.

But if Anglo-American trade were stopped, what would be done for the necessary manufactures, which along with the gewgaws were imported from England? First, Jefferson and Madison did not propose to develop domestic manufactures. They hoped instead by raising tariffs against England to shift America's dependence for essential manufactures to France. As Madison said in defense of his tonnage bill of 1789, "From artificial or adventitious causes, the commerce between America and Great Britain exceeds what may be considered its natural boundary." Since France had "relaxed considerably in that rigid policy it before pursued," he hoped that favors given to it and other nations in treaty with the United States would "enable them to gain their proportion of our direct trade from the nation who had acquired more than it is naturally her due." His introduction to that bill stated that its purpose was the regulation of commerce and the raising of a revenue; it made no mention of protective duties for manufacturers.

This was certainly in keeping with Madison's former ideas. In 1787 he had written, "There is a rage at present for high duties, partly for the purpose of revenue, partly for forcing manufacturers, which it is difficult to resist. . . . Manufacturers will come of themselves when we are ripe for them." Jefferson, whose agrarian bias exceeded even Madison's, certainly had no desire to "force" domestic manufactures. He was content to "let our workshops remain in Europe. It is better to carry provisions and material to workmen there, than to bring them to the provisions and materials, and with them their manners and principles. . . . The mobs of great cities add just so much to the support of pure government as sores do to the strength of the human body."

Jefferson and Madison were confident that France and other European nations could easily supply the few things that the United States really needed to import. The French and the Dutch had the capital to supply essential credit, and French manufactures were as good as the British while being generally cheaper, they thought. Should British shipping be unavailable to supplement American shipping in carrying off America's products, the Dutch would supply it. Also, distributing America's trade among several nations would eliminate American dependence on any one country and help maintain a balance of power in Europe.

Admittedly, however, diverting American trade from Britain to France and the Netherlands involved a decline in the import trade. This would diminish the source of 90 percent of the federal government's revenue which in turn paid the interest and principle on America's debts and established its credit. Jefferson and Madison were not too worried about this aspect. They thought Hamilton's funding and assumption schemes had drastically inflated the national debt, and that substantially less revenue was necessary to pay off the true debt. Nor did they favor extensive federal activities that might in themselves require large amounts of revenue.

As good agrarians, Jefferson and Madison concluded that the only potential benefit that British trade offered was to supply markets for America's agricultural surpluses. The most important of these markets were in the western hemisphere, particularly in the West Indies. "Access to the West Indies is indispensably necessary to us," said Jefferson. "The produce of the U.S. will soon exceed the European demand. What is to be done with the surplus, when there shall be one? It will be employed, without question, to open by force a market for itself with those placed on the same continent with us, and who wish nothing better."

Thus, changing British policy regarding the West Indies was vital not only to America's agricultural prosperity, but to peace as well. And commercial retaliation promised to do just that. . . . Restrictions on British trade would starve the West Indies, bankrupt British manufacturers, and undermine British finances. Great Britain would be forced to conclude a trade treaty opening its West Indies and evacuating the posts. Probably this would come about without much of a struggle. But if it did require a commercial war, the United States would certainly win. Besides, a commercial war would avoid the shooting war which could easily occur if appeasement led to British miscalculations, if the war with the Northwest Indians led to a clash with the British-occupied frontier posts, or if American surpluses brought about an attempt to open western hemisphere markets by force.

But what if they were wrong, and war with England did result from commercial retaliation? Would America then not require a powerful central government, revenue, credit, domestic manufactures, an army, and a navy? Jefferson and Madison answered that question in a slightly different way after Hamilton had shown his intentions as secretary of the treasury than they had before. At both times they relied primarily on the financial hardships that the expenses of the war and the loss of American trade would inflict on Great Britain to bring the war to a speedy and victorious conclusion. At both times they expected America's distance from Europe to make it impossible for England to send and supply an army large enough to conquer the United States. And at both times they expected to be forced to "abandon the ocean where we are weak, leaving to neutral nations the carriage of our commodities; and measure with [the British] on land where they alone can lose." America could safely rely on foreign shipping for vital supplies in times of war because "Neutral nations, whose rights are becoming every day more and more extensive, would not now suffer themselves to be shut out from our ports, nor would the hostile Nation presume to attempt it," predicted Madison. Meanwhile, the American merchants could turn their vessels into privateers to harass enemy trade. This reliance on neutral ships to supply vital materiel, a militia army and privateer navy to do the fighting, and distance and financial hardship to sap the spirit of Great Britain allowed Jefferson and Madison to minimize the necessity for a consolidated government, domestic manufactures, a standing army, and heavy expenditures.

. . . But after Hamilton took office, the two Virginians abandoned certain other war preparations they had advocated in the Confederation period. The first of these was the domestic manufacture of war implements. Neutral shipping could supply most of the goods America might need to import, but belligerent nations could legally intercept war materiel as contraband. Thus, in 1787, when Madison was rejecting the need for most domestic manufactures, he said that "As far as relates to implements of war which are contraband, the argument for our fabrication of them is certainly good." In 1788 Jefferson too thought that the United States should make provision for "magazines and manufacturers of arms." After these men began their opposition to Hamilton's policies, they promoted this idea no longer.

Far more important, they abandoned their support for a navy. Prior to Hamilton's taking office, Jefferson and Madison had zealously advocated a navy as the best means of defense involving the least danger to internal liberty. "I consider that an acquisition of maritime strength is essential to this country," said Madison; "what but this can defend our towns and cities upon the sea-coast? or what but this can enable us to repel an invading enemy?" Jefferson agreed; without "a protecting force on the sea . . . the smallest powers in Europe, every one which possesses a single ship of the line may dictate to us, and enforce their demands by captures on our commerce." Jefferson thought that a small navy of some eighteen ships of the line and twelve frigates would be about adequate. A small American navy could cope with even the strongest naval powers because

Providence has placed their richest and most defenceless possessions at our door; has obliged their most precious commerce to pass, as it were in review before us. To protect this, or to assail, a small part only of their naval force will ever be risked across the Atlantic. . . . A small naval force then is sufficient for us, and a small one is necessary.

Hamilton's policies evidently led Jefferson and Madison to fear federal taxation and power more than the lack of a navy. So they decided that privateers could threaten the West Indies, the fisheries, and the western trade routes as well as a regular navy. Madison signaled the retreat from his former ideas in 1790, when he told Congress that although he favored a maritime force, he did not favor a navy; he sought only to increase those resources that might be converted into such a marine force as would be absolutely necessary in an emergency. By the time of the Jay Treaty crisis, Jefferson had adopted the same policy, and it became an important plank in the platform of the nascent Republican party. Jefferson and Madison remained confident, however, that the United States had the power to challenge British policy even without a navy and domestic sources of war implements. America could still handle a shooting war with Great Britain in the unlikely event that commercial retaliation or other circumstances should lead to it.

.   .   .

If retaliation was undertaken, would the people support it, or would they undercut it by smuggling? Even if they did support it, could France and the Netherlands really supply credit and manufactures in sufficient quantity to maintain a reasonable occupation for American merchants and ships? Would there be sufficient imports to furnish a revenue capable of paying off America's debts and maintaining its credit? And if war should come, would the people be willing to endure the privations of a guerrilla war which destroyed their trade and subjected their coastal cities to naval bombardment?

Jefferson and Madison were confident that if the test came, these questions would all be answered in the affirmative. Perhaps these assumptions were wildly unrealistic. For to think that the people would unite behind a policy that forsook wealth and power in return for austerity and the risk of another guerrilla war, all in pursuit of a simple, republican, economically independent, agrarian nation might seem to verge on insanity to some. One can point to the reaction of the Northeast to Jefferson's embargo and the War of 1812 in support of this view. And certainly Great Britain's interruptions of neutral trade during the Anglo-French wars of the late eighteenth century demonstrate the folly of Jefferson and Madison in hoping that neutral nations could supply America with necessary imports in case of war with England.

Yet in these days we cannot so easily dismiss the dreams of Jefferson and Madison as hopelessly utopian. The examples of Cuba and Vietnam have shown that large groups of people will sometimes sacrifice the promise of greater wealth for national independence and an appealing political vision. Cuba and Vietnam also demonstrate that a people struggling on their home ground can resist the economic or military opposition of great powers for indefinite periods. Had the Americans been willing to make equivalent sacrifices, there is no doubt that they could have realized the dreams of Jefferson and Madison. The question the people of the United States had to decide was whether these goals were worth the sacrifice.

Undoubtedly most did not think so. They may have sympathized with the democratic tendencies and agrarian biases of Jefferson and Madison. But the American people's dreams were of a republicanism based on economic opportunity rather than austerity. In all probability, a commercial or shooting war with England in the 1790s would have resulted in the same kind of disaffection and consequent ineffectuality that characterized the foreign policy efforts of Jefferson and Madison during their administrations.

.   .   .

All in all, it seems that the policy advocated by Washington, Adams, and Jay and actually followed by the United States during the first twelve years of its existence was proper. Growing prosperity and the magnitude of the other problems facing the new government rendered an immediate settlement with Great Britain less urgent than it had been during the Confederation. To avoid challenging Britain and bringing on a crisis while building the strength of the new nation was undoubtedly the wisest course, especially in the light of our present knowledge that Great Britain would have retaliated rather than surrender to commercial discrimination. On the other hand, it was wise to avoid making all the concessions that Hamilton advocated in order to achieve a settlement and perhaps an alliance with England. Britain was as yet unready to give up its dreams of throttling America's chances to expand westward, and any settlement brought about by conciliation would have cost the United States dearly on the frontier. To hold matters with England in abeyance while building America's strength seems from a twentieth-century vantage point to have been the best possible course between 1789 and 1793.

Nationalists also argue that the War of 1812 is no proof of the excessive idealism and optimism of Jefferson and Madison. They point out that the embargo could well have succeeded if Federalist New England had supported instead of violated it. Even the less effectual commercial measures of Madison came close to succeeding, for Great Britain did ultimately abandon its commercial warfare against neutrals. The tragedy was that news of this retreat reached the United States several weeks after war had already been declared. Nationalists thus ascribe the failure of Republican foreign policy more to the treachery of the Federalists than to the supposed blundering of the Republicans. (See Louis M. Sears, Jefferson and the Embargo, and Marshall Smelser, The Democratic Republic.)

four
The Monroe
Doctrine

Nationalist

Nationalists regard the Monroe Doctrine as a nearly perfect example of what American foreign policy has been and should continue to be. By warning Europe away from the Western Hemisphere, the United States combined benevolence and idealism with a healthy regard for its own interests. Helping to prevent European intervention in the Western Hemisphere protected the rights of Latin American republics to self-determination, thus striking a blow for democracy against colonialism. At the same time, the security and prosperity of the United States were enhanced. With Europe out of Latin America, no major power could use the area as a staging ground to threaten the security of the United States. In addition, the United States would have an advantage over distant European nations in Latin American markets.

Samuel Flagg Bemis, author of the following selection, is the dean of American diplomatic historians. He is a professor emeritus of history at Yale University. Among his most noted publications is a biography of John Quincy Adams, the chief formulator of the Monroe Doctrine. Does Bemis see any aggressive intent or designs for empire in America's declaration of the Monroe Doctrine? How does he seem to weight the elements of ideology, trade, and security in the motivations of Monroe and Adams?

A Diplomatic History of the United States

Samuel Flagg Bemis

Recognition by the United States of the independence of the Latin-American states had been in the face of European and British disapproval. After the overthrow of Napoleon the Czar of Russia, Alexander I, had banded together the continental allies and the restored Bourbon monarchy of France in a Holy Alliance, the purpose of which was to protect the peace of Europe against another eruption of France and further to prevent any subversive or revolutionary movements in their own or other states which might threaten the tranquillity of the "legitimate" and absolute monarchies. Liberal insurrections were promptly crushed in Naples and Piedmont (1821) by Austrian armies under the mandate of the Holy Allies, and in Spain (1823) by a French army with similar authority.

Great Britain refused to be a party to the Holy Alliance and its repressive program. Her great foreign ministers Castlereagh and Canning held that British obligation to continental allies was limited to hold France to observance of the peace settlement of Vienna. They would not help the holy monarchs straitjacket the countries of Europe for absolute divine-right rulers. Besides, they looked skeptically upon the Holy Alliance as a scaffolding by which Russia might achieve a military authority over all Europe. It remained British policy to balance European powers in rivalry while Great Britain continued unmolested to consolidate her territorial gains of 1815 and ply the markets and maritime trade of the world. Following this sound policy the British Empire reached its apogee in the nineteenth century under the reign of Queen Victoria.

The intervention of the Holy Allies saved his throne for King Ferdinand VII of Spain in 1823. Might it not save him also his col-

From Samuel Flagg Bemis, *A Diplomatic History of the United States*, 5th ed., Chap. XII, pp. 202–208. Copyright 1936, 1942, 1950, 1955, © by Holt, Rinehart and Winston, Inc. Copyright © 1964 by Samuel Flagg Bemis. Reprinted by permission of Holt, Rinehart and Winston, Inc.

onies? He appealed to the banded monarchs of Europe to send armies and navies to the New World to put down his rebellious subjects and give him back his rich provinces. The Holy Allies were preparing to meet at another European congress in which this subject might be discussed. Great Britain was disturbed. She feared that any forcible settlement of Spain's colonial affairs by the Holy Alliance might close up the new commerce and give a political tutelage and commercial advantage to some continental power like France. That indeed was the ambition of French diplomacy: to set up in the former Spanish provinces a galaxy of new American monarchies under French Bourbon princes, with close political and commercial ties to France. Here was a remotely possible program of recovery from France's prostration of 1815 —an outlet in South America in nominal conjunction with Spain.

Investigation among the confidential archives of European powers by Professor Dexter Perkins reveals that there was not much likelihood of the Holy Allies helping Spain and furthering French ambitions. Though they frowned on independence of the Spanish provinces, neither Prussia, Russia nor Austria, for varying reasons of their own, was sufficiently interested to take forcible steps to prevent it. The only danger was that they might give France a free hand to work out with Spain some settlement. This Great Britain was determined to prevent.

The policy of Great Britain and the United States had had much in common in regard to Latin America. Both desired to continue their new and profitable trade with liberated Spanish colonies. But there was one difference between the two powers. Great Britain had hesitated at actual recognition of independence of the new republics and the Empire of Brazil. Castlereagh had striven to mediate between Britain's ally, Spain, and her colonies, without any sequence of force, on condition that trade should remain open to the outside world. Failing in this, he was preparing for British recognition of the Latin-American states when he died in 1822. If Castlereagh had lived Great Britain might have recognized the new republics and the world might never have heard of the Monroe Doctrine as we have come to know it from the message of 1823.

Spain now appealed to the Holy Alliance. Confronted with the possibility of European intervention, particularly of French intervention, Castlereagh's successor, George Canning, turned to the United States. In a memorable conversation with Richard Rush

(August 20, 1823) the famous Secretary for Foreign Affairs laid down the following propositions for an Anglo-American understanding:

1. For ourselves we have no disguise. We conceive the recovery of the Colonies by Spain to be hopeless.
2. We conceive the question of the recognition of them as independent states to be one of time and circumstances.
3. We are, however, by no means disposed to throw any impediment in the way of an arrangement between them and the mother country by amicable negotiation.
4. We aim not at the possession of any portion of them ourselves.
5. We could not see any portion of them transferred to any other Power with indifference.

If these opinions and feelings are, as I firmly believe them to be, common to your government with ours, why should we hesitate mutually to confide them to each other, and to declare them in the face of the world?

Rush on his own responsibility was ready to accept Canning's proposal if he would have altered it to include immediate British recognition of the new states of Latin America; without this, he referred the propositions home for advice. Canning was disappointed. He would not wait for uncertain and conditional American action. Though not wholly averse to recognition at this time, he did not want to have England seem to have been prompted to it by the United States, and he hesitated to take leadership even jointly in a step so disagreeable to his ally Spain. He wanted to use the Latin-American question, and the foreign policy of the United States, as an anvil on which to shatter the Holy Alliance. He decided to act alone, without waiting for an uncertain American cooperation. So he informed (October 9, 1823) the French Ambassador in London, Polignac, that England would recognize the independence of the Spanish colonies if attempt were made to restrict her existing trade with them, or in case any foreign power interfered in the contest between Spain and them; further, that England would not enter any joint deliberation with the European powers on this question unless the United States were invited to participate.

Canning's Polignac Memorandum was in effect an ultimatum to France and Europe to let Latin America alone. After it there was no substantial danger of European intervention to subdue the independence of the new states of the New World, so recently recognized by the United States, though not yet by Great Britain.

This did not mean that there was no likelihood of a British pre-dominance there.

Before we notice the reaction at Washington to Rush's des-patches containing the propositions of Canning, we must turn back to John Quincy Adams' interest in western territorial expan-sion. He was determined to preserve as much of North America as possible for the future sovereignty of his nation. We have already noted how in 1816 he secured a qualified disavowal from Castlereagh of British intentions to purchase or otherwise ac-quire a cession of Spanish territory in America. We have ob-served his treaties of 1818 and 1819 securing recognition of American territorial claims to the Oregon country to the north of 42°, claims which he aggressively defended in subsequent months in conversations with the British Minister in Washington. We have not failed to follow the evolution of Jefferson and Madi-son's policy of opposing the transfer of European colonial pos-sessions from one possessory power to another. This idea Adams embodied in instructions (April 28, 1823) to the minister in Spain. But he was to go further than this in his warnings to European powers. The occasion for vigorous pronouncements by the virile Secretary of State was the progress of Russian expansion from Alaska southward down the Pacific coast.

From its headquarters at Sitka the Russian-American Company (founded 1799) had been extending its activities. It established Fort Ross, a trading-post (1816) near Bodega Bay, in Spanish California just north of San Francisco. The Czar issued an impe-rial edict, or *ukase,* in 1821, by which he assumed as owner of the coast to exclude all foreigners from trading or fishing within 100 Italian miles of the northwest coast as far south as 51° north latitude. Both Great Britain and the United States pro-tested. At the Court of St. Petersburg in 1809–1810, Minister John Quincy Adams, acting under instructions, had refused to co-oper-ate with Russia to regulate the trade in firearms with the Indians of the northwest coast, because of reluctance to recognize thereby the Czar's sovereignty there. Russia's absorption in the distresses of the Napoleonic wars caused Alexander I's Govern-ment to drop the matter at that time. Secretary John Quincy Adams in July, 1823, declared to the Russian Minister at Wash-ington, Baron Tuyll, that the United States would contest the right of Russia, not only to the country covered by the new decree, but to *any* territorial establishment on this continent, and that "we should assume distinctly the principle that the American continents are no longer subjects for *any* new European colonial establishments." Thus had Adams' old anxieties about further extension of European power—anxieties sharpened by the long-standing closure of the existing European colonies to American navigation—crystallized into a dictum which presently he was to have opportunity to write into a formal pronouncement by the President. His attempt to contest Russia's title to *any* territorial establishments in North America was unsuccessful; but in 1824 the United States and Russia easily agreed in a practical way to a treaty restricting that empire from any *new* colonial establishments by accepting the southern boundary of Alaska at 54° 40″. Great Britain made a similar treaty with Russia in 1825, accepting the same southern limit and drawing a boundary line from there to the Arctic Ocean, the present boundary of Alaska.

The new dictum was fresh in Adams' mind and in the councils of the Government when despatches from Rush arrived in Washington describing Canning's propositions for a joint Anglo-American pronouncement on the status of the Spanish colonies. A serious question of state was thus posed. President Monroe sought the advice of two of the elder statesmen, ex-Presidents Jefferson and Madison (but not ex-President John Adams, father of the Secretary). These *genro*, who had grown up with American independence and were experienced with European diplomatic involvements, who had been anti-British in their foreign outlook for over half a century—these aged leaders advised the President to accept Canning's proposal, despite the danger of foreign entanglements.

The question of the British overture and Russia's new claims on the northwest coast was the subject of frequent deliberations in the Cabinet during November. Secretary Adams argued against accepting Canning's propositions. He thought the British Minister was trying to ensnare the United States into a public pledge against the future acquisition of any territory still held by Spain in the New World, Cuba for instance. Adams already (July 5, 1820) had instructed the Minister of the United States to Russia, Henry Middleton, to decline, with thanks, a formal invitation from the Czar to join the Holy Alliance. He had used language that recalled Washington's Farewell Address, reminding that "to stand in firm and cautious independence of all entanglements in the European system" had been a "cardinal point of American foreign policy since 1783." He had also said at that time: "For the repose of Europe as well as America, the European as well as the American systems should be kept as separate and distinct from each other as possible." He was none the more disposed to unite with England in 1823. Jefferson's advice to Monroe included this same principle, the principle of a separate American sphere, distinct from that of Europe. If we are to believe Adams' *Diary*, he convinced Monroe and his Cabinet against accepting; and he further urged taking an independent stand against European intervention in the New World. President Monroe decided to embody some such pronouncement in his next annual message. Meanwhile the Cabinet approved a note drafted by Adams to Baron Tuyll for the attention of the Russian Czar: "That the United States of America, and their government, could not see with indifference the forcible interposition of any European power, other than Spain, either to restore the dominion of Spain over the emancipated colonies in America, or to establish monarchical governments in those countries, or to transfer any of the possessions heretofore or yet subject to Spain in the American hemisphere, to any other European power."

Canning, with the force of the British navy behind him, in essence already had said this to Polignac. President Monroe and his advisers now put it forward as an independent American policy rooted in the thought and action of the people and government of the United States and in its diplomatic experience.

In his original draft of the momentous message Monroe was in favor of coupling some statement of sympathy for the struggle of the republican Spaniards and Greeks against arbitrary government in Europe while pronouncing against any interference of Europe in the affairs of the new states of the American continents. Prudently this was pruned out, on Adams' advice. As given to the world, through the message of President Monroe to Congress of December 2, 1823, the Monroe Doctrine declared:

(1) It did not comport with the policy of the United States to take any part in the politics or the wars of European powers in matters relating to themselves.

(2) The United States would regard as the manifestation of an unfriendly disposition to itself the effort of any European power to interfere with the political system of the American continents, or to acquire any new territory on these continents.

The Monroe Doctrine was a document rather of the future than of the time of its first utterance. Europe really paid little attention to it. Canning's ultimatum to France settled any possible danger of intervention in South America, and presently the European governments one after another (Great Britain first late in 1824—Spain last in 1836) began to recognize the independence of the new states. South America applauded the Doctrine, and the pecuniary bonds of the new states rose a few points. But the new Latin-American states were not in 1823 "saved" by the pronouncement of the Doctrine.

The significance in 1823 of the Monroe Doctrine is that it served as a capstone to a very positive structure of American foreign policy that had been built up from a half-century of independent dealing with foreign nations. It proclaimed in strong Republican tone an American system for the New World.

The Monroe Doctrine

Realist

Realists do not dispute the Nationalist account of the origins and intentions of the Monroe Doctrine. Their quarrel is with the delusions of later generations regarding its meaning and application. How do they believe the doctrine was misunderstood in later years? In what ways did misunderstandings lead to a lack of realism in American foreign policy? According to Bemis's previous account, does Lippmann overemphasize the realism of the originators of the Monroe Doctrine?

Walter Lippmann was for many years a syndicated columnist for the New York Herald Tribune. *He is the author of many works on political philosophy and is one of the most significant originators and popularizers of the Realist school.*

United States Foreign Policy: Shield of the Republic

Walter Lippmann

THE FUNDAMENTAL PRINCIPLE OF A FOREIGN POLICY

Before we examine the history of our insolvent foreign relations, we must be sure that we know what we mean by a foreign commitment and by the power to balance it.

I mean by a *foreign commitment* an obligation, outside the continental limits of the United States, which may in the last analysis have to be met by waging war.

I mean by *power* the force which is necessary to prevent such a war or to win it if it cannot be prevented. In the term *necessary* power I include the military force which can be mobilized effectively within the domestic territory of the United States and also the reinforcements which can be obtained from dependable allies.

The thesis of this book is that a foreign policy consists in bringing into balance, with a comfortable surplus of power in reserve, the nation's commitments and the nation's power. The constant preoccupation of the true statesman is to achieve and maintain this balance. Having determined the foreign commitments which are vitally necessary to his people, he will never rest until he has mustered the force to cover them. In assaying ideals, interests, and ambitions which are to be asserted abroad, his measure of their validity will be the force he can muster at home combined with the support he can find abroad among other nations which have similar ideals, interests, and ambitions.

For nations, as for families, the level may vary at which a solvent balance is struck. If its expenditures are safely within its assured means, a family is solvent when it is poor, or is well-to-do, or is rich. The same principle holds true of nations. The statesman of a strong country may balance its commitments at a high level or at a low. But whether he is conducting the affairs of Germany, which has had dynamic ambitions, or the affairs of Switzerland which seeks only to hold what it already has, or of the United States, he must still bring his ends and means into balance. If he does not, he will follow a course that leads to disaster.

.   .   .

The Western Hemisphere

This new and different and momentous chapter of our history begins in 1823. In that year the United States assumed an obligation outside of its continental limits. President Monroe extended the protection of the United States to the whole of the Western Hemisphere, and declared that, at the risk of war, the United States would thereafter resist the creation of new European empires in this hemisphere. The prohibition was directed at Spain, France, Russia, and Austria. This momentous engagement was taken by President Monroe, after he had consulted Madison and Jefferson. They approved it only after Canning, the British Foreign Secretary, had assured the American Minister, Richard Rush, that Britain and the British navy would support the United States. For the Founding Fathers understood the realities of foreign policy too well to make commitments without having first made certain they had the means to support them.

They knew, as John Quincy Adams put it, that at that time the naval power of the United States was to that of Great Britain "as a cockboat in the wake of the British man-of-war." The Latin Americans who had revolted from Spain were aware of this, and they looked, says [Dexter] Perkins, "for succor to the mistress of the seas rather than to the young republic of the North. This was true of Bolivar, the Liberator, who wrote in January of 1824 that only England could change the policy of the allies. It was true of Santander, the Vice President of Columbia. It was true of Alaman, the Mexican Foreign Minister. It was true of Rivadavia, the Foreign Minister of Argentina. And when the danger had defi-

nitely passed, all of these men recognized that the British attitude had been the really decisive one even though they did not
ignore the role of the United States. It is, after all, anachronistic
in the highest degree to give greater weight to the immature
American democracy in 1823 than to the power whose prestige
was never greater, whose force was never more impressive, than
eight years after the defeat of Napoleon at Waterloo."

Unfortunately, however, for the education of the American people in the realities of foreign policy—that commitments must be
balanced by adequate power—the understanding with Britain,
which preceded Monroe's Message, was never avowed. To this
day most Americans have never heard of it. Yet as a matter of
fact the two governments came very near making a joint declaration. On August 20, 1823, Canning, who was the British Foreign
Secretary, had proposed to Richard Rush, the American Minister
in London, that they sign a convention, or exchange ministerial
notes.

Rush held back from the joint declaration because there was a
difference in the position of the two countries. The United States
had recognized the independence of the Spanish-American nations in 1822, that is to say in the year before the negotiations
with England. Canning was not then willing to commit England
that far, and would only suggest that she might promise the *future* acknowledgment of the South American states. The project
of a joint declaration was rejected because the United States
was already irrevocably committed, whereas Rush feared that
Britain, being uncommitted, might alter her policy and bring it
into harmony with that of the Continental powers.

This was in September 1823. Yet in November when President
Monroe began the discussion with his Cabinet and with the two
ex-Presidents, Jefferson and Madison, he had before him the reports of Rush's negotiations with Canning. In the Cabinet discussions Calhoun, who was Secretary of War, and Southard, who
was Secretary of the Navy, wished to give Rush discretionary
power to act with Britain. John Quincy Adams, who was Secretary of State, objected that without British recognition of the independence of the South American republics "we can see no
foundation upon which the concurrent action of the two governments can be harmonized." He objected to joint action with Britain on the interesting and significant ground that Britain and
America, unless both recognized the Spanish republics, would
not be *"bound by any permanent community of principle,"* and

Britain would "still be free to accommodate her policy to any of those distributions of power and partitions of territory which have for the last century been the *ultima ratio* of all European political arrangements."

Adams prevailed, and the American position was stated, not jointly with Britain, but as a unilateral commitment of the United States. But it is clear from Monroe's correspondence with Madison and Jefferson that this bold commitment was made only because the three Virginian Presidents were sure, after studying Rush's report from London, that Britain in her own political and commercial interest would not permit the Holy Alliance (France, Spain, Austria, and Russia) to intervene in South America.

The failure to reach a clear and binding agreement with Britain, based upon a "permanent community of principle," had very serious consequences some years later. In 1858 Napoleon III decided to defy the Monroe Doctrine, and in 1861 sent an invading army into Mexico and established an empire on our southern frontier. He did this at a moment when there was a strong expansionist and annexationist movement in the United States which had led to sympathy with the Mexican revolution. From the point of view of France the time had come to put a stop to the aggrandizement of the American republics and to restore the rights of monarchy in the New World. From the American point of view the success of Napoleon III's venture would have meant the collapse of republicanism in most of this hemisphere and the beginning of a new era of imperialist rivalry.

The American Civil War broke out in April 1861. In October of that year, France induced Great Britain and Spain to agree to joint intervention against the revolutionary government of Juárez. This agreement, reached at a time when the United States was helpless, made it possible for Napoleon to invade Mexico and to enthrone Maximilian as Emperor. In the absence of a permanent binding agreement with the United States, Lord John Russell, who had no liking for the enterprise, nevertheless did not oppose Napoleon, and indeed joined in with him to the extent of sending a few hundred Marines to Mexico. However, soon thereafter Britain withdrew and then tried to persuade Napoleon to desist. Nevertheless, the enterprise went on while the United States was rent by civil war. We might well have had to fight an international war in Mexico as soon as our own Civil War had been concluded. That we did not have to do this was a matter of good luck in that

Maximilian was unfortunate in Mexico and Napoleon became involved in troubles at home.

This affair demonstrated how serious was the commitment of the Monroe Doctrine, and how difficult it was to sustain the commitment in the absence of a clear and dependable agreement with Britain. For if Britain had opposed Napoleon at the outset, he could not have ventured into Mexico. If Britain had really supported him effectively, the United States could not have forced him out.

Yet the American people, their minds on other things, never learned the lesson of this experience. Thus they were taught to believe that the immense obligation to protect the Western Hemisphere, and consequently almost any other obligation we chose to assume, could in the nature of things be validated by American forces alone. Because the informal alliance with British sea power was concealed, and was displeasing to their self-esteem, the American people lost the prudence, so consistently practised by the Founding Fathers, of not underestimating the risks of their commitments and of not overestimating their own power.

The Pacific

With this misunderstanding of the nature of foreign policy, the United States expanded its commitments far beyond the wide limits of the Monroe Doctrine. [Lippman goes on to discuss the expansion of American commitments to Alaska, Hawaii, the Philippines, Japan, China, and Europe, all without properly balancing America's goals with its available power.]

The Monroe Doctrine

Radical

Radicals see the Monroe Doctrine as a public pronouncement of an American empire. They regard it as an attempt to stake out an area of dominance and exploitation rather than as a measure to defend the stra-

tegic and commercial interests of the United States and the Latin American republics from European imperialism.

Compare the following essay by S. Gonionsky, a Soviet journalist, with that of Bemis. According to Gonionsky, was the real intent of the doctrine defensive or aggressive? Regardless of its original intent, does it seem that in later years the doctrine was used to establish an American empire? How would you expect Bemis and Lippmann to answer the Radicals' charges? (For one thing, Nationalists and Realists usually argue that Adams and Monroe expected Great Britain to dominate the markets of independent Latin American nations. They maintain that America's leaders hoped merely to increase the share of the United States in these markets, not to displace England.)

The Unburied Corpse of the Monroe Doctrine

S. Gonionsky

American diplomacy has long been renowned for its inexhaustible ingenuity in devising all sorts of "doctrines." Most of them, it is true, fade into oblivion as soon as they appear giving way to fresh and just as short-lived official definitions of U.S. foreign policy "principles."

But Washington diplomats have a "doctrine" that is 137 years old and not forgotten yet, although in fact, it is dead, because the situation in which it originated has long since changed. It is the Monroe Doctrine. The State Department stubbornly refuses to inter its corpse and even goes so far as to maintain that it is not

From S. Gonionsky, "The Unburied Corpse of the Monroe Doctrine," International Affairs (October 1960), pp. 60–63.

a corpse at all. Washington tries to galvanize it, falling back upon Monroe's formulas in "justifying" the present foreign policy of the United States—one that accords just as little with the present international scene as the Monroe Doctrine itself.

The latest effort to galvanize the Monroe Doctrine was made by the Department of State on July 14, 1960. Washington's diplomats claim in a blustering and unsubstantiated statement that "the principles of the Monroe Doctrine are as valid today as they were in 1823 when the Doctrine was proclaimed," and that "these principles are not professed by itself alone [i.e., by Washington—S. G.], but represent through solemn agreements the views of the American community as a whole." In other words, the top men in [Secretary of State] Herter's department maintain that the Monroe Doctrine, which is ultimately directed against the independence of the Latin American countries and personifies the policy which has turned the latter into semi-colonies of the United States, is now hailed and supported by those selfsame countries.

Needless to say, the State Department claim is false from start to finish. This is amply demonstrated by the application of the Monroe Doctrine throughout its history, and in particular by the "solemn agreements" imposed by the U.S.A. on the members of the "American community," i.e., the Governments of the Latin American countries. Let us examine the facts and pertinent documents. To begin with, let us look at President James Monroe's message to Congress of December 2, 1823.

The United States, wrote President Monroe, declares that the American continents are "henceforth not to be considered as subjects for future colonization by any European Power" and that the United States considers any attempt on the part of the European Powers "to extend their system to any portion of this hemisphere as dangerous to our peace and safety."

While declaring that the United States would not interfere in European affairs and with the colonies of the European Powers in America, the message went on to say:

"But with the Governments [of American states—S. G.] who have declared their independence and maintained it, and whose independence we have . . . acknowledged, we could not view any interposition . . . by any European Power in any other light than as the manifestation of an unfriendly disposition toward the United States."

Thus, Washington posed as an opponent of the avowed intention of the European Powers to suppress the national-liberation movement in the Spanish and Portuguese colonies of South and Central America. It acted against the French intentions of exploiting that movement to turn the Spanish colonies into French ones, and against British ambitions to dominate the new American states burgeoning in place of the liberated colonies. Last but not least, the United States feared that tsarist Russia, which then had colonies in North America (Alaska), would try to extend them, and it was determined to defeat Russia's plans.

Viewed from that angle, the Monroe Doctrine was defensive and in a way even progressive in character (inasmuch as the foreign policy of the European Powers was an incarnation of the darkest semi-feudal reaction). But the defensive aspect of the doctrine was unessential, since the European designs listed above (with the possible exception of the British) were scarcely feasible. The main purpose behind Washington's move was to proclaim the exclusive "right" of the United States to interfere in the affairs of any country in the Western Hemisphere, and to do so under the pretext of protecting the independence of the newly established Latin American states. It was not to prevent European expansion, but rather to facilitate the United States expansion throughout the whole of America, that was the guiding motive behind the Monroe Doctrine.

These very same Spanish possessions in the Western Hemisphere, for which President Monroe showed such touching "concern," have been the key objects of U.S. predatory ambitions years before 1823. As far back as 1786, one of the makers of U.S. foreign policy, Thomas Jefferson, defined the objectives of his country's ruling element in the following way:

"Our confederacy must be viewed as the nest from which all America, North and South, is to be peopled. We should take care too not to think it for the interest of that great continent to press too soon on the Spaniards. Those countries [the Spanish colonies in America—S. G.] cannot be in better hands. My fear is that they [the Spaniards—S. G.] are too feeble to hold them till our population can be sufficiently advanced to gain it [the continent—S. G.] from them piece by piece." Even Jefferson, as you see, whose name is associated with a number of democratic measures at home, favoured seizure of foreign territories.

In 1803, the United States took advantage of the fact that the British and French were embroiled in the Anglo-French war and closed a deal with Napoleon, "buying" Spanish Louisiana which did not belong to France, from him. In 1810–1812, the United States again profited by the wars in Europe to seize western Florida under the pretext that the Spanish possessions in America had become a seat of the "dangerous ideas" of the French Revolution, coming from Europe. In 1818, U.S. troops followed this up by seizing eastern Florida under the pretext of combatting "Indian raids" and these selfsame "dangerous ideas."

It should be noted that Jefferson directly advised President Washington to adopt the following tactics in making seizures of that sort: "I wish a hundred thousand of our inhabitants would accept the invitation [the reference is to a statement of the Spanish Governor of eastern Florida, Quesada, who invited foreigners to settle there—S. G.]. It may be the means of delivering to us peacefully what may otherwise cost a war." It was as early as the late 18th century that the United States took note of the possibilities of so-called "peaceful" annexations of foreign territories —later typical of U.S. methods of expansion.

It is interesting that while it seized one Spanish possession after another, the United States assured Spain of its most friendly sentiments, "guaranteed" her peace and "the strictest neutrality," and promised American assistance and good will. In his *Notes on Imperialism,* V. I. Lenin made the following comment concerning America's hypocrisy in seizing Florida, "Not bad! ('Alliance'—and 'sale')."

American history books still make free with the claim that the United States was well disposed to the struggle of the insurgents in the Spanish colonies. Yet the notorious "neutrality" which the United States proclaimed in the late 18th century was hostile to the independence of the Latin American countries. Under cover of "non-interference," the United States supplied Spanish troops in America with food and munitions, and refused the same to the insurgent Latin American juntas. Indeed, in pursuance of its masked intervention, it sought to stamp out the liberation movement through the Spanish royalists and colonialists, and its own agents.

In spite of this, it had become clear by 1822 that the days of the Spanish monarchy in Latin America were numbered, and that the independence of the new Latin American states was a matter of months. It was only at this point that the United States took account of the failure of its interventionist designs, tried to grab the lion's share of Latin American commerce and sought to win new territorial concessions by declaring that "the American provinces of Spain, which have declared their independence, and are in the enjoyment of it, ought to be recognized by the United States as independent nations."

But while recognizing their independence from Spain, Washington sought to make them dependent upon the United States, and, in the final analysis, to establish an "American political system," i.e., to build up its colonial empire of nominally sovereign Latin American countries weakened by the prolonged wars of liberation. It was this programme for the establishment of the "American political system" in the Western Hemisphere that was rounded out by the Monroe Doctrine, which consummated the aggressive and two-faced policy of the North American colonialists towards their neighbours in the South. It also ushered in a new phase in the development of the Latin American policy of the United States, the phase of intensified U.S. expansion.

In this new phase Washington continued to pose as the defender of the young Latin American republics from the predatory ambitions of the European colonial Powers. But history shows that whenever these countries really did need protection, the United States, far from providing it, frequently assisted the European colonialists. Here are a few examples.

In 1829, a Spanish army of 4,000 attacked Mexico from Cuba. The United States preferred "not to notice" this fact. In 1883, Britain seized the Malvinas (now Falklands) from the Argentine with U.S. help. In 1835, the United States refused support to the resistance put up by the Central American states against part of the Honduras being turned into a British colony. In 1837, the British navy blockaded Cartagena in Colombia, and in 1838, a French squadron blockaded the Mexican port of Vera Cruz. In both cases, the United States showed no inclination whatever to oppose these acts.

In 1847, the British made a landing in Nicaragua, and established a protectorate—the Mosquito Coast. In 1848, abetted by the United States, Britain extended the frontiers of British Guiana at the expense of Venezuela. In 1852, Britain founded a new colony in the Caribbean Sea, composed of the Bay Islands which belonged to Honduras. In 1861, Spain restored her rule in Santo Domingo, and that same year a French expeditionary corps established a monarchy in Mexico. In 1864, a Spanish flotilla captured the Peru islands of Chincha. In all these cases, the United States made no move to check the British, French, and Spanish colonialists, although the spirit and letter of the Monroe Doctrine prescribed it to do so.

Within a few years after proclaiming the Monroe Doctrine, the United States officially tried to evade the responsibilities following from that doctrine whenever this went against its interests.

In 1825, for example, the Brazilian Government proposed to the United States to conclude a defensive pact guaranteeing Brazil's independence in the event Portugal were to attack her with the support of other European Powers to restore Portuguese rule in that former colony. U.S. State Secretary Henry Clay refused, claiming that a pact of that kind did not accrue from the Monroe Doctrine, although, in substance, Brazil only wanted what was virtually a confirmation of the avowed principle of Washington's foreign policy as formulated in President Monroe's message.

At the same time, the United States tried to extend the sphere of its own colonialist "political system," on more than one occasion taking advantage of the situation created in Latin America by the aggressive acts of the European Powers.

The very next year after proclaiming the Monroe Doctrine, U.S. ruling elements gave a graphic demonstration of its true purpose by landing troops in Puerto Rico. In 1831, U.S. marines landed on the Malvina Islands, and four years later in Peru. In 1846, the United States saddled the viceroyalty of New Granada (later Colombia) with an "agreement" which gave it control over the Isthmus of Panama, part of the viceroyalty. From 1846 to 1848, the United States waged an aggressive war against Mexico, annexing nearly half of Mexico's territory.

In the subsequent period, the United States landed its troops in the Argentine (1852–1853 and 1890), Nicaragua (1853–1854, 1857, 1894), Uruguay (1855 and 1858), Colombia (1856, 1865, 1885), Paraguay (1859), again in Mexico (1873–1882), Chile (1891), and Brazil (1893–1894).

The insolence of American imperialism grew apace with the growth of its economic and military power. In 1898, the United States waged a successful war against Spain, seizing the Philippines, Guam and, in effect, Cuba. It compelled Spain to relinquish its rights to Puerto Rico. What is more, in 1901, Washington bullied Cuba into inserting the so-called "amendment" of U.S. Senator Platt into the Cuban Constitution, which turned the Cuban Republic, freshly liberated from Spanish rule and only just proclaimed independent, into a virtual colony of the United States.

In the 20th century, U.S. expansion in Latin America gained in scope, but its methods were modified to some extent. Open intervention alternated with the organization of *coups d'état*. But every time, whatever the method, the affair culminated in the placement of Washington's *protégé* at the helm and the entrenchment of North American capital in the country concerned. Here is the far from complete list of U.S. armed interventions in Latin American countries between 1904 and 1917:

Dominican Republic—1904 and 1916; Cuba—1906, 1912 and 1917; Honduras—1907 and 1912; Nicaragua—1909 and 1912; Haiti—1914 and 1915; Mexico—1914 and 1916 (etc., etc.).

The conclusion is self-evident. The Monroe Doctrine has never had anything in common with the interests of the Latin American countries, and has always been an instrument of oppression, plunder, and enslavement of Latin Americans. It is only natural that it has never been recognized in any of the Latin American countries, nor, for that matter, in any of the European countries, either at the time when it was proclaimed or at any later date. Even in the United States, Congress practically refused it legislative recognition by not adopting any resolution concerning the "principles" of foreign policy formulated in President Monroe's message. It would be so much labour lost to look for any endorsement of these "principles" in any international acts, and the recent attempts of the U.S. Government to assert the reverse are obviously meant to mislead public opinion.

Simon Bolivar, Jose de San Martín, and other outstanding fighters for the independence of Latin American countries grasped the aggressive nature of the Monroe Doctrine from the first. As early as the beginning of the 19th century, the Latin American countries sought safety in numbers against the aggressive policy of the United States, clearly aware of the threat to their independence contained in the "doctrine" that "substantiated" that policy.

These sentiments came to the fore at the congress of Latin American countries convened in Panama by Bolivar in 1826. The contemporary apologists of North American imperialism go out of their way to represent Bolivar as the father of pan-Americanism, i.e., of a political alliance of all American countries under the leadership of the United States. But in reality, he voiced the interests and sentiments of the peoples of Latin America, who were highly suspicious of the U.S.A. Bolivar was inclined to see only spokesmen of the Latin American republics at the congress, and to have it form a confederation for the purpose of jointly defending their independence against any possible enemy.

True, the confederation idea fell through. But by initiating a movement of the Latin American peoples for unity and defence of their independence, the Panama congress, in effect, condemned the Monroe Doctrine three years after it was proclaimed. The doctrine discredited itself entirely in the 19th century. All the more today, as N. S. Khrushchev pointed out, it has "outlived its time, has come to nought, and has, so to say, died a natural death."

five
Westward
Expansion
and the
Mexican War

Nationalist

Nationalist historians see America's westward expansion as the occupation and civilization of an almost empty continent—a thoroughly justifiable and praiseworthy enterprise. They argue that the West was occupied by no highly developed civilizations and by very few people; millions of acres of land lay fallow and unused. American conquest of the land was a tragedy for the Indians, but theirs was a doomed civilization in any case. If Americans had not taken their lands the British, the Mexicans, or some other powerful nation would have done so. At least the Americans admitted new territories into the union as equal, democratically ruled states. The wealth and power so gained were used to defeat the aggressive ambitions of the Kaiser, of Hitler, and of Stalin. In addition, most American expansion was accomplished peacefully, according to the Nationalists. The one major exception, the Mexican War, was as much the fault of the Mexicans as of the United States.

In the following essay, Samuel Flagg Bemis succinctly summarizes the Nationalist outlook on westward expansion and the Mexican War. In Bemis's eyes, what specific actions of Mexico justified America's declaration of war? Was America's willingness to fight the product of aroused public opinion or was it more the result of President James K. Polk's determination?

The Latin American Policy of the United States

Samuel Flagg Bemis

THE MANIFEST DESTINY
OF CONTINENTAL EXPANSION (1823–1860)

I

The Monroe Doctrine, which capped the foundations of American diplomacy in 1823, was not a self-denial ordinance. The last thing that the statesmen who formulated it would have wished to do was to deny to the United States any further expansion in that part of the world where the Doctrine said hands-off to Europe, particularly in contiguous regions of the former Spanish Empire in North America, and the island of Cuba. We have seen that one of the purposes of the independent pronouncement of the Doctrine was to avoid such a self-denial. At the same time there was no thought of other than peaceful expansion. John Quincy Adams had gone further than the strict requirements of national security against a sudden transfer of territory from one European monarchy to another. His treaties with Great Britain (1818) and Spain (1819) were deliberate steps of transcontinental expansion, taken in the seven-league boots of Adamsonian diplomacy. His goal was the Pacific Ocean. As during the Era of Emancipation the Latin American policy of the United States focused first and foremost on the Floridas and on Cuba, so after the settlement of the Florida question and the independence of continental Latin America it concentrated on the next contiguous borderland, and still on the island of Cuba. South America speedily slipped away from official interest and public notice. After 1823 we can no

From Samuel Flagg Bemis, *The Latin American Policy of the United States*, pp. 73–79, 82–92. Copyright 1943 by Samuel Flagg Bemis. Reprinted by permission of Harcourt Brace Jovanovich, Inc.

longer explain Latin American policy by the requirements of national security, that is security of the original territory of the republic of 1783, not to mention the Louisiana Purchase; we must interpret it in terms of the Manifest Destiny of a future Continental Republic and the larger problems of security that developed from that.

The actual phrase Manifest Destiny does not appear until the high-tide of the expansionist movement in 1845. The feeling of it was in the air and the meaning of it was in the minds of North American statesmen, and the people sensed it from the time of the Louisiana Purchase; in fact, it was as old as the westward-moving frontier. Jefferson, who had started Lewis and Clark across the continent before he knew he had bought Louisiana from Napoleon, had long believed that it was in the manifest course of events for the United States peaceably to displace Spain and even Britain in North America. We have seen that John Quincy Adams thought so too, that he believed that the world "[should] be familiarized with the idea of considering our proper dominion to be the continent of North America." Peaceful continental expansion came to be the most popular credo of American nationalism in the first half of the nineteenth century, and this despite the political division on the issue of slavery in the new territories. The United States acquired the whole western territory from the Mississippi River to the Pacific Ocean without unjustly despoiling any civilized nation, and this statement holds good for the war with Mexico presently to be discussed. From these territorial acquisitions there resulted no appreciable dominion over alien peoples (always excepting, of course, the aborigines, if they can be called alien).

There are those historical philosophers who deprecate the Manifest Destiny of an agrarian continental expansion equally with a later more spurious Manifest Destiny of twentieth-century imperialism. . . . These same thinkers would fain believe that the United States must exercise its power and its resources to lead the whole world toward great humanitarian ideals. They forget that such elements of greatness rest upon the position of the nation and the character of its people as a Continental Republic. The Manifest Destiny of continental expansion has been the strongest and most enduring expression of American nationalism, and nationalism is still the strongest historical force in the modern world.

2

When the United States recognized the independence of Mexico in 1822, the vast northern territories of that republic were almost devoid of civilized inhabitants—indeed the passes of the Rocky Mountains and the great interior basin between them and California (western Colorado, Utah, Nevada) were still unexplored. Filibustering raids and frontier anarchy had all but depopulated Texas of its frontier outposts of Spanish colonists. In the upper Rio Grande Valley, from El Paso north to Santa Fe and Taos, lived the most numerous population, about 40,000; of these a third were Pueblo Indians, the remainder mostly mestizo Spanish-speaking inhabitants. California contained about thirty-five hundred settlers who had gone there under Spanish sovereignty, grouped in little clusters at meager river valleys near the sea, from San Diego to San Francisco Bay, the most northern outpost of the old authority. On the eastern fringe, above the new States of Louisiana and Missouri, the great plains of the Louisiana Purchase stretched unsettled by civilized people. North of them the continent extended still empty of the freezing seas of the Arctic Ocean, except for a few score of British traders in the Columbia Valley and a handful of Russians at Sitka.

Mexico was the seat of an ancient aboriginal people upon whom the Spanish had imposed a feudal structure of colonial administration, replaced after 1822 by the rule of a narrow creole minority. There was little indication that independent Mexico would people and govern those empty areas of the north to which she had won unquestioned sovereignty by her successful revolution from Spain. She could populate them only by the risky expedient of inviting colonization from the outside. In Texas, California and New Mexico, the Mexican Government exerted only the feeblest authority.

There was little possibility of effectively administering or even policing capably the uninhabited appanages marked by the political frontier that Spain had ratified in 1821. From the Mississippi Valley into the Louisiana Purchase the advance pioneers of a westward-moving, state-making population were trekking toward that new frontier from the United States, with nothing but an unsurveyed boundary to bar them in those solitudes of the continent. It did indeed seem the manifest destiny of the United States to spill over into these empty western spaces and to push its political frontiers through at least to the Rio Grande River and the coast of California.

No sooner had Adams become President in 1825 than he tried to "rectify" the boundary of that Texas from which the advice of President Monroe and his Cabinet had deflected him in the negotiation of the Transcontinental Treaty. There was no longer any divided counsel on Latin American policy, for the new President had appointed his old rival Henry Clay as Secretary of State, thus apparently settling him in the traditional succession to the White House.

It was Clay who sent the instructions to Joel Poinsett, first Minister of the United States to Mexico, to approach that government. After failing to secure "rectification" by simply asking for it, the United States was willing in 1827 to offer graduated prices for a "rectification" of the frontier of 1819 as far westward as possible: to the Rio Grande and Pecos Rivers; if not, then the line of the Colorado River (of the Gulf of Mexico), or at least the Brazos. For the boundary of the Rio Grande Adams was willing to pay one million dollars, for the Colorado half a million. In any of these proposed rectifications the new boundary would run north from the river source to meet the old treaty boundary of 1819. Clay thought that the difficulties which Mexico was already having with American immigrants in Texas might induce her to sell to avoid later trouble. Poinsett sensed so much opposition to a rectification—unless it were to move the boundary back to the Mississippi!—that he refrained from making a formal proposal.

Of course it was not improper to offer to buy territory from a neighbor. The peaceful nature of the proposal is to be measured by the reaction to an unwillingness to sell. When it was apparent that Mexico would not sell, Adams gave up the idea, and Poinsett signed a treaty of limits which confirmed the boundary of the Transcontinental Treaty with Spain. If Mexico had been willing to sell she would have avoided the whole later Texas question, and the Mexican War that resulted from it, and the ensuing great territorial cession of 1848.

Andrew Jackson was a far more fiery apostle of Manifest Destiny than the peaceful Adams. As Clay had done in Congress, he blamed Adams for having lost Texas in 1819. As President he countenanced a boundary dispute with Mexico as to the identity of the Sabine River. He too tried in vain to buy Texas, and more than Texas, from Mexico. He authorized his minister plenipotentiary, Anthony Butler, to offer any reasonable price for a new transcontinental frontier below Adams's line of 1819: the Rio Grande north to 37° North Latitude and thence due west to the Pacific Ocean so as to include San Francisco Bay—a million square miles of territory which at that time seemed of little value. Mexico refused to sell even Texas, not to mention the territory to the west. She further refused to ratify a treaty of amity and commerce, which Jackson's plenipotentiary had signed in 1826, until the United States would ratify the boundary treaty of 1828. The two treaties received ratification together in 1832; this again evidenced the restraint of the United States even under President Jackson.

Meanwhile the Texas question had arisen in Mexico. One would suppose that with the example of the Floridas so fresh in the history of the borderlands, the Mexican Government would not repeat the mistake of Spanish policy and invite immigrants from the United States into Texas in order to plant a putatively loyal frontier colony that would defend Mexican sovereignty over those vast distant northern lands. As well might the United States today encourage Japanese immigration into Alaska or the Argentine Republic seek for such a reason to populate Patagonia with Nazi Germans, going through the forms of naturalization and oaths of allegiance. Mexico actually offered land bonuses, tax concessions, and other inducements to immigrants to settle in Texas, well realizing that they would come mostly from the adjacent southwestern States of the United States. While fearing such colonization, the Mexican Government really did invite it, cautiously reserving to itself the right later to take such precautionary measures as it might deem expedient for the security of the Mexican Confederation in respect to the foreigners settling within it. Of this policy, so strange and suicidal, the United States Government remained a passive spectator. It did nothing to check emigration in that direction. A nation of immigrant origin, it has been a constant champion of the right of expatriation.

The immigrants from the United States for the most part proved to be only nominal expatriates, inscribed as naturalized Mexican citizens and Catholics. As ranchers and farmers they scattered over the prairies of Texas. They retained their frontier habits, their American customs, their English language, their Protestant religion, their state-making proclivities. Some of them brought their slaves and were vexed by Mexican attempts to abolish slavery. All the elements of friction were present and none of effective control. Too late the Mexican Government realized its folly and began to restrict the privileges of the obnoxious immigrants. This only caused more trouble and in 1835 the sudden abolition by the dictator Santa Anna of the Federal Constitution of 1824, thus doing away with their constitutional state rights, gave to the eager Texans abundant justification for secession and a war for independence. Such an act would have caused secession and revolution even had the Texans lived in Ohio instead of the Mexican state of Coahuila y Texas. At the battle of San Jacinto, April 21, 1836, the Texans under General Sam Houston routed an army under General Santa Anna, and captured the dictator-President himself. Mexico was not able to exercise sovereignty in Texas after that date.

President Jackson has been loosely accused of plotting with his turbulent intimate and fellow-Tennessean, Sam Houston, who returned to Texas in 1833 promising revolution and annexation, but there is no convincing proof of this. We may doubt the actual existence of unproven complicity if only because there was no need to conspire if the President wanted a revolution. One was obviously in the making by spontaneous combustion. More serious are the charges that the United States violated the canons of neutrality in favor of the Texans during their war against Mexico.

No one can deny the good-will of the Government, and of the people particularly, for the embattled Texans. It reminds one of the partiality manifested toward the earlier patriots of Spanish America, notably of Mexico, in their struggle against Spain, although the aid to Texas was to closer kin and on a larger scale. But Jackson coldly refused the pleas of the Texans for armed help. He even refrained from a proclamation of neutrality, which would have given moral encouragement to the cause of Texan independence by recognizing belligerency. Thus there was no obligation on the United States as a neutral according to the requirements of international law. Nevertheless the President instructed the appropriate officials to enforce the neutrality laws, which have never prohibited citizens of the United States from expatriating themselves, or from enlisting in the service of a foreign state, prince, or people, once they find themselves outside the United States, or from exporting contraband of war.

We recall all the activity of this kind, doubtless so pleasing to the sensibilities of the reader, that went on during the Spanish American revolution two decades earlier. What the United States neutrality laws did prohibit was the fitting out within the United States of expeditions to go to fight in Texas. These the Federal

Government conscientiously prosecuted when evidence was presented, but it proved impossible to get convictions from sympathetic juries in the southwestern States just as it was difficult to get jury convictions of privateers illegally fitted out within the United States by South American revolutionary governments and by Mexico during the Latin American wars for independence from Spain. But the fact that the very next year, 1837, during a rebellion in Canada, the United States revised its enforcement legislation so as to enable the seizure of *vehicles* as well as ships suspected of being used to violate the law, is sufficient testimony to irresponsibility on this score in 1836. In the case of the Texans, public opinion would not have tolerated a neutrality stricter than that previously manifested toward the original Latin American patriots, including Mexico. The wonder is that, notwithstanding the sympathy and acts of its citizens, the Government of the United States itself furnished no aid, overt or covert, to Texas, and made not unreasonable efforts to prevent private individuals from violating the neutrality laws. [Bemis goes on to describe Jackson's decision to recognize Texas as an independent republic.]

.   .   .

We come now to annexation. Disappointed at being rejected by the United States, the Texans turned to the alternative career of an independent nation. The perennial political disturbances in Mexico and sporadic revolts in the northern States presented a likely field for Texan expansion by the erection of a new confederation stretching through from the Gulf of Mexico to the Pacific, another transcontinental republic, rich in natural resources, a rival cotton-producing nation possessing the finest port on the Pacific Coast, a natural medium for the diplomacy of European powers who preferred to see North America divided into several republics like South America rather than one strong continental union. Sam Houston in his most expansive flights of fancy imagined that if Texas remained independent it might some day include even Oregon! Discount as we may the diplomatic purpose of such dreams, the possibility of an independent Texas raised troublesome prospects for Manifest Destiny.

President John Tyler was responsible for the annexation of Texas in 1845, if it can be said to be due to any one man. After Van Buren's rejection of the Texan proposal of marriage, interest in the Lone Star State slumbered during the remainder of his Administration. The new Whig President of 1841, William Henry Harrison, and his Secretary of State, Daniel Webster, were both Northerners and antislavery men, and they were no more willing to stir up a convulsing sectional issue in their party than Van Buren had been in his.

The Whigs represented the brains of the country more than its heart. They were less interested in expansion than the Democrats, at any rate more in the acquisition of Oregon and California, which would not meet antislavery opposition, than Texas. They never were truly enough in tune with the national continental instinct to have any real hold on political power. Their first victory came only when they made no platform and appealed to the emotions of the people in the "log-cabin and hard-cider" campaign of 1840 ("Tippecanoe and Tyler too"). Then they floated into office on a tide of popular weariness with the party held responsible for panic and depression. To catch wavering votes they had nominated for Vice President the former Democrat, John Tyler, of Virginia.

As a result of Harrison's death a few weeks after his inauguration, Tyler unexpectedly became President. The Whigs promptly read him out of their party when he vetoed their favorite measure, Senator Henry Clay's bill to reëstablish a national bank. The Democrats whom he had deserted to become a Whig Vice President would not welcome Tyler back to their camp even after their opponents had made him President of the United States for them. Finding himself in this predicament of a man without a party, Tyler began to stimulate popular opinion in favor of the annexation of Texas, a measure which he believed would win him new political adherents. His Whig Secretary of State, Daniel Webster, was opposed to the annexation of Texas but eager to secure California. Tyler conceived the project of uniting the annexation of Texas with that of California and a settlement of the Oregon question in a projected tripartite agreement between the United States, Great Britain and Mexico: Britain would be conceded the Oregon country as far south as the Columbia River, except for the Olympic Peninsula; the United States would buy California from Mexico; and Mexico would set aside the purchase money to satisfy claims of both British subjects and American citizens.

Webster liked the California-Oregon part of this plan. He sounded Lord Ashburton informally on the idea and got a favorable response. Webster desired to go to London to put through such a deal, thus gracefully relieving himself of the office of Secretary of State, but he could not persuade his friend, Edward Everett, to be shifted from the London legation to China. So Webster fulfilled his party obligations by resigning anyway, now that his negotiations with Lord Ashburton over the northeastern boundary and other issues were successfully completed. Whether Webster in this proposed tripartite coup would have worked for Texas too, is a question.

Tyler now turned to Texas without California. He was certain that it would be popular with both parties in the South, and he expected that it would have so strong a national appeal that Clay and Northerners like Van Buren and Webster would not dare to oppose it. Further, it might rally the patriotic against a meddling England. Tyler feared the efforts of British diplomacy to abolish slavery in Texas by mediating between the new republic and Mexico on the basis of a recognition of independence by the parent state. Abolition in Texas would rob the South of political advantage from the absorption of that State, and a British ascendency in Texas might block annexation under any circumstances. Southern leaders professed to see in British policy a step toward abolition in the United States itself. In Webster's place Tyler appointed as Secretary of State a well-known annexationist, Abel P. Upshur of Virginia, close friend of John C. Calhoun, the proslavery leader and state's rights champion.

To Upshur fell the agreeable duty of negotiating a treaty of annexation. Andrew Jackson, in retirement, urged Tyler on to obtain Texas. The hero of New Orleans feared that, if that country should pass under the influence of British diplomacy, its capacious harbors and firm level plains would present an easy approach for a flank attack on the Mississippi Valley—to undo the Louisiana Purchase—just as once he feared, and with abundant reason, that Florida opened to the same danger from the other side of the river. Texas should be "re-annexed," said Old Hickory from his Hermitage in Tennessee, peaceably if we can, forcibly if we must. He urged Sam Houston to get Texas to accept the treaty. Upshur believed that he had lined up a constitutional majority of the Senate in favor of the treaty, when he perished suddenly in an accident before he had finished the negotiation. It was Calhoun who succeeded him and signed the treaty. Thus within a few months and without a national election did the great nullificationist follow in the office of Secretary of State the defender of national unity and international appeasement, Daniel Webster. Harrison's death had changed the whole aspect of foreign policy.

"This Texan question will ride down and ride over every other [question]," so Congressmen quoted the President as telling them. Tyler sensed more fully than his political opponents the national significance of Texas, as the events of the year 1844 will show, but his treaty unfortunately came before the Senate, and before the people, clothed, not in the radiant raiment of Manifest Destiny as Tyler intended, but in proslavery habiliments, dressed up by Calhoun. In an exchange of diplomatic correspondence, the Secretary of State declared publicly to Great Britain that the United States had signed the annexation treaty precisely for the purpose of preventing abolition of slavery there. He did this in order to identify annexation with a defense of slavery in foreign policy as well as in domestic affairs.

Thus did Calhoun ride away on Tyler's Texan mustang. The perverse display of sectionalism killed the treaty in what had been so recently a tolerably well-disposed Senate (35 votes against, 16 for it). But it did not kill annexation. While the treaty was under debate the Whigs nominated for the presidency Senator Henry Clay, who had led the attack on annexation, and the Democrats rejecting both Tyler and Van Buren put up James K. Polk of Tennessee, friend of Andrew Jackson, and a downright annexationist. Ardently and unequivocally he campaigned on the Democratic platform that called for the "reannexation" of Texas and the "reoccupation" of all of Oregon—"fifty-four forty or fight."

Old Andrew Jackson eagerly urged Polk on. Here was a double-barreled appeal, north and south. With weakening emphasis Henry Clay continued to oppose annexation. Too late he felt the ground-swell of the continent under him. Then his political knees buckled. He hesitated. In a conditional, equivocal way he declared at last for Texas: "without dishonor, without war, with common consent of the Union, and upon just and fair terms." He lost.

Had Clay stuck to his old popular ground as an original expansionist that first made him a rising leader of the West on the eve of the War of 1812 he might at last have become President. One cannot say, though, that the election of 1844 was a clean-cut national decision, because an independent Free-Soil candidate sprang up in New York State and split the antislavery opposition, throwing that decisive State's electoral votes to Polk. Nevertheless the country very definitely interpreted the election as the verdict for Manifest Destiny, just as many years later the people construed the curious election of 1920 as a repudiation of the League of Nations. Chastened by Polk's victory, the Senate that had so recently wrecked Tyler's treaty joined the House of Representatives to support the President's demand for annexation of Texas by act of Congress. The necessary joint resolution was carried just three days before Tyler left the White House. Texas now became an international issue between the United States and Mexico, and back of that, between the United States and Great Britain.

To block annexation, Anglo-French mediation had brought Texas to sign a protocol of preliminaries of peace by which Mexico would consent to acknowledge the independence of Texas and Texas would agree never to annex herself or be subject to any country whatever. After the passage of the resolution for annexation by the United States Congress, Mexico, by an act of her Congress, signed by her President, accepted this protocol. Mexico had proposed that the mediating states guarantee Texan independence forever. Great Britain was willing to do this, but France refused to go that far. The European rivalry of Great Britain and France prevented any genuine cooperation in the New World. France served to checkmate British diplomacy in North America; England acted as a brake on French designs in South America. This is another example of America's advantage from Europe's distresses.

The Texan Congress had a choice between annexation to the United States and the Mexican treaty of independence. Unanimously both houses voted for annexation, and unanimously the Senate rejected the proposed treaty with Mexico. Thus was Texas cleared of European influence.

The Mexican Secretary of Foreign Relations had delcared in 1843 that his government "would consider equivalent to a declaration of war against the Mexican Republic the passage of an act for the incorporation of Texas with the territory of the United States; the certainty of the fact being sufficient for the immediate proclamation of war." When the joint resolution passed Congress in the face of this declaration, the Mexican Government ended diplomatic relations with the United States but did not immediately declare war. Following the Mexican warning Polk sent troops into Texas to protect the country during the legislative process of annexation, and he made appropriate dispositions of naval forces.

During this critical period President Polk also had his eyes on the Pacific Coast. Like Tyler, Webster, and Jackson, not to mention John Quincy Adams, he coveted California. He feared that Great Britain was determined to possess that remote Mexican department. This would block the United States off from a window on the Pacific Coast and put British pincers on Oregon north and south. He instructed Larkin, the American consul at Monterey, to use the greatest vigilance to prevent any European nation from acquiring possession and said that he "could not view with indifference the transfer of California to Great Britain or any other European Power." This confirmed, under the mantle of the Monroe Doctrine, that interpretation which John Quincy Adams had given to the No-Transfer Policy in 1823: not only to stop the transfer of an American colonial possession (Polk restricted the Monroe Doctrine to North America) from one European sovereign to another, but also to prevent any (North) American state from annexing itself to a non-American power. Polk was determined not to admit the European system of the balance of power to North America. To offset this he hoped for an independence movement in California to be followed by annexation to the United States à la Texas.

Notwithstanding British attempts to block the annexation of Texas and of California, and the Mexican posture of war, President Polk made a decent effort to come to peaceful terms with Mexico. After being informed by his diplomatic agents that the Mexican Government would receive a "commissioner" empowered to discuss outstanding disputes, he sent to Mexico City a new minister plenipotentiary, John Slidell of Louisiana, to offer terms which stopped short of insistence upon any undisputed Mexican territory. Slidell was to try to get a new transcontinental frontier between Mexico and the United States on the line of the Rio Grande to El Paso and thence due west to the Pacific; for this he could offer $25,000,000. Indeed "money would be no object when compared with the value of the acquisition." If he could not get that he could offer $5,000,000 for New Mexico (that is, the watershed of the Rio Grande above El Paso). The indispensable minimum was the line of the Rio Grande which Texas had claimed as her boundary without being able to occupy it successfully; for Mexico's acceptance of this, Polk's minister could agree that the United States would release Mexico from completing payment of about $2,000,000 of adjudicated claims to citizens of the United States. This minimum demand is not far from what Mexico had been willing to accept at the hands of the Anglo-French mediation earlier in the same year 1845.

Reasonable as that was, President Polk did not get a chance to put his peace offer before Mexico. The Herrera Government hesitated to receive a diplomatic agent of the United States after the annexation of Texas, for fear that such an unpopular act would precipitate a revolution. When a revolution did occur without such incitement, the succeeding Paredes Government refused to see Slidell and resorted to the technical objection that he was a minister plenipotentiary and not a "commissioner" *ad hoc* such as the previous Mexican Government had agreed to receive. To have accepted Slidell as minister plenipotentiary would have seemed to tolerate the annexation of Texas, and this Mexico would not do, although she had been willing in the Anglo-French mediation to recognize Texan independence providing the new republic should never be annexed to any other power. The question was clear: was it to be the United States or Europe that was to decide the continental future of the United States?

Mexico had given formal notice that she would regard the annexation of Texas as equivalent to a declaration of war. Instead of taking this challenge at its face value, Polk had gone out of his way to procure a peaceful settlement. Only by refusing to acknowledge the undeniable fact of Texan independence and the consequent sovereign right of self-determination can one justify Mexico's quibble over a technicality, her reckless refusal to treat and her persistence in a posture of war. Below the Rio Grande many people believed that the numerically larger army of Mexico, particularly the reputed prowess of its cavalry, would be at least a match for such troops as the United States would be able to put in the field. They even hoped that Great Britain, then at odds with the United States over the Oregon question, would come to Mexico's aid. Was it not British policy to divide continents into as many nations as possible and keep these smaller units balanced against each other, as in South America?

It is true that it was British policy to lock the westward rolling wheels of American continental expansion: the diplomatic history of Texas shows that sufficiently; but Great Britain did not really want to fight to prevent the United States from acquiring Oregon or Texas or California. She was heavily involved in a joint intervention with France in Uruguay and the Plata River, and in Europe the two powers were at odds over Mediterranean questions. The British Empire was already in a state of wearied satiation. The Little Englanders were sounding the counsel of retreat. By 1845 London had decided to yield Oregon to the United States up to 49° North Latitude. President Polk's unflinching nerve had won the day for Manifest Destiny, his country's greatest urge.

Only when Polk heard that Mexico had refused to receive his emissary of peace did he fall back to the use of force. He sent troops under General Taylor from Texas proper well into the disputed area between the Nueces and the Rio Grande, with orders to repel force by force if Mexican troops should move north of the latter river. On April 23, 1846, President Paredes of Mexico declared war, and on April 25 some Mexican cavalry met Taylor's forces on the Texan side of the river. Today it seems fantastic that Mexico should have made Texan annexation a cause of war, after that republic had been so long independent and so widely recognized, and should have actually attacked United States troops on the disputed side of the Rio Grande. By doing so the Mexican Government played into Polk's hands, who, after failing to make peace, preferred to make a war—just as Napoleon III served Bismark's purposes in 1870.

In the ensuing war United States troops quickly and easily occupied California and New Mexico, meeting only a modicum of resistance. General Taylor's army penetrated northern Mexico, and General Scott's troops fought their way from Vera Cruz to the gates of Mexico City. The de facto government of Mexico had to make the best terms possible. That peace, imposed by a conquering army, corresponded to no more than the maximum terms which Polk had tried so patiently to offer through Slidell in 1845: the line of the Rio Grande to El Paso, and thence west to the Pacific, not as conquered soil but as a purchase. For this territory —the last real popular goal of Manifest Destiny, following the Oregon treaty of 1846—the United States, which had just defeated Mexico, actually paid $18,325,000. The war itself cost the United States $100,000,000 more, and a still greater loss: several thousand lives. Another article of the Treaty of Peace of Guadalupe Hidalgo of 1848 illustrated the continental purpose of Polk's policy. It provided for a future agreement for the construction and use of a road, canal, or railway via the Gila River valley. After surveys had established the desirability of this, Mexico sold the strip to the United States in 1853: the Gadsden Purchase, for $10,000,000 more.

The peace treaty contained an unique article, for those times, calculated to prevent any future wars between the two countries. Perhaps not because of the letter of this article, but because of the spirit that grew into it, it has been successful. Article XXI provided that in the case of a future dispute between the two parties, they would endeavor to settle it by peaceful process: "And if, by these means, they should not be enabled to come to an agreement, a resort shall not, on this account, be had to reprisals, aggression or hostility of any kind, by the one Republic against the other, until the Government of that which deems itself aggrieved, shall have maturely considered, in the spirit of peace and *good neighbourship,* whether it would not be better that such difference should be settled by the arbitration of Commissioners appointed on each side, or by that of a friendly nation. And should such course be proposed by either party, it shall be acceded to by the other, unless deemed by it altogether incompatible with the nature of the difference, or the circumstances of the case."

Sober reflections on the Texas question and the War with Mexico suggest that political anarchy and folly on the part of Mexico was as responsible for the conflict as much as was the urge of expansion in the United States; that the peace was not lacking in forbearance; and that James K. Polk correctly interpreted and achieved the Manifest Destiny of his country. The war between the United States and Mexico was only one of numerous wars fought in the New World as well as the Old World during the nineteenth century. It was by no means as disturbing to the nations of Central and South America as the contemporary British interventions in the Isthmus and the British and French interventions in the Plata River countries. Certain it is that no countryman of President Polk today would desire to undo either the annexation of Texas or the Mexican purchases of 1848 and 1853. They stand with the Louisiana Purchase and the Transcontinental Treaty as the most enduring expressions of American nationality. When in 1917 the German Government invited Mexico, in case of a war between Germany and the United States then impending, to make an alliance with Japan and to fall upon the "lost provinces" and recover them, it met no response either in Mexico or in Japan, and it threw the people of the United States into a paroxysm of uncompromising patriotism. So would any such suggestion result again.

Westward Expansion and the Mexican War

Radical

Radicals regard the Nationalist view of westward expansion as hypocritical. They see this expansion not as a natural and idealistic march into an empty continent, but as an aggressive conquest of foreign territory impelled by the contradictions of capitalism. American territorial expansion destroyed cultures and subjugated peoples in precisely the way European imperialism did. The Indians were decimated, Mexico despoiled, and the nonwhite remnants of these civilizations relegated to reservations or ghettos. The culmination of this course was the Mexican War, in which a group of politicians plotted and carried out a campaign of conquest.

Glenn W. Price, author of the following essay, is an associate professor of history at Sonoma State College in California. He is not really a Radical historian because he does not emphasize the role of capitalism in America's westward expansion. But his is one of the most effective attacks on the Nationalist defense of the Mexican War. How strong is Price's evidence that Polk plotted the war with Mexico? Why did Polk want such a war? What role, in Price's account, did popular opinion play? According to him, did Mexico bear any responsibility for the war?

Origins
of the War
with Mexico:
The Polk-Stockton
Intrigue

Glenn W. Price

James K. Polk was now in control of the power of the United
States government. In turning to an examination of his use of that
power in his relations with Mexico it is essential to understand
the status of the Texas question in March of 1845. The issue of
Texas annexation had been the most important single issue in
the presidential campaign of 1844, the campaign in which Polk
had been elected. It therefore might seem to follow that the annexation of Texas was the most important business in hand when
Polk assumed the executive leadership of the nation, and the
matter which required his closest attention.

That, however, was not the case. The struggle for the annexation of Texas had taken place before Polk's inauguration; the
issue had been decided, the Congress had acted, there remained
only the implementation of that action through the acceptance of
the offer by the government and by the people in convention of
the Republic of Texas. That acceptance was, in fact, no more
than a formality, and it was known to be so by qualified observers in Texas during this period, as will become quite clear in the
examination of the matter which follows. Some reluctance was
evident on the part of certain Texas leaders, efforts to prevent
annexation were made by representatives of the British and
French governments, and the Mexican government felt badly

From Glenn W. Price, *Origins of the War with Mexico: The Polk-Stockton Intrigue*, pp. 36–37, 47, 107–108, 110–115, 153–168, 171–172 (University of Texas
Press, 1967). ©1967 by Glenn W. Price. All rights reserved.

used and was disposed to threaten and bluster; but none of this mattered. Such a large majority in Texas was for joining the Union that there was no possibility that Texas would refuse the offer extended by the Congress. Some Texan leaders had doubts about the adequacy of the terms of annexation, the lack of assurance on the boundary and on the public debt, but these reservations were brushed aside by the overwhelming pressure of public opinion in Texas.

The acquisition of Texas, although it was completed in the first year of Polk's term, is properly attributed to the administration of John Tyler. Polk himself gave indirect agreement to this judgment when he formulated the objectives of his administration. George Bancroft, Secretary of the Navy in Polk's Cabinet and a prominent historian, recorded much later that soon after Polk took the oath of office he listed the items in his program in a conversation in the White House office: " 'There are four great measures,' said he, with emphasis, striking his thigh forcibly as he spoke, 'which are to be the measures of my administration: one, a reduction of the tariff; another, the independent treasury; a third, the settlement of the Oregon boundary question; and, lastly, the acquisition of California'."

The annexation of Texas does not appear on the list because that was a settled matter. In Polk's correspondence with his agents in Texas, however, and in the records of the State Department during the spring and early summer of 1845 great anxiety is frequently expressed about the uncertainty of success in the effort to secure Texas. It is the contention of this study that through that first year of Polk's term, until the beginning of hostilities with Mexico in May of 1846, the problem was not the annexation of Texas, not the protection of Texas from attack by Mexico, and not the boundary of Texas—although these pseudo issues dominated the official pronouncements of the Administration. These matters were a "cover" to shelter the actual objective of President Polk. The problem, and the opportunity, as Polk saw it, was how to use Texas as a means of achieving one of the "great measures" of his administration—the acquisition of California.

.   .   .

Before [the Mexican] war began, President Polk set in motion an intrigue in Texas. . . . The design was to initiate a war between Texas and Mexico prior to the completion of the annexation of Texas; the United States would then immediately come to the defense of the Texans and the responsibility for the war would not appear to rest with the United States. That war would enable Polk to accomplish one of the "great measures" of his administration, the acquisition of California.

As will be seen, the intrigue failed. Polk was then driven to preparation of a declaration of war on Mexico on the grounds of Mexico's failure to pay American claims, a measure of desperation from which he was saved by the beginning of hostilities that followed upon the sending of a United States army into Mexican settlements on the Rio Grande. But efforts which failed are often as valuable in the light which they throw upon the character of men and societies in the past as are the successes; not infrequently such abortive efforts guide us to some understanding of "the mind of the past"—which, after all, is the center of our interest. And the failed designs of those who have held supreme power in a society provide an essential check against the strong tendency to accept the past at its own evaluation, which is to say, to see the past through the eyes and the interests of those who were in control of power. Much has been said in condescending criticism of the muckrakers in history, but the dominant approach of historians is quite otherwise; the knees of historians naturally bend before the bitch-goddess success. If the human enterprise were a remarkable success in its foundations and superstructure in the middle of the twentieth century, something could be said for an attitude of acquiescence before past power; but that is not our present condition. It is not useful to go on celebrating the past, as the past celebrated itself. In our present situation it is neither pleasant nor amusing; it is feeble-minded frivolity.

.   .   .

The overwhelming sentiment in Texas in favor of annexation, and the knowledge of that fact by the Polk Administration through March, April, May, and June of 1845, must be constantly kept in mind if Polk's actions are to be understood. When the matter came to a vote by the Congress of Texas on 18 June, that vote was unanimous for annexation. But it is not necessary to merely assume that Polk should have been able to foresee this; he was constantly being told, both by Texans and by Americans who were reporting to him from Texas, that there was no question on the matter. Polk asked Charles H. Raymond, of the Texas

Legation in Washington, if he had "*any* doubts about the acceptance by the Government and people of Texas of the proposition for annexation now before them," and Raymond reported to his government: "I told him frankly and unhesitatingly that I entertained none whatever." One of Buchanan's informants wrote from Galveston to assure him that "nine tenths of all the people of Texas are in favor of annexation immediately." Polk's ostensible reason for sending [Commodore Robert Field] Stockton to Texas was concern over the acceptance of the United States offer; to accept that reason as the actual motivation for the mission would be very difficult, even in the absence of explicit documentation for another interpretation.

. . .

What Stockton proceeded to do was first described in some circumstantial detail by Anson Jones in a book published posthumously in 1859. In his *Memoranda and Official Correspondence Relating to the Republic of Texas, Its History and Annexation,* the former President of Texas wrote:

In May, 1845, Commodore Stockton, with a fleet of four or five vessels, arrived at Galveston, and with him Hon. C. A. Wickliffe, ex-Postmaster General of the United States. These gentlemen had various interviews with Major Gen. Sherman, the chief officer of the militia of Texas, the character of which is not precisely known to me; but the result of which was active preparations at Galveston for organizing volunteer forces, the ostensible (and no doubt real) object of which was an invasion of Mexico. A party [Jones thus seems to refer to President Polk], it appears, was anxious that the expedition should be set on foot, under the auspices of the Major-General and Com. Stockton; but these gentlemen, it appears, were unwilling to take so great a responsibility: it was therefore resolved that the plan should be submitted to me and my sanction obtained—(quere [sic], forced?) indeed such, as afterwards became apparent, were the Commodore's instructions; and the organizing, &c, had been gone into for the purpose of forcing my assent to the proposed scheme. On the 28th May, Gen. Sherman for himself and associates in the militia, and Dr. Wright, surgeon of the steamer Princeton, and secretary of the Commodore, (as he informed me) took three days in unfolding to me the object of their visit. Dr. Wright stated that he was sent by Com. Stockton to propose that I should authorize Major Gen. Sherman to raise a force of two thousand men, or as many as might be necessary, and make a descent upon the Mexican town of Matamoras, and capture and hold it; that Com. Stockton would give assistance with the fleet under his command, under the pretext of giving the protection promised by the United States to Texas by Gen. Murphy; that he would undertake to supply the necessary provisions, arms and munitions of war for the expedition, would land them at convenient points on our coast, and would agree to pay the men and officers to be engaged; that he had consulted Gen. Sherman, who approved the plan, and was present to say so; and, besides that, the people generally from Galveston to Washington [the city in Texas] had been spoken to about it, that it met their unanimous approval; and all that was now wanting was the sanction of the Government to the scheme. Gen. Sherman confirmed what Dr. Wright stated, said he had had various interviews with Com. Stockton, and hoped I would approve the expedition.

Throughout the intrigue, according to Jones, Dr. Wright was Stockton's spokesman in the attempts to reach an agreement with the President of Texas. Stockton's reports from Texas do not acknowledge such a role for Dr. Wright, but in the fall of 1845, when Stockton was preparing to leave in the *U.S.S. Congress* for the Pacific Coast, he wrote to Secretary Bancroft to ask that Dr. Wright accompany him: "He was with me in Texas and I think he is fitted in a remarkable manner to aid me in the duty of *information* and *conciliation.*"

In his interviews with President Jones, Dr. Wright had need of the ability to conciliate as he informed. It was apparent that Stockton had instructions to initiate an attack upon Mexico, instructions which could be given in such a matter to a naval officer only by the President of the United States. Jones pointed out to Dr. Wright that such an action was a very grave matter, and he said he needed some written evidence of Commodore Stockton's part in it; he asked if Stockton had sent any communication to him:

As I expected, he replied in the negative, but that if I wished, Com. Stockton would visit me in person, and give me the same assurances in person. I asked him if the Minister of the United States [Donelson] was cognizant of the matter. He then stated to me that the scheme was rather a confidential and secret one, that it was undertaken under the sanction of the United States Government, but that the President did not wish to be known in the matter, but approved Com. Stockton's plan;—that as an evidence of that to me, Mr. Wickliffe was associated with the Commodore; that the President of the United States, satisfied that annexation was in effect consummated, wished Texas to place herself in an attitude of active hostility towards Mexico, so that, when Texas was finally brought into the Union, *she might bring a war with her;* and this was the object of the expedition to Matamoras, as now proposed. He further stated that Com. Stockton was known to be, individually, very wealthy; that he had means of his own sufficient to support and carry on the expedition; and that it was desirable it should appear to the world as his individual enterprise, while at the same time I was given to understand that the Government of the United States was, in reality, at the bottom of it, and anxious for its accomplishment and for the reasons stated.

According to Jones, the proposed expedition against the Mexican forces on the Rio Grande was not designed to occupy the area between the Nueces and the Rio Grande, the land claimed but not occupied by the Republic of Texas; it was designed as an attack upon the Mexican city of Matamoros, on the right bank of the Rio Grande. The purpose of the action was not to protect Texas; it was not to defend her territory, however conceived; it was to begin a war.

Jones put the question to Dr. Wright and General Sherman in the most direct and unambiguous form: "I then said, smiling, 'So, gentlemen, the Commodore, on the part of the United States, wishes me *to manufacture a war* for them'; to which they replied affirmatively."

General Sherman, in a subsequent private interview with Jones, urged him to assent to Stockton's proposal, asserting that it was "extremely popular among the people, and that he would have no difficulty in obtaining the requisite number of men, upon the assurances of Stockton that they should be provisioned and paid."

Jones said he was "indignant at the proposition," but concealed his feelings and temporized for fear that Sherman, who was a popular leader, would concert with Stockton to take advantage of the hatred of Mexico and the desire for revenge among the people to start a movement against the government, resulting in anarchy and bloodshed. Jones adds that he was expecting within a few days the return of British Minister Elliot from Mexico, "with propositions of peace, and an acknowledgment of Texan independence." He calculated that such an offer from the Mexican government, even if conditional and therefore not acceptable to the Texans, would put a halt to any movement for an attack upon Mexico. Since he could "say nothing openly in regard to these expectations," he "answered Commodore Stockton [through Dr. Wright] that [he] would take a few days longer to reflect upon the matter." Jones gave as specific grounds for his hesitation the fact that Congress would soon convene (on 16 June) and he would seek the advice of that body on the matter. This delay gained him "breathing time." When Elliot returned from Mexico a few days later with the preliminary treaty and acknowledgment of Texas independence, Jones was able to "declare *my* independence of Com. Stockton, and Mr. Wright, Gov. Yell, Major Donelson, Mr. Polk, and Mr. Buchanan."

President Jones issued a proclamation announcing the Mexican offer and declaring a state of peace with Mexico until such time as the government of Texas should act on the matter. General Sherman and Dr. Wright were on their way back from consultations with Stockton at Galveston when they saw his proclamation; Sherman turned about, concluding that now no possibility remained of developing the attack, but Dr. Wright came on. Jones records, with evident satisfaction, his meeting with Wright: "*One word* settled Com. Stockton's business, and I assured [*sic*] him I never had the least idea of *manufacturing a war for the United States.* Soon after which he left our waters and sailed for the Pacific in search of the same *un*pacific object which had brought him to Texas, as I suppose."

Jones says he could have been very popular if he had sanctioned the "war scheme," and probably could have received great rewards from the United States government if he had agreed to "involve the country afresh in a war with Mexico." To leave no doubt that Stockton's plan was in fact President Polk's design, Jones writes that he had "the direct and positive assurance of the Texan chargé at Washington City in September, 1845," that "this scheme had the sanction of the United States."

The war which began the following year was, in the interpretation of President Jones, a consistent and logical development of United States policy. The United States "made the war *ostensibly* for the *DEFENCE* of Texas; but, in *reality,* to consummate views of conquest which had been entertained probably for many years, and to wage which, the annexation of Texas afforded a pretext long sought and wished for." Polk kept insisting upon forcing "protection" upon Texas, and finally "brought down an army and a navy upon us, when there was not a hostile foot, either Indian or Mexican, in Texas; not (as afterwards became apparent) to *protect* Texas . . . but to insure a *collision* with Mexico."

The government of Texas, Jones grants, had indeed asked for protection while in the process of accepting the offer of annexation, but "the protection asked for was only *prospective* and contingent," while the protection which the government of the United States had in view "was *immediate* and *aggressive.*"

Jones makes the flat charge that President Polk forced the war on Mexico. The Mexican government, "though she might bluster a little, had not the slightest idea of invading Texas either by land or water; and . . . nothing would provoke her to (active) hostilities, but the presence of troops in the immediate neighborhood of the Rio Grande, threatening her towns and settlements on the southwest side of that river."

That, indeed, was precisely the situation which existed when the War began in April of 1846, and Jones makes an explicit statement of the motivation of President Polk:

. . . I am bound to say, the war between the United States and Mexico grew directly out of annexation; that it was the "foregone conclusion" of Mr. Polk when he came into office, to have that war with Mexico; that, failing in his most cherished scheme of inducing me to the responsibility of provoking and bringing it about, *he blundered* into it by other means. . . . The war was begun without law, and in like manner ended without law; and a feeble, distracted, and imbecile nation, by it were [sic] divested of an immense territory, which, as a component part of Mexico, never could have been of use to her or anybody else, but which, in the possession of the United States, may and probably will become of incalculable importance to that country and the world—if it does not unfortunately dissolve the Union.

This account of President Polk's attempt to "annex a war," as told by the President of Texas, has been available to historians for over a century. If it had been accepted as an authentic and valid account the interpretation in American histories of the origins of the War with Mexico would have been significantly different; to portray Polk as being basically intent upon a peaceable solution of the financial claims and the boundary question would have been impossible. But the report of these events by President Jones has either been ignored, or denied and rejected in its essential points by all but a few American historians.

.   .   .

THE SUCCESSFUL USE OF THE BOUNDARY QUESTION: THE ACQUISITION OF CALIFORNIA

The Texas and American boundary claims provided the means by which the War with Mexico was initiated, but it should be noted at once that the responsibility for starting the War does not hinge on the question of the validity of those claims. The first indisputable act of war was an act of the United States, when its naval forces blockaded the Rio Grande on 12 April 1846. Even had the land on the left bank of that river been within the limits of the

United States, to blockade the river, which in that case would have been the international boundary, was an act of war. That conclusion needs no supporting argument, but it may be of interest to point out that the United States government was on record as stating that any attempt by Mexico to close the river to American traffic would justify hostilities. Instructions given General Zachary Taylor by the Department of War stated that "the Rio Grande, in a state of peace, may be regarded as equally open to navigation of the U.S. & Mexico," and should this "reciprocal right be resisted by Mexico," Taylor was at liberty to force it open by military power. The first military encounter took place on 25 April; it pleased Polk to describe that action as the shedding of American blood upon the American soil. Two weeks before that event, it bears repeating, the United States had committed an act of war against Mexico.

Nevertheless, the pretension of the Republic of Texas to the Rio Grande boundary, a claim taken up by the government of the United States after annexation, provided the ground upon which Polk was able to initiate the War in the spring of 1846, as it had provided the rationale for the scheme which Stockton had tried to develop in the summer of 1845. If the claim was valid, or even if it was based upon substantial considerations which would give it a reasonable basis for a judicial inquiry, the design to occupy the region would stand on a different footing than if it were a wholly unwarranted claim. President Polk and Commodore Stockton would still be subject to criticism for the use they had tried to make of the situation; but, in any case, they could be seen as working for a legitimate interest of Texas and of the United States. The substance of the claim to the Rio Grande boundary is therefore pertinent to an evaluation of President Polk's intrigues.

Most American historians have avoided formulating a clear statement on the disputed matter. An exception is found in the notable text by Samuel E. Morison and Henry S. Commager; they forthrightly state that when Polk sent the United States Army to the Rio Grande he "attempted to force the solution of a boundary controversy. That is the important point. It also happens that his view of the controversy was wrong."

Samuel F. Bemis, on the other hand, avoids criticizing the United States' claim by making a statement that is simply nonsensical: "The district of Texas when a part of the Mexican state of Texas and Coahuila had not extended beyond the Nueces River," he writes; "but the Texans after their Revolution had asserted their boundary to be the Rio Grande—without being able to establish real authority there, particularly on the upper reaches of the river in the region of Santa Fe and Taos." Texas, of course, had been unable to establish her authority anywhere along the Rio Grande; she had no more authority, "real" or otherwise, in Santa Fe, than she had in Mexico City.

Julius W. Pratt, in his *History of United States Foreign Policy*, says simply that the "soil in question was claimed with at least equal right by Mexico." Thomas A. Bailey writes that it was "soil to which Mexico perhaps had a better technical claim than the United States."

Such formulations by historians reveal a recognition of the impossibility of defending the American claim joined with a disinclination to state clearly that the claim was indefensible. No one has seriously tried to support the claim since George P. Garrison, sixty years ago, argued that although "it has been the commonly accepted view of American historians that Texas did not extend west of the Nueces," the treaty with Santa Anna, made when he was a prisoner following his capture at the battle of San Jacinto, provided for that boundary, and thus "there is much to be said in favor of its validity, and hence of the Texas claim to the Rio Grande subsequent to 1836." Garrison said "American historians have generally accepted the Mexican argument." Let this curious statement stand as the interesting result of the attempt to produce an "American argument" on the issue. No one takes it seriously.

.   .   .

The difficulty which historians have had in treating the Rio Grande border claim is very easily explained: it is impossible to make Polk's military and diplomatic moves in relation to Mexico appear to have a just and reasonable and "peaceable" character unless some case can be made for the American claim to the Rio Grande border; and it is impossible to make even the shadow of a case.

The Republic of Texas was the product of a revolution; since Texas lacked an agreement on the boundary with the former mother-country, the only basis for claim was that established by presence, occupancy, control and extension of government. The boundary then, was not difficult to determine: The Republic of Texas was bounded on the south and southwest essentially by the Nueces River, but had settlements in that river valley on the right bank—including the town of Corpus Christi—and for a short distance beyond; on the west very indefinitely, for much territory was occupied or controlled neither by Texas nor by the Mexicans in New Mexico, but the line of the one-hundredth parallel north to the Red River encroached on the settlements of neither. Indeed, a no-man's-land, of approximately two hundred miles in width, lay between Texas and Mexico from the Gulf of Mexico west and north; there were Mexican settlements in the Rio Grande Valley from the source of the river, above Taos, to the Gulf; on the lower river the settlements were spread over the delta north of the mouth of the river; on the upper river, above El Paso, the Rio Grande was the heart of the province of New Mexico, with extensive settlements on the east side.

The First Congress of Texas, on 19 December 1836, resolved that the boundary ran from the mouth of the Rio Grande to the source of that river and thence due north to the forty-second degree of north latitude and thence along the United States boundary line to the mouth of the Sabine. That resolution cast some light upon the state of mind of the Texans, and revealed something of their ambitions, but it had no more effect upon the matter of establishing an international boundary than if they had declared that Texas was composed of a half dozen other states of Mexico. In fact the Congress of Texas did just that in 1842, by a joint resolution to include portions of the states of Tamaulipas, Coahuila, Durango, Sinaloa, and all of Chihuahua, New Mexico, Sonora, and Upper and Lower California—some five hundred million acres of land; the resolution represented the decision of 100,000 Texans to govern some 2,000,000 Mexicans. The President of Texas at the time the measure was introduced, Mirabeau Buonaparte Lamar, had supported the bill; in his inaugural address of 10 December 1838 he had referred to the boundaries of Texas as "stretching from the Sabine to the Pacific and away to the South West as far as the obstinacy of the enemy may render it necessary for the sword to make the boundary." But Sam Houston was President when the bill came to the executive desk and he vetoed it as "visionary."

.   .   .

The United States government had taken a more reasonable and logical view of the appropriate boundary when it had been attempting to purchase Texas from Mexico prior to the Texas Revolution. On 25 August 1829, Secretary of State Martin Van Buren wrote to Joel Poinsett in Mexico:

The territory of which the cession is desired by the United States, is all that part of the Province of Texas which lies East of a line beginning at the Gulf of Mexico, in the centre of the desert of Grande Prairie which lies West of the Rio Nueces, and is represented to be nearly two hundred miles in width, and to extend north to the mountains, the proposed line following the course of the centre of that desert or prairie, north, to the mountains; thence, with a central line on the mountains dividing the waters of the Rio Grande del Norte, from those that run eastward to the Gulf, and until it strikes our present boundary at the 42nd degree of North latitude.

Van Buren said that this line might be considered too extensive by the Mexican government, since it included the "Spanish" settlements of La Bahía and San Antonio de Béxar. But he said this line would be the most desirable "to us," since it would constitute a natural separation of the resources of the two nations. "It is the centre of a country uninhabitable, on the Gulf; and, on the mountains, so difficult of access, and so poor, as to furnish no inducements for a land intercourse." As it happened, the revolution in Texas and subsequent development in that Republic did not affect in any significant way the situation which Van Buren described; the arguments for that line in 1829 were fully applicable in 1845 and 1846.

In the few years before the annexation of Texas the governments of both Mexico and Texas, in principle, had accepted the boundary as established by occupancy and control.

.   .   .

In response to this pressure from the most influential individual in Texas, Polk replied in a letter of 6 June: "You may have no apprehensions in regard to your boundary. Texas once a part of the Union & we will maintain all your rights of territory & will not suffer them to be sacrificed." Polk said it would be his duty and his pleasure "to guard your interests in that respect with vigilance & care." And Anson Jones said in December of 1845 that Polk had pledged to him, through Governor Yell—who had been instructed to give him the message verbally but not to put it in writing—that the government of the United States would establish the Rio Grande boundary.

Andrew Jackson Donelson, the official representative of the United States in Texas, stood for mediation, moderation, reason, and accommodation on this matter, as he had on all controverted questions during his mission in Texas. He encouraged the Texans in the belief that the United States government would "in good faith maintain the claim," and he said he had reason to believe that the claim could be supported successfully. Such a statement was the minimum required to hold support for annexation. But he constantly emphasized in his communications with his government that the boundary was a disputed question, and he argued strongly against military occupation of the contested territory.

But President Polk gave orders early in 1846 for American troops to march into the Mexican settlements north of the Rio Grande. When he gave the order he expected the consequence would be war. It was.

.   .   .

The political dynamics were aimed in the direction of expansion of demands, however, not of moderation and accommodation to reality; this was true both in Texas and in the United States. Senator Thomas Hart Benton's amendment to the joint resolution for annexation provided for negotiations with Texas on the boundary, as well as on other matters, and Benton proposed the between-the-rivers boundary: the boundary, he proposed, was "to be in the desert prairie west of the Nueces, and along the highlands and mountain heights which divide the waters of the Mississippi from the waters of the Rio del Norte, and to latitude forty two degrees north." The Tyler Administration ignored the Benton amendment and Polk never had any intention of moderating the untenable demands of the Texans; on the contrary, it was in the interest of his schemes to encourage excessive territorial claims. Not that the Texans needed encouraging: sentiment in Texas was almost unanimous for the Rio Grande border; what Texas had not been able to establish in a decade of independence, the United States, it was assumed, would now successfully assert.

So much public discussion of the vexed question of the boundary between Texas and Mexico had raged that President Polk could not simply publicly promise the government of Texas that he would accept their position and act on the boundary claim as Texas defined it, but he did so unofficially. On 6 April 1845 Samuel Houston wrote to Donelson insisting that the Rio Grande must be the boundary if Texas accepted annexation, and he wrote to Polk on the subject in May.

.   .   .

Indeed, a very considerable opposition to the President, and a very clear understanding of his design, was apparent, but his control of the armed forces and the boundary claim which provided a surface justification for his throwing the Army into the Mexican settlements kept the control of events in his hands. It does not follow that he wanted war; rather, he was determined to have the fruits of war. Polk would have preferred paying the Mexican government to dismember that nation, and he recognized that this would require giving money to certain Mexican officials so that they would perform that operation on their country. In March of 1846 he thought it would be necessary to give General Paredes, who had overthrown the civilian government, a half million or a million dollars to "pay, feed, and clothe the army, and maintain himself in power," between the time when the General should sign a treaty with the United States and the subsequent ratification of that treaty by the United States Senate.

The President talked to Calhoun at this time about the boundary which the United States should secure in such a treaty, and the exchange, as Polk recorded it in his Diary, makes it clear that the President's objectives required a war. Calhoun, he wrote,

concurred with me in the great importance of procuring by a Treaty with Mexico such a boundary as would include California. He said he had contemplated, when Secretary of State, as a very desirable boundary a line running from a point on the Gulf of Mexico through the desert to the Northward between the Nueces & the Del Norte to a point about 36° or 37° and thence West to the Pacific so as to include the Bay of San Francisco, and he said he would like to include Monterey also; and that for such a boundary we could afford to pay a large sum, and mentioned ten millions of dollars.

This boundary would have excluded the Mexican settlements on the lower Rio Grande and the settled portions of New Mexico; Polk was not prepared to be so considerate of foreign populations.

I told him that I must insist on the Del Norte as the line up to the Passo in about latitude 32°, where the Southern line of New Mexico crosses that River, and then if practicable by a line due West to the Pacific; but if that could not be obtained then to extend up the Del Norte to its source, including all New Mexico on both sides of it, and from its source to the source of the Colorado of the West and down that River to its mouth in the Bay of California.

President Polk appears to have had a rather uncertain grip on the geography of the Southwest—a condition he shared with many other politicians in Washington—but he had a firm, not to say convulsive, hold on his objectives: Upper California first, and New Mexico in addition, although the latter was always a secondary goal. His purpose in discussing the territorial objectives with Calhoun, as also with Senators Thomas Hart Benton, William Allen, and Lewis Cass, was to enlist support for an appropriation to be made giving the President a million dollars or more to be used in the negotiation of a treaty. Calhoun opposed it on the ground that in spite of the utmost care to prevent it, the object of the appropriation would become known. Polk gave up. . . .

By this time, in any event, Polk had concluded that neither money nor the threat of force, nor the careful mixture of the two, would suffice; force would be required. He failed, however, to avoid direct and personal responsibility for the forcing of the War, as he had long tried to do. General Taylor was first encouraged to take the responsibility for the march to the Rio Grande. A dispatch from Secretary of War Marcy to Taylor, dated 30 July 1845, supposedly directing him in the disposition of his troops, appears to have been deliberately designed to encourage the General to march to the Rio Grande while at the same time placing the burden of responsibility on him for that move:

The Rio Grande is claimed to be the boundary . . . and up to this you are to extend your position, only excepting any posts on the eastern side thereof, which are in the actual occupancy of Mexican forces. . . . It is expected that you will approach as near the boundary line—the Rio Grande—as prudence will dictate. . . .

The president desires that your position . . . should be near the river Nueces.

General Zachary Taylor was not very perspicacious, but Polk was so well known for devious and underhanded maneuvers that his scapegoats were forewarned. Taylor declined to march south from his Corpus Christi camp without specific orders; these came to him on 3 February 1846, having been issued by Polk on 13 January on the receipt of a dispatch from John Slidell, who was in Mexico trying to purchase territory. The refusal of the Mexican government to receive Slidell and to negotiate with him, convinced Polk that he must take the responsibility for moving the Army to the Rio Grande.

Taylor began the advance on 8 March and arrived on the Rio Grande opposite Matamoros on the twenty-eighth. The Mexican inhabitants had fled across the river on the approach of the American Army, many of them setting their buildings on fire before leaving. Two weeks after arriving at the river Taylor committed the first act of war (if the invasion of Mexican territory was not), by blockading the mouth of the Rio Grande. Another two weeks, 25 April, and the clash of arms took place on the left bank of the river. The blood was shed which Polk referred to in his war message as "American blood on the American soil."

News of the encounter did not reach Washington until 9 May and Polk's patience snapped just before that information arrived. He had been expecting for several weeks to hear that hostilities had begun; he had told his Cabinet on several occasions that the United States should "take redress for the injuries done us into our hands." On 21 April he said that he was thinking of preparing a message for Congress asking for authorization to wage war on Mexico; on 25 April Buchanan "concurred" with the President, and said he should recommend a declaration of war; on 28 April the Cabinet agreed that a message should be sent to Congress, but Polk kept delaying. On 6 May he noted the receipt of dispatches from General Taylor with news up to the fifteenth of April, and he commented in his Diary: "No actual collision had taken place, though the probabilities are that hostilities might take place soon." Finally, at a Cabinet meeting on Saturday, 9 May, Polk brought up "the Mexican question" again:

All agreed that if the Mexican forces at Matamoras committed any act of hostility on Gen'l. Taylor's forces I should immediately send a message to Congress recommending an immediate declaration of War. I stated to the Cabinet that up to this time, as they knew, we had heard of no open act of aggression by the Mexican army, but that the danger was imminent that such acts would be committed. I said that in my opinion we had ample cause of war, and that it was impossible that we could stand in *statu quo,* or that I could remain silent much longer; that I thought it was my duty to send a message to Congress very soon & recommend definitive measures.

Polk then polled the Cabinet on a declaration of war; Buchanan said he would be better satisfied if the Mexican forces should commit any act of hostility, but he supported a demand for war; Bancroft alone dissented. The decision was made for war. They adjourned at 2:00 P.M., and at 6:00 P.M. dispatches arrived from General Taylor with information of the fight of 25 April. The American government's decision for war was not changed by news of that event; but the argumentation, the justification for war was altered. Polk had been prepared to call for a declaration of war against Mexico on the ground that she had defaulted in payments due to citizens of the United States; now he asserted that the United States had been attacked. He spent 10

May, a Sunday, writing the war message—and remarked in his Diary that he "regretted the necessity which had existed to make it necessary for me to spend the Sabbath in the manner I have."

The message went to Congress on 11 May. Polk asserted that,

after reiterated menaces, Mexico has passed the boundary of the United States, has invaded our territory and shed American blood upon the American soil. . . .

As war exists, and, notwithstanding all our efforts to avoid it, exists by the act of Mexico herself, we are called upon by every consideration of duty and patriotism to vindicate with decision the honor, the rights, and the interests of our country.

Congress passed the war bill after two days of discussion and Polk signed the measure on 13 May. On that same date the President decided that his Secretary of State was so obtuse as not to understand the point of the War. In a Cabinet meeting Buchanan read the draft of a dispatch which he had prepared to be sent to the United States ministers at London, Paris, and other foreign capitals, announcing the beginning of the War against Mexico and providing the reasons for it, for their communication to the several governments. Polk recorded in his Diary: "Among other things Mr. Buchanan had stated that our object was not to dismember Mexico or to make conquests, and that the Del Norte was the boundary to which we claimed; or rather that in going to war we did not do so with a view to acquire either California or New Mexico or any other portion of the Mexican territory."

It is small wonder that Polk was, as he said, "much astonished at the views" Buchanan expressed. He enlightened his Secretary:

I told Mr. Buchanan that I thought such a declaration to Foreign Governments unnecessary and improper; that the causes of the war as set forth in my message to Congress and the accompanying documents were altogether satisfactory. I told him that though we had not gone to war for conquest, yet it was clear that in making peace we would if practicable obtain California and such other portion of the Mexican territory as would be sufficient to indemnify our claimants on Mexico, and to defray the expenses of the war which that power by her long continued wrongs and injuries had forced us to wage.

When Buchanan said that if the United States did not make it clear to Britain and France that there was no intention on our part to take California they almost certainly would join Mexico in the War, Polk replied that before he would pledge not to acquire California in this war he "would meet the war which either England or France or all the Powers of Christendom might wage, and that I would stand and fight until the last man among us fell in the conflict."

Polk thus clarified, finally and definitely, his position on a subject that needed no clarification: the acquisition of California. Two years later, with the ratification of the Treaty of Guadalupe Hidalgo, the United States acquired the Mexican territories along the lower Rio Grande, and New Mexico, and California.

. . .

Polk had discovered how vain diplomatic arts and intrigues could be. To secure California he had tried to bribe Mexican officials; he had sought to encourage revolutionary forces in that Mexican province; he had used the threat of force to frighten Mexico into selling the territory; and, as this study has shown in some detail, he had sought to initiate a war by proxy in order to achieve his ends without assuming the responsibility for aggressive war. Here was no fine Italian hand nor astute Prussian practitioner of *Realpolitik;* here was a determined, clumsy amateur whose every maneuver failed. The last resort was to begin the War by throwing American troops into Mexican settlements, having naval forces poised to occupy California as soon as the Mexican government should respond.

Westward Expansion and the Mexican War

Realist

The Realists admit that many of America's actions in its westward march to the sea were aggressive and indefensible by general standards of morality. They argue, however, that this movement was the inevitable result of a growing nation situated on the border of a vacuum of power. They regard national expansion into a vacuum of power as the natural outcome of the selfish nature of man and find no need to attribute it to the capitalist ethic, as Radicals do. They also reject the Nationalist claims as to the peaceful and moral nature of American expansion.

Norman Graebner, professor of history at the University of Virginia and author of Empire on the Pacific: A Study in American Continental Expansion, *claims that much of the impulse for expansion derived from a popular frenzy rather than from the manipulation of Polk and a power elite. He argues, in the following essay, that Polk and a conservative coalition in Congress actually restrained and harnessed the frenzy for expansion to limited, realistic goals. This, says Graebner, made for a successful policy, the moral transgressions of which were mitigated by the inevitability of a strong nation's being drawn into a vacuum of power.*

Manifest Destiny

Norman Graebner

MANIFEST DESTINY: A NATIONAL FORCE

Manifest destiny, a phrase used by contemporaries and historians to describe and explain the continental expansion of the United States in the 1840's, expressed merely a national mood. The belief in a national destiny was neither new nor strange; no nation or empire in history has ever been totally without it. But for its proponents of the 1840's the meaning conveyed by the phrase was clearly understood and peculiarly American. It implied that the United States was destined by the will of Heaven to become a country of political and territorial eminence. It attributed the probability and even the necessity of this growth to a homogeneous process created by certain unique qualities in American civilization—the energy and vigor of its people, their idealism and faith in their democratic institutions, and their sense of mission now endowed with a new vitality. It assigned to the American people the obligation to extend the area of freedom to their less fortunate neighbors, but only to those trained for self-government and genuinely desirous of entering the American Union.

Expansionists of the forties saw this self-imposed limitation on forceful annexation as no serious barrier to the Republic's growth. It was inconceivable to them that any neighboring population would decline an invitation to enter the realm of the United States. Eventually editors and politicians transformed the idea of manifest destiny into a significant expression of American nationalism.

Such convictions of destiny came easily to the American people in the mid-forties, for they logically emerged from the sheer size and dramatic achievements of the young Republic. . . .

The purchase of Louisiana, forty years earlier, enabled the United States to leap the Mississippi and extended its territorial claims westward to the shores of the Pacific. But, in the forties, the land resources of the nation no longer appeared as boundless as they once did to Thomas Jefferson. Augmented by Europe's ceaseless outpouring of humanity, the population of the United States had quadrupled in less than fifty years. Immigrants from Ireland and northern Europe flowed into the little settlements dotting the Mississippi Valley, and from these centers of trade they fanned out across the countryside, creating new markets and stimulating the region's industrial and agricultural expansion. Settlements extended as far west as the lower Missouri; beyond them stretched the treeless prairies inhabited by Indians and buffalo. Restless farmers, always reaching for the farthest frontiers, had begun the grand overland trek to the inland valleys of Oregon and California. The easy identification of sufficient land with opportunity and the absence of oppression quickly converted manifest destiny into a major reform movement. Through territorial expansion the Republic would guarantee humanity's future. "Long may our country prove itself the asylum of the oppressed," pleaded Congressman James Belser of Alabama in January, 1845. "Let its institutions and its people be extended far and wide, and when the waters of despotism shall have inundated other portions of the globe, and the votary of liberty be compelled to betake himself to his ark, let this government be the Ararat on which it shall rest."

This visible evidence of the nation's expanding power contrasted markedly with the relative absence of such progress elsewhere on the North American continent, and assured the Republic that one day it would surpass in strength and grandeur the great nations of Europe. As one British traveler warned his countrymen in the late forties:

We cannot conceal from ourselves that in many of the most important points of national capabilities they beat us; they are more energetic, more enterprising, less embarrassed with class interests, less burthened by the legacy of debt. This country, as a field for increase of power, is in every respect so infinitely beyond ours that comparison would be absurd. . . . They only wait for material power, to apply the incendiary torch of Republicanism to the nations of Europe.

However, manifest destiny's existence, as an organized body of thought, required more than a recognition and appreciation of national power and energy. It demanded above all a sense of mission, one anchored to political idealism. Americans of the early forties viewed their political system with a messianic consciousness, convinced that they held the future of republican government in their hands. Andrew Jackson asserted in his Farewell Address that Providence had selected the American people to be "the guardians of freedom to preserve it for the benefit of the human race." Even more grandiloquent was the phraseology of John L. O'Sullivan, editor of the *Democratic Review,* who reminded the American people in July, 1840, that to them much had been given and much would be required. Continued O'Sullivan:

We have been placed in the forefront of the battle in the cause of Man against the powers of evil which have so long crushed him to the dust. The problem of his capacity for self-government is to be solved here. . . . he [Man] should be left to the individual action of his own will and conscience. Let us but establish this, and the race will have made an advance from which nothing short of the hand of Omnipotence can force it to recede. To no other has been committed the ark of man's hopes. . . . Surely we cannot fail of success in such a cause! Surely we cannot falter when so much depends upon our perseverance to the end!

O'Sullivan, always in the vanguard of American expansionist thinking, had helped to found the *Review* in 1837 and remained its editor until 1846. With Samuel J. Tilden he founded the New York *Morning News* in 1844, and for the following two years as editor filled its pages with expansionist sentiment. It was O'Sullivan who, during the summer of 1845, first used the phrase "manifest destiny. . . ."

America's mission to humanity was not new, but the generation of the forties was the first to attach it to territorial expansion. The Founding Fathers had limited the nation's democratic mission to the creation and perpetuation of a model republic which might be worthy of emulation. Expansion, they feared, might disturb the federal structure of government by dispersing political authority too widely. The outspoken southern conservative of the Jeffersonian era, John Randolph, once observed, "We are the first people that ever acquired provinces . . . not for us to govern, but that they might *govern us*—that we might be ruled to our ruin by people bound to us by no common tie of interest or sentiment." With the passage of time, however, even conservative Easterners accepted the inevitability of American expansion and ceased to regard the westward-moving center of political power a threat to their estate. "We look forward to that event without alarm," the noted Massachusetts scholar and orator, Edward Everett, could assure a Tennessee audience in 1829, "as in the order of the natural growth of this great Republic. We have a firm faith that . . . if you prosper, we shall prosper. . . ."

By the forties the addition of new states from the Louisiana Purchase, all without subverting the American federal system, had dispelled completely such earlier fears of expansion. The reestablishment of the states-rights principle under Jacksonian rule destroyed what remained of the older institutional arguments against national growth. In January, 1838, the *Democratic Review* affirmed the compatibility between the expansion and the basic principles of American government: "The peculiar characteristic of our system,—the distinctive evidence of its divine origin . . . is, that it may, if its theory is maintained pure in practice, be extended, with equal safety and efficiency, over any indefinite number of millions of population and territory." Similarly Stephen A. Douglas of Illinois asserted in January, 1845, that "our federal system is admirably adapted to the whole continent." Indeed, to states-rights Democrats there was no better guarantee against federal consolidation than the addition of new states.

In essence, then, manifest destiny suggested that the American people were destined to extend their democratic principles over the North American continent. . . .

Historically, national ambition demanded no vindication beyond the demonstration of interest and the possession of the strength to achieve the objective. But no nation had ever embarked on a career of expansion so completely at the price of its own national ideology as did the United States in the 1840's. Its sense of mission collided sharply with its democratic doctrine of self-determination as well as its ideals of amity and peace. Morality among individuals is a rationale for self-sacrifice; among nations it often serves as a cloak for self-aggrandizement. Democratic idealism is easily transformed into an agency of imperialism when it attempts to deny opposing governments—because of their alleged corruption or immorality—the right to territories which they possess. It seeks to rationalize the removal of those who stand in the path of destiny by declaring them politically and morally inferior. Such an approach to the achievement of external ambitions may assure popular support for specific foreign policies formulated by the national government; it can do no more. National sentiment, unsupported by force or the threatened use of force, can wield no measurable influence in affairs among nations.

MANIFEST DESTINY: THE ABSENCE OF ENDS AND MEANS

Never in history could a people more readily accept and proclaim a sense of destiny, for never were a people more perfectly situated to transform their whims into realities. Expansion was rationalized so effectively at each point of conflict that it seemed to many Americans an unchallangeable franchise. Confronted by problems neither of conscience nor of extensive countering force, the American people could claim as a natural right boundaries that seemed to satisfy the requirements of security and commerce. Expanding as they did into a vacuum—vast regions almost devoid of population—they could conclude that they were simply fulfilling the dictates of manifest destiny. For them the distinctions between sentiment and action, between individual purpose and national achievement, appeared inconsequential.

Historians, emphasizing the expansive mood of the forties, have tended to identify the westward extension of the United States to the Pacific with the concept of destiny itself. Such identifications are misleading, for they ignore all the genuine elements of successful policy. Those regions into which the nation threatened to expand were under the legal jurisdiction of other governments. Their acquisition required the formulation of policies which encompassed both the precise definition of ends and the creation of adequate means. Manifest destiny doctrines—a body of sentiment and nothing else—avoided completely the essential question of *means,* and it was only the absence of powerful opposition on the North American continent that permitted the fallacy that power and its employment were of little consequence. Occupying a wilderness created the illusion that power was less important than moral progress, and that expansion was indeed a civilizing, not a conquering, process.

Jeremy Bentham once termed the concept of natural right pure nonsense, for the claims of nations were natural only when supported by superior force. The natural right of the United States to a continental empire lay in its power of conquest, not in the uniqueness of its political institutions. American expansionism could triumph only when the nation could bring its diplomatic and military influence to bear on specific points of national concern. What created the easy victory of American expansion was not a sense of destiny, however widely and dramatically it was proclaimed, but the absence of powerful competitors which might have either prevented the expansion entirely or forced the country to pay an exorbitant price for its territorial gains. The advantages of geography and the political and military inefficiency of the Indian tribes or even of Mexican arms tended to obscure the elements of force which were no less real, only less obtrusive, than that employed by other nations in their efforts at empire building. It was no wonder that British and French critics concluded that the American conquest of the continent was by pick and shovel.

Concepts of manifest destiny were as totally negligent of *ends* as they were of means. Expansionists agreed that the nation was destined to reach its natural boundaries. But what were these natural frontiers? For Benjamin Franklin and John Adams they comprised the Mississippi River. But when the United States, through the purchase of Louisiana, crossed the Mississippi, there was no end in sight. Expansionists now regarded Florida as a natural appendage—belonging as naturally to the United States, declared one Kentucky newspaper, as Cornwall did to England. John Quincy Adams observed in his diary that the acquisition of Florida in 1819 "rendered it still more unavoidable that the remainder of the continent should ultimately be ours." Eventually Europe would discover, he predicted, that the United States and North America were identical. But President James Monroe revealed no more interest in building a state on the Pacific than had Jefferson. Equally convinced that the distances to Oregon were too great to be bridged by one empire, Thomas Hart Benton of Missouri in 1825 defined the natural boundary of the United States as "the ridge of the Rocky Mountains. . . . Along the back of this ridge, the Western limit of this republic should be drawn, and the statue of the fabled god, Terminus, should be raised upon its highest peak, never to be thrown down." President John Tyler, in his message of December, 1843, perpetuated this limited view of the nation's future. And as late as 1845 Daniel Webster continued to refer to an independent republic along the distant Pacific coast. Meanwhile expansionists could never agree on the natural boundaries of Texas. Representative C. J. Ingersoll of Pennsylvania found them in the vast deserts between the Rio Grande and the Nueces. For others they comprised the Rio Grande itself, but James Gadsden discovered in the Sierra Madre mountains "a natural territorial boundary, imposing in its Mountain and Desert outlines."

Yet geographical predestination alone seemed sufficient to assure the sweep of the nation to the Pacific. As Lord Curzon once wrote, "Of all natural frontiers the sea is the most uncompromising, the least alterable, and the most effective." As early as 1823 Francis Baylies warned the nation not to terminate its westward march at the Rockies. "Sir, our natural boundary is the Pacific Ocean," he declared. "The swelling tide of our population must and will roll on until the mighty ocean interposes its waters, and limits our territorial empire." By the mid-forties the true proponents of manifest destiny had become continentalists. Stephen Douglas voiced these sentiments when he declared in January, 1845:

He would blot out the lines on the map which now marked our national boundaries on this continent, and make the area of liberty as broad as the continent itself. He would not suffer petty rival republics to grow up here, engendering jealousy at each other, and interfering with each others domestic affairs, and continually endangering their peace. He did not wish to go beyond the great ocean—beyond those boundaries which the God of nature had marked out. . . .

.   .   .

If the ultimate vision of American destiny in the forties comprised a vast federal republic that boasted continental dimensions and a government based on the principle of states rights, the future boundaries of the United States, as determined by the standards of geographical predestination, never seemed to possess any ultimate logic. Boundaries that appeared natural to one generation were rejected as utterly inadequate by the next. It was left for Robert Winthrop, the conservative Massachusetts Whig, in January, 1846, to reduce the doctrine of geographical predestination to an absurdity:

It is not a little amusing to observe what different views are taken as to the indication of "the hand of nature" and the pointings of "the finger of God," by the same gentlemen, under different circumstances and upon different subjects. In one quarter of the compass they can descry the hand of nature in a level desert and a second-rate river, beckoning us impatiently to march up to them. But when they turn their eyes to another part of the horizon the loftiest mountains in the universe are quite lost upon their gaze. There is no hand of nature there. The configuration of the earth has no longer any significance. The Rocky Mountains are mere molehills. Our destiny is onward.

Democratic idealism was even less precise as a guide to national action than the doctrine of geographical predestination. By 1845 such goals of reaching the waters of the Pacific were far too limited for the more enthusiastic exponents of the new expansionism. As they interpreted the expression of democratic idealism, the dogma represented an ever-expanding force. Indeed, for some it had no visible limit at all. It looked beyond the North American continent to South America, to the islands of the Pacific, and to the Old World itself. One editorial in the New York *Herald* (September 15, 1845), declared, "American patriotism takes a wider and loftier range than heretofore. Its horizon is widening every day. No longer bounded by the limits of the confederacy, it looks abroad upon the whole earth, and into the mind of the republic daily sinks deeper and deeper the conviction that the civilization of the earth—the reform of the governments of the ancient world—the emancipation of the whole race, are dependent, in a great degree, on the United States." This was a magnificent vision for a democratic purpose, but it hardly explains the sweep of the United States across the continent. It bears no relationship whatever to the actual goals which the Tyler and Polk administrations pursued in their diplomacy with Texas, Mexico, and England.

.   .   .

POLK'S WAR FOR CALIFORNIA

California no less than Oregon demanded its own peculiar expansionist rationale, for its acquisition confronted the United States with a series of problems not present in either the Texas or Oregon issues. If the government in Mexico City lacked the energy to control, much less develop, this remote province, its title was still as clear as its hold was ephemeral. The annexation of this outpost required bargaining with its owner. Even that possibility seemed remote in 1845, for the Mexican government had carried out its threat to break diplomatic relations with the United States rather than condone the American annexation of Texas. For a decade American citizens had drifted into the inland valleys and coastal villages of California, but in 1845 they still comprised an infinitesimal number, even when compared to the small Mexican and Indian population.

Obviously the United States could not achieve its continental destiny without embracing California. Yet this Mexican province had never been an issue in American politics; its positive contribution to American civilization had scarcely been established. California, moreover, because of its alien population, was by the established principles of American expansion less than acceptable as a territorial objective. American acquisitiveness toward Texas and Oregon had been ethnocentric; it rejected the notion of annexing allegedly inferior peoples. "There seems to be something in our laws and institutions," Alexander Duncan of Ohio reminded the House of Representatives early in 1845, "peculiarly adapted to our Anglo-Saxon-American race, under which they will thrive and prosper, but under which all others wilt and die." He pointed to the decline of the French and Spanish on the North American continent when American laws had been extended to them. It was their unfitness for "liberal and equal laws, and equal institutions," he assumed, that accounted for this inability to prosper under the United States.

Such inhibitions toward the annexing of Mexican peoples gradually disintegrated under the pressure of events. The decision to annex Texas itself encouraged the process by weakening the respect which many Americans held for Mexico's territorial integrity, and thus pointed the way to further acquisitions in the Southwest. Having, through the annexation of Texas, passed its arm "down to the waist of the continent," observed the *Dublin Freeman,* the nation would certainly "not hesitate to pass it round." That the United States was destined to annex additional portions of Mexican territory seemed apparent enough, but only when its population had been absorbed by the Anglo-Saxons now overspreading the continent. As early as 1845 the rapid migration of pioneers into California promised to render the province fit for eventual annexation. In July, 1845, the *Democratic Review* noted that Mexican influence in California was nearing extinction, for the Anglo-Saxon foot was on its border.

American acquisitiveness toward California, like that displayed toward Texas and Oregon, progressed at two levels—that of abstract rationalization and that of concrete national interest. Polk alone carried the responsibility for United States diplomacy with Mexico, and interpreted American objectives in the Southwest— like those in Oregon—as precise and determined by the sea. Travelers and sea captains of the early forties agreed that two inlets gave special significance to the California coast—the bays of San Francisco and San Diego. These men viewed San Francisco harbor with wonderment. Charles Wilkes assured the readers of his *Narrative* (Vol. V, p. 162) that California could boast "one of the finest, if not the very best harbor in the world." It was sufficiently extensive, he added, to shelter the combined navies of Europe. Thomas J. Farnham, the American traveler and writer, called it simply "the glory of the Western world." All who had visited the bay observed that it was the unqualified answer to American hopes for commercial greatness in the Pacific. To the south lay San Diego Bay—the rendezvous of the California hide trade. Here, all Boston firms maintained their coastal depots for cleaning, drying, and storing the hides until a full cargo of thirty to forty thousand had been collected for the long journey to Boston. The processing and storing of hides required a warm port, free from rain, fog, and heavy surf. San Diego alone met all these requirements. This beautiful bay, so deep and placid that ships could lie a cable's length from the smooth, hard-packed, sandy beach, became the chief point of New England's interest on the California coast. The bay was exposed to neither wind nor surf, for it was protected for its entire fifteen-mile length and possessed a narrow, deep entrance. Richard Henry Dana observed in *Two Years Before the Mast* (1840) that San Diego harbor was comparable in value and importance to San Francisco Bay. The noted sea captain, Benjamin Morrell, once termed San Diego "as fine a bay for vessels under three hundred tons as was ever formed by Nature in her most friendly mood to mariners."

During the autumn of 1845, even before his administration had disposed of the Oregon question, Polk embarked on a dual course to acquire at least a portion of California. English activity in that distant province convinced him that, in Great Britain, the United States faced a strong and determined competitor for possession, in particular, of San Francisco Bay.

.   .   .

Polk appointed Larkin as his confidential agent in California to encourage the Californians, should they separate from Mexico, to cast their lot with the United States. "While the President will make no effort and use no influence to induce California to become one of the free and independent states of the Union, yet," continued Buchanan's instructions, "if the people should desire to unite their destiny with ours, they would be received as brethren, whenever this can be done without affording Mexico just cause of complaint." Larkin was told to let events take their course unless Britain or France should attempt to take California against the will of its residents.

During November, 1845, Polk initiated the second phase of his California policy—an immediate effort to purchase the province from Mexico. [That effort failed.] . . .

From the defeat of their diplomacy to achieve a boundary settlement with Mexico Polk and his cabinet moved early in May, 1846, toward a recommendation of war, employing as the immediate pretext the refusal of the Mexican government to pay the claims of American citizens against it for their losses in Mexico. Before the cabinet could agree on such a drastic course of action, Polk received word that a detachment of General Zachary Taylor's forces stationed along the disputed Rio Grande boundary of Texas had been fired upon by Mexican forces. Armed with such intelligence, the President now phrased his message to obtain an immediate and overwhelming endorsement for a policy of force. Mexico, he charged, "has passed the boundary of the United States, has invaded our territory and shed American blood upon American soil." War existed, in short, by act of Mexico. Polk explained that his action of stationing Taylor on the Rio Grande was not an act of aggression, but merely the attempt to occupy a disputed territory. Yet the possibility that the President had sought to provoke a clash of arms left sufficient doubt in the minds of his Whig opponents to permit them to make the Mexican War the most bitterly criticized in American history.

. . .

CALIFORNIA WITHOUT MEXICO

Polk maintained control of United States military and diplomatic policy throughout the course of the Mexican War, despite the persistent opposition and ridicule that he faced. But his initial purpose of exerting vigorous, if limited, pressure on the Mexican government—just enough to gain his precise territorial objectives—ended in miscalculation simply because no Mexican government would come forth to treat with the agents of a victorious United States. By the autumn of 1847 this growing conviction that the ephemeral nature of the Mexican government might prolong an expensive war indefinitely convinced the expansionist press that the United States had no choice but to meet her destiny and annex the entire Mexican republic.

New manifest destiny doctrines swept aside the older arguments against the annexation of other than Anglo-Saxon peoples. Now Mexico, like California, would be rescued from inefficient and corrupt rule, and regenerated by an infusion of American power and influence. The regeneration that could not be achieved by the United States armed forces would be accomplished by a rapid migration of settlers into Mexico.

.   .   .

During December and January [1848], with Congress in session, Democratic orators seized control of the all-of-Mexico movement and carried this new burst of expansionism to greater heights of grandeur and extravagance. Their speeches rang with appeals to the nationalism of war and the cause of liberty. Cass observed that annexation would sweep away the abuses of generations. Senator Ambrose Sevier of Arkansas pointed to the progress that awaited the most degenerate Mexican population from the application of American law and education. In January, 1848, the Democratic Party of New York, in convention, adopted resolutions favoring annexation. The new mission of regeneration was proclaimed everywhere in the banquet toasts to returning officers. At one Washington dinner in January Senator Daniel Dickinson of New York offered a toast to "A more perfect Union: embracing the entire North American continent." In Congress that month Senator R. M. T. Hunter of Virginia commented on the fever annexationism had stirred up. "Schemes of ambition, vast enough to have tasked even a Roman imagination to conceive," he cried, "present themselves suddenly as practical questions." Both Buchanan and Walker of the cabinet, as well as Vice President Dallas, openly embraced the all-of-Mexico movement.

That conservative coalition which had upheld the Oregon compromise combined again early in 1848 to oppose and condemn this new crusade. This powerful and well-led group feared that the United States, unless it sought greater moderation in its external policies, would drift into a perilous career of conquest which would tax the nation's energies without bringing any commensurate advantages. Its spokesmen doubted that the annexation of Mexico would serve the cause of humanity or present a

new world of opportunity for American immigrants. Waddy
Thompson, the South Carolina Whig who had spent many years
in Mexico, warned in October against annexation: "We shall get
no land, but will add a large population, aliens to us in feeling,
education, race, and religion—unaccustomed to work, and accustomed to insubordination and resistance to law, the expense
of governing whom will be ten times as great as the revenues derived from them." Thompson, joined by Calhoun and other Southern antiannexationists, warned the South that no portion of Mexico was suitable for slavery. Mexico's annexation would merely
endanger the South's interests with a new cordon of free states.
In Congress Calhoun acknowledged the dilemma created by the
thoughtless decision to invade Mexico and recommended that
the United States withdraw all its military forces to a defensive
line across northern Mexico and maintain that line until Mexico
chose to negotiate a permanent and satisfactory boundary arrangement with the United States.

Neither the mission of regeneration nor its rejection by conser-
vatives determined the American course of empire. The great debate between those who anticipated nothing less than the
achievement of a continental destiny and those who, in the interest of morality or from fear of a bitter controversy over slavery
expansion, opposed the further acquisition of national territory,
was largely irrelevant. Polk and his advisers pursued a precise
vision, shared by those expansionists who searched the Mexican
borderlands for the American interest. In the mid-forties, when
the nation's agricultural frontier was still pushing across Iowa
and Missouri, the concern of those who knew California lay less
in land than in the configuration of the coastline and its possible
relationship to America's future in the entire world of the Pacific.
If American continentalism during the war years provided a substantially favorable climate for the acquisition of Mexican lands,
it contributed nothing to the actual formulation of the administration's expansionist program.

During the early weeks of the Mexican War the President
noted repeatedly in his diary that he would accept no treaty
which did not transfer New Mexico and Upper California to the
United States. It was left only to hammer out his precise war
aims. Initially, Polk and his cabinet were attracted to San Francisco and Monterey. Several days after the outbreak of war
George Bancroft, Secretary of the Navy, assured the Marblehead
merchant, Samuel Hooper, that by mid-June the United States

flag would be floating over these two northern California ports. "I hope California is now in our possession, never to be given up," he added. "We were driven reluctantly to war; we must make a solid peace. . . ."

But Hooper did not rest at Bancroft's promise. He prodded the administration to look southward along the California coast. Settlement at the thirty-second parallel, Hooper informed Bancroft, would secure both Los Angeles and the bay of San Diego. Such a boundary, moreover, would encompass all the Anglo-American population in the province and remove future annoyance by leaving a barren wilderness between Upper California and the larger Mexican cities to the south. Should the United States acquire San Diego as well as Monterey and San Francisco, continued Hooper, "it would insure a peaceful state of things through the whole country and enable [the Americans] to continue their trade as before along the whole coast. . . ." Thereafter the administration looked to San Diego. Bancroft assured Hooper in June, 1846, that the administration would accede to New England's wishes. "If Mexico makes peace this month," he wrote, "the Rio del Norte and the Parallel of 35° may do as a boundary; after that 32° which will include San Diego." This harbor remained the ultimate and unshakable territorial objective of Polk's wartime diplomacy.

Eventually the President achieved this goal through the efforts of Nicholas P. Trist. Unable after almost a year of successful fighting in Mexico to force the Mexican government to sue for terms, Polk, in April, 1847, dispatched Trist as a secret diplomatic agent to join General Winfield Scott's army in Mexico and await any sudden shift in Mexican politics. Trist's official baggage contained detailed instructions and the *projet* for a treaty which aimed pointedly at the acquisition of the entire coast of California to San Diego Bay. Trist's subsequent negotiations secured not only a treaty of peace with Mexico which terminated the war but also the administration's precise territorial objectives. Manifest destiny fully revealed itself in the Mexican War only when it clamored for the whole of Mexico, but even that final burst of agrarian nationalism was killed effectively by the Treaty of Guadalupe Hidalgo. American victories along the road to Mexico City were important only in that they created the force which permitted the President to secure through war what he had once hoped to achieve through diplomacy alone. It was Trist, working alone and unobserved, who in the final analysis defined the southern boundary of California.

six

The Spanish-American War and the Decision for Imperialism

Realist

Realists regard the Spanish-American War as the point at which American foreign policy began to move in a dangerously wrong direction. Earlier American actions may have sometimes been mistaken, but the United States had recovered from its mistakes quickly and had returned to its proper path. In 1898, however, the Realists believe the government allowed itself to be stampeded by the idealism and emotionalism of the populace into an unnecessary war. Then, to compound the error, the United States accumulated overseas territories that it was unable to govern and that constituted strategic liabilities.

George F. Kennan, author of the following essay, is the former ambassador to the U.S.S.R. and Yugoslavia. He is also a former chief of the policy planning section of the State Department and the author of many books on American diplomacy.

What specific departures from past policies does Kennan feel occurred during the Spanish-American War? What reasons does he offer for his belief that we could have avoided the war? How important were economic interests in bringing about United States intervention? How important were strategic considerations? Does idealism seem to play any role at all in Kennan's conception of a proper American foreign policy?

American Diplomacy, 1900—1950

George F. Kennan

I would like first to say a word about the concept of these six lectures. This concept stems from no abstract interest in history for history's sake. It stems from a preoccupation with the problems of foreign policy we have before us today.

A half-century ago people in this country had a sense of security vis-à-vis their world environment such as I suppose no people had ever had since the days of the Roman Empire. Today that pattern is almost reversed—our national consciousness is dominated at present by a sense of insecurity greater even than that of many of the peoples of western Europe who stand closer to, and in a position far more vulnerable to, those things that are the main source of our concern. Now, much of that change may be, and doubtless is, subjective—a reflection of the fact that in 1900 we exaggerated the security of our position and had an overweening confidence in our strength and our ability to solve problems, whereas today we exaggerate our dangers and have a tendency to rate our own abilities less than they actually are. But the fact remains that much of this change is also objectively real;

in 1900 the political and military realities were truly such that we had relatively little to fear in the immediate sense, whereas today we have before us a situation which, I am frank to admit, seems to me dangerous and problematical in the extreme.

What has caused this metamorphosis? How did a country so secure become a country so insecure? How much of this deterioration can be said to be "our fault"? How much of it is attributable to our failure to see clearly, or to take into account, the realities of the world around us?

What lessons, in other words, does the record of the external relations of the United States over the last fifty years hold for us, the generation of 1951, pressed and hemmed in as we are by a thousand troubles and dangers, surrounded by a world part of which seems to be actually committed to our destruction and another part to have lost confidence either in ourselves or in itself, or in both?

These are the questions which have taken me back, in the past few months, to a review of some of our decisions of national policy in these fifty years. I certainly cannot hold out to you the hope that this series of lectures will answer all these questions, or will answer any one of them in a manner beyond controversy.

But what we can hope, I think, is that it will be useful to turn again to certain of the major phases of national policy over this period and to look at them once more in the light of what seem in retrospect to have been their alternatives and their consequences. We have good reason for doing this. Not only is there much that should be visible to us now that was not visible to people as little as ten years ago; but I would hope that we might bring to such an inquiry a new sort of seriousness—a seriousness induced by our recollection of the vast destruction and the sacrifices we have witnessed in our lifetimes, a seriousness more thoughtful and sadder than most people would have been able to bring to these problems in the days before the two tragic world wars.

What I would like to talk about first is the Spanish-American War.

Today, standing at the end rather than the beginning of this half-century, some of us see certain fundamental elements on which we suspect that American security has rested. We can see that our security has been dependent throughout much of our history on the position of Britain; that Canada, in particular, has been a useful and indispensable hostage to good relations between our country and the British Empire; and that Britain's position, in turn, has depended on the maintenance of a balance of power on the European Continent. Thus it was essential to us, as it was to Britain, that no single Continental land power should come to dominate the entire Eurasian land mass. Our interest has lain rather in the maintenance of some sort of stable balance among the powers of the interior, in order that none of them should effect the subjugation of the others, conquer the seafaring fringes of the land mass, become a great sea power as well as land power, shatter the position of England, and enter—as in these circumstances it certainly would—on an overseas expansion hostile to ourselves and supported by the immense resources of the interior of Europe and Asia. Seeing these things, we can understand that we have had a stake in the prosperity and independence of the peripheral powers of Europe and Asia: those countries whose gazes were oriented outward, across the seas, rather than inward to the conquest of power on land.

Now we see these things, or think we see them. But they were scarcely yet visible to the Americans of 1898, for those Americans had forgotten a great deal that had been known to their forefathers of a hundred years before. They had become so accustomed to their security that they had forgotten that it had any foundations at all outside our continent. They mistook our sheltered position behind the British fleet and British Continental diplomacy for the results of superior American wisdom and virtue in refraining from interfering in the sordid differences of the Old World. And they were oblivious to the first portents of the changes that were destined to shatter that pattern of security in the course of the ensuing half-century.

There were, of course, exceptions. Brooks Adams, Henry's brother, probably came closer than any American of his day to a sort of an intellectual premonition of what the future had in store for us. But even he caught only a portion of it. He saw the increasing vulnerability of England—the increasing "eccentricity," as he called it, of her economic position, her growing economic dependence on the United States—and, conversely, the growing strategic dependence of the United States on England. He sensed the ultimate importance of the distinction between sea power and land power. Vaguely, he felt the danger of political collaboration between Russia and Germany and China. But his thinking was distorted by the materialism of the time: by the overestimation of economics, of trade, as factors in human events and by corresponding underestimation of psychological and political reactions—of such things as fear, ambition, insecurity, jealousy, and perhaps even boredom—as prime movers of events.

Mahan, too, was charting new paths at that time in the analysis of international realities—paths which led in the direction of a more profound appraisal of the sources of American security. And there were others who might be mentioned. But altogether they comprised only a tiny coterie of persons. Their efforts were not even followed up by others at the time or in the years that immediately ensued. Those efforts remained suspended, as it were, in the mid-air of history—an isolated spurt of intellectual activity against a background of general torpor and smugness in American thinking about foreign affairs. And all of them—all of these deeper and more observant minds of the turn of the century—stopped short of the projection of their inquiry onto the theater of European Continental rivalries where, as it happened, the events most fateful to American security were destined to occur and where we stood in the greatest need of profound analysis and careful identification of the elements of American interest.

It is plain, for this reason, that the incident I am talking about today—our brief war with Spain in 1898—occurred against a background of public and governmental thinking in this country which was not marked by any great awareness of the global framework of our security. This being the case, it was fortunate that both the situation out of which the war arose and, for the most part, the events and consequences of the war itself were largely local and domestic in their importance. As we proceed with these lectures and advance into the twentieth century, we shall see the global implications of our predicaments and actions growing apace with the passage of the years, until in the case of World War II they are positively overwhelming. But at the time of the Spanish-American War they were hardly present at all—the taking of the Philippines was the closest we came to them. And if a war so colorless from the standpoint of our world relationships is worth discussing at all this afternoon, it is because it forms a sort of preface to our examination of the diplomacy of this half-century, a simple, almost quaint, illustration of some of our national reactions and ways of doing business, and a revelation of the distance we were destined to have to come if we were ever to be a power capable of coping with the responsibilities of world leadership.

Our war with Spain, as you will recall, grew out of a situation in Cuba. It was one of those dreadful, tragic, hopeless situations which seem to mark the decline or exhaustion of a colonial relationship. We have seen other such situations since, and some of them not so long ago. Spanish rule on the island was challenged by Cuban insurgents, poorly organized, poorly disciplined, but operating on the classical principles of guerilla forces everywhere and enjoying all the advantages of guerillas operating on the home territory against an unpopular foreign enemy. The Spanish attempts to suppress the insurrection were inefficient, cruel, and only partly successful. The situation had been long developing; it had been growing sporadically for decades. President Grant had summed it up very well in a presidential message, over two decades earlier, in 1875:

> Each party seems quite capable of working great injury and damage to the other, as well as to all the relations and interests dependent on the existence of peace in the island; but they seem incapable of reaching any adjustment, and both have thus far failed of achieving any success whereby one party shall possess and control the island to the exclusion of the other. Under these circumstances, the agency of others, either by mediation or intervention, seems to be the only alternative which must sooner or later be invoked for the termination of the strife.

There had been some improvement, to be sure, in the two decades between 1875 and 1895. But in that latter year insurrection broke out again, this time on a bloodier and more tragic scale than ever before. And in the years 1896 and 1897 it brought increasing concern and dismay to the government, the press, and the public in our country.

Strictly speaking, of course, it would have been possible for us to have said that it was none of our business and to have let things take their course. Our national security, as we think of it today, was not threatened. But American property interests were damaged; the activities of American filibusterers and arms salesmen, on behalf of the insurgents, caused a lot of trouble to our government. And, above all, American public opinion was deeply shocked by the tales of violence and misery from the island. Our sensibilities were not yet jaded by the immense horrors and cruelties of the twentieth century. The sufferings of the Cuban people shocked our sensibilities, aroused our indignation. They gave American statesmen the conviction that a continuation of this situation in Cuba would be intolerable to our interests in the long run and that, if Spain did not succeed in putting an end to it, we should have to intervene in some way ourselves.

In the fall of 1897 things looked up a bit. A new and more moderate government came into power in Spain. This government showed a greater disposition to clear up the unhappy problems on the island than had its predecessor. In his message to Congress in December, 1897, President McKinley noted this improvement and recommended that we give the new Spanish government a chance. "I shall not impugn its sincerity," he said, "nor should impatience be suffered to embarrass it in the task it has undertaken." Certain difficulties, he said, had already been cleared up; there was reason to hope that, with patience on our part and continued good will on the part of the Spanish government, further progress might be made. Thus the year 1898 began with a renewed hope that the plight of the Cuban people might get better instead of worse.

Unfortunately, two things happened during the winter which changed the situation quite drastically. First, the Spanish minister in Washington wrote an indiscreet letter in which he spoke slightingly of President McKinley, calling him "a bidder for the admiration of the crowd" and "a would-be politician . . . who tries to leave a door open behind himself while keeping on good terms with the jingoes of his party." This letter leaked; it was published in the New York papers, causing much indignation and resentment. And a few days later the American public was profoundly shocked and outraged to hear that the battleship "Maine" had been sunk in Havana harbor with the loss of 266 American lives.

Now, looked at in retrospect, neither of these incidents seems to have been an adequate cause, in itself, for war. The Spanish government could not help its minister's indiscretion—even diplomats are constantly being indiscreet, this sort of thing happens in the best of families. It promptly removed him from his job and disavowed his offensive statements. And, as for the "Maine," there has never been any evidence that the Spanish government had anything to do with the sinking of the vessel or would have been anything but horrified at the suggestion that it should have anything to do with it. Spanish authorities, as well as our own consul-general in Havana, had begged us not to send the vessel there at that time for the very reason that they were afraid this might lead to trouble. The Spanish government did everything in its power to mitigate the effects of the catastrophe, welcomed investigation, and eventually offered to submit the whole question of responsibility to international arbitration—an offer we never accepted.

Nevertheless, it seems to be the judgment of history that these two incidents so affected American opinion that war became inevitable with the sinking of the "Maine." From that time on no peaceful solution was really given serious consideration in the American government. This is particularly significant and unfortunate, because during the nine weeks that intervened between the sinking of the "Maine" and the opening of hostilities the Spanish government came very far in the direction of meeting our demands and desires. It came so far that by April 10 (eleven days before hostilities began) our minister in Madrid—a wise and moderate man who had worked hard to prevent the outbreak of war—was able to report that, if the President could get from Congress authority to deal with the matter at his own discretion, he could have a final settlement before August 1 on one of the following bases: autonomy acceptable to the insurgents, independence, or cession to the United States. On the same day, the queen of Spain ordered a complete armistice on the island, and the Spanish minister in Washington promised to our government the early promulgation of a system of autonomy "such that no motive or pretext is left for claiming any fuller measure thereof."

These are of course isolated snatches out of a long and involved correspondence between the two governments. I cite them only to indicate that on paper, at least, the Spanish government was coming around very rapidly in those early days of April, 1898, to the sort of attitude and action we had been demanding of them. Yet, despite all that, one finds no evidence that the United States government was in any way influenced by these last-minute concessions. It made no move to prevent feeling and action in Congress from proceeding along a line that was plainly directed toward an early outbreak of hostilities.

Now, it is true that, as people then saw it, many of these Spanish concessions came too late and were not fully dependable. It is also true that the insurgents were by this time in no frame of mind, and in no state of discipline, to collaborate in any way with the Spanish authorities. But one does not get the impression that these were the things which dictated the decision of our government to go to war. This decision seems rather attributable to the state of American opinion, to the fact that it was a year of congressional elections, to the unabashed and really fantastic warmongering of a section of the American press, and to the political pressures which were freely and bluntly exerted on the President from various political quarters. (It is an interesting fact, incidentally, that financial and business circles, allegedly the instigators of wars, had no part in this and generally frowned on the idea of our involvement in the hostilities.)

The upshot of all this, as you know, was that on April 20 Congress resolved that "it is the duty of the United States to demand, and the Government of the United States does hereby demand, that the Government of Spain at once relinquish its authority and government in the island of Cuba and withdraw its land and naval forces from Cuba and Cuban waters." And it directed and empowered the President "to use the entire land and naval forces of the United States . . . to such extent as may be necessary" to enforce that requirement. We gave the Spaniards a flat three-day ultimatum for compliance with this resolution. We knew they would not, and could not, accept it. Early the following morning the Spaniards, without waiting for the delivery of the ultimatum, declared the resolution "equivalent to a declaration of war" and broke relations. On the same day, hostilities were inaugurated by the United States government. Thus our government, to the accompaniment of great congressional and popular acclaim, inaugurated hostilities against another country in a situation of which it can only be said that the possibilities of settlement by measures short of war had by no means been exhausted.

So much for the origin of the war. Now a few words about the way we fought it and particularly about the taking of the Philippines. You will recall that the wording of the congressional resolution which I just quoted mentioned only the island of Cuba. There was nothing in the resolution to indicate that Congress had any interest in any territory other than Cuba or that the President was authorized to use the armed forces for any purpose not directly related to the Spanish withdrawal from Cuba. Now, this resolution was passed on April 20, 1898. Yet it was only eleven days later that Admiral Dewey, sailing into Manila Bay in the early hours of morning, attacked and destroyed the Spanish fleet there. And only a few days later President McKinley authorized preparations for the dispatch of an army of occupation. The mission of this ground force was to follow up Dewey's victory, to complete "the reduction of Spanish power in that quarter," and to give "order and security to the islands while in the possession of the United States." This force proceeded to the Philippines and went into action there. By August it stormed and took the city of Manila. The effect of this action was later to constitute the most important and probably decisive consideration in our final decision to take the islands away from Spain and put them under the United States flag entirely; for this military operation shattered Spanish rule in the islands, made it impossible for us to leave them to Spain, and left us, as we shall see shortly, no agreeable alternative but to take them ourselves.

Now, why did all this happen? If there was no justification for the action against the Philippines in the origin of the war with Spain, what were the motives that lay behind it? Why, in other words, did we do things in May, 1898, that made it almost impossible for us later not to annex a great archipelago in the South Seas in which, prior to this time, our interest had been virtually nil? I ask this question not as one of moral judgment of American statesmen of the time but as one which may illumine the ways by which decisions are taken, and business done, by the United States government.

The fact of the matter is that down to the present day we do not know the full answer to this question. We know a number of things about it. We know that Theodore Roosevelt, who was then the young Assistant Secretary of the Navy, had long felt that we ought to take the Philippines; that he wangled Dewey's appointment to the command of the Asiatic fleet; that both he and Dewey wanted war; and that he had some sort of a prior understanding with Dewey to the effect that Dewey would attack Manila, regardless of the circumstances of the origin or the purpose of the war. We know that President McKinley, in defending Dewey's action at a later date, showed a very poor understanding of what was really involved and professed to believe a number of strategic premises that simply were not true. McKinley indicated that he had no thought of taking the Philippines at the time of the Battle of Manila and that Dewey's action was designed only to destroy the Spanish fleet and eliminate it as a factor in the war. But, if this is true, we are still mystified as to why McKinley authorized the sending of any army of occupation to the islands within a few days of Dewey's victory. We are not sure that we really know what passed between the government in Washington and Dewey prior to the battle. And we can only say that it looks very much as though, in this case, the action of the United States government had been determined primarily on the basis of a very able quiet intrigue by a few strategically placed persons in Washington, an intrigue which received absolution, forgiveness, and a sort of a public blessing by virtue of war hysteria—of the fact that Dewey's victory was so thrilling and pleasing to the American public—but which, had its results been otherwise, might well have found its ending in the rigors of a severe and extremely unpleasant congressional investigation.

So much, then, for the decisions underlying our conduct of hostilities. What about the broader political decisions connected with the war—the decisions which led to the final annexation not only of the Philippines but of Puerto Rico and Guam and the Hawaiian Islands? These were very important decisions from our own standpoint. They represented a turning point, it seems to me, in the whole concept of the American political system. These territorial acquisitions of the year 1898 represented the first extensions of United States sovereignty to important territories beyond the continental limits of North America, unless our share in the ruling of Samoa warranted such description. They represented the first instances of sizable populations being taken under our flag with no wide anticipation that they would ever be accepted into statehood. Prior to this time our territorial acquisitions had been relatively empty lands, too sparsely populated to be eligible at once for statehood. For them the territorial status was viewed as a temporary expedient, intended to tide them over until they were filled with our own sort of people and were prepared to come into the Union.

But here, in 1898, for the first time, territories were acquired which were not expected to gain statehood at all at any time but rather to remain indefinitely in a status of colonial subordination. The leading advocates of expansion were quite definite on this point. One of the most thoughtful and articulate of them, Whitelaw Reid, often expressed his anxiety lest people might think of the new territories as candidates for statehood, because he knew that, if they did, they would be less inclined to take them in. Andrew Carnegie, who was an opponent of expansionism, attacked Reid on precisely this point: "You will be driven off from your opposition to letting all these islands in as states," he said; "you'll have to swallow every last one of them." The question was thus squarely raised and faced as one of the admission of territories not intended for statehood.

The debate over this was long and voluminous. Much of it was concerned with legalities. But these were not the real issue. The real issue was one of expediency and wisdom. The proponents of expansion advanced a variety of arguments. Some said that it was our manifest destiny to acquire these territories. Others said that for one reason or another we had a paramount interest in them. Still others maintained that we, as an enlightened and a Christian nation, had a duty to regenerate their ignorant and misguided inhabitants. Another argument was that they were necessary to the defense of our continental territory. Finally, it was alleged by the commercially minded that we had to take them, Hawaii and the Philippines in particular, to assure ourselves of a fitting part in what was regarded as the great future trade with the Orient.

The opponents of expansionism argued partly in legal terms, challenging the constitutionality of such arrangements. But their most powerful arguments were those which asked by what right we Americans, who had brought our country into existence on the thesis that governments derive their just powers from the consent of the governed, could assume the rights of empire over other peoples and accept them into our system, regardless of their own feelings, as subjects rather than as citizens. To annex foreign territory and govern it without the consent of its population, said Senator Hoar of Massachusetts in the course of the debate over the ratification of the peace treaty with Spain, would be utterly contrary to the sacred principles of the Declaration of Independence and unconstitutional because it promoted no purpose of the Constitution. The Founding Fathers, said the Senator, had never thought that their descendants "would be beguiled from these sacred and awful verities that they might strut about in the cast-off clothing of pinchbeck emperors and pewter kings; that their descendants would be excited by the smell of gun powder and the sound of the guns of a single victory as a small boy by a firecracker on some Fourth of July morning."

The strongest argument of the imperialists was actually none of those that I mentioned but the argument of what has sometimes been called contingent necessity—the argument that, unless we took these territories, somebody else would and that this would be still worse. In the case of Puerto Rico and Hawaii, this argument seems to me to have been unsubstantial. There was no real likelihood of anybody else intervening. Puerto Rico could quite safely have been left with Spain, or given independence like Cuba, so far as our security was concerned. In the case of the Philippines the question was a more serious one. Once we had completed our defeat of the Spanish forces on the island

and the conquest of Manila, once we had shattered Spanish rule, there was no question of giving the islands back to Spain. It was also fairly clear that the inhabitants were hardly fit for self-rule, even if there had been a chance of their being let alone by other powers, which there was not. The alternative to our taking them would probably have been a tussle between England and Germany over their possession but with a reasonable likelihood that some sort of a *modus vivendi* and division of the territory would eventually have resulted. Sooner or later, the Japanese would also have become competitors for their possession. Whether this would have been unfortunate from the standpoint of later developments in the Southwest Pacific, I cannot say. The historian's power fails before such speculative questions. But if we today cannot see a likelihood that this would have been particularly unfavorable to America's interests, I doubt that the people of that time could have seen it very clearly themselves. And if they did not, one asks one's self, why did they need to destroy Spanish reign in the islands at all?

The Russian writer, Anton Chekhov, who was also a doctor, once observed that when a large variety of remedies were recommended for the same disease, it was a pretty sure sign that none of them was any good and that the disease was incurable. Similarly, when one notes the variety of arguments put up by the expansionists for the territorial acquisitions of 1898, one has the impression that none of them was the real one—that at the bottom of it all lay something deeper, something less easy to express, probably the fact that the American people of that day, or at least many of their more influential spokesmen, simply liked the smell of empire and felt an urge to range themselves among the colonial powers of the time, to see our flag flying on distant tropical isles, to feel the thrill of foreign adventure and authority, to bask in the sunshine of recognition as one of the great imperial powers of the world. But by the same right of retrospect one is impressed with the force and sincerity of the warnings of the anti-expansionists and the logic, as yet never really refuted, of their contention that a country which traces its political philosophy to the concept of the social compact has no business taking responsibility for people who have no place in that concept and who are supposed to appear on the scene in the role of subjects and not of citizens. Kings can have subjects; it is a question whether a republic can.

One remembers, in particular, the words of one of the anti-imperialists, Frederick Gookin: "The serious question for the people of this country to consider is what effect the imperial policy will have upon themselves if we permit it to be established." It is primarily in the light of this question that one thinks about our subsequent experience with these colonial possessions.

About Puerto Rico, I shall not speak. Recent events have surely been eloquent enough to cause us all to ask ourselves whether we have really thought through all the implications of a relationship so immensely important, so pregnant with possibilities for both good and evil, as the colonial tie between our country and the people of Puerto Rico. In the case of Hawaii, we see the outcome of the decision as a relatively successful one, but only, I fear, because American blood and American ways were able to dominate the scene entirely: because the native way of life was engulfed and reduced, as was the case with our American Indians, to the helpless ignominy of tourist entertainment. In the case of the Philippines, we recall that only a few years after their annexation the first and most eager protagonist of their acquisition, Theodore Roosevelt, was already disillusioned, was already repenting his initiative and wishing we could be rid of them. Finally, let us remember, in the thirties we decided to set them free, and we recently did so, but not really primarily for their sake—not primarily because we were sorry for them or thought them prepared for freedom and felt that we had an obligation to concede it to them—but rather because we found them a minor inconvenience to ourselves; because the economic intimacy that their existence under our flag implied proved uncomfortable to powerful private interests in this country; because, in other words, we were not ourselves prepared to endure for long even those rudimentary sacrifices implied in the term "the white man's burden." Remember Gookin's words which I just cited: "The . . . question . . . is what effect the imperial policy will have upon [ourselves.]"

When one thinks of these things, one is moved to wonder whether our most signal political failures as a nation have not lain in our attempts to establish a political bond of obligation between the main body of our people and other peoples or groups to whom, whether because we wished it so or because there was no other practical solution, we were not in a position to concede the full status of citizenship. There is a deep significance in the answer to this question. If it is true that our society is really capable of knowing only the quantity which we call "citizen," that it debauches its own innermost nature when it tries to deal with the quantity called "subject," then the potential scope of our system is limited; then it can extend only to people of our own kind— people who have grown up in the same peculiar spirit of inde- pendence and self-reliance, people who can accept, and enjoy, and content themselves with our institutions. In this case, the rul- ing of distant peoples is not our dish. In this case, there are many things we Americans should beware of, and among them is the acceptance of any sort of a paternalistic responsibility to any- one, be it even in the form of military occupation, if we can pos- sibly avoid it, or for any period longer than is absolutely neces- sary.

These, then, are some of the things that strike us when we think about the remote and picturesque conflict with Spain at the end of the last century. Let us recapitulate them.

We see that, in the reasons governing our resort to war and the determination of the character of our military operations, there was not much of solemn and careful deliberation, not much prudent and orderly measuring of the national interest. When it came to the employment of our armed forces, popular moods, po- litical pressures, and inner-governmental intrigue were decisive. McKinley did not want war. But, when the bitter realities were upon him, there is no indication that either he or his Secretary of State felt in duty bound to oppose the resort to war if this was advantageous to them from the standpoint of domestic politics. Having resorted to war for subjective and emotional reasons, we conducted it in part on the basis of plans which, as far as we know, had never been seriously examined and approved by any competent official body; which were known to, and understood by, only a tiny handful of individuals in the government service; and which obviously reflected motives ulterior to the announced purposes of the war as defined by Congress. When the success of the naval and military operations that flowed from these plans inflamed public imagination and led to important questions of the acquisition of foreign territory, the executive branch of the gov- ernment took little part in the debate. It made no serious effort to control the effects of popular reaction to the exploits of a popular commander far afield. It was only the obligation of the Senate to ratify treaties which caught the tremendous issues involved and brought them to the attention of the public in a senatorial debate as measured and enlightened as any we have ever had.

To my mind it seems unlikely, in the light of retrospect, that the conclusions which triumphed in that debate were the right ones. But we should not let that constitute a reproach to our forefathers, for we are poor judges of their predicaments. Let us content ourselves with recording that in the course of their deliberations they stumbled upon issues and problems basic to the health of our American civilization; that these issues and problems are ones which are still before us and still require answer; and that, whereas the men of 1898 could afford to be mistaken in their answers to them, our generation no longer has this luxury.

The Spanish-American War and the Decision for Imperialism

Radical

Radical historians believe that the Spanish-American War and the decision for imperialism were the culmination of trends long present in the United States and not a sudden departure from past precedent. They also argue that neither the war nor the decision for imperialism were foisted on the government by popular pressure, but were the products of rational and vigorous leaders in government and industry who recognized the need to expand foreign markets if they were to avoid revolution and the forcible redistribution of goods at home.

Walter LaFeber, author of the following, is a professor of history at Cornell University. What evidence does he give for the importance of economics in bringing about American intervention in Cuba? How does he dispute Kennan on the role of popular opinion? Even though LaFeber does not discuss the specific decision to keep the Philippines, can you deduce from the essay the reasons he might offer for that decision? How do these reasons differ from those of George Kennan?

The New Empire: An Interpretation of American Expansion, 1860–1898

Walter LaFeber

During this period [the 1890's] Brooks Adams, Roosevelt, and Lodge were, in the words of Arthur F. Beringause, "three musketeers in a world of perpetual war." Alfred Thayer Mahan became a fourth in 1897. Agreeing with much of Brooks's grand strategy, Mahan suggested the tactical details with which Brooks did not concern himself. Because of his technical knowledge as a naval officer, Mahan became not only the best known of the so-called intellectual expansionists of his time, but the most influential. Unlike Turner, Strong, and Adams, his significance for American foreign policy can be measured in such tangible terms as the 15,000-ton battleships built in the post-1889 period, which initiated the modern United States battleship fleet.

.   .   .

[But] [h]e did not define a battleship navy as his ultimate objective, nor did he want to create a navy merely for its own sake. In the 1890's he did not seek military power for the sake of military power.

Mahan grounded his thesis on the central characteristic of the United States of his time: it was an industrial complex which produced, or would soon be capable of producing, vast surpluses. In the first paragraph of his classic, *The Influence of Sea Power upon History, 1660–1783,* Mahan explained how this industrial expansion led to a rivalry for markets and sources of raw materials and would ultimately result in the need for sea power. He sum-

Reprinted from Walter LaFeber, *The New Empire: An Interpretation of American Expansion, 1860–1898,* pp. 85, 88–94, 397–406. © 1963 by the American Historical Association. Used by permission of Cornell University Press.

marized his theory in a postulate: "In these three things—production, with the necessity of exchanging products, shipping, whereby the exchange is carried on, and colonies . . . —is to be found the key to much of the history, as well as of the policy, of nations bordering upon the sea." The order is all-important. Production leads to a need for shipping, which in turn creates the need for colonies.

Mahan's neat postulate was peculiarly applicable to his own time, for he clearly understood the United States of the 1890's. His concern, stated in 1890, that ever increasing production would soon make necessary wider trade and markets, anticipated the somber, depression-ridden years of post-1893. Writing three years before Frederick Jackson Turner analyzed the disappearance of the American frontier, Mahan hinted its disappearance and pointed out the implications for America's future economic and political structure. He observed that the policies of the American government since 1865 had been "directed solely to what has been called the first link in the chain which makes sea power." But "the increase of home consumption . . . did not keep up with the increase of forth-putting and facility of distribution offered by steam." The United States would thus have to embark upon a new frontier, for "whether they will or no, Americans must now begin to look outward. The growing production of the country demands it. An increasing volume of public sentiment demands it." The theoretical and actual had met; the productive capacity of the United States, having finally grown too great for its continental container and having lost its landed frontier, had to turn to the sea, its omnipresent frontier. The mercantilists had viewed production as a faculty to be stimulated and consolidated in order to develop its full capabilities of pulling wealth into the country. But Mahan dealt with a productive complex which had been stimulated by the government for years and had been centralized and coordinated by corporate managers. He was now concerned with the problem of keeping this society ongoing without the problems of underemployment and resulting social upheavals.

Reversing the traditional American idea of the oceans as a barrier against European intrigue, Mahan compared the sea to "a great highway; or better, perhaps . . . a wide common, over which men pass in all directions." To traverse this "highway" a nation needed a merchant marine; Mahan made this the second part of his postulate. In his 1890 volume he expressed doubts whether a navy could be erected without the solid foundation of a carrying fleet. This, however, was one of the few times in the decade that Mahan emphasized the necessity of a merchant marine. As the 1890's progressed, he could look about him and conclude that in this respect his theory did not correspond to reality. Congress constructed a new battleship fleet, American businessmen focused their attention on foreign markets, the impetus for building an Isthmian canal accelerated, and Mahan himself became a prophet with honor in his own country. And all this occurred in spite of the minuteness of the American merchant marine.

Mahan's early theory had been misleading, for a nation no longer had to ship its goods in its own bottoms to become commercially prosperous. The exporting country only needed warships capable of protecting the carrying fleet, whether it be domestic or foreign. This was a crucial result of the industrial revolution; modern machinery and technological inventions had replaced the merchant marine as the process which determined the victors in the markets of the world. It is tempting to speculate that Mahan realized this, because after his initial outburst in 1890 he de-emphasized the merchant marine theme. But it is more probable that he neglected the middle link in his theory simply because he could see the third part (military sea power) becoming a reality without the second factor. In any case, this de-emphasis sharply differentiated Mahan's ideas from those of the early mercantilists. The latter not only were concerned about carrying their own goods, but encouraged their own nations to develop an entrepôt trade between foreign powers. When Mahan implicitly subordinated his merchant marine theme, he eliminated the central part of early mercantilist theory.

Most important, Mahan differed from the British and French mercantilists in the final part of his theory—the definition and purpose of colonies. The early writers wanted colonies as sources of raw materials, markets for surplus goods, and as areas for the settlement of a surplus or discontented population. They simply assumed the establishment of naval bases in these colonies. Mahan, however, separated these functions of colonies. They could serve "as outlets for the home products and as a nursery for commerce and shipping." He then stressed the second aspect (colonies as strategic naval bases) and set aside the first part (colonies as markets).

It is especially in this crucial area—the purpose of colonial possessions—that Mahan becomes so dissimilar to the mercantilists, but so representative of the special characteristics of American expansion in the 1890's. To Mahan, William McKinley, Theodore Roosevelt, and Henry Cabot Lodge, colonial possessions, as these men defined such possessions, served as stepping stones to the two great prizes: the Latin-American and Asian markets. This policy much less resembled traditional colonialism than it did the new financial and industrial expansion of the 1850–1914 period. These men did not envision "colonizing" either Latin America or Asia. They did want both to exploit these areas economically and give them (especially Asia) the benefits of western, Christian civilization. To do this, these expansionists needed strategic bases from which shipping lanes and interior interests in Asia and Latin America could be protected.

In outlining his tactics, Mahan first demanded that the United States build an Isthmian canal. This would be the channel through which the Atlantic coast could "compete with Europe, on equal terms as to distance, for the markets of eastern Asia" and the markets on the western coast of Latin America. He viewed Hawaii through the same lens. The islands, once in American hands, would not only offset British naval dominance in the Pacific, but, viewed in a positive way, be a major step in the "natural, necessary, irrepressible" American expansion into this western theater. But nothing better demonstrates Mahan's non-mercantilistic colonialism, strategic-bases philosophy than his view of the Philippines in 1898. As late as July, 1898, he still entertained doubts about annexing all the islands. He proposed to Lodge that the United States take only the Ladrones and Luzon (including, of course, the port of Manila), and allow Spain to keep the Carolines and the remainder of the Philippines. With the achievement of his double objectives of a battleship fleet and the occupation of strategic bases leading to the Asian and Latin-American markets, plus the writing of the Open-Door Notes to protect American commerce in China (Mahan actively advised John Hay while the State Department formulated the notes), the United States could repudiate once and for all a colonial empire in the mercantilist sense.

Mahan had actually supplied the rationale for the open-door philosophy several years before the State Department issued the notes. He foresaw the advantages which commercial expansion possessed over further landed expansion. Most important, perhaps, he believed that commercial expansion would not cause political upheaval. Using French policy in the eighteenth century as an abject example, Mahan condemned France for pursuing a policy of expansion through land warfare when it had outlets to the sea. He quickly pointed to the lesson:

A fair conclusion is, that States having a good seaboard . . . will find it to their advantage to seek prosperity and extension by the way of sea and of commerce, rather than in attempts to unsettle and modify existing political arrangements in countries where a more or less long possession of power has . . . created national allegiance or political ties.

Following these ideas to their conclusion, Mahan declared that, while financial and commercial control, rather than political, would lessen possible points of dispute, international conflict would not end. Here military sea power entered the theory, for "when a question arises of control over distant regions . . . it must ultimately be decided by naval power." Mahan emphasized that giant battleships, not commerce destroyers as American planners had earlier believed, would decide such conflicts, for only battleships could gain and maintain control of the sea. Mahan thus closed his circle: the foundation of an expansive policy is a nation's productive capacities that produce vast surpluses; these surpluses should preferably be sold in noncolonial areas in order to lessen political irritations; and sea power in the form of battleships enters the scheme to provide and protect lines of communication and to settle the conflicts which inevitably erupt from commercial rivalry, thus ensuring access to foreign markets for the surplus goods.

The policy makers and other influential Americans who embraced Mahan's teachings made them a central part of the expansionist ideology of the 1890's. Albert Shaw, a close friend of Lodge, Roosevelt, and Mahan, advanced the Captain's ideas through the widely read pages of his newly established *Review of Reviews.* Book reviewers in the most popular periodicals of the day warmly received Mahan's voluminous writings. Theodore Roosevelt, perhaps the most important of these reviewers, emphasized the Captain's basic ideas in the *Atlantic Monthly* and then put these ideas into practice as Assistant Secretary of the Navy in 1897–1898 and later as President. Mahan and Roosevelt were the closest of friends and could often be found in the company of Brooks Adams, John Hay, and Lodge. Congressmen paid homage by plagiarizing not only ideas but phrases and paragraphs from Mahan's works in order to substantiate their own arguments for expansion.

One of the more notable of Mahan's converts was Hilary Herbert, congressman from Alabama and then Secretary of the Navy in Cleveland's second administration. Herbert had been a devotee of small commerce-destroying cruisers, and deprecated both giant battleships and the training of men to operate these battleships in the newly established War College. After reading Mahan's work in 1893, Herbert reversed his opinion and saved the War College just as it was about to close its doors. More important, Mahan's books demonstrated to Herbert the superiority which a battleship fleet enjoyed over commerce-destroyers. By pushing through the naval appropriation acts of 1895 and 1896, Herbert can share with Benjamin Tracy the honor of being the founding father of the modern American navy. Mahan, in turn, can justly receive much of the credit for both Herbert's and Tracy's activities.

.   .   .

McKinley had had the choice of three policies which would have terminated the Cuban revolution. First, he could have let the Spanish forces and the insurgents fight until one or the other fell exhausted from the bloodshed and financial strain. During the struggle the United States could have administered food and medicine to the civilian population, a privilege which the Spanish agreed to allow in March, 1898. Second, the President could have demanded an armistice and Spanish assurances that negotiations over the summer would result in some solution which would pacify American feelings. That is to say, he could have followed Woodford's ideas. Third, McKinley could have demanded both an armistice and Spanish assurances that Cuba would become independent immediately. If Spain would not grant both of these conditions, American military intervention would result. The last was the course the President followed.

Each of these policy alternatives deserves a short analysis. For American policy makers, the first choice was the least acceptable of the three, but the United States did have to deal, nevertheless, with certain aspects of this policy. If Spain hoped to win such a conflict, she had to use both the carrot of an improved and attractive autonomy scheme and the stick of an increased and effective military force. Spain could have granted no amount of autonomy, short of complete independence, which would have satisfied the rebels, and whether Americans cared to admit it or not, they were at least partially responsible for this obstinacy on the part of the insurgents. The United States did attempt to stop filibustering expeditions, but a large number nevertheless reached Cuban shores. More important, when the Spanish Minister asked Day to disband the New York Junta, the financial taproot of the insurgent organization, the Assistant Secretary replied that "this was not possible under American law and in the present state of public feeling." Woodford had given the Spanish Queen the same reply in mid-January. It was perhaps at this point that Spain saw the last hopes for a negotiated peace begin to flicker away.

Seemingly unrelated actions by the United States gave boosts to the rebel cause. The sending of the "Maine," for instance, considerably heartened the rebels; they believed that the warship diverted Spanish attention and military power from insurgent forces. When the vessel exploded, the New York Junta released a statement which did not mourn the dead sailors as much as it mourned the sudden disappearance of American power in Havana harbor. The Junta interpreted the passage of the $50,-000,000 war appropriation measure during the first week of March as meaning either immediate war or the preparation for war. Under such conditions, it was not odd that the rebels were reluctant to compromise their objective of complete independence.

If the insurgents would not have accepted autonomy, no matter how liberal or attractive, then Spain might have hoped to suppress the rebels with outright force. To have done so, however, the Spanish government would have had to bring its army through the rainy season with few impairments, resume to a large extent the *reconcentrado* policies, and prevent all United States aid from reaching the rebels. The first objective would have been difficult, but the last two, if carried out, would have meant war with the United States. The State Department could not allow Spain to reimpose methods even faintly resembling Weyler's techniques, nor could the Department have allowed the searching of American vessels. McKinley and the American people hoped that Spain would stop the revolution, but they also insisted on taking from Spain the only tools with which that nation could deal with the Cubans.

Having found this first alternative impossible to accept, McKinley might have chosen a second approach: demand an armistice and ultimate pacification of the island, but attempt to achieve this peacefully over several months and with due respect for the sovereignty of Spain. This was the alternative Woodford [the American minister to Spain] hoped the administration would choose. He had reported during the two weeks before McKinley's message that the Spanish had given in time and time again on points which he had believed they could not afford to grant. In spite of the threat of revolution from the army, the Queen had granted a temporary truce. The American Minister continued to ask for more time to find a peaceful settlement. On April 11, the day the war message went to Congress, Woodford wrote the President, "To-day it is just possible that Moret and I have been right [in our pursuit of peace], but it is too soon to be jubilant." The American Minister sincerely believed that the negotiations during the period of truce could, with good faith on both the American and Spanish sides, result in Spain evacuating the island. This would have to be done slowly, however. No sovereign nation could be threatened with a time limit and uncompromising demands without fighting back. The fact that Spain would not grant McKinley's demand for immediate Cuban independence makes the Spanish-American War which began in April, 1898, by no means an inevitable conflict. Any conflict is inevitable once one proud and sovereign power, dealing with a similar power, decides to abandon the conference table and issue an ultimatum. The historical problem remains: which power took the initiative in setting the conditions that resulted in armed conflict, and were those conditions justified?

By April 10 McKinley had assumed an inflexible position. The President abjured this second alternative and demanded not only a truce, but a truce which would lead to a guarantee of immediate Cuban independence obtained with the aid of American mediation. He moreover demanded such a guarantee of independence before the Cortes or the Cuban parliament, the two groups which had the constitutional power to grant such independence, were to gather for their formal sessions.

The central question is, of course, why McKinley found himself in such a position on April 10 that only the third alternative was open to him. The President did not want war; he had been sincere and tireless in his efforts to maintain the peace. By mid-March, however, he was beginning to discover that, although he did not want war, he did want what only a war could provide: the disappearance of the terrible uncertainty in American political and economic life, and a solid basis from which to resume the building of the new American commercial empire. When the President made his demands, therefore, he made the ultimate de-

mands; as far as he was concerned, a six-month period of negotiations would not serve to temper the political and economic
problems in the United States, but only exacerbate them.

To say this is to raise another question: why did McKinley arrive at this position during mid-March? What were the factors
which limited the President's freedom of choice and policies at
this particular time? The standard interpretations of the war's
causes emphasize the yellow journals and a belligerent Congress. These were doubtlessly crucial factors in shaping the
course of American entry into the conflict, but they must be used
carefully. A first observation should be that Congress and the yellow press, which had been loudly urging intervention ever since
1895, did not make a maiden appearance in March, 1898; new elements had to enter the scene at that time to act as the catalysts
for McKinley's policy. Other facts should be noted regarding the
yellow press specifically. In areas where this press supposedly
was most important, such as New York City, no more than one-
third of the press could be considered sensational. The strongest
and most widespread prowar journalism apparently occurred in
the Midwest. But there were few yellow journals there. The papers that advocated war in this section did so for reasons other
than sensationalism; among these reasons were the influence of
the Cuban Junta and, perhaps most important, the belief that the
United States possessed important interests in the Caribbean
area which had to be protected. Finally, the yellow press obviously did not control the levers of American foreign policy.
McKinley held these, and he bitterly attacked the owners of the
sensational journals as "evil disposed . . . people." An interpretation stressing rabid journalism as a major cause of the war
should draw some link to illustrate how these journals reached
the White House or the State Department. To say that this influence was exerted through public opinion proves nothing; the next
problem is to demonstrate how much public opinion was governed by the yellow press, how much of this opinion was influenced by more sober factors, and which of these two branches of
opinion most influenced McKinley.

Congress was a hotbed of interventionist sentiment, but then it
had been so since 1895. The fact was the Congress had more
trouble handling McKinley than the President had handling Congress. The President had no fear of that body. He told Charles
Dawes during the critical days of February and March that if
Congress tried to adjourn he would call it back into session.

McKinley held Congress under control until the last two days of March, when the publication of the "Maine" investigation forced Thomas B. Reed, the passionately antiwar Speaker of the House, to surrender to the onslaughts of the rapidly increasing interventionist forces. As militants in Congress forced the moderates into full retreat, McKinley and Day were waiting in the White House for Spain's reply to the American ultimatum. And after the outbreak on March 31 McKinley reassumed control. On April 5 the Secretary of War, R. A. Alger, assured the President that several important senators had just informed him that "there will be no trouble about holding the Senate." When the President postponed his war message on April 5 in order to grant Fitzhugh Lee's request for more time, prowar congressmen went into a frenzy. During the weekend of April 8 and 9, they condemned the President, ridiculed Reed's impotence to hold back war, and threatened to declare war themselves. In fact, they did nearly everything except disobey McKinley's wishes that nothing be done until the following week. Nothing was done.

When the Senate threatened to overrule the President's orders that the war declaration exclude recognition of the Cuban insurgent government, McKinley whipped the doubters into line and forced the Senate to recede from its position. This was an all-out battle between the White House and a strong Senate faction. McKinley triumphed despite extremely strong pressure exerted by sincere American sentiment on behalf of immediate Cuban independence and despite the more crass material interests of the Junta's financial supporters and spokesmen. The President wanted to have a free hand in dealing with Cuba after the war, and Congress granted his wishes. Events on Capitol Hill may have been more colorful than those at the White House, but the latter, not the former, was the center of power in March and April, 1898.

Influences other than the yellow press or congressional belligerence were more important in shaping McKinley's position of April 11. Perhaps most important was the transformation of the opinion of many spokesmen for the business community who had formerly opposed war. If, as one journal declared, the McKinley administration, "more than any that have preceded it, sustains . . . close relations to the business interests of the country," then this change of business sentiment should not be discounted. This transformation brought important financial spokesmen, especially from the Northeast, into much the same position that had long been occupied by prointerventionist business groups and journals in the trans-Appalachian area. McKinley's decision to intervene placated many of the same business spokesmen whom he had satisfied throughout 1897 and January and February of 1898 by his refusal to declare war.

Five factors may be delineated which shaped this interventionist sentiment of the business community. First, some business journals emphasized the material advantages to be gained should Cuba become a part of the world in which the United States would enjoy, in the words of the New York *Commercial Advertiser,* "full freedom of development in the whole world's interest." The *Banker's Magazine* noted that "so many of our citizens are so involved in the commerce and productions of the island, that to protect these interests . . . the United States will have eventually to force the establishment of fair and reasonable government." The material damage suffered by investors in Cuba and by many merchants, manufacturers, exporters, and importers, as, for example, the groups which presented the February 10 petition to McKinley, forced these interests to advocate a solution which could be obtained only through force.

A second reason was the uncertainty that plagued the business community in mid-March. This uncertainty was increased by Proctor's powerful and influential speech and by the news that a Spanish torpedo-boat flotilla was sailing from Cadiz to Cuba. The uncertainty was exemplified by the sudden stagnation of trade on the New York Stock Exchange after March 17. Such an unpredictable economic basis could not provide the springboard for the type of overseas commercial empire that McKinley and numerous business spokesmen envisioned.

Third, by March many businessmen who had deprecated war on the ground that the United States Treasury did not possess adequate gold reserves began to realize that they had been arguing from false assumptions. The heavy exports of 1897 and the discoveries of gold in Alaska and Australia brought the yellow metal into the country in an ever widening stream. Private bankers had been preparing for war since 1897. *Banker's Magazine* summarized these developments: "Therefore, while not desiring war, it is apparent that the country now has an ample coin basis for sustaining the credit operations which a conflict would probably make necessary. In such a crisis the gold standard will prove a bulwark of confidence."

Fourth, antiwar sentiment lost much strength when the nation realized that it had nothing to fear from European intervention on the side of Spain. France and Russia, who were most sympathetic to the Spanish monarchy, were forced to devote their attention to the Far East. Neither of these nations wished to alienate the United States on the Cuban issue. More important, Americans happily realized that they had the support of Great Britain. The *rapprochement* which had occurred since the Venezuelan incident now paid dividends. On an official level, the British Foreign Office assured the State Department that nothing would be accomplished in the way of European intervention unless the United States requested such intervention. The British attitude made it easy for McKinley to deal with a joint European note of April 6 which asked for American moderation toward Spain. The President brushed off the request firmly but politely. On an unofficial level, American periodicals expressed appreciation of the British policy on Cuba, and some of the journals noted that a common Anglo-American approach was also desirable in Asia. The European reaction is interesting insofar as it evinces the continental powers' growing realization that the United States was rapidly becoming a major force in the world. But the European governments set no limits on American dealings with Spain. McKinley could take the initiative and make his demands with little concern for European reactions.

Finally, opposition to war melted away in some degree when the administration began to emphasize that the United States enjoyed military power much superior to that of Spain. One possible reason for McKinley's policies during the first two months of 1898 might have been his fear that the nation was not adequately prepared. As late as the weekend of March 25 the President worried over this inadequacy. But in late February and early March, especially after the $50,000,000 appropriation by Congress, the country's military strength developed rapidly. On March 13 the Philadelphia *Press* proclaimed that American naval power greatly exceeded that of the Spanish forces. By early April those who feared a Spanish bombardment of New York City were in the small minority. More representative were the views of Winthrop Chanler who wrote Lodge that if Spanish troops invaded New York "they would all be absorbed in the population . . . and engaged in selling oranges before they got as far as 14th Street."

As the words of McKinley's war message flew across the wires to Madrid, many business spokesmen who had opposed war had recently changed their minds, American military forces were rap-

idly growing more powerful, banks and the United States Treasury had secured themselves against the initial shocks of war,
and the European powers were divided among themselves and
preoccupied in the Far East. Business boomed after McKinley
signed the declaration of war. "With a hesitation so slight as to
amount almost to indifference," *Bradstreet's* reported on April
30, "the business community, relieved from the tension caused
by the incubus of doubt and uncertainty which so long controlled it, has stepped confidently forward to accept the situation
confronting it oweing to the changed conditions." "Unfavorable
circumstances . . . have hardly excited remark, while the stimulating effects have been so numerous and important as to surprise all but the most optimistic," this journal concluded. A new
type of American empire, temporarily clothed in armor, stepped
out on the international stage after a half century of preparation
to make its claim as one of the great world powers.

The Spanish-American War
and the Decision for Imperialism

Nationalist

*Some Nationalist historians do not attempt to defend America's decisions
for war and empire. Samuel Flagg Bemis considers actions taken to implement these decisions "the great aberration" and argues that, although
we did fight an unnecessary war and accumulate an empire, we quickly
repented and released most of our conquests. H. Wayne Morgan, professor of history at the University of Texas and biographer of McKinley,
argues otherwise in the following essay. He believes that the war was
justified, that it was the product of neither popular pressure nor of the
business elite, but the result of realistic and careful consideration by the
McKinley administration. He also maintains that, once in the war, the
United States had little alternative but to accept responsibility for the
Spanish colonies. Since our rule over those colonies was benevolent and
since we released most of them as soon as possible, he rejects the
charge that the United States is and was a rapaciously imperialist power.*

Why does Morgan believe that American intervention in Cuba was jus-

tified and necessary? What does he see as the role of economics, of strategy, of idealism, and of popular opinion in that decision? LaFeber and Kennan think the Spanish were willing to make sufficient concessions to avoid war. How does Morgan answer that contention? How does he justify the decision to keep the Philippines? What reasons does he offer for McKinley's decision? How do those reasons differ from those offered by Kennan and LaFeber?

America's Road to Empire: The War with Spain and Overseas Expansion

H. Wayne Morgan

The anti-autonomy riots in Havana of January 1898, the de Lome letter, and the *Maine* incident subtly but effectively turned American demands from Cuban autonomy to independence. It was now obvious to the administration that autonomy could not be instituted, and that it was not acceptable either to the Cubans or the American people. Spain must guarantee the final liberation of Cuba. The McKinley administration's historical reputation suf-

From H. Wayne Morgan, *America's Road to Empire: The War with Spain and Overseas Expansion*, 1965, pp. 49–62, 87–90, 96–97, 111–112. Reprinted by permission of John Wiley & Sons, Inc.

fered for the lack of clarity around the change in demands. But Spain understood the new policy, which was clarified on the war's eve. She continued to assume before the world, however, that autonomy could be implemented and would satisfy American demands. It was a false view, but it gave her the best of the historical argument.

To emphasize the stiffening American attitude, McKinley called Illinois' crusty Republican Representative Joseph G. "Uncle Joe" Cannon to the White House for a conference. He spoke briefly and sincerely with the powerful Cannon, outlining with many gestures of the hands, as he paced up and down the room, just what he thought Congress should do. He wanted both houses to be patient and not force his hand, but he also wanted patriotic support. He still did not think war was necessarily inevitable, but if it should come, the country ought to be better prepared. He sat down and wrote out on a piece of paper the title of a bill appropriating fifty million dollars for defense, to be used at his discretion. He handed the paper to Cannon. This would show the Spanish he meant business, and would pacify a good deal of American opinion. It would also give Congress something positive to do. He hoped it would be a bipartisan measure; it would be wise not to exclude the Democrats in case of either war or peace. Cannon spent the afternoon and evening conferring with colleagues. On March 9 the bill was law, passed to thunderous applause in the press and the courts of public and congressional opinion.

.   .   .

Public attention now turned to the elaborate report which the investigating commission was ready to send the President. The Spanish commission investigating the wrecked *Maine* reported that an internal accident destroyed the vessel, but American public opinion was in no mood to listen. The American court of inquiry reported that an external explosion sank the ship, assigning no blame. Most Americans would immediately assume that Spanish agents had planted a mine, without realizing that of all people involved, the Spanish had least to gain from such an incident. . . .

As the tension mounted in both capitals, Woodford finally admitted that hope of speedy action was illusory. He suggested that Washington insist bluntly on Spanish haste to show that "the United States means business and means it *now*. The Spanish mind is so ingrained with 'mananaism' that few Spaniards ever act until they have to act." Washington answered late in March, saying bluntly that the *Maine* incident could be arbitrated, as the Spanish had proposed; but "the general condition of affairs in Cuba" could not be tolerated any longer. The President finally set a deadline; April 15 would be "none too early for accomplishment of these purposes." He added an appendix that jolted Woodford: "It is proper that you should know that unless events otherwise indicate, the President having exhausted diplomatic agencies to secure peace in Cuba will lay the whole matter before Congress." Surely even the Spanish could see that meant war.

In the last days of March, McKinley entertained a long series of congressmen of all political persuasions, buying time and support from everyone he could impress. The pressure was such that he reluctantly agreed to send the relevant documents concerning Cuba to Congress if Spain did not act quickly. It was a last resort, which was not finally necessary.

. . . To the newspapers, discussion over guilt was academic. "Nine out of every ten American citizens doubtless believe firmly that the explosion which destroyed the *Maine* was the result of the cowardly Spanish conspiracy, and the Report of the Court of Inquiry will not tend to destroy that belief," trumpeted the Cleveland *Leader* on March 27. The Hearst press was even more rabid than usual, reveling in its own slogan: "Remember the *Maine* and to hell with Spain!"

For the first time the President was the target of violent public abuse. The widespread belief in his diplomacy and ability now began to crack. In Virginia a raging mob burned twin effigies of him and Hanna. McKinley's picture was hissed in theaters and torn from walls in some cities. Visitors to the Capitol saw jingoes sitting in the House and Senate galleries wrapped in American flags, and ladies who urged on their favorite demagogues with roses and smiles.

.   .   .

That tone now flavored all dispatches that went to Spain. As experts studied the commission's report [on the sinking of the Maine], Day cabled Woodford the President's last and most comprehensive plan, worked out in negotiation with congressional leaders and administration advisors. "A feeling of deliberation prevails in both houses of Congress," Day told Woodford, stretching the truth for diplomacy's sake, and outlined McKinley's plan: (1) Spain must freely grant an armistice to last until October, both sides to accept McKinley's good offices. (2) Spain would end reconcentration forever and undertake massive relief in Cuba. (3) If peace terms were not reached by October 1, McKinley would settle the Cuban problem as arbitrator. (4) If necessary, the President would approach the Cuban rebels directly for their participation in the plan if Spain first agreed. Implicit but not spelled out was the administration's central demand: Cuba must ultimately be independent. A mere cease-fire or suspension of hostilities would not be enough. The whole plan depended on speed.

This was an act of virtual desperation for McKinley, since the plan contained nothing new, except its half-stated insistence on Cuban independence; and Spain had refused to permit American intervention since the days of Grant and Fish. She could never reform the island by October 1, except by granting independence; at no time had she even entertained such an idea. The President probably knew this, but wished to make one last comprehensive effort for the sake of conscience and the historical record.

Both Woodford in Madrid and his superiors in Washington feared congressional opinion. Only a dramatic breakthrough in negotiations would satisfy either or both houses. As congressmen of both parties looked at Cuban intervention, its virtues grew. To the Democrats it would end the frustrations of domestic defeat with foreign victory. To the wavering Republicans it would remove the explosive issue from politics and save them from the steamroller of public clamor. To each party it seemed a unifying issue that would help win future elections. "I trust we shall escape without a war," Lodge wrote with tongue in cheek, "but if we should have war we will not hear much of the currency question in the elections." Congress always thought less of Spanish power than did the President. Senator Chandler snapped that any war with Spain would last between fifteen minutes and ninety days.

McKinley was certainly alive to the politics of the problem. He had already stretched his painfully built Republican coalition to the limit. If he resisted further, he might destroy his party and torpedo any future program of national development and international diplomacy. Though he did not say it, he knew of the feeling Senator Chandler expressed: "If [peace negotiations] had been prolonged the Republican party would have been divided, the

Democrats would have been united, nothing would have been done and our party would have been overwhelmed in November." It was pointless to quote Grover Cleveland to the effect that Congress might declare war but only the President could fight. If Congress declared war, what President would refuse to fight? Ugly scenes occurred at the White House and the State Department. An angry, cane-waving senator stormed into Day's office and pounded on the table. "By————!" he yelled, "Don't your President know where the war-declaring power is lodged? Well tell him, by————! that if he doesn't do something Congress will exercise the power and declare war in spite of him! He'll get run over and the party with him!" Would Congress have done so? It is history's question. The administration's lines were not quite broken; McKinley could rally Aldrich, Platt, Hanna, and other stalwarts. But what would it profit him if he fragmented the party in doing so?

There was infinite irony in reflecting that McKinley, among the most peace-loving of men, might be remembered chiefly as a war President. How bitter he must have felt at reflecting what had become of his hopeful beginning. And he also remembered something almost pathetic that Woodford once said in a dispatch from Madrid: ". . . you, as a soldier, know what war is, even when waged for the holiest of causes." The strain on him was obvious. His sleepless nights, long, hectic days, and endless worries cost him temper, nerves, and even affected his physical appearance.

Whatever his personal feelings, the processes of diplomacy now carried the President to the inevitable end. The last week of March brought a Spanish answer to American demands: yes, they would reform Cuba; yes, they would relieve reconcentration; yes, they would grant a cease-fire, but only if the rebels asked first; no, they would not accept presidential mediation. Woodford reported that the cabinet would confer on March 31, presumably to make a comprehensive reply to the President's demands. The message, which trickled over the cables in the small hours of March 31 and April 1, was not promising. Spain offered to arbitrate the *Maine* incident; to undertake relief; to accept American relief assistance; and to turn the Cuban problem over to the insular parliament, which would meet in Havana in May. But she would not accept mediation; there was no hint of granting Cuban independence. Woodford's disappointment shone through his dispatch. This was "the ultimate limit to which [Spain] can go in the way of concessions," but it was not enough. It did not immediately end reconcentration; promised only further delay on autonomy in a wrangling parliament; and was couched in such insulting tones that Long thought it ended McKinley's peace policy.

Facing the critical likelihood of war, Spain still showed the un-reality, confusion, and cross-purposes that always characterized her Cuban policy. Officials in the Colonial Office and even some men around Premier Sagasta admitted that Cuba was lost. They only wished to lose her in an honorable, face-saving manner. But Spanish domestic politics, national pride, and insular interests in Cuba forbade such a negotiated settlement. Court circles, con-servative politicians, and jingoistic nationalists preferred honor-able defeat in war to any surrender to American demands. Wood-ford was told that Maria Christina herself had said bluntly "that she wished to hand over his patrimony unimpaired to her son when he should reach his majority; and that she would prefer to abdicate her regency and return to her Austrian home rather than be the instrument of ceding or parting with any of Spain's colonies." Though a desire to end the Cuban problem peacefully had finally penetrated a small number of Spanish officials, no sig-nificant Spanish policy makers ever considered acceding to American demands. There was simply no way for a Spanish gov-ernment to solve the problem peacefully and remain in power or have any political future. "They know that Cuba is lost," Wood-ford cabled home, but he feared the ministry would seek honor-able defeat in war.

On April 4 Day delivered the expected answer which showed that American intervention was inevitable, barring total Spanish surrender:

We have received today from the Spanish Ministry a copy of the Manifesto of the Autonomy Government. It is not armistice. It proves to be an appeal by the Autonomy Government of Cuba urging the insurgents to lay down their arms and to join with the autonomy party in building up the new schemes of home rule. It is simply an invitation to the insurgents to sub-mit, in which event the autonomy government, likewise suspending hostilities, is prepared to consider what expansion, if any, of the decreed home-rule scheme is necessary or practicable. It need scarcely be pointed out that this is a very different thing from an offered armistice.

Woodford could only ask for time, with the familiar suggestion that he might work out something.

McKinley had no more time, and no more hope for a negotiated settlement. He set April 6 as the date his war message would go to Congress, but expectant crowds at the Capitol that day left disappointed. The President delayed until Lee evacuated American citizens in Cuba. Angry congressmen who crowded into his office demanding war met a rare show of presidential wrath. Calling his secretary, McKinley ordered the message locked in the White House safe until he was ready to send it.

On April 6 Woodford reported that the Spanish would consider papal intervention, and begged for a short delay. On that same day the ministers of the Great Powers arrived in McKinley's office to make a last gesture toward averting war. The President received the formal delegation in the Blue Room, gratefully noting Sir Julian Pauncefote, dean of the diplomatic corps, who represented an England widely known to favor American policies. Spain had conducted a long and complicated search for support among her continental neighbors, but despite anti-Americanism at some courts, no power was willing to act directly against either English or American interests. When the august delegation read its little speech deploring the coming conflict, McKinley tactfully read one of his own. They listened attentively and then withdrew. The New York *World* parodied the scene the next day. "We hope for humanity's sake you will not go to war," said the diplomats. "We hope if we go to war you will understand that it is for humanity's sake," McKinley replied.

Then the cables brought what appeared to be a fresh break on April 9: Spain would suspend hostilities in Cuba and extend the promises of reform, acting on the advice of the pope. Did it change anything? "I hope that nothing will now be done to humiliate Spain," Woodford urged in an accompanying dispatch, "as I am satisfied that the present Government is going and is loyally going to go as fast and as far as it can. With your power of action sufficiently free you will win the fight on your own lines." A quick talk with Lodge, Senator Aldrich, and others convinced McKinley that the answer was not sufficient. Events had passed them all by; it seemed doubtful now that such an armistice could be enforced. It would only prolong an intolerable situation. McKinley appended the last Spanish note to his war message and transmitted both to Congress on April 11, making it clear that he no longer believed in Spain's ability to end the Cuban problem peacefully:

The long trial has proved that the object for which Spain has waged the war cannot be attained. The fire of insurrection may flame or may smolder with varying seasons, but it has not been and it is plain that it cannot be extinguished by present methods. The only hope of relief and repose from a condition which can no longer be endured is the enforced pacification of Cuba. In the name of humanity, in the name of civilization, in behalf of endangered American interests which give us the right and the duty to speak and to act, the war in Cuba must stop.

And so it ended. Some said he should have accepted the final Spanish offer, since it surrendered to American demands. But it was a specious "surrender." It spurned American mediation or control of the process of suspending hostilities. It offered no genuine or enforceable program either to pacify Cuba or grant the island autonomy. It said nothing of ultimate Cuban independence, now the basic American demand. When Day asked the Spanish Minister if these last-minute concessions implied ultimate Cuban independence, he answered with a single word: "No." To assume that this cease-fire promised a peaceful long-term settlement was an act of faith which nothing in Spain's past diplomacy or present capabilities warranted. The measure of its hollowness lay in the failure even of McKinley's opponents to take it seriously. No substantial element of the press or Congress suggested that it marked a path to peace. The President no longer believed that Spain could carry out any promises she made. No historical evidence shows that he was wrong. Only two solutions were now possible: the war might continue indefinitely in Cuba, or the United States could intervene and expel Spain, reform the island, and end the issue once and for all. There was no middle ground. If McKinley delayed, his party would be defeated in the November elections. With jingoes packing both houses, an aroused press, and a people favoring war, conflict would come. But that entered into the President's thinking less than the final realization that the ideas he had hoped to implement peacefully could now be achieved only by force.

What went wrong? What ruined the President's painfully pursued hope of a peaceful settlement? The real fault in McKinley's diplomacy was not a lack of consistency or courage, but of imagination and alternatives. He sought peace by the only means available, threatening war, and continued Cleveland's policy of pressuring Spain, gambling that she would give way rather than face a war she could only lose. The basic problem was a lack of alternatives to intervention.

How easy it is to argue with all the textbooks that an addition to the President's spine would have averted the conflict, or that had Cleveland been President there would have been no war. The diplomacy of the two men was similar, but the conditions in which they worked greatly differed. Cleveland did not face the de Lome letter, the *Maine* incident, or the failure of autonomy; nor was the Cuban issue ablaze in the press and Congress as much as under McKinley.

McKinley's methods differed from Cleveland's, for he was more flexible in his approach and more responsible to his critics and supporters alike. But he did not "surrender" to public opinion. He merely accepted as inevitable what he had feared all along; intervention was necessary to free Cuba and to attain America's diplomatic and economic goals in the hemisphere. The chief personal weakness of his diplomacy was his silence. Fearful of being misunderstood or inflaming the issue, he remained silent during the whole long crisis. Had he defined his position publicly in 1897, and certainly in the great crises of 1898, he might have rallied some added public opinion to his side. He could not have prevented the war, but he could have clarified and justified his own record.

A bolder and more vigorous mind might have cut through the tedium of diplomacy with a striking idea to move ahead of both the Spanish and the Cuban rebels. McKinley might have called for an international meeting between his government and that of Spain, at which a settlement could at least have been proposed. But American public opinion would never have tolerated such a summit conference. It would have created more problems than it solved. What, for example, would be the Cubans' status at such a conference? Would not both Spain and the United States insist upon an agenda, consuming endless time, thus aiding Spain's policy of inaction? Could an award made at such a conference have been justified to the people of Spain, Cuba, or the United States? Probably not. In any event, McKinley was not the man to set such a startling precedent in American diplomacy. He might have served Spain with an ultimatum, but that would merely have accelerated war's arrival. He might have quietly asked the Powers to pressure Spain, but they were already more sympathetic to her than the United States. American public opinion would never have tolerated such an abandonment of freedom of action. He might have called for an investigation in Cuba by an international commission, its judgment to be final. But who involved would have agreed to such a commission, much less accepted its findings? All such suggestions seem unreal when set in their late nineteenth-century context.

What policy might have saved the peace? Inaction was impossible, and whatever McKinley did offended some strong body of opinion. If he could have conducted his policy alone; if Spain had been more amenable to rapid reform; if the Cubans had not been so irksome and had no influence in Congress and the press; if the American people had been more patient—the "ifs" mount up, showing the bleakness of the President's task. The problem was old, fraught with hidden complexities and unseen contingencies. If there be blame for the war, it should rest fairly with everyone concerned: the Spanish and Cubans, the American people and press, and the diplomatic policies of Cleveland and McKinley.

McKinley thus accepted the responsibilities of intervening in Cuba. Humanitarian desires to relieve the island's suffering, to make it free, and to establish a Latin-American democracy were uppermost in his own mind. Americans of a later generation will understand these motives. But the administration and influential blocs of public opinion also wanted to eliminate Spain from the New World. Future American influence in the Caribbean and all of Latin America required a free Cuba. Strategic interest in a two-ocean Navy, and an Isthmian canal unthreatened by a Spanish Cuba, figured in the minds of military and diplomatic planners. Rehabilitation of the Cuban economy and future trade with the island certainly moved many men.

.   .   .

McKinley lacked no advisors that hot summer. Nearly everyone who visited him offered a solution to the Philippine problem. Trends were already evident in many circles. Missionary elements wanted to take the islands and save them for Christianity, conveniently forgetting that they were in large part already Roman Catholic. Pride stirred many newspapers and politicians to retention as a matter of principle; who would now surrender the war's legacy? Though sentiment in the business community was blurred, more and more business spokesmen urged acquisition of the islands as a stepping stone to the supposedly lucrative Oriental trade. By October many businessmen seemed ready to take the islands on economic grounds.

A potentially tense problem confronted the peacemakers in the United States as they devised a course of action toward the Philippines. Foreign ships still lingered in Manila Bay, and intelligence reports from American embassies in Europe indicated a strong interest in many chancelleries over the islands' fate. If the United States did not take them, who would? Could the benevolent Americans return the Philippines to Spain, only to have them fall to Japan or Germany from Spain's feeble grasp? At home the expansionist press did not lessen these fears, and even Senator Hanna modified his doubts about expansion by remarking: "Hoar is crazy. He thinks Germany is just fooling." The Powers would not have risked a war with the United States over the islands, and were never as hostile to American ideas and actions as Americans thought. But was it not logical to assume that the Philippines would pass by default to a hostile nation if the United States refused them? That would be both economically and militarily unwise. In view of all the foreign interest in the Philippines, as the President said in his annual message of 1899, the country could not "fling them, a golden apple of discord, among the rival powers."

If the news from abroad fortified the President's desire to retain all the islands, that from home solidified it. While the war raged, McKinley wrote significantly on a scrap of paper: "While we are conducting war and until its conclusion we must keep all we get; when the war is over we must keep what we want." He digested all the intelligence reports and saw confirmation for his belief in many quarters. As early as July, 43 per cent of some sixty-five newspapers polled on the question favored acquiring empire; a mere quarter were undecided, while roughly a third were opposed.

.   .   .

What did the President think? He maintained his silence, listening rather than talking, carefully steering men toward the position his own acts had long since outlined. Allowing men to think they influenced him was his oldest talent, and one which had repaid its use many times in his political career. He followed it once more, listening to Lodge talk of empire and international power, assuring him in noncommittal tones that it was an interesting point. But as early as May, though he thought McKinley was "a little timid," Lodge convinced himself and his powerful friends that the President was in their camp. "I think his imagination is touched by the situation, and I think he grasps it fully."

The President had more to worry about and more to reinforce

his silence than his visitors knew. His chief worry focused not in Washington or Madrid, but in distant Manila, where confusion and delay heightened Aguinaldo's suspicions about American designs on his homeland. Would the natives oppose American acquisition, or would they be content as wards of their liberators? No one in Washington could be very sure, for military and diplomatic intelligence reports were confused, often inaccurate, and slow. The first military commanders on the scene thought that conservative Filipinos would welcome American rule if it brought peace and commercial prosperity. The insurgents, they insisted, were only a vocal minority, commanding no appreciable respect among the population. The archipelago consisted of thousands of islands and hundreds of tribes of varying states of civilization, religion, and well-being. Aguinaldo could not presume to speak for them all; his "Republic" was a house of cards.

But the complications were endless. In the year between December 1897 and December 1898, dozens of emissaries passed between Aguinaldo and the Americans. There was no doubt that many American diplomatic agents in effect promised the Filipinos that the Americans would free them. If they did not promise outright independence in return for rebel cooperation in ousting the Spanish, they implied it. That the American government always sternly forbade such an understanding made it no less real to those on either side who wanted to believe it.

Aguinaldo often did seem comical. His childish preoccupation with titles and etiquette obscured for many his talents as a leader. "They are big children whom one must treat as little ones," one correspondent wrote McKinley in words he must have rued a year later. The military, though naturally suspicious of any potential opponent, tended to brush aside Filipino pretentions to power. Though singularly opaque in his opinions, Dewey seemed to feel the islanders never wanted independence and would not oppose American rule.

Seeking to clarify his own situation, Aguinaldo sent a trusted advisor, Felipe Agoncillo, to Washington to ask McKinley personally just what his administration intended to do. On October 1 he met the President in his office. McKinley listened to a long recital of Filipino grievances against Spain, delivered tediously through an interpreter. Time passed slowly and the President shifted restlessly in his chair. He made no response to Agoncillo's talk of independence. When he had finished, McKinley tactfully suggested that he leave a copy of his speech which he could study at his leisure. Ten prosy-points resulted, and State Department officials took the memorandum from the little brown man with the chilly injunction that this did not imply recognition of his theoretical government.

.   .   .

. . . While the commissioners talked in Paris, and while he toured the country and then heard advice in Washington, he had weighed both his alternatives and his support. The choices were not happy ones. The people would never leave the islands to Spain. Taking just one island would merely deepen the problem, for divided sovereignty could be worse than no sovereignty. Proclaiming the islands autonomous under American authority was a makeshift which the President rejected, since it implied a shadow responsibility without power to control events in the islands. The only choice open was to take all the islands.

On paper, it was a prosaic decision, but it was not without its drama, as McKinley later revealed. With uncharacteristic self-revelation he told a group of ministers how he had reached his decision. "I have been criticized a good deal about the Philippines, but don't deserve it," he said. He explained that the islands had come as "a gift from the Gods" and outlined his dilemma and alternatives during the summer and fall of 1898. He had frankly thought at first of retaining only a part of the islands. He sought help from all parties but got little support. He was a deeply religious man. After much prayer and thought, it came to him one evening that he had four choices: (1) he could not return the islands to Spain, "that would be cowardly and dishonorable"; (2) he could not turn them over to another power, for "that would be bad business and discreditable"; (3) he could not leave them to themselves, for anarchy and bloodshed would follow in the wake of native ignorance and inability to govern; and (4) so "there was nothing left for us to do but to take them all, and to educate the Filipinos, and uplift and civilize and Christianize them, and by God's grace do the very best we could by them, as our fellowmen for whom Christ also died." His belief in the rightness of this course confirmed the choice.

What the ministers thought of this remarkable statement, they did not say. A later generation, not knowing McKinley's sincere Christianity, finds it easy to scoff. God, they note, was very clear that night. It is tempting to credit McKinley rather than the Deity with the decision, which is doubtless true. Few of the President's statements reveal so well his thought process and the forces he took into consideration. The statement is a classic outline of his alternatives, but McKinley prefaced them with a disingenuous explanation of how the islands came to the United States. He told many people that he had never wanted them. Yet the suspicion lingers that he knew the train of events Dewey's arrival in Manila Bay would set in motion. No man in politics as long as he could have thought otherwise. Acquisition of the islands was not an innovation; it merely helped confirm the fact of American imperial and economic and political interests in the Orient. Mixed motives produced the demand for the islands: duty to the Filipinos, fear of foreign control, the glittering prospects of trade and politics in the lucrative Eastern markets, and a strong feeling of destiny combined to make acquisition not merely logical but inevitable. Although he was not an emotional man, McKinley found the prospects of American expansion satisfying. In the summer of 1899, he told friends at his home in Ohio that "one of the best things we ever did was to insist upon taking the Philippines and not a coaling station or an island, for if we had done the latter we would have been the laughing stock of the world."

Did he and fellow expansionists understand the only half-hidden prospect of war in the Philippines, the enormous costs of empire, or the cold fact that much of their hope for Oriental trade would prove illusory? Probably not, for they were at the mercy of often erroneous information as well as hard events. To most expansionists, these considerations were not prohibitive. They were willing to risk immediate and temporary costs, believing that long-term results would repay them. America must be great, even if it meant sacrifice.

.   .   .

EPILOGUE

In the few years that followed the Spanish-American War, Americans often learned more than they cared to know about the problems of empire. They realized with bewildering suddenness that greatness brought unseen responsibilities, and that the status of a world power carried with it grave threats and expenses. The bitter fight over accepting the treaty in 1899 merely symbolized a deep division in American attitudes toward foreign responsibilities.

.   .   .

But the nation never abandoned empire. Nor did policy makers forget the high charge with which they acquired empire. "I cannot for the life of me see any contradiction between desiring liberty and peace here and desiring to establish them in the Philippines," John Hay wrote a critic. The war's end in the Philippines in 1902 brought peace to the islands, and a modicum of self-government and satisfaction among both the natives and their American rulers. In the half century that followed the United States was true to its promise, and in 1946 the Philippine Republic redeemed that hope of independence. Progress and innovation, success and plenty in the islands never followed any predictable course, but in retrospect the American colonial policy has much to recommend it. Compared to that of other nations, its basic altruism and success is obvious.

seven
The Open Door and American Policy in the Orient

Nationalist

Nationalist historians see the Open Door policy as another of those doctrines that combine American idealism with a realistic appreciation of the nation's interests. The Open Door helped maintain the territorial integrity of China against the rapaciousness of colonialism. Germany, Japan, and Russia were all warned against carving China into colonial domains. At the same time, such a policy protected American interests. The United States had neither the power nor the desire to share in the spoils of such a colonial division, but it did want to share in the markets of a nation containing nearly a fifth of the world's population. The Open Door policy aimed at providing the United States with just such an opportunity.

Tyler Dennett is the author of a biography of John Hay, as well as of the book from which the following essay is taken.

Americans in Eastern Asia

Tyler Dennett

OVERTURES FOR AN ALLIANCE

When the famous Hay notes of September 6, 1899 are isolated from the details of the international situation in which they were launched they lose much of their significance. As a definition of policy on the part of the United States we may think of them as the answer of the American Government to certain informal proposals from British sources which had invited an alliance of three or four powers for purposes very similar to those which were eventually expressed in the Anglo-Japanese alliance of 1902.

An Anglo-Japanese alliance was no new idea even in 1899. British writers had been proposing such a relationship intermittently for a quarter of a century. The steady advance of Japan had convinced many even before 1880 that the assumption of British foreign policy that Japan was a weak and negligible quantity while China was the only nation in the Far East worth cultivating, was erroneous.

The abrupt change of attitude on Japanese treaty revision in 1886 was an indication of changing British policy, but it was so little marked that until the outbreak of the war in 1894 Japan suspected that England was in secret alliance with China. When it became clear that there was no such pact Japanese statesmen would appear to have begun seriously to consider the possibility of some sort of an Anglo-Japanese convention. This was fully in line with the policy which had been suggested by Lord Hotta in 1858 and by Viscount Tani in 1887. The Japanese halted between an alliance with Russia and one with England. On the whole Japan had less to forgive if she chose Russia, but she also would have more to fear.

A new impetus to the discussion was given by the visit of Lord Charles Beresford, representing the Associated Chambers of Commerce of Great Britain, to China and Japan in the winter of

From Tyler Dennett, *Americans in Eastern Asia* (The Macmillan Company, 1922), pp. 640–654, 656–658. Reprinted by permission of Barnes & Noble, Inc.

1898–9. Both in China and in Japan in public addresses Lord Beresford developed at length the idea that the open door in China could not be maintained in the face of the opposition of France and Russia unless there was a combination of powers which were willing to fight to keep it open. Beresford proposed an elaborately devised scheme for the creation of a police force in China in which Chinese troops would be directed by British, German, Japanese and American military instructors. The open door, he thought, would be of little use "unless the room inside is in order." The proposed police force would operate in much the same way as the Ever-Victorious Army under Ward and Gordon had aided in the suppression of the Taiping Rebellion, but Beresford's plan would have involved placing the Chinese troops under foreign control. "Why," he asked in Japan, "should not the Japanese officers try to put the Chinese army in order, on the understanding that China will keep the door open? . . . I believe I personally was the first public man in England that ventured to suggest that what would be for the interest of your country and ours would be an alliance between the Empire of the West and the Empire of the East. (*Applause*.)"

The Beresford speeches were an exercise in diplomatic kite-flying. It was officially denied in Parliament that he was speaking in any other capacity than as a representative of the Chambers of Commerce, but it is to be noted that early in 1898, before Beresford departed from England, Joseph Chamberlain and others had supported a proposal for an alliance of Great Britain with both Germany and the United States. This semi-official proposal reached the form of actual conversations with the German ambassador in London and was even taken up officially with Mr. Hay. Lord Beresford returned from the Far East by way of America where he made many speeches in the early part of 1899. That the Beresford proposals as outlined in China and Japan found their way to President McKinley, Secretary Hay and Mr. Rockhill, there can be little doubt.

The Beresford plan accomplished nothing except the creation of a rumor that the Department of State had made a "secret alliance with England." How utterly baseless this rumor was ought to have been apparent when in April, 1899, Great Britain entered into a convention with Russia by which the two powers agreed to respect each other's spheres of influence in the Yangtze Valley and outside the Great Wall, respectively. This agreement was, in effect, a certificate of title granted by each to the other for special privileges in a very large part of the Chinese Empire. A similar agreement between Germany and England had been made the preceding year. Affairs in China were daily becoming more complicated and each new agreement was inimical to the United States as well as to China. It was quite true that England would have liked to save China for open trade but British diplomacy had no other resource than the alliance. British commerce was far better off with the existing low Chinese tariffs and an open door to the entire trade than it would have been with a part of China under exclusive British control and the other fragments closed to free commercial intercourse, but England apparently felt that she must fight fire with fire. If England could not rely upon the support of the United States, and apparently she could not, she was likely to adopt a policy in China which would be as objectionable to the United States as were the policies of Russia, France and Germany. For America to ignore the British calls for help and at the same time to offer no substitute for an alliance was to drive England still farther along towards the partition of China and render more certain the dismemberment of the Empire.

The choice before the United States in 1899 was just what it had been in the fifties: cooperation with Great Britain, or independent action. To reject an alliance and offer nothing in its place was a purely negative policy which only increased the difficulties and pitted the United States against not one, but all of the other powers. It is a significant fact that the rejection of the offer of an alliance in 1857 had accomplished nothing for China and had resulted in the eclipse of American prestige. In the settlement at Tientsin in 1858 the United States had no influence. Otherwise the Americans might have exercised a restraint upon the dictatorial and ruthless Lord Elgin. Again, in Japan the retirement of the United States from a cordial cooperation with England had resulted in the elimination of American influence in the final treaty revision. What it had accomplished for Japan might have been obtained by other means; it had been costly to the United States. So now in 1899 the United States was in grave danger of complete elimination from influence in China. The choice was really between cooperation with such powers as had similar interests and exercising upon them as much of a restraining influence as a powerful ally always possesses, or futilely opposing the entire company of the powers.

JOHN HAY AND THE OPEN-DOOR NOTES

England wanted an alliance. It is unlikely that Japan would have hesitated to join. Probably John Hay, had he been at liberty to make a perfectly free choice, would have favored it, although the Beresford plan was in its details open to the gravest of objections. Beresford's plan would have driven the Chinese into the arms of Russia and provoked a war terrible to contemplate. But an alliance to protect China rather than to destroy her had much to commend it. Those who talk so glibly about the superlative advantages of independent action in American foreign relations cannot bring to the support of their arguments any large array of facts gathered from American relations with the East since 1899. It seems highly probable that an alliance of Great Britain, Japan and the United States at that time in support of a common policy in China, such as Mr. Hay could have defined and the other powers would have accepted, would have been vastly preferable to the Anglo-Japanese alliance of 1902 which would have been rendered unnecessary.

The peculiar contribution of Hay at this critical moment was not the *invention* of the open door policy, for that was as old as our relations with China, but the directing of a diplomatic technique by which the open door could, in a measure, be guaranteed without actual resort to either force or alliances. It was not an adequate measure but it is difficult to see how any more effective measure could have been devised under the circumstances. Two factors contributing to the success of Hay's efforts were: the recent military successes of the United States and the presence in the East of a large expeditionary force with large reserves in the United States; and the natural identity of British, Japanese, and possibly German, interests in China. Although no shadow of treaty engagements existed, a certain amount of "give-and-take" had been going on between Japan, England and the United States for several months. The United States had declined to intervene in Korea after the murder of the queen, and had recalled an anti-Japanese American representative; Japan had withdrawn her protests at the annexation of Hawaii; England had stood by the United States in the Spanish-American War; and now the American Government was making the utmost effort to maintain the strictest neutrality in the Boer War in the face of no inconsiderable anti-British and pro-Boer American sentiment.

The Hay-Pauncefote treaty was in process of negotiation, and England had expressed willingness to make concessions to promote the construction of an American, rather than an Anglo-American Isthmian canal. In a word, the United States was now well embarked again upon a cooperative policy like that of Seward's.

But John Hay was a very different type of man from William H. Seward, and when he turned to the Chinese question he found the model not in Seward's bellicose policy in Japan but in the more direct, straightforward, irenic and independent course of Anson Burlingame, who had set out to save China from the rapacity of the powers by agreement. On September 6, 1899, Hay instructed the American representatives in London, Berlin and St. Petersburg (Joseph H. Choate, Andrew D. White and Charlemagne Tower, respectively) to approach the governments to which they were accredited with similar though not identic propositions concerning commercial rights in China. He pointed to the various verbal or written statements which had already been made by each power respecting freedom of trade for all nations on equal terms and asked for "formal declarations" to the following effect:

First. [That it] Will in no wise interfere with any treaty port or vested interest within any so-called 'sphere of influence' or leased territory it may have in China.

Second. That the Chinese tariff of the time being shall apply to all merchandise landed or shipped to all such ports as are within said 'spheres of interest' (unless they be 'free ports') no matter to what nationality it may belong, and that duties so leviable shall be collected by the Chinese Government.

Third. That it will levy no higher harbor dues on vessels of another nationality frequenting any port in such 'sphere' than shall be levied on vessels of their own nationality, and no higher railroad charges over lines built, controlled, or operated within its 'sphere' on merchandise belonging to citizens or subjects of other nationalities transported through such 'sphere' than shall be levied on similar merchandise belonging to its own nationals, transported over equal distances.

The propositions received immediate attention. The proposals were not entirely acceptable to any of the powers addressed. Even England wished to have exceptions made to meet the peculiar conditions of her own interests. It is notable that although the notes contemplated the application of the declaration to all leased territory, Lord Salisbury excluded the newly leased area at Kowloon from his assent. Great Britain really regarded this land as for all practical purposes a part of the ceded territory of Hongkong. It had been taken in the form of a lease rather than as a cession in order that Germany, Russia and France might not have precedent for transmuting their respective leases into actual cessions of territory. With this single, and in principle not unimportant exception, England agreed to the declaration (November 30). Germany stated (December 4) that she "would raise no objection" if the other powers agreed. France, which was approached November 22, replied December 16. Russia gave a very evasive declaration two days later. Japan and Italy, which were approached after the other powers, agreed promptly December 26 and January 7, respectively. The news of the negotiations was released to the press January 3, 1900.

WHAT WAS OBTAINED?

What had been obtained? Not so much as is popularly supposed. The United States had not secured more than already accrued to it under the "most-favored-nation" clauses in the treaties. The preferential railway and mining privileges had in no way been disturbed. Although the United States expressly stipulated that it did not recognize the spheres of influence the replies to the notes had in each case afforded an opportunity of reaffirming that there were such spheres. There remained no good harbor on the entire coast of China where the American Government could have leased a port had it so desired. On March 20, 1900, Secretary Hay announced that he regarded as "final and definitive" the declarations of the several powers that the open door would be maintained and that China would continue to collect the customs and therefore exercise the rights of sovereignty in the sphere of influence, but as a matter of fact only the partition of the Empire had been halted. The Hay notes, which are believed to have been drafted by Rockhill, were as significant in their omissions as in their contents. By their omissions they marked virtual surrenders which the American traders in the forties and fifties would probably have contemplated with little satisfaction. These notes have been popularly mislabeled. They did not secure a completely open door. But they did avert the immediate partition of the Empire, for the Powers assented to the recognition of the sovereign tax-collecting rights of China. They also averted the accomplishment of any scheme of foreign-officered police such as Lord Beresford had proposed.

The Hay notes may be best appreciated when they are regarded as a purely temporary expedient to meet a specific situation. As such they were a success. As a permanent measure they are less to be commended for they did not secure the open door as had been hoped and they did not avert further threatening engagements among the powers, notably the Anglo-Japanese Alliance. The United States had, in fact, missed a great opportunity to serve both its own interests and those of China, but the failure cannot be ascribed to John Hay.

The open door policy has become so much a phrase to conjure with in American politics that a definition of it as it was in 1899 is in order. Based on sixty years of history and on the circumstances as well as the text of the notes the definition was as follows: The United States still adhered to the policy, to which Seward alone had made exception, of independent rather than allied action. This independence was not, however, to preclude cooperation. The American Government relinquished the right to lease a port in China like Kiaochow or Port Arthur for all the good ports were either leased or preempted by non-alienation agreements. The United States was making no specific demand for the open door for investments; there was not enough American money seeking investment to make it worth while to quarrel about the preferential rights to construct railways or operate mines which had already been given to the other powers. The United States merely demanded an open door for trade in that part of China in which American merchants were already interested, viz., the area westward from Kwangtung on the South to Manchuria on the North. As for Korea, the United States was not politically or commercially interested. And as for those parts of the traditional Chinese Empire in the extreme south where France had already carved out an empire, or along the Amur where Russia had begun the partition of China in 1860, the United States had never murmured a protest.

What the American Government would have done had the powers withheld assent from the Hay proposals is a speculative, yet interesting and important question. It seems clear that the United States would not have taken up arms either to enforce assent to the open door policy, or to prevent the partition of the Empire. On the other hand, had the dismemberment of China been started, there would have been a very strong sentiment in the

United States against remaining aloof from the division of the spoils. Considering what John Hay had to work with, and what he had to work against, his must be regarded as, if not a famous victory, then at least an important diplomatic coup. The United States had not secured a great deal, as the next score of years revealed, but what it had obtained cost nothing, was accompanied by the assumption of no obligations, and was in return for no actual concessions.

. . .

THE BOXER INSURRECTION

The disturbances in China which culminated in the Boxer affair had been approaching for many years. For three quarters of a century the alien Manchu dynasty had been losing the loyalty and confidence of the Chinese people. The Chinese entertained no special dislike for the Manchus as aliens or as conquerors, but the corruption and weakness of their government made them objectionable as rulers.

. . .

The powers sustained the Manchu government not because they respected it, but because they did not dare to take the risk of permitting successful revolution which would have resulted either in the separation of the Empire into fragments, or the establishment of some new vigorous central authority which, while restoring order and promoting the development of the country, would likewise have been able to set up an effective opposition to the encroachment of the powers. To the latter it was most profitable to sustain a weak government which they could intimidate and control. The policy of the foreign governments was to crowd the Chinese to a compliance with every foreign demand, but to stop just short of creating the causes for successful revolution. A weak, disintegrating China made possible the continuance of extraterritoriality, an absurdly low tariff, and a hundred kindred privileges such as the Japanese, who were eluding the grasp of the powers, were more and more able to escape. Probably the most effective ally of China was the mutual jealousies of the powers.

. . .

The weakness of the Empire, the growing ambitions of Japan, the political rivalries of Europe and the overflowing coffers of European money-lenders, created conditions favorable for a stampede among the powers. The leasing of ports, the acquirement of spheres of influence, the non-alienation compacts followed. The Manchu government was being treated with derision by the powers, and the Chinese people saw themselves the present and future victims. They would have to pay. They were therefore ready to turn upon the Manchus not because they were Manchus but because they were collecting taxes under false pretenses. They were rendering poor government and surrendering their domain. The Chinese were also ready to turn against the foreigners, not because they were foreigners, but because they were secondarily the disturbing influence.

Following the Sino-Japanese War the powers, had they been united in a desire to help China, might have given support to a reform movement which would have resulted in a better government and set the Chinese people on the path of advance. But the powers were utterly divided. Only the United States wanted a strong China and the United States was after all only slightly interested. The Empress Dowager therefore seized the opportunity. She, also, was not conspicuously anti-foreign, but she was shrewd enough to see that her best hope of sustaining the Manchu dynasty and her own influence was to exterminate or expel the foreigners. This program, successfully carried through, would restore the vanished prestige of her government. The powers, by their jealousy of each other and by their unvarnished greed, played directly into her hand by furnishing her each day with fresh illustrations of rapacity. The foreigners, from the Parsee opium trader up the scale to the most unselfish and untiring Christian missionary, owed their lodgment in the Empire to the "naked force" of some foreign vessel of war which had never been out of call since 1842. Between the muzzle of these guns and the people at whom they were aimed were a multitude of foreigners, many of them seekers after peace, honest and kindly in their dealings, but no amount of uprightness could conceal the guns which supported them and which were each month becoming more numerous. The people, ignorant and incredibly superstitious, were goaded to desperation. While the foreigner remained aloof, the Empress Dowager, "Old Buddha," skillfully diverted from herself and her dynasty to the foreigner the wrath which in spite of its horrible manifestations was none the less the proof of the innate vitality of the Chinese people. Thus the Manchus escaped a few years longer. The foreigners became the victims.

Collectively they richly deserved their fate; but as so often happens the individuals who paid the terrible price were in equal measure innocent.

.   .   .

THE DESIRES OF THE AMERICAN GOVERNMENT

When the true nature of the insurrection became known the American Government naturally shared to the fullest extent in the common desire of the powers to effect the rescue of their Legations, to make sure of reparations for the damage done and for the expense of their naval and military forces, but on the question of the correction of the conditions which had made possible the insurrection, the agreement among the powers was less marked.

The American Government had already defined the general principles of its political and commercial policy in the Hay notes, but now something more specific was required. Secretary of State Hay addressed a circular note to the powers on July 3, which became the base-line for all subsequent American policy.

In this critical posture of affairs in China it is deemed appropriate to define the attitude of the United States as far as the present circumstances permit this to be done. We adhere to the policy initiated by us in 1857 of peace with the Chinese nation, of furtherance of lawful commerce, and of protection of lives and property of our citizens by all means guaranteed under extraterritorial treaty rights and by the law of nations. If wrong be done to our citizens we propose to hold the responsible authors to the uttermost accountability. We regard the condition at Peking as one of virtual anarchy, whereby power and responsibility are practically devolved upon the local provincial authorities. So long as they are not in overt collusion with rebellion and use their power to protect foreign life and property, we regard them as representing the Chinese people, with whom we seek to remain in peace and friendship.

The reference to the policy of 1857 is illuminating, and recalls the continuity of American policy. Hay did not conceive himself to be the originator of new principles. Great Britain, France, Russia and Japan had all been at war with China; the United States, never. But the kernel of the policy in 1900 was to forestall a declaration of war and a military movement by one or more of the powers against the Chinese Empire. "Anarchy" at Peking might be dealt with locally and was susceptible of settlement by reparations, but war against the Empire would probably involve permanent occupation or the surrender of territory. A declaration of war against China by any one of them would quite probably have been followed in a short time by hostilities between rival powers. Hay, greatly aided by the jealousies of the other powers, was entirely successful in this phase of his policy. It cannot be asserted that Hay was solely responsible for no declaration of war against China, but it seems fair to rate the circular note of July 3 as an important contribution to the peaceful solution of the Chinese problem. It was unaccompanied by any compromising acquiescence in the programs of other powers such as in 1857 had rendered the policy of Buchanan and Cass so futile and hypocritical.

Hay elaborated in a few carefully phrased sentences the general policy of the United States adding both definiteness and scope to what had been stated in the notes of the previous year:

. . . the policy of the Government of the United States is to seek a solution which may bring about permanent safety and peace to China, preserve Chinese territorial and administrative entity, protect all rights to friendly powers by treaty and international law, and safeguard for the world the principle of equal and impartial trade with all parts of the Chinese Empire.

Such phrases as "territorial and administrative entity" and "all parts of the Chinese Empire" reveal a certain vigor and precision of purpose which were lacking in the Open Door Notes. One has a feeling that since September 6, of the year previous, American policy in China had been taking shape and stiffening.

Hay's broad purpose as revealed in the course of the Protocol negotiations was substantially as follows: to maintain harmony among the Powers and by united action to secure as quickly as practical the removal of the foreign military forces from Chinese territory; to secure adequate reparations and adequate punishments for the responsible instigators of the insurrection and yet to prevent the imposition upon China of injustices which would be fruitful of new antagonisms and sow the seeds for an even more formidable popular uprising; and to secure such administrative and fiscal reforms as would make China in the future the best possible market for international trade. He viewed China as the weak link in the international political and commercial system. Enlightened self-interest dictated that the powers should unite to strengthen this link. The American policy in 1900 has since been clothed with a garb of altruism which it could not properly claim. Its motive was not conspicuously benevolent, but its object was, nevertheless, highly beneficent.

The Open Door and American Policy in the Orient

Realist

Realist historians see the Open Door as a romantic foray into Asian politics, an adventure that vastly overrated American power, greatly overestimated American interests in Asia, and ultimately led the United States into a war with Japan. In the following essay, Louis Halle puts particular emphasis on the folly of the Open Door notes and the consequences of such wild idealism. He does not, however, take up the question of American interests in the markets of China.

Paul Varg, the most influential Realist historian writing on this subject, argues that the "great China market" was a myth. According to him, the public at large was bewitched by this myth, but the American government recognized it for what it was. Varg attempts to demonstrate that, despite the pressures from some businessmen, missionaries, and members of the diplomatic corps, the government did very little to aid businessmen in their attempts to exploit the markets of China, at least until John Hay issued the Open Door notes. Until then, Varg claims, the government realized that China's poverty and different cultural attitudes made it a poor customer not only for the present, but for the future as well. Thus America's interest in China was altogether insufficient to justify the assertion of the Open Door policy.

As one can see from Varg's argument and the following essay of Louis Halle, Realist historians regard the declaration of the Open Door policy as one of America's most stupid blunders. Halle was a member of the State Department for thirteen years. For part of that time he served in the policy planning section with George Kennan.

Dream and Reality:
Aspects of American
Foreign Policy

Louis J. Halle

The acquisition of the Philippines made Washington's Fare-well Address and the Monroe Doctrine inapplicable to the chief problems of our foreign affairs. They would, in any case, have become obsolete in the years that followed, with the passing of the *Pax Britannica* and the technological development of war and communications. Our acquisition of the Philippines, however, had the effect of making them obsolete overnight rather than grad-ually. The situation is summed up in a single sentence from the Sprouts' *Rise of American Naval Power*: The annexation of the Philippines transformed the United States "from a geographically isolated continental Power into a scattered empire with a strate-gic problem virtually insoluble without recourse to alliances abso-lutely incompatible with the traditions of American foreign policy."

Until 1898 the United States had an established foreign policy, rooted in tradition, enshrined in the sacred writings of the Found-ing Fathers, and accepted as dogma. With Dewey's stroke at the Philippines that policy became irrelevant overnight. But it took us fifty years to accept this fact and to do the rethinking which it re-quired. As humanity goes, fifty years is not bad, especially for a people altogether inexperienced in the intricate and deceptive field of foreign policy. But during those fifty years, inevitably, we floundered.

Our unexpected acquisition of the Philippines embroiled us permanently in the Far East. It required us to maintain power overseas, in alien territory, or to ally ourselves with power over-seas, in order to meet our new commitment.

In actual fact, however, our commitment to defend the Philip-

From pp. 216–228, 233 in *Dream and Reality: Aspects of American Foreign Pol-icy* by Louis J. Halle. Copyright © 1958, 1959 by Louis J. Halle, Jr. Reprinted by permission of Harper & Row, Publishers, Inc.

pines does not play the dominant role in our Far Eastern affairs which one might expect from all that I have written. Our great disputes of the twentieth century in this area do not revolve around the Philippines at all, so that one might think I had been exaggerating the importance of the commitment. But the only reason why this particular commitment does not loom larger in the subsequent record is that, almost immediately after assuming it, we embarked on a course of policy by which we gradually assumed a still larger commitment in the Far East—a commitment that at first was vague and rather rhetorical, but that hardened with the passage of time. Our commitment to defend the Philippines was dwarfed by our subsequent commitment to defend the administrative and territorial integrity of China itself, that vast and crumbling empire which reached into the remotest parts of Asia. It was this commitment that was the direct cause of our long quarrel with Japan.

I wish I could offer a simple strategic explanation of such a staggering undertaking, pointing out that the integrity of China had, for us, some such strategic significance as the integrity of Belgium had for the British in 1914. But there is no such explanation, and one may as well say at the start that this can hardly be explained except as the impulsive commitment of a Don Quixote. We saw China as a lovely lady by the wayside beset by bullies, and we gallantly interfered. We didn't draw our sword, because we had none to draw, but we said we would defend her against the bullies who did have swords. The consequences of this gallantry, undertaken so casually and with so little thought of where it would lead, have been far-reaching. For half a century the lady looked to us for a protection which we were hardly prepared to give her.

The most significant thing about our position in the Far East, then, has been the fact that throughout the present century we have looked upon half of Asia as something approaching an American protectorate. All of us Americans were brought up assuming that of course it was the duty of the United States to defend the integrity of China. If anyone had asked why, I suppose we would have said that China was our special friend. But this would simply have begged the question. Once a man has committed matrimony he has no choice but to defend his wife, but the decision to marry her was presumably taken freely. The fact is, however, that none of us appear ever to have asked why we got ourselves into this position. We have simply accepted, as in the nature of things, our moral obligation to defend China from those who wanted to exploit her. Most of us have been proud of the idealism which this represents in our conduct.

But this moral obligation still seems strange to me, because we never felt obliged to protect the Sudan, say, from the British, or the Congo from the Belgians. Perhaps the explanation is, in part at least, that we had so many missionary societies operating in China. Their own paternalistic attitude toward the Chinese communicated itself to our whole nation. We came to cherish the Chinese as our pupils. Whatever the explanation, the fact is that this relationship of ours to China became dogma in our American thinking. Entanglement with China, just like non-entanglement with Europe, came to be traditional. By what course of events did this happen?

One of the most dangerous of the standard situations which occur again and again in history is that created by the disintegration of great empires. The disintegration of the Turkish Empire produced a whole series of conflicts from the Crimean War to World War I. The disintegration of the Spanish Empire brought about the Spanish-American War and that rivalry for possession of the Philippines which forced us to take them for ourselves. The disintegration of the ancient Chinese Empire produced great disorder in the Far East, beginning with the Opium War of 1840 and continuing to the victory of the Chinese Communists in 1949.

It seems to me a standard mistake, in these situations, to attribute the disintegration primarily to external rather than to internal forces—to suppose, for example, that Turkey would be all right if Russia were not bullying her, that the Spanish Empire would be sound if the United States left it alone, that the Middle Kingdom of China would go on as it has been for another couple of thousand years if only the greedy imperialistic powers were restrained, or that the Nationalist regime of China is suffering from nothing except Communist aggression. The failure to realize that the basic weakness is internal, and perhaps incurable, may lead to the mistake of guaranteeing what cannot be guaranteed, the survival and integrity of the crumbling structure.

China at the turn of the century was disintegrating of its own internal weakness. The incursions of the powers were secondary. A vacuum of effective authority had developed in an area in which the powers had nationals in residence and large interests, so that they were drawn almost irresistibly to set up their own authority. The danger of committing oneself to maintain the territorial and administrative integrity of China was that, even though one was able to hold back the vultures, the sick empire would continue to disintegrate. If the Chinese were unable to maintain their own integrity, no outsider would be able to do it for them.

Everyone judges the world by his own experience. He reads his experience into what is happening to others. Accordingly, it has been the tendency of us Americans to equate imperialistic conflicts in other parts of the world with our own heroic struggle for independence against King George and his redcoats. There could be no doubt, under the circumstances, where American sympathies would be when the European powers moved to partition China among themselves. As early as the 1850's, when the Taiping rebellion threatened anarchy in China, Mr. Humphrey Marshall, our American commissioner on the scene, reported to Washington his opinion of what our policy should be. Referring to "the avarice or the ambitions of Russia or Great Britain," he said that the fate of Asia would be sealed "unless *now* the United States shall foil the untoward result by adopting a sound policy." And what was Mr. Marshall's notion of "a sound policy"? "It is my opinion," he wrote, "that the highest interests of the United States are involved in sustaining China—maintaining order here and engrafting on this worn out stock the healthy principles which give life and health to governments, rather than to see China become the theater of widespread anarchy, and ultimately the prey of European ambitions."

Here, at the outset of the contest among the great powers for influence in China, Mr. Marshall proposed that the United States, which was still fighting Indians and seeking to establish order on its own continent, intervene to sustain the integrity of China and halt any aggression by Britain or Russia. I call attention not only to his total disregard of the power factors involved, but also to that optimism which is native to us and which makes it seem a casual undertaking to maintain order in China and to engraft on the Chinese nation "the healthy principles which give life and health to governments." When we were still struggling to dominate our own continent, we were to undertake the establishment of order among hundreds of millions of alien people on the other side of the globe—and to re-educate them.

The policy advocated by Mr. Marshall was the one that we actually adopted, and with the same insouciance, at the turn of the century. The innocence in which we undertook the commitment to defend and support China is represented by the way we went about it. Because we had been an isolationist nation for so long, our government was not organized, at the turn of the century, for the responsible formulation of foreign policy by men with professional knowledge. Our best statesmen were amateurs recruited from the fields of belles-lettres, scholarship, or domestic politics. Our policy toward China in the twentieth century was initially the creation of two Sinologists without official position in our government, one an Englishman who happened to be passing through Baltimore, the other an American who had been brought up in France, who had been an officer in the French Foreign Legion, and who, in the entire span of his life, spent only thirteen years in the United States. Both were moved by a nostalgic regard for the old Chinese civilization, which they wanted to save as one might wish to save a Ming porcelain.

W. W. Rockhill, the former French officer, was of misanthropic disposition. All his life he tried to escape from the ordinary society of men either in his study or in expeditions through Mongolia and Tibet. His avocation was the study of oriental languages and religions. He was already known through his books and lectures on the Far East, and a certain glamour must have attached itself to him in the eyes of Washington society. It is not always that one can produce in one's own drawing room an explorer of Tibet—a man, moreover, with a mandarin moustache, a foreign accent, and an air of eccentricity.

When Rockhill's friend John Hay, an American poet and essayist, became Secretary of State at a time when it appeared that we had suddenly become a Far Eastern power, he seems to have seen the usefulness of having close by an authority on the Far East. After an effort to have Rockhill appointed Librarian of Congress failed, he was given instead the post of director general of the Pan American Union (then called the Bureau of American Republics). Though this was an international office, Rockhill found himself serving as a confidential private consultant to the Secretary of State, a rather informal arrangement by which he became the key figure in the shaping of our new Far Eastern policy.

This was at a time when the final partitioning of China appeared about to take place. Since mid-century the United States had had a policy which seemed well adapted to this situation and which President McKinley saw no reason to change. By that policy the United States disclaimed all ambition for territory, spheres of influence, or any special privileges in China. It asked only that its citizens be allowed to share on a basis of equality any privileges accorded to the citizens of other foreign powers in China. If other foreign powers got trading privileges for their nationals, then America should have them too. In other words, we asked for most-favored-nation treatment.

The imminent establishment of the spheres of influence by which China would be partitioned required that we assure ourselves that the rights of our nationals would be preserved under the new dispensation. There was the danger that the partitioning powers would establish commercial monopolies from which American traders would be excluded. What, if anything, ought we to be doing about this? Hay relied on Rockhill to answer the question.

At this time there was considerable expansionist sentiment in the United States that, flushed by our acquisition of the Philippines, saw the American flag advancing around the world. It was also a common belief that commercial opportunities in China were boundless, although our actual commerce with China was insignificant. But Rockhill had nothing to do with commerce, as a Sinologist he tended to be hostile to missionaries, and he was not a flag-waving patriot. He had in his mind no clear motive for an American policy except his scholar's desire to see a precious ruin preserved.

The picture of Rockhill's mind comes out in the memoranda he wrote. It was an earnest mind, full of information in disarray. It had trouble when it tried to put things together, or follow a line of thought, or grasp a general idea. His memoranda are full of sentences that get nowhere, of paragraphs that wander from the path and meet other paragraphs coming back along the line of argument. They are too long, and one keeps on reading them only in the hope that eventually they will find a way of revealing what it is they want to say.

Rockhill was saved from the fate of having to depend on his own mind, in his contingency, by the fortuitous advent of an English acquaintance whose mind had all the clarity which his own lacked. Alfred E. Hippisley, an Englishman resident in China, had stopped over in Baltimore to visit his wife's family on his way back to England for home leave. With Washington only forty miles away, he thought he would drop in on his old friend Rockhill, too, the more so because he wanted to talk about what was happening in China.

Hippisley was a commissioner of the imperial maritime customs service in China and an authority of Chinese ceramics. He was able to bring Rockhill up to date on developments across the Pacific. Matters had already gone so far, he reported, that the division of China had to be accepted as an accomplished fact. The thing to do now was somehow to persuade the powers involved not to close the door against the commerce of others in their respective spheres of influence. This was perfectly in keeping with our American policy of seeking most-favored-nation treatment. The only real novelty was in generalizing it, in proposing equal treatment for all comers rather than for American interests alone. This, however, was a fateful novelty because of the effect it would have on public opinion in the United States. By virtue of it, what had been a selfish interest became the general moral principle of the "Open Door."

The proposal was that the United States address notes to the powers that were dividing China asking them to agree to the "Open Door." How casually this was approached is indicated by the form of Secretary Hay's assignment of the matter to Rockhill. Hay was spending the summer of 1899, as he spent every summer, at his country estate in New Hampshire. From there he wrote to Rockhill: "If you have time between now and next Wednesday to set down your views on this question—in the form of a draft instruction to Mr. Choate, Mr. White, Mr. Tower and General Porter—I would be greatly obliged. . . . But if it should not be convenient, all right." One may judge from this that the Secretary of State did not yet regard the proposed "Open Door" notes as having historic significance for the development of American foreign policy.

On the face of it, one may well ask, even today, why they should be regarded as a turning point in the history of our policy. They represented no radical departure from our position, merely the generalizing of it in the form of the "Open Door" proposal to the partitioning powers. However, once the "Open Door" notes had been sent, and replies to them received, they were publicized as an achievement of our diplomacy, they were theatrically identified with American morality in opposition to Old World chicanery, and the American electorate was encouraged to take a magnified view of them in connection with the 1900 elections. The McKinley administration was tempted to present itself to the voters as one that had, in the name of a newly arisen America, brought the slinking dogs of European imperialism to heel in Asia. It did not resist the temptation.

Here was a demonstration, to be repeated at every crisis in the following half century, of the disposition among our people to support foreign policies only when they are presented in the guise of great principles. Defense merely of our own commercial rights in China had no such appeal as the "Open Door" for all nations (semanticists and politicians should note the special magic in the word "open"); protection of our shipping, in 1914–17, had no such appeal as "Freedom of the Seas." "Don't tread on me!" has never aroused us as have "self-determination," "open convenants openly arrived at," or universal "freedom from want and freedom from fear." Policies given such names as "containment," however creditable, have been regarded as being, somehow, wicked. In this sense the Eisenhower administration was well advised when it undertook to continue the Truman administration's policy of "containment" under the new name of "liberation."

The fact is that Hippisley's "Open Door" policy, so far from frustrating the imperialistic designs of the powers on China, represented the acceptance of China's partitioning. It did not seek guarantees from the government of China but, rather, from the governments of the powers that were replacing Chinese authority with their own. It recognized the new authority and acquiesced in it. If the purpose had been to forbid encroachment by the powers, then it would have made strange sense to seek guarantees from those powers for the treatment of others in the areas in which they encroached.

All this was made explicit for Rockhill's understanding by Hippisley. "Spheres of interest," he wrote, ". . . must be treated as existing facts. . . . I venture therefore to suggest that the U.S. loses [sic] no time in calling the attention of all the Powers to the changes now taking place in China, and—while disclaiming any desire on her own part to annex territory—in expressing her determination not to sacrifice for her annually increasing trade any of the rights or privileges she has secured by treaty with China. . . ." But Rockhill had difficulty in grasping the idea. He told Hippisley, in reply, that he would like to see the United States "make a declaration in some form or other, which would be understood by China as a pledge on our part to assist in maintaining the integrity of the Empire." In addition to telling the powers to leave the door open behind them when they trespassed, Rockhill wanted to put up a "No Trespassing" sign.

Rockhill's intellectual confusion, combined with the administration's desire to appear before the voters as the slayer of the dragon of imperialism, ultimately determined our policy and so became enshrined in history. This is why the original "Open Door Notes" are regarded to this day as the notes by which we undertook to slam the door to China shut in the face of the great imperialistic powers.

Hay and McKinley, finding themselves publicly regarded by the American people as knights in shining armor, and that on the eve of a presidential election, can hardly be blamed for failing to insist on a more modest view. Instead, they seized the next occasion to send out a second round of "Open Door Notes"— this time, and for the first time, explicitly identifying the United States with the preservation of China's "territorial and administrative entity." The United States, unwittingly, had set its foot on the path that would lead, step by step, to the disaster at Pearl Harbor in 1941.

The original "Open Door Notes," as we have seen, were Hippisley's conception. He virtually wrote them, since Rockhill largely accepted his language and Hay—who was, as usual, spending the summer in New Hampshire—signed substantially what Rockhill put before him.

What was Hippisley's interest in all this? The evidence indicates that he was not serving and, in some instances, was even opposing British policy. The point of departure for his thinking was acceptance of China's partitioning. This does not mean that he did not, like Rockhill, have the welfare of China at heart. He simply did not think Rockhill was being realistic in his suggestion that the United States pledge itself to maintain the integrity of an empire which had already lost its integrity.

Hippisley did, however, contribute one rather odd item to the original Notes, in response to Rockhill's desire to support the integrity of China. The Notes asked the powers to agree not only that the Chinese tariff of the time should apply in any treaty port, but also "that duties so leviable shall be collected by the Chinese Government." And what was the agency of "the Chinese Government" responsible for collecting duties in the ports? It was the Chinese Maritime Customs Service, a foreign board of customs inspectors established in 1854 to collect customs on behalf of the Chinese government. One of its officers was Mr. Hippisley, who by including this provision in the Notes of the United States government contributed to keeping his agency in business.

So the policy of the United States was made. The Notes were sent out, and the powers, momentarily glancing aside from their struggles to maintain or upset the balance of power, made polite replies that were chiefly designed to prevent any appearance that they were not on the side of the angels. The administration, in its public treatment of these replies, gave the impression that the powers would not have been on the side of the angels had it not been for its action in recalling them to the paths of moral duty. Hay appears to have had few illusions about what the replies really meant. Living in a world of his own, however, Rockhill was moved to see in them evidence that, as he put it in a private letter, "this country holds the balance of power in China." If a feather could have held the balance of power in China Rockhill might have been right.

In point of fact, it is hard to see any effect that our publicized exchange of notes had on the foreign situation to which it was addressed. When, exhilarated by the domestic success of the Notes, the administration in June of that election year, 1900, sent out the second round of "Open Door Notes," this time calling upon the powers to respect China's "territorial and administrative" integrity, the foreign effect appears to have been no greater. If the final partitioning of China was not carried through at this time, it was, as Professor Griswold has pointed out, "a case of political stalemate rather than conversion to principle."

Only a few months after we had announced to the great powers our policy of supporting the integrity of China the Russians virtually grabbed China's richest province, Manchuria, and made it their own. "I take it for granted," Secretary Hay wrote to President Theodore Roosevelt, "that Russia knows as we do that we will not fight over Manchuria, for the simple reason that we cannot." When Russia refused to get out of Manchuria in deference to our policy, Hay wrote the President: "I am sure you will think it is out of the question that we should adopt any scheme of concerted action with England and Japan. Public opinion in this country would not support such a course, nor do I think it would be to our permanent advantage . . ." Here we see the persistence of the dogma of "no entangling alliances" in an altered situation to which it no longer had any relevance.

A few years later, when Japan ousted Russia from Manchuria, we again placed that province under the nominal protection which we extended to all the territory of China; and when again it was taken from China, this time by Japan, we found it more embarrassing to do nothing about it. Finally, almost a century after Mr. Marshall first proposed that the United States protect China against aggression, his policy involved us in the war which, surely, had been implicit in it from the beginning.

. . .

What Hay did elicited public praise. Therefore, he and his successors were tempted to do it again and again, each time to the applause of the electorate. So we embarked and continued on the road to Pearl Harbor.

. . .

The notion that diplomacy calls for an equation of means with objectives, which had been vivid to our Founding Fathers, did not enter our minds. Part of the reason that it did not enter our minds was that, as the century advanced, we came to think of our own self-contained strength as practically unlimited, while hardly appreciating the weight of the charges against that strength which we had been incurring in the world overseas.

What could one expect, after all? If the National City Bank were suddenly put into the hands of people like me, with no banking experience at all, and they had to run it by themselves, they would commit follies which would seem inexcusable to any seasoned banker. The conduct of foreign relations is not a less subtle and complex business than banking. It calls for sophisticated skill and knowledge based on long experience. This in turn requires such a professional corps and such professional thinking as can be built up only over the generations. We emerged from our isolation in 1898 without this indispensable equipment for playing an active and responsible role in the world, and it took us half a century to develop it.

The Open Door and American Policy in the Orient

Radical

Radical historians see the Open Door policy as the embodiment of American diplomacy not only in China, but throughout the world. In their view it marked the beginning of a new imperialism that sought to control for-

eign nations by dominating their economies instead of conquering them militarily. Radicals argue that America's economic power has been so great since the turn of the twentieth century that it could win any economic competition in an open market. Thus, they contend, American demands for open markets and free competition are really attempts to provide conditions for American economic domination. Obviously, Radicals regard this as a highly realistic and unromantic policy. Surely this was the case in China, they declare. Policy there was dictated almost solely by the need for new markets to absorb the immense production of America's rising industry. The men who controlled industry (and the politicians who were beholden to them) were interested in profits and the avoidance of revolution at home, according to the Radicals, and were almost totally uninfluenced by a desire to protect China's territorial integrity from European imperialism.

Thomas McCormick, author of the following essay, is a professor of history at the University of Wisconsin; he replaced his friend and mentor, William Appleman Williams. How does he answer the Realists' contention that the China market was a myth? What evidence does he have for the influence of economic considerations on the declaration of the Open Door? What evidence does he present to show that the desire for open markets in China was dictated by the expectation that the United States would ultimately dominate those markets? Does he successfully deal with the charge that the Open Door failed to balance America's power with its goals?

China Market:
America's Quest
for Informal Empire,
1893–1901

Thomas J. McCormick

We believe that 'a fair field and no favor' is all we require, and with less we cannot be satisfied. . . . We believe our interests in the Pacific Ocean are as great as those of any other power, and destined to infinite development.

—*John Hay,* 1901

One year after the armistice with Spain, America sent forth into the world the then-famous, now-denigrated Open Door Notes. In and of themselves, they established no new policy lines. Both Cleveland's response to the Sino-Japanese War and McKinley's stance during peace talks with Spain make it abundantly clear that the open door in China was already cardinal American policy long before the 1899 notes appeared.

But the promulgation of the Hay Doctrine did pass the sceptre of open door champion from Great Britain to the United States. For a half-century the British had successfully used an open door policy to create and sustain their economic (and diplomatic) supremacy in the Chinese Empire; the Americans, as "hitchhiking imperialists," gathered the commercial leavings. Now, as Britain's power wavered—and with it her commitment to the open door, the United States made a concerted effort to adapt the nineteenth-century policy to the expansive needs of a twentieth-century industrial America.

This dramatic departure and its timing have long been the source of interpretive controversy. For example, George F. Kennan, in a capsule version of A. Whitney Griswold's work, has viewed the Open Door Notes as a rather haphazard product, sold by an English member of the Chinese Customs Service indirectly to a somewhat disinterested and quickly disillusioned Secretary of State. On the other hand, Charles S. Campbell, Jr., has stressed the midwife role played by special business interests in bringing the policy to life. Yet each analysis, in its own way, has trivialized an event of enormous importance. The first grossly overestimates the influence of a quite peripheral figure, whose ideas were wholly unoriginal (and well known to every journeyman diplomat) and whose efforts in no way affected the timing of the Open Door Notes. The other bases its provocative interpretation upon a too narrow segment of the national community. Both inadequately appreciate that the Open Door Policy accurately reflected the widely shared assumptions and analyses of most social elements in America (including many without special vested interests); that both individual and group pressures were at best minor catalytic factors. Both, by focusing on the particular, miss the really substantive thing about the Open Door Policy—that it represented America's basic response to the methodological question of how to expand. Instead of closed doors, open markets; instead of political dominion, economic hegemony; instead of large-scale colonialism, informal empire. In short, a most interesting hybrid of anti-colonialism and economic imperialism.

On October 19, 1898, President McKinley told a Citizens' Banquet of Chicago that "territorial expansion is not alone and always necessary to national advancement" and the "broadening of trade." Before another year had passed, his State Department was feverishly at work trying to transform this unilateral sentiment into a universally accepted tenet—at least so far as the Chinese Empire was concerned. Behind this belated effort to make the open door a multilateral vehicle were two seemingly contradictory factors: a sense of power and a sense of impotence.

Latter-day critics of the Open Door Policy have managed to evade one central truth—that the policy was one of strength as well as weakness. A less confident nation might easily have joined in the partitioning scramble in China, content to have an assured but fragmentary slice of the market. But America wanted more, much more than that, and was certain of her ability to get it. When Brooks Adams wrote in 1899 that "East Asia is the prize for which all the energetic nations are grasping," few of his readers doubted who would win that prize. When William McKinley told Congress in that same year that "the rule of the survival of the fittest must be . . . inexorable" in the "rivalry" for "mastery in commerce," most of his listeners were doubtless sure who would be the fittest. In each instance, the certitude grew from that sense of American economic supremacy born in the export revival of 1897, nourished by the retooling and refinancing of American industry, and confirmed by the return of full prosperity. Viewed from this vantage, the open door became appropriate means for the most advanced and competitive industrial nation to grab the lion's share of the China market instead of settling for a pittance. No one saw this more clearly or said it more forcefully than the influential *Bankers' Magazine,* when it exclaimed that "without wars and without military aggression that nation will secure the widest and best markets which can offer the cheapest and best goods." "If China was open to trade with all the world . . . the United States and England need not be afraid of any competitors. But Russia, Germany and France . . . are more or less at a disadvantage when they meet either English or American goods. They therefore do not take the philosophical view at all."

.   .   .

In view of subsequent developments, such glowing optimism about the future of the China trade appears naive, misguided, and grotesquely overdrawn—much flap about nothing. But the *potential* for trade expansion was real, and it remained so (enough to exercise vast impact upon American policy-makers for the four decades that preceded Pearl Harbor). In 1899 there were signs—however small—that the penetration of the China market was already underway. For one thing, in the relative sense, manufactured products began to account for more than 90 per cent of American exports to China—a fact of some significance to those preoccupied with *industrial* overproduction. (By 1906, 96 per cent of all United States exports to China were finished products, as compared to 27 per cent for Europe.) The absolute volume of manufactured exports also experienced a sharp rise (albeit from a small base), multiplying four times between 1895 and 1899, from $3.2 million to $13.1 million. (Seven years later, despite a Chinese boycott and persistent obstacles from both Russia and Japan, the total had reached nearly $42 million.) Particularly blessed were the iron and steel industry and cotton textile enterprises, both key elements in the American economy.

The latter's exports to China, for example, grew from less than $2 million in 1895 to almost $10 million in 1899 (and reached $30 million by the Panic of 1907, accounting for 56.5 per cent of all American cotton textile exports). The figures lent an air of credence to one southern group's assessment that "[the China trade] is everything." All these facts were, to be sure, small straws in the wind and easily written off in retrospect. But in the expansionist psychology of the 1890's they were eagerly seized upon to bolster the widespread expectation that given equal, open door access, the United States could and would win economic dominion in China.

If American commercial ascendancy made the Open Door Policy a fruitful one, American weaknesses made it nearly unavoidable.

Political power was the prime deficiency. The Far East was no Latin America, where, after 1895, American hegemony was seldom challenged and usually acknowledged. In China the United States faced all the handicaps of the latecomer to a game already in play with a full lineup of great powers. America did have the capacity to play a significant role in Chinese affairs, and its words and acts now carried substantially more weight, thanks to the Spanish-American War. As the American Ambassador to France reported to McKinley: "we did in three months what the great powers of Europe had sought in vain to do for over a hundred years . . ." and "the most experienced statesmen here envy our transcendent achievements and see clearly the future benefits." Still, heightened power and all, the United States was in no position to issue any Olney Corollaries for the Chinese Empire; to make American word fiat; to manipulate with relative impunity and success. Here more subtle methods would be demanded.

The instances are many (and well known) of America's inability to control events in the western Pacific. Significantly, these failures came despite "the President's most serious consideration" of Chinese instability; despite Secretary Hay's "serious attention" to the famous petition of cotton textile spokesmen, exhorting that something be done to keep the door open in northern China; despite Hay's assurances to Paul Dana of the *New York Sun* that "we are keenly alive to the importance of safeguarding our great commercial interests in that Empire." For all this accumulated anxiety, America's newly won status in the

Pacific could not prevent Germany's acquisition of Spain's old insular empire in Micronesia. It could not prevent Japan from occupying Marcus Island (a cable point upon which the American Navy had tentative designs) or from establishing an extraterritorial settlement in Amoy (important for its geographic relationship to Manila). It could do little to stop Russia's apparent drift toward trade discrimination in Manchuria. It could do nothing, one way or another, about the rumored impending war between Russia and Japan. Finally, it could not block Italy's far-reaching demands for a sphere of influence in San Mun Bay and Che-Kiang province—demands that ominously had the support of Great Britain; that threatened to set off another whole round of partitioning in China; that led the *New York Times* to conclude that the disintegration of China (and the open door) was "inevitable," and the *Chicago Inter-Ocean* to guess that "the end may be at hand." All the administration did was to watch, wait, and hope—a policy (better, a stance) that offered little hope for the future.

Financial weakness, another marked American liability, was in part an extension of political weakness. Simply put, American commercial expansion could not encompass financial expansion. In the realm of investments (chiefly railroads and mines) no open door existed, and no American syndicate seemed likely to compete on equitable grounds with its European peers. None of this was exactly new, of course; the move toward a "modified" open door (one that concerned only commerce, not investment) had begun in 1895 and, as already noted, accelerated sharply in 1898. But it did not reach its climax until the Anglo-Russian agreement of April 1899. In effect, Great Britain promised not to compete for railroad concessions north of the Great Wall, while Russia made a similar pledge for the Yangtze basin. All that remained between them for open competition was a buffer zone between the Russian and British spheres—and much of this was already covered by the earlier Anglo-German agreement.

This tightly constricted area of activity left American investors with little more than hope of a junior partnership with the British. This would be by no means inconsequential, and in early 1899 there was some optimism along these general lines. On February 1 the American China Development Company and the British and Chinese Corporation agreed on paper to share in each other's future concessions. One day later the *New York Times* reported that yet another British syndicate had agreed to give American capital a one-quarter share of investment in the railroads and mines of Szechwan province. But in fact British support was seldom vigorous, and American financiers fared poorly in competition with their politically and financially subsidized opponents. A prime example was the glaring failure of the American China Development Company to secure the Hankow-Canton concession, despite initially high hopes. The syndicate's inability to meet the rigorous Chinese terms was probably the major reason for the contract loss, but the company, in its frustration, blamed it on inadequate governmental support. In the end the concession "went thataway" while the State Department and the company engaged in futile backbiting as to why. Overall the episode was more souring than cathartic and played no small role in the administration's later attitude toward American investment in China.

A realistic foreign policy is an exact blend of means and ends —it knows what is vital to the national interest, whether that interest can be fulfilled within the framework of national power and ideology, and precisely how. By 1899 the makers of American foreign policy had long since defined marketplace expansion into China as an important element in their variegated effort to stabilize the political economy. But they had to adopt means that would make the best use of American commercial power while minimizing American liabilities: a still inadequate power base and financial frailty.

There were only three viable choices, and the McKinley administration considered them all. One obvious alternative was to accept the disintegration of China as inevitable (even beneficial) and join in the partitioning. In 1899 there were repeated rumors that the United States would take precisely this course. The *New York Times,* during the San Mun Bay crisis, reported that the administration had already determined to have Pechihli province for an American sphere, while at the same time the actions of the American Consul in Amoy seemed designed to convert that port and its environs into an American entrepôt. But the rumors were untrue and the American Consul's efforts repudiated, and both for the same reason: the administration felt that partitioning was an ineffectual vehicle for American trade expansion. For one thing, it would intensify anti-imperialist criticism while adding bureaucratic and military burdens that McKinley wished to avoid (a view shared with his anti-imperialist critics). For another, American sales and arteries of distribution were largely centered in zones controlled by Russia and Germany, and to relocate these in an American sphere would be expensive and time consuming —far better to keep open existing channels if possible. And finally, to re-emphasize an earlier point, a small slice of the pie (which is all partitioning could offer) held little attraction for men who wanted (and thought they could get) the major share of the market.

The second policy possibility was to make common cause with other open door supporters, presumably England and Japan, and use force if necessary to keep trade entrées open. This was the method that Theodore Roosevelt later tried informally, and it did have the merit of reflecting one vital truth—that in the last analysis only force could make the open door work. But this technique also raised basic objections which ultimately made it an impractical choice for the administration. To begin with, no military alliance (especially one with the English) was likely to enhance the political popularity of the McKinley administration. Moreover, such a formal commitment would deprive the United States of complete freedom of action, and the President (far more than his Anglophile Secretary of State) disliked tying American national interests too rigidly to the foreign policies of countries whose own shifting interests might not always coincide with those of the United States. He already had sufficient evidence (and more was to come) of British and Japanese ambivalence toward the Open Door Policy—enough to make them seem somewhat uncertain allies. Finally, any policy predicated upon the *possible* use of force might eventually require its *actual* use, and the use of force in China (save against Chinese themselves) was considered out of the question. A Far Eastern war would be an unpopular war; it might lead to the very consequence one wished to avoid—the fragmentation of China; and it might ignite the general world holocaust that all the great powers feared at the turn of the century. No, this would not do. What the United States wanted was not force but coexistence and economic competition for open markets; an "eat-your-cake-and-have-it-too" policy of peace and market domination. That America could not have both was, again, the certain fallacy of informal marketplace expansionism and the insoluble dilemma that American policy-makers vainly struggled with for the first half of the twentieth century.

There was of course some informal tripartite consultation and cooperation, and some public figures (generally outside the government) did refer to an "open door entente" of Great Britain,

Japan, and the United States. But such collusion never aimed at the use of force, and moreover it was generally an on-again-off-again sort of thing, a tactical strategem employed when it was advantageous to American interests and ignored when it was not —which was frequently.

The third policy alternative—and the one embodied in the Open Door Notes—was to gain common agreement among a concert of powers that China would be exempted from imperial competition. This course obviously begged the whole question of force and has been rightly criticized on that ground. But, on the other hand, it was hardly the legalistic-moralistic anachronism that some have made it seem. On the contrary, as we shall see, it tried to make use of two very real and interrelated factors: (1) the *de facto* balance of power that existed between the Russo-French entente and the emerging Anglo-Japanese bloc; and (2) the intense fear of possible world war that preoccupied the foreign offices of Europe. In this framework of balance and fear, the policies of each power were likely to be flexible and even a bit tentative, for rigidity could be disastrous. (Certainly British action was chameleonic, and students of Russian policy in the Far East at the turn of the century find it so baffling and contradictory that there is doubt one existed.) Furthermore, any changes in the status quo were likely to be cautious ones, undertaken on a quid pro quo basis, lest imbalance lead to conflict. Under these circumstances, if a third force dramatically insisted that the status quo (the open door and Chinese sovereignty) be universally accepted, and if that force had the capacity to upset the delicate equilibrium of power (as the United States certainly had in Europe's eyes after 1898), then there was a good chance the powers would acquiesce. The agreement might be more rhetorical than real, but it would (and did) offer useful leverage in exploiting Europe's fears and occasionally manipulating the scale of power.

These were the realities that produced the Open Door Notes. Neither partitioning nor military alliance offered practical means to realize the desired American ends; only the consensus neutralization held any glimmer of hope. That such hope was illusory, that indeed it *had* to be illusory, is worth analyzing later at length. But for the moment it ought to be emphasized that, given America's commitment to economic penetration in China, given the peculiar combination of American strengths and weaknesses, the Open Door Policy was the most *realistic* one at hand.

eight

World War I and the Treaty of Versailles

Realist

Realist historians believe that the United States was correct to enter World War I. They argue, however, that the nation fought the right war for the wrong reasons. The United States should have fought it to prevent Germany from conquering Europe and from upsetting the European balance of power. Instead, Woodrow Wilson made the war a crusade to avenge Germany's barbarous violation of American neutral rights and, in the process, to make the world safe for democracy. In so doing, he and the American people lost sight of the realities of international politics.

After destroying Germany, Wilson tried unrealistically at Versailles to supersede power politics by creating the League of Nations. Even more serious, Wilson's failure to explain to the American people the significance of the war for American interests and the importance of the collapse of the European balance of power destroyed his base of support at home. As a consequence, Congress and the people failed to support American participation in the League and destroyed whatever hopes even that flimsy agent might have held for maintaining peace and stability in Europe. Thus the war and the treaty helped create both a vacuum of power in central Europe and an embittered Germany ready to take advantage of it.

Robert Osgood, author of the following essay, is a professor of American diplomacy and director of the Washington Center of Foreign Policy Research at Johns Hopkins University.

Ideals and Self-Interest in America's Foreign Relations

Robert Endicott Osgood

World War I is a crucial period in the evolution of America's attitude toward international relations. It provides a highly significant context of events in which to examine the real conditions for reconciling national self-interest with universal ideals.

As we now know, but as few foresaw in 1914, the United States entered World War I on the side of British sea power and played a decisive part in preventing Germany from gaining control of Continental Europe. Twenty-five years later, when Germany had once more swept across the Lowlands and upset the balance of power, some American observers, anxious to support their arguments for intervention with the sanction of history, contended that the nation had joined forces with Great Britain during the previous world conflict because the people and their leaders had perceived America's enduring strategic interest in the preservation of the Atlantic System espoused by Henry Adams.

From Robert Endicott Osgood, *Ideals and Self-Interest in America's Foreign Relations,* pp. 111–112, 172, 174–175, 178–194, 283–288, 298–299. Copyright 1953 by the University of Chicago Press. All rights reserved.

This contention has very important implications concerning America's outlook upon world politics. If it is a true explanation of American intervention in World War I, it suggests a sharp break with traditional conceptions of national self-interest. If, on the other hand, the explanation is an unwarranted projection of contemporary circumstances upon past history, then it involves a substantial misinterpretation of the whole significance of World War I in the course of America's adaptation to its international environment.

It is true that a number of American publicists, politicians, diplomats, and scholars during 1914–17 believed that a German victory would directly endanger the nation's security. If a German victory had at any time before April, 1917, seemed imminent, their apprehensions might possibly have seized the general public and become a major factor in American intervention; but, actually, this circumstance never developed; and the nation as a whole, even including some of the most prominent Realists, supported America's intervention for reasons quite different from national self-preservation. Because of the inertia of traditional attitudes toward world politics, because of the character of American leadership, and, above all, because of the circumstances of the war itself Americans, as a whole, entered the war without a clear and reasoned perception of any enduring self-interest, such as their national survival. Instead, they drifted into war, largely oblivious of the practical consequences of momentary impulses, out of an aroused sense of national honor, combined with a missionary zeal to achieve world peace and democracy.

The practical demands of national self-interest were further obscured by the exacerbation of an underlying temperamental and ideological conflict, personified in the antipathy of Theodore Roosevelt toward Woodrow Wilson, between those most conscious of the imperatives of power and those most anxious to subordinate national egoism to universal moral values. This conflict was suspended momentarily in the common embrace of a new crusade, but, as in 1898, it flared up with increasing heat as the issues of war aims and the peace settlement arose. Largely because the circumstances of the war failed to provide the incentive for subjecting either militant or pacific sentiments to the test of expediency, the deep-rooted struggle for public opinion between the Rooseveltians and the Wilsonians, instead of bringing about a fusion of realism with idealism, actually exacerbated their dissociation.

As it was, neither the egoistic nor the idealistic motives which led the United States to intervene in the European contest were sufficiently rooted in a consciousness of compelling self-interest to sustain beyond victory the break with the nation's pacific ideals and its traditional sense of self-interest in isolation. This fact was concealed during the period of American intervention by the nation's preoccupation with the overriding object of victory and by President Wilson's success in reconciling even the tenderest consciences to warfare through the identification of intervention with America's altruistic mission. However, when victory was achieved, altruism collapsed, and the nation reverted to its normal isolationist behavior in the society of nations. Those with the greatest inhibitions toward intervention became impatient with the frustration of their proportionately lofty expectations; the most militant interventionists became apprehensive lest idealism get out of hand and hamstring the nation's power of independent action; and with the immediate object of winning the war removed, the nation as a whole relaxed its moral muscles and began comparing the human and material sacrifices of war with its meager rewards, both tangible and spiritual.

.   .   .

WOODROW WILSON

Wilson's Independence

Even if it were true that a number of high officials and advisers to the administration favored America's entrance into the war primarily in order to redress the balance of power and to safeguard the Atlantic lines of communication, it would not follow that their views were a decisive cause of American intervention. That is quite another proposition.

The influence of these men upon the course of the nation during 1914–17 would be difficult to determine with any assurance. However, it is reasonable to assume that a major share of their influence would have had to be transmitted through the thoughts and actions of the nation's Chief Executive, for no President was ever in more complete control of the conduct of the nation's foreign affairs than Woodrow Wilson. Therefore, it is pertinent to inquire about the relation of the President to his advisers.

In the broad outlines of his foreign policy and the principal decisions implementing it, Wilson was remarkably independent of his advisers. These men have testified to their inability to change the President's mind upon important issues. Partly because of his innate stubbornness but largely because of his steadfast resolve to make scholarly and impartial decisions, Wilson was extremely cautious and deliberate in forming his opinions and quite tenacious of them once they were formed. He might listen patiently to a variety of advice, and he often appeared to accept the views of others without question; but because he tended to lose confidence in those who differed with him very often, most members of his cabinet were careful not to dissent too frequently, lest they lose what influence they had; and on crucial issues his seemingly unquestioning acceptance of the views of others was more the pose of impartiality than the reality of acquiescence.

. . . If this is true, the key to American intervention must lie in the thoughts and actions of the Chief Executive more than in the purposes of any other individual or group of individuals.

Wilson's Indifference Toward Power and Strategy

Before the war in Europe broke out Wilson had demonstrated, especially in his policy toward Latin America, his profound dedication to America's mission of bringing constitutional and democratic liberty, universal peace, and the Golden Rule to all the peoples of the world. He had proclaimed that Americans were placed on earth as mankind's shining example of the subordination of material and national interests to the highest moral values and the service of humanity. By 1914 Wilson had formulated and had begun to put into practice certain ideal principles of American foreign policy. On the other hand, he had given very little thought to problems of national security and the exigencies of power politics. And as for the balance of power, he abhorred it as a tool of militarists and despots.

Wilson was not blind to America's strategic interests. His policy toward Mexico, Nicaragua, San Domingo, Haiti, and Latin America in general, like the hemispheric policy of his predecessors in office, was motivated, in part, by a desire to safeguard American security by keeping the Western Hemisphere free from opportunities for European interference. Moreover, he seems to have believed at one time that the nation's hemispheric defense would be jeopardized by a German victory in the European war. The British ambassador Spring-Rice, in a letter to Sir Edward Grey early in September, 1914, reported a conversation with the President in which Wilson expressed the opinion that if Prussian militarism won the war, the United States would have to take such measures of defense as would be fatal to its form of government and its ideals. Harley Notter, in a studious examination of the philosophical bases of Wilson's foreign policy, has said that, undoubtedly, an "impelling consideration" in Wilson's desire to purchase the Danish West Indies was the threat to the Monroe Doctrine which would follow transfer of the islands to a Germany victorious in Europe; and that the "dominant factor" in Wilson's policy toward these islands was the general protection of the Canal and America's strategic interests in the Caribbean.

Yet Wilson's private correspondence contains only a hint here and there of any fear of the impact of a German victory upon America's position in world politics, while his public pronouncements are almost totally devoid of strategic considerations. Moreover, on numerous occasions he specifically disavowed the existence of any German threat to the national security. For example, Colonel House records Wilson's opinion in the fall of 1914 that "even if Germany won, she would not be in a condition seriously to menace our country for many years to come. . . . He did not believe there was the slightest danger to this country from foreign invasion, even if the Germans were successful."

After the first half-year of the war Wilson steadfastly maintained that, no matter which side won, the warring nations of the world would be so utterly exhausted that, for a generation at least, they could not possibly threaten the United States, even economically; but that, on the contrary, they would desperately need America's healing influence.

Those who had direct access to the President during the neutrality years have testified to their inability to impress upon him the gravity of the German threat. Thus Lansing in a memorandum to himself early in the summer of 1916 expressed his amazement at Wilson's inability to grasp the real issues of the war: "That German imperialistic ambitions threaten free institutions everywhere apparently has not sunk very deeply into his mind. For six months I have talked about the struggle between Autocracy and Democracy, but do not see that I have made any great impression."

Actually, Wilson was impressed by the struggle between autocracy and democracy; and, eventually, in his War Message he placed American might on the side of democracy; but, far from implying the preservation of a balance of power, as Lansing hoped, Wilson's pronouncement heralded the death of this iniquitous system and the birth of a new order in international relations, in which power politics and the pursuit of selfish national interests would be supplanted by the higher moral standards of personal conduct. In fact, Wilson's conception of foreign relations was remarkable not so much for its neglect of the problems of power as for its conscious subordination of national expediency to ideal goals. Above all, he coveted for America the distinction of a nation transcending its own selfish interests and dedicated in altruistic service to humanity.

.   .   .

Wilson's Ideal of Neutrality

From the moment President Wilson learned of the outbreak of war in Europe he looked to America to exemplify that self-control and dispassionate idealism which he believed was indispensable for the fulfilment of her historic mission to serve humanity. As the German Army advanced through neutralized Luxemburg he told newspaper correspondents, "I want to have the pride of feeling that America, if nobody else, has her self-possession and stands ready with calmness of thought and steadiness of purpose to help the rest of the world." It was in response to this aspiration, as well as to America's traditional policy toward European belligerents and to the overwhelming weight of public opinion, that he issued a proclamation on August 4, explicitly stating the duties imposed upon Americans as citizens of a neutral nation. Two weeks later he evoked the full measure of self-possession implied in this proclamation by asking Americans not only to observe their legal obligations but to "act and speak in the true spirit of neutrality, which is the spirit of impartiality and fairness and friendliness to all concerned."

My thought is of America. . . . She should show herself in this time of peculiar trial a Nation fit beyond others to exhibit the fine poise of undisturbed judgment, the dignity of self-control, the efficiency of dispassionate action; a Nation . . . which keeps herself fit and free to do what is honest and disinterested and truly serviceable for the peace of the world.

In accordance with this ideal Wilson rejected all suggestions that he protest Germany's violation of Belgian neutrality. His refusal to pass moral judgment on the belligerents was strengthened by his belief that the whole war was such a tremendous evil that it was the part of discretion to remain impartial until all the pertinent facts were available.

However, as reports of the German invasion of helpless Belgium flowed in and the German Chancellor referred contemptuously to Belgium's treaty of neutrality as a "scrap of paper," Wilson, like the majority of the nation, began to draw a moral distinction between the Allied cause, which was identified in a general way with the cause of democracy, and the cause of the German rulers, who were seen as exhibiting the inevitable wickedness of militarism and autocracy. Wilson's private condemnation of Germany's part in the war was consistent with his early antipathy toward her philosophy of materialism and her political system of military despotism. His general approval of British aims reflected a long-standing preference for Anglo-Saxon philosophy and institutions. Wilson's secretary, Tumulty, writing after the war, reported a conversation in which Wilson, referring to Lord Grey's remark to Page that England was fighting to save civilization, stated, "He was right. England is fighting our fight and . . . I shall not . . . place obstacles in her way. Many of our critics suggest war with England in order to force reparation in these matters. War with England would result in a German triumph." Whether or not one places credence in the absolute accuracy of Tumulty's recollections, one can take the reported conversation as an authentic representation of Wilson's belief, which he reached during the first year of war, that an English victory was desirable, whereas a German victory would be a disaster for civilization.

However, this belief failed to modify the President's public and official neutrality. More than ever, as the trials of neutrality set in, Wilson's old suspicion of British diplomacy, his determination to reserve judgment until all the facts were available, and, above all, his desire to keep America impartial and self-possessed in order that she might reconstruct world peace led him to stress America's independence from the Old World conflict.

We can only speculate about the nature of Wilson's position had he foreseen the probability of a German victory, but it is clear that, as a matter of fact, he did not feel that he was confronted with the alternative of choosing a British or a German victory. Thus, in spite of his advisers' warnings about the German threat to American security that would follow a British defeat, he reassured the nation in his annual message on December 8, 1914, that there was no need for additional military prepared- ness, since there was no "reason to fear that . . . our indepen- dence or the integrity of our territory is threatened. . . ." This was "a war with which we have nothing to do, whose causes cannot touch us." Live and let live, was his motto. Wilson later changed his view on military preparedness, but he changed it in order to prepare the nation for the defense of its rights, not its security. He continued to repeat his assurances that America's interests—aside from its honor and rights, which he interpreted as the larger interests of humanity—were in no way involved.

President Wilson's more bellicose critics denounced his posi- tion on neutrality as a transparent rationalization of timidity and moral myopia, but in Wilson's mind neutrality did not mean sim- ply keeping out of trouble; it meant self-control and service to humanity. As he said in this same message, America's purpose in staying out of the war was to bring peace to the belligerents, for this was a war "whose very existence affords us opportunities of friendship and disinterested service which should make us ashamed of any thought of hostility or fearful preparation for trouble." America, he declared, had been "raised up" to "exem- plify the counsels of peace."

Wilson's position appears in its true perspective when it is placed beside his preoccupation during the autumn of 1914 and thereafter with bringing about peace through mediation.

According to Stockton Axson's memorandum of his conversa- tion with the President in August, 1914, Wilson, even at this early date, had definite ideas about the kind of peace the world needed. His plan included prohibition of the acquisition of land by conquest, "a recognition of equal rights between small na- tions and great," the manufacturing of munitions by public enter- prise only, and, finally, "an association of nations, all bound to- gether for the protection of the integrity of each, so that any one nation breaking from this bond will bring upon herself war; that is to say, punishment, automatically." It was such far-sighted vi- sions as these that moved Wilson to seek the role of mediator through the private negotiations of Colonel House with Jusse- rand, Spring-Rice, and Bernstorff. It was the ideal of world peace which led him to send House to Europe at the end of January,

1915, in order to discover the peace terms upon which the belligerents would accept American mediation.

Nothing concrete came of House's mission, since neither of the belligerents was willing to call a halt to hostilities while the hope of victory remained. But Wilson did not surrender his peace ambitions. Addressing the Associated Press on April 20, 1915, he asserted that the three thousand miles between the United States and Europe gave Americans a unique calm and detachment, and he noted that by force of circumstances the nation was becoming a focus of financial power. "Therefore, is it not likely that the nations of the world will some day turn to us for the cooler assessment of the elements engaged?" He was at pains to assure his audience that America did not assume her isolated position in a mean and petty spirit.

> . . . I am not speaking in a selfish spirit when I say that our whole duty, for the present at any rate, is summed up in the motto, "America first." Let us think of America before we think of Europe, in order that America may be fit to be Europe's friend when the day of tested friendship comes. The test of friendship is not now sympathy with the one side or the other, but getting ready to help both sides when the struggle is over. The basis of neutrality, gentlemen, is not indifference; it is not self-interest. The basis of neutrality is sympathy for mankind. . . .
>
> We are the mediating Nation of the world. . . . We are compounded of the nations of the world. . . . We are, therefore, able to understand all nations. . . . It is in that sense that I mean that America is a mediating nation. . . .
>
> My interest in the neutrality of the United States is not the petty desire to keep out of trouble. . . . I am interested in neutrality because there is something so much greater to do than fight; there is a distinction waiting for this Nation that no nation has ever got. That is the distinction of absolute self-control and self-mastery.

Here was the perfect expression of Wilsonian idealism. The principles he voiced in this address formed the core of his whole foreign policy during the neutrality years and, eventually, became the basis for American intervention when neutrality became untenable.

Compared to the goal of world peace and democracy, national self-interest seemed an ignoble consideration. Wilson may have entertained some vague apprehensions of the practical effect of a German victory upon America's strategic position in the world, but these apprehensions were insignificant when measured against his concern for America's moral position. In Wilson's philosophy it was the things of the spirit that counted, and how could America serve as an impartial peacemaker if she placed her own self-interest above the interests of mankind and adopted national expediency rather than Humanity as her guide? Wilson was determined that Americans should not lose sight of their mission in the world by abandoning their self-composure and falling victim to the alarms of German peril sounded by the jingoes and militarists. Americans were different; they created their nation, not to serve themselves, but to serve mankind.

Wilson's Practice of Neutrality

In Wilson's view neutrality was never an end in itself. It was the traditional way of getting along with belligerents, and it seemed to be a means of keeping the United States sufficiently aloof to enable it to serve as an impartial mediator. But if neutrality should become incompatible with his ultimate ideal objectives, it was likely that Wilson would abandon its substance, if not its form. The events of 1914–17 rapidly conspired to make this hypothesis a reality.

As long as the war did not vitally concern America's own interests and as long as the ideal objectives of neutrality seemed more important than the victory of one belligerent over the other, Wilson was, apparently, willing to discharge America's obligations under international law impartially, regardless of his preference for British over German culture and institutions. However, the laws of neutrality not only imposed legal obligations upon Americans; they also granted legal rights; and this was where Germany's submarine warfare entered to confound the issue of neutrality as Wilson had conceived it.

Briefly, the confounding circumstances were these: America's merchant marine at the beginning of the war was small, and, after August, 1914, Great Britain was the undisputed ruler of the high seas; consequently, the United States was almost wholly dependent upon British ships and the British Navy for the transportation of its goods and its citizens across the Atlantic. At the same time, the safety of American goods and citizens transported on Allied vessels was seriously jeopardized when, on February 4, 1915, Germany announced that it would sink all enemy ships found within a war zone established around the British Isles, pointing out that neutrals on board enemy merchantmen might incidentally suffer the same fate as enemies. The primacy of the issue of submarine warfare in America's foreign policy became inevitable when, on February 10, 1915, the State Department delivered a note, devised jointly by Wilson and Lansing, strongly protesting Germany's proclamation and solemnly declaring that the German government would be held to "strict accountability" for acts jeopardizing American property and lives by "unprecedented" methods. From this moment on, the relation of the United States to the belligerents was bound to be determined primarily by events on the sea, over which Americans had little or no control.

If the American government had had only its neutral obligations to consider, Wilson might have enjoyed a large measure of freedom in choosing the methods by which he sought his ultimate objectives in the European conflict. In Wilson's view the traditional objectives of the American mission would have been served best by remaining aloof from the war. But, as long as the nation was determined to demand observance of its neutral rights, its freedom of choice was circumscribed by the extent to which the belligerents chose to conform to America's conception of legal and humanitarian conduct. By holding Germany strictly accountable to a rigid standard of conduct Wilson greatly increased the difficulty of his problem of reconciling America's role as a peacemaker with the maintenance of her honor and her rights. From the first he realized that this difficulty might be insurmountable.

Wilson's dilemma was sharpened by the difficulties of applying the uncertain rules of international law to unprecedented circumstances. The conventional law that forbade a belligerent warship from destroying an enemy merchantman without first stopping it, ascertaining its identity, and making adequate provision for the safety of passengers and crew had not anticipated the predicament of the small and vulnerable submarine. Yet the American government would not admit that unusual conditions justified a departure from the rules, especially when that departure involved such gross inhumanity. At the same time, it was unwilling to avoid serious incidents arising from the loss of American lives at sea at the price of abnegating the legal right of neutral citizens to take passage on belligerent vessels.

There is a good deal in the record of American diplomacy during 1914–17 to indicate that Wilson's administration met the unprecedented circumstances of submarine warfare by insisting upon the observance of the nation's rights on the high seas with something less than perfect impartiality or a rigid adherence to the spirit of neutrality. For instance, the government was certainly on shaky legal and practical ground when it defended the immunity of Great Britain's armed merchantmen by drawing a distinction between defensive and offensive armament and yet, at the same time, denied Germany the right to attack any armed merchantman without warning. However, the inconsistencies and incongruities of the government's legal position had much less to do with America's relation to the European conflict than some postwar critics of intervention claimed. They do explain something about the way in which the administration chose to rationalize America's fateful course; but that course itself—once the basic decision to hold Germany strictly accountable had been made—was determined largely by the vicissitudes of submarine warfare.

Germany's policy toward Allied ships was governed by the exigencies of war rather than by the legality or absence of legality with which the United States executed its policy toward the belligerents. It was unrestricted submarine warfare against neutral as well as belligerent ships that eventually brought America into the war; and the decision to wage that kind of warfare was made on the basis of a cold military calculation that the advantages of destroying all commerce flowing to Great Britain outweighed the disadvantages of a war with the United States. Under these circumstances the United States could have avoided intervention only if Americans had been willing to accept unparalleled destruction of their lives and property without retaliating or else to renounce the right of all her citizens and ships to travel on the high seas. Americans were unalterably opposed to either course.

Wilson's Rationalization of a Dilemma

The government's original stand on neutral rights and the widespread public support of this stand made America's relation to the European conflict largely dependent upon events beyond American control. However, the grounds upon which the government based its policy toward that conflict were well within President Wilson's power to choose and explain and rationalize. The grounds which Wilson chose were the grounds upon which he eventually led the nation into war. They had a very significant impact upon America's international conduct both during and after the period of intervention. Therefore, it is important to examine their origin in the tortuous process by which Wilson strove to evoke a consistent and high-principled concept of American purpose amid the ironic contradictions between the ideal and the practice of neutrality.

With the sinking of the *Lusitania* Wilson confronted the first great test of his firm resolve to lead the nation to exemplify the reasonableness, nobility, and calm moral courage befitting its world mission. His emotional reaction to the *Lusitania* disaster was in harmony with the reaction of the majority of the American people. He was indignant and deeply shocked, but he was strongly opposed to flying into a rage or resorting to war. His self-control was steeled not only by an aversion toward violence but also by a conviction that the world would need America to mediate for peace. It was with this mission in mind that, three days after the *Lusitania* disaster, addressing a large gathering in Philadelphia, he asserted,

> The example of America must be a special example. The example of America must be the example not merely of peace because it will not fight, but of peace because peace is the healing and elevating influence of the world and strife is not. There is such a thing as a man being too proud to fight. There is such a thing as a nation being so right that it does not need to convince others by force that it is right.

In his Flag Day address on June 15, 1915, Wilson said much the same thing, but more pointedly, as though in answer to those demanding strong action. "I sometimes wonder why men even now take this flag and flaunt it. If I am respected, I do not have to demand respect. If I am feared, I do not have to ask for fear. If my power is known, I do not have to proclaim it." The flag, he asserted, "is henceforth to stand for self-possession, for dignity, for the assertion of the right of one nation to serve the other nations of the world. . . ." In other words, genuine power used for altruistic purposes did not need bluster or force to vindicate it.

The jingoes, the Rooseveltian nationalists, and the pro-Ally patriots largely ignored this latter speech, but they seized upon the phrase "too proud to fight" in the May 10 address and flaunted it across the nation as the motto of a coward and a moral weakling. To anyone sympathetic with Wilson's constant assertion of national self-control this much-distorted statement was, obviously, an expression of the highest idealism, which posited the superior power of justice over force and morality over national self-interest.

Nevertheless, American lives had been lost as the result of a frightful violation of American rights; and the President of a great nation could not honerably dismiss the incident without a protest, no matter how proud and self-possessed he might be, especially since he had taken the position that Germany should be held strictly accountable. Moreover, Wilson's own stiff sense of national honor and self-respect would not permit him to turn the other cheek. Therefore, he also pursued another policy toward the problems of neutrality, and that was forthrightly to condemn any violation of what he considered the nation's just rights and steadfastly to refuse any modification of his original conception of these rights.

In accordance with this policy, the first American note of protest over the *Lusitania* vigorously upheld the right of noncombatants to travel on "unarmed" belligerent merchantmen; demanded disavowal, reparation, and assurance against repetition of the sinking; and declared that the United States would omit no act "necessary to the performance of its sacred duty of maintaining the rights of the United States and its citizens."

But Wilson was not content to meet alleged violations of American rights with a mere assertion of a legal case; for America, as the mediating nation of the world, had more at stake in the war than its own rights and interests. Moreover, he was painfully aware of the uncertainties of interpreting international law under unprecedented circumstances, and he had no desire to base his foreign policy upon complex legal disputation. Consequently, in response to an inveterate proclivity for moralizing national ends, he sought to place American protests on the highest possible ethical ground. He contended that it was not just American rights and honor that were involved but the rights of humanity itself, not just a legal case but a supreme moral issue. In this vein he wrote to Bryan, explaining his position on a note of protest over the death of the American citizen Thrasher on the British ship *Falaba,* sunk on March 28. "My idea, as you will see, is to put the whole note on very high grounds,—not on the loss of this single man's life, but on the interests of mankind which are involved and which Germany has always stood for."

In the series of notes on the *Lusitania* incident Wilson based his case on these lofty grounds. Bryan, who was no mean moralist himself, could see neither principle nor vital interest at stake in taking the risk of plunging the whole nation into war in order to support the right of a few citizens to expose themselves to known dangers by traveling on foreign ships, which might or might not be armed; and, accordingly, he resigned his position as Secretary of State when the second *Lusitania* note, of June 9, 1915, took such a resolute stand as to convince him it would bring war. But Wilson was intent upon the moral issue at stake. Brushing aside German allegations that the *Lusitania* carried contraband, the second note declared,

The sinking of passenger ships involves principles of humanity which throw into the background any special circumstances of detail that may be thought to affect the cases. . . . The Government of the United States is contending for something much greater than mere rights of property or privileges of commerce. It is contending for nothing less high and sacred than the rights of humanity. . . .

While this moralistic position may have helped Wilson reconcile his conscience with the contradictions of neutrality, it did not solve his basic problem of securing the observance of America's rights and still remaining at peace. In fact, it only heightened his dilemma. By generalizing American honor and rights Wilson succeeded in elevating a tenuous legal position and a dubious neutrality into a matter of high principle; but in doing so he, in effect, sublimated his stubborn adherence to a policy which, though seemingly wise and far-sighted at the beginning of the war, now promised to become more and more inconsistent with its original objective of making the United States the world's impartial mediator. For if the administration would not compromise a position which it had erected into a moral issue, and if Germany would not meet the crippling conditions this position imposed, the nation would inevitably drift toward war. In other words, as long as Wilson was honor-bound to pursue the logic of his chosen policy, its ultimate success rested not upon his decisions but upon the fortunes of war and the military calculations of the German leaders. At the same time, the more the United States was forced to defend its policy, the more difficult it became to alter it. And once Wilson had taken his stand on the grounds of international law and humanity, it was natural that he should regard any diminution of American rights as an appeasement of evil leading to the destruction of the whole principle of international morality, since to allow expediency to take the place of principle in one case would only invite further transgression.

Therefore, it is understandable that President Wilson felt bound to oppose the McLemore resolution of early 1916, which would have prohibited American travel on belligerent ships passing through the war zone. On February 24, 1916, he wrote a letter to Senator Stone defending his opposition and admirably expressing his whole philosophy of national honor.

For my own part, I cannot consent to any abridgement of the rights of American citizens in any respect. The honor and self-respect of the nation is involved. We covet peace and shall preserve it at any cost but the loss of honor. To forbid our people to exercise their rights for fear we might be called upon to vindicate them would be a deep humiliation indeed. . . . It would be a deliberate abdication of our hitherto proud position as spokesmen . . . for the law and right. It would make everything this Government has attempted and everything that it has achieved during this terrible struggle of nations meaningless and futile. . . . Once accept a single abatement of right, and many other humiliations would certainly follow, and the whole fine fabric of international law might crumble under our hands piece by piece. What we are contending for in this matter is of the very essence of the things that have made America a sovereign nation. She cannot yield them without conceding her own impotency as a nation, and making virtual surrender of her independent position among the nations of the world.

In an address before the Gridiron Club at Washington, D.C., two days later, Wilson made it clear that the principles embodied in this letter might logically become the basis for intervention. "America ought to keep out of this war. She ought to keep out at the sacrifice of everything except this single thing upon which her character and history are founded, her sense of humanity and justice."

It was on the same basis that Wilson went before Congress on February 26, 1917, to ask for authority to arm American merchant ships.

I have spoken of our commerce and of the legitimate errands of our people on the seas, but you will not be misled as to my main thought, the thought that lies beneath these phrases and gives them dignity and weight. It is not of material interests merely that we are thinking. It is, rather, of fundamental human rights, chief of all the right of life itself. . . . I am thinking of those rights of humanity without which there is no civilization.

After the *Lusitania* disaster Wilson fully realized the dilemma which this stand upon fundamental human rights imposed upon him. He confessed, both privately and in public, that he might not be able to grant the "double wish" of the American people that the nation might rigidly maintain its national honor and, at the same time, keep out of the war. Even a highly moralized stand on the laws of neutrality was not easily squared with his vision of an impartial, self-possessed nation, subordinating its own rights and interests to the welfare of humanity in order to bring about a new era of peace and unity. It is probable that Wilson was sensitive to charges by both critics and advocates of neutrality that his policy was not truly neutral but benevolently neutral. At any rate, it was the fear that he might not be able to resolve this dilemma short of war that moved him during 1916 to fall back upon America's ultimate objective, world peace, as the major criterion of the nation's policy toward the belligerents; for as the contradictions between the ideal and the practice of neutrality grew deeper and the incompatibility of American and German policy became manifest, Wilson reached the conclusion that the best way for America to keep out of the European conflict was to bring it to an end.

America's Goal: World Peace

Behind House's famous peace mission in 1916 there was a background of Wilson's growing interest in the bases of a just and lasting peace. During the autumn of 1915 his ideas on this subject matured to the stage of specific provisions, including a league of nations. In January, 1915, as a first step toward permanent peace, he sent House to sound out the belligerents concerning American mediation. House's mission failed, but Wilson continued to ponder the bases of peace. Throughout 1915 his interest in world organization increased, along with the growing concern of a large body of highly educated Americans with such projects as the League to Enforce Peace. He rejected House's advice that the United States discard its neutrality and throw its whole weight behind a demand for a just peace based on a world league; but during the fall of 1915 he did decide that the nation should become a partner in an organization for world peace, and to that end he encouraged House and Sir Edward Grey to develop their ideas on the subject of the formation of a league after the war.

Early in 1916 the mounting hazards of neutrality placed a new urgency upon ending the war, and once more Colonel House went to Europe to work for mediation. This time Wilson authorized him to urge peace negotiations and to promise that America would throw her moral force—he did not say her physical force —against Germany if she should refuse to co-operate. To this extent Wilson expressed his preference for the Allied cause in the war; but he was far from subscribing to House's interpretation of mediation as an adjunct of an Allied victory, for he harbored a lingering distrust of Allied war aims, and he believed that no peace that resulted in the crushing of the vanquished could endure. Moreover, whereas House's version of mediation involved American intervention on the side of the Allies if Germany refused a settlement, Wilson regarded mediation as a means of enabling America to avoid intervention.

As it developed, House's second mission of peace became an imbroglio of misunderstanding between Wilson and House, and House and Grey. But coincident with the rising interest in both England and the United States in linking a peace settlement with a league of nations, the President became more determined than ever to bring about American mediation. This was the period when the *New Republic* issued its appeal to the President to link a peace plan with the breaking of relations with Germany. However, Wilson, who was reaching a peak of exasperation over England's interference with American rights on the high seas, was in no mood to predicate peace upon an Allied victory. He was, if anything, more insistent than ever upon the necessity of American neutrality and impartiality, more firmly convinced that only a settlement that transcended the selfish advantage of all parties concerned could attain the spiritual strength to resolve international dissension. Therefore, mediation was still precluded by Sir Edward Grey's determination to make a settlement contingent upon British victory.

However, Wilson could at least affirm America's moral commitment to an association of nations founded on the principles of self-determination, the equality of small states, and the prevention of aggression. And this he accomplished in his significant address of May 27, 1916, before the League to Enforce Peace. The United States, he announced, was willing to become a partner in a universal association of nations

to maintain the inviolate security of the highway of the seas for the common and unhindered use of all nations of the world, and to prevent any war begun either contrary to treaty covenants or without warning and full submission of the causes to the opinion of the world—a virtual guarantee of territorial integrity and political independence.

Wilson had long been convinced of the interdependence of the peoples of the world. Now, for the first time, he clearly challenged America's political isolation and acknowledged the revolutionary character of the movement for a league to enforce peace. "We are participants, whether we would or not, in the life of the world. The interests of all nations are our own also. . . . What affects mankind is inevitably our affair as well as the affair of the nations of Europe and Asia." But Wilson was referring to moral interdependence, not strategic interdependence. America's mission was conceived in altruism, not self-interest. Americans, he said, wanted to end the war because it affected their rights and interests, but they approached the task of establishing permanent peace as an opportunity to replace the selfish struggle among nations and the balance-of-power system with a "new and more wholesome diplomacy," as an opportunity to realize among nations the same standards of honor and morality that were demanded of individuals. He expected an association of nations to come about as a great moral awakening rather than as a response to new conditions of national security. The war had disclosed "a great moral necessity," but he said nothing about strategic necessity.

As for America's part in bringing about an association of nations, in Wilson's view she remained an impartial, magnanimous bystander, ready to apply her moral weight to the service of humanity whenever the warring nations were willing to accept it. With the "causes" and "objects" of the war she had no concern. "We have nothing material of any kind to ask for ourselves, and are quite aware that we are in no sense or degree parties to the present quarrel. Our interest is only in peace and its future guarantees." This principle of disinterested service to the cause of world peace dominated Wilson's foreign policy thereafter.

Wilson's determination to keep the nation out of war in order that it might fulfill its mission was symbolized by the Democratic campaign slogan "He Kept Us out of War." With this slogan still ringing in his ears the President entered upon one final desperate effort to achieve its implied promise. On December 18, 1916, he sent identical notes to the belligerents asking them to state the terms upon which they would be willing to stop fighting. While his advisers were urging him to align the country on the side of the democracies, and while Roosevelt was fairly apoplectic over his refusal to abandon neutrality, Wilson was more soberly resolute than ever in his determination to refrain from moral judgments that might distract the nation from its goal of impartial mediation. Thus he pointed out in his note that "the objects which the statesmen of the belligerents on both sides have in mind in this war are virtually the same, as stated in general terms to their own people and to the world." America, he said, had no interest in the outcome of the war except the achievement of these objects, including a league of nations "to insure peace and justice throughout the world." But Americans were interested in the immediate ending of the war "lest it should presently be too late to accomplish the greater things which lie beyond its conclusion, lest the situation of neutral nations be rendered altogether intolerable, and lest, more than all, an injury be done civilization itself which can never be . . . repaired."

When this final attempt to achieve a peace based upon the principles proclaimed in the May 27 address failed to elicit a favorable response from the belligerents, Wilson went before the Senate, on January 22, 1917, and in a classic expression of America's moral leadership announced to the peoples of the world his own conception of an enduring peace.

Chief among the indispensable elements of peace which he set forth was a concert of nations to guarantee liberty and justice throughout the world. "It is inconceivable," he said, "that the people of the United States should play no part in that great enterprise." But Wilson did not look upon this concert as an arrangement of power to assure Anglo-American supremacy, nor was he interested in the victory of one belligerent over the other. Quite the contrary. If "the guarantees of a universal covenant" were to result in permanent peace, he believed that the peace terms would have to "win the approval of mankind." Therefore, the settlement should replace the balance of power with a "community of power"; and, lest harsh terms create resentment in the defeated nations, the war should end in a "peace without victory."

Wilson's critics were incensed at this maddeningly exalted assertion of national altruism, but Americans in general welcomed the speech as evidence that the President was doing everything in his power to keep the nation out of the war. Moreover, there were some grounds for confidence that he would succeed. Ever since Germany's so-called *Sussex* pledge of May 4, 1916, diplomatic relations with Germany had been more amicable than with the Allies. By that pledge Germany acceded to the United States' demand that no more merchantmen should be sunk without warning and without humanitarian precautions, even though it qualified its assurance by making it contingent upon the other belligerents' respect for the "laws of humanity." Therefore, on the face of things, the administration had averted war, maintained American prestige, and exacted assurances from Germany that it would perpetrate no further incidents involving innocent neutrals traveling aboard belligerent vessels. And the President himself was, evidently, more determined than at the beginning of the war to enforce the nation's rights impartially. From all appearances, Wilson had succeeded in surmounting the inconsistencies and dangers of his original stand upon neutral rights. He had done so by urging self-restraint and abstention from the war, by sublimating his interpretation of American rights as the cause of humanity, and, above all, by elevating America's neutrality into the instrument of a new world order of peace and brotherhood.

As for the threat of a German victory to American security, this was not a consideration in his mind. His devotion to America's mission of serving humanity led him to minimize such matters of expediency, while his aversion to the balance-of-power system and to all elements of force in international relations caused him to depreciate strategic calculations as a basis for national action. And as long as a German victory did not seem imminent, it remained possible that he might continue to reconcile America's honor and rights with the highest sort of idealism and still keep the nation free from the holocaust of war without jeopardizing American security.

Intervention

On January 31, 1917, the foundation of American neutrality collapsed, for on that date the German government announced that U-boat commanders would henceforth sink all ships—neutrals included—within the war zone. Before the American government had extracted the *Sussex* pledge it had unequivocally stated, "Unless the Imperial Government should now immediately declare and effect an abandonment of its present methods of submarine warfare against passenger and freight-carrying vessels, the Government of the United States can have no choice but to sever diplomatic relations." It was evident that the government could not now consistently or honorably avoid carrying out this threat. Reluctantly, Wilson returned to his dogged defense of

American rights. On February 3 he told Congress that the nation was severing relations with Germany. The American people well-nigh unanimously supported him. On February 26, 1917, he asked Congress for authority to provide arms for American merchant-men. The House passed a bill for this purpose, but eleven Senators, whom Wilson branded as "a little group of wilful men," filibustered it to death. Wilson found authority to arm American vessels anyhow, and it then became just a question of time before a German submarine commander would commit an "overt act" that would bring the United States into the war. A number of such acts occurred before the middle of March. By March 21 Wilson had finally made the fateful decision to ask Congress to declare that a state of war existed.

To the last, Wilson was oppressed by the thought of taking America into war. He could find no solace in the ecstasy of patriotism. His bellicosity was too refined. He had reached his decision simply because he could find no alternative. In his final reckoning with the logic of strict accountability, which he had constantly feared but which he was powerless to escape, there is an element of the high tragedy that befalls men who, due to the inevitable choices dictated by their nature, become the victims of events beyond their control.

However, if Wilson could finally choose no other course but intervention, he would, at least, lead America into war upon the highest possible moral ground: the service of others. He had always believed in a holy war to vindicate spiritual conceptions and set men free. For a man with his strong emotional and intellectual revulsion toward international conflict, war had to be holy in order to be justifiable. Wilson was following a higher consistency than his opposition to war when he based his War Message of April 2 on the very principles for which he had sought to keep America a disinterested bystander.

I have exactly the same things in mind now that I had in mind when I addressed the Senate on the twenty-second of January last; the same that I had in mind when I addressed Congress on the third of February and on the twenty-sixth of February. Our object now, as then, is to vindicate the principles of peace and justice in the life of the world as against selfish and autocratic power and to set up amongst the really free and self-governed peoples of the world such a concert of purpose and of action as will henceforth insure the observance of those principles.

He explained that America had taken up arms as a last resort. "We enter this war only where we are clearly forced into it because there are no other means of defending our rights." And he reviewed the events on the high seas that made neutrality untenable, also mentioning the spies and "criminal intrigues" which Germany had set loose upon the nation. But it was not just American rights which he was considering; it was the fundamental rights of all peoples. "The present German submarine warfare against commerce is a warfare against mankind. It is a war against all nations. . . . The challenge is to all mankind."

Wilson further generalized America's cause by presenting it as the cause of democracy against autocracy. He said that only an autocratic government, in which the moral voice of the people was suppressed, could perpetrate such crimes against international law and humanity. He avowed that neutrality was no longer feasible or desirable where peace and freedom of peoples were menaced by autocratic government. Therefore, the only remedy was a peace founded upon a concert among democratic nations.

Some Realists had been saying the same thing ever since the *Lusitania* sank; however, when they talked about autocracy, they referred not only to the principle of autocracy but to the fact of German military power; when they talked about democracy, they were thinking not only of the ideal but, in particular, of the mutual political interests of Great Britain and the United States; and when they talked about a concert among democratic nations, they did not anticipate the end of power politics but rather the beginning of a larger political arrangement, through which America could secure its power and its vital interests. But Wilson was bound to dwell upon the spiritual aspects of America's cause, simply because he believed that it was the things of the spirit that gave the American mission its power. He was bound to stress the democratic basis of a concert of nations, because he believed, "Only free peoples can hold their purpose and their honor steady to a common end and prefer the interests of mankind to any narrow interest of their own."

Wilson would not taint America's mission with the suggestion of self-interest, for he believed that only in proportion as the nation was disinterested could it serve the rest of the world. Therefore, he declared that Americans sought nothing material for themselves. They would fight only for the ultimate peace and liberation of others. Nor would he have the nation forsake that magnanimity and self-control which it had exemplified during the trials of neutrality. He pleaded that the war be conducted without rancor toward the German people. America would fight only the selfish and irresponsible German leaders. It would fight only for the privilege of all men, including Germans, to be free. "The world must be made safe for democracy. Its peace must be planted upon the tested foundations of political liberty."

Concluding his address, in solemn tones Wilson spoke again of the reluctance with which he had reached his fateful decision.

> But the right is more precious than peace, and we shall fight for the things which we have always carried nearest our hearts—for democracy, for the rights and liberties of small nations, for a universal dominion of right by such a concert of free peoples as shall bring peace and safety to all nations and make the world itself at last free. To such a task we can dedicate our lives and our fortunes, everything that we are and everything that we have, with the pride of those who know that the day has come when America is privileged to spend her blood and her might for the principles that gave her birth and happiness and the peace which she has treasured. God helping her, she can do no other.

Amid the orgy of rejoicing and congratulation that followed this pronouncement, Wilson stood pale and silent. He later remarked to his secretary, Tumulty, "My message today was a message of death for our young men. How strange it seems to applaud that." Only a holy war could vindicate a message so elevated and yet so tragic.

.   .   .

The Egoistic Defection From Wilson's Program

Woodrow Wilson viewed the making of peace as a fulfilment of the purpose for which America had waged war, and he relied upon the common people of America, with their tremendous resources of idealism, to support his plans for peace with the same zeal they had spent upon war. On the day of the Armistice, November 11, 1918, he told a joint session of Congress that victory was no mere military decision, no mere relief from the trials of war, but a divine vindication of universal principles and a call to greater duties ahead. Two days before he sailed for the Paris peace conference he proclaimed the continuation in peace of America's disinterested service to humanity during war: "We are about to give order and organization to this peace not only for ourselves but for the other peoples of the world as well, so far as they will suffer us to serve them. It is international justice that we seek, not domestic safety merely."

Wilson forgot—if, indeed, he ever realized it—that America, as a whole, had not entered the war in the spirit of altruism; that there was implicit in American intervention no acceptance of revolutionary international commitments; that the nation's war-born enthusiasm for a world made safe for democracy and the end of all wars gained a good part of its inspiration from a simple desire to lick the Hun and stay out of future trouble. However fervent America's belief in the righteousness of its cause may have been, the general approval of Wilson's war aims implied no eagerness to sacrifice traditional modes of national conduct for the sake of other nations and peoples.

Nevertheless, one cannot deny that the American people had come to believe that their war was a crusade for a freer, more democratic, and more peaceful world. This vague aspiration would somehow have to be fulfilled in order to justify the sacrifices of war. For by the time the German Army was defeated, the principal reasons which had justified intervention in April, 1917 —the maintenance of neutral rights and the vindication of national honor—had all but disappeared from popular discussion. The war had been fought for a different set of reasons from those that had led to intervention; and these reasons, however imperfectly conceived, raised expectations of a nature that could not be satisfied by mere military victory.

Wilson counted upon the fundamental altruism of the people to bridge the gap between the League and tradition. But with the strongest basis for popular idealism removed by victory, it seems likely that only some persuasive appeal to fundamental national self-interest could have sustained America's crusade into the period of peacemaking. Yet Wilson, by his very nature, could appeal only for an even greater subordination of self-interest to moral principle.

Wilson insisted that the League of Nations was pre-eminently a moral conception, an organization to turn the "searching light of conscience" upon wrong and aggression wherever it might be contemplated. It followed from his faith in the moral sense of the masses that the American people were bound to embrace this plan once they understood its lofty nature. Therefore, he expounded its transcendent idealism in the confidence that Americans would prefer the interests of mankind to all other interests. While this approach made American membership in an international league seem less and less compelling to the great body of Americans as war-born idealism subsided, it positively assured a mounting hostility toward the project on the part of Realistic national egoists like Roosevelt and Lodge.

Although Wilson was not ignorant of the practical national advantages to be gained through membership in a league, his whole nature rebelled at a frank acknowledgment of expediency as a basis for national action. He preferred to emphasize the universal moral principles that bound men together as human beings rather than the fine adjustments of self-interest among nations, which might disintegrate into violent jealousies with a slight change of circumstance. Consequently, he presented the League as a substitute for the balance-of-power system, not as a supplementation or extension of it. As he told an English audience on December 30, "If the future had nothing for us but a new attempt to keep the world at a right poise by a balance of power, the United States would take no interest, because she will join no combination of power which is not the combination of all of us."

Roosevelt, on the other hand, took just the opposite view. In his opinion it was folly to join a concert of nations that did not reflect the actual power situation. As far as he was concerned, both practical and idealistic considerations pointed to the wisdom of an Anglo-American alliance. On November 19 he wrote Arthur Lee that he had become more convinced than ever that "there should be the closest alliance between the British Empire and the United States." To George Haven Putnam, who had solicited his membership in the English-Speaking Union, he wrote,

I regard the British Navy as probably the most potent instrumentality for peace in the world. . . . Moreover, I am now prepared to say what five years ago I would not have said. I think the time has come when the United States and the British Empire can agree to a universal arbitration treaty.

In one of his last editorials Roosevelt declared that he strongly shared the feeling that there should be some kind of international league to prevent a recurrence of war, but he warned his readers not to be deceived by sham idealism, by high-sounding and meaningless phrases, such as those embodied in the Fourteen Points. Let us face the facts, he wrote. The first fact is that nations are not equal. Therefore, let us limit the league to the present Allies and admit others only as their conduct warrants it. Let us specifically reserve certain rights from the jurisdiction of any international body. America should be very careful about promising to interfere with, or on behalf of, "impotent or disorderly nations and peoples outside this league" where they lie "wholly outside our sphere of interest." Roosevelt concluded with a plea for universal military training.

Actually, Roosevelt's conception of a peace settlement as one phase of a continuing accommodation of power was as remote from the popular view as Wilson's vision of the selfless submerging of national sovereignty in a community of interest. Both views involved a serious break with traditional conceptions of America's relation to world politics. However, in his strong assertion of national prerogatives Roosevelt was joined by parochial nationalists, such as Borah and Beveridge, who were unalterably opposed to all involvements in power politics, including those for limited national ends, on the grounds that nothing that happened overseas could be of enough concern to the United States to warrant contaminating the nation by association with the evil balance-of-power system. While Lodge and Roosevelt had never been opposed to joining an international organization that would redound to the national interest, Beveridge and Borah were convinced, as a matter of principle, that the national interest and membership in a league were mutually contradictory. But, whatever their differences, both groups were agreed that American interests came first; and, if only for this reason, Wilsons' persistent association of the League with altruism proved as repelling to Realistic as to parochial nationalists.

Moreover, the President's moralistic approach gave the nationalists a distinct tactical advantage in the debate over the terms of America's membership in the League; for if America's entrance into the League of Nations were purely a philanthropic gesture, then there was strength in the argument that the nation ought to be able to determine, independently of others, the proper extent of its own generosity. On this basis Lodge argued for his reservations to the League Covenant. In an address before the Senate on February 28, 1919, he accepted Wilson's contention that American participation in the League would be almost wholly for the benefit of others and asserted that, therefore, the United States had a right to limit the sacrifice of its sovereignty as it pleased. On August 12 he argued, "Surely it is not much to insist that when we are offered nothing but the opportunity to give and to aid others we should have the right to say what sacrifices we shall make and what the magnitude of our gifts should be.''

Senator Borah had presented the same thesis of limited philanthropy the week before.

> I may be willing to help my neighbor, though he be improvident or unfortunate, but I do not necessarily want him for a business partner. I may be willing to give liberally of my means, of my council and advice, even of my strength or blood, to protect his family from attack or injustice, but I do not want him placed in a position where he may decide for me when and how I shall act or to what extent I shall make sacrifice.

If the majority of the nation were willing to grant philanthropy a greater scope than Borah, it was not because they were more idealistic but simply because they were less apprehensive of the sacrifice demanded of them.

The Idealistic Defection From Wilson's Program

In urging the nation to sustain its crusade at a wartime pitch and subordinate its own interests to the interests of mankind Wilson greatly overestimated the idealism of the great majority of his countrymen; but there was at least one group of Americans as altruistic as he, and this was that small but articulate band of liberals and intellectuals in the vanguard of the nation's pacific idealists, which had long constituted itself as a sort of guardian of the American conscience. These men yearned for the fulfilment of America's crusade with that passion for perfection which obsessed the prewar anti-imperialists and peace advocates. In a sense, their very self-respect depended upon the achievement of Wilson's goals, for nothing much short of those goals could have vindicated their personal concessions to the war spirit. Unfortunately, their exalted aspirations were not balanced by a comprehension of the rigid limitations upon altruism in international relations. It is not strange that this group of ardent idealists should have become the most bitterly disillusioned in the 1920's.

The sources of disillusionment were apparent before the completed draft of the Versailles Treaty was made public, for it became obvious almost from the start of the Paris peace conference that most of the Fourteen Points—which, contrary to the opinion of many idealists, was a unilateral statement of general principles by Woodrow Wilson and not a contract signed by the Allies—would be carried out only imperfectly, if at all. The idealists who had given Wilson his strongest support were the first to be shocked by the inevitable deviations from his war aims amid the post-armistice reassertion of nationalism throughout the world.

Wilson's astounding pinnacle of world leadership in November, 1918, represented the triumph of Wilson the Conqueror, not Wilson the Peacemaker. The Armistice filled Wilson with a sober anticipation of great world responsibilities, but hundreds of thousands of his own countrymen were merely exultant over the vanquishing of the Hun and the end of the trials of war. In view of the disillusionment of the 1920's and 1930's, it is interesting to recall that the great majority of Americans in the autumn of 1918 had no doubts whatsoever that Germany was guilty of perpetrating the war and ought to be punished accordingly. If Americans were worried about the peace terms, it was because they feared that the settlement would be too soft, not too tough.

Abroad the spirit of vengeance was, quite naturally, even more intense. And one had but to read the front page of the newspapers to discover that the Fourteen Points had no more abolished the national egoism of foreigners than of Americans. Winston Churchill, then British Minister of Munitions, announced that the League of Nations could be no substitute for the supremacy of the British fleet and should not interfere with Great Britain's retention of the German colonies or the conquered parts of Turkey. Lloyd George won a sweeping victory in the general elections on the issue of "Hang the Kaiser and make the Germans pay the cost of the war." French patriots were talking of reconstructing Central Europe in accordance with French interests. Italian patriots were talking about acquiring the Dalmatian Coast and control of the Adriatic. Leaders of all nations were advancing their territorial and financial claims. Evidently, hundreds of millions of peoples of conflicting hopes and ambitions regarded Wilson as the Messiah of their special national concerns and theirs only.

In January the wily French Premier, Clemenceau, who had privately ridiculed Wilson for claiming four more points than the Lord Himself, shocked American idealists and overjoyed the Chamber of Deputies when he unequivocally asserted, "There is an old system of alliances called the Balance of Power—this system of alliance, which I do not renounce, will be my guiding thought at the Peace Conference."

These revelations, supplemented by additional evidence at the peace conference that Wilson's New Diplomacy had failed to transform the world, had a devastating effect upon the moral optimism of the most ardent apostles of the American mission. Their early defection, and not the nationalist assault, was the real beginning of the general repudiation of America's second crusade that swept the nation in the 1920's; for it was they, and not the nationalists, who were chiefly responsible for associating American intervention with altruistic goals, and it was they who first became disillusioned with their handiwork.

.   .   .

The Idealistic Rejection of Versailles

By insisting that acceptance of the Versailles Treaty was essential to fulfil America's whole purpose in entering the war, Wilson seemed to be asserting, in effect, that intervention could be justified only if America achieved the loftiest objectives in peace. It was precisely this belief that became the basis for postwar disillusionment with American intervention. America, it was said, had fought to save the world, but the world, lapsing into its wicked habits, had rejected American generosity and subjected its savior to a campaign of vilification and slander; therefore, America had been played for a sucker; American beneficence had been turned to the evil advantage of selfish and unenlightened forces. Never again! This sullen and peevish paranoia gained its original impetus from the more creditable moral indignation of idealists who had staked their reluctant support of the war upon the expectation of achieving the full measure of Wilson's Fourteen Points.

The Versailles Treaty, in the perspective of a second effort at settling a world conflict, seems now much less iniquitous than it seemed in the light of the disappointed hopes following World War I; and it is right that it should. Certainly, Woodrow Wilson's role in drafting that treaty was admirable and sometimes skilful, barring a few blunders and considering the almost insuperable obstacles beyond his control, or for that matter beyond the control of any of the much-maligned statesmen and politicians at the peace conference. In any case, no peace is achieved with the signing of a document. The preservation of peace is a continuous process and an arduous one. Wilson understood this, and he was aware of the treaty's imperfections; but he regarded the League machinery as the instrument through which these imperfections might be eliminated.

Nevertheless, it was true that the treaty was a bundle of compromises, and in world politics and international reform American idealists were far less tolerant of compromise than in the sphere of domestic politics and national reform. Their intolerance of the half-loaf of Versailles was sharpened by their anticipation of Wilson's whole loaf; and Wilson heightened their dissatisfaction by insisting that the treaty was, in principle, the whole loaf, even though he himself had obviously been willing to accept many half-loaves during the hectic negotiations of the treaty.

World War I and the Treaty of Versailles

Radical

Radicals maintain that Woodrow Wilson was far more self-interested and realistic than the Realists admit. In the Radicals' view Wilson entered the war not to protect some ideal of American neutral rights, but to protect America's prosperity. This prosperity was dependent on the war trade with the Allies. The critical factor in America's decision for war was not Germany's use of submarine warfare in violation of the neutral rights Wilson had idealistically declared he would protect; instead it was the Wilson administration's decision to loan money to the belligerents so they could continue to order American goods. Since Great Britain controlled the seas, only the Allies could benefit from American trade and loans. As Radicals see it, America's defense of such a lopsided neutrality virtually compelled Germany to respond with submarine warfare.

Charles A. Beard, the author of the following essay on American intervention in World War I, is one of the "greats" of American historical writing and the intellectual father of the Radical school of American diplomatic history. In this essay he argues not only with the Nationalists and Realists, but also with some of the earlier Radical critiques of the war that blamed American intervention on very narrow economic élites, such as munitions makers or Wall Street bankers.

Radicals also attribute much of Wilson's conduct at Versailles to American economic interests, in this case Wilson's desire to expand America's Open Door Empire. They believe that Wilson was more concerned about the rise of revolutionary socialism than about the problems of peace with Germany and argue that his major hope at Versailles was to contain Russian expansion, prevent revolutions, and maintain democratic free-enterprise governments in Europe. This would permit American exports to penetrate and dominate the markets and politics of Europe. While Wilson might cast such ambitions in idealistic terms and even believe himself that they were altruistic, as radicals see it, they were still part and parcel of an advancing American imperialism. N. Gordon Levin's account of Wilson's antirevolutionary policy, which follows Beard's essay, is a very restrained statement of this view. Doctor Levin is an associate professor of history at Amherst College.

The Devil Theory of War

Charles A. Beard

The Devil Theory of War and History

At the outset we must get rid of a false notion of human affairs.

Widespread is the conviction that wicked men make war—political or economic men or both. Under this conception, the masses of the people are viewed as loving peace. They want to go about their daily work, to earn a good living, to get along with their neighbors and to see everybody prosperous.

Cherishing good will, they pursue their callings, occupations, professions and interests, without thought of stirring up domestic or foreign troubles. If let alone in their pacific pursuits, war will never come. In every referendum on war in the abstract, they vote overwhelmingly against it, just as they vote against sin at church on Sunday.

But into this idyllic scene of the people engaged in "peaceful" pursuits, wicked politicians, perhaps shoved along by wicked bankers, burst with their war cries. They stir up the people. They thrust arms into their hands and marshal them off to war. The politician, with the banker in the background, is a kind of *deus ex machina,* a strange kind of demon, coming from the nether region and making the people do things they would never think of doing otherwise. Or if the source of the trouble is not some wicked person, it is a wicked "force"—an impersonal "cause" of war. If this force could be eliminated or "cured" the cause of war would be removed, and the people would keep their Utopia in everlasting peace. All we need to do, then, is to drive the wicked from power or exorcise the evil spirit. This done, peace will reign.

Support for this simple view of peace and war comes from many economists. They seem to regard the politician as a kind of evil shaman that intervenes in economic affairs, without rhyme or reason or for selfish reasons of his own. Where he comes from, how he gets his power and why he interferes—these are questions seldom explored by theorists of this persuasion. Politicians interfere with the people in business. If they would stop, enterprise would boom along and everybody (almost) would be employed and happy. But this *deus ex machina* keeps breaking into the blissful domestic scene and upsetting the perfect balance of "the delicately adjusted economy."

Besides making domestic troubles, politicians willfully lead countries into war. And war is a senseless, uneconomic performance that destroys the balance of world economy and brings on panics. If politicians would stop interfering at home and stop making wars, the whole world would be busy, employed and (almost) happy.

Of course economists do not always put the case in these brief terms, but this is what their speculations amount to when boiled down to fundamentals. Politicians upset things at home, make wars abroad and disarrange the balance of production and exchange. Otherwise, peace and prosperity.

The Devil Theory Will Not Hold Water

Anybody who will stop singing this old tune for a few minutes and examine it in the light of a few facts will see how childish it is. In the pursuit of peace, people are doing things that have a direct bearing on war. They are producing goods and offering them for sale. And such is the nature of machine industry under capitalist propulsion that there are usually a lot more goods to sell than buyers can pay for. These are the so called "surpluses" of industry and agriculture. In some lines they may be small, in others, large. If these surpluses are not large at the moment, the potentials for increasing them are always present in machine industry. Given a chance to "make a profit," the owners of land and industries can usually manage to expand on short notice and pour out as many goods as the market will take.

Now it generally happens, even in the best of times, that the peaceful people, engaged in pursuing ways of peace, are looking hungrily for buyers—foreign as well as domestic. As a matter of fact, it is as patriotic to sell to a foreigner as to a fellow citizen. The pressure for opportunities to sell goods is an enormous peacetime pressure that comes out of the peaceful pursuit of peaceful pursuits.

The politicians and the bankers who are often accused of making wars do not come from some nether region, under this world of peaceful people so busily engaged in peaceful pursuits. They all come from among these very people. Apart from the chronic professionals, most politicians have engaged at one time or another in some peaceful pursuit. Often they are lawyers who have labored hard for business men and corporations devoted to turning out goods and making profits. Bankers are as a rule middlemen. Their function is to facilitate the operations of making and selling goods. They are in constant touch with such operations. They lend money to set them in motion. They smooth the ways of exchange, both domestic and foreign.

Neither politicians nor bankers operate in a vacuum. They do not intrude themselves upon the people from some magic world of their own. The politician seldom if ever conjures up any measure or scheme of action from the vasty deeps of his own mind. He works on suggestions from people engaged in one or more pursuits of peace, or on threats, pressures and orders from them. Whether he keeps the peace or goes to war he is acting under the stimulus of demands from groups, classes and interests. His strokes of state do not come out of an empty sky. He dwells in no ivory tower. He reflects the ideas and wishes of his constituents. The banker also lives right down in the middle of things, amid the pushing and shoving of the market-place. He, too, doesn't play pinochle in an ivory tower. He watches for chances to speed

up the business of making goods and selling them at a profit—
this being the great peacetime pursuit of the nation at large.

War as an Outcome of Peacetime Pursuits

In the summer of 1914 the American people were busy as ever
making and trying to sell goods at an advantage. But things were
not going at top-notch speed. Business had slowed down in the
preceding winter, notwithstanding the New Freedom. There was a
great deal of unemployment in the cities. Manufactures were not
moving swiftly enough to suit the makers. The prices of farm produce did not satisfy farmers.

In other words, Americans could do a lot more business than
they were doing—peaceful business of making and selling
goods, at an advantage. They had no idea, it is true, of going out
frankly with a battle axe to drive bargains with other nations, but
they were looking for customers. That was what they imagined
themselves to be here for, at least principally. After all, what
other purpose would more firmly engage the affections of a
peaceful and practical people?

Then the big war broke with a bang. The American people got
excited about it and evolved all kinds of passions, sentiments
and theories pertaining thereunto. But in general they were
peaceful and wanted to go on making and selling goods, at an
advantage. They had been doing that before the War came, and
to continue the performance seemed as natural as sunrise.

Very soon the Allies, for whom the seas were open, began to
buy steel, manufactures and farm produce rather heavily. Indus-
trialists and farmers were pleased to sell. Workers were pleased
to have jobs. Merchants and bankers were pleased to facilitate
the transactions of purchase and payment. The Wilson administration was not unpleased to have business looking up. A congressional election was approaching and the sign of the full dinner pail would help keep Democrats in power. Keeping Democrats in power was deemed for the good of the country, by
Democrats.

Of course there was a lot of confusion in the beginning. American short-term loans had to be paid in London. The stock market
was bewildered. And the wise prognosticators in Wall Street
could not forecast the future to their satisfaction. But after the
first confusions were over, the peaceful business of making and
selling goods spurted forward. It just so happened, perhaps un-

fortunately, that the best of new customers were the Allied governments engaged in an unpacific enterprise. But they were good customers. They were in a hurry. They needed goods, in fact, very badly, and were not inclined to haggle too much over prices, commissions and fees.

At first also they could pay for their purchases. They had gold to send over. They could muster American, Canadian and other foreign securities, and sell them to raise cash. Despite the War, some British, French and Russian goods were imported into the United States, and these imports provided credits for paying export bills. But there was a limit to the gold, securities and imports available to pay for American goods and keep Americans busy at peacetime pursuits.

Apparently a pinch was felt very early in the rush, for the French government soon sounded out the National City Bank on the possibility of a loan or credit. That would help. It would make American money available to pay American business men and farmers, engaged in peacetime pursuits. Bigger sales, bigger profits, bigger wages, bigger prices and bigger prosperity. It looked good to everybody—manufacturers, farmers, bankers, wage-earners and politicians who wanted to stay in office. Perhaps some tears were shed, but they were not as big as millstones and did not get in the way of making and selling at an advantage.

To those Americans who, for one reason or another, sympathized with the Entente Allies, the boom in business was doubly sweet. It piled up profits and commissions; it meant strength for the Allies' cause; it helped "to save civilization." But very few Americans engaged in the peaceful pursuit of making and selling had any thought at first of getting into the war. They were all for more and better business. It was nearly as simple as that, apart from the uproar of propagandists, sentimentalists and the intelligentsia.

The Democrats knew the country when in 1916 they flung up the slogan "He kept us out of war." The great majority of the American people doubtless wanted to continue their peaceful pursuit, making and selling goods.

It was simple and natural. But few realized how fateful in outcome their peaceful pursuit was to be. Few realized that war is not made by a *deus ex machina,* but comes out of ideas, interests and activities cherished and followed in the preceding months and years of peace. The notion that peace might make war did not enter busy heads.

The big question in 1915 was: How can the Allies "pay" for more and more goods, and enable Americans to follow peaceful pursuits happily?

New York bankers found the answer. They communicated it to Robert Lansing, Secretary of State, to William G. McAdoo, Secretary of the Treasury, to Colonel House, confidential adviser to the President of the United States. The question reached Woodrow Wilson. The answer reached him. Finding the solution agreeable, he approved it. The bankers' solution worked—for a time. Americans bought bonds to pay themselves for goods sold to the Allies. It was wonderful, the way it worked—for a time. Americans could keep on with their peaceful pursuits, with bigger and better prospects—for a time, for a time.

But in time the Allies were in another jam. They were in danger of losing the War or entering a stalemate that would defeat their ambitions. As Ambassador Page informed President Wilson in March, 1917, defeat for the Allies meant an economic smash for the United States. The following month, President Wilson called on Congress to declare war on the German Empire. So the United States entered the War and was at war.

War is not the work of a demon. It is our very own work, for which we prepare, wittingly or not, in ways of peace. But most of us sit blindfolded at the preparation.

.   .   .

THE FOURTH ACT IN THE WAR DRAMA—THE PLUNGE

Having broken down the ban on credits and then on loans, bankers made the most of their opportunity. Loan after loan was floated to pay Americans for American goods. As the days and weeks passed the fate of American bankers, manufacturers, farmers, merchants, workers, and white-collar servants became more deeply entangled in the fate of the Allies on the battlefield —in the war.

Act IV. September, 1915—April, 1917. Deep in the Mire of War Through Loans, Credits, and Sales, the Government of the United States Enters the War

By the opening of 1917 the Allies had stretched their borrowing power—perhaps not to the limit. Who knew the limit? But it was stretched. On the field of battle things were not going well. In March, 1917, the Tsar's government collapsed, threatening to take Russia out of the War. Defeat was possible for the Allies or a stalemate equivalent to a defeat of their ambitions expressed in the Secret Treaties dividing the spoils of victory in advance of victory.

Again, the Wilson administration faced a crisis such as it had faced in October, 1914 and again in August, 1915. If the war stopped, American business would slow down from prosperity to dullness, if not calamity. If the Allies were defeated, things would be worse. American millions were at stake. What other things were really at stake no one knew.

But a crisis was there—cold, brutal, remorseless. Economic leaders as well as political leaders, now all entangled in the same fateful web, were under a great strain. The propaganda for American participation in the War increased. Much could be said for it, and was said. Immediate advantages to stake-holders were apparent, surrounded by dark shadows of uncertainty.

Amid this tension, the German government renewed its submarine warfare. This action has been called "the primary and final cause" of the American declaration of war.

Why call it "the" cause? Why not make "the" cause the action of the Allied governments in imposing an "illegal" blockade on Germany? Germany alleged that this was the cause of her action called the cause of President Wilson's action. Why stop in the search for causes with the British action? Why not attribute the cause to the action of the United States government in acquiescing in British action? Why stop anywhere along the "chain of causes" short of the "first cause"? Nobody knows or will ever know "the" cause of Woodrow Wilson's decision in favor of war.

But we do know a great deal about the economic conditions and pressures that made his decision possible and the execution of that decision possible. The Nye revelations portray them in multitudinous detail and show powerful leaders in banking and politics taking actions that facilitated the slide toward the war abyss. In the letters and papers of these leaders written for private consumption the burden of all arguments was the maintenance of American prosperity and the fear of domestic calamity: Goods must be sold and paid for in some way or the swollen structure of prosperity would burst.

The President of the United States and his advisers knew this. They had weathered two crises by yielding to the demands of bankers for a free hand with credits and loans. Each time they had been told that it was a question of favorable action or an economic explosion at home. They knew in the spring of 1917 that a still greater crisis of the same kind was at hand, and that there was choice between an economic explosion at home and making war abroad.

These were the circumstances in which the decision to enter the war was made. Walter Hines Page, American ambassador in Great Britain, set the circumstances clearly before President Wilson in the following cable, dated March 5, 1917. The situation could not be more accurately described. As Mr. Page put the case, the J. P. Morgan Company seemed to be near the end of its power to keep the finances of the Allies going in the United States. The country faced an economic smash at home or intervention in war on the side of the debtors.

Document 13 Ambassador Page States the Dilemma

London, March 5, 1917—1 p. m. (Received March 6, 3:20 a. m.)

The financial inquiries made here reveal an international condition most alarming to the American financial and industrial outlook. England is obliged to finance her allies as well as to meet her own war expenses. She has as yet been able to do these tasks out of her own resources. But in addition to these tasks she cannot continue her present large purchases in the United States without shipments of gold to pay for them, and she cannot maintain large shipments of gold for two reasons: First, both England and France must retain most of the gold they have to keep their paper money at par; and, second, the submarine has made the shipping of gold too hazardous, even if they had it to ship. The almost immediate danger, therefore, is that Franco-American and Anglo-American exchange will be so disturbed that orders by all the allied governments will be reduced to the minimum, and there will be almost a cessation of trans-Atlantic trade. This will, of course, cause a panic in the United States. The world will be divided into two hemispheres, one of which has gold and commodities, and the other, which needs these commodities, will have no money to pay for them and practically no commodities of their own to exchange for them. The financial and commercial result will be almost as bad for one as for the other. This condition may soon come suddenly unless action is quickly taken to prevent it. France and England must have a large enough credit in the United States to prevent the collapse of world trade and of the whole European finance.

Charles A. Beard

If we should go to war with Germany, the greatest help we could give the Allies would be such a credit. In that case our Government could, if it would, make a large investment in a Franco-British loan or might guarantee such a loan. All the money would be kept in our own country, trade would be continued and enlarged till the war ends, and after the war Europe would continue to buy food and would buy from us also an enormous supply of things to re-equip her peace industries. We should thus reap the profit of an uninterrupted, perhaps an enlarging, trade over a number of years, and we should hold their securities in payment.

But if we hold most of the money and Europe cannot pay for re-equipment, there may be a world-wide panic for an indefinite period.

Unless we go to war with Germany our Government, of course, cannot make such a direct grant of credit, but is there no way in which our Government might indirectly, immediately, help the establishment in the United States of a large Franco-British credit without a violation of armed neutrality? I am not sufficiently acquainted with our own reserve bank law to form an opinion, but if these banks were able to establish such a credit, they would avert this danger. It is a danger for us more real and imminent, I think, than the public on either side of the ocean realizes. If it be not averted before its symptoms become apparent, it will then be too late to avert it. I think that the pressure of this approaching crisis has gone beyond the ability of the Morgan Financial Agency for the British and French Governments. The need is becoming too great and urgent for any private agency to meet, for every such agency has to encounter jealousies of rivals and of sections.

Perhaps our going to war is the only way in which our present prominent trade position can be maintained and a panic averted. The submarine has added the last item to the danger of a financial world crash. During a period of uncertainty about our being drawn into the war, no more considerable credit can be privately placed in the United States and a collapse may come in the meantime.

                                                                        Page

    Such were certain phases of American history immediately preceding the entrance of the United States into the war. Such were certain back-stage negotiations among heavily interested parties—bankers and politicians. Leaders in political affairs knew that a domestic crisis would flow, in all probability, from the defeat of the Allies or a stalemate that thwarted their ambitions. This is not to say that fear of the crisis was the "cause" of American intervention in the war. But indisputable evidence shows that in the autumn of 1914 and again in the summer of 1915 the issue of crisis or concession was put up to President Wilson by bankers and political advisers, and that President Wilson had yielded . . . had chosen concession rather than crisis.

Evidence so far unearthed does not show that bankers put the issue of crisis or war up to President Wilson in the spring of 1917. What was said privately by bankers and advisers we do not know. They did not have to "see" him personally about this issue. Since President Wilson was a man of intelligence and knowledge, it is reasonably certain that he was then aware of the economic dilemma before him. If he had not developed that awareness out of his experience in the autumn of 1914 and the summer of 1915, then he could scarcely have escaped it on reading Ambassador Page's precise description of the dilemma in his message of March 5.

Yet we are told that "the" cause of American intervention was the renewal of the German submarine campaign. "There," says Charles Seymour, "lay the basic cause of American intervention. It is historically isolated, as one isolates a microbe." If there had been no German submarine campaign, there would have been no war.

Now it is possible to isolate a microbe, but it is not possible to isolate any event in history from other events, except in one's mind and theoretically. Events in history as reality are connected with other events, past and contemporaneous. The renewal of the German submarine campaign was one of the events that may have predisposed President Wilson in the direction of war. How "heavily" it "weighed" in his mind we do not know. Nor could President Wilson himself have known precisely.

One need only to try to imagine such an operation to discover the absurdity of the very idea. The idea is an analogy borrowed from physics—a kind of animism. To carry it out we must conclude that a net weight of some kind tipped the "balance" in President Wilson's mind to war. Let us say that it was twelve ounces. If so, did the submarine event weigh two ounces, eight ounces, ten ounces, eleven ounces, twelve ounces?

Such an analogy is simply preposterous as a description of mental operations. Resort to astrology is quite as "reasonable."

All that we can say realistically is that the German submarine campaign was one of the events in a vast concatenation of events that shortly preceded American intervention in the war. It was one event in a total situation of events that made possible President Wilson's decision and action.

To travel beyond that is to express a mere opinion. To say that President Wilson could and would have taken the country into war on the submarine issue, if the posture of economic interests had not been favorable, is also to express an opinion—a dubious opinion. Indeed, why was the German submarine campaign followed by repercussions in the United States? In part, at least, for the reason that it smashed into the "profitable" business which American bankers and traders had built up with the Allies, and it threatened American bankers, traders, and other immediately and remotely interested parties with a crisis in domestic economy. In other words, the German submarine campaign was not an action from the blue sky which merely offended "American honor." It was part and parcel of the total military and economic situation. It was not isolated from the context of the times. The historian who isolates it in his mind is merely performing a mental trick that does not correspond to known realities.

Thus it is impossible to determine that the submarine campaign was "the" cause of American intervention. The case is not helped by adding question-begging adjectives, such as "basic," "immediate," "primary," or "fundamental." What is a "basic" cause, as distinguished from a cause? If such an adjective means anything, it means that the "basic" cause was not the whole or total cause. How does one discover the respective weights or values of the several parts of "the cause?" Let the proponents of the hypothesis make a demonstration. When they try to make answer they will discover the unreality of their figurative language.

This is not all. Historians who call the German submarine campaign "the basic cause" of American intervention must admit that they rely on evidence, on testimony of some kind. Well, on this point we have testimony of such high authority that few will dispute it. During its hearings, the Nye munitions committee introduced files of the Senate Foreign Relations Committee giving a colloquy between Senator McCumber and President Wilson shortly after the close of the war. It ran as follows:

Senator McCumber—Do you think that if Germany had committed no act of war or no act of injustice against our citizens we would have gotten into the war?
President Wilson—I think so.
Senator McCumber—You think that we would have gotten in anyway?
President Wilson—I do.

What becomes of the German submarine campaign as "the basic or primary or fundamental cause" of American intervention? Such is the testimony of the President who went before Congress and asked for a declaration of war. Surely his testimony is to be taken as against the testimony of historians who imagine that they know the determining influence that operated in President Wilson's mind.

So we are back where we started. We do not know the "cause" of American intervention. We do know something about the operations of bankers and politicians which verged in the direction of war, which were favorable to war. We know that these operations were carried on secretly, that knowledge of them was not then revealed to the people of the United States or to the Congress of the United States. We know that these operations helped to entangle the fate of American economy in the fate of the Allied belligerents. We know that bankers and politicians knew this, and had been active in creating the situation.

The question before us is not the question of their honor or wisdom or virtue. The question is simply this: Do we want, for the future, discussions and decisions of this character to be carried on secretly behind closed doors or openly in the Congress of the United States? In fine, are bans on loans, credits, and sales to belligerents to be raised clandestinely in huddled conferences of bankers and politicians or publicly by the representatives of the American people in Congress assembled?

That is the "lesson" of the last World War. That is the issue to be decided now.

Woodrow Wilson and World Politics

N. Gordon Levin Jr.

WAR AND REVOLUTION: WILSONIANISM AND LENINISM, THE IDEOLOGICAL SETTING OF CONFLICT

The world views of both Woodrow Wilson and Vladimir I. Lenin, like those of most messianic political thinkers, were centered on a dominant faith or myth. At the core of Wilson's political creed was a conception of American exceptionalism and of the nation's chosen mission to enlighten mankind with the principles of its unique liberal heritage. In Lenin's case, the central myth concerned the imminent liberation of mankind from liberalism, capitalism, and imperialism through the means of a proletarian revolution led by a knowledgeable socialist vanguard. From this basis, Leninist ideology would challenge not only Wilson's ultimate goal of a capitalist-international system of free trade and liberal order, but also the President's final decision to achieve this aim by fighting a liberal war against Germany in the interests of universalizing self-determination and democracy throughout Europe. In 1917, these two mutually exclusive visions of world history came directly into conflict when Lenin and Wilson both became, almost simultaneously, major historical actors.

Liberal and Revolutionary Socialist Critiques of Imperialism

Woodrow Wilson's vision of a liberal world order of free trade and international harmony did not oppose but rather complemented his conception of the national interests of American capitalism. By the turn of the century it was clear to Wilson that the growth of the American economy, especially in heavy industry, meant that America would soon be competing for the markets of the world with the other major industrialized powers. The future President also correctly saw that the Spanish-American War and the subsequent annexation of the Philippines marked the realization by the nation that

From N. Gordon Levin Jr., *Woodrow Wilson and World Politics*, 1968, pp. 13–14, 254–257, 260. Copyright ©1968 by Oxford University Press, Inc.

the next frontier to be conquered consisted of the fertile export market of Asia. Indeed, this new frontier had to be conquered lest the United States burst with the goods its new industrial system was capable of creating. On the eve of his first presidential campaign, Wilson told the Virginia General Assembly that "we are making more manufactured goods than we can consume ourselves . . . and now, if we are not going to stifle economically, we have got to find our way out into the great international exchanges of the world."

A constant *leitmotif* in Wilson's speeches both before and during his campaign for the presidency in 1912 was the concern that recession and stagnation might overtake the American economy if exports were not drastically increased.

.   .   .

It is little wonder that Wilson's speeches and letters in 1916 radiated pride in what his first Administration had done to promote American trade abroad. Time and again Wilson stressed the aid given by the Federal Reserve Act, the Federal Trade Commission, and the Commerce Department to American exporters, and called on the nation's business leaders to rise to their global opportunities. It should be noted, however, that the Wilsonian program of commercial expansion did not go uncriticized domestically. On the Right, some Republican and Progressive nationalist spokesmen, such as Theodore Roosevelt, Albert Beveridge, George Perkins, and Henry Cabot Lodge, were not willing to see tariffs lowered as a means of increasing exports, and they were not averse to having exports expanded by the alternate method of international economic rivalry backed by naval preparedness. On the Left, socialists questioned the very concept of trade expansion itself, arguing that there was no real surplus to export, but only those goods which the lower classes were not able to consume at existing price and income levels. Beyond the question of underconsumption, socialists and some radical liberals also saw a danger of navalism, imperialism, and war in any vigorous program of export expansion. In the Center, however, the Wilsonian position implicitly held, against both conservative and radical critics, that it was possible to have economic expansion and yet to avoid such traditional imperialistic practices as protection, economic warfare, and navalism. Yet, in order fully to understand how Wilson could ideologically fuse commercial expansionism with a form of anti-imperialism, it is now important to grasp that, for the President, export was the necessary material aspect of a national mission to spread the values of American liberalism abroad in the interests of world peace and international liberal-capitalist order.

At the heart of Wilson's defense of the Versailles Treaty and the League of Nations Covenant lay his idea that the results of the Paris Peace Conference represented the fulfillment of America's liberal-exceptionalist mission to liberate oppressed peoples and to reform the traditional war-producing diplomacy of the European balance of power. In the President's view, it was fitting for an American nation-state, whose own national tradition was based on an original triumph of progressive liberal values over European reaction, to be the disinterested and trusted leader of mankind at the moment of liberal-internationalism's final victory over the atavistic restraints of traditional reaction. For Wilson, the United States had a moral duty to participate in the American-inspired League of Nations, not only to ensure fully the triumph of world democracy and Slavic self-determination over German imperialism, but, more broadly, to support a new "Lockeanized" world order, under international law, within which American liberal values would remain victorious over Europe's traditional balance of power diplomacy. For all these reasons, the President sought to commit America to give its liberal leadership to the League of Nations, thereby ensuring that the triumph of world liberalism over German and/or European imperialism would remain a permanent triumph.

Yet, while the main emphasis in Wilson's defense of the Versailles Treaty and the League Covenant was on America's responsibility to fulfill its liberal anti-imperialist mission through leadership in the League, the President did not ignore the related function of the progressive League program in containing revolutionary-socialist pressures. Time and again during our analysis of the theory and practice of Wilsonian diplomacy, we have had occasion to remark upon the manner in which the Administration's liberal anti-imperialism also served a related anti-Bolshevik function. Indeed, it is clear that the essential Wilsonian endeavor to reform international politics from within in a non-revolutionary manner was implicitly anti-Leninist in its values and assumptions. It is not surprising, then, that on several occasions, during his final speaking tour in early autumn 1919, Wilson chose to defend the Treaty and the League as liberal barriers to possible revolutionary-socialist tendencies among the world's restless masses. In his speeches the President often argued that America had a duty to support a progressive liberalization of the old imperialistic world power structure, partly to show restive peoples everywhere that the evils of international politics could be reformed without socialist revolution.

At Bismarck, North Dakota, on September 10, 1919, Wilson made quite explicit his sense of the relationship between America's missionary anti-imperialism and America's liberal anti-Bolshevism:

It is a noble prospect. It is a noble opportunity. My pulses quicken at the thought of it. I am glad to have lived in a day when America can redeem her pledges to the world, when America can prove that her leadership is the leadership that leads out of these age-long miseries into which the world will not sink back, but which, without our assistance, it may struggle out of only through a long period of bloody revolution. The peoples of Europe are in a revolutionary frame of mind. They do not believe in the things that have been practiced upon them in the past, and they mean to have new things practiced. In the meantime they are, some of them, like pitiful Russia, in danger of doing a most extraordinary thing, substituting one kind of autocracy for another. Russia repudiated the Czar, who was cruel at times, and set up her present masters, who are cruel all the time and pity nobody, who seize everybody's property and feed only the soldiers that are fighting for them; and now, according to the papers, they are likely to brand every one of these soldiers so that he may not easily, at any rate, escape their clutches and desert. Branding their servants and making slaves of a great and loveable people! There is no people in the world fuller of the naive sentiments of good will and of fellowship than the people of Russia, and they are in the grip of a cruel autocracy that dares not, though challenged by every friendly Government in Europe, assemble a constituency; they dare not appeal to the people. They know that their mastery would end the minute the people took charge of their own affairs. Do not let us expose any of the rest of the world to the necessity of going through any such terrible experience as that, my fellow countrymen. We are at present helpless to assist Russia, because there are no responsible channels through which we can assist her. Our heart goes out to her, but the world is disordered, and while it is disordered—we debate!

Obviously, the Wilsonian liberal struggle against imperialism and war was ideologically fused with the Wilsonian liberal struggle against Leninist revolutionary-socialism.

Finally, however, it must be re-emphasized that Wilson's anti-imperialist and anti-Bolshevik sense of America's liberal-exceptionalist missionary idealism was perfectly compatible with his sense of America's national self-interest. It is clear, for instance, that the President saw America's future commercial expansion as assured, providing that the United States chose to maintain its moral and financial world leadership by doing its part, through the League of

Nations, to support an economically stable and nonrevolutionary liberal-international order. On September 5, 1919, speaking in St. Louis, Wilson succinctly conveyed his sense of the inseparable relationship between, on the one hand, America's economic and political national interests and, on the other, America's missionary liberal duty to the rest of mankind:

I have sometimes heard gentlemen discussing the questions that are now before us with a distinction drawn between nationalism and internationalism in these matters. It is very difficult for me to follow their distinction. The greatest nationalist is the man who wants his nation to be the greatest nation, and the greatest nation is the nation which penetrates to the heart of its duty and mission among the nations of the world. With every flash of insight into the great politics of mankind, the nation that has that vision is elevated to a place of influence and power which it cannot get by arms, which it cannot get by commercial rivalry, which it can get by no other way than by that spiritual leadership which comes from a profound understanding of the problems of humanity.

In sum, then, the President envisioned America as the moral and the commercial leader of a new liberalized international order, safe both from traditional imperialism and from revolutionary-socialism, in which world trade and world politics would henceforth be conducted on America's liberal terms.

.   .   .

. . . Yet looking back, what seems clear is that Wilsonianism, even while losing the battle over the League of Nations, eventually triumphed in the more long-term struggle over the ultimate definition of the nature of twentieth century American foreign policy. Wilson established the main drift toward an American liberal globalism, hostile both to traditional imperialism and to revolutionary-socialism. Many who had been associated with Wilson, or who accepted the essentials of his world view, such as Herbert Hoover, Cordell Hull, Franklin Roosevelt, and John Foster Dulles, would continue in later periods to identify America's expansive national interest with the maintenance of a rational and peaceful international liberal order. Ultimately, in the post-World War II period, Wilsonian values would have their complete triumph in the bi-partisan Cold War consensus.

World War I and the Treaty of Versailles

Nationalist

Nationalist historians argue that Wilson and his advisors, while idealistic, were also quite conscious of America's economic and strategic interests when they led the United States into World War I. These historians believe that America's leaders took the balance of power firmly into account. Nationalists admit the importance of the broad economic interests depicted by Charles Beard in the motives of Wilson and his advisors, but they argue that this was only one of several equally important factors, such as a concern for national security, national honor, and human rights.

They point to the same factors as influencing Wilson at Versailles. They argue that fear of revolutionary socialism did not loom nearly so large in Wilson's mind as Radicals maintain and that his primary concern was with an arrangement in Europe that would provide fair treatment for Germany, a lasting peace, and the end of militarism and autocracy. Nationalists believe that Wilson took full account of the balance of power and conflicts of national interest in his negotiations. They blame the failure of the Treaty of Versailles on the selfishness and shortsightedness of America's vengeful allies, the partisanship of Wilson's Republican critics in the United States, and the ultimate failure of the League and the Allies to enforce the treaty's provisions during the 1930s.

Daniel M. Smith is professor and chairman of the history department at the University of Colorado and author of Robert Lansing and American Neutrality, 1914–1917.

The Great Departure: The United States and World War I, 1914–1920

Daniel M. Smith

I

The European war also gave a severe shock to the American economy. A recession had been underway prior to August 1914, and the outbreak of hostilities at first caused a further deterioration. International exchanges were disrupted, stock market prices tumbled, the cotton market nearly collapsed with the threatened loss of the German and Austrian market, and many European investors liquidated their American holdings. Thousands of frantic citizens were stranded in Europe, temporarily bereft of credit and with their relatives in America bombarding officials with inquiries as to their safety. American export trade with Europe, in large part dependent on British and other foreign shipping, was adversely affected. The Wilson administration reacted with speed to cushion the impact of war, adopting measures ranging from the issuance of special credits to citizens stranded in Europe to use of emergency currency at home.

Within a short time the economy began to adjust to the war and under the impetus of Allied war purchases recovered from the recession and began an upward spiral of prosperity. War orders flooded in for foodstuffs, raw materials, and munitions. American production of iron, steel, copper, oil, meat, wheat, and other materials was vastly increased and the value of exports to Europe steadily mounted. Despite the virtual loss of the German market and Allied controls over European neutral imports, American exports to Europe rose from an excess over imports of 500

From Daniel M. Smith, *The Great Departure: The United States and World War I, 1914–1920*, 1966, pp. 6–7, 9, 13–27, 80–82, 174–176. Reprinted by permission of John Wiley & Sons, Inc.

million dollars in 1914 to three and a half billion in 1917. Trade with the Allies increased 184 per cent over peacetime. A virtually new munitions industry was created by Allied purchases, and by 1917 America had exported over one billion dollars' worth of explosives and arms to Europe.

In view of these facts, it was not surprising that many citizens and scholars in the 1930's, disillusioned by the war and affected by the sensational Nye Committee investigation of the munitions industry, concluded that the country had been pulled into World War I by the golden chain of economic forces. It was alleged that the one-sided American war trade with the Allies and the vast loans of money had made the United States a silent member of the Allied camp. Involvement in the war had been the inevitable result, since an enraged Germany had been driven to ruthless U-boat warfare in order to halt the burgeoning flow of war supplies to its enemies. Some also suggested that the United States had entered the fray as an active belligerent in order to prevent an Allied defeat and the consequent loss of American loans. Little evidence exists to substantiate these interpretations. Although the Wilson administration was seriously concerned with the health of the American economy and defended the war trade as legitimate, it never contemplated hostilities to ensure continued prosperity or to protect the American stake in the Allies. Most citizens and high officials in the government were confident throughout the neutrality period that the Allied powers would eventually triumph over Germany. In any case, the majority of the loans to the Allies were amply secured by pledged collateral, regardless of the outcome of the war. And as for Germany's adoption of unrestricted submarine warfare, the evidence reveals conclusively that the motive was not merely to sever the war trade between America and England but was to cut off all trade with the British Isles and to starve that nation into submission.

.   .   .

AMERICAN INTERESTS AND THE WORLD WAR

In recent years historians have examined closely the role of national self-interest in propelling the United States into World War I. For two decades after that war ended, the scholarly debate was centered on the question of whether the country had been genuinely neutral in 1914–1917, with the defenders of the Wilson administration contending that hostilities had resulted only because of German submarine attacks on American rights and lives on the high seas, while critics ("revisionists") attributed involvement to the administration's allegedly unneutral policies favoring the Allied cause. The coming of World War II, when the Axis powers posed a manifest threat to American security and national values, suggested the need for a reevaluation of the causes of the earlier struggle. Wartime books, like Walter Lippmann's *U.S. Foreign Policy: Shield of the Republic,* reinterpreted the decision for war in 1917 as necessitated by the German challenge to Anglo-American control of the north Atlantic and to the security of the United States in the Western Hemisphere. A decisive German victory would have supplanted British with German naval power and would have constituted a real and immediate danger to North America. Since 1945 a number of scholars have reexamined President Wilson's foreign policies and have inquired into the role of considerations of the national economic and security interests in the decision for war. The answers reveal that realistic concepts of the national interests were held by Wilson and his principal advisers and were involved to a degree in the formulation of basic neutrality policies and the ultimate transition to belligerency.

.   .   .

The outbreak of war in 1914 enhanced the belief of a number of citizens that the national interest required an Allied victory. Editorials and letters in the *New York Times,* and several articles by historians George Louis Beer, George Burton Adams, and Albert Bushnell Hart, contended that security and maintenance of the Monroe Doctrine required the preservation of British naval supremacy. To Beer, "German ambitions in South America have been dormant only because the British fleet was an insuperable barrier. . . . Similar dangers threaten our economic interests in the Far East." Hart pointed out the nation's stake in the existing world equipoise, which affected the country's ability to defend the Monroe Doctrine: "Peace can be maintained only by convincing Germany and Japan, which are the two Powers most likely to be moved by an ambition to possess American territory." To Adams, apart from valid idealistic and ideological factors, "political and military expediency" justified intervention to preclude a German triumph over the Allies. A sweeping German success would leave no power in Europe able to restrain its ambitions; the United States at the minimum would have to exist in a hostile world as a result and probably would face direct Teutonic challenges. Other well-known scholars and commentators, such as Walter Lippmann of the *New Republic,* presented papers on these themes at the 1916 assembly of the American Academy of Political and Social Science. Books and articles by H. H. Powers, Roland G. Usher, and Hudson Maxim also warned of the dangers of a German victory.

The great majority of Americans, however, were not accustomed to the contemplation of foreign policy based on realistic appraisals of economic and political interests. Instead, popular reactions in 1914–1917 largely reflected traditional isolationist attitudes, modified by some emotional and ideological sympathy with the Allies. It is clear, nevertheless, that for over a decade a minority of informed citizens had been exposed to repeated warnings that an aggressive Germany potentially endangered an Anglo-American community of interests. They had come to view Great Britain as the bulwark standing between the Western Hemisphere and Europe, whose removal would expose the United States to great peril. Such views were particularly prevalent in the eastern part of the United States, and were held by people with considerable influence in the molding of public opinion. Existence of these attitudes and convictions made it inestimably easier to condemn Germany on moral and idealistic grounds and probably facilitated the ultimate entry into war.

The most influential advisers of President Wilson shared a "realistic" appraisal of the significance of the European war for the United States. Robert Lansing, counselor of the State Department and its second in command, presidential adviser Edward M. House, and ambassadors Walter Hines Page in London and James W. Gerard in Berlin, together with several cabinet members, fused pro-Ally sentiments and ideological considerations with apprehensions that a German victory would affect adversely American economic and political interests. These views, however, were most emphatically not held by William Jennings Bryan, Wilson's first secretary of state.

.   .   .

As secretary of state, Bryan, like Wilson, was determined to use the nation's influence for good in world affairs. Historian Arthur S. Link has aptly described their approach as a "missionary diplomacy" of moral exhortation and example. Bryan was especially interested in the cause of world peace. In addition to supplementing previous arbitration treaties with thirty "cooling-off" pacts, designed to resolve crises through investigation and delay, he repeatedly pledged the American people that the nation would not become involved in war while he was in charge of the State Department.

Bryan had less of a policy and more of an emotional reaction toward the European war. He took a firmly moral view of American neutrality from the first days of the conflict. Deeply shocked by the carnage and without concern for the practical portents of the war, he saw no danger to the United States if Germany emerged the master of Europe. After one conversation on the subject with Bryan, House noted with near incredulity that the secretary "did not believe there was the slightest danger to this country from foreign invasion, even if the Germans were successful. . . . He talked as innocently as my little grandchild. . . ." Bryan viewed the war as merely a temporary reversal in the universal march toward peace and he was passionately convinced that the role for the United States should be to restore sanity by remaining neutral and mediating the struggle. America, he believed, was the foremost Christian spokesman for democracy, which would ultimately bring peace and progress to all peoples. The nation, therefore, must offer a moral example to the world.

The secretary was untiring in his advocacy of mediation. He hailed Wilson's formal tender of good offices in August 1914 in biblical language: "He has sent the dove out of the ark in search of dry land—God speed its return with the olive leaf." Repeatedly Bryan called Wilson's attention to the possibilities of further peace efforts. At his suggestion, October 4, 1914, was designated as a national day of prayer for peace. In a moving address in New York City on the proclaimed day, Bryan emphasized the economic interdependence of all nations and asserted that a peace based on territorial aggrandizement and a continued arms race could not long endure. Reflecting the current concepts of the peace movement, the secretary argued to Wilson that the most desirable peace settlement would be one that reduced armaments to the level of mere national police forces, with a mutual pledge by the nations to respect the territorial integrity of others. This vision of an ideal peace appealed strongly to the president but he judged the time inopportune for a renewed effort at mediation. Acting upon House's advice that the Allies would probably reject any overture while the military situation strongly favored Germany, Wilson reluctantly declined to act.

Unlike many Americans, Bryan was not persuaded that Germany alone was responsible for the initiation of hostilities. In any case, he was less interested in distributing guilt for the outbreak of war and more in determining the responsibility for continuation of the struggle. From that point of view he held the Allies to be equally as selfish as the Central powers. It would be better, therefore, for America not to wait until the Allied states had won enough victories to restore the military balance before making a strong peace effort. The holocaust, he argued, should be ended by immediate efforts toward a restoration of peace. Wilson and House, however, were then convinced not only that untimely overtures for mediation would be foredoomed but that it was unwise from the American viewpoint to embarrass the Allies while Germany held the upper hand and would emerge with the largest gains. Such considerations of expediency and interests left Bryan unaffected. Peace, whatever its dimensions, was his sole aim.

II

Robert Lansing, the counselor of the State Department, held diametrically opposed views of the war. A descendant of a distinguished New York family and trained in international law, Lansing had traveled extensively abroad and by 1914 had participated in more international arbitrations than probably any other living American. As a result of training and experience, he was eminently practical and "hard-headed" in his approach to world affairs and questions of foreign policy. Although he shared the American faith in the efficacy and future of democracy and as a devout Presbyterian believed in the moral imperative, Lansing recognized that amoral physical power was the underlying reality in international relations. Moral law did and should govern domestic society, but unfortunately relations between states were characterized by materialistic and selfish motives and conflicts usually were resolved by violence. In essence a nation dealt with other nations in a savage manner, regardless of how enlightened the conduct of its domestic affairs might be. To assume otherwise, to believe that foreign policy should be founded solely on altruistic motives, was fallacious and a grave error. Idealism had an important place in American foreign policy but it needed to be harmonized with common sense.

The initial response of Lansing to the war was one of relief that his country was spared the waste and sufferings of the con-

flict. Yet he was pro-Ally from the first, in part because of emotional and cultural attachments to Great Britain, and in part because of his conviction that the Allies represented the
democratic impulse against the aggressive autocracy of the Central powers. He assumed, as many others, that the war would
soon end in an Allied triumph, and at first he concentrated on
perfecting American neutrality. By early 1915, however, he perceived that the war would be a long and bitter one seriously affecting the economic and political interests of the United States.
Submarine warfare, a novel and rude challenge to trade and past
international practices, seemed to Lansing to portend a possible
German victory. The destruction of British passenger liners with
American travelers aboard removed all doubt from his mind and
underscored America's interest in the outcome of the war. Germany, he believed, was a very real danger to American ideals
and to its economic interests and security.

On July 11, 1915, a few days after he had succeeded Bryan as
secretary of state, Lansing recorded in his private notebook his
views on policy:

I have come to the conclusion that the German Government is utterly
hostile to all nations with democratic institutions because those who
compose it see in democracy a menace to absolutism and the defeat of
the German ambition for world domination. Everywhere German agents
are plotting and intriguing to accomplish the supreme purpose of their
Government. . . . Germany must not be permitted to win this war and to
break even, though to prevent it this country is forced to take an active
part. This ultimate necessity must be constantly in our minds in all our
controversies with the belligerents. . . .

If Germany should win, the United States would be confronted
with a hostile naval power threatening its interests in the Caribbean, in Latin America generally, and perhaps in the Far East as
well. The United States had already experienced sharp controversies with an expansionist Japan, frequently rumored to be on
the verge of deserting the Allies and realigning with the Central
powers. Lansing could envision, therefore, the possibility of a future grand alliance between the three autocratic empires of Germany, Russia, and Japan, which would isolate the United States
in a menacing world.

The new secretary was also imbued with the American faith in
democracy and its eventual universal triumph. Democratic states
were inherently peace-loving, he believed, because the ordinary
citizen presumably never desires war and its costly sacrifices,

which fall heaviest on the average man, whereas autocratic states with dynastic rivalries were basically aggressive and militaristic. From the point of view of Lansing and others similarly inclined, imperial Germany, the leading representative of a militaristic and statist philosophy, could be said to be a triple threat to the United States: ideologically it menaced democratic institutions and values, militarily it endangered the nation's security, and it was the most serious rival of the United States for economic and political influence in Latin America. To cope with these dangers, Lansing resolved to endeavor to watch carefully German activity in Latin America, especially in turbulent Mexico and the Caribbean area, to take steps to forestall possible German acquisition of bases by American purchase of the Danish West Indies (done in 1916–1917), to keep the submarine issue clearly defined, and to enter the war if it became necessary to avert a Teutonic victory.

Although ideological factors figured prominently in Lansing's thought, at least as important were considerations of the country's economic and security needs. In his private memoranda he repeatedly recorded the conviction that a German conquest in Europe would dangerously expose the United States. On the eve of America's entry into the war, he wrote: "The Allies must *not* be beaten. It would mean the triumph of Autocracy over Democracy; the shattering of all our moral standards; and a real, though it may seem remote, peril to our independence and institutions." In 1915–1916, however, he appreciated the fact that public opinion was divided, with pacifist and isolationist traditions still strong, and that the president was most reluctant to contemplate actual hostilities. Insofar as he was able, therefore, he tried to shape the American course so that dangerous disputes with the Allies would be avoided, while the submarine issue was clearly delineated and the American people were slowly prepared by events for the great leap into belligerency. Lansing usually did not speak to Wilson directly of his belief that the nation's vital self-interests required preparation for war, but with an understanding of the presidential psychology he instead used moralistic and legalistic arguments to justify what he viewed as the correct policy. Often working in close cooperation with the similarly inclined Colonel House, Lansing was able to achieve a large measure of influence on Wilsonian foreign policy.

Other officials within the State Department and the foreign service held comparable views on the meaning of the war. James

Brown Scott, William Phillips, and Frank L. Polk (later undersecretary) were also pro-Ally in sympathies and were persuaded that a German triumph would endanger America. Chandler P. Anderson, a legal adviser on problems of neutrality, remarked after a discussion with Lansing of a recent German note that it was surly in tone and "a good example of the sort of lecturing and regulating that all nations might expect if Germany succeeded in its ambition to rule the world." From London, Ambassador Walter Hines Page sought to convince Wilson and top administration figures that Britain's fight against Germany was in the best interests of the United States. Only if the Allies won, he wrote, would a favorable power balance be preserved in the Far East and in the Atlantic. Ambassador James W. Gerard in Berlin had similar apprehensions and predicted that if the Central powers emerged victorious "we are next on their list. . . ."

III

Edward M. House of Texas, usually referred to by his honorary title of colonel (which he disliked), is generally conceded to have had the greatest individual influence on President Wilson's domestic and foreign policies. Born into a wealthy Texas family, young House had been frail of health but intensely ambitious and he early turned to politics as his *metier*. Confining his role to that of a behind-the-scenes manipulator, he helped direct several successful campaigns in his native state before applying his talents to the national stage. He attached himself to Wilson's cause in 1912 and speedily became the intimate friend and counselor of the professor in politics. A very intelligent and able man, House asked no political office for himself and desired only the role of a privy counselor. He understood well the psychology of the new president and sought to influence him by quiet suggestion and indirect recommendations. House avoided arguing with Wilson and usually lapsed into silence when he strongly disagreed with some action or view. For reasons of health, and apparently because he realized it was the wisest approach, he continued to live in New York City during the Wilson administration and maintained contact with the president through letters, telephone conversations, and occasional visits. He also relied upon certain administration officials to keep him informed of developments and *au courant* with presidential thinking. As a result, Wilson viewed House as a selfless and devoted friend upon whom he could depend for counsel and encouragement. So close was the relationship that Wilson referred to House as his second personality, whose thought almost automatically coincided with his own. Time was to reveal some pronounced divergencies but until the Paris Peace Conference the friendship flourished. House's ambition was to make an impression on history, but it was selfless in the sense that he desired to do so by making the administration of his friend preeminently successful in all areas. Some writers have been inclined to exaggerate his role and to attribute to House most of Wilson's notable achievements. Perhaps House's biographer, Charles Seymour, described his role more accurately when he depicted the colonel not as the master strategist but rather as the expediter and tactician who linked the recluse in the White House with the outside world.

Although lacking experience in foreign affairs prior to 1913, House had given some thought to the most desirable general policies for the United States. In his utopian novel *Philip Dru,* published anonymously in 1912, he sketched a foreign policy based on a world system of spheres of influence and a balance of power, with the United States playing a much larger role in the Western Hemisphere. He also expressed distrust of Russia and the hope that Japan would curb that nation in the Far East. House traveled to Europe in the summer of 1913 and established a close relationship with British Foreign Secretary Sir Edward Grey and other English leaders. In the months thereafter he planned another trip, on what he called his "Great Adventure," to "bring about an understanding between France, Germany, England, and the United States regarding a reduction of armaments . . ." and the development of backward areas of the world. He was in Europe on this mission, with Wilson's encouragement, when the events occurred that plunged the world into the great war.

The 1914 trip and subsequent journeys not only familiarized House with the principal belligerent leaders but did much to convince him that the German government represented unrestrained militarism threatening the peace and welfare of the world. As a consequence he shared Lansing's views on the political and ideological connotations of the war. He differed, however, in that Lansing soon came to believe that only a decisive German defeat would suffice, whereas House long preferred a more limited Allied victory which would preserve the existing equipoise and leave Germany sufficiently strong to check the equally dangerous expansionist tendencies of czarist Russia. Consequently he later urged Wilson to undertake a form of mediation-intervention, but by early 1917 he had come to support active American involvement and the defeat of Germany.

In the early months of the war, House advised a benevolent neutrality of acquiescence in the Allied system of maritime warfare. With the advent of the U-boat issue, he joined Lansing in recommending a strong policy of opposition even at the risk of war. In the fall of 1915, House and Lansing conferred at length on foreign policy problems and agreed that the Allies should be reassured that "we considered their cause our cause, and that we had no intention of permitting a military autocracy [to] dominate the world if our strength would prevent it." House, like Lansing, was fully aware that American neutrality favored the Allied cause, and he once complained to French Ambassador Jules Jusserand that "The United States had practiced benevolent neutrality toward the Allies which the Allies in no way appreciated." As issues with Germany became clearly insoluble and after the failure of his own efforts at mediation-intervention, House cooperated with Secretary Lansing in support of a firmer stand toward Berlin and entry into the war.

IV

President Wilson entered office surprisingly uninformed about foreign affairs. What was striking about this was not its novelty, since most presidents after the Civil War had been similarly ill-equipped, but was, as Arthur Link has pointed out, that it should have been true of Wilson, a professional historian and political scientist, author of a number of books and former president of Princeton University. Yet his publications indicated little interest in foreign affairs, and prior to 1898 he had written of diplomatic problems and machinery as almost a minor aspect of government. After the "passing" of the frontier and the Spanish-American War, he like others was made aware that the isolation of the nineteenth century was no longer possible and that the nation would perforce play an ever larger role in world affairs. Nothing indicated, however, that his knowledge and interest in international relations was more than perfunctory and superficial. In an oft-quoted remark, on the eve of his presidential inauguration, Wilson confessed to a friend that his primary interests were in domestic reform and that it would be "the irony of fate" if he should be compelled to concentrate on foreign affairs.

Wilson has been described by many scholars as primarily an idealist unresponsive to practical considerations in foreign relations and as unusually independent of his pro-Ally advisers in shaping America's course during the great war. Later studies have substantially modified such estimates. He was deeply moralistic in his approach, the result of being steeped in Calvinistic piety and training during his youth. Idealism usually meant for him, however, not the ignoring of practical considerations but the exalting of noble purposes and goals. He has been aptly described as a "romantic moralist, who . . . raised every issue and conflict to a high stage. . . ." He was capable of sometimes being blinded to reality by his faith and goals, as was painfully clear after the 1919 peace conference, but in the neutrality period his moralistic impulses usually were reenforced rather than contradicted by practical considerations of the national interest. Recent historians have revealed also that Wilson was by no means impervious to the counsel of his close advisers and that he shared to a degree their analyses of the meaning of the war to America's economic, security, and ideological interests.

When the war began, Wilson's first reactions were based on emotional sympathy for England and its allies, and he tended to attribute to Germany primary responsibility for beginning the struggle. Within a few months, however, he had recovered emotional balance and had come to realize that the causes of the war were complex and that guilt was more evenly distributed than he had at first suspected. Yet he remained sympathetic toward the Allies, especially Great Britain and its leaders in whom he had much trust and whom he long believed were pursuing more reasonable goals than were the other belligerents. He also came to appreciate the view that a decisive German victory would pose some danger for the United States. He indicated agreement with House that "if Germany won it would change the course of our civilization and make the United States a military nation." Later in the fall of 1914, he told his private secretary Joseph Tumulty, that he would not pressure England to a dangerous point on the issue of neutral rights because Britain was fighting for the life of the world. During the *Arabic* crisis in mid-1915, he surprised House by stating that he had never been certain that America would not have to intervene in order to prevent a German victory. In 1916, in an effort to promote greater defensive military preparedness, Wilson repeatedly revealed in his public addresses serious concern for the national security and the long-range safety of Latin America. In these speeches he justified heavier expenditures on the army and navy as necessitated in part to protect American trade on the high seas and to avert possible dangers to the Western Hemisphere. Thus at Pittsburgh he asked rhetorically:

What is it that we want to defend? . . . We want to defend the life of this Nation against any sort of interference. We want to maintain the equal right of this Nation as against the action of all other nations, and we wish to maintain the peace and unity of the Western Hemisphere.

Again, at Cleveland, he warned his audience that the United States "must play her part in keeping this conflagration from spreading to the people of the United States; she must also keep this conflagration from spreading on this side of the sea. These are matters in which our very life and our whole pride are embedded. . . ."

It must be emphasized, however, that in general Wilson did not believe that a German victory, undesirable though it would be, would pose an immediate threat to the United States. Like most of his fellow citizens, he was confident of an eventual Allied triumph. But if the opposite should result, he thought that Germany probably would be too weakened by the European war to offer more than a future menace to the security of the Western Hemisphere. He remarked to a sceptical Colonel House, in late 1914, that Germany would need at least several years for recuperation before it could undertake a direct challenge to the United States. He adopted policies, therefore, which protected those national interests that were immediately affected by the war (commerce, legal rights, and prestige), and relied upon such measures as purchase of the Danish West Indies and increased military preparations to ward off future dangers to the national security and to the Monroe Doctrine. He was long convinced, in fact, that neutrality was the wisest course for America and that peace without victory for either belligerent side would alone make possible a just and stable postwar world. The mission of the United States, therefore, was to stand as a bastion of liberty and peace, and to serve all mankind by helping to mediate this terrible struggle whenever events proved favorable. Not until early 1917, after the failure of his two peace overtures and the renewal of submarine warfare, did he accept the necessity for intervention in the war.

.   .   .

American involvement in World War I, as in most other wars, defies simplistic explanations. In the 1930's the historical debate was polarized into the "submarine school," best represented by Charles Seymour, and the "revisionists," with Charles C. Tansill as the most effective spokesman. Seymour dismissed political and economic factors as at most peripheral causes of the war entry and instead emphasized the submarine challenge to American rights and lives. Tansill overlooked security aspects of the war and emphasized American unneutrality, the economic and sentimental ties to the Allies, as pulling the United States into conflict. Neither approach suffices to explain so complex an event. Seymour probably was right in the contention that there would have been no war without the submarine issue, for otherwise Germany and America would not have had a direct clash of interests and power. But the U-boat challenge alone does not explain why the United States adopted the strict accountability policy, since other alternatives were at least theoretically possible. As for the revisionist charges of unneutrality, it seems clear that American neutrality in fact was benevolent toward the Allies and grudgingly technical toward Germany. This did not result from deliberate planning, however, but rather from previous emotional and cultural affinities and from wartime economic connections with the Allies. In any case, Germany did not launch unrestricted submarine warfare merely from anger at the United States or just to cut off the arms trade. Although a different American posture perhaps could have influenced German policy along a more moderate course, the final decision for full underseas warfare was undertaken as the best remaining hope for decisive victory over the Allies through starving Britain into submission.

Just as clearly the hypothesis that the United States went to war in 1917 primarily to protect an endangered security against an immediate threat is not satisfactory. Although Lansing and House, and occasionally Wilson, thought of Germany as a menace to American security and stability, it was primarily as a future danger rather than an imminent peril. Yet Wilson was indeed far more practical in his policies and thinking than many scholars formerly believed, and he sought to promote the national interests as he envisioned them. Aided by his advisers, who exerted considerable influence on him, Wilson adopted policies that embodied economic and prestige interests, as well as moral considerations. The tacit acquiescence in the war trade and the permission of credits and loans to the belligerents reflected primarily

372 Daniel M. Smith

economic interests; whereas the strict accountability policy toward U-boat warfare combined economic and moralistic factors with a desire to uphold the nation's prestige and honor as essential to any worthwhile diplomatic endeavors in the future including mediation of the war. Thus policies toward the Allies were favorable or benevolent because America's basic interests were essentially compatible with British control of the seas and Allied utilization of the American market. The course adopted toward Germany, on the other hand, was firmly nonacquiescent. Submarine warfare endangered American economic connections with Europe and as well violated moral sensibilities and affronted the national honor.

Among high administration officials, Lansing appears to have held the clearest conviction that American security would be endangered by a German triumph and that intervention in the struggle might be necessary—by late 1916 he believed it *was* necessary—to prevent that possibility. Although he sometimes indicated complete concurrence with Lansing's views, Colonel House believed that the most desirable culmination of the war would be enough of an Allied victory to check German ambitions but with Germany left sufficiently strong to play its proper role in the balance of power and to check Russian expansionism. A desire to preserve the balance of power, in the sense of ending the war short of victory for either side, was a factor behind the mediation plans of House and Wilson in 1915 and 1916.

Why did the reluctant president finally decide that belligerency was the only possible answer to unrestricted U-boat warfare? Why did he not rest content with the diplomatic rupture, or with armed neutrality or a limited naval war? The answer seems to have been that the prestige and honor of the nation were so committed as the result of previous policies that nothing less than a diplomatic break and a forceful defense of American interests were possible. By 1917 the evidence suggests that Wilson feared that a German victory was probable and that it would disturb the world balance, and although he was not apprehensive about an immediate threat to the United States, he did believe that such a result would endanger his idealistic hopes for a just peace and the founding of a new and stable world order. He referred to Germany as a madman who must be restrained. He finally accepted the necessity for actively entering the war, it would appear, with the submarine as the precipitant, only because he believed that larger reasons of national prestige, economic interests, and future security so demanded, and above all because of his commitment to the cause of an enduring world peace.

.   .   .

Debate about the nature of the Versailles Treaty began even before it had been completed. Many disillusioned idealists branded it a Carthaginian peace, dictated to the beaten foe and designed to keep Germany prostrate indefinitely. Germany was stripped of its colonies, navy, and merchant marine; deprived of extensive territories inhabited by Germans, in violation of the principle of self-determination; and forced to acknowledge its war guilt while assuming the burden of large but as yet unfixed reparations. Moreover, Germany alone was to be disarmed and left to the mercy of a vengeful France. Why, many asked, had the Fourteen Points been so flagrantly violated? The answer of some critics was expressed by John Maynard Keynes, a British economist at the peace conference and a former admirer of Wilson. In *The Economic Consequences of the Peace,* published in 1920, Keynes attributed the failure to Wilson's moral collapse at Paris. The philosopher-king from the West, he wrote, had turned out to be merely a stubborn Presbyterian theologian in politics, whose very rigidity of mind and lack of detailed preparation had rendered him vulnerable to the agilities of Lloyd George and the cynical determination of Clemenceau. The president had been confused and deceived by these adept Old World leaders and, obsessed with his dream of a league of nations, had sacrificed most of his own Fourteen Points. After the outbreak of World War II, scholars became less concerned with whether Wilson had achieved all that was possible in behalf of a liberal peace and instead began to criticize the Wilsonian peace program as too idealistic for the painful realities of the modern world. George F. Kennan, in a series of stimulating lectures on American diplomacy since 1900, summed up the view of the realists who deplored the marriage of war hysteria and utopian idealism with which Wilson and his fellow Americans had turned World War I into a holy crusade for a world without conflict and injustice.

The judgment of most students of the period, however, is that neither the disillusioned liberals nor the realistic critics have presented a balanced and fair appraisal of Wilson's efforts at Paris. It was true that the Wilsonian peace program was highly idealistic and was only sketchily outlined in his wartime addresses. Yet that which in the abstract appears visionary sometimes can be eminently practical in application. Thus the principle of self-determination, regardless of the many difficulties in applying it to concrete cases, expressed the realization that any peace treaty which did not accord a very large measure of satisfaction to nationalistic aspirations was doomed to an early demise. Wilson realized, perhaps not as much as he should have, that he would experience great difficulty in implementing his goals against the more narrowly conceived national interests of the Allies at the peace conference. Far from being unprepared, he had created a body of scholars, the Inquiry, to gather information and suggest solutions for the problems likely to arise at the peacemaking.

At Paris, Wilson drove himself almost to the point of exhaustion in conscientious application to the tasks of the conference. He consistently revealed a depth of knowledge and understanding beyond that of his counterparts, Lloyd George, Orlando, and Clemenceau. In retrospect, he appears to have been far more realistic than Clemenceau in his opposition to excessive reparations and efforts to dismember Germany, and the same was true of his objections to many of the boundary changes proposed by the various powers at the conference. Wilson undoubtedly was an idealist at Paris, but he combined with idealism a high degree of practicality and stood firmly for a reasonable and workable peace.

The Versailles Treaty was harsh in many of its provisions and it definitely fell short of a complete realization of the liberal peace goals. Wilson had experienced a defeat in the reparations settlement, though he hoped that American participation in the commission which would determine the actual amount Germany would pay could keep the total bill to a reasonable level. Only Germany was disarmed, but the Covenant of the League did pledge future efforts at significant general reductions. The demilitarization and occupation of the Rhineland and French exploitation of the Saar Valley seemed draconian in German eyes, yet France in view of the past was entitled to reasonable safeguards against a renewed invasion. Moreover, Wilson had successfully defended his principles when he and Lloyd George dissuaded France from insisting on the dismemberment of Germany. The peace undoubtedly would have been an even poorer prospect of permanence if German nationalism had been affronted by partition.

Self-determination, although necessarily transgressed in certain areas because of the intermixtures of population and considerations of economic and strategic factors, was generally honored in the drawing of the boundaries of the new states. Italy had been conceded some areas not inhabited by a majority of Italians, but Wilson had resisted the claim to Fiume, vital to the new state of Yugoslavia, even to the point of an open rupture with the Italian delegation. As for Shantung, it was more an apparent than a real defeat, whatever the political repercussions in America. The mandate solution for Germany's colonies in one sense only put a respectable facade over their acquisition by the victors; yet the new system subjected the mandatory powers to legal and moral restrictions and it symbolized the end of the era of nineteenth-century imperialism. Finally, Wilson undoubtedly regarded the creation of the League of Nations as more than justifying all the defeats and compromises at Paris. Whatever the defects of that global collective security organization which time was to reveal—it broke down in the 1930's primarily because it was not supported—it did offer man's best hope for a more secure and progressive world and it would probably not have been achieved, or at least not then, without the American president's determined efforts. A peace admittedly less than perfect would be preserved and improved, Wilson hoped, through the operations of the League.

nine
The Entry
of the
United States
into
World War II

Radical

Radicals view America's entry into World War II as largely dictated by its desire to protect its Open Door Empire. They do not deny that Americans opposed Nazi Germany for other reasons; they admit that the United States had reason to dislike Hitler's government and to fear Germany as a military threat. They argue, however, that a major ingredient in the American government's decision to oppose Hitler was a desire to keep the markets of Europe from falling into the hands of a hostile power. If these markets had been closed to American trade, the consequences would have been disastrous.

If economic motives were important in America's policy toward Europe, Radical historians see them as even more important in this nation's Far Eastern policy. As we have already seen, the United States had committed itself to a policy of free trade in China. In 1931 Japan defied America's Open Door policy by conquering Manchuria; in 1937 Japan invaded China. American attempts to prevent the Japanese conquest of China ultimately caused Japan to attack Pearl Harbor, and our entry into World War II was assured. Radicals hold that American opposition to Japan

was primarily the result of America's desire to protect her economic interests in China by maintaining the Open Door and preventing China from
becoming a province of Japan.

For many years critics of American entry into World War II claimed
that Franklin D. Roosevelt had maneuvered the United States into it. First
he supposedly tried to force Germany into a declaration of war. When
Germany failed to oblige, these critics charge, Roosevelt tried "the back
door to war" by inviting the Japanese to attack Pearl Harbor. (Some of
these charges will be taken up and answered later in an essay by Dexter
Perkins.) Most historians, including the Radical and Realist critics of
Roosevelt, have abandoned these accusations. Today Radical historians
base their criticisms of American entry into World War II on a much
broader economic analysis of American foreign policy.

Lloyd Gardner, author of the following essay, is a professor of history
at Rutgers, the State University of New Jersey. Does he argue that the
United States could or should have avoided participation in World War
II? If this is not his argument, what does he criticize in American policy?
Does the fact that American trade with Japan was far greater than that
with China at the outbreak of World War II necessarily contradict Gardner's interpretation of the economic motives behind America's policy?

Economic Aspects of New Deal Diplomacy

Lloyd Gardner

Unwilling to see Germany and Italy establish a joint hegemony in Europe, the United States finally plunged into the very fields of political involvement it had hoped to avoid through neutrality.

Hitler's military challenge forced the issue. The strain of finding a way to meet it cracked and shattered domestic political alliances, especially after the Administration called for serious rearmament in 1938. The Progressive-Northern Democrat front fell into many fragments. Although not all Progressives refused to follow the Administration, many did, including some of Roosevelt's strongest allies on social legislation.

Undoubtedly many former opponents of the New Deal found the growing emphasis on foreign affairs to their liking. The militancy of Southern conservative Democrats has long been a feature of American politics. The isolationist wing of Progressivism in the Republican party, on the other hand, was much less happy at sharing a bed with the *Chicago Tribune* and the Hearst Press.

Thoughtful interventionists had concluded, perhaps reluctantly, that America could not work out its destiny in the same world with the Axis—the world could not endure, Stimson had said in a radio address, half-slave and half-free. Some isolationists admitted the force of this argument, but replied that even if the country could lead a crusade against the Axis, it would surely lose its soul in the process. A few conservative isolationists, however, did not hesitate to advocate a Fortress America that would have imitated fascist economic—and perhaps later on political—methods

From Lloyd Gardner, *Economic Aspects of New Deal Diplomacy* (Madison: The University of Wisconsin Press; © 1967 by the Regents of the University of Wisconsin), pp. 152–154, 168–174, 133–138, 141–151.

in the Western Hemisphere. Socialists had a vision of the Western Hemisphere, too. But whatever their disagreements on the future, both believe the interventionists exaggerated the threat and that a strong America need not fear for its existence·as a free nation.

This brings one to the question of New Deal shortcomings and specific failures in the recession of 1937–38. The recurrent specter of unemployment and low prices did hover over the New Dealers well into the period when the Administration was aiding the Allies with "everything short of war," but to blame this spirit's influence, at least in the narrow sense, or to call it the demon which drove Roosevelt into the war, simply is not warranted.

One of Roosevelt's ablest defenders, Basil Rauch, quite rightly pointed out that although domestic economic problems sharpened many issues, they did not make the Axis challenge "either more or less minatory." Rauch goes on, however: "Besides, Roosevelt had made it clear from the beginning of his administration that the danger was real to him." Now whether one agrees with Rauch that this was the role Roosevelt essayed or not, he has raised an important question: When and for what reasons did the New Deal undertake political involvement in Europe? To answer simply in order to stop Hitler's military thrust is right but only the first cut in a probe that should go much deeper. The Anglo-American conservative poet-intellectual T. S. Eliot had some scathing words for contemporaries which represented a thoughtful corrective to the growing emotionalism of the times, but far more importantly, to the idealization of the Anglo-American Alliance after the war. He said in his *Idea of a Christian Society* (1940): "Sometimes we are almost persuaded that we are getting along very nicely, with a reform here and a reform there, and would have been getting along still better, if only foreign governments did not insist upon breaking all the rules and playing what is really a different game."

Whether one agrees even partially with Eliot, there is another point to be made: the years before and after World War II demonstrated that the United States regarded the defense of its liberal trade system as central to the conduct of its foreign policy and the stem of that policy's ideology. This is not to say that Americans did not regard Germany as primarily a military threat, especially after the violation of the Munich promise, but when the United States looked to the postwar world, it planned for one that was liberal economically and politically.

And of course Cordell Hull always led the Administration in linking foreign and domestic matters under the umbrella of his reciprocal trade agreements program. He remarked to Henry Stimson in 1938 that he had truly hoped to force Germany back into line through the creation of a trading bloc of twenty or thirty nations, but national economic difficulties stemming from the recession were choking both the domestic economy and his foreign economic policy.

But the Secretary's troubles in pre-war years more generally resulted from an inability to sustain neutrality, matched with a reluctance to involve the United States, and though Sumner Welles and William Bullitt criticized Hull for wanting his cake and eating it too, the Secretary's attitude better typified the country as a whole.

The gold problem and the question of the Spanish Civil War were good examples of the American predicament. These were two issues among many which led American leaders to the conclusion that intervention was the only way out of the world of the 1930's, for it was impossible to accept the possibility of an Axis victory. Committed to defeating the Axis, the United States at once began postwar planning for a better world. The State Department was determined that the economic reorganization of the peace should follow the broad outlines of the Reciprocal Trade Agreements Act, and there should be no political deals between other members of the Grand Alliance to mar the vision of an open world.

.   .   .

The Last Great Debate Ends—Lend-Lease

The State Department first greeted the Munich Pact with a "sigh of relief and pleasure," though only a few in that department thought that a chance would now arise for "real appeasement on sound economic foundations."

But, *pro forma,* the department kept up its pressure to bring Germany back into line, and goods from the Sudeten area were separated from those coming from the rest of Czechoslovakia. A few months later, countervailing duties were reimposed on all German goods. The German chargé told Sumner Welles that the duties would upset his government. "To this I made no reply," Welles recorded coldly. The German diplomat then reported to Berlin that Secretary Hull believed that all political problems were capable of an economic solution. "The preponderance of the economic over the political is the result of the involvement of American commerce with the whole world," cabled the German. "Hence the national interest of America is in the greatest possible encouragement of international trade and in the maintenance of peace. She feels that both are threatened by the totalitarian powers."

As 1939 began, the Administration was indeed responding to this dual threat. Rearmament continued, of course, and the President launched a campaign, not successful until November, to repeal the arms embargo; he also took personal responsibility for selling military airplanes to the French government. When a public storm arose over this issue, Roosevelt called the Senate Foreign Relations Committee to a White House conference, where he tried to satisfy his critics among them and in the nation. He discussed the world in geopolitical terms: If "one nation dominates Europe, that nation will be able to turn the world sphere." The current struggle was one "between different kinds of economies"—between the have nations and the have-nots.

"Why dammit," exclaimed Secretary Hull about this time, "these nations have told us again and again what they mean to do. . . . If they succeed, we will have to transact our business with the rest of the world through Tokyo and Berlin."

In March, Hitler moved his legions all the way into Czechoslovakia. The American President asked Hitler and Mussolini to guarantee the rest of Europe that there would be no more territorial rearrangements. If Berlin and Rome would do that, then "the United States would be prepared to take part in discussions looking towards the most practical manner of opening up avenues of international trade to the end that every nation of the earth may be enabled to buy and sell on equal terms in the world market as well as to possess assurance of obtaining the materials and products of peaceful economic life." Hitler laughed; Mussolini sarcastically called it "a result of progressive paralysis."

On September 1, German armies rolled into Poland and the war began. Within three months, Congress had repealed the arms embargo and the United States was selling war goods and munitions to the Allies. If only to keep the record straight, the President sent Sumner Welles to Europe the following spring to see if there was any basis at all for a negotiated peace. Welles found none.

Traveling to the capitals of each belligerent, Welles repeated the President's long-standing economic offers. In Berlin the German Foreign Minister reasserted his country's claim to close economic and political ties with Central Europe, but more ominous was the dark declaration which stayed in Welles's mind that the United States should not "forget that one thousand years ago German Emperors had been crowned in Prague."

Without doubt the Lend-Lease discussion and debate climaxed the Great Debate over foreign policy in the 1930's. It was Welles's answer to the German foreign minister, and it was the nation's decision to oppose the Axis—and to make a commitment to that goal. At the end of 1940 Great Britain declared that its dollar supplies had fallen too low to permit further purchases on the cash and carry plan. Even if there were some differences of opinion about this claim, and some downright skepticism, everyone in the Administration accepted the broad conclusion that if aid to Britain was essential to victory over the Axis, then it had to be given. On December 18, 1940, the British government was told to go ahead and place orders totaling over three billion dollars; a way would be found to pay for them.

House Resolution 1776 was introduced in January, 1941, to provide that way. Administration spokesmen explained that this Lend-Lease idea and its fulfillment was fully as vital to American security as the creation of the army and navy at the time of independence. Navy Secretary Knox referred also to another historic time and act—the Monroe Doctrine of 1823—and he said that for 118 years that Doctrine had prevented non-American military and political intervention in the Western Hemisphere. It had been "enunciated for preserving the territorial, economic, and social integrity of the United States." Germany threatened that integrity and had to be stopped.

Secretary of War Stimson described Lend-Lease as a "skillful Yankee bargain." To begin with, Great Britain had already spent over 605 million dollars in cash and had thereby provided "our manufacturers working capital with which to build factories and take care of her orders." Consequently, England had contributed "vitally" to our productive capacity. And finally, since management of the new aid program would always be in American hands, it would make for a coordinated and effective war effort.

Before workers in the offices of the War Department, the Secretary called it unprecedented and magnificent realism. Furthermore, if any one asked them if Congress' war-making power had been bypassed, his personal reply would be, "Congress has declared war to this extent at least." And the President reportedly told the Polish Ambassador on March 6, 1941: "We Americans will have to buy this war as such. Let us hope at the price of Lend-Lease only. But who can say what price we may ultimately have to pay?"

Acting partly upon the momentum supplied by the passage of Lend-Lease, President Roosevelt now began that last series of "complicated maneuvers" which revisionist-minded historians have so belabored. And it is noteworthy that even Secretary Stimson considered the April, 1941, decision to order the navy to report German ship movements to the world a "disingenuous" means of supporting British convoys: "I wanted him to be honest with himself. To me it seems a clearly hostile act to the Germans and I am prepared to take the responsibility of it." Roosevelt may have assumed that Hitler still did not want to risk a shooting war with the United States even after this "clearly hostile act." Nonetheless, Stimson was justly worried about the President's haphazard approach to such an important matter of peace and war. This sterile debate on Roosevelt's personal morality, though barely relevant, has thus taken precedence over the political economy of American foreign policy.

Incidents did occur on the Atlantic between German and American ships, but war came from the other direction. On September 11 the President told the American people in a "fireside chat" about the decision to convoy Lend-Lease ships to England. For if the Axis won, he said, the "Atlantic Ocean which has been, and which should always be, a free and friendly highway for us would then become a deadly menace to the commerce of the United States, to the coasts of the United States and even to the inland cities of the United States."

Turning the Challenge into Opportunity

Planning for the postwar period had already begun; the Atlantic Conference between Roosevelt and Churchill, for example, was divided into strategy sessions on how to deal with Germany and forestall Japan and sessions devoted to more long-range matters, such as the disarmament of the aggressors and prospects for continuing the Anglo-American alliance.

A letter from former President Herbert Hoover to Secretary Hull in March, 1941, typified the American mood in approaching these problems. Though discredited by the New Dealers and turned down by the voters, Hoover's summary of the alternatives before the United States, like his earlier one in 1933, ably outlined the situation: "The passage of the Lend-Lease Act obviously involves us deeply in the consequences of the war. But it also gives our government a measure of responsibility to see that the policies pursued by the British are in the interest of both winning the war and winning a peace, and in the interests of the United States." Hoover was particularly worried that the British food blockade "negatived" all the principles England had advanced in war propaganda against fascism. These were exactly the same arguments Mr. Hoover had advanced to Woodrow Wilson just after World War I when he described how Central Europe was "rumbling with social explosion" and on the verge of "total collapse." Then, as in 1941, Hoover sought to "use food control to aid in winning the war and peace and in the special interest of the United States."

Great Britain would have to follow policies not incompatible with American plans, it was contended: "No help to Germany," one State Department official said in September, 1939, "but no dominion status for ourselves." Most of the officers in the Department suspected that London wanted to organize a huge trading orbit after the war, to the exclusion of American interests.

Compared to the protests and sanctions against Germany before the United States entered the war, those sent to Great Britain were mild and they could have been simply for the record, but past experience with British trade policies made them more important than that. Indeed, they were like Woodrow Wilson's protests against British naval policies before American entrance into World War I, which he tried to eliminate in the Fourteen Points. "This Government has made it clear," read a typical protest against restrictions on American exports to British Africa, "that it attaches the highest importance to the sanctity of treaties and that violations of treaty rights wherever they occur tend to spread still further the forces of disorder."

In plainer language still, Secretary of Commerce Hopkins reported to the Cabinet on April 4, 1940: "There is no doubt that relative to our pre-September position we stand to increase our net exports because of the war." Since the British were being forced to buy more from the United States, "We are, of course, in a position to exercise considerable influence upon [them] in decisions of policy which affect us."

385 Economic Aspects of New Deal Diplomacy 385

Lend-Lease was the best lever to use to achieve this goal, and from the beginning the State Department wanted to use it to pry open the Ottawa Agreements. These developments will be considered in a later chapter; suffice it here to indicate that President Roosevelt thought a framework agreement on Lend-Lease repayment should be made first, while the details could be left to continuing negotiations.

Sumner Welles tried to establish such a framework at the Atlantic Conference, and he and Roosevelt spent much time on their way to meet Churchill discussing the problem of opening trade so that underdeveloped countries could help themselves and increase their standards of living. The more prosperous nations would then enjoy the reciprocal benefit of larger foreign markets for their goods. Without the cooperation of the British Empire this was useless talk, and Wells realized it clearly. Lord Halifax, the British Ambassador to the United States, confirmed that Roosevelt had spoken "earnestly" to Churchill about economic matters and noted that the President and Welles seemed worried already about a possible rebirth of isolationism in America. Halifax gave it as his opinion that the two American leaders were determined to have a share in "moulding and running the world" after the war.

A key example of this determination was Washington's flat opposition to Anglo-Russian preliminary attempts to define possible spheres of influence in Europe. This question was touched on at the Atlantic Conference, but the very urge to join with the British in making a generalized postwar statement like the Atlantic Charter had come partly from Roosevelt's concern about Churchill's unilateral pronouncements on the postwar world. On July 14, for instance, the President had sent a message to the Prime Minister disclosing his interest in "rumors regarding trades or deals" in Anglo-Russian talks. He asked for a public statement from London, which he would then back up, reassuring the world that "no post-war peace commitments as to territories, populations or economics have been given." The Atlantic Charter was just such a statement.

American leaders decided from 1938 to 1941 that the country could not achieve its destiny in a closed world dominated by the Axis. Having gone that far with its assumptions, the Administration had to accept political commitments, not only for the war period but also in order to restore an open world society. The doubts and uncertainties since 1933 in European policy were gone; World War II provided a new chance to reshuffle for another "deal" both in domestic and in foreign policy.

In this changed world and in a changed mood, Adolf Berle felt exhilarated about the future: "There is no need to fear. Rather, we shall have an opportunity to create the most brilliant economic epoch the U.S. has yet seen. It is entirely feasible to make the country at once more prosperous and more free than it has ever been. And . . . without sacrificing any of the essential freedoms."

Berle's new optimism presupposed (perhaps unconsciously) the extension of American commitments far beyond anything in American diplomacy before 1941. Were Americans up to that challenge as well as to the lesser, immediate one?

. . .

JAPAN TRIES TO CLOSE THE DOOR IN ASIA

In the case of China our chief object should be, not a favorable balance of trade, but a strong China. A strong China, able and willing to defend the principle of the open market in the Far East, would be worth billions of dollars to the U.S., not alone in terms of exports, but in terms of the security of the system under which we want to live.

Fortune, May, 1941

When I said that the matter depended entirely on the President's statesmanship, he replied that the United States was not in favor of the "closed door" and that it was Japan's turn to figure out ways and means of opening it.

Ambassador Nomura to Tokyo, 1941

Prior to World War II and Japan's decision to join the Tripartite Pact a year later in September, 1940, some American diplomats still hoped that the Far Eastern problem would remain manageable within traditional limits. Events since 1933 had dented badly, but not yet demolished, that hope. Economic pressure probably would have to be brought into play, maybe even military displays, but few—at least before 1939—really expected anything like an attack on Pearl Harbor.

The war in Europe changed Washington's attitude: Japan's somewhat reluctant (but complete) turn to Berlin and Rome enlarged the dimensions of the problem, making it part of the European struggle. Perhaps the Tripartite Pact made a Japanese-

American war inevitable; a strong case can be made for that point of view, but it is probably a nearsighted one. This Pact might better be understood as a sudden-recognition scene, where tensions which have been rising in the early acts of a tragedy are finally resolved.

Japan's membership in the Axis Pact did encourage Tokyo to strike southward in 1940 and 1941, not only endangering British imperial lifelines but also cutting American security lines. And in explaining his reasons for aiding Great Britain in its war with Germany, President Roosevelt, in a letter to Ambassador Grew, linked Europe and the Far East: "We must . . . recognize that our interests are menaced both in Europe and in the Far East. We are engaged in the task of defending our way of life and our vital national interests wherever they are seriously endangered."

The President did not mean simply the preservation of the British Empire in the Far East. "Something bigger is at stake," wrote Admiral Harold Stark to a colleague. "So far as China is concerned, we have 'our foot in the door—the door that once was "open," ' and if I had the say so, it would remain there until I was ready to withdraw it—or until the door opened to such a point that I could withdraw if and when I saw fit."

Though not so pugnacious, Secretary Hull was equally determined. A few days after the European war started, the Japanese Foreign Office presented a note to the American Embassy suggesting the prompt removal of all the belligerent's troops from China. America was not directly concerned, since it was not at war, but like Roosevelt in his letter to Grew, Hull feared that a challenge to Britain or France was only a way to get rid of all Occidental influence in China: "Not since the middle of the nineteenth century has any one power claimed a right of preponderance or predominance of influence there. The United States has its rights and interests there just as Japan."

A few months later, the State Department rejected out of hand a British suggestion that London and Washington work to achieve a compromise peace between Japan and China. Washington felt that the British wanted to surrender too much to Japan, and the State Department was unwilling, possibly even for the sake of easing Britain's situation in the war with Germany, to agree to any scheme by which Japan might solidify its forward position in China.

From 1933 to 1937 the United States had sought a way out of the dilemma in attempting to convince Japan that its best interests would be served by subscribing to the Open Door Policy. That effort continued, but after the failure at Brussels it became more legalistic, more moralistic, and more persistent. Put another way, Stimson had first labeled Japan a defendant in a civil suit; after 1937, the Administration came to see Japan as a criminal offender and therefore subject to restraint.

Some recorders of these events have rightly stressed Japanese militarism and duplicity, especially in connection with the negotiations leading to the Tripartite Pact and in general right up to the day of the attack at Pearl Harbor. Others have pointed out that American insistence that Japan conform to its way of thinking and give up the path of empire was of equal importance—if not more so.

However that may be, these two things are certain: Japan wanted an Asian Empire, and the United States would not yield it. The United States firmly insisted that all nations would prosper through the Open Door Policy; Japan just as firmly denied it.

Nor were the Japanese army warrior-politicians the only ones, as some have contended, who denied the universal value of the Open Door Policy and set out to destroy it. Japanese naval officers made this fact plain to Norman Davis and Admiral Standley at the time of the London Naval talks, when they protested that Japan desired a navy equal to that of the United States primarily because of America's defense of the Open Door Policy by using its navy. Japanese statesmen such as Prince Fuminaro Konoye, Hachiro Arita, and Yosuke Matsuoka had held similar views for a long time. Japanese liberals, on the other hand, were unable to convince these fellow countrymen that Tokyo should stay away from an alliance with Berlin and Rome and stay with London and Washington.

Herbert Feis unintentionally, but precisely, gave the best reason for the defeat of the Japanese liberals. American policy, he wrote in *The Road to Pearl Harbor,* offered Japan no rewards, no advantages for returning to the "company of peaceful and orderly states and accepting a place below the salt." Certainly a Japanese chauvinist could point to Hull's March, 1938, speech to the National Press Club on American overseas interests and rights as contradictory of the principles Washington was pressing upon Tokyo, if not in letter then in spirit. The Secretary had avowed that the United States could not adopt isolationism without "incalculable injury to the standard of living" or exposing its

nationals and "legitimate interests abroad" to injustice and out-
rage.

But America's advance into Asia had been a peaceful one
through the Open Door (with the somewhat embarrassing exception of the pacification of the Philippines after the Spanish-American War), and Japan employed ruthless military conquest. A sympathetic account of the last talks between Secretary Hull and the
Japanese touched upon these differences, and the mental barrier
between them: Secretary Hull's mind was that of the "orderly
nineteenth century when imperial ambitions could be satisfied
without provoking war . . . and the powers professed regard for
the law of nations." "Nomura's world stretched back to the Emperor Jimmu, traversing centuries of samurai militarism, unmodi-
fied by Christian idealism and scarcely touched by democratic individualism."

A significant contrast in method—yet in each instance, the
dynamic force was expansion. And Japan *did* imitate Western
imperialism from the 1890's on into the next century. Hull strove
mightily to convince the Japanese to accept an orderly framework for its expansionism, but buried within scattered State Department reports on Japanese-American relations were precise
refutations of the arguments he was using. "The evidence advanced in this report," said an American vice-consul in Osaka,
"demonstrates that Japan has not derived any material benefits
from the trade agreements program of the United States, either
in its trade with the agreement countries or with the United
States. It is believed that the trade agreements have been largely
responsible for Japan's inability to secure advantages from the
so-called 'free gift of reduced duties.' " Perhaps this should not
be surprising. After all, Sayre and Hull had promised Roosevelt
that third nations would not benefit greatly from the reduced duties that the United States granted to trade agreement countries.

The Vice-Consul's report was supported by the director of the
Trade Agreements Division of the State Department, Harry Hawkins, in a memorandum to the Far Eastern Division as late as November 10, 1941. It was clear, asserted Hawkins, that most nations which had recently negotiated trade agreements with the
United States discriminated against Japan in one way or another.
Even the United States itself did not really give Japan an open
door into the Philippines or into Cuba. Hawkins recommended
that Washington consider the situation and then open these mar-

kets, for the small losses it would suffer there would be far out-weighed by the advantages the United States might then expect in China if a *quid pro quo* could be arranged.

Japan's union with Germany and Italy had raised additional political questions that precluded such an understanding. But Japan's choice had been influenced by an increasingly militant economic policy the United States had pursued since the summer of 1938, in response to Japan's forward movement in China. The "moral embargo" of that year was followed in 1939 by the failure to renew the Japanese-American Commercial Treaty. In the summer of 1940 Japan's quest for raw materials and economic self-sufficiency motivated a drive into Indo-China; from then on, there was really no turning back for either side. A year more of conflict followed. On July 2, 1941, Japanese leaders declared in secret: "We will not be deterred by the possibility of being involved in a war with England and America."

Japanese militarism was a brutal and ugly thing; it cannot be justified, for the same reason that American excesses against the Indians and questionable motives in the Mexican War and the Spanish-American War cannot be. But in each instance some factors behind the expansionist drive can be identified. The starting point is obvious: Japan opposed American presence in China, and perhaps in all of the Far East.

Reasserting the Traditional American Policy

Critics of American Far Eastern policy prompted Secretary Hull to reassert its fundamentals in an open letter to Vice-President Garner on January 8, 1938. The failure of the Brussels Conference frustrated and rankled American diplomats in these months, probably because of the bad press Davis had received near the end, but also because of the inability to find any kind of answer to the Far Eastern dilemma. Like Secretary Stimson's letter to Senator Borah announcing the nonrecognition doctrine, Hull emphasized United States support "by peaceful means [of] influences contributing to preservation and encouragement of orderly processes."

Having cast this moral cloak over his policy, Hull continued to play down direct material interests in the Far East which had brought American gunboats to Chinese rivers, a successful demand for extra-territorial rights, or marines to various treaty ports since the Allied defeat of the Boxers.

The following excerpts from Ambassador Grew's diplomatic records provide much more evidence that the cloak Hull had thrown over American policy had a very materialistic lining. On March 4, 1937, he called on the vice-minister for foreign affairs: "I spoke of the fundamental basis of the commercial policy of the United States as favoring the maintenance and extension of the open door. . . ." On November 28, 1937: "I . . . went into an extensive explanation of the American government's interest in the preservation of the integrity of the Chinese Maritime Customs presenting every possible argument to the effect that the Japanese military in Shanghai must not tamper therewith." On December 28, 1937: "I said to the Vice Minister that in my opinion the integrity of the Chinese customs certainly represented one of the American interests envisaged in the final paragraph of our PANAY note of December 14. . . ." On May 17, 1938: "I said that American missionaries and businessmen are becoming increasingly restive at this arbitrary interference with their legitimate interests which cannot be explained by pleading the dangers of the war zone. . . ." And finally, on July 4, 1938, Grew presented the Japanese Foreign Office a twenty-two page list of depredations against American businessmen, churches, schools, and individual nationals.

"It is inconceivable to me," Admiral Leahy wrote to the President two days before Hull's letter to Garner, "that we as a nation are going to give up our rights of trading or living in China and confine our activities to our own continental limits." The similarity to Hull's speech to the National Press Club of this letter from Leahy is striking, and the Admiral gained a chance to support his contentions publicly when Roosevelt sent an Administration bill to Congress calling for an enlarged navy. "At the present time," Leahy testified before a Congressional committee, "it is the national policy to protect our commerce. The naval policy is designed to support the known national policies, such as the Monroe Doctrine, the protection of nationals abroad, the protection of American shipping, and the protection of American territory, including island possessions, against invasion."

.   .   .

Economic Warfare Against Japan

In January, 1939, Secretary Hull was still trying to dissuade Japan. Referring to the recently concluded Lima Foreign Ministers Conference, he described its trade resolutions to the Japanese Ambassador as the "only basis for real commercial progress." The Ambassador replied simply that he hoped that the question of discrimination against American rights would be solved soon, so that the two nations could go ahead with the development of China. That was an interesting thought, said Hull, but of course the United States stood, as it always had both in Europe and Asia, for broad equality of opportunity.

The year just passed had indeed been a disturbing one. However one interpreted it, Japan's surpassing for the first time the volume of American trade with China could not be ignored. Nelson Johnson informed Hull on March 30, 1938, that his talks with some businessmen had left him with the feeling that they still failed to understand what Japanese dominance would mean. He knew well enough that the "respect extended to foreign interests will be the respect which is given to exhibits in a museum retained because of their historic value."

As worried, yet as reluctant to face a final break as Hull, Stanley Hornbeck could not avoid the thought in February, 1939, that "military opposition" might have to be mounted against Japan. Economic Adviser Herbert Feis suggested a less militant course, proposing that the 1911 Commercial Treaty with Japan should be allowed to lapse. This would give Washington direct control on a day-to-day basis over Japanese-American trade and serve to put Japan on notice. Adolf Berle turned over this idea and mused: "It is a curious fact that the United States, which bolts like a frightened rabbit from every remote contact with Europe, will enthusiastically take a step which might well be a material day's march on the road to a Far Eastern War."

Hull hesitated, considered for a time allowing only part of the treaty to lapse, became concerned with Roosevelt that Congress was going to force their hands, and finally gave notice in July that the Commercial Treaty would be allowed to lapse, though he carefully explained that the action meant no immediate change. The United States had decided to conduct its relations with Japan on an *ad hoc* basis. During that month the Japanese Ambassador had proposed to a skeptical Hull another reason for his country's continuing military actions in Asia: Japan was preventing the spread of Bolshevism. The Secretary turned the point beautifully by replying that although the United States also "fights Bolshevism," Japan by "steadily lowering the standards of life of their own and other peoples by a course of militarism and military conquest," had become the greatest supporter of Bolshevism.

A few months later, Roosevelt had a related point to make to Ambassador Grew. The President denied that a point of no return had been reached in Japanese-American relations; the United States was more incensed for the moment by Russia's attack upon Finland, "but things might develop into such a feeling if the Japanese Government were to fail to speak as civilized twentieth century human beings."

To Tokyo the European war seemed a perfect opportunity to advance Japan's cause, and at the outset of 1940 its foreign policy became much more militant. For example, the Japanese began demanding of the Dutch government in the East Indies unlimited access to that colony's oil resources. To the United States this was a clear indication of what even indirect cooperation between Germany and Japan would mean.

In a letter to the *New York Times,* Henry Stimson called for an end to scrap-iron sales to Japan. "We think Mr. Stimson is right," editorialized the New York *Daily News,* "and we hope Congress takes his advice. This country has a golden opportunity to put the squeeze on the Japanese military caste now, the proper object being to squeeze the Japanese out of China with economic pincers. If we let the chance slide for the sake of a few dollars for a few people, we'll be inviting a Japanese onslaught on us after Japan has conquered and reorganized huge, rich and industrious China."

Japan's leaders did not intend to be caught in an economic pincers, nor did they think of getting out of China. Grew reported that new trade negotiations had begun with France, Argentina, and Paraguay. Mexico and Spain had also been invited to send trade missions to Tokyo. There remained a few among Japan's leaders, continued the American Ambassador, who realized that only the large volume of Japanese-American trade prevented a complete break, but they were losing out to the extremists.

On the Fourth of July, 1940, Hull sent one of his longest appeals to the Japanese Foreign Office. He stressed the similarities between the two nations instead of the known differences. Each attached great importance to foreign trade, for instance; and both had a large stake in maintaining that trade through the Open Door Policy. In both countries respect for private property rights constituted the "foundation of the social and economic system."

This message arrived as Japan was getting ready to make demands upon French Indo-China. When it went ahead and asked for the placement of military observers in the colony to counter Anglo-American "encirclement," Hull urged the Vichy French government to resist. If Japan ruled supreme over the Pacific area, he warned the French, "all foreigners would be driven out and could return only by paying sky-scraping preferences." The Vichy French set a high price on their cooperation, the kind of economic and political guarantees that Washington could not make or even bargain about.

In September, 1940, Japan adhered to the Triparite Pact. There had been a long debate in Tokyo; and even those who were strongest for the Axis Alliance wanted to limit Japan's commitment to as vague a one as possible. In theory, at least, Tokyo did reserve the right to determine when the pact should come into play militarily if the United States should enter the European war. This did nothing to calm Washington's anger—and fear.

Sumner Welles responded in a speech at Cleveland, Ohio, which summarized the Administration's feelings. He had already stated in policy memoranda that the Tripartite Pact elevated China to a position of equal importance to Great Britain in American security planning. At Cleveland he began by reviewing the events of the past few months in the Far East and American objectives in the light of those events. Nothing had changed; the United States still demanded complete "respect by all powers for the legitimate rights of the United States" and "equality of opportunity for the trade of all nations" and Japan's "new order in Asia" had violated all international treaties and law. Welles concluded with references to Japanese pressures on the East Indies and Indo-China, where the events of even the last few weeks had "culminated in measures undertaken by Japanese military forces which threaten the integrity of the French Colony."

In Administration discussions, Roosevelt raised the question whether Russia might be wooed a little. Hull jumped all over the idea, exclaiming that the Soviet Union could never be trusted. But newly appointed War Secretary Stimson defended the suggestion against Hull's battering, remarking that the Russians and the Americans had parallel interests in Asia. Then Stimson began recalling past plans for dealing with the Japanese. In 1918, he told the meeting, Woodrow Wilson became infuriated at Japanese actions in Siberia and imposed an economic boycott against that country, "with the result that she crawled down within two months and brought all her troops out again from Siberia like whipped puppies."

Left unsatisfied and still searching, the President mulled over his next move. A day or two after this Cabinet meeting, he casually remarked to Admiral James Richardson that he had considered stringing light ships across the Pacific to enforce a boycott of Japan. But as he went on talking to the Admiral, he grew less and less positive and admitted that he did not know if America would fight if Japan attacked other European colonial possessions or even the Philippines.

On September 27 Roosevelt had advised Stimson and Knox that he did not intend to pick quarrels with Japan, but he would not back down on any key issue. Economic pressure was still the best weapon, and the door should remain open for "discussion and accommodation within the framework of our historic position in the Far East."

Acting upon this premise and his hunch that something had better be done about direct aid to China, Roosevelt asked Sumner Welles to clear the way for a large loan to Chiang Kai-shek. Years later, staff writers for the *Reporter* magazine called this loan the first victory of the China lobby, and so it may have been; but America's "historic position" in Asia was of long standing. Moreover, Chiang always assumed that he should give a prominent place to economic arguments when appealing to the United States for funds. In asking for this loan, he cited the dangers of trade disturbances and discriminations "against American economic interests" which would follow a collapse of the Chinese economy. The American Information Committee at Shanghai, added the Chinese leader, was undoubtedly supporting the loan because of the realization that "Japan's renewed attack on Chinese currency is seriously detrimental to American trade."

Besides the loan, Washington also cleared the way for volunteer pilots to join the famous Flying Tigers squadron and cut off shipments of scrap iron.

A State Department memorandum of December 10, 1940, set forth the reasons why the United States had stepped up its economic warfare to stop Japan: Tokyo has made its choice for Germany. If the Japanese should succeed in driving out the British from the Far East, "our general diplomatic and strategic position would be considerably weakened—by our loss of Chinese, Indian and South Seas markets (and by our loss of much of the Japanese market for our goods, as Japan would become more and more self-sufficient) as well as by insurmountable restrictions upon our access to the rubber, tin, jute, and other vital materials of the Asian and Oceanic regions."

Prolonging The Agony—The Hull-Nomura Talks

Out of contacts some American clergymen had with Japanese leaders came an opportunity (the last one, as it turned out) to resolve the dispute short of war. These men carried to the State Department certain ideas for a *modus vivendi* which they had received in Tokyo. Hull and Roosevelt accepted the gambit and so informed the new Japanese Ambassador, Kichisaburo Nomura, who had been selected for just such work because of his acquaintance with America, its naval officers, and President Roosevelt. Perhaps with a wave of the hand, the American Commander-in-Chief had been reassuring and confident at their first interview, saying: "there is plenty of room in the Pacific for everybody." Hull, who was making these notes on the conversation, said that here the President "elaborated a little in order to emphasize this suggestion."

In his *Memoirs* the Secretary revealed his own state of mind at the outset of these prolonged discussions with the Japanese Ambassador. Japan wanted a direct bilateral negotiated settlement in Asia, but he would accept nothing short of a broad agreement on the rights of all nations there and the Open Door Policy.

Hull then asked Nomura to meet him at the Wardman Park Hotel in his apartment on April 14, 1941, for the first of a continuing series of meetings which lasted almost to the very day Japan bombed Pearl Harbor. The Secretary posited four principles as the only satisfactory basis for negotiations; in fact, as Nomura learned, Hull would not even begin serious talks until Tokyo had accepted them. These were:

1. Respect for the territorial integrity and the sovereignty of each and all nations.
2. Support of the principle of non-interference in the internal affairs of other countries.
3. Support of the principle of equality, including equality of commercial opportunity.
4. Non-disturbance of the status quo in the Pacific except as the status quo may be altered by peaceful means.

Later on, the question of Japan's membership in the Tripartite Pact became a fifth principle. Nomura apparently failed to report these American prerequisites in full until some months later, out of fear that they were so objectionable to Tokyo that his superiors would call off the discussions immediately.

Four days after this first meeting, recalled Ambassador Grew, a Strictly Confidential memorandum on Japanese-American relations was circulated within the State Department. Its main point was that Japanese expansion would be curtailed only when Tokyo had been made to understand that its militant policy and leaders could not take and keep an area against the wishes of the United States and other powers.

Not all advisers in the State Department agreed that Japan could be forced to retreat. "Japan is making a bid to establish itself as a major power," Maxwell Hamilton observed. "To do that, supplies of certain commodities are essential. A conclusion that Japan is likely, in the present world situation, to acquiesce in measures which would deny Japan essentials would not seem to be well-founded."

Hamilton's dissent was swallowed up in the emotional and ever more rigid atmosphere of the State Department, just as dissenters in Tokyo lost out to the war-planners. When Nomura, for example, asked that the principle of equality of opportunity be made part of the negotiations proper, the Secretary retorted that the United States would not even consider entering into discussions if Japan "should even hesitate in agreeing" to this principle.

Through its "Magic" formula the United States had broken the Japanese code and therefore knew Nomura's instructions at the same time he did. The State Department learned thereby of a new move into Indo-China scheduled for mid-July. When it came, the United States nearly broke off the talks completely. A State Department press release spoke gravely of "the vital problems of our national security" raised by the Japanese action and of the danger of the loss of such "essential materials . . . as tin and rubber which are necessary for the normal economy of this country and the consummation of our defense program."

Then the last economic shot was fired: Washington froze Japanese assets on July 26, 1941. Sumner Welles accused the Japanese of supporting Nazi Germany and he and Hull agreed privately that "nothing will stop them except force." "The point is how long we can maneuver the situation until the military matter in Europe is brought to a conclusion. . . ."

Playing for time was the primary tactic from now on, but Roosevelt did suggest to Ambassador Nomura that his country should accept a neutralized Indo-China from which foodstuffs and raw materials would be guaranteed to all nations by international agreement. In response to this suggestion, Tokyo instructed Nomura to ask for a meeting between the President and Prime Minister Konoye. The ambassador raised this question at an interview after Roosevelt's return from the Atlantic Conference with Prime Minister Winston Churchill in August, 1941. Roosevelt seemed taken with the idea at first, but Hull and other Cabinet officers opposed it unless the Japanese first agreed to the four principles. The President's reply, therefore, was restricted to stressing Japan's responsibility for peace in Asia, and to warning that if Tokyo continued its movement into Thailand, the United States would have to take steps to "preserve its security and safety." This was the carefully phrased statement that Churchill and Roosevelt had worked out at the Atlantic Conference. They hoped it would forestall Japanese action for at least a few months.

Some later interpretations of this document insist that it was an ultimatum, or nearly so, but a more critical historical question centers in how much Secretary Hull expected from the Japanese before agreeing to a Konoye-Roosevelt conference. Stimson noted, for example, that the Secretary of State was firmly set on achieving a Japanese evacuation of China up to Manchuria as a prior condition. The evacuation of the latter area would be discussed afterwards. Moreover, Japan would also have to promise not to attack Russia.

Konoye's shaky government could not end the China Incident that way; and Ambassador Grew also felt this was too much to expect before even beginning negotiations, and he had been one who felt that Hull was not tough enough back in the mid-1930's. If the idea had been to bring the Japanese leaders to a willingness to compromise with the United States, then that end had been accomplished by August, 1941. Sending reports to the State Department during these months seemed to him "like throwing pebbles into a lake at night; we were not permitted to see even the ripples."

Tokyo's response to the freezing order reaffirmed its position, with an added twist of fatalism: "In an atmosphere of world crisis and international confusion, it is sometimes difficult to ascertain when an event is a cause and when it is a consequence." As Grew could attest, the remark suited the occasion. But when he had presented a copy of the freezing order, such bothersome questions were put aside, and he made the point plainly: "The American freezing order in effect works along lines similar to the restrictions and handicaps which American business and trade and commerce have encountered in Japan and Japan occupied areas during the last several years."

During October ahd November, Washington continued to stall, as Secretary Stimson put it, "so as to be sure that Japan was put in the wrong and made the first bad move—overt move," and so as to "get that big stick in readiness."

Hull, fatalistically, like the Japanese Foreign Office, played out the tragedy of the Open Door Policy. "It cannot be doubted for a moment," he said, going over past ground with Nomura on October 17, that if Japan "adopts this basic policy" of peaceful change, "she will have the advantage over all countries in her area because of her geographical position, her race, and because of her business acumen." Japanese leaders had by this time decided, however, that United States policy would soon strangle Japan unless a sharp blow could force the United States to let go its economic grip. It is unlikely that the more realistic leaders in Japan expected to gain more than an extended breathing space during which they could build up their defenses in depth and discourage the United States from fighting a long and difficult war.

A few Administration policy makers thought about proposing a short truce to the Japanese. At worst it would give Stimson and Knox more time; at best it might even cool off things enough so that negotiations might begin again. Stimson was adamantly against the idea; and when Roosevelt mentioned it to him, he retorted that "it has always been our historic policy since the Washington Conference not to leave the Chinese and Japanese together, because the Japanese were always able to overshadow the Chinese and the Chinese knew it."

Even so, Hull came close to making such an offer for a three month's truce on November 25, 1941. In exchange for United States resumption of limited economic relations with Japan, Tokyo was to have promised to send no more troops into areas it then occupied and not to invoke the Tripartite Pact if the United States entered the European War. Finally, the United States would "introduce" Chinese and Japanese representatives to one another, so that they could begin talks anew. The Chinese opposed the truce scheme; there was confusion in the British cabinet, and at least one negative response was received from London; and various cabinet members were against it; so that Hull and Roosevelt decided against making the offer. It may be that Hull never fully believed in the idea anyway.

Hence the Secretary of State informed his two colleagues of the War and Navy Departments that "we were likely to be attacked perhaps next Monday." On November 26, the Secretary of War prepared his now famous message to the Western Defense Command: "Negotiations with Japan have been terminated without an agreement on disputed points. Japanese future action unpredictable but action possible any moment. If hostilities cannot, repeat cannot, be avoided the United States desires that Japan commit the first overt act."

In the Pearl Harbor investigations, this message became an important piece of evidence. Senator Homer Ferguson pressed Sumner Welles about this decision:

Well, do you agree that we did turn it over to the Army and the Navy on the 27th as indicated by Colonel Stimson's note or language?

Mr. Welles: I think that is a question only Mr. Hull himself could answer.

Around the possible answers to this question has spun a whirlpool of argument over American entry into World War II. This question and others like it have been debated and argued without any satisfaction and have only resulted in limiting American political thought and attitudes even today. The debate picks up the issues too late; it assumes that American policy was either narrowly moral or unmoral; it concerns itself too much with the irrelevant idea of a huge conspiracy to lead America into war; and it obscures many other issues entirely. Harry Hopkins probed to the nexus of the Japanese-American dialogue:

Apropos of the Roberts report, which indicates that the State Department had given up all hope of coming to an agreement with Japan, it seems to me that hardly squares with the facts. It is true that Hull told the Secretaries of War and Navy that he believed Japan might attack at any moment. On the other hand, up to the very last day, he undoubtedly had hopes that something could be worked out at the last moment. Hull had always been willing to work out a deal with Japan. To be sure, it was the kind of deal that Japan probably would not have accepted but, on the other hand, it was also the type of a deal which would have made us very unpopular in the Far East.

Hopkins missed the point only by failing to stress more plainly that Hull always insisted upon prior acceptance of American principles. In the ten years before Pearl Harbor, and not just from November 25, 1941, the United States feared that Japan would attack the Washington treaties, and then American interests. Tokyo's 1931 assault on the Washington treaties met an uncertain response. Stimson and Hull both hoped (along with many others) that something could be worked out. Secretary Hull was hardly as alone as Hopkins' statement would indicate in trying to achieve a settlement.

From 1931 to 1937, Washington tried logic and persuasion. The Brussels Conference demonstrated how unsatisfactory this approach had become. After that the United States firmly reasserted its position, began a series of economic measures, and kept hoping this would be enough. Japan responded with increased belligerency, and climaxed its opposition by joining the Axis Tripartite Pact. When President Roosevelt told the Japanese it was their turn to figure out ways and means of keeping the door open in Asia, the attack on Pearl Harbor was Tokyo's answer.

The Entry of the United States into World War II

Realist

Realist historians have no quarrel with America's entry into the war in Europe, but they argue that a more realistic Asian policy might have avoided war with Japan. Such a policy would have permitted the United States to concentrate its force against the Nazi conquest of Europe, a far greater threat to American interests and security than that which Japan offered in the Far East. While Radicals see a solid economic interest behind America's defense of the Open Door against Japan, Realists tend to see American protection of China as a romantic escapade dictated by a foolish and maudlin view of China rather than by true national interest. They point out that the attempt to rescue China failed in the long run anyway, for the regime of Chiang Kai-shek soon went down before the Communist revolution.

Paul W. Schroeder, author of the following essay, is a professor of history at the University of Illinois at Champagne. Is his argument that the

United States could and should have avoided war with Japan convincing? Do the Realists have a different attitude toward American interests in Asia than toward United States interests in Europe? If so, what do you think is behind that difference? What weight do the Realists seem to place on economics as the motivation for American policy? What part do they think economics should play? How important is it compared with strategic interests in the Realist scheme of things?

The Axis Alliance and Japanese-American Relations, 1941

Paul W. Schroeder

In judging American policy toward Japan in 1941, it might be well to separate what is still controversial from what is not. There is no longer any real doubt that the war came about over China. Even an administration stalwart like Henry L. Stimson and a sympathetic critic like Herbert Feis concur in this. Nor is it necessary to speculate any longer as to what could have induced Japan to launch such an incredible attack upon the United States and Great Britain as occurred at Pearl Harbor and in the south Pacific. One need not, as Winston Churchill did in wartime, characterize it as "an irrational act" incompatible "with prudence or even with sanity." The Japanese were realistic about their position throughout; they did not suddenly go insane. The attack was an act of desperation, not madness. Japan fought only when she

Reprinted from Paul W. Schroeder: *The Axis Alliance and Japanese-American Relations, 1941*, pp. 200–216. © 1958 by the American Historical Association. Used by permission of Cornell University Press.

had her back to the wall as a result of America's diplomatic and economic offensive.

The main point still at issue is whether the United States was wise in maintaining a "hard" program of diplomatic and economic pressure on Japan from July 1941 on. Along with this issue go two subsidiary questions: the first, whether it was wise to make the liberation of China the central aim of American policy and the immediate evacuation of Japanese troops a requirement for agreement; the second, whether it was wise to decline Premier Konoye's invitation to a meeting of leaders in the Pacific. On all these points, the policy which the United States carried out still has distinguished defenders. The paramount issue between Japan and the United States, they contend, always was the China problem. In her China policy, Japan showed that she was determined to secure domination over a large area of East Asia by force. Apart from the legitimate American commercial interests which would be ruined or excluded by this Japanese action, the United States, for reasons of her own security and of world peace, had sufficient stake in Far Eastern questions to oppose such aggression. Finally, after ten years of Japanese expansion, it was only sensible and prudent for the United States to demand that it come to an end and that Japan retreat. In order to meet the Japanese threat, the United States had a perfect right to use the economic power she possessed in order to compel the Japanese to evacuate their conquered territory. If Japan chose to make this a cause for war, the United States could not be held responsible.

A similar defense is offered on the decision to turn down Konoye's Leaders' Conference. Historians may concede, as do Langer and Gleason, that Konoye was probably sincere in wanting peace and that he "envisaged making additional concessions to Washington, including concessions on the crucial issue of the withdrawal of Japanese troops from China." But, they point out, Konoye could never have carried the Army with him on any such concession. If the United States was right in requiring Japan to abandon the Co-Prosperity Sphere, then her leaders were equally right in declining to meet with a Japanese Premier who, however conciliatory he might have been personally, was bound by his own promises and the exigencies of Japanese politics to maintain this national aim. In addition, there was the serious possibility that much could be lost from such a meeting—the confidence of China, the cohesiveness of the coalition with Great Britain and

Russia. In short, there was not enough prospect of gain to merit taking the chance.

This is a point of view which must be taken seriously. Any judgment on the wisdom or folly of the American policy, in fact, must be made with caution—there are no grounds for dogmatic certainty. The opinion here to be developed, nonetheless, is that the American policy from the end of July to December was a grave mistake. It should not be necessary to add that this does not make it treason. There is a "back door to war" theory, espoused in various forms by Charles A. Beard, George Morgenstern, Charles C. Tansill, and, most recently, Rear Admiral Robert A. Theobald, which holds that the President chose the Far East as a rear entrance to the war in Europe and to that end deliberately goaded the Japanese into an attack. This theory is quite different and quite incredible. It is as impossible to accept as the idea that Japan attacked the United States in a spirit of overconfidence or that Hitler pushed the Japanese into war. Roosevelt's fault, if any, was not that of deliberately provoking the Japanese to attack, but of allowing Hull and others to talk him out of impulses and ideas which, had he pursued them, might have averted the conflict. Moreover, the mistake (assuming that it was a mistake) of a too hard and rigid policy with Japan was, as has been pointed out, a mistake shared by the whole nation, with causes that were deeply organic. Behind it was not sinister design or warlike intent, but a sincere and uncompromising adherence to moral principles and liberal doctrines.

This is going ahead too fast, however; one needs first of all to define the mistake with which American policy is charged. Briefly, it was this. In the attempt to gain everything at once, the United States lost her opportunity to secure immediately her essential requirements in the Far East and to continue to work toward her long-range goals. She succeeded instead only in making inevitable an unnecessary and avoidable war—an outcome which constitutes the ultimate failure of diplomacy. Until July 1941, as already demonstrated, the United States consistently sought to attain two limited objectives in the Far East, those of splitting the Axis and of stopping Japan's advance southward. Both aims were in accordance with America's broad strategic interests; both were reasonable, attainable goals. Through a combination of favorable circumstance and forceful American action, the United States reached the position where the achievement of these two goals was within sight. At this very moment, on the verge of a major diplomatic victory, the United States abandoned her original goals and concentrated on a third, the liberation of China. This last aim was not in accord with American strategic interests, was not a limited objective, and, most important, was completely incapable of being achieved by peaceful means and doubtful of attainment even by war. Through her single-minded pursuit of this unattainable goal, the United States forfeited the diplomatic victory which she had already virtually won. The unrelenting application of extreme economic pressure on Japan, instead of compelling the evacuation of China, rendered war inevitable, drove Japan back into the arms of Germany for better or for worse, and precipitated the wholesale plunge by Japan into the South Seas. As it ultimately turned out, the United States succeeded in liberating China only at great cost and when it was too late to do the cause of the Nationalist Chinese much real good.

This is not, of course, a new viewpoint. It is in the main simply that of Ambassador Grew, who has held and defended it since 1941. The arguments he advances seem cogent and sensible in the light of present knowledge. Briefly summarized, they are the following: First is his insistence on the necessity of distinguishing between long-range and immediate goals in foreign policy and on the folly of demanding the immediate realization of both. Second is his contention that governments are brought to abandon aggressive policies not by sudden conversion through moral lectures, but by the gradual recognition that the policy of aggression will not succeed. According to Grew, enough awareness of failure existed in the government of Japan in late 1941 to enable it to make a beginning in the process of reversal of policy—but not nearly enough to force Japan to a wholesale surrender of her conquests and aims. Third was his conviction that what was needed on both sides was time—time in which the United States could grow stronger and in which the tide of war in Europe could be turned definitely against Germany, time in which the sense of failure could grow in Japan and in which moderates could gain better control of the situation. A victory in Europe, Grew observed, would either automatically solve the problem of Japan or make that problem, if necessary, much easier to solve by force. Fourth was his belief that Japan would fight if backed to the wall (a view vindicated by events) and that a war at this time with Japan could not possibly serve the interests of the United States. Even if one considered war as the only final answer to Japanese militarism, still, Grew would answer, the United States stood to gain nothing by seeking a decision in 1941. The time factor was entirely in America's favor. Japan could not hope to gain as much from a limited relaxation of the embargo as the United States could from time gained for mobilization; Roosevelt and the military strategists were in fact anxious to gain time by a *modus vivendi.*

There is one real weakness in Grew's argument upon which his critics have always seized. This is his contention that Konoye, faced after July 26 with the two clear alternatives of war or a genuine peace move, which would of necessity include a settlement with China, had chosen the latter course and could have carried through a policy of peace had he been given the time. "We believed," he writes, "that Prince Konoye was in a position to carry the country with him in a program of peace" and to make commitments to the United States which would "eventually, if not immediately" meet the conditions of Hull's Four Points. The answer of critics is that, even if one credits Konoye's sincerity and takes his assurances at face value, there is still no reason to believe that he could have carried even his own cabinet, much less the whole nation, with him on any program approximating that of Hull. In particular, as events show, he could not have persuaded the Army to evacuate China.

The objection is well taken; Grew was undoubtedly overoptimistic about Konoye's capacity to carry through a peaceful policy. This one objection, however, does not ruin Grew's case. He countered it later with the argument that a settlement with Japan which allowed Japanese garrisons to remain in China on a temporary basis would not have been a bad idea. Although far from an ideal solution, it would have been better, for China as well, than the policy the United States actually followed. It would have brought China what was all-important—a cessation of fighting—without involving the United States, as many contended, in either a sacrifice of principle or a betrayal of China. The United States, Grew points out, had never committed herself to guaranteeing China's integrity. Further, it would not have been necessary to agree to anything other than temporary garrisons in North China which, in more favorable times, the United States could work to have removed. The great mistake was to allow American policy to be guided by a sentimental attitude toward China which in the long run could do neither the United States nor China any good. As Grew puts it:

Japan's advance to the south, including her occupation of portions of China, constituted for us a real danger, and it was definitely in our national interest that it be stopped, by peaceful means if possible, by force of arms if necessary. American aid to China should have been regarded, as we believe it was regarded by our Government, as an indirect means to this end, and not from a sentimental viewpoint. The President's letter of January 21, 1941, shows that he then sensed the important issues in the Far East, and that he did not include China, purely for China's sake, among them. . . . The failure of the Washington Administration to seize the opportunity presented in August and September, 1941, to halt the southward advance by peaceful means, together with the paramount importance attached to the China question during the conversations in Washington, gives rise to the belief that not our Government but millions of quite understandably sympathetic but almost totally uninformed American citizens had assumed control of our Far Eastern policy.

There remains the obvious objection that Grew's solution, however plausible it may now seem, was politically impracticable in 1941. No American government could then have treated China as expendable, just as no Japanese government could have written off the China Affair as a dead loss. This is in good measure true and goes a long way to explain, if not to justify, the hard American policy. Yet it is not entirely certain that no solution could have been found which would both have averted war and have been accepted by the American people, had a determined effort been made to find one. As F. C. Jones points out, the United States and Japan were not faced in July 1941 with an absolute dilemma of peace or war, of complete settlement or open conflict. Hull believed that they were, of course; but his all-or-nothing attitude constituted one of his major shortcomings as a diplomat. Between the two extremes existed the possibility of a *modus vivendi,* an agreement settling some issues and leaving others in abeyance. Had Roosevelt and Konoye met, Jones argues, they might have been able to agree on a relaxation of the embargo in exchange for satisfactory assurances on the Tripartite Pact and southward expansion, with the China issue laid aside. The United States would not have had to cease aid, nor Japan to remove her troops. The final settlement of the Far Eastern question, Jones concludes,

would then have depended upon the issue of the struggle in Europe. If Germany prevailed, then the United States would be in no position to oppose Japanese ambitions in Asia; if Germany were defeated, Japan would be in no position to persist in those ambitions in the face of the United States, the USSR, and the British Commonwealth.

Such an agreement, limited and temporary in nature, would have involved no sacrifice of principle for either nation, yet would have removed the immediate danger of war. As a temporary expedient and as an alternative to otherwise inevitable and useless conflict, it could have been sold by determined effort to the public on both sides. Nor would it have been impossible, in the writer's opinion, to have accompanied or followed such an agreement with a simple truce or standstill in the China conflict through American mediation.

This appraisal, to be sure, is one based on realism. Grew's criticism of Hull's policy and the alternative he offers to it are both characterized by fundamental attention to what is practical and expedient at a given time and to limited objectives within the scope of the national interest. In general, the writer agrees with this point of view, believing that, as William A. Orton points out, it is foolish and disastrous to treat nations as morally responsible persons, "because their nature falls far short of personality," and that, as George F. Kennan contends, the right role for moral considerations in foreign affairs is not to determine policy, but rather to soften and ameliorate actions necessarily based on the realities of world politics.

From this realistic standpoint, the policy of the State Department would seem to be open to other criticisms besides those of Grew. The criticisms, which may be briefly mentioned here, are those of inconsistency, blindness to reality, and futility. A notable example of the first would be the inconsistency of a strong no-compromise stand against Japan with the policy of broad accommodation to America's allies, especially Russia, both before and after the American entrance into the war. The inconsistency may perhaps best be seen by comparing the American stand in 1941 on such questions as free trade, the Open Door in China, the territorial and administrative integrity of China, the maintenance of the prewar *status quo* in the Far East, and the sanctity of international agreements with the position taken on the same questions at the Yalta Conference in 1945. . . .

The blindness to reality may be seen in the apparent inability of American policy makers to take seriously into account the gravity of Japan's economic plight or the real exigencies of her military and strategic position, particularly as these factors would affect the United States over the long run. Equally unrealistic and more fateful was the lack of appreciation on the part of many influential people and of wide sections of the public of the almost certain consequences to be expected from the pressure exerted on Japan—namely, American involvement in a war her military strategists considered highly undesirable. The attitude has been well termed by Robert Osgood, "this blind indifference toward the military and political consequences of a morally-inspired position."

The charge of futility, finally, could be laid to the practice of insisting on a literal subscription to principles which, however noble, had no chance of general acceptance or practical application. The best example is the persistent demand that the Japanese pledge themselves to carrying out nineteenth-century principles of free trade and equal access to raw materials in a twentieth-century world where economic nationalism and autarchy, trade barriers and restrictions were everywhere the order of the day, and not the least in the United States under the New Deal. Not one of America's major allies would have subscribed wholeheartedly to Hull's free-trade formula; what good it could have done to pin the Japanese down to it is hard to determine.

But these are all criticisms based on a realistic point of view, and to judge the American policy solely from this point of view is to judge it unfairly and by a standard inappropriate to it. The policy of the United States was avowedly not one of realism, but of principle. If then it is to be understood on its own grounds and judged by its own standards, the main question will be whether the policy was morally right—that is, in accord with principles of peace and international justice. Here, according to its defenders, the American policy stands vindicated. For any other policy, any settlement with Japan at the expense of China, would have meant a betrayal not only of China, but also of vital principles and of America's moral task in the world.

This, as we know, was the position of Hull and his co-workers. It has been stated more recently by Basil Rauch, who writes:

No one but an absolute pacifist would argue that the danger of war is a greater evil than violation of principle. . . . The isolationist believes that appeasement of Japan without China's consent violated no principle worth a risk of war. The internationalist must believe that the principle did justify a risk of war.

This is not an argument to be dismissed lightly. The contention that the United States had a duty to fulfill in 1941, and that this duty consisted in holding to justice and morality in a world given to international lawlessness and barbarism and in standing on principle against an unprincipled and ruthless aggressor, commands respect. It is not answered by dismissing it as unrealistic or by proscribing all moral considerations in foreign policy. An answer may be found, however, in a closer definition of America's moral duty in 1941. According to Hull, and apparently also Rauch, the task was primarily one of upholding principle. This is not the only possible definition. It may well be contended that the moral duty was rather one of doing the most practical good possible in a chaotic world situation and, further, that this was the main task President Roosevelt and the administration had in mind at least till the end of July 1941.

If the moral task of the United States in the Far East was to uphold a principle of absolute moral value, the principle of nonappeasement of aggressors, then the American policy was entirely successful in fulfilling it. The American diplomats proved that the United States was capable of holding to its position in disregard and even in defiance of national interests narrowly conceived. If, however, the task was one of doing concrete good and giving practical help where needed, especially to China, then the American policy falls fatally short. For it can easily be seen not only that the policy followed did not in practice help China, but also that it could not have been expected to. Although it was a pro-China and even a China-first policy in principle, it was not in practical fact designed to give China the kind of help needed.

What China required above all by late 1941 was clearly an end to the fighting, a chance to recoup her strength. Her chaotic financial condition, a disastrous inflation, civil strife with the Communists, severe hunger and privation, and falling morale all enfeebled and endangered her further resistance. Chiang Kai-shek, who knew this, could hope only for an end to the war through the massive intervention of American forces and the consequent liberation of China. It was in this hope that he pleaded so strongly for a hard American policy toward Japan. Chiang's hopes, however, were wholly unrealistic. For though the United States was willing to risk war for China's sake, and finally did incur it over the China issue, the Washington government never intended in case of war to throw America's full weight against Japan in order to liberate China. The American strategy always was to concentrate on Europe first, fighting a defensive naval war in the Far East and aiding China, as before, in order to keep the Japanese bogged down. The possibility was faced and accepted that the Chinese might have to go on fighting for some years before eventual liberation through the defeat of Japan. The vehement Chinese protests over this policy were unavailing, and the bitter disillusionment suffered by the Chinese only helped to bring on in 1942 the virtual collapse of the Chinese war effort during the latter years of the war.

As a realistic appraisal of America's military capabilities and of her world-wide strategic interests, the Europe-first policy has a great deal to recommend it. But the combination of this realistic strategy with a moralistic diplomacy led to the noteworthy paradox of a war incurred for the sake of China which could not then be fought for the sake of China and whose practical value for China at the time was, to say the least, dubious. The plain fact is that the United States in 1941 was not capable of forcing Japan out of China by means short of war and was neither willing nor, under existing circumstances, able to throw the Japanese out by war. The American government could conceivably have told the Chinese this and tried to work out the best possible program of help for China under these limitations. Instead, it yielded to Chinese importunities and followed a policy almost sure to eventuate in war, knowing that if the Japanese did attack, China and her deliverance would have to take a back seat. It is difficult to conceive of such a policy as a program of practical aid to China.

The main, though not the only, reason why this policy was followed is clearly the overwhelming importance of principle in American diplomacy, particularly the principle of nonappeasement of aggressors. Once most leaders in the administration and wide sections of the public became convinced that it was America's prime moral duty to stand hard and fast against aggressors, whatever the consequences, and once this conviction became decisive in the formulation of policy, the end result was almost inevitable: a policy designed to uphold principle and to punish the aggressor, but not to save the victim.

It is this conviction as to America's moral duty, however sincere and understandable, which the writer believes constitutes a fundamental misreading of America's moral task. The policy it gave rise to was bad not simply because it was moralistic but because it was obsessed with the wrong kind of morality—with that abstract "Let justice be done though the heavens fall" kind which so often, when relentlessly pursued, does more harm than good. It would be interesting to investigate the role which this conception of America's moral task played in the formulation of the American war aims in the Far East, with their twin goals of unconditional surrender and the destruction of Japan as a major power, especially after the desire to vindicate American principles and to punish the aggressor was intensified a hundredfold by the attack on Pearl Harbor. To pursue the later implications of this kind of morality in foreign policy, with its attendant legalistic and vindictive overtones, would, however, be a task for another volume.

In contrast, the different kind of policy which Grew advocated and toward which Roosevelt so long inclined need not really be considered immoral or unprincipled, however much it undoubtedly would have been denounced as such. A limited *modus vivendi* agreement would not have required the United States in any way to sanction Japanese aggression or to abandon her stand on Chinese integrity and independence. It would have constituted only a recognition that the American government was not then in a position to enforce its principles, reserving for America full freedom of action at some later, more favorable time. Nor would it have meant the abandonment and betrayal of China. Rather it would have involved the frank recognition that the kind of help the Chinese wanted was impossible for the United States to give at that time. It would in no way have precluded giving China the best kind of help then possible—in the author's opinion, the offer of American mediation for a truce in the war and the grant of fuller economic aid to try to help the Chinese recover—and promising China greater assistance once the crucial European situation was settled. Only that kind of morality which sees every sort of dealing with an aggressor, every instance of accommodation or conciliation, as appeasement and therefore criminal would find the policy immoral.

What the practical results of such a policy, if attempted, would have been is of course a matter for conjecture. It would be rash to claim that it would have saved China, either from her wartime collapse or from the final victory of communism. It may well be that already in 1941 the situation in China was out of control. Nor can one assert with confidence that, had this policy enabled her to keep out of war with Japan, the United States would have been able to bring greater forces to bear in Europe much earlier, thus shortening the war and saving more of Europe from communism. Since the major part of the American armed forces were always concentrated in Europe and since in any case a certain proportion would have had to stand guard in the Pacific, it is possible that the avoidance of war with Japan, however desirable in itself, would not have made a decisive difference in the duration of the European conflict. The writer does, however, permit himself the modest conclusions that the kind of policy advocated by Grew presented real possibilities of success entirely closed to the policy actually followed and that it was by no means so immoral and unprincipled that it could not have been pursued by the United States with decency and honor.

The Entry of the United States into World War II

Nationalist

Nationalist historians believe that the United States had little choice but to enter World War II. They regard selfish economic interests as relatively unimportant motives for American policy. They argue that it was impossible for the United States to have abandoned China and that the American refusal to do so meant, inevitably, war with Japan. In the following selection, Dexter Perkins responds to the criticisms of the two preceding articles and answers some of the more extreme denunciations of American policy that have circulated in the United States for the past twenty-five years.

Why does Perkins believe that the United States had to oppose Hitler? If Hitler had no plans to conquer the United States, could we have abstained from the war in Europe? What evidence does Perkins cite to answer Schroeder's argument that the United States could have avoided war with Japan?

Foreign Policy and the American Spirit

Dexter Perkins

It seems to me fair to say at the outset that it is impossible to avoid the conclusion that revisionism is essentially history by hypothesis. It suggests—indeed in some instances it almost claims —that the world would have been a better place, or that at any rate the present position of the United States would have been happier, if this country had not intervened in the Second World War. Such a proposition can be put forward, but it cannot be established like a theorem in geometry. We cannot go back to 1939 or 1941 and re-enact the events of those stirring and tumultuous years. In a sense, we are bound by the past.

None the less, it seems worth while, even though we are in the realm of speculation rather than scientific history, to state the revisionist point of view. First, with regard to Germany, the point of view is advanced that the United States was in no essential danger from Adolf Hitler, that he demonstrated no very great interest in the American continents, that he desired until almost the day of Pearl Harbor to keep out of trouble with the United States, that there is no reliable evidence that he meditated an assault upon the New World. It is possible for the revisionist to go further. The ambitions of Hitler, it would be maintained, would have been checked and contained within limits by the presence of the great totalitarian state to the East. The two colossi would act each as a restraint on the other. It needed not the intervention of the American government to preserve the safety of the New World. As to Asia, the argument runs somewhat differently. Less emphasis is placed on the question of national security and more on a certain interpretation of national interest. The United States, we are told, had only a meager interest in China; its trade and investments

Reprinted from Dexter Perkins, *Foreign Policy and the American Spirit*, Glyndon G. Van Deusen and Richard Wade, eds., pp. 109–124. © 1957 by Cornell University. Used by permission of Cornell University Press.

there were insignificant, and were likely to remain so. They were distinctly inferior to our trade and investments in Japan. The shift in the balance of the Far East that might come about through a Japanese victory over Great Britain was no real concern of the United States. As to the Philippines, they might have been left alone had we stayed out of the war, or conversely, they were not worth the sacrifice involved in maintaining our connection with them. Such are the assumptions, implied, if not always expressed, in the revisionist view of the problem of the Orient.

Now some of the assertions in this rationale are unchallengeable. It is true that Hitler desired to avoid a clash with the United States until just before Pearl Harbor. It is true that the economic interests of the United States in China were inferior to our interests in Japan. These are facts, and must be accepted as facts. But there still remain a good many questions about the revisionist assumptions. For example, was there in 1940 and 1941 no danger of the destruction of British naval power, and would that destruction have had no unhappy consequences for the United States? Granted that the documents show great reluctance on the part of the Fuehrer to challenge the United States, would this reluctance have outlasted the fall of Great Britain? Granted that the Kremlin might have exercised a restraining influence on the Germans, is it certain that the two powers might not have come to an understanding as they did in 1939, and had at other periods in the past? Just how comfortable a world would it have been if the psychopathic leader of Germany had emerged from the Second World War astride a large part of the Continent, with the resources of German science at his command? There are questions, too, that can be asked about the Orient. Did the United States have no responsibility for the Philippines, and would the islands have been safe for long if the Japanese had dominated the Far East? Could the United States divest itself of all concern for China, abandoning a policy of nearly forty years duration and a deep-seated American tradition? Was the destruction of British power in this part of the world a matter of no concern to this country? Could the defeat of Britain in the East be separated from the fate of Britain in the world at large? These are extremely large questions, and it is a bold man who will brush them aside as inconsequential or trivial, or who will reply to them with complete dogmatism. Indeed, it is because they raise so many problems cutting to the root of our feelings, as well as our opinions, that they arouse so much controversy. Nor is there any likelihood that we can ever arrive at a complete consensus with regard to them.

We must, I think, seek a somewhat narrower frame of reference if we are to answer the revisionists with facts, and not with speculations. One of the ways to answer them, and one particularly worth pursuing with regard to the war in Europe, is to analyze the policy of the Roosevelt administration in its relation to public sentiment.

Foreign policy, in the last analysis, depends, not upon some logical formula, but upon the opinion of the nation. No account of American diplomacy in 1940 and 1941 can pretend to authority which does not take into account the tides of sentiment which must always influence, and perhaps control, the course of government. It is not to be maintained that a President has no freedom of action whatsoever; he can, I think, accelerate or retard a popular trend. But he does not act independently of it; the whole history of American diplomacy attests the close relationship between the point of view of the masses and executive action. A peacefully-minded President like McKinley was driven to war with Spain; a President who set great store by increasing the physical power of the nation, like Theodore Roosevelt, was limited and confined in his action; and Franklin Roosevelt himself, when, in the quarantine speech of October, 1937, he sought to rouse the American people against aggression, was compelled to admit failure, and to trim his sails to the popular breeze. These things are of the essence; to fail to observe them is to fail to interpret the past in the true historical spirit.

Let us apply these conceptions to the period 1939 to 1941. It will hardly be denied that from the very beginning of the war public sentiment was definitely against Germany. Indeed, even before the invasion of Poland, the public opinion polls show a strong partiality for the democratic nations. As early as January, 1939, when asked the question whether we should do everything possible to help England and France in case of war, 69 per cent of the persons polled answered in the affirmative, and the same question in October produced a percentage of 62 per cent on the same side. No doubt this sentiment did not extend to the point of actual participation in the war, but it furnished a firm foundation for the action of the President in calling Congress in special session, and in asking of it the repeal of the arms embargo on shipments of war in the interest of the Allies. The measure to this effect was introduced in the Congress towards the end of September; and it was thoroughly debated. There are several things to be said in connection with its passage. The first is that after its introduction there was a consistent majority of around 60 per cent in the polls in favor of passage. The second is that, though there was a strong partisan flavor to the debate, the defections when they came were more numerous on the Republican than on the Democratic side. It is true that, without the leadership of the President, the repeal could not have been enacted. But also it did not fly in the face of public sentiment (so far as that can be measured), but on the contrary reflected it.

With the fall of France there took place a deep and significant development in public opinion. This change the revisionists usually do not mention. They prefer to treat of American policy as if it were formed in a vacuum without regard to the moving forces that have so much to do with the final decisions. Yet the evidences are ample that in June of 1940 the American people were deeply moved. Take, for example, the action of the Republican nominating convention. There were several outstanding professional politicians in the running in 1940, Senator Taft, Senator Vandenberg, Thomas E. Dewey. Each one of these men represented a policy of caution so far as Europe was concerned. Yet what did the convention do? It turned to a relatively unknown figure, to a novice in politics who had, however, more than once declared himself as advocating extensive assistance to the democracies. The choice of Wendell Willkie as the Republican candidate for the Presidency is a fact the importance of which cannot be denied. It is worth while calling attention to other like phenomena. One of these is the overwhelming majorities by which the Congress appropriated largely increased sums for the armed forces, not only for the navy but for the army and the air force as well. Perhaps the American people, or the representatives of the American people, ought not to have been perturbed at what was happening in Europe. But the fact is that they were perturbed. They were perturbed in a big way. And the votes in the legislative halls demonstrate that fact.

Or take another example. The movement for a conscription law in time of peace developed rapidly after June of 1940. It developed with very little assistance from the White House. It cut across party lines. And it resulted in a legislative enactment which reflected the excitement of the public mind. How can we interpret the measure otherwise? Was there not a substantial body of opinion in the United States that feared a German victory?

Another important factor to be noted is the formation in June of 1940 of the Committee to Defend America by Aiding the Allies. It is highly significant that this movement arose at all. It is doubly significant that it found a leader in a Kansan Republican such as William Allen White. It is trebly significant that, once initiated, it spread like wild-fire, and that by September there were more than 650 chapters in the United States. And it is also to be noted that in New York there soon came into being a more advanced group, the so-called Century Group, which advocated war if necessary to check the aggressions of Germany.

And it is further to be observed that out of the Committee to Defend America came an agitation for what was eventually to be the bases-destroyer deal of September 2, 1940. This deal, by the way, was approved by 62 per cent of the persons polled on August 17, 1940, two weeks before it was actually consummated.

Let us go further. The next important step forward in American policy was the lend-lease enactment of the winter of 1941. This measure, it would appear from the polls, was based on a very distinct evolution of public sentiment. In July of 1940 59 per cent of the persons polled preferred to keep out rather than to help England at the risk of war, and 36 per cent took the contrary view. In October the percentages were exactly reversed: they were 36 to 59. By January of 1941 68 per cent of those interviewed thought it more important to assist Great Britain than to keep out of war. And the lend-lease enactment, when presented to the Congress, passed the Lower House by the impressive vote of 317 to 71 and the Senate by 60 to 31. As in the legislation of 1939, though the vote again had a partisan flavor, there were more defections from the Republicans in favor of the measure than of Democrats against it. And there is something more to be added to the account in this instance. By the winter of 1941 the America Firsters had appeared upon the scene. A counter-propaganda was now being organized against the administration. Yet this new group, despite its vigorous efforts, failed signally to rally majority opinion. And Senator Taft, who represented the most thoughtful opposition to the administration, himself proposed a measure of assistance to Great Britain.

I shall treat a little later of the various measures requiring no legislative sanction which the President took in the course of the year 1941. But it is important to observe that throughout the period there was a strong public sentiment that believed that it was more important to defeat Germany than to keep out of war. This view was held, according to the polls, by 62 per cent of those interrogated in May of 1941 and by 68 per cent in December of 1941. As early as April, 1941, 68 per cent of the pollees believed it important to enter the war if British defeat was certain.

We should next examine the legislation of the fall of 1941. By this time the Congress was ready to authorize the arming of American merchant ships, and this by a heavy vote. The measure was passed by 259 to 138 in the House and the Senate amended it and passed it by 50 to 37. Congress was ready, more reluctantly, to repeal those provisions of the neutrality acts which excluded American vessels from the so-called war zones. It was moving in the direction of fuller and fuller engagement against Hitler. We shall never know, of course, what the next step would have been had not that step been taken by Germany. It was the dictator of the Reich who declared war on the United States, not the American national legislature that declared war on the Fuehrer and his minions. But in the period between 1939 and 1941 it seems safe to say that the foreign policy of the Roosevelt administration was in accord with the majority public opinion of the nation. It seems incontestable that the President was acting on assumptions which majority opinion accepted, and pursuing a course of action which majority opinion approved.

This circumstance is naturally either ignored or obscured in the revisionist literature. And what makes it easier to forget is the undeniable fact that Franklin Roosevelt was unhappily sometimes given to equivocation and shifty conversation. Very early, it is true, as early as the quarantine speech of October, 1937, he sounded the alarm against the totalitarians. Very often he stated his conviction that their continued progress presented a threat to the United States. On occasion he took his courage in his hands as, when at Charlottesville in June of 1940, in an election year, he came out frankly in favor of aid to the democracies, or in the declaration of unlimited emergency in the address of May 27, 1941. There is little doubt that he deemed the defeat of Hitler more important than the avoidance of war (as did many other Americans, as we have seen). Yet he was often less than frank in his approach, and the emphasis he laid on his devotion to peace was often excessive. He shocked even his ardent admirer, Robert Sherwood, in the election of 1940. His presentation of the case for lend-lease does not at all times suggest candor; indeed, the very phrase seems a bit of cajolery. With regard to the question of convoy, in the spring of 1941, he was clever and, though verbally correct, hardly wholly open in his approach to the problem. In the famous episode of the *Greer* (an attack by a German submarine on a vessel which was reporting its position to a British destroyer), he misrepresented the facts, or spoke without full knowledge of them. All this it is only right to admit. Yet we must not exaggerate the importance of these considerations. The country knew where it was going with regard to Germany. It accepted lend-lease as desirable. Of the patrolling of the ocean lanes which followed, the President spoke candidly in the speech of May 27, 1941. There was nothing clandestine about the occupation of Greenland or Iceland. The pattern in the fall of 1941 would most probably not have been much altered if Roosevelt had been more scrupulous with regard to the *Greer*. In the last analysis we come back to the essential fact that Roosevelt represented and expressed in action the mood of the country with regard to Germany.

The question is, I believe, more difficult when we come to examine American policy towards Japan. We can say with some assurance that the denunciation of the treaty of commerce of 1911, undertaken by the administration in July of 1939 as an indication of American displeasure with Japanese policy, was distinctly well received. Indeed, if the State Department had not acted, the legislature might have. We can also say that in August of 1939 there was an overwhelming feeling against sending war materials to Nippon. When in September of 1940, an embargo on the export of scrap iron was imposed, 59 per cent of the persons polled on this issue approved the step that had been taken. And in 1941 the number of persons who believed that some check should be put on Japan even at the risk of war rose from 51 per cent to 70 per cent between July and September, and stood at 69 per cent at the time of Pearl Harbor.

But we have fewer indications of the direction of public sentiment in the action of Congress, and no actual votes on which to base our estimate of how the representatives of the American people felt with regard to the important problem of our course of action in the Orient. We must, I think, speak less confidently on this question of public opinion than in the case of Germany. We must turn rather to an analysis of the policy of the administration, and to revisionist criticism of that policy.

First of all, let us look at some of the uncontroverted facts. We know that there were militarist elements in Japan. We know that as early as 1934 Japan proclaimed its doctrine of a Greater East Asia in the famous Amau statement. We know that in the same year it upset the naval arrangements made at Washington and London. We know that it set up a special régime in North China in 1935. We know that it became involved in a war with China in 1937. This, of course, was only prelude. The outbreak of the European conflict in Europe, and the collapse of France, offered to the sponsors of further aggressive action a great opportunity. The occupation of northern Indo-China followed. In the summer of 1940, the impetuous and aggressive Matsuoka came to the Foreign Office. On September 27, 1940, there was signed a tripartite pact with Japan, which bound Nippon to come to the assistance of the Axis powers if they were attacked by a power then at peace with them. In other words, the Tokyo government sought to confine and limit American policy. In April of 1941 came a neutrality pact with Russia which freed the hands of the Japanese militarists for a policy of advance towards the south. In July came the occupation of the rest of Indo-China. The occupation of *northern* Indo-China made some sense from the point of view of blocking the supply route to the Chinese Nationalists. The occupation of *southern* Indo-China made no sense, except as the prelude to further acts of aggression. And in due course the aggression came.

Admittedly, this is only one side of the story. The question to be examined is, did these acts take place partly as a result of American provocation? Was it possible for a wiser and more prudent diplomacy to have avoided the rift that occurred in December, 1941? Revisionist criticism of our Oriental policy has been expressed in a variety of ways. In its most extreme form, it suggests that the President and his advisers actually plotted war with Japan. In its less extreme form, it directs its shafts at a variety of actions, of which I shall examine the most important. They are the conversations with the British as to the defense of the Far East, the commitments made to China, the severance of commercial relations, the failure to accept the proposals of Prince Konoye for direct conversations with the President, and the breakdown of the *modus vivendi* proposal of November, 1941. I shall examine each of these briefly, but let us first turn to the accusation that American policy was directed towards producing and not avoiding an armed conflict in the Orient.

It seems quite impossible to accept this view on the basis of the documentation. During the greater part of 1940 and 1941, it was certainly not the objective of the Roosevelt administration to bring about a clash in the Far East. On the contrary such a clash was regarded as likely to produce the greatest embarrassment in connection with the program of aid to Britain. The military and naval advisers of the President were opposed to it, and said so again and again. Even on the eve of Pearl Harbor this was the case. In addition, Secretary Hull was opposed to it. Even the apostle of caution, he made his point of view quite clear almost up to the end. And as for the President, it is worth pointing out that on the occasion of the Japanese occupation of southern Indo-China he came forward with a proposal for the neutralization of that territory in the interests of peace, and that in August he frankly stated it to be his purpose to "baby the Japanese along." That he feared Japanese aggression is likely, almost certain; that he desired it is something that cannot be proved.

But let us look at the various specific actions which have awakened criticism on the part of the revisionists. In the first place I cannot see that staff conversations with the British were open to any objections whatsoever. If the object of the Roosevelt administration was to limit Japanese aggression in the Far East, then it seems wholly rational to take precautions against such aggression, and surely it could reasonably be expected that such precautions would serve as a deterrent rather than as an incitement to action. It is, in my judgment, rather distorted thinking that regards such action as provocation. This is precisely the point of view of the Kremlin today with regard to the North Atlantic treaty and the European defense pact, or, to take another example, very like the contention of the Germans when they invaded Belgium in 1914. Because the British had engaged in military conversations with the Belgians looking to the possible violation of the neutrality treaty of 1839, it was claimed by apologists for Germany that the violation of neutrality was defensible. Where is the possible justification for such reasoning?

There is more to be said with regard to the breaking off, by the United States, of commercial and financial relations with Japan on the heels of the Japanese occupation of southern Indo-China in the summer of 1941. Undoubtedly this created an extraordinarily difficult situation for the government in Tokyo. Undoubtedly the cutting off of the oil supply from the United States gave great additional force to the arguments of the militarists. Undoubtedly, in the absence of a far-reaching diplomatic arrangement, it presented a strong reason for "bursting out" of the circle, and going to war. If the administration put faith in this measure of economic coercion as a substitute for physical resistance, its faith was to turn out to be groundless. For myself, I have for a long time believed that economic coercion against a strong and determined power is more likely to produce war than to prevent it. But there are circumstances that ought to be mentioned in favor of the action of the administration. It is to be emphasized that the severance of commercial and financial relations resulted not in a breach of the negotiations with Japan but in a resumption of those negotiations. It is to be remembered that Prince Konoye's proposal for a personal conference with the President came after and not before the President's action. American policy by no means put an end to the efforts of those substantial elements in Japan who feared a clash with this country and who were laboring to prevent it. It must be pointed out, also, that the alternative was by no means a pleasant one. At a time when we were deeply engaged in the Atlantic, when we were being more and more deeply committed with regard to the war in Europe, when our domestic supply of oil might have to be substantially curtailed, the continuation of our exports to the Far East to assist Japan in possible projects of aggression was a very difficult policy to follow. It may even be that it would have proven to be totally impracticable from a political point of view.

We come in the third place to the efforts of Premier Konoye to establish direct contact with President Roosevelt. It is well known that Ambassador Grew believed at that time, and that he has more than once stated since, that a good deal was to be hoped from such a meeting. And it is by no means clear why, if the objective were the postponement of a crisis, the experiment should not have been tried. Secretary Hull brought to this problem, as it seems to me, a rigidity of mind which may properly be criticized. In insisting on a previous definition of the issues before the meeting was held, he was instrumental in preventing it. While we cannot know what the result of such a meeting would have been, we are entitled, I think, to wish that it had been held. All the more is this true since it would appear likely that Prince Konoye was sincere in the effort which he made to avoid war.

But there is another side to the matter. We cannot be absolutely sure of Konoye's good faith. We can be still less sure of the willingness of the Tokyo militarists to support him in the far-reaching concessions that would have been necessary. And in the final analysis we cannot be sure of the ability of the American government to make concessions on its own part.

And here we come, as it seems to me, to the crux of the matter. It was the American policy in China that created an impassable barrier in our negotiations with Japan. It is necessary to examine that policy. From one angle of vision the patience of the American government in dealing with the China incident seems quite remarkable. There was a good deal to complain of from 1935 onward, certainly from 1937 onward, if one were to think in terms of sympathy for an aggressed people and in terms of the traditional policy of the United States with regard to this populous nation. The Roosevelt administration moved very slowly in its opposition to Japan. It made its first loan to Chiang Kai-shek in the fall of 1938. It denounced the commercial treaty of 1911 with Nippon only in the summer of 1939. And it embarked upon a policy of really substantial aid to China only contemporaneously with the signing of the tripartite pact in the fall of 1940. Its increasing assistance to Chiang is intelligible on the ground that to keep the Japanese bogged down in China was one means of checking or preventing their aggressive action elsewhere.

The fact remains, however, that it was the Chinese question which was the great and central stumbling block in the long negotiations that took place in 1941. Though the Japanese had entered into an alliance with the Axis powers, it seems not unlikely that, in 1941, as the issue of peace or war defined itself more clearly, they would have been willing to construe away their obligations under that alliance had they been able to come to terms with the United States on the Chinese problem. But by 1941 the American government was so far committed to the cause of Chiang that it really had very little freedom of maneuver. The various Japanese proposals for a settlement of the China incident would have involved a betrayal of the Chinese Nationalist leader. The proposal for a coalition government, a government of the Nationalists and the puppet régime of Wang Ghing-wei, could hardly have been accepted. The proposal that America put pressure on Chiang to negotiate, and cut off aid to him if he refused, was by this time equally impracticable. And the question of the withdrawal of the Japanese troops in China presented insuperable difficulties. True it is that in October of 1941 the idea of a total withdrawal seems to have been presented to Mr. Welles by Mr. Wakatsuki, Admiral Nomura's associate in the negotiations. But the idea was emphatically rejected by the militarists in Tokyo, and perhaps there was never a time when they would have agreed to any proposal that at the same time would have been acceptable to Chungking. The American government had been brought, by its policy of association with the Chinese Nationalists, to the point where understanding with Japan was practically impossible.

This fact is dramatically illustrated by the negotiations over the *modus vivendi* in November, 1941. At this time, as is well known, proposals were brought forward for the maintenance of the *status quo,* and a gradual restoration of more normal relations through the lifting of the commercial restrictions, and through the withdrawal of the Japanese from southern Indo-China. At first it seemed as if there were a possibility of working out some such proposal. But the Chinese objected most violently, and Secretary Hull dropped the idea. In the face of Chinese pressure, and of the possible popular indignation which such a policy of concession might produce, and acting either under the orders or at least with the assent of the President, he backed down. We must not exaggerate the importance of this. There is no certainty that the *modus vivendi* would have been acceptable to Tokyo, and, judging by the Japanese proposals of November 20, there is indeed some reason to think otherwise. But the fact remains that our close association with Chiang was a fundamental factor in making the breach with Japan irreparable. And it seems fair to say in addition that our hopes with regard to Nationalist China were at all times, in 1941 as later, very far removed from political reality.

Let us not, however, jump to absolute conclusions with regard to questions that, in the nature of the case, ought not to be a matter of dogmatic judgment. If there was a party in Japan, and a substantial one, which feared war with the United States and earnestly sought for accommodation, there was also a party which regarded the course of events in Europe as a heaven-sent opportunity for national self-aggrandizement. That this party might in any case have prevailed, whatever the character of American policy, does not seem by any means unlikely. It is significant that in July of 1941 the fall of Matsuoka brought no change in policy in the Far East, and that the so-called moderate, Admiral Toyoda, gave the orders for the crucial and revealing occupation of southern Indo-China in the summer of 1941.

Let us not forget, either, that after all it was the Japanese who struck. The ruthless act of aggression at Pearl Harbor was no necessary consequence of the breakdown of negotiations with the United States. If new oil supplies were needed, they were, of course, to be secured by an attack on the Dutch East Indies, not by an attack on Hawaii. Though there were strategic arguments for including America in any war-like move, there were strong political reasons for not doing so. No greater miscalculation has perhaps ever been made than that made by the militarists at Tokyo in December, 1941. By their own act, they unified American opinion and made their own defeat inevitable. It will always remain doubtful when the decisive involvement would have come for the United States had the bombs not dropped on Pearl Harbor on the 7th of December of 1941.

ten
Origins
of the
Cold War

Nationalist

The Nationalists trace the origins of the cold war to the messianic expansionism of Communist Russia. They argue that Russian attempts following World War II to dominate Eastern Europe and Asia were preludes
to the subversion of a prostrate Western Europe and to ultimate world
domination. They argue that this expansionism was almost totally unpro-
voked since the United States had made obvious its willingness to abide
by the peaceful, democratic rules of the United Nations. With the clear
demonstration of Russia's intentions in Poland and elsewhere, however,
the United States had no choice but to rearm and contain Communist aggression.

John Spanier, author of the following essay, is a professor of political
science at the University of Florida. Although Professor Spanier's article
contains some of the phraseology of the Realists, the difference between
his view and that of the Realists will become clear in the succeeding article. What evidence does Spanier present to show that Russia sought
domination of Eastern Europe? Of Western Europe? Did the United
States, in his view, bear any responsibility at all for the coming of the
cold war?

American Foreign Policy Since World War II

John Spanier

THE BEGINNING OF THE COLD WAR
American Wartime Illusions

Before one of the wartime conferences between Prime Minister Winston Churchill and President Franklin Roosevelt, an American Intelligence forecast of Russia's postwar position in Europe concluded that the Soviet Union would be the dominant power on the continent of Europe: "With Germany crushed, there is no power in Europe to oppose her tremendous military forces. . . . The conclusions from the foregoing are obvious. Since Russia is the decisive factor in the war, she must be given every assistance, and every effort must be made to obtain her friendship. Likewise, since without question she will dominate Europe on the defeat of the Axis, it is even more essential to develop and maintain the most friendly relations with Russia."

The importance of this estimate lies less in its prediction of the Soviet Union's postwar position—which was, after all, fairly obvious—than in its reflection of American expectations about future Russo-American relations. American policy-makers were apparently unable to conceive of the Soviet Union, the acknowledged new dominant power in Europe, replacing Nazi Germany as a grave threat to the European and global balance of power. Yet, the United States had already twice in this century been propelled into Europe's wars at exactly those moments when Germany became so powerful that she menaced—indeed, almost destroyed—this balance. The lessons of history—specifically, the impact of any nation's domination of Europe upon American security—had not yet been absorbed. President Roosevelt and the American Government did not aim at re-establishing a bal-

From John Spanier, *American Foreign Policy Since World War II*, 3rd rev. ed., 1968, pp. 18–37. Reprinted by permission of Praeger Publishers, Inc.

ance of power in Europe to safeguard the United States; they expected this security to stem from mutual Russo-American goodwill, unsupported by any power considerations. This reliance upon mere goodwill and mutual esteem was to prove foolish at best and, at worst, might have been fatal.

Indeed, the expectation of a postwar "era of good feeling" between the Soviet Union and the United States was characteristic of the unsuspecting and utopian nature of American wartime thinking, which held that war was an interruption of the normal state of harmony among nations, that military force was an instrument for punishing the aggressor or war criminals, that those who cooperated with this country in its ideological crusade were equally moral and selfless, and that once the war was finished, the natural harmony would be restored and the struggle for power ended. The implication was clear: the United States need take no precautionary steps against its noble wartime allies in anticipation of a possible disintegration of the alliance and potential hostility among its partners. Instead, it was hoped that the friendly relations and mutual respect which American leaders believed had matured during the war would preserve the common outlook and purposes and guarantee an enduring peace.

These optimistic expectations of future Russo-American relations made it necessary, however, to explain away continuing signs of Soviet hostility and suspicion. Throughout the war, the Russians constantly suspected the United States and Britain of devious intentions. This was particularly true with regard to the Western delay in opening up a second front. When the front was postponed from 1942 to 1943 to 1944, Stalin, Russia's dictator, became very bitter. He brusquely rejected Allied explanations that sufficient invasion barges for such an enormous undertaking were not available; and he especially denounced Prime Minister Churchill for declaring that there would be no invasion until the Germans were so weakened that Allied forces would not have to suffer forbiddingly high losses. To Stalin, this was no explanation, for the Russians accepted huge losses of men as a matter of course. "When we come to a mine field," Marshal Zhukov explained to General Eisenhower after the war, "our infantry attacks exactly as if it were not there. The losses we get from personnel mines we consider only equal to those we would have gotten from machine guns and artillery if the Germans had chosen to defend that particular area with strong bodies of troops instead of with mine fields." It was no wonder, then, that the Russians should dismiss these Allied explanations and fasten instead upon a more reasonable interpretation which, to them, would account for American and British behavior. From the Marxist viewpoint, the Allies were doing exactly what they should be doing—namely, postponing the second front until the Soviet Union and Germany had exhausted one another. Then the two Western powers could land in France, march bloodlessly into Germany, and dictate the peace to both Germany and Russia. The Western delay was, in short, apparently seen as a deliberate attempt by the world's two leading capitalist powers to destroy both of their two major ideological opponents at one and the same time. Throughout the war, the Russians displayed again and again this almost paranoid fear of hostile Western intentions.

American leaders found a ready explanation for these repeated indications of Soviet suspicion. They thought of Soviet foreign policy not in terms of the internal dynamics of the regime and its enmity toward all non-Communist nations, but solely in terms of Russian reactions to Western policies. The Soviet attitude was viewed against the pattern of prewar anti-Soviet Western acts: the Allied intervention in Russia at the end of World War I in order to overthrow the Soviet regime, and, after the failure of that attempt, the establishment by France of the *cordon sanitaire* in Eastern Europe to keep the Soviet virus from infecting Europe; the West's rejection of Soviet efforts in the mid- and late 1930's to build an alliance against Hitler; and especially, the Munich agreement in 1938, which, by destroying Czechoslovakia, in effect opened Hitler's gateway to the East. In short, Western efforts to ostracize and ultimately destroy the Soviet Union, as well as attempts to turn the Hitlerian threat away from the West and toward Russia, were considered the primary reasons for the existence of Soviet hostility. To overcome this attitude, the West had only to demonstrate its good intentions and prove its friendliness. The question was not *whether* Soviet cooperation could be won for the postwar world, only *how* it could be gained. And if Western efforts did bear fruit and create goodwill, what conflicts of interest could not be settled peacefully in the future? Various Soviet policies and acts during the war—the disbanding of the Comintern (the instrument of international Communism), the toning down of Communist ideology and new emphasis placed on Russian nationalism, the relaxation of restrictions upon the Church, the praise of the United States and Britain for also being democratic, and, above all, the statement of Russian war aims in the same language of peace, democracy, and freedom used by the West—all seemed to prove that if the Western powers demonstrated their friendship, they could convert the Russians into friends.

President Roosevelt and his advisers certainly believed that they had firmly established such amicable relations with the Soviet Union at the Yalta Conference in February, 1945. Stalin had made concessions on a number of vital issues and promised goodwill for the future. On United Nations membership, Stalin had reduced his claim from sixteen seats (one for each of the Soviet Republics) to only three (for the Soviet Union, the Ukraine, and Belorussia) and stated he would support an American claim for parity. He had also accepted the American formula that the veto in the Security Council should be applied only to enforcement action, and not to peaceful attempts at the settlement of disputes. On Germany, he had agreed to a zone of occupation and seat on the Control Commission for France, and to a single administration for all the occupation zones. Moreover, in the "Declaration on Liberated Europe" he had promised to support self-government and allow free elections in Eastern Europe. And regarding the Far East, he had responded to the wishes of the American military and promised to enter the war against Japan. Finally, he had repeatedly expressed his hope for fifty years of peace and "big power" cooperation.

It is little wonder that at the end of the conference the American delegation felt a mood of "supreme exaltation." The President's closest adviser, Harry Hopkins, later recounted: "We really believed in our hearts that this was the dawn of the new day we had all been praying for and talking about for so many years. We were absolutely certain that we had won the first great victory of the peace—and, by 'we,' I mean *all* of us, the whole civilized human race. The Russians had proved that they could be reasonable and far-seeing, and there wasn't any doubt in the minds of the President or any of us that we could live with them and get along with them peacefully for as far into the future as any of us could imagine."

This new era of goodwill was to be embodied in the United Nations. Here the peoples of the world could exercise vigilance over the statesmen in their dealings with one another and prevent them from striking any wicked bargains which might erupt into another global war. The United Nations was regarded as an example of democracy on an international scale: just as the people within democratic states could constantly watch their representatives and prevent them from effecting compromises injurious to their interests, so the people of all countries would now be able to keep an eye on their statesmen, making it impossible for them to arrange any secret deals which would betray the people's interests and shatter the peace of the world. Peace-loving world public opinion, expressing itself across national boundaries, would maintain a constant guard over the diplomats and hold them accountable. Covenants were to be open, and openly arrived at, as President Wilson had once expressed it. Power politics would then be banned once and for all. In the words of Secretary of State Cordell Hull: "There will no longer be need for spheres of influence, for alliances, balance of power, or any other of the special arrangements through which, in the unhappy past, the nations strove to safeguard their security or promote their interests." Reliance would instead be placed upon sound principles and good fellowship. Again, in Hull's words: "All these principles and policies [of international cooperation] are so beneficial and appealing to the sense of justice, of right and of the well-being of free peoples everywhere that in the course of a few years the entire international machinery should be working fairly satisfactorily." The Advisory Commission on Postwar Foreign Policy had been even more emphatic in its stress on the subordination of power politics to principles: "International security was regarded as the supreme objective, but at the same time the subcommittee held that the attainment of security must square with principles of justice in order to be actual and enduring . . . the vital interests of the United States lay in following a 'diplomacy of principle'—of moral disinterestedness instead of power politics." No comment could more aptly have summed up the American habit of viewing international politics in terms of abstract moral principles instead of clashes of interest and power.

SOVIET POSTWAR EXPANSION

The American dream of postwar peace and Big Three cooperation was to be shattered as the Soviet Union expanded into Eastern and Central Europe, imposing its control upon Poland, Hungary, Bulgaria, Romania, and Albania. (Yugoslavia was already under the Communist control of Marshal Tito, and Czechoslovakia was living under the shadow of the Red Army.) In each of these nations of Eastern Europe where the Russians had their troops, they unilaterally established pro-Soviet coalition governments. The key post in these regimes—the ministry of the interior, which usually controlled the police—was in the hands of the Communists. With this decisive lever of power in their grasp, it was an easy matter to extend their domination and subvert the independence of these countries. Thus, as the war drew to a close, it became clear that the words of the Yalta Declaration, in which the Russians had committed themselves to free elections and democratic governments in Eastern Europe, meant quite different things to the Russians than to Americans. To the Russians, "democratic governments" meant Communist governments, and "free elections" meant elections from which parties not favorable to the Communists were barred. The peace treaties with the former German satellite states (Hungary, Bulgaria, Romania), which were painfully negotiated by the victors in a series of Foreign Ministers' conferences during 1945 and 1946, could not reverse the tight Soviet grip on what were by now Russian satellite states. Democratic principles could not be extended beyond Western power. Russian dominance in the Balkans and Poland was, in short, firmly established, and Russian power now lapped the shores of the Aegean, the Straits of Constantinople, and—through its close relationship with Yugoslavia—the Adriatic.

Greece, Turkey, and Iran were the first states beyond the confines of the Red Army to feel the resulting expansionist pressure of the Soviet Union. In the period from the end of the war to early 1947, the Russians attempted to effect a major breakthrough into the Middle East. Every would-be world conqueror—Napoleon, Kaiser Wilhelm II, and Hitler, to mention only a few of the more recent ones—has tried to become master of this area. Napoleon called the Middle East the key to the world, and well he might, for the area links Europe, Africa, and Asia. The power that dominates the Middle East is in an excellent position to expand into North Africa and South Asia, and thereby gain control of the World-Island.

The pressure on Iran began in early 1946 when the Russians refused to withdraw their troops from that country. These troops had been there since late 1941, when Russia and Britain had invaded Iran in order to forestall increased Nazi influence and to use Iran as a corridor for the transportation of military aid shipped by the West to the Persian Gulf for transit to Russia. The Russians had occupied northern Iran, the British the central and southern sections. The Tripartite Treaty of Alliance signed in early 1942 by Iran, Britain, and Russia specified that within six months of the cessation of hostilities all troops would be withdrawn; the Allies also pledged themselves to respect Iran's sovereignty and territorial and political independence.

The final date set for evacuation from Iran was March 2, 1946. British and United States troops—the latter had arrived after America's entry into the war, to help move the lend-lease supplies to Russia—had already left. Only the Soviet troops still remained. Indeed, the Russians were sending in more troops and tanks. Their goal: to reduce Iran to a Soviet satellite. The Russians had, in fact, begun their campaign in late 1944, when they demanded exclusive mineral and oil rights in northern Iran and offered to supply the Iranians with experts to help administer their government. When the Iranian Government rejected these demands, the Russians had organized a revolt by the Communist-controlled Tudeh Party in the north. The revolt began openly in November, 1945, and the Red Army prevented the Iranian Army from quelling it. The Tudeh Party, renamed the Democratic Party, then formed a government in Azerbaijan. The Russian game was clear: to force the Iranian Government to recognize the Soviet puppet regime in Azerbaijan, which would then send "elected representatives" to the legislature in Teheran. These would then exert pressure on the government to grant Russia the economic and political control it wanted in Iran. The result would have been the conversion of Iran into a Soviet satellite. It was imperative, therefore, that Soviet troops be forced to withdraw. Not until then could the national government and troops attempt to cope with the Communist government in the north.

During this period, the Soviet Union also put pressure on Turkey. Indeed, the Russians had begun to do this as early as June, 1945, when they suddenly demanded the cession of several Turkish districts lying on the Turkish-Russian frontier, the revision of the Montreux Convention governing the Dardenelles Straits in favor of a joint Russo-Turkish administration, Turkey's abandonment of her ties with Britain and the conclusion of a treaty with the Soviet Union similar to those which Russia had concluded with its Balkan satellites, and finally, the lease to the Soviet Union of bases for naval and land forces in the Straits for its "joint defense." In August, 1946, the Soviet Union renewed its demand, in a note to the United States and Britain, for a new administration of the Straits. In effect, this would have turned Turkey, like Iran, into a Soviet satellite.

In Greece, too, Communist pressure was exerted on the government through wide-scale guerrilla warfare, which began in the fall of 1946. Civil war in Greece was actually nothing new. During the war, the Communist and anti-Communist guerrillas fighting the Germans had spent much of their energy battling each other. When the British landed in Greece and the Germans withdrew from the country, the Communists had attempted to take over the capital city of Athens. Only after several weeks of bitter street fighting and the landing of British reinforcements was the Communist control of Athens dislodged and a truce signed in January, 1945. Just over a year later—in March, 1946—the Greeks held a general election in which right-wing forces captured the majority of votes.

The Greek situation did not improve, however. The country was exhausted from the Italian and German invasions, the four years of occupation, and the Germans' scorched-earth policy as they retreated. Moreover, Greece had always been dependent upon imports that were paid for by exports; but her traditional market in Central Europe was now closed. While the masses lived at a bare subsistence level, the black market flourished. The inability of any government to deal with this situation aroused a good deal of social discontent. And the large, 100,000-man army which Greece needed to protect her from her Communist neighbors (Albania, Yugoslavia, and Bulgaria) had brought the country to near-bankruptcy. If Britain had not helped finance—as well as train and equip—the army and kept troops in the country to stabilize the situation, Greece would in all probability have collapsed. It was in these circumstances that in August, 1946, the Communists began to squeeze Greece by renewing the guerrilla warfare in the north, where the guerrilla forces could be kept well supplied by Greece's Communist neighbors.

In all these situations, the American Government was suddenly confronted with the need for action to support Britain, the traditional guardian of this area against encroachment. In the case of Iran, the United States and Britain delivered firm statements which strongly implied that the two countries would use force to defend Iran. The Soviet response in late March, 1946, was the announcement that the Red Army would be withdrawn during the next five to six weeks. In the Turkish case, the United States sent a naval task force into the Mediterranean immediately after the receipt of the Soviet note on August 7. Twelve days later, the United States replied to the note by rejecting the Russian demand to share sole responsibility for the defense of the Straits with Turkey. Britain sent a similar reply. The Greek situation had not yet come to a head, and the need for American action could be postponed for a while longer. But it should be pointed out that the Administration's actions in Iran and Turkey were merely swift reactions to immediate crises. They were not the product of an over-all American strategy. Such a coherent strategy could only arise from a new assessment of Soviet foreign policy.

The Strategy of Containment

A period of eighteen months passed before the United States undertook that reassessment—from the surrender of Japan on September 2, 1945, until the announcement of the Truman Doctrine on March 12, 1947. Perhaps such a reevaluation could not have been made any more quickly. Public opinion in a democratic country does not normally shift drastically overnight. It would have been too much to expect the American public to change suddenly from an attitude of friendliness toward the Soviet Union —inspired largely by the picture of Russian wartime bravery and endurance and by hopes for peaceful postwar cooperation—to a hostile mood. The American "reservoir of goodwill" for the Soviet Union could not be emptied that quickly. Moreover, the desire for peace was too strong. The United States wished only to be left alone to preoccupy itself once more with domestic affairs. The end of the war signaled the end of power politics and the restoration of normal peacetime harmony among nations. In response to this expectation, the public demanded a speedy demobilization. The armed forces were thus reduced to completely inadequate levels of strength. In May, 1945, at the end of the war with Germany, the United States had an army of 3.5 million men organized into 68 divisions in Europe, supported by 149 air groups. Our allies supplied another 47 divisions. By March, 1946, only ten months later, the United States had only 400,000 troops left, mainly new recruits; the homeland reserve was six battalions. Further reductions in Army strength followed. Air Force and Navy cuts duplicated this same pattern.

The Eightieth Congress, which convened in Washington in January, 1947, represented this postwar mood of withdrawal well.

The Senate was divided into 51 Republicans and 45 Democrats. House Speaker Joseph Martin stated Republican intentions in his opening address to his colleagues: a reduction in government expenditures to allow for a 20 per cent income tax reduction. The Congress thereupon cut the President's budget from $41 billion to $31.5 billion. The Secretary of War denounced the cut and warned that the United States might have to withdraw its troops from Germany and Japan; and the Secretary of the Navy announced that the cut would render the Navy impotent. This deliberate and unilateral disarmament could not have failed to encourage Russian intransigence in Europe and increased Soviet pressure in southeast Europe and the Middle East. As this pressure increased in intensity and scope, however, American policy toward the Soviet Union began to be re-evaluated.

Three positions became clear during this period. At one extreme stood that old realist Winston Churchill. At the end of the European war, he had counseled against the withdrawal of American troops. He had insisted that they stay, together with British troops, in order to force the Soviet Union to live up to its Yalta obligations regarding free elections in Eastern Europe and the withdrawal of the Red Army from Eastern Germany. The United States had rejected Churchill's plea. In early 1946, at Fulton, Missouri, Churchill took his case directly to the American public. The Soviet Union, he asserted, was an expansionist state. "From Stettin in the Baltic to Trieste in the Adriatic, an iron curtain has descended across the continent. Behind that line lie all the capitals of the ancient states of Central and Eastern Europe. Warsaw, Berlin, Prague, Vienna, Budapest, Belgrade, Bucharest, and Sofia, all the famous cities and populations around them lie in the Soviet sphere and all are subject in one form or another, not only to Soviet influence but to a very high and increasing measure of control from Moscow." Churchill did not believe that the Russians wanted war: "What they desire is the fruits of war and the indefinite expansion of their power and doctrines." This could be prevented only by the opposing power of the British Commonwealth and the United States. Churchill, in short, said bluntly that the cold war had begun, that Americans must recognize this fact and give up their dreams of Big Three unity in the United Nations. International organization was no substitute for the balance of power. "Our difficulties and dangers will not be removed by closing our eyes to them. They will not be removed by mere waiting to see what happens; nor will they be relieved by a policy of appeasement." An alliance of the English-speaking peoples was the prerequisite for American and British security and world peace.

At the other extreme stood Secretary of Commerce Henry Wallace, who felt it was precisely the kind of aggressive attitude expressed by Churchill that was to blame for Soviet hostility. The United States and Britain had no more business in Eastern Europe than had the Soviet Union in Latin America; to each, the respective area was vital for national security. Western interference in nations bordering on Russia was bound to arouse Soviet suspicion, just as Soviet intervention in countries neighboring on the United States would. "We may not like what Russia does in Eastern Europe," said Wallace. "Her type of land reform, industrial expropriation, and suspension of basic liberties offends the great majority of the people of the United States. But whether we like it or not, the Russians will try to socialize their sphere of influence just as we try to democratize our sphere of influence (including Japan and Western Germany)." The tough attitude that Churchill and other "reactionaries" at home and abroad demanded was precisely the wrong policy; it would only increase international tension. "We must not let British balance-of-power manipulations determine whether and when the United States gets into a war . . . 'getting tough' never bought anything real and lasting— whether for schoolyard bullies or world powers. The tougher we get, the tougher the Russians will get." Only mutual trust would allow the United States and Russia to live together peacefully, and such trust could not be created by an unfriendly American attitude and policy.

The American Government and public wavered between these two positions. The Administration recognized that Big Three cooperation had ended, and it realized that the time when the United States needed to demonstrate goodwill toward the Soviet Union in order to overcome the latter's suspicions had passed. No further concessions would be made to preserve the surface friendship with the Soviet Union. We had tried to gain Russia's amity by being a friend; it was now up to her leaders to demonstrate a similarly friendly attitude toward us as well. Paper agreements, written in such general terms that they actually hid divergent purposes, were no longer regarded as demonstrating such friendship. Something more than paper agreements was needed: Russian words would have to be matched by Russian deeds.

The American Secretary of State, James Byrnes, called this

new line the "policy of firmness and patience." This phrase meant that the United States would take a firm position whenever the Soviet Union became intransigent, and that we would not compromise simply in order to reach a quick agreement. This change in official American attitude toward the Soviet Union was not, however, a fundamental one. A firm line was to be followed only on concrete issues. The assumption was that if the United States took a tougher bargaining position and no longer seemed in a hurry to resolve particular points of tension, the Soviet rulers would see the pointlessness of their obduracy and agree to fair compromise solutions of their differences with the United States and the West. In short, American firmness would make the Russians "reasonable." For they were regarded as "unreasonable" merely on particular issues; that this "unreasonableness" might stem from the very nature of the Communist regime had not yet occurred to American policy-makers. They did not yet agree with Churchill's position that the Soviet government was ideologically hostile to the West and that it would continue to expand until capitalism had been destroyed. The new American position, as one political analyst has aptly summed it up, "meant to most of its exponents that the Soviet Union had to be induced by firmness to play the game in the American way. There was no consistent official suggestion that the United States should begin to play a different game." The prerequisite for such a suggestion was that American policy-makers recognize the revolutionary nature of the Soviet regime.

This recognition came with increasing speed as the Greek crisis reached a peak. By early 1947, it was obvious that the United States would have to play a different game. It was George Kennan, the Foreign Service's foremost expert on the Soviet Union, who first presented the basis of what was to be a new American policy. Kennan's analysis began with a detailed presentation of the Communist outlook on world affairs. In the Soviet leaders' pattern of thought, he said, Russia had no community of interest with the capitalist states; indeed, they saw their relationship with the Western powers in terms of an innate antagonism. Communist ideology had taught them "that the outside world was hostile and that it was their duty eventually to overthrow the political forces beyond their borders. The powerful hands of Russian history and tradition reached up to sustain them in this feeling. Finally, their own aggressive intransigence with respect to the outside world began to find its own reaction. . . . It is an undeniable privilege for every man to prove himself right in the thesis that the world is his enemy; for if he reiterates it frequently enough and makes it the background for his conduct, he is bound to be right." According to Kennan, this Soviet hostility was a constant factor; it would continue until the capitalist world has been destroyed: "Basically, the antagonism remains. It is postulated. And from it flow many of the phenomena which we find disturbing in the Kremlin's conduct of foreign policy: the secretiveness, the lack of frankness, the duplicity, the war suspiciousness, and the basic unfriendliness of purpose." Kennan did suggest, however, that Soviet tactics might change, depending upon circumstances: "And when that happens, there will always be Americans who will leap forward with gleeful announcements 'that the Russians have changed,' and some who will even take credit for having brought about such 'changes.' But we should not be misled by tactical maneuvers. These characteristics of Soviet policy, like the postulates from which they flow, are basic to the *internal* nature of Soviet power, and will be with us . . . until the nature of Soviet power is changed. [Italics added]" Until that moment, he said, Soviet strategy and objectives would remain the same.

The struggle would thus be a long one. Kennan stressed that Soviet hostility did not mean that the Russians would embark upon a do-or-die program to overthrow capitalism by a fixed date. They had no timetable for conquest. In a brilliant passage, Kennan outlined the Soviet concept of the struggle:

The Kremlin is under no ideological compulsion to accomplish its purposes in a hurry. Like the Church, it is dealing in ideological concepts which are of a long-term validity, and it can afford to be patient. It has no right to risk the existing achievements of the revolution for the sake of vain baubles of the future. The very teachings of Lenin himself require great caution and flexibility in the pursuit of Communist purposes. Again, these precepts are fortified by the lessons of Russian history: of centuries of obscure battles between nomadic forces over the stretches of a vast unfortified plain. Here caution, circumspection, flexibility, and deception are the valuable qualities; and their value finds natural appreciation in the Russian or the Oriental mind. Thus the Kremlin has no compunction about retreating in the face of superior force. And being under the compulsion of no timetable, it does not get panicky under the necessity of such a retreat. Its political action is a fluid stream which moves constantly, wherever it is permitted to move, toward a given goal. Its main concern is to make sure that it has filled every nook and cranny available to it in the basin of world power. But if it finds unassailable barriers in its path, it accepts these philosophically and accommodates itself to them. The main thing is that there should always be pressure, increasing constant pressure, toward the desired goal. There is no trace of any feeling in Soviet psychology that the goal must be reached at any given time.

How could the United States counter such a policy—a policy that was always pushing, seeking weak spots, attempting to fill power vacuums? Kennan's answer was that American policy would have to be one of "long-term, patient, but firm and vigilant containment." The United States would find Soviet diplomacy both easier and more difficult to deal with than that of dictators such as Napoleon or Hitler. "On the one hand, it [Soviet policy] is more sensitive to contrary force, more ready to yield on individual sectors of the diplomatic front when that force is felt to be too strong, and thus more rational in the logic and rhetoric of power. On the other hand, it cannot be easily defeated or discouraged by a single victory on the part of its opponents. And the patient persistence by which it is animated means that *it can be effectively countered not by sporadic acts which represent the momentary whims of democratic opinion, but only by intelligent long-range policies on the part of Russia's adversaries—policies no less steady in their purpose, and no less variegated and resourceful in their application, than those of the Soviet Union itself.* [Italics added]" Kennan thus envisaged containment as the test of American democracy, with our very survival as the stake. If the United States failed to meet the strict requirements of this test, it would suffer the same fate as previous civilizations, becoming no more than a name in history books.

On the other hand, if American society rose to the challenge, it could ensure its future. For containment could contribute to changes within the Soviet Union which might bring about a moderation of its revolutionary aims. The United States, Kennan emphasized, "has it in its power to increase enormously the strains under which Soviet policy must operate, to force upon the Kremlin a far greater degree of moderation and circumspection than it has had to observe in recent years, and in this way to promote tendencies which must eventually find their outlet in either the breakup or the gradual mellowing of Soviet power. For no mystical, messianic movement—and particularly not that of the Kremlin—can face frustration indefinitely without eventually adjusting itself in one way or another to the logic of that state of affairs." Kennan's theory was thus not so new. He was, in effect, asserting the old thesis that within an authoritarian or totalitarian society there are certain strains and stresses, and that these give rise to frustrations which can only be relieved by being channeled into an aggressive and expansionist foreign policy. Kennan's remedy was to prevent this expansion, thereby aggravating the internal tensions in such a way that they would either destroy the Soviet system or force the Soviet leaders to placate the domestic dissatisfaction. Assuming that the Soviet leaders preferred to remain in power and that they would therefore be compelled to adopt the second course, they would have no alternative but to moderate their foreign policy. For a relaxation of international tensions was the prerequisite for coping with their domestic problems. Thus, the Kremlin would have no choice but to surrender its revolutionary aims and arrange a *modus vivendi* with the Western powers—above all, with the United States.

The Truman Doctrine

Whether the United States could meet this Soviet challenge became a pressing question when, on the afternoon of February 21, 1947, the First Secretary of the British Embassy in Washington visited the State Department and handed American officials two notes from His Majesty's Government. One concerned Greece, the other Turkey. In effect, they both stated the same thing: that Britain could no longer meet its traditional responsibilities in those two countries. Since both were on the verge of collapse, the import of the British notes was clear: that a Russian breakthrough could be prevented only by an all-out American commitment.

February 21 was thus a historic day. On that day, Great Britain, the only remaining power in Europe, acknowledged her exhaustion. She had fought Philip II of Spain, Louis XIV of France, Kaiser Wilhelm II and Adolf Hitler of Germany. She had preserved the balance of power which protected the United States for so long that it seemed almost natural for her to continue to do so. But her ability to protect that balance had steadily declined in the twentieth century. Twice she had needed American help. Each time, however, she had fought the longer battle; on neither occasion had the United States entered the war until it became clear that Germany and its allies were too strong for her and that we would have to help her in safeguarding our own security. Now, all of a sudden, there was no power to protect the

United States but the United States itself; no one stood between this country and the present threat to its security. All the other major powers of the world had collapsed—except the Soviet Union, which was the second most powerful nation in the world and was wedded to an expansionist ideology. The cold fact of a bipolar world suddenly faced the United States. The country could no longer shirk the responsibilities of its tremendous power.

The immediate crisis suddenly confronting the United States had its locale in the eastern Mediterranean. Direct Soviet pressure on Iran and Turkey had temporarily been successfully resisted. The Russians had now turned to outflanking these two nations by concentrating their attention on Greece. If Greece collapsed—and all reports from that hapless country indicated that it would fall within a few weeks—it would only be a question of time until Turkey and Iran would crumble before Soviet power. But the fall of Greece would not only affect its neighbors to the east; it would also lead to an increase of Communist pressure on Italy. Italy would then be faced with two Communist states to its east—Yugoslavia and Greece—and with the largest Communist party in Western Europe in its own midst. And to the northwest of Italy lay France, with the second largest Communist party in the West. Thus, the security of all of Western Europe would be endangered as well. The immediate danger, however, remained in the eastern Mediterranean; and the Soviet desire for control over this area was underlined by its demands that the city of Trieste at the head of the Adriatic be yielded to Yugoslavia and that Italy's former colonies of Tripolitania and Eritrea in North Africa be placed under Soviet trusteeship.

The United States had no choice but to act in this situation. The results of inaction were only too clear: the collapse of Europe's flank in the eastern Mediterranean, the establishment of Communist dominance in the Middle East, and a Soviet breakthrough into South Asia and North Africa. The psychological impact upon Europe of such a tremendous Soviet victory over the West would have been disastrous. For Europeans already psychologically demoralized by their sufferings and fall from power and prestige, this would have been the final blow. In short, what was at stake in Greece was America's survival itself.

President Truman was quick to recognize this stark fact. On March 12, 1947, he went before a joint session of Congress and delivered a speech which must rank as one of the most important in American history. The President first outlined the situation in Greece: her lack of natural resources; the cruel German occupation, resulting in widespread destruction; her inability to import the goods she needed for bare subsistence, let alone reconstruction; the Communist efforts to exploit these conditions by spreading political chaos and hindering any economic recovery; and the guerrilla warfare in northern Greece, where the Communist forces were receiving aid from Yugoslavia, Albania, and Bulgaria.

Then Truman came to the heart of his speech. Here he spelled out what was to become known as the Truman Doctrine. The United States, he emphasized, could survive only in a world in which freedom flourished. And we would not realize this objective

. . . unless we are willing to help free peoples to maintain their institutions and their national integrity against agressive movements that seek to impose upon them totalitarian regimes. *This is no more than a frank recognition that totalitarian regimes imposed on free peoples, by direct or indirect aggression, undermine the foundations of international peace and hence the security of the United States.* [Italics added.]

The peoples of a number of countries of the world have recently had totalitarian regimes forced upon them against their will. The Government of the United States has made frequent protests against coercion and intimidation, in violation of the Yalta agreement, in Poland, Romania, and Bulgaria. I must also state that in a number of other countries there have been similar developments.

At the present moment in world history nearly every nation must choose between alternative ways of life. The choice is often not a free one.

One way of life is based upon the will of the majority, and is distinguished by free institutions, representative government, free elections, guarantees of individual liberty, freedom of speech and religion, and freedom from political oppression.

The second way of life is based upon the will of a minority forcibly imposed upon the majority. It relies upon terror and oppression, a controlled press and radio, fixed elections, and the suppression of personal freedoms.

I believe it must be the policy of the United States to support free peoples who are resisting attempted subjugations by armed minorities or by outside pressure.

I believe that we must assist free peoples to work out their own destinies in their own way.

I believe that our help should be primarily through economic and financial aid which is essential to economic stability and orderly political processes.

Stressing the impact of Greece's collapse upon Turkey and the Middle East, as well as upon Europe, the President then brought the Congress and the American people face to face with their responsibility. "Should we fail to aid Greece and Turkey in this fateful hour," he said, "the effect will be far-reaching to the West as well as to the East. We must take immediate and resolute action."

Truman asked Congress to appropriate $400 million for economic aid and military supplies for both countries, and to authorize the dispatch of American civilian and military personnel in order to help the two nations in their tasks of reconstruction and provide their armies with appropriate instruction and training. Truman ended on a grave note:

This is a serious course upon which we embark.

I would not recommend it except that the alternative is much more serious . . .

The seeds of totalitarian regimes are nurtured by misery and want. They spread and grow in the evil soil of poverty and strife. They reach their full growth when the hope of a people for a better life has died.

We must keep that hope alive.

The free peoples of the world look to us for support in maintaining their freedoms.

If we falter in our leadership, we may endanger the peace of the world—and we shall surely endanger the welfare of our nation.

Great responsibilities have been placed upon us by the swift movement of events.

I am confident that the Congress will face these responsibilities squarely.

The Congress and the American people did. History had once more shown that when a great and democratic people is given decisive and courageous leadership, the people will respond quickly and wisely. Under Truman's leadership, the American public had made a decisive commitment. The United States was now a full participant in the international arena. There could no longer be any retreat. The survival of freedom was dependent solely upon the United States. The only question was how responsibly and honorably this country would bear its new burden of world leadership.

Origins of the Cold War

Realist

Realist historians agree with the Nationalists that the primary responsibility for the cold war lies at the door of the U.S.S.R., but they have some major quarrels with the way the United States has conducted the cold war and with the Nationalist historians' defense of it. In the following selection George F. Kennan, the major architect of the containment policy followed by the United States and defended by the Nationalists, spells out his objections to the way his policy has been carried out.

Kennan argues that the threat Russia posed to the West after World War II was far more political than military. He believes that Stalin had neither the power nor the intentions to conquer Western Europe, let alone the world. But the chaos in war-torn Europe invited political subversion; if the Communists in these European countries could have taken power by internal revolutions, they would have allied themselves with Russia, thus destroying the balance of power and threatening American prosperity and security. Kennan bemoans the turning of his containment policy from political to military purposes and argues that this decision was responsible at least for prolonging the duration of the cold war. He especially decries the unrealistic anti-Communist fanaticism that grew out of his containment policy.

What evidence does Kennan give in his essay of Russia's original aggressive intent? Of the limits of that intent? How and when does Kennan think we should have dealt with Russia's aggression? Why does he think it was necessary to respond to Russian policy at all?

Memoirs

George F. Kennan

Mr. Joseph Jones, in his excellent book *The Fifteen Weeks,* has described in great and faithful detail the various discussions, consultations, clearances, and literary struggles that took place within the government in the ensuing days before the President was in a position to present to the Congress, two weeks later, his famous Truman Doctrine message. It was (I learn from Mr. Jones's book) on the day before the State Department's final draft of this message went to the White House, presumably about March 6, that I came over to the department to have a look at the paper. What I saw made me extremely unhappy. The language to which I took particular exception was not the product of Henderson's pen or of any of his associates in the geographic divisions. It had been produced, at the initiative of the department's public relations office, in a subcommittee of the State-War-Navy Coordinating Committee (SWNCC), which evidently felt itself under the necessity of clothing the announced rationale for the President's decision in terms more grandiose and more sweeping than anything that I, at least, had ever envisaged. (More about that later.) I remonstrated, by my own recollection, to Henderson. Mr. Jones says I also remonstrated to Mr. Acheson; and I have no doubt that I did, although I do not specifically recall it. I produced, in any event, some alternative language, though I have no record of what it was. Whether these remonstrations met with much understanding in substance, I cannot remember. In any case, they came too late. No one wanted to repeat the agony of collective drafting that had been invested over the preceding days in the production of this historic piece of paper.

Faced, as any autobiographer is, with the danger of mistaking hindsight for recollection, I am fortunate in finding among my papers one that not only sets forth in detail the reasons, as I saw them at the time, why it was desirable that our government should respond to the challenge of the British move but also explains, by clear implication, the reasons for my unhappiness over the wording of the President's message. We in the faculty of the

From *Memoirs: 1925–1950* by George F. Kennan, pp. 314–324, 357–367. By permission of Atlantic-Little Brown and Co. Copyright ©1967 by George F. Kennan.

War College used the Greek crisis, just at that time, as the basis for a problem which we assigned to various committees of the students. We asked them, in effect, to supply some of the individual components of the President's decision on this question. Twice, on the heels of the President's presentation to Congress, I discussed this problem informally before the student body. On the first of these occasions, March 14, two days after presentation of the President's message, I commented on the terms of the War College problem itself. On March 28, after the student answers were in, I discussed the solutions to it and gave the reasons why I, personally, had felt that we had been right to accept the challenge of the British action. It is the stenographic records of these two statements that I find in my papers.

First, as to my understanding of the background of the decision: I accepted the conclusion, to which many others in the government had arrived, that (and I use the words of the War College presentation) "if nothing were done to stiffen the backs of the non-Communist elements in Greece at this juncture the Communist elements would soon succeed in seizing power and in establishing a totalitarian dictatorship along the lines already visible in other Balkan countries." I did not view the prospect of such a Communist takeover as *"in itself* any immediate and catastrophic setback to the Western world." I considered that the Russians and their Eastern European associates were poorly set up to take responsibility either for the governing of Greece or for the support of the Greek economy. Eventually, I thought, all this might boomerang on them in the form of serious economic difficulties and other problems, which the West might even ultimately exploit to good advantage. But Communist rule, I thought, "would probably be successfully consolidated in the long run and might some day have most unfortunate strategic consequences from the standpoint of any military adversary of the Soviet Union." And more important still were the probable repercussions which such a development would have on neighboring areas.

In this last connection, I took up first the question of Turkey. I pointed out that the situation of Turkey differed quite fundamentally from that of Greece. There was no serious Communist penetration in Turkey—no comparable guerrilla movement. The Turks had nothing to fear but fear. "If . . . the Turks do not lose their nerves, if they keep their internal political life relatively clean and orderly and refuse to become involved in negotiations with the Russians on a bilateral basis over complicated questions such as that of the Straits, they will probably continue to enjoy a temporary and precarious immunity to Russian pressure." But, I pointed out, should they be increasingly encircled by Communist-dominated entities, it would plainly be harder for them to maintain this stance. Aid to Greece was therefore important as a support for stability in Turkey as well.

It should be noted that this view of the problem of Turkey afforded no rationale for the mounting of a special aid program for Turkey itself. The accent was put on internal morale and on firmness of diplomatic stance, not on military preparations. It was for this reason that I was not happy to find in the draft of the President's message to Congress a proposal for aid to Turkey as well as to Greece. I suspected that what was intended primarily was military aid, and that what had really happened was that the Pentagon had exploited a favorable set of circumstances in order to infiltrate a military aid program for Turkey into what was supposed to be primarily a political and economic program for Greece. Since it was important, in my view, that the Soviet threat be recognized for what it was—primarily a political one and not a threat of military attack—it seemed unfortunate that the picture of what was needed in Greece should be confused by association with something that was not needed—or, if needed, was needed for entirely different purposes—in Turkey.

To return to the exposé at the War College: From Turkey, I moved on to the subject of the Middle East. What would be the repercussions there of a Communist takeover in Greece? Here again my conclusions were somewhat different from those of other people. I did not underrate the seriousness of Russian-Communist penetration among the restless intelligentsia of the Moslem capitals. But I questioned the ultimate ability of the Russians to disaffect and dominate the entire Moslem world. Not only was their ideology in conflict with the Moslem faith, but they were just not that good. Even in northern Iran and among the Kurds their recent performance, as political intriguers, had not been impressive. If they were to expand still further in this area they would "soon encounter the far more vigorous political society of Arabia itself and contiguous areas, where the fire of Moslem ideology burns with a purer and fiercer flame, and where resistance to Communist political pressure would be of a far sterner quality than in the lands to the north and east." It was not, then, for the long term that I feared the fillip to Soviet penetration of the Middle East which a Communist coup in Greece would certainly provide. But I had to recognize that the immediate repercussions might be ones unsettling to such fragile stability as the region then enjoyed. And this in turn might have effects in relation to the situation in an area even more important from the standpoint of our security: Western Europe.

It was hard to overestimate, in those days of uncertainty and economic difficulty, the cumulative effects of sensational political events. People were influenced, as I pointed out on that occasion to the War College, not just by their desires as to what *should* happen but by their estimates of what *would* happen. People in Western Europe did not, by and large, want Communist control. But this did not mean that they would not trim their sails and even abet its coming if they gained the impression that it was inevitable. This was why the shock of a Communist success in Greece could not be risked.

In Western Europe, too, I added, it was not likely that Communist domination could last indefinitely. But while it lasted, it could do great damage.

Because floodwaters must—by the laws of nature—some day subside is no reason that one should welcome them on his place. . . . We have no cause to assume that Europe as we know it—and as we need it—would never recover from the blow which even a brief period of Russian control would deal to her already weakened traditions and institutions. . . . The waves of Communist authority might some day recede but we could have no reason to expect that American prestige and influence could easily reenter the territories thus liberated. . . .

I went on, then, to point out that if we were to leave Europe to the Communists, the resulting problem of security for the United States "might not be one of external security alone."

Remember that in abandoning Europe we would be abandoning not only the fountainheads of most of our own culture and tradition; we would also be abandoning almost all the other areas in the world where progressive representative government is a working proposition. We would be placing ourselves in the position of a lonely country, culturally and politically. To maintain confidence in our own traditions and institutions we would henceforth have to whistle loudly in the dark. I am not sure that whistling could be loud enough to do the trick.

I know that there are many people—and probably some among you— who will reply indignantly that I am selling short the strength and soundness of our institutions—who will maintain that American democracy has nothing to fear from Europe's diseases and nothing to learn from Europe's experiences.

I wish I could believe that that were true. I wish I could believe that the human impulses which give rise to the nightmares of totalitarianism were ones which Providence had allocated only to other peoples and to which the American people had been graciously left immune. Unfortunately, I know that that is not true. After all, most of us are only Europeans once or twice removed; and some of us are less removed than that. There are openly totalitarian forces already working in our society. Do you think that they could fail to derive new confidence and new supporters from such a series of developments? And it is not even with these small existing groups of extremists that the real danger lies. The fact of the matter is that there is a little bit of the totalitarian buried somewhere, way down deep, in each and every one of us. It is only the cheerful light of confidence and security which keeps this evil genius down at the usual helpless and invisible depth. If confidence and security were to disappear, don't think that he would not be waiting to take their place. Others may lull themselves to sleep with the pleasing assumption that the work of building freedom in this country was accomplished completely and for all time by our forefathers. I prefer to accept the word of a great European, the German poet, Goethe, that freedom is something that has to be reconquered every day. And in that never-ending process of reconquest, I would hate to see this country lose all its allies.

So much for the reasons for our limited intervention in Greece. Why, then, approving this action, did I take exception to the language of the President's message?

I took exception to it primarily because of the sweeping nature of the commitments which it implied. The heart of the message and the passage that has subsequently been most frequently quoted was this:

I believe it must be the policy of the United States to support free peoples who are resisting subjugation by armed minorities or by outside pressures.
I believe that we must assist free peoples to work out their own destinies in their own way.

This passage, and others as well, placed our aid to Greece in the framework of a universal policy rather than in that of a specific decision addressed to a specific set of circumstances. It implied that what we had decided to do in the case of Greece was something we would be prepared to do in the case of any other country, provided only that it was faced with the threat of "subjugation by armed minorities or by outside pressures."

It seemed to me highly uncertain that we would invariably find it in our interests or within our means to extend assistance to

countries that found themselves in this extremity. The mere fact
of their being in such a plight was only one of the criteria that
had to be taken into account in determining our action. The establishment of the existence of such a threat was only the beginning, not the end, of the process of decision. I listed, in my presentation to the War College, three specific considerations that
had supported our decision to extend assistance to Greece:

A. The problem at hand is one within our economic, technical, and financial capabilities.
B. If we did not take such action, the resulting situation might redound very decidedly to the advantage of our political adversaries.
C. If, on the other hand, we do take the action in question, there is
good reason to hope that the favorable consequences will carry far beyond the limits of Greece itself.

These considerations, I pointed out, did not necessarily apply
to all other regions. I doubted, for example, that any of them
would fully apply in the case of China: the first most definitely
would not. But if this was the case, then why use language that
suggested that all that was required was proof of the existence
of a threat of "subjugation by armed minorities or by outside
pressure"—that this was the sole criterion of our response?
Were I reacting today to the Truman Doctrine message, I
would certainly have added to this list of specific requirements
the willingness and ability of the threatened people to pick up
and bear resolutely the overwhelming portion of the responsibility
and effort in their own defense against both direct and indirect
aggression—not just to sit back and hedge against the possibility
that resistance might not be effective and leave the burden of the
struggle to us. I would also take exception to the repeated
suggestions, in the text of that message, that what we were concerned to defend in Greece was the democratic quality of the
country's institutions. We would find it necessary to give aid, over
the ensuing years, to a number of regimes which could hardly
qualify for it on the basis of their democratic character. It was
unwise to suggest that this, too, was an essential criterion. But
these omissions, the recognition of which does indeed reflect the
promptings of hindsight, only reinforce the validity of the objections to the language of the message that suggested themselves
at the time.
I was not alone in my awareness of the danger that the sweeping language of the message might be subject to misinterpre-

tation. Mr. Acheson was himself at pains to try to dispel among the members of the Congress the impression that what the President had said represented some sort of a blank check. The fact that we were prepared on principle to extend aid in such situations did not mean, he explained in his testimony before the Senate Committee on Foreign Relations on March 24, 1947, that our action in other instances would always be the same as in Greece. "Any requests of foreign countries for aid," he said in his opening statement,

will have to be considered according to the circumstances in each individual case. In another case we would have to study whether the country in question really needs assistance, whether its request is consistent with American foreign policy, whether the request for assistance is sincere, and whether assistance by the United States would be effective in meeting the problems of that country. It cannot be assumed, therefore, that this government would necessarily undertake measures in any other country identical or even closely similar to those proposed for Greece and Turkey.

Nevertheless, the misapprehension already conveyed was, as I see it, never entirely corrected. Throughout the ensuing two decades the conduct of our foreign policy would continue to be bedeviled by people in our own government as well as in other governments who could not free themselves from the belief that all another country had to do, in order to qualify for American aid, was to demonstrate the existence of a Communist threat. Since almost no country was without a Communist minority, this assumption carried very far. And as time went on, the firmness of understanding for these distinctions on the part of our own public and governmental establishment appeared to grow weaker rather than stronger. In the 1960s so absolute would be the value attached, even by people within the government, to the mere existence of a Communist threat, that such a threat would be viewed as calling, in the case of Southeast Asia, for an American response on a tremendous scale, without serious regard even to those main criteria that most of us in 1947 would have thought it natural and essential to apply.

On many occasions, both before and after this Greek-Turkish episode, I have been struck by the congenital aversion of Americans to taking specific decisions on specific problems, and by their persistent urge to seek universal formulae or doctrines in which to clothe and justify particular actions. We obviously dis-

454   George F. Kennan

like to discriminate. We like to find some general governing norm
to which, in each instance, appeal can be taken, so that individual decisions may be made not on their particular merits but automatically, depending on whether the circumstances do or do
not seem to fit the norm. We like, by the same token, to attribute
a universal significance to decisions we have already found it
necessary, for limited and parochial reasons, to take. It was not
enough for us, when circumstances forced us into World War I,
to hold in view the specific reasons for our entry: our war effort
had to be clothed in the form of an effort to make the *world*
(nothing less) "safe for democracy." It was not enough for us, in
World War II, that the Japanese attacked us at Pearl Harbor and
that both Japanese and German governments declared war on
us: we did not feel comfortable until we had wrapped our military
effort in the wholly universalistic—and largely meaningless—
generalities of the Atlantic Charter. Something of this same compulsion became apparent in the postwar period in the tendency
of many Americans to divide the world neatly into Communist
and "free world" components, to avoid recognition of specific differences among countries on either side, and to search for general formulas to govern our relations with the one or the other. I
think, in this connection, of the periodic wrangling in Congress,
in connection with the annual aid bills, over the question whether
most-favored-nation treatment should be extended, or various
forms of aid be granted, to "Communist" countries or to countries "forming part of the Communist conspiracy" or whatever
general language one chose to employ—the idea being always to
define a category of states and to compel the executive to be-
have in a uniform way with relation to all of them. Seldom does it
seem to have occurred to many congressional figures that the
best thing to do would be to let the President, or the Secretary of
State, use his head.

To this day I am uncertain as to the origins of this persistent
American urge to the universalization or generalization of decision. I suspect it to be a reflection of the extent to which we are
a people given to government by laws rather than by executive
discretion. Laws, too, are general norms, and Congress, accustomed to limiting executive discretion through the establishment
of such norms in the internal field, obviously feels more comfortable when its powers with relation to foreign policy can be exercised in a similar way. Unable to control executive decisions on a
day-to-day basis, many Congressmen and Senators feel, I sus-

pect, a need for general determinations defining the latitude within which those decisions may be taken.

Whatever the origins of this tendency, it is an unfortunate one. It confuses public understanding of international issues more than it clarifies it. It shackles and distorts the process of decision-taking. It causes questions to be decided on the basis of criteria only partially relevant or not relevant at all. It tends to exclude at many points the discrimination of judgment and the prudence of language requisite to the successful conduct of the affairs of a great power.

.   .   .

Measured against the interpretations that were at once attached to it [the X-Article], and have continued to a considerable extent to surround it ever since, the article that appeared in *Foreign Affairs,* in June 1947, suffered, unquestionably, from serious deficiencies. Some of these I might have corrected at the time by more careful editing and greater forethought, had I had any idea of the way it was to be received. But I cannot lay these failures exclusively to the innocent and unsuspecting manner in which the article was written. Certain of the public reactions were ones I would not, in any event, have foreseen.

A serious deficiency of the article was the failure to mention the satellite area of Eastern Europe—the failure to discuss Soviet power, that is, *in terms of* its involvement in this area. Anyone reading the article would have thought—and would have had every reason to think—that I was talking only about Russia proper; that the weaknesses of the Soviet system to which I was drawing attention were ones that had their existence only within the national boundaries of the Soviet state; that the geographic extension that had been given to the power of the Soviet leaders, by virtue of the recent advances of Soviet armies into Eastern Europe and the political exploitation of those advances for Communist purposes, were irrelevant to the weaknesses of which I was speaking. Obviously, in mentioning the uncertainties of the Soviet situation—such things as the weariness and poor morale among the population, the fragility of the constitutional arrangements within the party, etc.—I would have had a far stronger case had I added the characteristic embarrassments of imperialism which the Soviet leaders had now taken upon themselves with their conquest of Eastern Europe, and the unlikelihood that

Moscow would be permanently successful in holding this great area in subjection.

To this day, I am not sure of the reason for this omission. It had something to do, I suspect, with what I felt to be Mr. Forrestal's needs at the time when I prepared the original paper for him. I have a vague recollection of feeling that to go into the problems of the satellite area would be to open up a wholly new subject, confuse the thesis I was developing, and carry the paper beyond its intended scope. Whatever the reason, it was certainly not that I underrated the difficulties with which the Soviet leaders were faced in their attempt to exercise political dominion over Eastern Europe. It has been noted above, in Chapter 9, that even as early as V-E Day, two years before, I had expressed the view that the Russians were overextended in this area. Without Western support, I had written at that time

Russia would probably not be able to maintain its hold successfully for any length of time over all the territory over which it has today staked out a claim. . . . The lines would have to be withdrawn somewhat.

Similarly, in the long telegram I had sent to Washington from Moscow, in February 1946, I had pointed out that the Soviet internal system

will now be subjected, by virtue of recent territorial expansions, to a series of additional strains which once proved a severe tax on Tsardom.

Had I included these appreciations in the X-Article, and added to the description of the internal weaknesses of Soviet power a mention of the strains of Moscow's new external involvement in Eastern Europe, I would have had a far stronger case for challenging the permanency of the imposing and forbidding facade which Stalin's Russia presented to the outside world in those immediate postwar years.

A second serious deficiency of the X-Article—perhaps the most serious of all—was the failure to make clear that what I was talking about when I mentioned the containment of Soviet power was not the containment by military means of a military threat, but the political containment of a political threat. Certain of the language used—such as "a long-term, patient but firm and vigilant containment of Russian expansive tendencies " or "the adroit and vigilant application of counterforce at a series of constantly shifting geographical and political points"—was at best ambiguous, and lent itself to misinterpretation in this respect.

A third great deficiency, intimately connected with the one just mentioned, was the failure to distinguish between various geographic areas, and to make clear that the "containment" of which I was speaking was not something that I thought we could, necessarily, do everywhere successfully, or even needed to do everywhere successfully, in order to serve the purpose I had in mind. Actually, as noted in connection with the Truman Doctrine above, I distinguished clearly in my own mind between areas that I thought vital to our security and ones that did not seem to me to fall into this category. My objection to the Truman Doctrine message revolved largely around its failure to draw this distinction. Repeatedly, at that time and in ensuing years, I expressed in talks and lectures the view that there were only five regions of the world—the United States, the United Kingdom, the Rhine valley with adjacent industrial areas, the Soviet Union, and Japan—where the sinews of modern military strength could be produced in quantity; I pointed out that only one of these was under Communist control; and I defined the main task of containment, accordingly, as one of seeing to it that none of the remaining ones fell under such control. Why this was not made clear in the X-Article is, again, a mystery. I suppose I thought that such considerations were subsumed under the reference to the need for confronting the Russians with unalterable counterforce *"at every point where they show signs of encroaching upon the interests of a peaceful world."*

So egregious were these errors that I must confess to responsibility for the greatest and most unfortunate of the misunderstandings to which they led. This was the one created in the mind of Mr. Walter Lippmann. It found its expression in the series of twelve pieces attacking the X-Article (later published in book form as *The Cold War, A Study in U.S. Foreign Policy,* New York: Harper and Brothers, 1947) which he published in his newspaper column in the late summer and autumn of 1947. As I read these articles over today (and they are well worth the effort), I find the misunderstanding almost tragic in its dimensions. Mr. Lippmann, in the first place, mistook me for the author of precisely those features of the Truman Doctrine which I had most vigorously opposed—an assumption to which, I must say, I had led squarely with my chin in the careless and indiscriminate language of the X-Article. He held up, as a deserved correction to these presumed aberrations on my part, precisely those features of General Marshall's approach, and those passages of the Harvard speech, for which I had a primary responsibility. He interpreted the concept of containment in just the military sense I had not meant to give it. And on the basis of these misimpressions he proceeded to set forth, as an alternative to what I had led him to think my views were, a concept of American policy so similar to that which I was to hold and to advance in coming years that one could only assume I was subconsciously inspired by that statement of it—as perhaps, in part, I was. He urged a concentration on the vital countries of Europe; he urged a policy directed toward a mutual withdrawal of Soviet and American (also British) forces from Europe; he pointed with farsighted penetration to the dangers involved in any attempt to make of a truncated Western Germany an ally in an anti-Soviet coalition. All these points would figure prominently in my own later writings. He saw them, for the most part, long before I did. I accept the blame for misleading him. My only consolation is that I succeeded in provoking from him so excellent and penetrating a treatise.

Nevertheless, the experience was a painful one. It was doubly painful by reason of the great respect I bore him. I can still recall the feeling of bewilderment and frustration with which—helpless now to reply publicly because of my official position—I read these columns as they appeared and found held against me so many views with which I profoundly agreed. A few months later (April 1948), lying under treatment for ulcers on the sixteenth floor of the Naval Hospital in Bethesda, very bleak in spirit from the attendant fasting and made bleaker still by the whistling of the cold spring wind in the windows of that lofty pinnacle, I wrote a long letter to Mr. Lippmann, protesting the misinterpretation of my thoughts which his articles, as it seemed to me, implied. I never sent it to him. It was probably best that I didn't. The letter had a plaintive and overdramatic tone, reflecting the discomfort of flesh and spirit in which it was written. I took a more cruel but less serious revenge a year or two later when I ran into him on a parlor car of the Pennsylvania Railroad, and wore him relentlessly down with a monologue on these same subjects that lasted most of the way from Washington to New York.

But the terms of the unsent letter still hold, as I see them, a certain interest as expressions of the way the Lippmann columns then affected me.

I began, of course, with a peal of anguish over the confusion about the Truman Doctrine and the Marshall Plan. To be held as the author of the former, and to have the latter held up to me as the mature correction of my youthful folly, hurt more than anything else.

I also naturally went to great lengths to disclaim the view, imputed to me by implication in Mr. Lippmann's columns, that containment was a matter of stationing military forces around the Soviet borders and preventing any outbreak of Soviet military aggressiveness. I protested, as I was to do on so many other occasions over the course of the ensuing eighteen years, against the implication that the Russians were aspiring to invade other areas and that the task of American policy was to prevent them from doing so. "The Russians don't want," I insisted,

to invade anyone. It is not in their tradition. They tried it once in Finland and got their fingers burned. They don't want war of any kind. Above all, they don't want the open responsibility that official invasion brings with it. They far prefer to do the job politically with stooge forces. Note well: when I say politically, that does not mean without violence. But it means that the violence is nominally *domestic,* not *international,* violence. It is, if you will, a police violence . . . not a military violence.

The policy of containment related to the effort to encourage other peoples to resist this time of violence and to defend the *internal* integrity of their countries.

I tried, then, to explain (I could have done it better) that the article was in reality a plea—addressed as much to our despairing liberals as to our hotheaded right-wingers—for acceptance of the belief that, ugly as was the problem of Soviet power, war was not inevitable, nor was it a suitable answer; that the absence of war did not mean that we would lose the struggle; that there was a middle ground of political resistance on which we could stand with reasonable prospect of success. We were, in fact, already standing on that ground quite successfully. And I went ahead to point proudly (and rather unfairly, for after all, Lippmann had approved and praised the rationale of the Marshall Plan in his articles) to what had already been accomplished. I cite this passage here, not as a correction to Mr. Lippmann, to whose arguments it was not really an answer, but as a sort of epilogue to the discussion of both Marshall Plan and X-Article.

Something over a year has now gone by since General Marshall took over his present job. I would ask you to think back on the state of the world, as he faced it last spring. At that time, it was almost impossible to see how Europe could be saved. We were still caught in the fateful confusion between the "one-world" and the "two-world" concepts. The economic plight of the continent was rapidly revealing itself as far worse than anyone had dreamed, and was steadily deteriorating. Congress was in an ugly frame of mind, convinced that all foreign aid was "operation rathole." The Communists were at the throat of France. A pall of fear, of bewilderment, of discouragement, hung over the continent and paralyzed all constructive activity. Molotov sat adamant at the Moscow council table, because he saw no reason to pay us a price for things which he thought were bound to drop into his lap, like ripe fruits, through the natural course of events.

Compare that with today? Europe is admittedly not over the hump. But no fruits have dropped [into Molotov's lap]. We know what is West and what is East. Moscow was itself compelled to make that unpleasant delineation. Recovery is progressing rapidly in the West. New hope exists. People see the possibility of a better future. The Communist position in France has been deeply shaken. The Western nations have found a common political language. They are learning to lean on each other, and to help each other. Those who fancied they were neutral are beginning to realize that they are on our side. A year ago only that which was Communist had firmness and structure. Today the non-Communist world is gaining daily in rigidity and in the power of resistance. Admittedly, the issue hangs on Italy; but it hangs, in reality, on Italy alone. A year ago it hung on all of Europe and on us.

You may say: this was not the doing of US policy makers; it was others who worked this miracle.

Certainly, we did not do it alone; and I have no intention of attempting to apportion merit. But you must leave us some pride in our own legerdemain. In international affairs, the proof of the pudding is always in the eating. If the development of the past year had been in the opposite direction—if there had been a deterioration of our position as great as the actual improvement—there is not one of you who would not have placed the blame squarely on the failure of American statesmanship. Must it always, then, be "heads you win; tails I lose" for the US Government?

In the years that have passed since that time, the myth of the "doctrine of containment" has never fully lost its spell. On innumerable occasions, I have been asked to explain it, to say whether I thought it had been a success, to explain how it applied to China, to state a view as to whether it was still relevant in later situations, etc. It has been interpreted by others in a variety of ways. Pro-Soviet writers have portrayed it as the cloak for aggressive designs on the Soviet Union. Right-wing critics have assailed it precisely for its lack of aggressiveness: for its passivity, for its failure to promise anything like "victory." Serious commentators have maintained that it was all very well in 1947 but that it lost its rationale with the Korean War, or with Stalin's death, or with the decline of bipolarity.

It is hard for me to respond to all these criticisms. What I said in the X-Article was not intended as a doctrine. I am afraid that when I think about foreign policy, I do not think in terms of doctrines. I think in terms of principles.

In writing the X-Article, I had in mind a long series of what seemed to me to be concessions that we had made, during the course of the war and just after it, to Russian expansionist tendencies—concessions made in the hope and belief that they would promote collaboration between our government and the Soviet government in the postwar period. I had also in mind the fact that many people, seeing that these concessions had been unsuccessful and that we had been unable to agree with the Soviet leaders on the postwar order of Europe and Asia, were falling into despair and jumping to the panicky conclusion that this spelled the inevitability of an eventual war between the Soviet Union and the United States.

It was this last conclusion that I was attempting, in the X-Article, to dispute. I thought I knew as much as anyone in the United States about the ugliness of the problem that Stalin's Russia presented to us. I had no need to accept instruction on this point from anybody. But I saw no necessity of a Soviet-American war, nor anything to be gained by one, then or at any time. There was, I thought, another way of handling this problem—a way that offered reasonable prospects of success, at least in the sense of avoiding a new world disaster and leaving the Western community of nations no worse off than it then was. This was simply to cease at that point making fatuous unilateral concessions to the Kremlin, to do what we could to inspire and support resistance elsewhere to its efforts to expand the area of its dominant political influence, and to wait for the internal weaknesses of Soviet power, combined with frustration in the external field, to moderate Soviet ambitions and behavior. The Soviet leaders, formidable as they were, were not supermen. Like all rulers of all great countries, they had their internal contradictions and dilemmas to deal with. Stand up to them, I urged, manfully but not aggressively, and give the hand of time a chance to work.

This is all that the X-Article was meant to convey. I did not suppose, in saying all this, that the situation flowing immediately from the manner in which hostilities ended in 1945 would endure forever. It was my assumption that if and when the Soviet leaders had been brought to a point where they would talk reasonably about some of the problems flowing from the outcome of the war, we would obviously wish to pursue this possibility and to see what could be done about restoring a more normal state of affairs. I shared to the full, in particular, Walter Lippmann's view of the importance of achieving, someday, the retirement of Soviet military power from Eastern Europe, although I did not then attach quite the same political importance to such a retirement as he did. (In this he was more right than I was.)

No one was more conscious than I was of the dangers of a permanent division of the European continent. The purpose of "containment" as then conceived was not to perpetuate the status quo to which the military operations and political arrangements of World War II had led; it was to tide us over a difficult time and bring us to a point where we could discuss effectively with the Russians the drawbacks and dangers this status quo involved, and to arrange with them for its peaceful replacement by a better and sounder one.

And if the policy of containment could be said in later years to have failed, it was not a failure in the sense that it proved impossible to prevent the Russians from making mortally dangerous encroachments "upon the interests of a peaceful world" (for it did prevent that); nor was it a failure in the sense that the mellowing of Soviet power, which Walter Lippmann took me so severely to task for predicting, failed to set in (it did set in). The failure consisted in the fact that our own government, finding it difficult to understand a political threat as such and to deal with it in other than military terms, and grievously misled, in particular, by its own faulty interpretations of the significance of the Korean War, failed to take advantage of the opportunities for useful political discussion when, in later years, such opportunities began to open up, and exerted itself, in its military preoccupations, to seal and to perpetuate the very division of Europe which it should have been concerned to remove. It was not "containment" that failed; it was the intended follow-up that never occurred.

When I used the term "Soviet power" in the X-Article, I had in view, of course, the system of power organized, dominated, and inspired by Joseph Stalin. This was a monolithic power structure, reaching through the network of highly disciplined Communist parties into practically every country in the world. In these circumstances, any success of a local Communist party, any advance of Communist power anywhere, had to be regarded as an extension in reality of the political orbit, or at least the dominant influence, of the Kremlin. Precisely because Stalin maintained so jealous, so humiliating a control over foreign Communists, all of the latter had, at that time, to be regarded as the vehicles of his will, not their own. His was the only center of authority in the Communist world; and it was a vigilant, exacting, and imperious headquarters, prepared to brook no opposition.

Tito's break with Moscow, in 1948, was the first overt breach in the monolithic unity of the Moscow-dominated Communist bloc. For long, it remained the only one. It did not affect immediately and importantly the situation elsewhere in the Communist world. But when, in the period between 1957 and 1962, the differences between the Chinese and Russian Communist parties, having lain latent in earlier years, broke to the surface and assumed the form of a major conflict between the two regimes, the situation in the world Communist movement became basically different. Other Communist parties, primarily those outside Eastern Europe but partly the Eastern European ones as well, had now two poles —three, if Belgrade was included—to choose among. This very freedom of choice not only made possible for them a large degree of independence; in many instances it forced that independence upon them. Neither of the two major centers of Communist power was now in a position to try to impose upon them a complete disciplinary control, for fear of pushing them into the arms of the other. They, on the other hand, reluctant for the most part to take the risks of total identification with one or the other, had little choice but to maneuver, to think and act for themselves, to accept, in short, the responsibilities of independence. If, at the end of the 1940s, no Communist party (except the Yugoslav one) could be considered anything else than an instrument of Soviet power, by the end of the 1950s none (unless it be the Bulgarian and the Czech) could be considered to be such an instrument at all.

This development changed basically the assumptions underlying the concept of containment, as expressed in the X-Article. Seen from the standpoint upon which that article rested, the Chinese-Soviet conflict was in itself the greatest single measure of containment that could be conceived. It not only invalidated the original concept of containment, it disposed in large measure of the very problem to which it was addressed.

Efforts to enlist the original concept of containment with relation to situations that postdate the Chinese-Soviet conflict, particularly when they are described in terms that refer to some vague "communism" in general and do not specify what particular communism is envisaged, are therefore wholly misconceived. There is today no such thing as "communism" in the sense that there was in 1947; there are only a number of national regimes which cloak themselves in the verbal trappings of radical Marxism and follow domestic policies influenced to one degree or another by Marxist concepts.

If, then, I was the author in 1947 of a "doctrine" of containment, it was a doctrine that lost much of its rationale with the death of Stalin and with the development of the Soviet-Chinese conflict. I emphatically deny the paternity of any efforts to invoke that doctrine today in situations to which it has, and can have, no proper relevance.

Origins of the Cold War

Radical

Radicals blame the United States more than they do Russia for the development of the cold war. They argue, along with the Realists, that Russia had no intentions of conquering the world; but they argue further that the United States was well aware of this all along. Radicals point out that until 1949 the United States had sole possession of the atomic bomb. Thus the American withdrawal of troops from Europe constituted neither a gesture of peace nor a concession to Russia of superior strength in Europe. With the bomb, the United States and Western Europe had no reason whatever to fear Russia. Rather, it was the other way around.

Radical historians argue that the United States and its allies had agreed at the Yalta conference and elsewhere to concede Eastern Europe to Russia as a sphere of influence. A security zone would then be formed to protect Russia from any renewed German aggression. But when the United States exploded the atomic bomb, Radicals argue, its leaders decided to renege on their previous agreements. Hoping to force

*open Eastern European markets for American goods and influence, the
United States attempted to use fear of the bomb to roll back Russian
control of the area. Stalin was forced to react, and the cold war was on.*

*Gar Alperovitz, author of the following article, is president of the Cam-
bridge Institute in Massachusetts and the author of* Atomic Diplomacy:
Hiroshima and Potsdam. *What evidence does Alperovitz have for American agreement to a Russian sphere of influence in Eastern Europe? How
does he support his contention that Russian intentions at the end of
World War II were limited to attaining a security zone bordering Germany? What areas of agreement do you see between Kennan and Alperovitz?*

How the
Cold War Began

Gar Alperovitz

Writing as "Mr. X," George Kennan suggested twenty years ago
that the mechanism of Soviet diplomacy "moves inexorably along
the prescribed path, like a persistent toy automobile wound up
and headed in a given direction, stopping only when it meets
with some unanswerable force." A generation of Americans
quickly embraced Kennan's view as an explanation of the tension, danger, and waste of the Cold War. But was his theory of
inexorable Soviet expansion—and its matching recommendation
of "containment"—correct? A cautious but important book, *Beginnings of the Cold War,* suggests we might well have been
more critical of so mechanistic an idea of the way Great Powers
act and how the Cold War began.

From Gar Alperovitz, "How the Cold War Began," *The New York Review of
Books* (March 23, 1967), pp. 6–12. Reprinted by permission of Gar Alperovitz %
IFA. Copyright ©1967 by The New York Review.

Any examination of the very earliest postwar period forces us to think about developments *before* 1947 when it was decided to contain the Soviet Union by "unanswerable force." Herz's study is important because it makes two serious judgments about this period: first, that in 1945 Soviet policy was by no means inexorably prescribed and expansionist; second, that mistakes made by American officials just after the war may well have prevented the kind of compromise and accommodation which is just beginning to emerge in Europe today.

These suggestions recall Walter Lippmann's *The Cold War,* published in 1947, which also argued—with greater candor and less detail—that the Russians might have been willing to accept a negotiated settlement in 1945 and 1946, but that US policy ignored opportunities to meet them halfway. Lippman's now little-remembered book offered a powerful critique of Kennan's theory of Soviet expansion and American containment. If Herz's view is correct, accepted interpretations of American-Russian relations are called into question. And if Lippmann was right in saying that American policy helped to prevent an accommodation in 1945 and 1946, the Cold War itself must be regarded, at least in part, as the result of fundamental errors of American diplomacy. These are startling conclusions, but anyone willing to bring an open mind to Herz's book or to Lippmann's will find that they have exposed many weaknesses in the usual explanations of early events in the Cold War.

No one, of course, can be certain of "what might have been." But Herz refutes at least one accepted myth. Contrary to current historical reconstructions, there is abundant evidence that American leaders in 1945 were not much worried about the expansion of communism into *Western* Europe. That worry came later. In the days just after the war, most Communists in Italy, France, and elsewhere were cooperating with bourgeois governments. At Potsdam, in 1945, Truman regarded the Russian's desires for concessions beyond their area of occupation as largely bluff. The major issues in dispute were all in Eastern Europe, deep within the zone of Soviet military occupation. The real expansion of Soviet power, we are reminded, took place in Poland, Hungary, Bulgaria, Rumania, Czechoslovakia, and the eastern regions of Germany and Austria.

The US in 1945 wanted Russia to give up the control and influence the Red Army had gained in the battle against Hitler. American demands may have been motivated by an idealistic desire to foster democracy, but Herz's main point is that in countries like Rumania and Bulgaria they were about as realistic as would be Soviet demands for changes in, say, Mexico. Any such parallel has obvious limits, the most significant of which is not that democracy and communism cannot so easily be compared, but that Eastern Europe is of far greater importance to Soviet security than is Mexico to American security: from the time of Napoleon—and twice in the lifetime of millions of present-day Russians—bloody invasions have swept through the area to their "Middle West."

In the early spring of 1945, negotiations concerning one border state—Poland—brought the main issue into the open. At Yalta and immediately thereafter, the US had mainly mediated between Stalin and Churchill on Poland; Roosevelt had warned Churchill that to make extreme demands would doom the negotiations. A month later, in the faltering last days of Roosevelt's life, the US itself adopted a new tough line, demanding that pro-Western and openly anti-Russian Polish politicians be given more influence in negotiations to set up a new government for Poland. As was predicted, the Russians balked at the idea of such an expansion of anti-Soviet influence in a country so important to their security, and the negotiations ground to a halt. Moreover, at this precise moment, Russian suspicions about the West deepened with Allen Dulles's concurrent but unrelated secret negotiations with Nazi generals in Switzerland. The result was a violent quarrel which shook the entire structure of American-Soviet relations. But this was only the beginning. The demands on the Polish question reflected the ideas of the men who were to surround the new President; led by Joseph Grew and James F. Byrnes, they soon convinced Truman to attempt to make stronger demands elsewhere in Eastern Europe.

For most of the war Roosevelt had been highly ambivalent toward such matters. By late 1944, however (in spite of wavering on the politically sensitive Polish issue in his dying days), Roosevelt concluded it would be a fundamental error to put too much pressure on Russia over other regions vital to her security. In September and October 1944, and in early January 1945, he gave form to his conclusion by entering into armistice agreements with Britain and Russia, which gave the Soviet military almost complete control of internal politics in each Eastern European ex-Nazi satellite. It was understood, for instance, that the Soviets would have authority to issue orders to the Rumanian government, and that, specifically, the Allied Control Commission would be "under the general direction of the Allied (Soviet) High Command acting on behalf of the Allied Powers." The Rumanian accords, and the similar but slightly less severe Bulgarian and Hungarian armistice agreements, served to formalize the famous Churchill-Stalin spheres-of-influence arrangement which, without FDR's agreement, had previously given the Russians "90 per cent" influence in Rumania, "80 per cent" influence in Bulgaria, and "75 per cent" influence in Hungary, in exchange for "90 per cent" British influence in Greece and a "50–50" split of influence in Yugoslavia. The armistice accords were also modeled after a previous understanding which had contained Soviet endorsement of dominant American-British influence in Italy. The Eastern European armistice agreements have been available to the public for years, but have been successfully buried, or avoided by most scholars. Herz has exhumed them, and he shows that they contain American endorsement of dominant Soviet influence in the ex-Nazi satellites.

At Yalta, in early February, 1945, Roosevelt pasted over these specific texts the vague and idealistic rhetoric of the famous Declaration on Liberated Europe. The President apparently wished to use the Declaration mainly to appease certain politically important ethnic groups in America; he devoted only a few minutes to the matter at the Yalta Conference, and the familiar rhetoric promising democracy was almost devoid of practical meaning. For example, who was to decide in given instances between the American and Soviet definitions of common but vague terms like "democratic"? Much more important, as Herz shows, in the broad language of the Declaration the Allies agreed merely to "consult" about matters within the liberated countries, not to "act," and they authorized consultations only when all parties agreed they were necessary. Thus the United States itself confirmed the Russians' right to refuse to talk about the ex-Nazi satellites. The State Department knew this and, in fact, had tried to insert operative clauses into the Declaration. But Roosevelt, having just signed the armistice agreements, rejected this unrealistic proposal. Moreover, when the Soviets after Yalta crudely tossed out a Rumanian government they did not like, the President, though unhappy that he had not been consulted, reaffirmed his basic position by refusing to intervene.

Ironically, Herz's book lends credence to the old Republican charge that Roosevelt accepted a compromise at Yalta which bolstered Stalin's position in Eastern Europe. The charge, while correct in essentials, was silly in assuming that much else, short of war, could have been done while the Red Army occupied the area. The Republican politicians also ignored the fact that at Yalta Roosevelt could not expect a continued American military presence in Europe for very long after the war. This not only deprived him of leverage, it made an accommodation with Russia much more desirable for another reason: Red Army help became essential as a guarantee that Germany would not rise from defeat to start yet a third World War. Stalin also needed American help, as he too made clear, to hold down the Germans. Hence, underlying the American-Soviet plans for peace at Yalta was not "faith" but a common interest—the German threat—which had cemented the World War II alliance. From this 1945 perspective the crucial portion of the Yalta agreement was not the Declaration on Liberated Europe, nor even the provisions on Poland, but rather the understanding that the United States and Russia (with Britain and France as minor partners) would work together to control Germany. This meant, among other things, joint action to reduce Germany's physical power by extracting reparations from German industry.

Although Herz tends to play down the German issue, he does take up important economic matters that relate to it. He understands that Moscow was in a cruel dilemma which, had the US been shrewd enough, might have been resolved to the benefit of both American diplomacy and the economic health of Europe. The Russians were greatly in need of aid for their huge postwar reconstruction program. Importing industrial equipment from Eastern Europe was a possible solution, though a doubtful one, for taking this equipment would inevitably cause political problems. Reparations from Germany were another, but the key industrial sectors were in American hands. Finally, the United States itself was a potential source. Herz argues (as did Ambassadors Harriman and Winant at the time) that a US reconstruction loan for Russia would have been wise: it would have given US diplomacy strong leverage in a variety of negotiations. (Without other sources of reconstruction to aid them the Russians were almost inevitably reduced to extracting industrial goods from either Germany or Eastern Europe.) American officials seriously considered such a loan, but, as Herz shows, they did not actively pursue it with the Russians—though one or two crude attempts were made to use a loan as a bludgeon in negotiations. With a future US troop commitment unlikely, and a large loan ruled out, the United States had no real bargaining power. Hence its attempts at intervention in Eastern Europe amounted to little more than bluster.

The State Department wanted to have it both ways: it wanted to hold the Russians to the vague promises of the Yalta Declaration; it also wanted to avoid the specific texts of the armistice agreements. But the Republicans, and even Secretary Byrnes in his later writings, understood the weakness of this position. The Republicans, for their part, also wanted to have it both ways. They wanted to argue both that Roosevelt gave the Russians all the authority they needed for their actions *and* that the Russians broke their agreements.

The Republican attack on Yalta came late in the Cold War, and was combined with a new demand that the US "roll back" Soviet influence. Few now realize how unoriginal the demand was, for a "roll back" effort—without its latter-day label—was, in fact, at the center of Harry Truman's first postwar policy. The President, we now know, made this effort in a spurt of confidence derived from the new atomic bomb. But the policy failed in its continuing attempt to reduce Soviet control by expanding Western influence in Poland. It also failed in its bold follow-up effort to force the Russians to change the Bulgarian and Rumanian governments. Nevertheless, these opening moves of the postwar period helped to set the tone of the new Administration's attitude toward Russia. Truman, although publicly proclaiming his adherence to Roosevelt's policy of cooperation, seems to have understood that his approach differed fundamentally from his predecessor's. (In private, as Secretary of State Stettinius has written, he complained that the intervention in Poland rested on rather shaky diplomatic ground.) Indeed, by September 1945, the basic change in US policy was so clearly defined that, as Secretary of State Byrnes later wrote, the Russian complaint that Roosevelt's policy had been abandoned was "understandable." [In his book *Atomic Diplomacy*, Alperovitz expands on this point. He charges that the real reason for dropping the atomic bombs on Hiroshima and Nagasaki was not to force the surrender of Japan but "to make Russia more manageable in Eastern Europe." It is a fascinating if horrifying argument with sufficient documentation to make the charge at least plausible.]

What was the result? Like Herz, John Foster Dulles (who assisted Byrnes at the time) also believed that the Cold War began in 1945. Dulles emphasized in his book *War or Peace* (1950) that a new tough line of US policy was adopted at this time over dimly remembered issues deep within the Soviet-controlled Balkans. Herz prints almost the full text of the crucial 1945 Hopkins-Stalin talks, which reveal the equally important point that, in Russia, the change in American policy produced what Stalin termed "a certain alarm." A few thoughtful US officials recognized the significance of these developments. Secretary of War Henry L. Stimson, for example, tried to block the campaign to engage American prestige in Eastern Europe. In White House discussions he argued, first, that the demand for more Western influence in Poland was a mistake: "The Russians perhaps were being more realistic than we were in regard to their own security. . . ." He then tried to cut short efforts to intervene elsewhere, reminding Truman, as Stimson's diary shows, that "we have made up our minds on the broad policy that it was not wise to get into the Balkan mess even if the thing seemed to be disruptive of policies which the State Department thought were wise." Stimson pointed out that "we have taken that policy right from the beginning, Mr. Roosevelt having done it himself or having been a party to it himself."

When Stimson failed in his conservative effort to limit American objectives, the stage was set for one of the great tragedies of the Cold War. As Stimson understood, the Russians, though extremely touchy about the buffer area, were not impossible to deal with. Had their security requirements been met, there is evidence that their domination of Eastern Europe might have been much different from what it turned out to be. Churchill, too, thought the Russians were approachable. Obviously, conditions in Eastern Europe would not meet Western ideals; but Churchill judged, in late 1944 and early 1945, that Moscow was convinced it would be much easier to secure its objectives through moderate policies. In Greece at this time, as Churchill was to stress in *Triumph and Tragedy,* Stalin was "strictly and faithfully" holding to his agreement *not* to aid the Greek Communists. Even in much of the border area the Russians seemed willing to accept substantial capitalism and some form of democracy—with the crucial proviso that the Eastern European governments had to be "friendly" to Russia in defense and foreign policies. Finland serves as a rough model of a successful border state. Here, too, the armistice made the Soviets supreme, giving rights parallel to the Bulgarian and Rumanian accords plus the right to maintain Soviet military installations. However, the US made no independent effort to intervene; Finland maintained a foreign policy "friendly" to Russia; and the Russians were—as they still seem to be—prepared to accept a moderate government.

Although it is often forgotten, a modified application of the Finnish formula seemed to be shaping up elsewhere in 1945 and much of 1946. In Hungary, Soviet-sponsored free elections routed the Communist Party in 1945. In Bulgaria, a country with rather weak democratic traditions, the 1945 elections were complicated by competition for Great Power support among the various internal factions. Certainly the results were not perfect, but most Western observers (except the State Department) felt they should have been accepted. In Austria, the Communists were swamped in Soviet-run free elections in their zone in 1945, and, after a hesitant start, a free democratic government emerged for the entire country. In Czechoslovakia, from which the Red Army withdrew in December of 1945, democracy was so clearly acceptable to Soviet policy that the US had little to protest at the time.

Almost all of this was to change, of course. The freedoms in Hungary were to end in 1947. The initial pattern in Czechoslovakia was to be reversed in 1948. But writers who focus only on the brutal period of totalitarian control after 1947 and 1948 often ignore what happened earlier. The few who try to account for the known facts of the 1945–46 interlude usually do so in passing, either to suggest that the democratic governments "must have been" mere smoke-screens, formed while Moscow waited for the US to leave the Continent; or that the Russians "must have been" secretly planning to take full control, but were methodically using the early period to prepare the groundwork for what came later. (Communists, too, like to ignore the 1945–46 period, for it suggests the possibility that Soviet Russia was more interested in an old-fashioned *modus vivendi* with the capitalists than in spreading World Communism. This was the essence of Tito's bitter complaint that Stalin tried to turn back the Yugoslav revolution.)

The Russians have displayed so much duplicity, brutality, and intransigence that it is easy to imagine the 1945–46 interlude as a mere smokescreen. But they have also a long history of protecting "Socialism in one country" in a rather conservative, nationalistic way: the moderation of the 1945–46 interlude can be viewed as a logical extension of this tradition. That at least two quite different interpretations of their 1945–46 policy are conceivable is now rarely admitted, and the relative merits of each have not been seriously examined. Herz's study calls for a careful reappraisal of early postwar Soviet objectives. If the Russians were secretly harboring plans for an ultimate takeover, they certainly were preparing a lot of trouble for themselves by sponsoring free politics, by pulling out the Red Army (it is not particularly shrewd to have to re-introduce foreign troops), by ripping up the Red Army's main rail connections across Poland—as they did in the fall of 1945. As well-informed an observer as Averell Harriman believed, as he once testified to Congress, that Soviet policy in 1945 was ambivalent, that it could have become either more moderate within a framework of security and understanding with the West, or that it could have become hard-line and totalitarian, within the framework of insecurity and conflict. Harriman, though puzzled by the ultimate Russian decision in favor of the iron-fisted policy, clearly saw that Soviet expansion was neither inexorable nor inevitable.

At least one reason for Russia's shift to a tough line may be traced to mistakes made by US officials. As Stimson argued—and as history later showed—the demand for more influence in Soviet-controlled areas was almost certainly doomed from the start. This basic miscalculation stemmed, finally, from an attempt to overextend *American* diplomatic sway. Lippmann was, I believe, correct in seeing that the other error was the failure of US policy makers to turn their energies to an early solution of the crucial German problem. Bolstered by the atomic bomb, which eliminated the threat that had been Roosevelt's central concern, American leaders dallied over Germany. Moreover, by refusing to hold to Roosevelt's agreement that a specific target for German reparations would be set (July, 1945), by permitting France to hamstring the German Control Commission (fall, 1945), by halting German reparations shipments (spring, 1946)—US policy suggested the very prospect Russia feared most: The abandonment of economic and political controls and the possibility that a new and powerful Germany would rise from the ashes of Nazism to become the bastion of Western capitalistic aggression in Europe. The United States had no such aggressive intent. Nonetheless, the US chose not to negotiate seriously on Germany until a full year-and-a-half after the war's end. Especially after Secretary

Byrnes's tough speech in Stuttgart in the Fall of 1946, American policy was short-sighted enough to suggest a threat to Russia at the very time it was attempting to weaken Soviet control in the vital area which lay—protectively or threateningly—between German power and the Russian heartland. The Russians, who had no nuclear weapons, were far less casual about the question of security; their grip seemed to tighten in the buffer area month by month, as their worst fears about Germany seemed to come true.

The Russians were not easy to deal with, either in Germany or elsewhere. Nevertheless, if the hypothesis suggested by Lippmann's book is correct—and Herz's study indirectly supports it—there are reasons to believe that US policy itself may have to share responsibility for the imposition of totalitarian control in Eastern Europe, and possibly also for the subsequent expanding Communist agitation in Western Europe. The *addition* of increased insecurity to known Soviet tendencies may explain the rigidity which Soviet leaders displayed in their satellite policy after 1946. The first pattern seemed crudely similar to the Finnish or Austrian models. Would it have been reversed had the US seriously tried from the first to resolve the European security problem—as Lippmann urged? That Soviet actions may have been in part reactions to their judgments of American intentions may also help to explain why sustained Communist opposition developed in the West only after the clear breakdown of German control arrangements. It was not in 1945, but late in 1946 and in 1947 that the Italian and French Communists began to reverse their initial policy of cooperation with bourgeois governments. Was the changed focus of Communist politics part of the inexorable plan? Or was it primarily a rather shortsighted response to American policy itself?

Once the Communists became active in Western Europe, of course, the United States was faced with quite another set of issues. Disputes with Russia moved out of the border regions. The threat some officials had anticipated while reading Marx and listening to Communist propaganda began to become a political reality. In 1947, those who proposed a mechanical theory of Soviet expansion had to deal with expanding Communist political activity in the West. And it was in July of that year, precisely two years after Truman faced Stalin in his first Potsdam showdown over Eastern Europe, that Kennan's containment recommendation was publicly offered.

We do not yet have answers to all the questions about postwar American-Russian relations, but we know enough to consider afresh whether either of the Great Powers ever really did move inexorably, like a wound-up toy automobile, as "Mr. X" argued. Herz's sturdy little book suggests they did not, and is at least the beginning of a more subtle explanation of the complex sequence of interacting events which produced the Cold War.

eleven
The United States and the Third World — Vietnam as a Case Study

Nationalist

Nationalists argue that America's role in the "third world" should be the same one the United States played so successfully in Europe—the containment of Communism. The Korean War, the Southeast Asia Treaty Organization, the intervention in the Dominican Republic, the economic and diplomatic isolation of Cuba, and the war in Vietnam are defended as necessary to resist Communist aggression and subversion. Reasoning from the events at Munich before World War II, Nationalists argue that to allow Communist aggression to succeed anywhere in the world invites further aggression.

Formerly, aggression had taken the form of direct invasion. It was easily recognized and the tactics necessary to stop it were well known. Recently, however, Communists have turned to "wars of national liberation" to accomplish their aims; these wars have involved aid to internal revolutions. Such aggression has been more difficult both to prove and to counteract. Yet, the Nationalists argue, it has to be met and stopped. They regard Communism as hostile to all forms of capitalism and democracy. Thus each government that falls to the Communists adds its re-

sources to a group of the world's nations bent on the destruction of America and its way of life.

Former Secretary of State Dean Rusk, in testimony before the Senate Foreign Relations Committee, justified American actions in Vietnam in these terms. He argued that South Vietnam was the victim of Communist aggression. This aggression took the form of an invasion disguised as an internal revolution, one of Communism's wars of national liberation. If the Communists were not defeated in Vietnam, they would continue these tactics until all the countries of Asia fell like a row of dominoes.

In his testimony, which follows, what evidence does Mr. Rusk offer to show that the war was exported from North Vietnam? How does he connect America's policy in Vietnam with past American policies? What evidence does he have of Communist intentions to revolutionize the world?

Testimony Before the Senate Foreign Relations Committee

Dean Rusk

Since World War Two, which projected the United States into the role of major world power, we Americans have had to face a series of difficult tasks and trials. On the whole we have faced them very well. Today we are facing another ordeal in Southeast Asia which again is costing us both lives and treasure. South Vietnam is a long way from the United States, and the issues posed may seem remote from our daily experience and our immediate interests. It is essential, therefore, that we clearly understand—and so far as possible agree—on our mission and purpose in that faraway land.

Why are we in Vietnam? Certainly we are not there merely be-

cause we have power and like to use it. We do not regard ourselves as the policeman of the universe. We do not go around the
world looking for quarrels in which we can intervene. Quite the
contrary. We have recognized that, just as we are not gendarmes
of the universe, neither are we the magistrate of the universe. If
other governments, other institutions, or other regional organiza-
tions can find solutions to the quarrels which disturb this present
scene, we are anxious to have this occur. But we are in Vietnam
because the issues posed there are deeply intertwined with our
own security and because the outcome of the struggle can profoundly affect the nature of the world in which we and our children will live. The situation we face in Southeast Asia is obviously complex but, in my view, the underlying issues are
relatively simple and are utterly fundamental. I am confident that
Americans, who have a deep and mature understanding of world
responsibility, are fully capable of cutting through the underbrush
of complexity and finding the simple issues which involve our
largest interests and deepest purposes. I regard it, therefore, as
a privilege to be able to discuss these problems with the Committee this morning—to consult with you—and at the same time
to try to clarify for the American people the issues we must
squarely face.

I do not approach this task on the assumption that anyone,
anywhere, has all the answers or that all wisdom belongs to the
Executive branch of the government, or even to the government
itself.

The questions at issue affect the well-being of all Americans
and I am confident that all Americans will make up their own
minds in the tradition of a free and independent people. Yet
those of us who have special responsibilities for the conduct of
our foreign policy have had to think hard and deeply about these
problems for a very long time. The President, his Cabinet colleagues, and the Congress, who share the weightiest responsibilities under our constitutional system, have come to certain conclusions that form the basis for the policies we are now pursuing.
Perhaps it is worth pointing out that those who are officially
responsible for the conduct of our public affairs must make
decisions—and must make decisions among existing alternatives. None of us in the Executive or the Legislative branch has
fulfilled our responsibilities merely by formulating an opinion; we
are required to decide what this nation shall do and shall not do

and are required to accept the consequences of our determination.

What are our world security interests involved in the struggle in Vietnam? They cannot be seen clearly in terms of Southeast Asia only or merely in terms of the events of the past few months. We must view the problem in perspective. We must recognize that what we are seeking to achieve in South Vietnam is part of a process that has continued for a long time—a process of preventing the expansion and extension of Communist domination by the use of force against the weaker nations on the perimeter of Communist power. This is the problem as it looks to us. Nor do the Communists themselves see the problem in isolation. They see the struggle in South Vietnam as part of a larger design for the steady extension of Communist power through force and threat.

I have observed in the course of your hearings that some objection has been raised to the use of the term "Communist aggression." It seems to me that we should not confuse ourselves or our people by turning our eyes away from what that phrase means. The underlying crisis of this postwar period turns about a major struggle over the very nature of the political structure of the world. Before the guns were silent in World War Two, many governments sat down and thought long and hard about the structure of international life, the kind of world which we ought to try to build, and wrote those ideas into the United Nations Charter. That Charter establishes an international society of independent states, large and small, entitled to their own national existence, entitled to be free from aggression, cooperating freely across national frontiers in their common interests, and resolving their disputes by peaceful means. But the Communist world has returned to its demand for what it calls a "world revolution," a world of coercion in direct contradiction to the Charter of the United Nations.

There may be differences within the Communist world about methods and techniques and leadership within the Communist world itself, but they share a common attachment to their "world revolution" and to its support through what they call "wars of liberation." So, what we face in Vietnam is what we have faced on many occasions before—the need to check the extension of Communist power in order to maintain a reasonable stability in a precarious world. That stability was achieved in the years after

the war by the valor of free nations in defending the integrity of
postwar territorial arrangements. And we have achieved a certain
stability for the last decade and a half. It must not be overthrown
now.

Like so many of our problems today, the struggle in South
Vietnam stems from the disruption of two world wars. The Second
World War completed a process begun by the first. It ripped
apart a structure of power that had existed for a hundred years.
It set in train new forces and energies that have remade the map
of the world. Not only did it weaken the nations actively engaged
in the fighting, but it had far-reaching secondary effects. It undermined the foundations of the colonial structures through which a
handful of powers controlled one third of the world's population.
And the winds of change and progress that have blown fiercely
during the last twenty years have toppled those structures almost
completely. Meanwhile, the Communist nations have exploited
the turmoil of the time of transition in an effort to extend Communist control into other areas of the world.

The United States first faced the menace of Communist ambition in Europe when one after another of the nations on the
boundaries of the Soviet Union fell under the dominion of Moscow through the presence of the Red Army. To check this tidal
wave the U.S. provided the Marshall Plan to strengthen the nations of Western Europe, and then moved to organize with those
nations a collective security system through NATO. As a result,
the advance of Soviet Communist power was stopped and the
Soviet Union gradually adjusted its policies to this situation. But
within a year after the establishment of NATO, the Communists
took over China. This posed a new and serious threat, particularly to those weak new nations of the Far East that had been
formed out of colonial empires. The problems in Asia were, of
course, different from those in Europe. But the result was much
the same—instability, uncertainty, and vulnerability to both the
bully and the aggressor.

Western Europe, with its established governmental and traditional social institutions, recovered quickly. But certain of the
new nations of Asia—particularly those that had not known self-
government for a century or more—continued to face a far more
formidable problem which they still face. The first test in Asia
came in Korea when the United Nations Forces—predominantly
American—stopped the drive of Communist North Korea supported by material aid from the Soviet Union. It stopped the

Chinese Army that followed. It brought to a halt the Communist effort to push out the line that had been drawn and to establish Communist control over the Korean peninsula. We fought the Korean War—which like the struggle in Vietnam occurred in a remote area thousands of miles away—to sustain a principle vital to the freedom and security of America, the principle that the Communist world should not be permitted to expand by overrunning one after another of the arrangements built during and since the war to mark the outer limits of Communist expansion by force.

Before the Korean War had ended, the United States, under President Truman, moved to settle and consolidate the situation in the Pacific through a peace treaty with Japan, and through bilateral security treaties with Japan and the Philippines, and through the ANZUS Treaty with Australia and New Zealand. Hardly had the Korean War been finished when France, which had been fighting a protracted struggle in Indochina, decided to relinquish its political presence in Southeast Asia. After a brief negotiation it came to terms with the Communist forces that had captured the Nationalist movement. The result was the division of Indochina into four parts: a Kingdom of Cambodia, a Kingdom of Laos, and Vietnam divided at the 17th Parallel between the Communist forces in the North and a non-Communist Vietnamese government in the South.

Recognizing that the Communists had not abandoned their ambitions, the U.S. government under President Eisenhower took steps to secure the situation by further alliances. Bilateral treaties were concluded with the Republic of Korea and the Republic of China on Formosa. In the Middle East the so-called "northern tier" of countries lying to the south of the Soviet Union entered into the Baghdad Pact which established what is now known as CENTO, the Central Treaty Organization. The United States did not become a formal member of this alliance, which is composed of Great Britain, Turkey, Iran, and Pakistan. But we are closely associated with CENTO and have bilateral military assistance agreements with its regional members, concluded by the Eisenhower Administration.

In order to give support to the nations of Southeast Asia, the United States took the lead in the creation of an alliance embodied in a treaty and reinforced by a collective security system known as SEATO, the Southeast Asia Treaty Organization. In this alliance the United States joined with Great Britain, France, Australia, New Zealand, Thailand, Pakistan, and the Philippines to guarantee the security not only of the member nations but also to come to the aid of certain protocol states and territories if they so requested. South Vietnam was included in this protocol. The United States had not been a party to the Agreements made in Geneva in 1954, which France had concluded with the Communist Vietnamese forces known as the Viet Minh. But the Under Secretary of State, Walter Bedell Smith, stated under instructions that the U.S. would not disturb the Agreements and "would view any renewal of the aggression in violation of the . . . Agreements with grave concern and as seriously threatening international peace and security." Under Secretary Smith's statement was only a unilateral declaration, but in joining SEATO, the United States took a solemn treaty engagement of far-reaching effect. Article IV, paragraph one, provides that "each party recognizes that aggression by means of armed attack . . . would endanger its own peace and safety, and agrees that it will in that event act to meet the common danger in accordance with its constitutional processes." It is this fundamental SEATO obligation that has from the outset guided our actions in South Vietnam.

The language of this treaty is worth careful attention. The obligation it imposes is not only joint but several; that is, not only collective, but individual. The finding that an armed attack has occurred does not have to be made by a collective determination before the obligation of each member becomes operative. Nor does the Treaty require a collective decision on actions to be taken to meet the common danger. If the United States determines that an armed attack has occurred against any nation to whom the protection of the Treaty applies, then it is obligated "to act to meet the common danger" without regard to the views or actions of any other Treaty member.

The far-reaching implications of this commitment were well understood by this Committee when it recommended, with only the late Senator Langer dissenting, that the Senate consent to the ratification of the Treaty. The Committee's report states, in its conclusion, that "The Committee is not impervious to the risks which this treaty entails. It fully appreciates that acceptance of these additional obligations commits the U.S. to a course of action over a vast expanse of the Pacific. Yet these risks are consistent with our own highest interests. There are greater hazards," the Committee's conclusions stated, "in not advising a potential enemy of what he can expect of us, and in failing to disabuse him of assumptions which might lead to a miscalculation of our intentions."

Following this Committee's recommendation, the Senate gave its advice and consent to the Treaty by a vote of eighty-two to one, the late Senator Langer voting against; all members of this distinguished Committee who were then Senators voted for. . . .

Our multilateral engagement under the SEATO treaty had been reinforced and amplified by a series of bilateral commitments and assurances directly to the government of South Vietnam. On October 1, 1954, President Eisenhower wrote to President Diem offering, and I quote, "to assist the government of Vietnam in developing and maintaining a strong, viable state, capable of resisting attempted subversion or aggression through military means." In 1957 President Eisenhower and President Diem issued a joint statement which called attention to "the large buildup of Vietnamese Communist military forces in North Vietnam," and stated, and I quote: "Noting that the Republic of Vietnam is covered by Article IV of the Southeast Asia Collective Defense Treaty, President Eisenhower and President Ngo Dinh Diem agreed that aggression or subversion threatening the political independence of the Republic of Vietnam would be considered as endangering peace and stability."

On August 2, 1961, President Kennedy declared that "the United States is determined that the Republic of Vietnam shall not be lost to the Communists for lack of any support which the United States can render." On December 14, 1961, President Kennedy wrote to President Diem, recalling the United States declaration made at the end of the Geneva Conference in 1954. The President once again stated that the United States was "prepared to help the Republic of Vietnam to protect its people and to preserve its independence." This commitment has been reaffirmed many times since.

These then are the commitments we have taken to protect South Vietnam as a part of protecting our own "peace and security." We have sent American forces to fight in the jungles of that beleaguered country because South Vietnam has, under the language of the SEATO Treaty, been the victim of "aggression by means of armed attack." There can be no serious question as to the existence and nature of this aggression. The war is clearly an "armed attack," cynically and systematically mounted by the Hanoi regime against the people of South Vietnam. The North Vietnamese regime has sought deliberately to confuse the issue by seeking to make its aggression appear as an indigenous revolt. But we should not be deceived by this subterfuge. It is a familiar Communist practice. Impeded in their efforts to extend their power by the use of classical forms of force, such as the invasion of Korea, the Communists have, over many years, developed an elaborate doctrine for so-called "wars of national liberation" to cloak their aggressions in ambiguity.

A "war of national liberation," in the Communist lexicon, depends on the tactics of terror and sabotage, of stealth and subversion. It has a particular utility for them since it gives an advantage to a disciplined and ruthless minority, particularly in countries where the physical terrain makes clandestine infiltration from the outside relatively easy. At the same time the Communists have a more subtle reason for favoring this type of aggression. It creates in any situation a sense of ambiguity that they can exploit to their own advantage. Yet, in spite of Communist efforts to confuse the issue, the nature of the conflict in South Vietnam is very clear.

Let me review briefly the facts. With the benefit of hindsight no one can doubt that in agreeing to the 1954 Accords, the regime in Hanoi fully expected that within a relatively short period the South Vietnamese would fall under their control. The South seemed overburdened with troubles; its formidable economic problems were complicated by the need to absorb almost one million North Vietnamese, who, having seen the true face of Communism, fled South after the 1954 Accords. The North moreover had concealed resources in the South. At the time of the Accords in 1954, many Communists fighting with the Viet Minh had been directed by the Lao Dong Party in Hanoi to stay in the South, to hide their arms, and to devote their efforts to undermining the South Vietnamese government. These efforts of subversion were in the initial years quite unsuccessful. Much to the dismay of the Hanoi regime, South Vietnam made substantial progress in spite of the extraordinary problems it faced, while North Vietnam lagged far behind. As a consequence the Communist leaders in North Vietnam were forced to conclude that more active measures were necessary if the subversion of South Vietnam were to succeed.

During the five years following the Geneva Conference the Hanoi regime developed a secret political-military organization in South Vietnam based on the cadres who had been ordered to stay in the South. Many of the activities of this organization were directed toward the assassination of selected South Vietnamese civilians. More than a thousand civilians were murdered or kidnaped from 1957 to 1959. In 1960 alone terrorists assassinated fourteen hundred local government officials and kidnaped some seven hundred others, while armed guerrillas killed twenty-two hundred military and security personnel.

In September, 1960, the Lao Dong Party—the Communist Party in North Vietnam—held its Third Party Congress in Hanoi. That congress called for the creation of a front organization to undertake the subversion of South Vietnam. Three months thereafter, the National Liberation Front was established to provide a political façade for the conduct of an active guerrilla war. Beginning in 1960 the Hanoi regime began to infiltrate into South Vietnam the disciplined adherents whom the Party had ordered north at the time of the settlement. In the intervening period since 1954, these men had been trained in the arts of sabotage and subversion; now they were ordered to conscript young men from the villages by force or persuasion, and to form cadres around which guerrilla units could be built. All of this was documented by the Legal Committee of the International Commission for Supervision and Control. That body, established to supervise the performance of the Vietnam cease-fire, is composed of Indian, Polish, and Canadian members. The Legal Committee, with Poland objecting, reported in 1962: "There is evidence to show that arms, munitions, and other supplies have been sent from the zone in the North to the zone in the South with the objective of supporting, organizing, and carrying out hostile activities, including armed attacks, against the armed forces and administration of the zone in the South.

"There is evidence that the PAVN (i.e., the North Vietnamese Army) has allowed the zone in the North to be used for inciting, encouraging and supporting hostile activities in the zone in the South, aimed at the overthrow of the administration in the South." That is the end of the quotation.

In the three-year period from 1959 to 1961 the North Vietnam regime infiltrated ten thousand men into the South. In 1962 thirteen thousand additional personnel were infiltrated; and by the end of 1964 North Vietnam may well have moved over forty thousand armed and unarmed guerrillas into South Vietnam. But beginning over a year ago the Communists apparently exhausted their reservoir of Southerners who had gone north. Since then the greater number of men infiltrated into the South have been native-born North Vietnamese. Most recently Hanoi has begun to infiltrate elements of the North Vietnamese Regular Army in increasingly larger numbers. Today there is evidence that nine regiments of regular North Vietnamese forces are fighting in organized units in the South.

I have reviewed these facts, Mr. Chairman, which are familiar enough to most of you, because it seems to me they demonstrate beyond question that the war in Vietnam is as much an act of outside aggression as though the Hanoi regime had sent an army across the 17th Parallel rather than infiltrating armed forces by stealth. This point is important, since it goes to the heart of our own involvement. Much of the confusion about the struggle in South Vietnam has arisen over a failure to understand this aspect of the conflict. For if the war in South Vietnam were, as the Communists try to make it appear, merely an indigenous revolt, then the United States would not have its own combat troops in South Vietnam. But the evidence is overwhelming that it is in fact, something quite different: a systematic aggression by Hanoi against the people of South Vietnam. It is one further effort by a Communist regime in one half of a divided country to take over the people of the other half at the point of a gun and against their will.

Up to this point I have tried to describe the nature of our commitments in South Vietnam and why we have made them. I have sought to put those commitments within the framework of our larger effort to prevent the Communists from upsetting the arrangements which have been the basis for our security. These policies have sometimes been attacked as static and sterile. It has been argued that they do not take account of the vast changes which have occurred in the world and indeed are still in train. These contentions seem to miss the point. The line of policy we are following involves far more than a defense of the status quo. It seeks rather to ensure that degree of security which is necessary if change and progress are to take place through consent and not through coercion. Certainly, as has been frequently pointed out, the world of the mid-twentieth century is not standing still: movement is occurring on both sides of the Iron Curtain. Communism today is no longer monolithic; it no longer wears one face but many; and the deep schism between the two great power centers of the Communist world—Moscow and Peiping—is clearly one of the major political facts of our time.

There has been substantial change and movement within the

Soviet Union as well, and perhaps even more among the countries of Eastern Europe. These changes have not been inhibited because of our efforts to maintain our postwar arrangements by organizing the Western Alliance. They have taken place because of internal developments as well as because the Communist regime of Moscow has recognized that the Western Alliance cannot permit it to extend its dominion by force. Over time the same processes, hopefully, will work in the Far East. Peiping, and the Communist states living under its shadow, must learn that they cannot redraw the boundaries of the world by force.

What we are pursuing, therefore, is not a static concept. For unlike the Communists, we really do believe in social revolution and not merely in power cloaked as revolution. We believe in constructive change and encourage it. That was the meaning of President Johnson's initiatives at the Honolulu Conference—to encourage the efforts of the South Vietnamese government to transform the country in a way that will correct ancient injustices and bring about a better life for all the people.

In meeting our commitments in South Vietnam, we are using substantial military forces. At the same time we are making it quite clear to North Vietnam and to the world that our forces are being employed for a limited and well-defined objective. What we seek in South Vietnam is to bring about a restoration of the conditions contemplated by the Accords of 1954. We seek, in other words, to restore the integrity of the settlement made between the French government and the Communist forces under Ho Chi Minh—a settlement which was joined in by the United Kingdom, Communist China, the Soviet Union, Laos, and Cambodia. This settlement forms a part of the structure of arrangements that are the key to stability in the present-day world.

Unfortunately, the limited nature of our purpose is foreign to the philosophy of the Communist world. It may be hard, therefore, for them to realize that the United States seeks no territorial aggrandizement in South Vietnam or anywhere in Southeast Asia. We do not wish to maintain our troops in that area any longer than is necessary to secure the freedom of the South Vietnamese people. We want no permanent military bases, no trade advantages. We are not asking that the government of South Vietnam ally itself with us or be in any way beholden to us. We wish only that the people of South Vietnam should have the right and opportunity to determine their future in freedom without coercion or threat from the outside.

For months now we have done everything possible to make clear to the regime in Hanoi that a political solution is the proper course. If that regime were prepared to call off the aggression in the South, peace would come in almost a matter of hours. When that occurred, the people of North Vietnam could safely go about their business. For we do not seek to destroy the Hanoi regime or to force the people of North Vietnam to accept any other form of government. And, under conditions of peace, we would be quite prepared for the North Vietnamese people to share with the other peoples of Southeast Asia in the economic and technical help that we and other nations are extending on a regional basis to that area.

This is the simple message that we have tried to convey to Hanoi through many channels. We have sought in every way to impress upon the Communist world the ease with which peace could be attained if only Hanoi were willing. We have used every resource of diplomacy. I know of no occasion in history where so much effort has been devoted—not only on the part of the United States but of many other nations—in an effort to bring about a political solution to a costly and dangerous war. . . . But to this point the sounds from the other side have been harsh and negative. The regime in Hanoi has been unwilling to accept any of the possibilities open to it for discussion. All we have heard is the constant insistence that they will not negotiate unless we accept in advance their Four Points. Yet the effect of those Four Points, as propounded by Hanoi, would be to give away the very purposes for which we are fighting and to deliver the people of South Vietnam against their will to the domination of a Communist regime. To understand the situation realistically, we should not underestimate the harshness of the Communist side or overestimate the ease of a political solution.

From time to time we have heard it suggested that we should seek a Geneva Conference or enlist the good offices of the Conference co-chairmen or take the problem to the United Nations or invite the mediation efforts of neutral nations. Well, we have done all of these things, and in most cases we have done them repeatedly, with no result. We have heard it suggested also, by governments and individuals on both sides of the Iron Curtain, that no peace was possible so long as American planes were flying bombing missions over North Vietnam, but that negotiations might be possible if the bombing were discontinued. We did that also, not once but twice. The last pause, as this committee will recall, lasted more than thirty-seven days. And again with no response. Certainly, we shall do everything consistent with our national objectives to seek a solution through diplomacy. There is no doubt as to the elements for an honorable peace as we see it. We have made them clear again and again. Most recently we have summarized them in the form of fourteen points:

1. The Geneva Agreements of 1954 and 1962 are an adequate basis for peace in Southeast Asia;
2. We would welcome a conference on Southeast Asia or on any part thereof;
3. We would welcome "negotiations without preconditions," as the seventeen nations put it;
4. We would welcome unconditional discussions, as President Johnson put it;
5. A cessation of hostilities could be the first order of business at a conference or could be the subject of preliminary discussions;
6. Hanoi's Four Points could be discussed along with other points which others might wish to propose;
7. We want no U.S. bases in Southeast Asia;
8. We do not desire to retain U.S. troops in South Vietnam after peace is assured;
9. We support free elections in South Vietnam to give the South Vietnamese a government of their own choice;
10. The question of reunification of Vietnam should be determined by the Vietnamese through their own free decision;
11. The countries of Southeast Asia can be nonaligned or neutral if that be their option;
12. We would much prefer to use our resources for the economic reconstruction of Southeast Asia than in war. If there is peace, North Vietnam could participate in a regional effort to which we would be prepared to contribute at least $1 billion;
13. The President has said, "The Viet Cong would not have difficulty being represented and having their views represented if for a moment Hanoi decided she wanted to cease aggression. I don't think," he said, "that would be an insurmountable problem";
14. We have said publicly and privately, and since this particular point was put through there were thirty-seven days of action, that we could stop the bombing of North Vietnam as a step toward peace although there has not been the slightest hint

or suggestion from the other side as to what they would do if the bombing stopped.

These fourteen points are on the public record. Our government has made quite clear what kind of peace we are prepared to accept—a peace that will guarantee the security of South Vietnam, a peace that will stop armed aggression in violation of international agreements and international law. This is the position that we have made known to the other side, both directly and through intermediaries. How does this compare with the position of the Hanoi regime? Both Hanoi and Peiping have repeatedly rejected our proposal for unconditional discussions. They have insisted instead that before any discussions can take place our side must agree in advance to the Four Points of Hanoi's program. The words that they have used have differed from formulation to formulation. Sometimes they have said their points are the "sole basis" for negotiations, sometimes "the most correct basis." But the effect is the same. What they are insisting upon is that we accept in advance their substantive position and then discuss only the ways in which it shall be given effect. The technique of demanding such substantive agreement in advance is a familiar Communist negotiating tactic. It does not mean that the basic points are open for discussion or that they can be loosely interpreted. It means just what it says.

We have subjected these Four Points to the most careful scrutiny. What do they reveal? The first point calls for "recognition of the fundamental rational rights of the Vietnamese people: sovereignty, independence, unity, and territorial integrity." This point also calls for the withdrawal of U.S. forces, dismantling of our military bases, and abolition of our military alliance with the government of South Vietnam, "in strict conformity with the Geneva Agreements." The United States has made clear that we, too, are prepared to support a restoration of the provisions of the Geneva Agreements and that we are prepared to withdraw our troops and dismantle military bases once there is compliance with the Accords by all parties. We have said also that we would not expect or require a military alliance with a free South Vietnam.

The second point relates to the military clauses of the Geneva Agreements, and these, too, we could agree to under the conditions I have indicated.

The fourth point provides that the issue of peaceful reunification should be settled by the Vietnamese people without foreign intervention. This also we could accept if it be clearly understood that conditions must first be created both in the North and South that will make it possible for truly free elections to be held.

It is in the third point that the core of the Communist position is disclosed. That point provides that "The Internal affairs of South Vietnam must be settled by the South Vietnamese people themselves in accordance with the program of the National Liberation Front." To understand the significance of this point, it is necessary not only to examine what is meant by the "Program of the National Liberation Front" but to explore somewhat further the character of the Front itself and the purposes it serves in the tactics of the North Vietnamese regime.

Let us turn first to the Front itself. Both Hanoi and Peiping have made clear again and again, and they have been joined in this by other Communist powers, that negotiations will be possible only when the United States recognizes the National Liberation Front as the "sole genuine representative of the entire South Vietnamese people."

What are the implications of this proposal and why are the Communists urging it so insistently? The evidence is overwhelming that the National Liberation Front is exactly what its name implies—a Communist front organization intended to give support to the deliberate fiction that the war in Vietnam is an indigenous revolt. The Front is, as the facts make clear, an invention of the Communist Party of North Vietnam, to serve as a political cloak for its activities in the South.

As I have noted earlier, the Front was created by the North Vietnamese Communist Party, the Lao Dong Party, in 1960, soon after North Vietnam's military leader, General Giap, announced: "The North is the revolutionary base for the whole country."

The individuals proclaimed as leaders of the Front are not personalities widely known to the Vietnamese people, either in the North or in the South. To suggest that they represent the aspirations of the Vietnamese people is absurd. The significant fact is that at no time has any single individual of political significance in South Vietnam adhered to the Front or to its policies. While some Vietnamese leaders and groups may differ among themselves on how the country is to be led, none of them differs on the fact that the Front does not speak for them.

In 1961 Hanoi sought to strengthen the fiction of the Front's indigenous origins by creating a seemingly independent Communist Party as the principal element of the Front. It therefore established the People's Revolutionary Party. A secret Lao Dong circular dated December 7, 1961, advised Party members that "The People's Revolutionary Party has only the appearance of an independent existence. Actually our Party is nothing but the Lao Dong Party of Vietnam unified from North to South under the Central Executive Committee of the Party, the chief of which is President Ho. . . ." During these explanations, take care to keep this strictly secret, they said, "especially in South Vietnam, so that the enemy does not perceive our purpose."

The People's Revolutionary Party has not concealed its role at the front. It has frankly stated that it is the dominant element. On February 15, 1961, the Viet Cong Committee for the South went even farther, stating that in time the Communist Party would "act overtly to lead the revolution in South Vietnam." In other words, the Communists have told their followers that at the proper moment they would emerge from cover and cast off the disguise of the National Liberation Front. And so the Communists have a clear purpose in insisting that we recognize the National Liberation Front as the sole representative of the South Vietnamese people. For them this is not a procedural question but a major question of substance. They insist on our recognition of the Front as the sole spokesman for the people of South Vietnam, since our acceptance of the Front in that capacity would in effect mean our acceptance of the Communist position as to the indigenous nature of the conflict and thus our acceptance of a settlement on Hanoi's terms, which would mean delivering South Vietnam into the control of the Communist North.

In spite of these clear realities, we have not asserted nor do we assert an unreasoning attitude with regard to the Front. The President said in his State of the Union Message, you will recall, that we will meet at any conference table, we will discuss any proposals—four Points or fourteen or forty—and we will consider the views of any group; and that, of course, includes the Front along with other groups. To the extent then that the Front has any validity as a representative of a group, the views of that group can be heard and the issue of the Liberation Front should, as the President has said, not prove "an insurmountable problem." It remains a problem only because Hanoi insists on using it to establish its own substantive position—that the Front represents the hopes and aspirations of the South Vietnamese people, and hence should control them.

The significance of this issue is clearly seen when one examines the so-called "Program of the National Liberation Front," as it was announced from Hanoi on January 29, 1961, and revised and amplified in a second publication on February 11 that same year. The first point of this program discloses the full Communist intention. It calls for the overthrow of the South Vietnamese government in Saigon and the establishment of a coalition government from which the government in Saigon would be totally excluded.

In other words the Hanoi regime is demanding the following preconditions to which the United States must agree before the Communists will even condescend to negotiate: First, that the South Vietnamese government be overthrown; second, that the Liberation Front, the creature and agent of Hanoi, be accepted as the sole bargaining representative for the South Vietnamese people; third, that South Vietnam be put under the control of a coalition government formed by the Communists and from which the South Vietnamese government would be excluded.

May I conclude, therefore, Mr. Chairman, with certain simple points which are at the heart of the problem and at the heart of United States policy in South Vietnam.

One, the elementary fact is that there is an aggression in the form of an armed attack by North Vietnam against South Vietnam. Two, the United States has commitments to assist South Vietnam to repel this aggression. Three, our commitments to South Vietnam were not taken in isolation but are part of a systematic effort in the postwar period to assure a stable space. Four, the issue in Southeast Asia becomes worldwide because we must make clear that the United States keeps its word wherever it is pledged. Five, no nation is more interested in peace in Southeast Asia or elsewhere than is the United States. If the armed attack against South Vietnam is brought to an end, peace can come very quickly. Every channel or forum for contact, discussion, or negotiation will remain active in order that no possibility for peace may be overlooked. . . .

The United States and the Third World— Vietnam as a Case Study

Realist

Realists concede the wisdom of attempting to contain the expansion of Communist Russia and China in the third world, but they argue that the Nationalists are going about it all wrong. By attempting to stop every revolution that might install a Communist government, the United States is far exceeding the limits of its power. Besides, they say, Communism is no longer monolithic. Because the resources of many Communist nations are no longer automatically at the beck and call of China or Russia, not every Communist revolution poses a threat to the United States.

Finally, Realists caution against using containment in Europe as a model for policy in the third world. The nations we aided in Europe were already developed and anxious to defend themselves against Russia. They also shared our cultural heritage and political outlook. Economic and military aid were therefore put to good use. Economic aid helped revive their economies, thus preventing internal revolution; military aid helped protect them against direct invasion.[1] In the third world, the economies cannot merely be revived. They must be built almost from scratch, which requires far more time and money. Third-world nations are not threatened so much by invasion as by internal unrest, which requires little aid from Communist nations to flare into armed rebellion. In addition, differences in race, culture, and historical outlook make American intervention in these nations far more difficult than it was in Europe.

Realists argue that American policy in the third world must be far more cautious, more political, and less military than it has been in the past. The United States must intervene only where American security and vital interests are directly threatened. They do not think that American interests justified intervention in Vietnam. They see participation in an endless war there as the consequence of a failure to balance America's interests with its power, a tragic example of the fruits of Nationalist policy in the third world.

[1] Notice that although Kennan and Lippmann emphasize the political and internal threat of Russia to Western Europe, Hans Morgenthau in the following essay accepts the idea that Russia's military threat was very real.

In the following essay, Hans J. Morgenthau illustrates the Realists' ap-
proach to American policy in Vietnam and in the third world generally.
Why does he deny that Communism in Vietnam is a threat to the United
States? How does he deal with the Nationalists' "domino theory"?

Vietnam and
the United States

Hans J. Morgenthau

The address President Johnson delivered on April 7, 1965 at
Johns Hopkins University is important for two reasons. On the
one hand, the President has shown for the first time a way out of
the impasse in which we find ourselves in Vietnam. By agreeing
to negotiations without preconditions he has opened the door to
negotiations which those preconditions had made impossible
from the outset.

By proposing a project for the economic development of
Southeast Asia—with North Vietnam a beneficiary and the Soviet
Union a supporter—he has implicitly recognized the variety of
national interests in the Communist world and the need for varied
American responses tailored to those interests. By asking "that
the people of South Vietnam be allowed to guide their own country in their own way," he has left all possibilities open for future
evolution of relations between North and South Vietnam.

On the other hand, the President reiterated the intellectual assumptions and policy proposals which brought us to an impasse
and which make it impossible to extricate ourselves. The Presi-

From "We Are Deluding Ourselves in Vietnam" by Hans Morgenthau, *The New York
Times Sunday Magazine,* 18 April 1965. © 1965 by The New York Times Company.
Reprinted by permission.

dent has linked our involvement in Vietnam with our war of independence and has proclaimed the freedom of all nations as the goal of our foreign policy. He has started from the assumption that there are two Vietnamese nations, one of which has attacked the other, and he sees that attack as an integral part of unlimited Chinese aggression. Consistent with this assumption, the President is willing to negotiate with China and North Vietnam but not with the Viet Cong.

Yet we cannot have it both ways. We cannot at the same time embrace these false assumptions and pursue new sound policies. Thus we are faced with a real dilemma. This dilemma is by no means of the President's making.

We are militarily engaged in Vietnam by virtue of a basic principle of our foreign policy that was implicit in the Truman Doctrine of 1947 and was put into practice by John Foster Dulles from 1954 onward. This principle is the military containment of Communism. Containment had its origins in Europe; Dulles applied it to the Middle East and Asia through a series of bilateral and multilateral alliances. Yet what was an outstanding success in Europe turned out to be a dismal failure elsewhere. The reasons for that failure are twofold.

First, the threat that faced the nations of Western Europe in the aftermath of the Second World War was primarily military. It was the threat of the Red Army marching westward. Behind the line of military demarcation of 1945 which the policy of containment declared to be the westernmost limits of the Soviet empire, there was an ancient civilization, only temporarily weak and able to maintain itself against the threat of Communist subversion.

The situation is different in the Middle East and Asia. The threat there is not primarily military but political in nature. Weak governments and societies provide opportunities for Communist subversion. Military containment is irrelevant to that threat and may even be counter-productive. Thus the Baghdad Pact did not protect Egypt from Soviet influence and SEATO has had no bearing on Chinese influence in Indonesia and Pakistan.

Second, and more important, even if China were threatening her neighbors primarily by military means, it would be impossible to contain her by erecting a military wall at the periphery of her empire. For China is, even in her present underdeveloped state, the dominant power in Asia. She is this by virtue of the quality and quantity of her population, her geographic position, her civilization, her past power remembered and her future power anticipated. Anybody who has traveled in Asia with his eyes and ears open must have been impressed by the enormous impact which the resurgence of China has made upon all manner of men, regardless of class and political conviction, from Japan to Pakistan.

The issue China poses is political and cultural predominance. The United States can no more contain Chinese influence in Asia by arming South Vietnam and Thailand than China could contain American influence in the Western Hemisphere by arming, say, Nicaragua and Costa Rica.

If we are convinced that we cannot live with a China predominant on the mainland of Asia, then we must strike at the heart of Chinese power—that is, rather than try to contain the power of China, we must try to destroy that power itself. Thus there is logic on the side of that small group of Americans who are convinced that war between the United States and China is inevitable and that the earlier it comes, the better will be the chances for the United States to win it.

Yet, while logic is on their side, practical judgment is against them. For while China is obviously no match for the United States in overall power, China is largely immune to the specific types of power in which the superiority of the United States consists— that is, nuclear, air and naval power. Certainly, the United States has the power to destroy the nuclear installations and the major industrial and population centers of China, but this destruction would not defeat China; it would only set her development back. To be defeated, China has to be conquered.

Physical conquest would require the deployment of millions of American soldiers on the mainland of Asia. No American military leader has ever advocated a course of action so fraught with incalculable risks, so uncertain of outcome, requiring sacrifices so out of proportion to the interests at stake and the benefits to be expected. President Eisenhower declared on February 10, 1954, that he "could conceive of no greater tragedy than for the United States to become involved in an all-out war in Indochina." General MacArthur, in the Congressional hearings concerning his dismissal and in personal conversation with President Kennedy, emphatically warned against sending American foot soldiers to the Asian mainland to fight China.

If we do not want to set ourselves goals which cannot be attained with the means we are willing to employ, we must learn to accommodate ourselves to the predominance of China on the Asian mainland. It is instructive to note that those Asian nations which have done so—such as Burma and Cambodia—live peacefully in the shadow of the Chinese giant.

This *modus vivendi,* composed of legal independence and various degrees of actual dependence, has indeed been for more than a millennium the persistent pattern of Chinese predominance in Southeast Asia. The military conquest of Tibet is the sole exception to that pattern. The military operations at the Indian border do not diverge from it, since their purpose was the establishment of a frontier disputed by both sides.

On the other hand, those Asian nations which have allowed themselves to be transformed into outposts of American military power—such as Laos a few years ago, South Vietnam and Thailand—have become the actual or prospective victims of Communist aggression and subversion. Thus it appears that peripheral military containment is counterproductive. Challenged at its periphery by American military power at its weakest—that is, by the proxy of client-states—China or its proxies respond with locally superior military and political power.

In specific terms, accommodation means four things: (1) recognition of the political and cultural predominance of China on the mainland of Asia as a fact of life; (2) liquidation of the peripheral military containment of China; (3) strengthening of the uncommitted nations of Asia by nonmilitary means; (4) assessment of Communist governments in Asia in terms not of Communist doctrine but of their relation to the interests and power of the United States.

In the light of these principles, the alternative to our present policies in Vietnam would be this: a face-saving agreement which would allow us to disengage ourselves militarily in stages spaced in time; restoration of the status quo of the Geneva Agreement of 1954, with special emphasis upon all-Vietnamese elections; cooperation with the Soviet Union in support of a Titoist all-Vietnamese Government, which would be likely to emerge from such elections.

This last point is crucial, for our present policies not only drive Hanoi into the waiting arms of Peking, but also make it very difficult for Moscow to pursue an independent policy. Our interests in Southeast Asia are identical with those of the Soviet Union: to prevent the expansion of the military power of China. But while our present policies invite that expansion, they make it impossible for the Soviet Union to join us in preventing it. If we were to reconcile ourselves to the establishment of a Titoist government in all of Vietnam, the Soviet Union could successfully compete with China in claiming credit for it and surreptitiously cooperate with us in maintaining it.

Testing the President's proposals by these standards, one realizes how far they go in meeting them. These proposals do not preclude a return to the Geneva agreement and even assume the existence of a Titoist government in North Vietnam. Nor do they preclude the establishment of a Titoist government for all of Vietnam, provided the people of South Vietnam have freely agreed to it. They also envision the active participation of the Soviet Union in establishing and maintaining a new balance of power in Southeast Asia. On the other hand, the President has flatly rejected a withdrawal "under the cloak of meaningless agreement." The controlling word is obviously "meaningless," and only the future can tell whether we shall consider any face-saving agreement as "meaningless" regardless of its political context.

However, we are under a psychological compulsion to continue our military presence in South Vietnam as part of the peripheral military containment of China. We have been emboldened in this course of action by the identification of the enemy as "Communist," seeing in every Communist party and regime an extension of hostile Russian or Chinese power. This identification was justified 15 to 20 years ago when Communism still had a monolithic character. Here, as elsewhere, our modes of thought and action have been rendered obsolete by new developments.

It is ironic that this simple juxtaposition of "Communism" and "free world" was erected by John Foster Dulles's crusading moralism into the guiding principle of American foreign policy at a time when the national Communism of Yugoslavia, the neutralism of the third world and the incipient split between the Soviet Union and China were rendering that juxtaposition invalid.

Today, it is belaboring the obvious to say that we are faced not with one monolithic Communism whose uniform hostility must be countered with equally uniform hostility, but with a number of different Communisms whose hostility, determined by different national interests, varies. In fact, the United States encounters today less hostility from Tito, who is a Communist, than from de Gaulle, who is not.

We can today distinguish four different types of Communism in view of the kind and degree of hostility to the United States they represent: a Communism identified with the Soviet Union—e.g., Poland; a Communism identified with China—e.g., Albania; a

Communism that straddles the fence between the Soviet Union and China—e.g., Rumania; and independent Communism—e.g., Yugoslavia. Each of these Communisms must be dealt with in terms of the bearing its foreign policy has upon the interests of the United States in a concrete instance.

It would, of course, be absurd to suggest that the officials responsible for the conduct of American foreign policy are unaware of these distinctions and of the demands they make for discriminating subtlety. Yet it is an obvious fact of experience that these officials are incapable of living up to these demands when they deal with Vietnam.

Thus they maneuver themselves into a position which is antirevolutionary per se and which requires military opposition to revolution wherever it is found in Asia, regardless of how it affects the interests—and how susceptible it is to the power—of the United States. There is a historic precedent for this kind of policy: Metternich's military opposition to liberalism after the Napoleonic Wars, which collapsed in 1848. For better or for worse, we live again in an age of revolution. It is the task of statesmanship not to oppose what cannot be opposed without a chance of success, but to bend it to one's own interests. This is what the President is trying to do with his proposal for the economic development of Southeast Asia.

Why do we support the Saigon Government in the Civil War against the Viet Cong? Because the Saigon Government is "free" and the Viet Cong are "Communist." By containing Vietnamese Communism, we assume that we are really containing the Communism of China.

Yet this assumption is at odds with the historic experience of a millennium and is unsupported by contemporary evidence. China is the hereditary enemy of Vietnam, and Ho Chi Minh will become the leader of a Chinese satellite only if the United States forces him to become one.

Furthermore, Ho Chi Minh, like Tito and unlike the Communist governments of the other states of Eastern Europe, came to power not by courtesy of another Communist nation's victorious army but at the head of a victorious army of his own. He is, then, a natural candidate to become an Asian Tito, and the question we must answer is: How adversely would a Titoist Ho Chi Minh, governing all of Vietnam, affect the interests of the United States? The answer can only be: not at all. One can even maintain the proposition that, far from affecting adversely the interests of the United States, it would be in the interest of the United States if the western periphery of China were ringed by a chain of independent states, though they would, of course, in their policies take due account of the predominance of their powerful neighbor.

The roots of the Vietnamese civil war go back to the very beginning of South Vietnam as an independent state. When President Ngo Dinh Diem took office in 1954, he presided not over a state but over one-half of a country arbitrarily and, in the intentions of all concerned, temporarily severed from the other half. He was generally regarded as a caretaker who would establish the rudiments of an administration until the country was united by nationwide elections to be held in 1956 in accordance with the Geneva accords.

Diem was confronted at home with a number of private armies which were politically, religiously or criminally oriented. To the general surprise, he subdued one after another and created what looked like a viable government. Yet in the process of creating it, he also laid the foundations for the present civil war. He ruthlessly suppressed all opposition, established concentration camps, organized a brutal secret police, closed newspapers and rigged elections. These policies inevitably led to a polarization of the policies of South Vietnam—on one side, Diem's family, surrounded by a Pretorian guard; on the other, the Vietnamese people, backed by the Communists, declaring themselves liberators from foreign domination and internal oppression.

Thus, the possibility of civil war was inherent in the very nature of the Diem regime. It became inevitable after Diem refused to agree to all-Vietnamese elections and, in the face of mounting popular alienation, accentuated the tyrannical aspects of his regime. The South Vietnamese who cherished freedom could not help but oppose him. Threatened by the secret police, they went either abroad or underground where the Communists were waiting for them.

Until the end of last February [1965], the Government of the United States started from the assumption that the war in South Vietnam was a civil war, aided and abetted—but not created—from abroad, and spokesmen for the Government have made time and again the point that the key to winning the war was political and not military and was to be found in South Vietnam itself. It was supposed to lie in transforming the indifference or hostility of the great mass of the South Vietnamese people into positive loyalty to the Government.

To that end, a new theory of warfare called "counterinsurgency" was put into practice. Strategic hamlets were established, massive propaganda campaigns were embarked upon, social and economic measures were at least sporadically taken. But all was to no avail. The mass of the population remained indifferent, if not hostile, and large units of the army ran away or went over to the enemy.

The reasons for this failure are of general significance, for they stem from a deeply ingrained habit of the American mind. We like to think of social problems as technically self-sufficient and susceptible of simple, clear-cut solutions. We tend to think of foreign aid as a kind of self-sufficient, economic enterprise subject to the laws of economics and divorced from politics, and of war as a similarly self-sufficient, technical enterprise, to be won as quickly, as cheaply, as thoroughly as possible and divorced from the foreign policy that preceded and is to follow it. Thus our military theoreticians and practitioners conceive of counterinsurgency as though it were just another branch of warfare, to be taught in special schools and applied with technical proficiency wherever the occasion arises.

This view derives of course from a complete misconception of the nature of civil war. People fight and die in civil wars because they have a faith which appears to them worth fighting and dying for, and they can be opposed with a chance of success only by people who have at least as strong a faith.

Magsaysay could subdue the Huk rebellion in the Philippines because his charisma, proven in action, aroused a faith superior to that of his opponents. In South Vietnam there is nothing to oppose the faith of the Viet Cong and, in consequence, the Saigon Government and we are losing the civil war.

A guerrilla war cannot be won without the active support of the indigenous population, short of the physical extermination of that population. Germany was at least consistent when, during the Second World War, faced with unmanageable guerrilla warfare throughout occupied Europe, she tried to master the situation through a deliberate policy of extermination. The French tried "counterinsurgency" in Algeria and failed; 400,000 French troops fought the guerrillas in Indochina for nine years and failed.

The United States has recognized that it is failing in South

Vietnam. But it has drawn from this recognition of failure a most astounding conclusion.

The United States has decided to change the character of the war by unilateral declaration from a South Vietnamese civil war to a war of "foreign aggression." "Aggression from the North: The Record of North Vietnam's Campaign to Conquer South Vietnam" is the title of a white paper published by the Department of State on the last day of February, 1965. While normally foreign and military policy is based upon intelligence—that is, the objective assessment of the facts—the process is here reversed: a new policy has been decided upon, and intelligence must provide the facts to justify it.

The United States, stymied in South Vietnam and on the verge of defeat, decided to carry the war to North Vietnam not so much in order to retrieve the fortunes of war as to lay the groundwork for "negotiations from strength." In order to justify that new policy, it was necessary to prove that North Vietnam is the real enemy. It is the white paper's purpose to present that proof.

Let it be said right away that the white paper is a dismal failure. The discrepancy between its assertions and the factual evidence adduced to support them borders on the grotesque. It does nothing to disprove, and tends even to confirm, what until the end of February had been official American doctrine: that the main body of the Viet Cong is composed of South Vietnamese and that 80 per cent to 90 per cent of their weapons are of American origin.

This document is most disturbing in that it provides a particularly glaring instance of the tendency to conduct foreign and military policy not on their own merits, but as exercises in public relations. The Government fashions an imaginary world that pleases it, and then comes to believe in the reality of that world and acts as though it were real.

It is for this reason that public officials are so resentful of the reporters assigned to Vietnam and have tried to shut them off from the sources of news and even to silence them. They resent the confrontation of their policies with the facts. Yet the facts are what they are, and they take terrible vengeance on those who disregard them.

However, the white paper is but the latest instance of a delusionary tendency which has led American policy in Vietnam astray in other respects: We call the American troops in Vietnam "advisers" and have assigned them by and large to advisory functions, and we have limited the activities of the Marines who have now landed in Vietnam to guarding American installations. We have done this for reasons of public relations, in order to spare ourselves the odium of open belligerency.

There is an ominous similarity between this technique and that applied to the expedition in the Bay of Pigs. We wanted to overthrow Castro, but for reasons of public relations we did not want to do it ourselves. So it was not done at all, and our prestige was damaged far beyond what it would have suffered had we worked openly and single-mindedly for the goal we had set ourselves.

Our very presence in Vietnam is in a sense dictated by considerations of public relations; we are afraid lest our prestige would suffer were we to retreat from an untenable position.

One may ask whether we have gained prestige by being involved in a civil war on the mainland of Asia and by being unable to win it. Would we gain more by being unable to extricate ourselves from it, and by expanding it unilaterally into an international war? Is French prestige lower today than it was 11 years ago when France was fighting in Indochina, or five years ago when France was fighting in Algeria? Does not a great power gain prestige by mustering the wisdom and courage necessary to liquidate a losing enterprise? In other words, is it not the mark of greatness, in circumstances such as these, to be able to afford to be indifferent to one's prestige?

The peripheral military containment of China, the indiscriminate crusade against Communism, counterinsurgency as a technically self-sufficient new branch of warfare, the conception of foreign and military policy as a branch of public relations—they are all misconceptions that conjure up terrible dangers for those who base their policies on them.

One can only hope and pray that the vaunted pragmatism and common sense of the American mind—of which the President's new proposals may well be a manifestation—will act as a corrective upon those misconceptions before they lead us from the blind alley in which we find ourselves today to the rim of the abyss. Beyond the present crisis, however, one must hope that the confrontation between these misconceptions and reality will teach us a long-overdue lesson—to rid ourselves of these misconceptions altogether.

The United States and the Third World—Vietnam as a Case Study

Radical

Radicals assert that American policy in the third world is designed to protect America's Open Door empire. This means not only containing Communism but crushing any revolution that threatens to expropriate American property, close markets to the United States, or divert necessary raw materials from our economy. Radicals see Vietnam as a particularly vicious, but in no way unique, example of this policy. They believe that a policy of global hegemony is necessary for expansive capitalism to survive. Communist expansion seems to them a myth conjured up by America's power elite to convince the people of the United States that it is necessary to intervene in popular revolutions all over the world.

Gabriel Kolko, author of the following essay, is a professor of history at York University in Toronto, Canada. He is the author of several books on American domestic policy as well as a book on American diplomacy during World War II, The Politics of War. *How does Kolko deal with the charge that the war in South Vietnam was imported from the North? What is his attitude toward the domino theory? What particular economic and strategic interests does he think inspired American intervention in Vietnam?*

The Roots
of American
Foreign Policy

Gabriel Kolko

THE UNITED STATES IN VIETNAM, 1944–66: ORIGINS AND OBJECTIVES

The intervention of the United States in Vietnam is the most important single embodiment of the power and purposes of American foreign policy since the Second World War, and no other crisis reveals so much of the basic motivating forces and objectives —and weaknesses—of American global politics. A theory of the origins and meaning of the war also discloses the origins of an American malaise that is global in its reaches, impinging on this nation's conduct everywhere. To understand Vietnam is also to comprehend not just the present purposes of American action but also to anticipate its thrust and direction in the future.

Vietnam illustrates, as well, the nature of the American internal political process and decision-making structure when it exceeds the views of a major sector of the people, for no other event of our generation has turned such a large proportion of the nation against its government's policy or so profoundly alienated its youth. And at no time has the government conceded so little to democratic sentiment, pursuing as it has a policy of escalation that reveals that its policy is formulated not with an eye to democratic sanctions and compromises but rather the attainment of specific interests and goals scarcely shared by the vast majority of the nation.

The inability of the United States to apply its vast material and economic power to compensate for the ideological and human superiority of revolutionary and guerrilla movements throughout the world has been the core of its frustration in Vietnam. From a

From Gabriel Kolko, *The Roots of American Foreign Policy*, pp. 88–100, 102–118, 132. Reprinted by permission of the Beacon Press, copyright © 1969 by Gabriel Kolko.

purely economic viewpoint, the United States cannot maintain its existing vital dominating relationship to much of the Third World unless it can keep the poor nations from moving too far toward the Left and the Cuban or Vietnamese path. A widespread leftward movement would critically affect its supply of raw materials and have profound long-term repercussions. It is the American view of the need for relative internal stability within the poorer nations that has resulted in a long list of United States interventions since 1946 into the affairs of numerous nations, from Greece to Guatemala, of which Vietnam is only the consummate example—but in principle no different than numerous others. The accuracy of the "domino" theory, with its projection of the eventual loss of whole regions to American direction and access, explains the direct continuity between the larger United States global strategy and Vietnam.

Yet, ironically, while the United States struggles in Vietnam and the Third World to retain its own mastery, or to continue that once held by the former colonial powers, it simultaneously weakens itself in its deepening economic conflict with Europe, revealing the limits of America's power to attain its ambition to define the preconditions and direction of global economic and political developments. Vietnam is essentially an American intervention against a nationalist, revolutionary agrarian movement which embodies social elements in incipient and similar forms of development in numerous other Third World nations. It is in no sense a civil war, with the United States supporting one local faction against another, but an effort to preserve a mode of traditional colonialism via a minute, historically opportunistic *comprador* class in Saigon. For the United States to fail in Vietnam would be to make the point that even the massive intervention of the most powerful nation in the history of the world was insufficient to stem profoundly popular social and national revolutions throughout the world. Such a revelation of American weaknesses would be tantamount to a demotion of the United States from its present role as the world's dominant superpower.

Given the scope of United States ambitions in relation to the Third World, and the sheer physical limits on the successful implementation of such a policy, Vietnam also reveals the passivity of the American Military Establishment in formulating global objectives that are intrinsically economic and geopolitical in character. Civilians, above all, have calculated the applications of American power in Vietnam and their strategies have prompted each military escalation according to their definitions of American interests. Even in conditions of consistent military impotence and defeat, Vietnam has fully revealed the tractable character of the American military when confronted with civilian authority, and their continuous willingness to obey civilian orders loyally.

It is in this broader framework of the roots of United States foreign policy since 1945 that we must comprehend the history and causes of the war in Vietnam and relate it to the larger setting of the goals of America's leaders and the function of United States power in the modern world.

Throughout the Second World War the leaders of the United States scarcely considered the future of Indo-China, but during 1943 President Roosevelt suggested that Indo-China become a four-power trusteeship after the war, proposing that the eventual independence of the Indo-Chinese might follow in twenty to thirty years. No one speculated whether such a policy would require American troops, but it was clear that the removal of French power was motivated by a desire to penalize French collaboration with Germany and Japan, or De Gaulle's annoying independence, rather than a belief in the intrinsic value of freedom for the Vietnamese. Yet what was critical in the very first American position was that ultimate independence would not be something that the Vietnamese might take themselves, but a blessing the other Great Powers might grant at their own convenience. Implicit in this attitude was the seed of opposition to the independence movement that already existed in Vietnam. Indeed, all factors being equal, the policy toward European colonialism would depend on the extent to which the involved European nations accepted American objectives elsewhere, but also the nature of the local opposition. If the Left led the independence movements, as in the Philippines, Korea, or Indo-China, then the United States sustained collaborationist alternatives, if possible, or endorsed colonialism.

Although Roosevelt at Yalta repeated his desire for a trusteeship, during March 1945 he considered the possibility of French restoration in return for their pledge eventually to grant independence. But by May 1945 there was no written, affirmative directive on United States political policy in Indo-China. The gap was in part due to the low priority assigned the issue, but also reflected growing apprehension as to what the future of those countries as independent states might hold.

At the Potsdam Conference of July 1945, and again in the General Order Number 1 the United States unilaterally issued several weeks later, the remaining equivocation on Indo-China was resolved by authorizing the British takeover of the nation south of the 16th parallel and Chinese occupation north of it, and this definitely meant the restoration of the French whom the British had loyally supported since 1943. One cannot exaggerate the importance of these steps, since it made the United States responsible for the French return at a time when Washington might have dictated the independence of that nation. By this time everyone understood what the British were going to do.

Given the alternative, United States support for the return of France to Indo-China was logical as a means of stopping the triumph of the Left, a question not only in that nation but throughout the Far East. Moreover, by mid-August French officials were hinting that they would grant the United States and England equal economic access to Indo-China. Both in action and thought the United States Government now chose the reimposition of French colonialism. At the end of August De Gaulle was in Washington, and the President now told the French leader that the United States favored the return of France to Indo-China. The decision would shape the course of world history for decades.

. . .

. . . By the end of the Second World War the Vietnamese were already in violent conflict not only with the representatives of France, but also England and the United States, a conflict in which they could turn the wartime political rhetoric against the governments that had casually written it. But, at no time did the desires of the Vietnamese themselves assume a role in the shaping of United States policy.

1946–49: United States Inaction and the Genesis of a Firm Policy

It is sufficient to note that by early 1947 the American doctrine of containment of communism obligated the United States to think also of the dangers Ho Chi Minh and the Vietminh posed, a movement in the United States analyzed as a monolith directed from Moscow. It is also essential to remain aware of the fact that the global perspective of the United States between 1946 and 1949 stressed the decisive importance of Europe to the future of the world power. When the United States looked at Indo-China they saw France, and through it Europe, and a weak France would open the door to communism in Europe. But for no other reason, this meant a tolerant attitude toward the bloody French policy in Vietnam, one the French insisted was essential to the maintenance of their empire and prosperity, and the political stability of the nation. Washington saw Vietnamese nationalism as a tool of the Communists.

In February 1947 Secretary of State George C. Marshall publicly declared he wished "a pacific basis of adjustment of the difficulties could be found," but he offered no means toward that end. Given the greater fear of communism, such mild American criticisms of French policy as were made should not obscure the much more significant backing of basic French policy in Washington. By early 1949 Washington had shown its full commitment to the larger assumptions of French policy and goals, and when Bao Dai, the former head of the Japanese puppet regime, signed an agreement with the French in March 1949 to bring Vietnam into the French Union, the State Department welcomed the new arrangement as ". . . the basis for the progressive realization of the legitimate aspirations of the Vietnamese people." Such words belied the reality, for the course of affairs in Asia worried Washington anew.

The catalysis for a reconsideration of the significance of Vietnam to the United States was the final victory of the Communists in China. In July 1949 the State Department authorized a secret reassessment of American policy in Asia in light of the defeat of the Kuomintang, and appointed Ambassador-at-Large Philip Jessup chairman of a special committee. On July 18th Dean Acheson sent Jessup a memo defining the limits of the inquiry: "You will please take as your assumption that it is a fundamental decision of American policy that the United States does not intend to permit further extension of Communist domination on the continent of Asia or in the southeast Asia area. . . ." At the end of 1949 the State Department was still convinced the future of world power remained in Europe, but, as was soon to become evident, this involved the necessity of French victory in Vietnam. Most significant about the Jessup Committee's views was the belief, as one State Department official put it, "In respect to Southeast Asia we are on the fringes of crisis," one that, he added, might involve all of Asia following China. It appears to have been the consensus that Bao Dai, despite American wishes for his success, had only the slimmest chance for creating an effective alternative to Ho in Vietnam. The Committee compared French prospects to those of Chiang Kai-shek two years earlier, and since they acknowledged that the Vietminh captured most of their arms from the French, the likelihood of stemming the tide seemed dismal.

There were two dimensions to the Vietnam problem from the United States viewpoint at the end of 1949. First, it was determined to stop the sweep of revolution in Asia along the fringes of China, and by that time Vietnam was the most likely outlet for any United States action. Second, it was believed that small colonial wars were draining France, and therefore Europe, of its power. Yet a Western victory had to terminate these struggles in order to fortify Europe, the central arena of the Cold War. "I found all the French troops of any quality were out in Indo-China," Marshall complained to the Jessup Committee, ". . . and the one place they were not was in Western Europe. So it left us in an extraordinarily weak position there. . . ." Massive American intervention in Vietnam was now inevitable.

.   .   .

Suffice it to say, the French were hard-pressed economically, and they needed United States aid on any terms, and in May 1950 direct United States economic aid was begun to Cambodia, Laos, and Vietnam. Immediately after the Korean affair Truman pledged greater support to the French and the Bao Dai regime.

During mid-October 1950, shortly after some serious military reverses, Jules Moch, the French Minister of National Defense, arrived in Washington to attempt to obtain even greater United States military aid. By this time, despite earlier reticence, the French had come to realize that the key to their colonial war was in Washington.

The aggregate military aid the United States contributed to the French effort in Vietnam is a difficult matter of bookkeeping, but total direct military aid to France in 1950–1953 was $2,-956,000,000, plus $684 million in 1954. United States claims suggest that $1.54 billion in aid was given to Indo-China before the Geneva Accords, and in fact Truman's statement in January 1953 that the United States paid for as much as half of the war seems accurate enough, and aid rose every year to 1954. The manner in which this aid was disbursed is more significant.

The United States paid but did not appreciate French political direction, though no serious political pressure was put on the French until 1954. Dulles, for one, was aware of Bao Dai's political unreliability and inability to create an alternative to the Vietminh, and he regretted it. "It seems," he wrote a friend in October 1950, "as is often the case, it is necessary as a practical matter to choose the lesser of two evils because the theoretically ideal solution is not possible for many reasons—the French policy being only one. As a matter of fact, the French policy has considerably changed for the better. . . ." It was Dulles, in the middle of 1951, who discovered in Bao Dai's former premier under the Japanese, Ngo Dinh Diem, the political solution for Indo-China. At the end of 1950 he was willing to content himself with the belief that the expansion of communism in Asia must be stopped. The French might serve that role, at least for a time.

In developing a rationale for United States aid three major arguments were advanced, only one of which was later to disappear as a major source of the conduct of United States policy in Vietnam. First of all, the United States wished to bring France back to Europe via victory in Vietnam: "The sooner they bring it to a successful conclusion," Henry Cabot Lodge explained in early 1951, "the better it would be for NATO because they could move their forces here and increase their building of their army in Europe. . . ." The French insistence until 1954 of blocking German rearmament and the European Defense Community until they could exist on the continent with military superiority over the Germans, a condition that was impossible until the war in Vietnam ended, gave this even more persuasive consideration special urgency. From this viewpoint, Vietnam was the indirect key to Germany. In the meantime, as Ambassador to France David Bruce explained it, "I think it would be a disaster if the French did not continue their effort in Indo-China."

Victory rather than a political settlement was necessary because of the two other basic and more permanent factors in guiding United States policy. The United States was always convinced that the "domino" theory would operate should Vietnam remain with the Vietnamese people. "There is no question," Bruce told a Senate committee, "that if Indo-China went, the fall of Burma and the fall of Thailand would be absolutely inevitable.

No one can convince me, for what it is worth, that Malay wouldn't follow shortly thereafter, and India . . . would . . . also find the Communists making infiltrations. . . ." The political character of the regime in Vietnam was less consequential than the larger United States design for the area, and the seeds of future United States policy were already forecast when Bruce suggested that ". . . the Indo-Chinese—and I am speaking now of the . . . anti-Communist group—will have to show a far greater ability to live up to the obligations of nationhood before it will be safe to with-draw, whether it be French Union forces or any other foreign forces, from that country." If the French left, someone would have to replace them.

Should Vietnam, and through it Asia, fall to the Vietminh, then the last major American fear would be realized. ". . . [Of] all the prizes Russia could bite off in the east," Bruce also suggested, "the possession of Indo-China would be the most valuable and in the long run would be the most crucial one from the standpoint of the west in the east. That would be true not because of the flow of rice, rubber, and so forth . . . but because it is the only place where any war is now being conducted to try to suppress the overtaking of the whole area of southeast Asia by the Com-munists." Eisenhower and Nixon put this assumption rather dif-ferently, with greater emphasis on the value of raw materials, but it has been a constant basis of United States policy in Vietnam since 1951. "Why is the United States spending hundreds of mil-lions of dollars supporting the forces of the French Union in the fight against communism?" Vice President Richard Nixon asked in December 1953. "If Indo-China falls, Thailand is put in an al-most impossible position. The same is true of Malaya with its rubber and tin. The same is true of Indonesia. If this whole part of Southeast Asia goes under Communist domination or Commu-nist influence, Japan, who trades and must trade with this area in order to exist, must inevitably be oriented towards the Commu-nist regime." "The loss of all Vietnam," Eisenhower wrote in his memoir, "together with Laos on the west and Cambodia on the southwest, would have meant the surrender to Communist en-slavement of millions. On the material side, it would have spelled the loss of valuable deposits of tin and prodigious supplies of rubber and rice. It would have meant that Thailand, enjoying buffer territory between itself and Red China, would be exposed on its entire eastern border to infiltration or attack. And if Indo-China fell, not only Thailand but Burma and Malaya would be threatened, with added risks to East Pakistan and South Asia as well as to all Indonesia."

.   .   .

. . . Given the larger regional, even global, context of the question of Vietnam for the United States, a peaceful settlement would have undermined the vital premise of Washington since 1947 that one could not negotiate with communism but only contain it via military expenditures, bases, and power. In February 1954, as Eden records, ". . . our Ambassador was told at the State Department that the United States Government was perturbed by the fact that the French were aiming not to win the war, but to get into a position from which they could negotiate." The United States was hostile to any political concessions and to an end to the war. To the French, many of whom still wished to fight, the essential question was whether the United States Government would share the burden of combat as well as the expense. The French would make this the test of their ultimate policy.

At the end of March the French sought to obtain some hint of the direction of United States commitments, and posed the hypothetical question of what United States policy would be if the Chinese used their aircraft to attack French positions. Dulles refused to answer the question, but he did state that if the United States entered the war with its own manpower, it would demand a much greater share of the political and executive direction of the future of the area.

It is probable the United States Government in the weeks before Geneva had yet to define a firm policy for itself save on one issue: the desire not to lose any part of Vietnam by negotiations and to treat the existing military realities of the war as the final determining reality. Eden's memory was correct when he noted that in April the Undersecretary of State, Walter Bedell Smith, informed the English Government ". . . that the United States had carefully studied the partition solution, but had decided that it would only be a temporary palliative and would lead to Communist domination of South-East Asia."

During these tense days words from the United States were extremely belligerent, but it ultimately avoided equivalent actions, and laid the basis for later intervention. On March 29th Dulles excoriated Ho and the Vietminh and all who ". . . whip up the spirit of nationalism so that it becomes violent." He again reiterated the critical value of Vietnam as a source of raw materials and its strategic value in the area, and now blamed China for the continuation of the war. After detailing the alleged history of broken Soviet treaties, Dulles made it clear that the United States would go to Geneva so that ". . . any Indo-China discussion will serve to bring the Chinese Communists to see the danger of their apparent design for the conquest of Southeast Asia, so that they will cease and desist." Vice President Richard Nixon on April 16th was rather more blunt in a press conference: Geneva would become an instrument of action and not a forum for a settlement. ". . . [The] United States must go to Geneva and take a positive stand for united action by the free world. Otherwise it will have to take on the problem alone and try to sell it to others. . . . This country is the only nation politically strong enough at home to take a position that will save Asia. . . . Negotiations with the Communists to divide the territory would result in Communist domination of a vital new area."

The fact the United States focused on Chinese "responsibility" for a war of liberation from the French that began in 1945, years before the Chinese Communists were near the south, was not only poor propaganda but totally irrelevant as a basis of military action. There was at this time no effective means for United States entry into the war, and such power as the Americans had would not be useful in what ultimately had to be a land war if they could hope for victory. War hawks aside, the Pentagon maintained a realistic assessment of the problem of joining the war at this time from a weak and fast-crumbling base, and for this reason the United States never implemented the much publicized schemes for entering the war via air power. The United States Government was, willy-nilly, grasping at a new course, one that had no place for Geneva and its very partial recognition of realities in Vietnam.

On April 4th Eisenhower proposed to Churchill that the three major NATO allies, the Associated States, the ANZUS countries, Thailand, and the Philippines form a coalition to take a firm stand on Indo-China, by using naval and air power against the Chinese coast and intervening in Vietnam itself. The British were instantly cool to the amorphous notion, and they were to insist that first the diplomats do their best at Geneva to save the French from their disastrous position. Only the idea of a regional military alliance appealed to them. Despite much scurrying and bluster,

Dulles could not keep the British and French from going to Geneva open to offers, concessions, and a *détente*.

On May 7th, the day before the Geneva Conference turned to the question of Vietnam, Laos, and Cambodia, Dien Bien Phu fell to the victorious Vietnamese. Psychologically, though not militarily, the United States saw this as a major defeat in Vietnam. Militarily, about three-quarters of Vietnam belonged to the Vietnamese and imminent French defeat promised to liberate the remainder. That same evening Dulles went on the radio to denounce Ho as a "Communist . . . trained in Moscow" who would ". . . deprive Japan of important foreign markets and sources of food and raw materials." Vietnam, Dulles went on, could not fall "into hostile hands," for then "the Communists could move into all of Southeast Asia." Nevertheless, "The present conditions there do not provide a suitable basis for the United States to participate with its armed forces," and so the hard-pressed French might wish an armistice. "But we would be gravely concerned if an armistice or cease-fire were reached at Geneva which would provide a road to a Communist takeover and further aggression."

The United States position meant an explicit denial of the logic of the military realities, for negotiations to deprive the Vietminh of all of their triumphs was, in effect, a request for surrender. Even before the Conference turned to the subject, the United States rejected—on behalf of a larger global view which was to make Vietnam bear the brunt of future interventions—the implications of a negotiated settlement.

The Geneva Agreement

Others have authoritatively documented the United States role during the Geneva Conference discussion of May 8–July 21—the indecision, vacillation, and American refusal to acknowledge the military and political realities of the time. The British, for their part, hoped for partition, the Russians and the Chinese for peace —increasingly at any price—and the Vietnamese for Vietnam and the political rewards of their near-military triumph over a powerful nation. The American position, as the *New York Times* described it during these weeks, was ". . . driving the U.S. deeper into diplomatic isolation on Southeast Asian questions," and "Though the U.S. opposes . . . these agreements, there appears to be little the U.S. can do to stop them."

To the Vietnamese delegation led by Pham Van Dong, the

question was how to avoid being deprived of the political con-
comitant of their military triumph, and they were the first to
quickly insist on national elections in Vietnam at an early date—
elections they were certain to win. As the Conference proceeded,
and the Russians and then the Chinese applied pressure for Vietnamese concessions on a wide spectrum of issues—the most important being the provisional zonal demarcation along the 17th
parallel—the importance of this election provision became ever
greater to the Vietminh.

To both the Vietnamese and the United States partition as a
permanent solution was out of the question, and Pham Van Dong
made it perfectly explicit that zonal regroupments were only a
temporary measure to enforce a cease-fire. Had the Vietminh felt
it was to be permanent they unquestionably would not have
agreed to the Accords. When Mendès-France conceded a specific date for an election, the world correctly interpreted it as a
major concession to Vietnamese independence. By the end of
June, the Vietnamese were ready to grant much in the hope that
an election would be held. During these very same days, Eden finally convinced the United States that a partition of Vietnam was
all they might hope for, and on June 29th Eden and Dulles issued
a statement which agreed to respect an armistice that "Does not
contain political provisions which would risk loss of the retained
area to Communist control." Since that loss was now inevitable,
it ambiguously suggested that the United States might look
askance at elections, or the entire Accord itself. When the time
came formally to join the other nations at Geneva in endorsing
the Conference resolutions, the United States would not consent
to do so.

The final terms of the Accords are too well known for more
than a contextual résumé here. The "Agreement on Cessation of
Hostilities" that the French and Vietnamese signed on July 20th
explicitly described as "provisional" the demarcation line at the
17th parallel. Until general elections, the Vietnamese and French
respectively were to exercise civil authority above and below the
demarcation line, and it was France alone that had responsibility
for assuring conformity to its terms on a political level. Militarily,
an International Control Commission was to enforce the terms.
Arms could not be increased beyond existing levels. Article 18
stipulated ". . . the establishment of new military bases is prohibited throughout Viet-Nam territory," and Article 19 that "the two
parties shall ensure that the zones assigned to them do not ad-

here to any military alliance," which meant that Vietnam could not join the Southeast Asia Treaty Organization the United States was beginning to organize. The Final Declaration issued on July 21st "takes note" of these military agreements, and ". . . that the essential purpose of the agreement relating to Viet-Nam is to settle military questions with a view to ending hostilities and that the military demarcation line is provisional and should not in any way be interpreted as constituting a political or territorial boundary." Vietnam was one nation in this view, and at no place did the documents refer to "North" or "South." To achieve political unity, ". . . general elections shall be held in July 1956, under the supervision of an international control commission . . . ," and "Consultations will be held on this subject between the competent representative authorities of the two zones from 20 July 1955 onwards."

To the United States it was inconceivable that the French and their Vietnamese allies could implement the election proviso without risk of total disaster. It is worth quoting Eisenhower's two references to this assumption in his memoir: "It was generally conceded that had an election been held, Ho Chi Minh would have been elected Premier." "I have never talked or corresponded with a person knowledgeable in Indo-Chinese affairs who did not agree that had elections been held as of the time of the fighting, possibly 80 percent of the population would have voted for the Communist Ho Chi Minh as their leader rather than Chief of State Bao Dai."

The United States therefore could not join in voting for the Conference resolution of July 21st, and a careful reading of the two United States statements issued unilaterally the same day indicates it is quite erroneous to suggest that the United States was ready to recognize the outcome of a Conference and negotiated settlement which it had bitterly opposed at every phase. Eisenhower's statement begrudgingly welcomed an end to the fighting, but then made it quite plain that ". . . the United States has not itself been a party to or bound by the decisions taken by the Conference, but it is our hope that it will lead to the establishment of peace consistent with the rights and needs of the countries concerned. The agreement contains features which we do not like, but a great deal depends on how they work in practice." The ". . . United States will not use force to disturb the settlement. We also say that any renewal of Communist aggression would be viewed by us as a matter of grave concern." Walter Bedell Smith's formal statement at Geneva made the same points, but explicitly refused to endorse the 13th article of the Agreement requiring consultation by the members of the Conference to consider questions submitted to them by the I.C.C., ". . . to ensure that the agreements on the cessation of hostilities in Cambodia, Laos and Viet-Nam are respected."

The Aftermath of Geneva: The U.S. Entrenchment, 1955–59

The United States attached such grave reservations because it never had any intention of implementing the Geneva Accords, and this was clear from all the initial public statements. The *Wall Street Journal* was entirely correct when on July 23rd it reported that "The U.S. is in no hurry for elections to unite Viet Nam; we fear Red leader Ho Chi Minh would win. So Dulles plans first to make the southern half a showplace—with American aid."

While various United States missions began moving into the area Diem controlled, Dulles addressed himself to the task of creating a SEATO organization which, as Eisenhower informed the Senate, was ". . . for defense against both open armed attack and internal subversion." To Dulles from this time onward, the SEATO treaty would cover Vietnam, Cambodia, and Laos, even though they failed to sign the Treaty and in fact the Geneva Agreement forbade them to do so. Article IV of the SEATO treaty extended beyond the signatories and threatened intervention by the organization in case of aggression "against any State or territory" in the region, or if there was a threat to the "political independence . . . of any other State or territory. . . ." Under such an umbrella the United States might rationalize almost any intervention for any reason.

The general pattern of United States economic and military aid to the Diem regime between 1955 and 1959, which totaled $2.92 billion in that period, indicates the magnitude of the American commitment, $1.71 billion of which was advanced under military programs, including well over a half-billion dollars before the final Geneva-scheduled election date.

That elections would never be held was a foregone conclusion, despite the efforts of the North Vietnamese, who on the first of January 1955 reminded the French of their obligations to see the provision respected. Given the internecine condition of the local opposition and its own vast strength among the people, the Democratic Republic of Vietnam had every reason to comply with the

Geneva provisos on elections. During February 1955 Hanoi proposed establishing normal relations between the two zones preparatory to elections, and Pham Van Dong in April issued a joint statement with Nehru urging steps to hold elections to reunify the country. By this time Diem was busy repressing and liquidating internal opposition of every political hue, and when it received no positive answer to its June 6th pleas for elections, the D.R.V. again formally reiterated its opposition to the partition of one nation and the need to hold elections on schedule. During June the world turned its attention to Diem's and Dulles' response prior to the July 20th deadline for consultations. Diem's response was painfully vague, and the first real statement came from Dulles on June 28th when he stated neither the United States nor the regime in the south had signed the Agreement at Geneva or was bound to it, a point that Washington often repeated and which was, in the case of the south, patently false. Nevertheless, Dulles admitted that in principle the United States favored ". . . the unification of countries which have a historic unity," the myth of two Vietnams and two nations not yet being a part of the American case. "The Communists have never yet won any free election. I don't think they ever will. Therefore, we are not afraid at all of elections, provided they are held under conditions of genuine freedom which the Geneva armistice agreement calls for." But the United States, it was clear from this statement, was not bound to call for the implementation of the agreement via prior consultations which Diem and Washington had refused until that time, nor did Dulles say he would now urge Diem to take such a course.

Diem at the end of April 1955 announced he would hold a "national referendum" in the south to convoke a new national assembly, and on July 16th he categorically rejected truly national elections under the terms of Geneva until ". . . proof is . . . given that they put the superior interests of the national community above those of Communism. . . ." "We certainly agree," Dulles stated shortly thereafter, "that conditions are not ripe for free elections." The response of the D.R.V. was as it had always been: Geneva obligated the Conference members to assume responsibility for its implementation, including consultations preparatory to actual elections, and in this regard Diem was by no means the responsible party. But the English favored partition, and the French were not about to thwart the United States Government. The fraudulent referendum of October 23rd which Diem organized in the south gave Diem 98 percent of the votes for the Presidency of the new "Government of Vietnam." Three days later Washington replied to the news by recognizing the legitimacy of the regime.

In reality, using a regime almost entirely financed with its funds, and incapable of surviving without its aid, the United States partitioned Vietnam.

To the D.R.V., the United States and the Diem Administrations' refusal to conform to the Geneva Accords was a question for the members of the Geneva Conference and the I.C.C. to confront, and while it had often made such demands—during June and again November 1955, and directly to Diem on July 19th—in September and again on November 17, 1955, Pham and Ho publicly elaborated their ideas on the structure of an election along entirely democratic lines. All citizens above eighteen could vote and all above twenty-one could run for office. They proposed free campaigning in both zones and secret and direct balloting. The I.C.C. could supervise. On February 25, 1956, Ho again reiterated this position.

On February 14, 1956, Pham Van Dong directed a letter to the Geneva co-chairmen pointing to the repression in the south, its de facto involvement in an alliance with the United States, and the French responsibility for rectifying the situation. He now proposed that the Geneva Conference reconvene to settle peacefully the problem of Vietnam. The British refused, and again on April 6th the Diem government announced that "it does not consider itself bound by their provisions." On May 8th the Geneva co-chairmen sent to the north and south, as well as to the French, a demand to open consultations on elections with a view to unifying the country under the Geneva Accords. Three days later the D.R.V. expressed readiness to begin direct talks in early June at a time set by the Diem authorities. Diem refused. The D.R.V. continued to demand consultations to organize elections, submitting notes to this effect to the Geneva co-chairmen and the Diem government in June and July 1957, March and December 1958, July 1959 and July 1960, and later, for arms reduction, resumption of trade, and other steps necessary to end the artificial partition of Vietnam. These proposals failed, for neither Diem nor the United States could survive their successful implementation.

Washington's policy during this period was clear and publicly stated. On June 1, 1956, after visiting Diem with Dulles the prior March, Walter S. Robertson, Assistant Secretary of State, attacked the Geneva Accords, which ". . . partitioned [Vietnam] by fiat of the great powers against the will of the Vietnamese people." He lauded Diem's rigged "free election of last March" and stated the American determination "To support a friendly non-Communist government in Viet-Nam and to help it diminish and eventually eradicate Communist subversion and influence. . . . Our efforts are directed first of all toward helping to sustain the internal security forces consisting of a regular army of about 150,000 men, a mobile civil guard of some 45,000, and local defense units. . . . We are also helping to organize, train, and equip the Vietnamese police force." Such policies were, of course, in violation of the Geneva Accords forbidding military expansion.

The term "eradicate" was an apt description of the policy which the United States urged upon the more-than-willing Diem, who persecuted former Vietminh supporters, dissident religious sects, and others. An estimated 40,000 Vietnamese were in jail for political reasons by the end of 1958, almost four times that number by the end of 1961. Such policies were possible because the United States financed over 70 percent of Diem's budget, and the main United States emphasis was on the use of force and repression. There were an estimated minimum of 16,600 political liquidations between 1955–59, perhaps much higher. Suffice it to say, every objective observer has accepted *Life* magazine's description in May 1957 as a fair estimate:

Behind a facade of photographs, flags and slogans there is a grim structure of decrees, "re-education centers," secret police. Presidential "Ordinance No. 6" signed and issued by Diem in January, 1956, provides that "individuals considered dangerous to national defense and common security may be confined on executive order" in a "concentration camp." . . . Only known or suspected Communists . . . are supposed to be arrested and "re-educated" under these decrees. But many non-Communists have also been detained. . . . The whole machinery of security has been used to discourage active opposition of any kind from any source.

The International Control Commission's teams complained of these violations in the south, and in the north they claimed that the only significant group to have its civil liberties infringed was the Catholic minority, approximately one-tenth of the nation. The cooperation of the D.R.V. with the I.C.C. was a critical index of its intentions, and an example of its naïve persistence in the belief Geneva had not in reality deprived them of its hard-fought victory. The vast military build-up in the south made real cooperation with the I.C.C. impossible, and its complaints, especially in regard to the airfields and reprisals against civilians, were very common. In certain cases the Diem regime permitted I.C.C. teams to move in the south, but it imposed time limits, especially after 1959. Although there is no precise way of making a count of what figures both Diem and the United States were attempting to hide, by July 1958 the D.R.V.'s estimate that Diem had 450,000 men under arms was probably correct in light of Robertson's earlier estimate of United States plans and the $1.7 billion in military expenditures for Diem through 1959.

Although the large bulk of American aid to Diem went to military purposes, the section devoted to economic ends further rooted an entirely dependent regime to the United States. That economic aid was a total disaster, exacerbated a moribund economy, ripped apart the urban society already tottering from the first decade of war, and enriched Diem, his family, and clique. Yet certain germane aspects of the condition of the southern economy are essential to understand the next phase of the revolution in Vietnam and further American intervention, a revolution the Americans had frozen for a time but could not stop.

The Vietminh controlled well over one-half the land south of the 18th parallel prior to the Geneva Conference, and since 1941 they had managed to introduce far-reaching land reform into an agrarian economy of grossly inequitable holdings. When Diem took over this area, with the advice of United States experts he introduced a "land reform" program which in fact was a regressive "modernization" of the concentrated land control system that had already been wiped out in many regions. Saigon reduced rents by as much as 50 percent from pre-Vietminh times, but in fact it represented a reimposition of tolls that had ceased to exist in wide areas. In cases of outright expropriation, landlords received compensation for property that they had already lost. In brief, the Diem regime's return to power meant a reimposition of a new form of the prewar 1940 land distribution system in which 72 percent of the population owned 13 percent of the land and two-thirds of the agricultural population consisted of tenants ground down by high rents and exorbitant interest rates. For this reason, it was the landlords rather than the peasantry who supported "agrarian reform."

Various plans for resettling peasants in former Vietminh strongholds, abortive steps which finally culminated in the strategic hamlet movement of 1962, simply helped to keep the countryside in seething discontent. These *agrovilles* uprooted traditional villages and became famous as sources of discontent against the regime, one which was ripping apart the existing social structure. In brief, Diem and the United States never established control over the larger part of south Vietnam and the Vietminh's impregnable peasant base, and given the decentralization and the corruption of Diem's authority, there was no effective basis for their doing so. The repression Diem exercised only rekindled resistance.

In the cities the dislocations in the urban population, constantly augmented by a flow of Catholic refugees from the north, led to a conservative estimate in 1956 of 413,000 unemployed out of the Saigon population of two million. The $1.2 billion in non-military aid given to the Diem regime during 1955–59 went in large part to pay for its vast import deficit which permitted vast quantities of American-made luxury goods to be brought into the country's inflationary economy for the use of the new *comprador* class and Diem's bureaucracy.

The United States endorsed and encouraged the military build-up and repression, but it did not like the strange mélange of mandarin anti-capitalism and Catholic feudalism which Diem jumbled together in his philosophy of personalism. Diem was a puppet, but a not perfectly tractable one. The United States did not appreciate the high margin of personal graft, nor did it like Diem's hostility toward accelerated economic development, nor his belief in state-owned companies. Ngo Dinh Nhu, his brother, regarded economic aid as a cynical means of dumping American surpluses, and the United States had to fight, though successfully, for the relaxation of restrictions on foreign investments and protection against the threat of nationalization. Ultimately Diem was content to complain and to hoard aid funds for purposes the United States thought dubious.

The U.S. thought of Vietnam as a capitalist state in Southeast Asia. This course condemned it to failure, but in April 1959, when Eisenhower publicly discussed Vietnam, ". . . a country divided into two parts," and not two distinct nations, he stressed Vietnam's need to develop economically, and the way ". . . to get the necessary capital is through private investments from the outside and through government loans," the latter, insofar as the United States was concerned, going to local capitalists.

1959–64: The Resistance Is Rekindled

Every credible historical account of the origins of the armed struggle south of the 17th parallel treats it as if it were on a continuum from the war with the French of 1945–54, and as the effect rather than the cause of the Diem regime's frightful repression and accumulated internal economic and social problems. The resistance to Diem's officials had begun among the peasantry in a spontaneous manner, by growing numbers of persecuted political figures of every persuasion, augmented by Buddhists and Vietminh who returned to the villages to escape, and, like every successful guerrilla movement, it was based on the support of the peasantry for its erratic but ultimately irresistible momentum. On May 6, 1959, Diem passed his famous Law 10/59 which applied the sentence of death to anyone committing murder, destroying to any extent houses, farms, or buildings of any kind, means of transport, and a whole list of similar offenses. "Whoever belongs to an organization designed to help to prepare or perpetuate crimes . . . or takes pledges to do so, will be subject to the sentences provided. . . ." The regime especially persecuted former members of the Vietminh, but all opposition came under the sweeping authority of Diem's new law, and the number of political prisoners between 1958 and the end of 1961 quadrupled. The resistance that spread did not originate from the north, and former Vietminh members joined the spontaneous local resistance groups well before the D.R.V. indicated any support for them. Only in 1960 did significant fighting spread throughout the country.

At the end of 1960 the United States claimed to have only 773 troops stationed there. By December 1965 there were at least fourteen major United States airbases in Vietnam, 166,000 troops, and the manpower was to more than double over the following year. This build-up violated the Geneva Accords, but that infraction is a fine point in light of the fact that the United States always had utter contempt for that agreement. In reality, the United States was now compelled to save what little it controlled of the south of Vietnam from the inevitable failure of its own policies.

It is largely pointless to deal with the subsequent events in the same detail, for they were merely a logical extension of the global policies of the United States before 1960. One has merely to juxtapose the newspaper accounts in the United States press against the official rationalizations cited in Washington to realize how very distant from the truth Washington was willing to wander to seek justification for a barbaric war against a small nation quite unprecedented in the history of modern times. To understand this war one must always place it in its contextual relationship and recall that the issues in Vietnam were really those of the future of United States power not only in Southeast Asia but throughout the entire developing world. In Vietnam the United States Government has vainly attempted to make vast power relevant to international social and political realities that had bypassed the functional conservatism of a nation seeking to save an old order with liberal rhetoric and, above all, with every form of military power available in its nonnuclear arsenal.

Ultimately, the United States has fought in Vietnam with increasing intensity to extend its hegemony over the world community and to stop every form of revolutionary movement which refuses to accept the predominant role of the United States in the direction of the affairs of its nation or region. Repeatedly defeated in Vietnam in the attainment of its impossible objective, the United States Government, having alienated most of its European allies and a growing sector of its own nation, is attempting to prove to itself and the world that it remains indeed strong enough to define the course of global politics despite the opposition of a small, poor nation of peasants. On the outcome of this epic contest rests the future of peace and social progress in the world for the remainder of the twentieth century, not just for those who struggle to overcome the legacy of colonialism and oppression to build new lives, but for the people of the United States themselves.